THE
ROANOKE VOYAGES

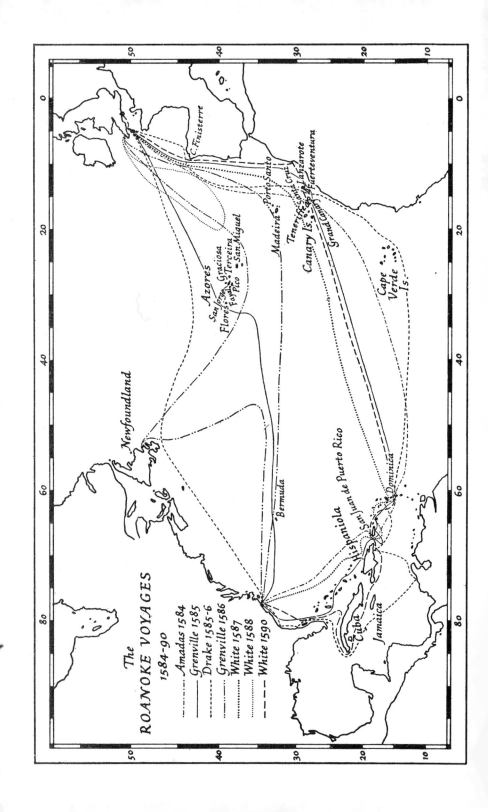

The
ROANOKE VOYAGES
1584-90

— · — Amadas 1584
——— Grenville 1585
— — — Drake 1585-6
········ Grenville 1586
·········· White 1587
··· ··· White 1588
— — — White 1590

Newfoundland

Azores
San Jorge Graciosa
Flores Terceira
Fayal Pico San Miguel

Madeira
Porto Santo
Teneriffe Santa Cruz
Canary Is. Lanzarote
Grand Canary Fuerteventura

Cape
Verde
Is.

C. Finisterre

Bermuda

Hispaniola
San Juan de Puerto Rico
Dominica

Cuba
Jamaica

THE
ROANOKE VOYAGES

1584-1590

DOCUMENTS TO ILLUSTRATE
THE ENGLISH VOYAGES TO NORTH AMERICA
UNDER THE PATENT GRANTED
TO WALTER RALEIGH
IN 1584

EDITED BY

DAVID BEERS QUINN

VOLUME I

DOVER PUBLICATIONS, INC.
NEW YORK

This Dover edition, first published in 1991, is an unabridged republication of the work first published by The Hakluyt Society, London, in 1955 (Second Series, No. CIV). Illustrations #6 and #7 which appeared as folding plates in the first edition are reproduced here on double-page spreads, #7 reduced in size.

Manufactured in the United States of America
Dover Publications, Inc.
31 East 2nd Street
Mineola, N.Y. 11501

Library of Congress Cataloging-in-Publication Data

The Roanoke voyages, 1584-1590 : documents to illustrate the English voyages to North America under the patent granted to Walter Raleigh in 1584 / edited by David Beers Quinn.
    p.   cm.
    Reprint. Originally published: London : Hakluyt Society, 1955.
Originally published in series: Works issued by the Hakluyt Society, 2nd ser., no. 104.
    Includes bibliographical references and index.
    ISBN 0-486-26512-9 (v. 1 : pbk.). — ISBN 0-486-26513-7 (v. 2 : pbk.)
    1. Roanoke Colony (N.C.)—History-Sources. 2. America—Discovery and exploration—English—Sources. I. Quinn, David B.
F229.R76   1991
973.1'7—dc20   90-24655
                                   CIP

TO THE MEMORY OF

A. P. NEWTON   J. E. TODD
EDWARD LYNAM

PREFACE

The voyages to North America made between 1584 and 1590 under the auspices of Sir Walter Raleigh have been named for convenience 'the Roanoke voyages' since they centred on Roanoke Island in the modern state of North Carolina. Though they lack the world-encompassing novelty of those of Drake and Cavendish, the Roanoke voyages were a significant episode in the sea-war between Elizabethan England and Spain, since it is now clear that their short-term objective was to facilitate privateering by the establishment of a mainland base in North America from which the Spanish Indies and the fleets coming from them might be more effectively attacked. They have, too, some appreciable scientific interest. In the course of them Englishmen for the first time set out seriously to explore, map and survey the natural resources and native society of any part of North America. The methods employed illustrate the process of technical and scientific development in the later sixteenth century, while the results, so far as they became known in Europe, appreciably enlarged and corrected existing knowledge of that part of the New World which was still least known and understood in the Old. The voyages, further, stand at the threshold of the period of English settlement in North America and represent the first English attempts to plant garrisons and enduring communities on North American soil. Though the colonial experiments failed, they are of considerable interest in revealing the economic and social factors involved in overseas settlement, and a study of them should lie at the foundations of any history of the first British empire or of the United States. It is for such reasons that their documentation has been attempted in so great detail in these volumes.

The younger Richard Hakluyt regarded the Roanoke voyages as being of so much promise for the ultimate settlement of North America that he published very full accounts of them in the

Principall navigations in 1589. These texts, which have not been republished *verbatim* before, together with the items added by him in 1600, form the basis of the present collection. Increase N. Tarbox annotated a number of them in detail in 1884 for his *Sir Walter Ralegh and his colony in America*. This has now been again attempted for all. Through the efforts of Edward Everett Hale, Henry Stevens, Charles Deane and Edward Eggleston additional documents and drawings were brought to light in the nineteenth century, while, in the twentieth, Laurence Binyon, Professor G. B. Parks, Professor E. G. R. Taylor, Dr J. A. Williamson, Randolph G. Adams, and Miss Irene A. Wright have uncovered new material and helped to reinterpret the old. An attempt has now been made to knit together what was already known and to add to it both by the publication of additional documents and of explanatory notes. At the same time, the present collection is not inclusive of all the known materials on the Roanoke voyages. The younger Richard Hakluyt's *Discourse of western planting* (as his 'Particuler discourse' has come to be called), and the elder Richard Hakluyt's 'Inducements to the liking of the voyage intended towards Virginia', are already available in Professor Taylor's collection of Hakluyt material in the Society's publications, as are Miss Wright's most valuable recent additions to the documentation of the Roanoke voyages from Spanish sources, only two of which are duplicated in this collection. There are, besides, many contemporary publications inspired or translated by the Hakluyts which throw some incidental light on the voyages from which only the most strictly relevant extracts are reprinted below. Above all, though a new catalogue of John White's drawings and maps is included, in an attempt to show how they can be used as historical documents, the full facsimile reproduction of the drawings now in preparation will, undoubtedly, add much to the appreciation of the English achievement in the 1585–6 survey, and give as well a vivid visual impression of the America seen by Elizabethan Englishmen. With these exceptions the collection is as comprehensive as it has been possible to make it, although a few documents have been given in summary form rather than in full.

Historical students in the present century have too often assumed that there are no more documents to be found on the Roanoke ventures. This collection should dissipate any such assumptions, even though many of the new additions made here are, individually, of minor significance. It should be stressed, however, that while a fairly wide search has been made for additional material, and the help of many scholars enlisted, there is no reason to believe that the work of collection is finished. Public and private collections in England and Spain alike may still contain important additions to a series of documents which remains, in many respects, tantalizingly incomplete.

The method adopted below is to provide in the introduction a critical discussion of the documents, followed by a chapter-by-chapter presentation of the materials, preceded in each case by a short narrative or other appropriate foreword, with explanatory notes. Special topics are dealt with in a series of appendices. The wide range of the annotation is intended to go some way towards satisfying inquiries of many kinds, but it raises many more questions than it answers and, on account of its range, is specially vulnerable both to error and inadvertence on the part of the editor. The intention of these volumes is to contribute to the full documentation of the English voyages to and colonizing ventures in North America before 1607. They have been preceded by a collection on *The voyages and colonising enterprises of Sir Humphrey Gilbert*, published by the Society in 1940, and more modestly annotated. It is expected to follow them with a further volume or volumes taking the series down to the foundation of the Virginia Company. This publication will afford an opportunity for collecting and publishing *addenda* and *corrigenda*, and it is earnestly hoped that contributions will be sent to the editor or to the Honorary Secretary of the Society.

These volumes owe much to the help that has been received from many sources. They could not have taken shape without

Preface

the encouragement and assistance of the late Edward Lynam and they would never have appeared if it had not been for the expert advice and hard labour of Mr R. A. Skelton, his successor as Honorary Secretary, who devoted an immense amount of time and skill to their production. Amongst other officers of the Society special thanks are due to Professor E. G. R. Taylor and to Dr Walter Muir Whitehill, the Society's Honorary Secretary in the United States. To Lord Haden Guest and the Leverhulme Fellowships Committee thanks are due for enabling the editor to visit the United States. Dr Carl Bridenbaugh and Professor Douglass Adair provided at the Institute of Early American History and Culture in Williamsburg an admirable headquarters from which research could be continued. Admiral J. F. Farley, Commandant, U.S. Coast Guard, generously made it possible for Dr Bridenbaugh, Mr John Gordon and the editor to use the Coast Guard vessels and stations in a visit to the Carolina Outer Banks. Mr Charles Rush, Director of the University of North Carolina Library, introduced the editor to Chapel Hill where he found so much assistance, while Dr Christopher Crittenden and Mr Harry T. Davis opened the resources of the State institutions at Raleigh to him. Dr Lawrence C. Wroth gave invaluable bibliographical counsel. Other detailed acknowledgements are made elsewhere, but institutional assistance was given with special generosity by the British Museum, the Smithsonian Institution, and the British Museum (Natural History). The Rev. James A. Geary has made original linguistic contributions to the appendices which have proved invaluable. Alison Quinn has worked closely on the collection and has had a greater share in its preparation than she would care to admit.

DAVID B. QUINN

UNIVERSITY COLLEGE
SWANSEA
September 1953

CONTENTS

VOLUME I

CHAPTER I

THE DISCOVERY OF RALEIGH'S VIRGINIA

Contents

xiv

Contents

CHAPTER III

THE 1585 VIRGINIA VOYAGE

Contents

Contents

Contents

CHAPTER IV

THE FIRST COLONY: LANE AND DRAKE, 1585–6

Contents

Contents

CHAPTER VII

THE 1586 VENTURES

Contents

Contents

VOLUME II

CHAPTER VIII

THE 1587 VOYAGES

Contents

Contents

Contents

CHAPTER XI

SPAIN AND THE ROANOKE VOYAGES, 1584–8

Contents

Contents

xxvii

Contents

Contents

CHAPTER XII

SPAIN AND VIRGINIA, 1588–1600

Contents

ILLUSTRATIONS AND MAPS

ABBREVIATIONS USED IN
THE FOOTNOTES

Amphibians and reptiles of N.C. C. S. Brimley, 'Revised key and list of the amphibians and reptiles of North Carolina', in *Journal of the Elisha Mitchell Scientific Society,* XLII, 75–93.

Andrews, 'Elizabethan privateering'. K. R. Andrews, 'The economic aspects of Elizabethan privateering' (London University thesis).

Beverley, *Hist. and present state.* Robert Beverley, *The history and present state of Virginia.* 1947.

Binyon, *Catalogue.* Laurence Binyon, *Catalogue of drawings by British artists in the British Museum,* IV. 1907.

Birds of N.C. T. G. Pearson, C. S. Brimley, and H. Brimley, *Birds of North Carolina.* 1942.

Bond, *Field guide.* James Bond, *Field guide to birds of the West Indies.* 1947.

Brit. Mus. British Museum, London, W.C. 1.

Brit. Mus. (N.H.) British Museum (Natural History), London, S.W. 7.

Childs, *Malaria.* St J. R. Childs, *Malaria and colonization in the Carolina Low Country, 1526–1696.* 1940.

Coker and Totten, *Trees of N.C.* W. C. Coker and H. R. Totten, *Trees of the southeastern states.* 1937.

Corbett, *Drake.* Sir J. S. Corbett, *Drake and the Tudor navy.* 2 vols. 1899.

Corbett, *Spanish war.* Sir J. S. Corbett, *Papers relating to the navy in the Spanish war, 1585–7.* 1898.

D.N.B. Dictionary of national biography.

Fernald and Kinsey, *Edible plants.* M. L. Fernald and A. C. Kinsey, *Edible wild plants of eastern North America.* 1943.

Fishes of N.C. H. M. Smith, *The fishes of North Carolina.* 1907.

Flannery, *Analysis.* R. Flannery, *Analysis of coastal Algonquian culture.* 1939.

Harrington, 'Report', I. J. C. Harrington, 'Archaeological explorations at Fort Raleigh National Historic Site', in *North Carolina Historical Review,* XXVI (1949), 127–49.

Harrington, 'Report', II. Typescript report of the excavations at the Fort Raleigh site, 1949–50, lent by Mr J. C. Harrington.

H.C.A. High Court of Admiralty.

H.R.T. Information supplied by Professor H. R. Totten, University of North Carolina, Chapel Hill.

H.T.D. Information supplied by Mr Harry T. Davis, Director, State Museum, Raleigh, N.C.

Abbreviations

Kearney, 'Ecology'. T. H. Kearney, 'The plant covering of Ocracoke Island; a study in the ecology of the North Carolina strand vegetation', in *Contributions from the U.S. National Herbarium*, v, 261–319.

Lewis and Loomie, *Spanish Jesuit mission*. C. M. Lewis and A. J. Loomie, *The Spanish Jesuit mission in Virginia, 1570–1572*. 1953.

Lorant, *New world*. Stefan Lorant, *The new world. The first pictures of America*. 1946.

Mammals of N.C. C. S. Brimley, *The mammals of North Carolina*. [1945.]

Mook, 'Algonkian ethno-history'. M. A. Mook, 'Algonkian ethno-history of the Carolina Sound', in *Journal of the Washington Academy of Sciences*, XXXIV, 182–97, 213–28.

Monardes, *Joyfull newes*. N. Monardes, *Joyfull newes out of the newe founde worlde....Englished by John Frampton*. 2 vols. Ed.Sir Stephen Gaselee. 1925.

O.E.D The Oxford English dictionary. 13 vols. 1933.

Oré, *Relación*. Luis Gerónimo de Oré, *Relación histórica de la Florida*. 2 vols. 1931–3.

P. and D. Department of Prints and Drawings in the British Museum.

Percyvall, *Dictionary*. R. Percyvall, *Bibliotheca Hispanica*. 1591.

Percyvall-Minsheu, *Dictionary*. R. Percyvall, *A dictionarie in Spanish and English....Now enlarged...by John Minsheu*. 1599.

Porcher, *Resources*. F. P. Porcher, *Resources of the southern fields and forests*. 1869.

P.R.O. Public Record Office, London.

Prospectus. Prospectus of John White, *The pictures of sondry things collected.... 1585*, issued by the British Museum in 1936.

Purchas, *Pilgrims*. S. Purchas, *Hakluytus posthumus or Purchas his pilgrimes*. 20 vols. 1905–7.

Quinn, *Gilbert*. *The voyages and colonising enterprises of Sir Humphrey Gilbert*, ed. D. B. Quinn. 2 vols. 1940.

Rowse, *Grenville*. A. L. Rowse, *Sir Richard Grenville*. 1937.

Seville, A.G.I. Archivo General de Indias, Seville.

Simancas, A.G. Archivo General de Simancas.

Smith, *Works*. John Smith, *Travels and works*, ed. E. Arber. 1884. 2 vols. 1910 (with same pagination).

S.P. State Papers.

Strachey, *Hist. of travell*. William Strachey, *Historie of travell into Virginia Britania*, ed. L. B. Wright and V. Freund. 1953.

Swanton, *Indians*. J. R. Swanton, *Indians of the United States*. 1946.

Swanton, *Indian tribes*. J. R. Swanton, *Indian tribes of North America*. 1952.

W.C.C. Information supplied by Professor W. C. Coker, University of North Carolina, Chapel Hill.

W.L.H. Information supplied by Mr William L. Hunt, Chapel Hill, N.C.

Wright, *Further English voyages*. *Further English voyages to Spanish America, 1583–94*, ed. I. A. Wright. 1951.

Yanovsky, *Food plants*. E. Yanovsky, *Food plants of the United States*. 1936.

NOTE ON EDITING

Texts printed directly from the manuscripts have been given as nearly as possible as they read, with a minimum of alterations in spelling and punctuation, except that expansions have been expanded and italicized, and a few misprints silently corrected. Elsewhere, italics are used for side notes and for those foreign words which stand in isolation, and italic type from printed texts is, normally, given in roman.

Dates for the day and month are Old Style, as used in England, with New Style (ten days in advance) added for Continental sources. English Style for the beginning of the year was 25 March, but the calendar year, beginning on 1 January, was sometimes used by Englishmen and, invariably, by Europeans represented in these documents.

'Virginia', as referred to in these documents, comprised parts of the modern states of North Carolina and Virginia. It is effectively defined, for the purpose of this collection, in the map at the end of the second volume, and any ambiguity in the use of the name should be resolved by reference to the map, where the relevant parts of the modern states are shown, overprinted with the sixteenth-century coastline and nomenclature.

INTRODUCTION

Atque his conatibus minus succedentibus, gens nostra nauibus abundans otij impatiens, in alias partes suas nauigationes instituerunt. Humfredus Gilbert Eques, Americae oras Hispanis incognitas, magno animo & viribus, successu non aequali nostris aperire conatus est. Id quod tuis postes auspicijs (vir honoratissime) felicius susceptum est quibus Virginia nobis patefacta est, praefecto classis Richardo Grinuil nobili equite, quam diligentissime lustrauit & descripsit Thomas Hariotus.

ROBERT HUES, dedicatory epistle to Sir Walter Raleigh, in *Tractatus de globis et eorum usu* (1594), sigs. ★★★2–4.

A CRITICAL ASSESSMENT OF
THE MATERIAL

The English progress towards the exploration and settlement of North America was a slow one and it is not until 1582 that propaganda for American colonization becomes overt. So far as printed material is concerned, the younger Richard Hakluyt's *Divers voyages touching the discoverie of America* is the first major landmark, and this was brought forth largely, if not wholly, by Sir Humphrey Gilbert's plans for a series of voyages for the detailed exploration and the extensive settlement of eastern North America.[1] The first work specifically to praise Gilbert's project was a rhetorical poem by the Hungarian Stephen Parmenius,[2] but it was not the sort to attract many adventurers. It was followed by Christopher Carleill's *A discourse upon the entended voyage to the hethermoste partes of America: written by Captaine Carleill, for the better inducement to satisfie suche Marchauntes, as in disburcing their money towardes the furniture of the present charge: doe demaunde forthwith a present returne of gaine: albeit their saied perticler disbursementes are in such slender sommes, as are not worth the speakyng of,*[3] written in April 1583, which is most specific and practical. Thirdly, there was Sir George Peckham's *A true reporte, of the late discoveries,* with its dedication to Walsingham, dated at Oxford, 12 November 1583,[4] after news of Gilbert's failure

[1] See Quinn, *Gilbert,* I, 62–4.

[2] *De navigatione...Humfredi Gilberti.* Ap. T. Purfutium, 1582.

[3] The unique copy in the John Carter Brown Library was brought to my attention by Dr Lawrence C. Wroth after my republication of Hakluyt's 1589 text in *Gilbert,* II, 351–64. It has no title-page, and apart from two ornamental initials and a conventional ornament it has nothing by which the printer might be identified. The collation is A⁴–B⁴.

[4] The British Museum copy (with ten preliminary poems) is printed in Quinn, *Gilbert,* II, 435–80, the New York Public Library one (with seven poems) in *Magazine of History,* XVII (1920), while the Britwell Library copy with ten had also 'A duplicate of the sheet containing the 4 leaves of commendatory poems,

and probable death had reached England. This, combining a highly academic approach with a frank request for subscriptions, probably appeared in December 1583 or January 1584, the object being to fit out an expedition before 20 March 1584. But this was not done.[1]

It is now known that there was also published 'A true discourse of the aduentures & travailes of David Ingram being sett on shore with 100 more of his fellowes by Captaine Hawkins in the heathen Countries in 8° 1583', so described in Humphrey Dyson's notebooks in All Souls College, Oxford;[2] no copy of this is now known to exist.[3] It was the first account of exploration of North America by an Englishman, even if the stories he tells are often too tall to be believed. In the autumn of 1582 he had answered various inquiries about his travels made by Gilbert and Sir Francis Walsingham, and it may be that his discourse was published during the calendar year 1583 as propaganda for Gilbert's voyage or for one of those directly connected with it. In the Sloane manuscript,[4] however, Ingram's relation is associated with a tract entitled 'Inducements to the lykinge of the voyadge intended to that parte of America which lyethe betwene 34. and 36. degree of Septentrionall Latytude'.[5] Gilbert's voyage and the plans of most of his associates were directed towards southern New England

but differently printed and omitting one poem' (Sotheby's *Catalogue*, 15–17 Aug. 1916, no. 248). Dr G. B. Parks ('George Peele and his friends as "ghost"-poets', in *Journ. of English and Germanic Philology*, XLI (1942), 527–36) argues that Sir George Peckham had a collaborator who wrote, amongst other things, the dedication and the poems, which is probable, but it appears to me more likely that this was George Peckham the younger rather than George Peele, Dr Parks's candidate.   [1] Cp. Quinn, *Gilbert*, I, 90–3.

[2] This entry was first published by Dr William A. Jackson, 'Humphrey Dyson's library, or, Some observations on the survival of books', *Papers of the Bibliographical Society of America*, XLIX (1949), 285.

[3] It was printed by Hakluyt in 1589 (cp. Quinn, *Gilbert*, I, 64–5, II, 283–96), but not reprinted in 1600.

[4] Brit. Mus., Sloane MS 1447, fos. 1–11, used for collation with Hakluyt in *Gilbert*, II, 283–96. The Bodleian Library copy, Tanner MS 79, fo. 172, was published in *Magazine of American History*, IX (1883), 200–8.

[5] Sloane MS 1447, fos. 12–15 v., first printed in P. C. G. Weston, *Documents connected with the history of South Carolina* (1856), pp. 20–4.

in higher latitudes. Professor Taylor sees in its language the expression of the views of both the elder and the younger Hakluyt, and regards it as part of the propaganda of 1584–5 for the 1585 Virginia venture.[1] It may here be suggested tentatively that the 'Inducements' may have been published along with Ingram's relation, bearing the date (English style) 1583, in February or March 1584 as propaganda for the first of Raleigh's Virginia ventures, that led by Amadas and Barlowe.

Thereafter, until 1586, publicity in print for the western ventures languished, 1586–7 sees some direct and indirect propaganda published, and finally between 1588 and 1590 the main bulk of our sources appeared, to be supplemented in certain respects in 1600. Why should this have been so? It may be suggested that the absence at the time of printed publicity for Raleigh's ventures of 1584, 1585 and 1586 was partly due to the ill success of printed matter such as has been noticed for the years 1582–3. It provided too ready a target for criticism: it gave too full and too specific details of what was proposed to be done in circumstances where so much in practice had to be left to improvization: it was not yet sufficiently authoritative. By the latter part of 1586 enough was known of North American conditions to justify more intelligent publicity, though even then it was used over a somewhat limited field. From 1588 to 1590 the dual motives of stirring up a flagging public to fresh enterprises, and getting the widest publicity for considerable achievements in exploration, if not in settlement, led to very substantial publication of results. Thereafter, the projects flagged. Hakluyt's republication of his earlier material in 1600, together with some additions, was partly due to his hope of reviving the American plantation movement for which economic and social conditions were becoming again more propitious.

Such a case is worth making, but it cannot stand in isolation. With it, though not contrary to it, runs an argument based on political conditions. When Gilbert was projecting his American

[1] Taylor, *Hakluyts*, I, 39. She says it can safely be attributed to the elder.

colonies between 1578 and 1583 there was little fear of Spanish intervention. Little was known of the Spanish colony in Florida. The main emphasis was on settlement somewhere well to the north of any possible Spanish centres. But during the preparations of 1582–3 it became clear that Spanish hostility might be a factor in wrecking English plans. It certainly played a part in preventing the scheme for enlisting the English Catholic gentry in the colonizing venture from coming to fruition. From the beginning of 1584 the cloud over Anglo-Spanish relations darkened with the expulsion of the Spanish envoy. The Spanish seizure of English shipping in Iberian ports in May 1585 brought a clear break, and began the openly-waged sea war in which English privateers were loosed against Spanish commerce. Drake's West Indian voyage represented a further intensification of the struggle, paralleled at home by the proceedings against Mary, Queen of Scots. By the autumn of 1586 the war, if not official, was quite open, and the Armada was well under way. Right through this phase, from 1584 to 1586, it was in the interests of English security to keep as quiet as possible about the North American plans of Raleigh and his associates. There is a substantial amount of evidence that the Roanoke voyages had as one of their aims the establishment of a strongly-fortified base on the shores of America at which privateers and other shipping operating against the Spanish Indies could assemble and refit, so as to keep up a continuous instead of an intermittent campaign in the west. It was thus essential that Spain should be prevented from finding out where this base was, what strength the English settlement could muster, and what arrangements were made for supplying it with reinforcements and stores. In any event, even if the establishment of a colony with the objective of exploiting local trade and natural resources had been the sole consideration, the Spaniards were, during this period, much more likely to intervene, or were thought more likely to do so, than they had been during the earlier phase. Thus Raleigh had to prepare the first three expeditions with a minimum of publicity which could be useful to the enemy. This is, in my opinion, the major reason why there was no printed publicity for the Roanoke ventures during the years 1584-6.

As a result of Grenville's expedition of 1585, however, it was realized that Roanoke Island and the unsatisfactory havens in the Carolina Banks could not serve adequately as such a base. It remained important to keep the site of the colony hidden from the Spaniards, but it was scarcely vital to attempt any longer to keep the colonizing project secret. Hakluyt, therefore, began in 1586 his campaign of assisting the enterprises by publishing or inspiring the publication of foreign texts about North America which usually had dedications containing some praise or propaganda for Raleigh's enterprise in sending out the expeditions. The first of these, Basanier's edition (1 March 1586) of Laudonnière's Florida narrative, with its dedication to Raleigh, gave little away; it had been carefully screened by Hakluyt. His edition of the Spanish text of Espejo's New Mexico expedition, followed by Basanier's French version, did not, he considered, need introductions. By 1587 he felt he could be more open. War with Spain was now in progress, and anything that could be said about English overseas enterprise was good propaganda against Spain abroad and might stimulate continuing interest in the colonies at home. Moreover, as from the beginning of 1587, Raleigh was making assignments to colonists and releasing himself from some of his direct responsibilities for the voyages. He therefore needed all the assistance that could be whipped up by publicity. Hakluyt's dedication (written in February) to the Latin edition of Peter Martyr's *Decades* was, therefore, more flamboyant, though it remained discreet about the precise location of the colonies. When he revised his dedication to the English translation in the autumn he felt still freer to express himself and would, indeed, have conveyed some general idea of the location of the settlement or settlements to a Spanish reader, while by this time too there had appeared in the second edition of Holinshed's *Chronicles* several brief factual accounts of the Virginia enterprises. Ortelius, moreover, added the name 'Wingandekoa' to a revised version of his North American map in

1587, but this, in view of its scale, was unlikely to help the Spaniards to locate the site of the colony.

By 1588 the need for reticence had almost passed. Drake's attack on the Spanish ports in 1587 had damaged the enemy's sea-power: the defeat of the Armada in 1588 had apparently crippled it. The Latin and French editions of the Bigges account of Drake's voyage of 1585–6, therefore, described clearly Drake's removal of the first colony from Roanoke Island in June 1586, though some specific detail was excluded until the English editions appeared in 1589, adding the general map (perhaps suppressed until then for security reasons) to a fuller text. Early in 1588 also, Thomas Hariot's *Briefe and true report* appeared in its first English version. Though it had no maps it contained a detailed picture of the economic resources of the area in which the English had been active, though perhaps one can still sense here and there some reluctance to be specific about places, which may probably be put down to its composition in 1587. Hakluyt had by then made great progress with his collections for the *Principall navigations* which was printing during 1589 and, perhaps, early in 1590. In that volume were almost all the major texts on the Virginia ventures of 1584–9, while at the same time Theodor de Bry was printing at Frankfort editions of Hariot in Latin, English, French and German, together with his notes to the engravings of White's drawings, and a map which was more detailed and more accurate than any that had yet appeared for any part of North America. The site and surroundings of Raleigh's Virginia were no longer a secret. What remained unknown was whether the 1587 colony had survived. The publications on the Virginia voyages down to the end of 1590 demonstrated fully to European readers the capacity of Englishmen to explore and to experiment with colonies in North America, while they gave so much practical and specific detail that little ambiguity was left about the general lines of English enterprise, and the belief was kept current that the 1587 settlers had survived. White's failure to find them in 1590 and the abandonment of the enterprise received no similar publicity, though Hakluyt in 1593 had the foresight to obtain from White an account of his last voyage. When he republished his collection he retained the bulk of the Virginia texts of 1589, added some incidental material which threw light on contiguous parts of North America, and rounded the story off with the new material from White, together with a plea for the resumption of the Virginia enterprises. *The principal navigations*, completed in their second edition in 1600, bring to an end the publication of material on the Roanoke ventures down to the nineteenth century.

In all this it is the younger Richard Hakluyt who is the great initiator, selecting for publication texts with a direct or indirect bearing on the Virginia enterprise, carrying through in them both broad and narrowly-based propaganda campaigns, and subjecting them to a detailed, scrupulous editing which is well illustrated in the collated texts which follow. It is to him that we owe the survival of practically everything we know of the voyages themselves. It is difficult to say to what extent he was aided or circumscribed in his choice of documents by Raleigh and, possibly, by Grenville. It is reasonably certain that he owed Arthur Barlowe's account of the 1584 expedition to Raleigh, as he did Lane's account of the 1585-6 colony. The journal of the 1585 voyage may have come from Grenville rather than Raleigh, while White's 1587 and 1588 journals are equally likely to have been given him by Raleigh or by their author, as was that of 1590. We cannot say exactly how Hakluyt pruned and trimmed his material for security purposes or to meet the desires of Raleigh or Grenville. We know that he consulted Raleigh about what he should print in the dedication to Peter Martyr in 1587, and there is also evident in all the material presented in the *Principall navigations* a desire to avoid overt or implied criticism of Raleigh, though the additional White material added in 1600 is not to the same degree inhibited. Moreover, the absence of certain documents, for example, any adequate account of the 1586 voyage or the major Hariot chronicle of the first three expeditions, may be the result of Raleigh withholding material for one reason or another.

As we survey the field in more detail it is possible to ask a series of questions which point to some degree of suppression within the documents printed by Hakluyt, though whether on his own initiative or at the insistence of Raleigh or Grenville we cannot tell. It is not, of course, always possible to say whether Hakluyt was suppressing evidence because it might still be of special value to Spain, to other foreign or to possible English competitors; or because he considered that it was undesirable to put too much discouragement in the way of later adventurers by stressing the unfavourable as well as the favourable aspects of the expeditions; or, finally, whether some of his presumed excisions were due merely to the desire to cut out detail which he did not consider significant, being unable to anticipate the hunger of subsequent investigators for business and biographical *minutiae*.

It is only now that we are beginning to get an inkling of what we have not hitherto been told about the Roanoke voyages. Materials to supplement the narratives in Hakluyt have been very scanty and they are still inadequate in many respects, but those from Spanish archives printed by Miss Wright and supplemented in these volumes do throw a substantial amount of new light on the ventures, even though they raise at least as many new problems as they solve. On the English side the main handicap is our lack of any of the large collections of private papers made by the main participants—Raleigh (one item only apart from what he gave Hakluyt), Hariot (a few scraps only, but nothing of the natural history and ethnological notes and collections he made or of his chronicle of the voyages from 1584 to 1587), Grenville (nothing of his own), White (no papers; a large and rather tangled collection of his drawings and of copies from them). Even Hakluyt has left us nothing of his own though it is possible that Purchas would have printed something additional from his papers if there had been anything there of outstanding interest. The group of Walsingham papers in the Public Record Office still forms the most valuable addendum to Hakluyt on the achievements of the 1585 expedition, but our knowledge of the business relations of

Raleigh, Walsingham, William Sanderson and Thomas Smythe is still quite inadequate. Although the memoranda which preceded the 1585 expedition have now been increased in number by one, we have still not a single manuscript set of instructions for any of the voyages, nor any log, journal or narrative which can be checked against Hakluyt's published versions. Yet with scraps from various sources, especially from the records of the High Court of Admiralty, it is possible at least to ask many additional questions, although, of course, any further accession of material, however small, is liable to upset the articulation of what we have already.

With all these qualifications it is perhaps worth while asking a number of questions. Did Hakluyt suppress the unpleasant features of the 1584 voyage so idyllically presented by Arthur Barlowe? Specifically, did the Indians kill and eat some of the sailors? Did the expedition leave two Englishmen behind and did the Indians kill them? Did Hakluyt refrain from any indication that Grenville intended to remain in America in 1585 because it would have meant a critical discussion of the failure to find an adequate harbour? Did he prune the *Tiger* journal of its later entries for this purpose, or was it because he hoped to obtain a fuller account of the expedition's proceedings between June and August 1585 from another source? Why did he omit reference to Raymond's marooning of men on Jamaica and Croatoan, and to Bernard Drake's squadron which was intended to follow Grenville's? Why is there so little reference, and that a one-sided one, to the divisions and quarrels inside the 1585 expedition? Did he omit a section in Lane's account of the 1585-6 colony, dealing with the Chesapeake Bay expedition, in view of Raleigh's desire to keep his precise plans for this region a secret? Did he know anything of Drake's plans, in so far as they involved clearing the Spaniards out of Florida and aiding the Roanoke settlement, before his departure in September 1585? Why did he not publish the agreement of January 1587 setting out the precise terms entered into between Raleigh and White over the City of Raleigh settlement? Did he suppress the real reasons for the White-Fernandez quarrels on the 1587 expedition and for the dumping of the colonists at Roanoke Island instead of bringing them on to Chesapeake Bay? What were the precise reasons for Hariot's suppression of information on certain natural products of North America? Why did Hakluyt not explain the agreement between White and the merchants in 1589 more fully, and why did he not give an account of their reasons for failing to provide aid in 1589? Why did he not check White's account of the circumstances of the setting out of the 1590 expedition? Is it not likely that Raleigh deliberately did nothing after 1590 to search for the 'lost colony' because its continued presumed existence after that date validated his continued use of his patent? Alternatively, was there anything in what the sailors on the 1590 expedition told the Spaniards about the intention to send out further expeditions so as to revive the 1584-6 project of using a North American base for further attacks on the Spanish Indies?

These are only a selection of the queries which will be found embedded in the notes to the following documents. They may well represent questions which Hakluyt did not feel inclined to ask, or to which he did not know the answers. To ask them here and to suggest that the necessity for asking some of them, at least, arises from suppressions by Hakluyt himself, does not oblige us to devalue the documents which he did preserve. They are in fact quite invaluable. It may indeed be argued that Hakluyt's policy was to let his informants tell their own stories and not always to intrude his own knowledge, even if he knew something which qualified the information they gave.

These general queries, however, pave the way for some more detailed examination of Hakluyt's activities as an editor. In his dealings with documents he was, in many respects, well in advance of his contemporaries. So far as he could conscientiously do so he respected the sanctity of the text he was given and tried to present it 'warts and all'. Yet he was not, of course, an editor with modern criteria. He did some things which would not now be considered desirable in an editor, making certain alterations in his texts without indicating that he had done so. There are few manuscripts extant for the texts which he printed and there has not, of course, ever been a critical edition of all his texts. Something can, however, be learnt of his editorial methods by a collation of the two editions of the *Principall navigations*, as is done in these volumes for a particular group of documents, where the 1589 text has been taken as basic. For only two of his documents have we other texts, the patent of 1584, and Hariot's *Briefe and true report*. A comparison with the patent as enrolled (and ignoring passages abbreviated in the enrolment) shows that there are seven instances where there are in Hakluyt changes of order, twenty-four alterations of words, sixteen omissions and eleven additions. Not all of the variations may be due to Hakluyt, some may be due to the transcriber of his copy, some to the vagaries of the clerk who made the enrolment, some to the printer. All are minor matters, though the alteration of 'alliance' into 'allegiance' involves a change of sense, and many are intended to make the formal legal language of the patent a little more readable. The conclusion here would appear to be that Hakluyt respected the sense of his text, but not its precise wording.

In comparing the 1588 Hariot with Hakluyt's versions it is necessary to proceed by two stages, first of all by a comparison with the 1589 text, then with that of 1600. Changes in the order of words can be ignored. Alterations of words are frequent, but they are designed mainly to improve the sense or the grammar; 'venemous' becomes 'venimous beasts'; 'vnknowen' is corrected to 'knowen', though 'Equieres' (correct) becomes 'Esquiers' (incorrect); 'violently' becomes 'vehemently'; 'thrise' becomes 'twise'. There are a few omissions. One is of a paragraph, another of 'in some sixtie' in a list, another of 'salt' in 'of salt waters'; but in 1589 there were no additions. If we carry the comparison on to the 1600 version we find further alterations. There are more changes of words to improve the sense: 'is' to 'are' several times; 'twoes' to 'two dayes'; 'that must' to 'of that which must', and some others of the same type. The changing of '1588' into '1587' is more serious, while there is an addition ('Monardes calls these roots Beads or Pater nostri of Santa Helena') without any indication that it is not in Hariot. If it were not for one other reference this might be taken as misleading evidence about Hariot's use of Monardes's *Joyfull newes*. In 1600 also there are a number of additional marginal notes, five of them containing information or comment of some significance.

It would be unnecessarily tedious to go through the results of the collation of the further eight documents which are contained in both editions of the *Principall navigations*, but the same editorial process is seen to be at work. There are frequent small alterations, a good deal of attention being paid to altering Indian place and personal names, presumably to fit them to the latest versions supplied by Hariot or White. There are occasional omissions, and some additions. Amongst the latter may be noted the addition of a final sentence to Barlowe's narrative of the 1584 expedition, recording the names of the Indians brought home by the explorers, and also the additions made to Lane's letter to the elder Hakluyt in 1585 regarding maize. There are, too, a substantial number of new marginal notes, some of considerable interest. We may then conclude that Hakluyt was a most conscientious editor, that his respect for his texts was great (even though he did not regard them as sacrosanct), and that his respect for his reader was rather greater. The edition of 1600 was not a mere reprint of that of 1589, but a careful revision with a very large number of small alterations the object of which was, in general, to improve the accuracy and readability of the narratives. Hakluyt clearly took down many of the texts which he published from illiterate men, or had to polish the crude versions of the semi-literate. In the documents on the Virginia voyages he was fortunate in having an eloquent Barlowe, an accurate Hariot and a common-sense White to follow. He may have had to doctor the journal of the 1585 voyage to make it read effectively, and it is highly likely that he had to 'improve' Lane, whose style as illustrated in his letters was decidedly shaggy. We could do with much more in the way of close study of Hakluyt's editorial methods, but this is not the place for it. Enough has been said to let the sample of Hakluyt's work collated in these volumes speak for itself.

THE 1584 VOYAGE

The documentation of the Amadas-Barlowe voyage of April-September 1584 remains unfortunately very meagre. Apart from the Chancery Warrant which brings Raleigh's association with the project back to March 16,[1] there are no new documents to add in this collection to those already known.[2] The earliest dateable references to the results of the voyage are the observations of a German traveller, Lupold von Wedel, on 18 October, and the bill for confirming Raleigh's title placed before Parliament in December following.[3] The first published notice appeared in the 1587 edition of Holinshed's *Chronicles*,[4] and this may have been by William Camden; it is of some slight independent value.

The main source still remains the discourse written by Arthur Barlowe and first published by Hakluyt in 1589.[5] This has many attractions of style and temper and well deserves its high reputation as one of the clearest contemporary pictures of the contact of Europeans with North American Indians. Its ethnological value is substantial,[6] but for the historian its omissions are exasperating. Of its author we know nothing, except that he is likely to have travelled in the Mediterranean and possibly in eastern Europe.[7] Its defects arise largely from the fact that we have no surviving journal of the expedition. Barlowe had clearly such a journal at his disposal but he omitted the details deliberately as 'unnecessarie'.[8] He is concerned with the results and not merely with the incidents of the voyage. In form the document is a 'briefe discourse' addressed to Raleigh as sponsor of the voyage.

[1] P. 82 below.
[2] Apart from the Spanish document printed by Miss Wright and discussed below, pp. 80–1.   [3] Pp. 116, 127 below.
[4] Document no. 3, pp. 90–1 below.   [5] Document no. 4, pp. 91–116 below.
[6] Cp. pp. 99–114 below.   [7] Cp. pp. 96–7 below.   [8] P. 92 below.

In fact, it would appear to be a carefully selective narrative designed to further the passage of the Raleigh bill through parliament in December and to serve as propaganda for the 1585 expedition during the months between December 1584 and February 1585. It puts on record the formal taking of possession of the land discovered but is studiously vague about its location, since it would at that time not suit Raleigh to be too specific about its whereabouts. It gave a glowing account of the natural resources of the land and a careful and perceptive narrative of dealings with the local Indians designed to show that subsequent expeditions would find a ready welcome and ample commerce.

Much of what Barlowe says about the structure of the Indian polity[1] is gained from men who have first-hand knowledge of it. Since there is no evidence that any member of the expedition could speak the southern Algonquian tongues the informants must have been the two Indians, Manteo and Wanchese, brought from the Carolina Banks. As they learnt English, or taught the Englishmen their own language, so gradually a body of information was built up which Barlowe incorporated in his discourse. This cannot have happened as soon as the expedition returned in mid-September as it is unlikely that sufficient linguistic progress would by then have been made. The suggestion is made elsewhere[2] that Thomas Hariot was probably given the task of interrogating these Indians and, at the same time, teaching them English and learning some Algonquian. There is evidence that the Indians were used as propagandists for the 1585 enterprise, and this as early as December 1584.[3] It is unlikely that Barlowe's discourse is earlier, and it is highly probable that it was circulated in manuscript—or even possibly printed[4]—about this time as part

---

[1] Pp. 110–14 below in particular.   [2] Pp. 37, 119, 368 below.
[3] Pp. 127, 232 below.
[4] There is no evidence for this, but the fact that Ingram's account (p. 4 above) was published has only recently been discovered from an incidental reference: the same may possibly be true of Barlowe's. Certainly its form and content would indicate quite clearly to the present editor that it was intended for propaganda purposes.

of a concerted campaign to whip up support for the second expedition. If this opinion is justified it might be possible to go a little further and to suggest that the discourse was possibly polished by Hariot himself, although many passages in it were clearly the result of direct personal experience. The text which Hakluyt incorporated in his 1589 edition was probably acquired directly from Raleigh but it was an unrevised one. Before reprinting it in 1600 Hakluyt had it carefully revised so that the nomenclature accorded with that established by the colonists of 1585-6. Again the hand of Hariot may possibly be seen, though White or Lane could have given Hakluyt the requisite advice or he may even have derived the alterations from White's maps.

The necessary evidence has not yet been found to prove that Barlowe's narrative suppressed unfavourable incidents of the voyage, but a story told by an English member of the 1585 expedition would indicate that the expedition had made a landing prior to that noted by Barlowe, that it was met with hostility by the Indians, who killed some of its members, and that the ships sailed on to find a more auspicious welcome elsewhere. This was expressed in ambiguous language in Spanish, after an interrogation in which there had been some language difficulties, and in circumstances in which the Englishmen may have given a garbled tale.[1] At the same time it does suggest that Barlowe did not tell the whole story, and it emphasizes our need for a more objective narrative, which we are not at all likely to be able to find.

PREPARATIONS FOR THE 1585 EXPEDITION

On the preparation of the most famous of the expeditions sent by Raleigh to North America, that of 1585, the materials vary very much in adequacy. We have substantial works by both Richard Hakluyts, which are deservedly famous, on the more general considerations involved in colonial settlement, and there is a new document, more limited in scope and in value, to add to them.

---

[1] Wright, *Further English voyages*, pp. 174-6; cp. pp. 80-1 below.

But on the planning of propaganda, the raising of money and of volunteers, the organization of personnel, shipping and supplies, and the detailed programme with which the Grenville expedition embarked, we are still left with a collection of pieces, which together take the story somewhat further than before, but which are still sadly incomplete.[1]

The younger Richard Hakluyt's 'A particular discourse concerninge the great necessitie and manifolde comodyties that are like to growe to this Realme of Englande by the Westerne discoueries latcly attempted, Written in the yere 1584. by Richarde Hackluyt of Oxforde at the requeste and direction of the righte worshipfull *Master* Walter Raghley nowe knight, before the commynge home of his Twoo Barkes', best known as *The discourse of western planting*, survives in a manuscript in the New York Public Library,[2] formerly Phillipps MS 14097, the descent of which has not yet been traced back beyond Sir Peter Thomson (d. 1770). As the title contains a reference to Raleigh being knighted, it was written not earlier than January 1585.[3] It has one passage probably inserted after the return of Amadas and Barlowe in mid-September 1584,[4] while the twenty-first chapter, 'A note of some thinges to be prepared for the voyadge'[5] may well also have been a subsequent addition. This strongly suggests that here is a copy of 'the first excription' brought in May 1585 to Walsingham by Hakluyt,[6] who also sent over a list of chapter headings to another gentleman, promising him a full copy later.[7] The significance of this latter information is that this document was not used for public propaganda for the expedition, though it was possibly employed privately in some way by Raleigh who

---

[1] A preliminary survey of them was given in D. B. Quinn, 'Preparations for the 1585 Virginia voyage', in *William and Mary Quarterly*, 3rd ser., VI (1949), 208–36.

[2] First printed in Charles Deane, *Documentary history of the state of Maine*, II (1877), new edition in Taylor, *Hakluyts*, II, 211–326.

[3] Cp. p. 145 below.   [4] Taylor, *Hakluyts*, II, 279.

[5] Ibid. II, 320–6.

[6] Ibid. II, 344, 346; Parks, *Hakluyt*, p. 248.

[7] Taylor, *Hakluyts*, II, 346.

is likely to have kept a draft. Hakluyt wrote it, in its unmodified
form, as it is now agreed,[1] between July and September 1584, in
order to present to the queen as full a statement as possible of
Raleigh's case that North American colonization ought to be an
affair for the English state and not be left to chartered private
enterprise alone. Unfortunately this manuscript is not now extant
in the royal collections.

'Inducements to the liking of the voyage intended towards
Virginia in 40. and 42. degree of latitude, written 1585. by M*aster*
Richard Hakluyt the elder', extant only in the published version
of 1602,[2] are more simply and directly aimed at publicity.
Covering the arguments of the younger Hakluyt with some
variations of emphasis, they were suited to circulation, and may
have been used in manuscript, or even printed, form to encourage
subscribers and volunteers. A third tract[3] with a very similar
title, which is associated in Sloane MS 1447 with David Ingram's
'Relation', is discussed above. If it was not published in 1584 it
may well have been used for propaganda for the 1585 venture.

The new document, published below,[4] which belongs with the
others of this group is a set of notes headed 'For m*aster* Rauleys
Viage' and endorsed 'Notes geuen to M*aster* Candishe'. The association of Thomas Cavendish with Raleigh places it as belonging
to the 1584–5 preparations while the absence of any recognition
of Raleigh's knighthood suggests, though it does not prove, that
it is not later than early January 1585. The paper contains advice
on what military forces should be taken, the kind of fort which
should be built, the choice and duties of officers and specialists,
and the outlines on which a code of laws should be based. It is
a draft, which may have been elaborated somewhat before it was
passed on to Cavendish and Raleigh. Now in the Essex County
Record Office, it comes from the papers of John Horace Round

[1] Taylor, *Hakluyts*, I, 34; II, 343–4; Parks, *Hakluyt*, pp. 87, 248.
[2] In John Brereton, *A briefe and true relation* (1602); reprinted Taylor, *Hakluyts*,
II, 327–38.
[3] Ibid., II, 339–43; P. C. G. Weston, *Documents connected with the history of
South Carolina* (1856), pp. 20–4.   [4] Document no. 8, pp. 130–9 below.

the historian, who lived at Colchester. Since it was evidently written by a professional soldier and probably one of some seniority, a possible author for it is Sir John Smythe (1534–1607), whose home was at Baddow in Essex and whose papers might have come into Round's possession. In the same file are a number of drafts relating to matters in the Low Countries, particularly the draft of a letter to Leicester of about October 1586, which may well be in the same hand, and which shows the author to have been a strong partizan of Leicester in his quarrels with the Dutch. This, in turn, links up with an endorsement, signed by John Smythe, apparently Sir John, which indicates a similar alignment of views.[1] Sir John was a military writer whose *Certain discourses ...concerning the formes and effects of divers sorts of weapons* (1590), and *Instructions, observations, and orders mylitarie* (1595) provide many parallel passages to suggestions in the 'Notes'. One or two of these are particularly suggestive as to authorship,[2] as is the high proportion of bowmen included in the list of soldiers,[3] since Smythe was a passionate advocate of archery. Of the possible authors so far investigated Smythe is the most likely, though this is far from saying that his authorship is proved.

Another candidate is Sir Roger Williams (1540?–1595).[4] There are again passages in his *A briefe discourse of warre* (1590) which very closely parallel certain passages in the notes, particularly those regarding fortification. He was, however, anxious to minimize the use of the bow, though perhaps not for American ventures. He was available about the appropriate time, leaving for the Low Countries during 1585. However, the 'Notes' are written in a fairly good hand, though, being hasty and unpolished, some words are difficult to read. Williams speaks in one place of

[1] 'An act of the states generall derogating from the aucthoritie of his Ex-cellencie / Io. smythe', 30 January 1586–7 (P.R.O., State Papers, Foreign, Holland and Flanders, S.P. 84/12, 57 (c)).

[2] Cp. pp. 130–1.

[3] 150 out of 800.

[4] He was first suggested as a possible author by Mr Irvine Gray, formerly of the Essex County Record Office.

'my foule hand'[1] and he usually employed an amanuensis for his letters.[2]

He may, of course, have been neither of these men. Both advocated the use of large companies of soldiers, for example, whereas in the 'Notes' a large number of small companies is suggested.[3] Again this may have been an adaptation to American conditions. Captain Humphrey Barwick, who, in his *A briefe discourse concerning the force and effect of all manuall weapons of fire* (*c.* 1591), criticized both Smythe and Williams, declaring that the size of companies should be governed by circumstances,[4] but this alone does not admit him to serious consideration as a possible author of the 'Notes'.

Thomas Digges can also be included as a possible author of the 'Notes'. Associated with John Dee over many years, involved with Grenville in the Terra Australis project in the 'seventies, and knight of the shire (with Sir George Carey) for Hampshire in the 1584 parliament, he was well placed to give advice on the formation of the first North American colony. He had finished and published in 1579 a treatise begun by his father Leonard, *An arithmeticall militare treatise, named Stratioticos*, which covered a number of the military topics touched on in the 'Notes', although his main interests were in navigation and surveying. He was, moreover, involved in Leicester's venture in the Netherlands at a later stage.[5] However, neither his italic[6] nor his secretary hand[7] has any similarity to that of the 'Notes' and his style is much smoother and more polished. At the present stage of our knowledge these considerations do not rule him out, but they place him

---

[1] *A briefe discourse of warre*, p. 61.

[2] E.g. his letter to Walsingham, 4 September 1584, asking for employment and suggesting an Anglo-Dutch expedition to the West Indies (*Cal. S.P., Foreign, 1584–5*, pp. 50–1).

[3] Cp. p. 32 below.   [4] Idem.

[5] Cp. *DNB*; Rowse, *Grenville*, p. 95; Taylor, *Tudor geography, 1485–1583*, pp. 42, 91, 97, 104, 124, 152, 154, 263.

[6] E.g. Brit. Mus., Lansdowne MS 37, fo. 153 (1583).

[7] E.g. Brit. Mus., Lansdowne MSS 19, no. 30 (1574); 72, no. 63 (1592); 73, no. 6 (1593).

lower on the list of possible authors than his contacts with the organizers of the 1585 expedition would otherwise indicate.

The interest of the document is mainly that it emphasizes the military considerations which lay at the back of the 1585 expedition. There is little doubt that a primary consideration in the plans of Raleigh and Grenville was the creation of a strong military base at a reasonable distance from Spanish Florida, but capable of protecting vessels assembling for raids on the Indies and refitting after their return.[1] The consultation of a military expert by Cavendish on Raleigh's behalf, of which the 'Notes' are evidence, did bear fruit both in the composition of the expedition and in the actions of its members in America, even though the precise prescriptions of the author were not followed in every case.

The remaining sources are miscellaneous in character. They illustrate the proceedings in parliament during the abortive attempt to have Raleigh's acquisition of the new American territories confirmed by a private act.[2] Following that, there is a draft commission for granting him authority to levy men and shipping,[3] and another for the supply of powder from the Tower for his expedition,[4] as well as one for authority to release Ralph Lane from service in Ireland to take part in the voyage.[5] The queen's permission to use the name of 'Virginia' for the new territories is illustrated by Raleigh's seal as Lord and Governor of Virginia.[6] There are glimpses of volunteers coming forward for the venture,[7] and, more significant, of the seizure of foreign shipping and the impressment of foreign seamen.[8] In Cornwall, Sir Richard Grenville is seen making preparations to lead the expedition

[1] Cp. pp. 173–4, 200, 721 below.
[2] Document no. 6, pp. 122–6 below.
[3] Document no. 10, pp. 144–5 below. Signet letters for the implementing of what was probably a subsequent, but similar, commission were issued on June 10 following (Document no. 20, p. 156–7) in connection with the Newfoundland venture (cp. pp. 234–52).
[4] Document no. 13, p. 148 below.   [5] Document no. 14, pp. 149–50 below.
[6] P. 147 below.
[7] Documents nos. 11 and 12, p. 146 below.
[8] Documents nos. 16 and 17, pp. 151–5 below.

Preparations for the 1585 Expedition

to America,[1] while an incident in the Thames which led to litigation in the High Court of Admiralty throws some light on the preparations which were taking place in the river and on the personality of Captain Philip Amadas.[2] Richard Hakluyt is seen keeping a close watch over the expedition from Paris,[3] while the Spaniards attempt to obtain information there about English preparations.[4] Not all the documents are entirely self-explanatory and some readers may wish to doubt the evidence which links them with the expedition, but in each case the strength and weakness of that evidence is set out in the notes.[5] With what can be gathered, we are still without adequate evidence of how the expedition was financed,[6] of precisely what the queen's adventure was,[7] and how the shipping was collected at London, possibly Bideford, and finally Plymouth for the voyage.[8] Lacking any sailing directions or any general statement of objectives to be achieved, we are left to fill them in from what is known of events on the voyage. Drafts of Raleigh's instructions would, if they were found, clear up many problems.

THE 1585 VOYAGE

The main authority for the 1585 voyage is the journal printed by Hakluyt.[9] It is by an anonymous member of the *Tiger's* company and, for convenience, is referred to subsequently as the '*Tiger* journal'. No evidence survives to indicate who its author was,[10] nor any information about him except that he was a member of the pro-Grenville and anti-Fernandez faction, and that he sailed back to England with the *Tiger*. It is clearly based on a more detailed journal of the expedition, the official one kept on the

---

[1] P. 151 below.
[2] Document no. 9, pp. 139–44 below. [3] Document no. 18, p. 155 below.
[4] Cp. pp. 155–6 below. [5] Cp. pp. 146, 153–5 below.
[6] Cp. pp. 220–6 below. [7] Cp. pp. 148, 178–9, 237 below.
[8] Pp. 139–44, 151, 173, 178, 728–30.
[9] Document no. 23, pp. 178–93 below.
[10] The suggestion that he may possibly have been Arthur Barlowe (p. 175, n. 2) is not made with any confidence.

ship, but the selection of information it contains clearly represents, on the positive side, the interests of the compiler, and, on the negative side, his desire, or that of Raleigh, Grenville, or Hakluyt, to suppress a certain amount of information which it was not desired should be widely known. It is highly probable that, approximately in its present form, it was prepared for Raleigh with the intention of giving him a fairly full picture of happenings in the West Indies, with an outline of other events, shortly after the return of the expedition. It is likely to have been trimmed by or for him shortly afterwards, perhaps with the object of publishing it as publicity for the venture. When and in what circumstances it was turned over to Hakluyt is not known.

While it provides a list of ships, mention of the principal persons in the company is perfunctory, and no clear indication is given of who sailed in which vessel. Nothing is said directly of the circumstances in which the vessels parted company off Portugal, or of what were the arrangements for a rendezvous off the Puerto Rico coast. A fair amount of detail is given of the actions of the *Tiger's* company on Puerto Rico between 11 and 23 May, but again little explanation. We lack precise information on why such elaborate defences were considered necessary. Was it because a holding party was intended to maintain it until Drake's force should have arrived in the West Indies? Or was it merely because, in the interval since 1584, the Spaniards were found to have installed a garrison in nearby San German?[1] No mention is made of the name of Cavendish's ship which joined them on the 19th, nor of the affixing of a message—which the Spaniards removed—giving a note of their arrival and departure.[2] The story from 23 to 29 May, when the ships remained off the south-western end of Puerto Rico, is not told clearly.[3] Possibly it was Hakluyt who suppressed the details about their trade with the Spaniards, including their offer to sell back one of their prizes. Nor is anything said about the quarrel between Lane and Grenville which

[1] Cp. pp. 181, 734, 740 below.   [2] P. 183 below.
[3] Compare the English and Spanish evidence, pp. 183–5, 733–43 below.

arose from the sending of Lane with one of the prizes to take off salt from Cape Rojo.[1] The visit to the north coast of Hispaniola is described with some colourful detail, but no explanation is given of the Englishmen's contacts there which enabled them to trade on such a friendly footing. After leaving there, a Portuguese, not named, is charged with having misled them about salt-ponds on one of the Caicos Islands. There seems little doubt that this was Simon Fernandez, the master and chief pilot, who was Lane's protégé.[2] He is again blamed, this time by name, for the grounding of the *Tiger* at the inlet of Wococon after the ships—the two English vessels, the new pinnace and two prizes—had arrived at the Carolina Banks. From this point onwards the journal gives only a perfunctory record of events. Elsewhere we learn that Grenville met there other vessels from which he had parted in European waters, but we are told that one (the *Lion*) had landed thirty-two men some three weeks before his own arrival and had then departed, while the name of the captain of the fly-boat, presumably the *Roebuck*, appears in a list a little later.[3] No clarity about these arrangements can be obtained. Rather more detail is given about Grenville's expedition to Secotan between 11 and 18 July, which fits in with the sketch-map now identified as showing some of the results of the exploration down to September.[4] It is not explained why Roanoke Island was chosen as a site for the fort or why Grenville did not stay himself, nor is it made clear what vessels remained behind at the *Tiger's* departure on 25 August.[5] Only the outlines of the chase and capture of the *Santa Maria* are given with the dates of the return of the *Tiger* and her prize.[6]

A second account of the expedition was contributed by Abraham Fleming to the second edition of Holinshed's *Chronicles* and published in 1587.[7] He may have had a narrative by Grenville

[1] Pp. 184–5, 228–9 below.   [2] Cp. p. 188 below.
[3] Cp. pp. 198–9 below.
[4] Document no. 30, pp. 215–17 below.   [5] Cp. pp. 192, 210–11 below.
[6] Pp. 192–3 below; Wright, *Further English voyages*, pp. 12–15.
[7] Document no. 22, pp. 173–8 below.

himself before him. If so he was rather careless about dates. Otherwise a more coherent story is given—though with less detail—than is provided by the *Tiger* journal. It is this account which supplies, for example, the information that Grenville was to decide, in the light of what he found there, whether to remain himself in America or to return, and the fact that his other vessels were found awaiting him on his arrival at the Carolina Banks. It does not, unfortunately, give additional information on the arrangements made for the conduct of Lane's colony, but little was said on this subject because it was probably thought unwise to publish at this time too specific details about its location and purpose.

What neither narrative discloses is that a second squadron was preparing to follow Grenville, but, in June, was diverted to Newfoundland. The documents from the High Court of Admiralty records which link Bernard Drake's Newfoundland voyage integrally with the Virginia venture are of considerable interest.[1]

For the West Indies part of the expedition there is now available a fair amount of Spanish official correspondence[2] which fills out the *Tiger* journal quite adequately as regards the visits to Puerto Rico and Hispaniola. There is also a report of the interrogation of an English prisoner at Jamaica which raises a number of problems.[3]

John White's drawings of plants, fish and animals which he made in the West Indies, together with his plans of the camps on Puerto Rico, form a valuable supplement to the written evidence for this part of the expedition.[4]

In the Public Record Office there is another valuable group of material, three letters from America by Lane to Sir Francis

[1] Document no. 44, pp. 234–42 below.

[2] Pp. 733–43, 747 below; Wright, *Further English voyages*, pp. 7–16.

[3] Ibid., pp. 174–6; cp. pp. 164–5 below.

[4] Document no. 55, pp. 403–9 below. The descriptions of the picture plans, in particular, fit in with the narrative evidence, while the evidence of the flora and fauna drawn by White is of much incidental significance on the activities of the voyagers.

The 1585 Voyage

Walsingham, and one to Sir Philip Sidney, Walsingham's son-in-law,[1] to which can now be added a sketch-map,[2] formerly misdated, which shows roughly what had been discovered by Grenville and the intending settlers down to early September 1585. These five items are all of the greatest interest since they represent original correspondence from the first English settlement in North America. Lane's letters have all the rough authenticity of the pioneer's hand. The map is crude but effective. Our only regret must be that Lane spent so much of his space in polemic against Grenville and comparatively so little in description of the new land where he was to bear so much responsibility. Yet, merely as sources of information, much can be gleaned from these items. With them belongs a letter to Walsingham from Sir Richard Grenville after his return.[3] This is clearly a group of Walsingham papers kept together by him either because of their intrinsic interest, or on account of the evidence they contained of dissensions on the voyage which he may well have investigated. The depositions made by Lane and his friends and sent to Walsingham[4] might have been expected to appear in this same group, but they have disappeared, although it is not impossible that they may yet be found. Lane's letter to Queen Elizabeth[5] is likewise lost, but Hakluyt preserved one to his elder cousin,[6] and also the valuable list of settlers[7] which he is almost certain to have had from Raleigh. One additional contribution by Lane[8] appears in a later treatise written by him.

The remaining materials are miscellaneous in character. News about the prize;[9] an incidental letter about the distribution of

---

[1] Documents nos. 25–7, 29, pp. 197–206, 210–14 below.
[2] Document no. 30, pp. 215–17 below.
[3] Document no. 34, pp. 218–21 below.
[4] See pp. 212, 214 below.
[5] It is referred to in Document no. 36, pp. 222–3; and Document no. 60, p. 474, is a brief summary of the queen's reply.
[6] Document no. 28, pp. 207–10 below.
[7] Document no. 24, pp. 194–7 below.
[8] Document no. 42 (a), pp. 228–9 below.
[9] Documents nos. 33, 35, 37, pp. 218, 221–2 below.

27

some of the spoil;[1] a remark that Grenville and Raleigh should not be allowed to retain such a treasure, combined with a fresh suggestion that Elizabeth should take over the responsibility for colonizing the American shore;[2] together with a recollection, not perhaps precisely true, that the queen seized the bulk of the spoil[3] —these make up the bulk of the additional documents. With them are indications of a French pilot being on the voyage;[4] some details[5] about a Danish member of the expedition, Martin Laurentson, who went to learn about maritime warfare and returned to beg his fare home; and, finally, evidence[6] about the circumstances in which the cape merchant of the expedition, Thomas Harvey, came to invest in the venture and to remain in the colony. To them we can add the story of one of the colonists, Darby Glande (or Glavin), told long afterwards to the Spaniards.[7]

What we lack most are a set of instructions for Grenville,[8] an estimate of the strategic and commercial results of the expedition, and an assessment of precisely what the voyage did to encourage or discourage Raleigh and his backers.[9] For example, was Walsingham's apparent withdrawal from the scheme brought about by lack of confidence in its ultimate results, or by the hostility which the members of his household who accompanied Grenville developed towards their commander?[10]

[1] Document no. 39, p. 224–5 below.
[2] Document no. 40, pp. 225–6 below.
[3] Document no. 42 (*e*), pp. 230–1 below.
[4] Document no. 42 (*b*), p. 229 below.
[5] Document no. 41, pp. 226–8 below.
[6] Document no. 43, pp. 232–4 below.
[7] Document no. 158, pp. 834–8 below.   [8] Cp. pp. 51–4 below.
[9] My own opinion is that Raleigh was somewhat disappointed by the failure to find a suitable harbour on which Indies raiders could be based, and was not unduly excited about the specimens and news which Grenville brought of his Virginia, but that he maintained a modest confidence in the project. So far as his associates are concerned they are certain to have made a profit (cp. p. 220), and most of them are likely to have subscribed once more towards the 1586 ventures.
[10] Cp. pp. 197–8, 210–14 below.

For the events of 1585-6 after the departure of the *Roebuck* in September our main, practically our only, source is Lane's account.[1] Written soon after his return to England at the end of July 1586, it is likely to have been somewhat reshaped in detail by Hakluyt or another before it appeared in print in 1589. Lane was an untidy writer and thinker, while the account, though providing some difficulties of interpretation, is in general lucidly expressed. The polishing, however, may not have interfered substantially or at all with its contents. Like Barlowe's before, it was written for Raleigh, though whether for his private consideration or in a form which could be handed round as publicity for further enterprises is not so clear. One thing, however, is certain. It was Lane's apologia for returning when he did, and for his actions during his residence on Roanoke Island. In both respects it carries a reasonable degree of conviction. Lane is, one feels, being honest, even if, in some respects, mistaken. It must be remembered too that many of his men, at the time it was being written,[2] were busily running down Raleigh's Virginia and no doubt also the leadership of the governor.

These circumstances explain what Lane's account is and what it is not. It is not a chronicle of events based closely on journals kept on the spot; some of these had been lost.[3] Hariot was, at the time Lane was writing, composing a history of the voyages since 1584 and doing so, no doubt, with considerable attention to chronology.[4] Indeed, Lane assumes in Raleigh so much knowledge of events in the colony that he may have known—or believed—that he already had a journal to hand. Lane is attempting four things: first, to give an account of the layout of the Indian tribes and villages, which he does very perfunctorily,[5] secondly, to state what were the prospects arising out of his visits to the Chowan and Roanoke Rivers,[6] thirdly, to demonstrate the circum-

---

[1] Document no. 45, pp. 255-94 below.   [2] Cp. pp. 232-4, 320-4 below.
[3] P. 293 below.   [4] P. 387 below.
[5] Pp. 256-9 below.   [6] Pp. 259-75 below.

stances of his final breach with the Roanoke Indians,[1] and, finally, to give a clear idea of why he left with Drake on 18 June.[2] In the course of the second he is led into a narrative of his explorations on the Roanoke River, but his main aim is to point towards the possibilities of a deep-water settlement, evidently on Chesapeake Bay. His elaboration of a plan to reach there overland and his failure to discuss the sea approach adequately, even though he clearly hoped to be able to make one, showed that he retained a very imperfect conception of the topography of the country north of that which he actually visited; this again argues an incomplete understanding of what information had been brought back by the Chesapeake Bay exploring party, to which he pays no adequate attention and for which we are largely dependent on John White's maps.[3] His next main point in this section is that it was reasonable for him to attempt to ascend the Roanoke River since there appeared a good prospect of reaching larger sources of gold or copper in its upper reaches. He is able to show adequate reasons for his failure to carry through his exploration.[4] In the course of these explanations he leaves the chronology in several places in some confusion, and he assumes a knowledge of events which Raleigh may well have had but which we do not possess. It has, however, proved possible to make some sense out of his references. His account of the final clash with Wingina-Pemisapan likewise lacks background. We are not given sufficient information on the relations between the Roanoke Indians and the settlers to be able to estimate judicially to what degree the latter were at fault.[5] Lane's narrative of the plot and counter-plot which led to Pemisapan's death is, however, a well-told and exciting story. Finally, he ends with a full account of his taking off by Drake. He shows that he was prepared to stay and that Drake was ready to make it possible for him to stay until at least his investigation of a deep-water harbour on Chesapeake Bay had been completed.

[1] Pp. 275–88 below.   [2] Pp. 288–94 below.
[3] See pp. 460–2, 854–6 below.   [4] Cp. pp. 266–75 below.
[5] Pp. 248–9, cp. pp. 259, 264–6, 276.

The storm which scattered the fleet, he convinces us, made a further stay impossible, unless they were to depend on what may have seemed the forlorn hope of supplies from home.[1] Had Lane been a shade tougher and hung on with a small party of his best men it would have paid very high dividends,[2] but he could not know that, and it must be admitted that he makes his case.

Owing to the limitations of Lane's account we have no full story of the colony and to some extent it has, therefore, to be supplemented by more or less informed speculation. John White's pictures, however, and his maps even more, do enable us to fill out the story,[3] while Hariot's tract is not only a record of a remarkable piece of investigation but also contains, here and there, valuable information on happenings during the course of the year.[4] Darby Glande's story,[5] told long after, in 1600, gives a few useful sidelights, but also a certain amount of cloudy misinformation. Our greatest lack, which we feel the more as we are told it once existed, is Hariot's chronicle of the events of 1584–7. As his own reference to it is the only surviving record of its existence, speculation about the causes of its disappearance does not take us very far. The simplest explanation is that it went to Raleigh and was lost in the wreck of all but one of his Virginia papers.[6] Why, however, it was not shown to Hakluyt—as I am convinced it was not—and why Hariot failed to publish it, or, perhaps, to get Raleigh's permission to do so, remains very much of a mystery. It is very often unwise to assert that a manuscript is irretrievably lost, but it is difficult to imagine where such a document could still lie buried, without a single reference being made to it for nearly 400 years, and considering the great interest there has been in its field and subject.

[1] The sources for Drake's visit (Documents nos. 46–49, pp. 294–312 below) do not reveal any significant discrepancies from Lane's account and, in general, support it, though his remains the fullest.

[2] Cp. pp. 465–9 below.   [3] Pp. 413–62 below.

[4] Note especially incidents on pp. 331–4, 377–9 below.

[5] Document no. 158, pp. 834–8 below.

[6] P. 387 and document no. 54, p. 389 below.

The Roanoke Voyages

DRAKE AND THE ROANOKE COLONY

Sir Francis Drake's West Indian voyage of 1585–6 has now been lavishly and effectively documented from Spanish sources by Miss Wright,[1] so that its significance as one of the major Elizabethan ventures and a prelude to the Armada emerges much more clearly than hitherto. Its full evaluation does not, however, lie to be made here. There are two questions which we may expect our sources to answer. First, how far was Drake committed to visit and assist the colonists before he left England and to what extent, during his Caribbean adventures, did he prepare to do so? And second, what precisely did he do when he eventually found Lane's men on the Carolina Banks in June 1586? It must be admitted that we do not know how far the two ventures were co-ordinated in detail and it would be most valuable if any further material turned up which could settle this point, but there is no doubt that the gradual accumulation of material tends to show that there was some over-all co-ordination between what Francis Drake planned for the Indies, Raleigh and Grenville for Virginia, and Bernard Drake for Virginia and Newfoundland, and that it was this which pushed the Spaniards from what would now be called a policy of containment into one of 'liberation' or aggression.[2] However, Miss Wright's documents do bring out the fascinating story of how, when Drake abandoned his plans for the crossing of the Isthmus, he kept his negroes and Indians for the stocking of the Virginia colony and busily collected at San Agustín all kinds of equipment which might conceivably be useful to the settlers. Unfortunately, our evidence does not go so far as to explain what he did with this material, human and other, when Lane decided to abandon the settlement;[3] English narratives confine themselves to some account of the taking off of Lane's men.

[1] Wright, *Further English voyages*, pp. 16–174, 176–228.
[2] Cp. D. B. Quinn, 'Some Spanish reactions to Elizabethan colonial enterprises', in *Trans. R. Hist. S.*, 5th ser., I, 8–13; pp. 249–50 below.
[3] Cp. pp. 251–5 below.

Drake and the Roanoke Colony

No evidence has yet appeared to explain fully why the narrative by Walter Bigges,[1] finished by Lieutenant Crofts and possibly Walter Cates, should have appeared at Leyden in 1588, first in a Latin dress as *Expeditio Francisci Draki* and then in French, before it was published in England. The two issues in 1589 by Richard Field are generally taken to be the first appearances of *A summarie and true discourse of Sir Francis Drakes West Indian voyage* in English, but a note to Roger Ward's edition of the same year suggests that it was this edition which first began printing some time before July 1588 and was delayed through accident, being apparently in the meantime forestalled by Field. The desire to publish any available narratives on Drake's successes against the Spaniards, whether in England or on the continent, following his 1587 attack on Spain and at a time when the sailing of the Armada was imminent, is obviously understandable.

What is most interesting for our purpose is that the 1588 publications gave only a brief summary of the removal of the Virginia colonists. Perhaps this was because those who prepared the Latin edition considered the episode one of minor importance, unlikely to interest Dutch and French readers, or it may have been because it was thought to give the Spaniards too precise details about the location and circumstances of the English settlement. By 1589 it could be argued that, once the Armada had been defeated, the chances of publicity injuring the English settlement in North America were much reduced.[2] At the same time, the detail published in the English versions was not too specific, apart from the situation of Roanoke Island.[3] The French manuscript account of Drake's voyage[4] is evidently closely associated with the *Expeditio*, even though it has some independent value, but it also regarded the Virginia episode as worthy of only very brief treatment.

---

[1] See Document no. 46, pp. 294–303 below. The bibliographical detail is outlined on p. 294.

[2] Cp. pp. 5–8 above.   [3] Pp. 301–3 below.

[4] See Document no. 48, pp. 309–11 below.

More interesting are the map and plans associated with the *Expeditio*.[1] They comprise four town plans illustrating Drake's attacks—Santiago, Cape Verde Islands; Santo Domingo; Cartagena; and San Agustín—and a map.[2] The plans were prepared with Latin inscriptions and appeared in the Leyden editions and subsequently in those of Field and Ward, published in London. The map shows Drake's outward and homeward course, including his call at Virginia, though in doing so it does not add anything to our information. Bearing an inscription in English, it was clearly intended to be used as a separate publication since letterpress was printed, to be attached to it, giving a brief summary of the voyage, including mention of the call at Virginia. It is probable, however, that it was also included with the plans in one or more of the English editions.[3] Like the plans, it was compiled by Baptista Boazio,[4] but it is not known if he was the artist who accompanied Drake and who drew them. The composition of all five is closely associated with the Virginia visit, however, since the *fauna* which adorn them have the closest links with some of John White's drawings.[5] From this we might well conclude that White and the artist travelled together from Virginia to England and collaborated in their preparation of the map and plans on the voyage or subsequently. The alternative explanation

[1] See pp. 294, 311 below.

[2] They are, conveniently, reproduced in Miss Wright's *Further English voyages*.

[3] Dr Lawrence C. Wroth and Mr J. C. Wheat do not think this likely, cp. pp. 311–12 below and Wright, *Further English voyages*, p. xiii. In view of the close association of all five with Boazio—and with John White—it would appear somewhat surprising if at some point it was not intended to use them together in a single publication. It might tentatively be suggested that the map was not ready by the time the plans were called for at Leyden, and that consequently it was issued in England with the letterpress during 1588 as a preliminary to an English edition of the narrative. If the latter was delayed by accident then it is probable that the map was added to the four plans, but without the letterpress, for either Field's edition or Ward's in order to make the publication as complete as possible. The state of surviving copies does not, in my opinion, provide conclusive evidence either way.

[4] One of his earliest datable productions (cp. Edward Lynam, *The mapmaker's art*, p. 75).

[5] Pp. 42, 398, 406–7, 411–12 below.

—that White copied the relevant drawings from those made by Drake's artist—is not so likely. But the collaboration completes an association between Drake's expedition and the Virginia settlement on which we could well do with further information.

The final document in the series is the journal kept by an unidentified 'Henrey' in the *Primrose*.[1] This '*Primrose* log', as Corbett called it, was not published until 1898.[2] It adds variety and detail to the *Summarie and true discourse*, but its treatment of the Virginia episode is brief. It does, however, add a few points, the most significant being Lane's desertion of three men because they were not on the spot when the colonists decided to go with Drake.[3]

THOMAS HARIOT AND JOHN WHITE

Two men, Thomas Hariot and John White, occupy a special place in the history of the Roanoke voyages, for between them they compiled the first detailed records to be assembled by Englishmen of the natural relations and resources of any part of North America, and in so doing gave a new content to English overseas discovery. The high degree of objectivity and the painstaking accuracy which they brought to their tasks make their work (though much of it has been lost) a landmark in the history of English cartography and the natural sciences, as well as, almost incidentally, in the development of a native school of watercolour painting. It is these circumstances which call for a rather different treatment here of their work. Something needs to be said about their respective careers and about the problem, in particular, of identifying White, to which no solution has yet been found. Furthermore, something needs to be said about the history and character of White's drawings, no full description of which is readily available. Finally, the work of both needs to be fitted into the contemporary situation in the natural sciences in

---

[1] See Document no. 47, pp. 303–8 below.

[2] Corbett, *Spanish war*, pp. 1–27, in modernized spelling.

[3] P. 307 below.

England. To do this adequately would require much more space than is here available, but at least there is enough to state the major problems which arise in connexion with both men.

Thomas Hariot, though we know little of his early life, does not, so far as the outlines of his career are concerned, provide a biographical problem of much magnitude. Born in 1560 in the parish of St Mary, Oxford, nothing appears yet to have been found about his background. At the age of seventeen he entered at St Mary's Hall, at that time very closely associated with Oriel College, and he took his B.A. in 1580. Mr C. S. Emden suggests that Richard Pigot, Fellow of Oriel and Principal of St Mary's Hall, was probably Raleigh's tutor (1572–4), and that it was probably he who recommended Thomas Hariot to Raleigh in 1580 or soon afterwards.[1] Hariot entered Raleigh's household and was well paid to teach him 'the mathematical sciences', chiefly, we may suggest, astronomy and navigation, and also to instruct the sea-captains who later frequented his household and were in his service, so as, in Hakluyt's words, to 'link theory with practice, not without almost incredible results',[2] a most modern scientific (or should it be Marxist?) sequence! It may be suggested that Raleigh's experience at sea in 1578–9 had shown him the need for theoretical and practical seamanship in a captain, even if it were not essential, and that, after he returned from Ireland in December 1581 and began to go into Sir Humphrey Gilbert's plans for further North American ventures, he began his mathematical studies and first employed Hariot, either in 1582 or 1583. It was not until after Gilbert's death that Raleigh took up, independently, plans for American colonies, and though we do not hear of Hariot being employed on the Amadas-Barlowe voyage in 1584, he drew up instructions on navigation for this and the following expeditions. Professor E. G. R. Taylor's recent work on his papers has shown that not only had he worked out a course of

[1] C. S. Emden, *Oriel papers* (1948), pp. 18–19.
[2] Hakluyt's dedication to Raleigh of his edition of Peter Martyr's *Decades*, 1587 (Taylor, *Hakluyts*, II, 360, 366–7).

navigational instruction by 1584 in his lost book, the 'Arcticon', but that it clearly contained many ideas much in advance of his time.[1]

As Hariot went out in 1585 with special instructions to study the native Indians[2] it appears at least highly probable that when Amadas came home in September 1584 with Manteo and Wanchese he was given the task of teaching them English, learning as much as he could of the local language from them, and interrogating them about the resources, economic and other, of their homeland. They were by December able to give some account of themselves in English and were clearly used to make propaganda for the 1585 expedition.[3] Hariot's task when he sailed with Grenville in April 1585 was to take astronomical observations at sea[4] and to act as a consultant on navigation. Once the North American mainland was reached he was to take on responsibility for studying the Indians and also for supervising the mapping of the new territories, noting natural phenomena such as comets[5] and storms, and above all making a survey, with any assistance he could obtain, of the economic resources of the region—metals, minerals, timber, wild or cultivated plants, and all living creatures likely to affect or be useful to man. How he did this between April 1585 and July 1586 will be discussed below. Once he returned to England his main task was to write up his material (some of which was lost at the hurried departure from Roanoke Island). His interrogation, with Hakluyt, of the Frenchman Nicholas Burgoignon, whom Drake rescued at San Agustín, probably took place soon after his return.[6]

The 1588 quarto Hariot is the most delectable of Americana, but it cannot be said that it now presents any bibliographical problems. The late Randolph G. Adams adequately described all

---

[1] See E. G. R. Taylor, 'Hariot's instructions for Ralegh's voyage to Guiana, 1595', in *Jnl of the Inst. of Navigation*, v, 345, discussing Brit. Mus., Additional MS 6788, fos. 468–92 (fo. 487 'my Arcticon'); E. G. R. Taylor and D. H. Sadler, '"The Doctrine of Nauticall Triangles Compendious"', *J. Inst. Nav.* VI, 131–4.

[2] P. 321 below. [3] Cp. pp. 127, 232. [4] P. 380 (cp. p. 53).
[5] Pp. 763–6 below. [6] P. 381 below.

surviving copies of *A briefe and true report of the new found land of Virginia* in 1931, and although some further checking has been done not a single additional copy has appeared, nor is there any technical addition to be made to his work. What is much less clear is when it was written in its present form. The published version gave on the last page its date of completion as February 1588. This was not 1588 English style, i.e. 1589. De Bry and Hakluyt in 1589–90 retained '1588' but in 1600 Hakluyt substituted '1587'. Now the earliest reference to the tract is that by Hakluyt, written either at the beginning of May, if it was in the first draft, or in October, if it was in the final revision, of his introduction to his edition of Laudonnière. Internal evidence does not point to a date necessarily later than February 1587. The document is essentially a plea for further support for the Virginia venture and it refers to land grants by Raleigh to White's intending settlers. These derived, however, it would seem, from the missing agreement of 7 January 1587 on the establishment of the City of Raleigh colony. The other evidence is a reference to 'the Gouernour and assistants of those alreadie transported'. While this might appear to place it later, it is consistent with a date late in February when White had brought some of his squadron out of the Thames, before putting in at Portsmouth, or else with a later date when the tract was under final revision for publication. If this passage is put on one side, however, the tract is entirely appropriate to one written for the encouragement of intending settlers and investors in the 1587 venture. This argument cannot be pressed, but it might be suggested that Hakluyt, who was himself very much addicted to the calendar year, though he did use English style as well, may have put in '1587' in 1600 with the purpose of showing that the tract belongs essentially to the propaganda for the 1587 expedition. The fact that it was not published in 1587 could have been due to a continued reluctance on Raleigh's part to engage on too detailed publicity, or to a number of other reasons, such as the finding of an adequate number of settlers by other means.

As the tract was, in fact, published in 1588 it is worth asking what purposes it was then intended to serve. Primarily, the encouragement of subscribers and volunteers for a further expedition for 1588, which Grenville was busy assembling in the West Country, though it is likely to have appeared too late to be of any value. It may be noted that Hariot added nothing to suggest that the 1587 colony might possibly be in difficulties and that he does not mention White's return. He concerned himself wholly with explaining the uncalled-for adverse publicity which the return of the 1585 colony had received, and dealing in detail with a number of practical problems: what crops the Indians grew, what wild plants and animals could be utilized for food or commerce, what European crops were likely to flourish, how to build, what the minerals prospects were; and, crudely, how to get on with the Indians. That he did these things with a temper which we can recognize as scientific was incidental to the main purpose of the tract.

After the English edition he was induced by Theodor de Bry and Richard Hakluyt[1] to agree to a multilingual edition of his pamphlet being published in Frankfort; Charles de l'Écluse, the eminent botanist, was to do the Latin translation.[2] Hariot was, himself, induced to supply a rather hasty set of explanatory notes in Latin to the collection of White's Indian drawings which De Bry intended to engrave, and of these Hakluyt did an English translation.[3] The appearance of part i of the *America*, in 1590, in

[1] The precise dates of De Bry's two visits to London remain obscure. The first was in 1587, and the second, when the meetings with Hakluyt, Hariot and White took place, late in 1588 or early in 1589 (cp. A. M. Hind, *Engraving in England in the sixteenth and seventeenth centuries*, I (1952), 22–4, 124–37). Henry Stevens (*Thomas Hariot* (1900), p. 57) maintained that the meeting took place about November 1588, when Hakluyt returned from Paris escorting Lady Sheffield. Dr G. B. Parks (*Hakluyt*, p. 251) will not commit himself to a date for Hakluyt's return beyond saying that it was late in 1588 or early in 1589. De Bry succeeded on the first occasion in obtaining the drawings of French Florida from the widow of Jacques le Moyne de Morgues (*America*, pt. ii (1591), sig. ***3 v.–4 v., cp. pp. 546–7 below).

[2] P. 401; *America*, pt. i (Lat.), title page: 'nunc...latio donata á C.C.A. [Carolo Clusio Atrebatense].'

[3] Pp. 399–400; *America*, pt. i (Eng.), sig. 3*4.

Latin, English, French and German, was a source of pride to Hariot and he noted long after in a list of allusions in print to himself 'My discourse of Vir*ginia* in 4 languages'.[1] His later career need not concern us here. Versatility is the keynote of the large number of miscellaneous papers of his which have come down to us,[2] but his primary interests and his main achievements in his later life were in astronomical observation and in mathematics.[3]

The biography of John White, the surveyor and painter of the 1585 expedition and the governor of the 1587 colony, remains largely a series of unresolved questions. If the voyage of 1590 to Virginia was his fifth, as he himself said,[4] then we must take it that he accompanied Amadas and Barlowe in 1584, even though he was not among the ten named participants.[5] We know that he accompanied Grenville in 1585. He is mentioned, though not by name, drawing plants on Puerto Rico in May.[6] He is named, along with Francis Brooke, treasurer of the expedition, as heading the crew of a ship's boat which set out with Grenville from Wococon Island for Pomeiooc, Aquascogoc, and Secoton (on the Pamlico River) on 11 July, returning a week later.[7] The fact that he is included among the ten principal members of this expedition indicates that his standing was a reasonably high one. The sketches of Indian life in the villages visited, on which a number of his drawings were based, were in all probability made then.[8]

[1] Petworth House, Leconfield MS no. 241, last folio.

[2] Brit. Mus., Additional MSS 6785–9, Harleian MSS 6001–3; Leconfield MSS 240–1.

[3] A useful brief estimate of his scientific achievement is Frank Vigor Morley, 'Thomas Hariot, 1560–1621', in *Scientific Monthly*, Jan. 1922, pp. 60–6. Dr John W. Shirley's forthcoming study of Hariot will be based on a large amount of new material. An engraving of 1602 (with which can be associated a portrait in Trinity College, Oxford) is believed to be of him (Jean Robertson, 'Some additional poems by George Chapman', in *The Library*, 4th Ser., XXII (1941–2), 168–76).

[4] P. 715 below. [5] Cp. pp. 115–16 below. [6] P. 742 below.

[7] P. 190. See also the sketch-map (p. 215) and the route of the expedition on the general map at end.

[8] Nos. 37–44, in particular (cp. pp. 420–32).

Thomas Hariot and John White

If White made all the drawings ascribed to him below it would be very difficult for him to have left the Virginia settlement between 25 August and mid-September 1585.[1] If he had a hand in the maps, other than the first preliminary sketch-map,[2] there is no doubt that he stayed with Lane until June 1586. But his name does not appear in the list of the 108 settlers. Simple omission is not impossible.[3] There may be a printer's error in the 'William White' on the list.[4] Or the 'John Twit' or 'Twyt' may be a slip for 'White',[5] as indeed could 'John Wright'.[6]

White next appears in a different guise, as the John White of London, gentleman, who, by the agreement of 7 January 1587, was to be the governor of the City of Raleigh colony on Chesapeake Bay, and to whom a grant of arms was made by the College of Heralds. His quarterings comprise arms of White, Wymarke, Wyat, Kyllyowe, Saker, Buddyer and Buttler,[7] but Mr Anthony R. Wagner, Richmond Herald, is not inclined to think that these names throw light on White's place of origin. White brought his settlers, including his son-in-law Ananias Dare and his daughter Elyoner, from Portsmouth to Roanoke Island, not Chesapeake

[1] Professor Wesley Frank Craven first put forward this view tentatively in the *Dictionary of American Biography*, xx, 110–11 (*s.v.* White, John), and makes it more positively in *The southern colonies in the seventeenth century* (1949), p. 52. The Indian drawings would, from their geographical distribution, lend some plausibility to this theory, but the fish and bird drawings, apart from the maps, would explode it since they fit in with Hariot's account of the total achievements of the colonists (cp. pp. 358–60). The support, too, which it might gain from the title to the collection of White drawings in the British Museum is not borne out by the contents (cp. pp. 391, 398).

[2] The preliminary sketch-map includes the information gathered down to the departure of the last vessels in September 1585 (cp. pp. 215–17), the general maps (pp. 460–2) all that collected down to June 1586.

[3] Pp. 194–7, more especially likely if White compiled the list himself.

[4] P. 196 below.

[5] De Bry turns 'White' into 'With' (p. 399). Yet Twit, like Withe, was a surname in its own right. Tudor spellings must always leave a margin of doubt, especially where surnames are concerned.

[6] P. 196, though the same name, with John White's, appears on the 1587 list of colonists (p. 541 below).

[7] Pp. 509–10 below.

Bay, in 1587, returned himself to speed up supplies, and landed in England on 5 November,[1] meeting Raleigh on 20 November.[2] His failure to do more in 1588 than attempt to cross the Atlantic with two small pinnaces, an attempt in which he failed, belongs to the general story of the ventures.[3] In 1589 he found as associates Richard Hakluyt and a number of London merchants who promised to back the settlement,[4] but only one of them, William Sanderson, did anything to help, so far as is known, and that in 1590, when he contributed a ship to John Watts's privateers who brought White with them to search for the colonists at Roanoke Island.[5] The failure of an inconclusive search discouraged White, who went to Ireland and who is last heard of in February 1593, having settled at Newtown, near the modern town of Charleville, in co. Cork.[6] This is all that is positively known, apart from what can be adduced from the drawings, about John White.

One small piece of knowledge already mentioned is that White closely co-operated with the artist of Drake's expedition. His name is not known, but he included fish and amphibians in his drawings, three of which bear such a close resemblance to known drawings by White that there is little doubt about their association. We may suggest that White and the artist travelled from Virginia to England in June and July 1586 on the same ship, and exchanged drawings and natural history notes. Whether all three drawings derived originally from White is not clear, since the copy of one or more may have come to him from the other artist.[7]

John White is a common name and this is the main obstacle to his identification; it led P. Lee Phillips to argue in 1896 that the presumably humble painter was not the same as the presumably important governor of 1587.[8] This argument has been taken

[1] P. 538 below   [2] P. 563 below.   [3] Pp. 562–9 below.
[4] Pp. 569–78 below.   [5] Pp. 704–10 below.   [6] P. 716 below.
[7] Cp. pp. 406–7, 410–13 below. I am much indebted to Mr P. H. Hulton for his assistance in this identification.
[8] 'Virginia cartography', in *Smithsonian Misc. Collns.*, xxxvii (no. 1039), pp. 1–17, adopted by Woodbury Lowery, *Spanish settlements*, I, 414.

seriously in America[1] though not in England, but there is nothing positive to support it. The main argument against it is that Hakluyt, careful editor that he was, would have almost certainly made the distinction clear.[2] The American argument based on social position has very little to be said for it. The surveyor, which was undoubtedly what White was, was a new kind of technician who might have been of gentle or merchant stock, and who required, as several writers of the time tell us, some education if he was to be efficient.[3] There is, too, White's statement that he had been on all five voyages, his presentation of the drawing of a butterfly to Thomas Penny in 1587,[4] and the mention of his maps and pictures among his damaged possessions which he found on Roanoke Island in 1590[5]—all pointing the other way, while such little evidence as we have about the 1587 settlers points to their being humble people under a simple (though perhaps well-born) leader who intended to lead a primitive, hard-working life in America. For De Bry there was one John White only.[6]

If we leave ourselves with a single John White, how far can conjecture bring us towards an identification? Only so far as to suggest some alternatives which may provide a later searcher with possible clues for linking up one or more of the John Whites mentioned below with John White, surveyor, painter and governor.

The 'John White of London, Gentleman' of the Herald's description would suggest that London would be the first place to look, though the attachment of the same description to the Azorean Portuguese, Simon Fernandez, would indicate that White

---

[1] Cp. R. G. Adams, 'An attempt to identify John White', in *American Hist. Rev.*, XLII (1935–6), pp. 87–91; Craven, *Southern colonies*, pp. 51–2; and W. P. Cumming, 'The identity of John White governor of Roanoke and John White the artist', in *North Carolina Hist. Rev.*, XV (1938), 197–203, the last being the best-balanced discussion of the evidence.

[2] Cp. his marginal note to 'Captain Lane' in 1590 (p. 603) making it clear that William, not Ralph, Lane was meant.

[3] Cp. E. G. R. Taylor, 'The surveyor', in *Econ. Hist. Rev.*, 1st ser., XVII (1947), 121–31.   [4] But see pp. 458–9 below.

[5] P. 615 below.   [6] Cp. p. 399, n. 6.

was not necessarily a Londoner.[1] There was a John White, fish-monger, of London who in 1591 was named as captain of a ship, the *Balinus*, 40 tons, of London, to which letters of reprisal against the Spaniards were granted, and which subsequently took a prize of wines. Her owner, George Bassett, was also a fishmonger, but neither he nor the master of the vessel, John Graunt, have been found associated with the Virginia ventures.[2] This could represent a final unsuccessful attempt by our John White to get to Roanoke Island on a privateer under his own command, but it is highly probable that he would have mentioned it in his letter of 1593[3] unless it was in some way particularly discreditable to him. Nor does it fit in with his known attitude to privateering.

It would be reasonable to investigate the possible Devonshire origin of John White, since many of the promoters came from the south-west, but no likely candidate has appeared. One of Raleigh's principal agents in the south-west was Martin White of Plymouth,[4] and it is not impossible that John White was his brother. If so, could he have been the John White who was Mayor of Plymouth in 1583–4?[5]

The uncovering of some parts of Sir George Carey's association

---

[1] P. 508 below. He was not the John White of London who was trading in tin in May 1585 (S.P. 15/29, 17), as he was then in the West Indies.

[2] H.C.A. 14/29, 165 (bis); H.C.A. 25/3, pkt. 9, 8 June 1591 (out of place); Brit. Mus., Lansdowne MS 142, fo. 109 (these documents being first referred to in K. R. Andrews, 'Elizabethan privateering', p. 230). Dr Andrews shows that a John White, who may have been the same man, owned the privateer *Fortunatus* (40 tons) of London in 1593 (ibid.; Harleian MS 598). No John White was a member of the Fishmongers' Company in 1600 (W. P. Haskett-Smith, *Lists of apprentices and freemen...of the Worshipful Company of Fishmongers* (1916)).

[3] Pp. 712–16, where all the indications are that his voyage of 1590 was his last; but if he went out in 1591, not intending to make the Atlantic crossing, there is no need for him to have mentioned it.

[4] See pp. 218, 475; Edwards, *Ralegh*, I, 173; Inq. P.M., Devon, 41 Eliz., C. 142/258, 135 (Martin White having died on 2 November 1598).

[5] R. N. Worth, *Cal. Plymouth municipal records* (1893), p. 125. Mr P. H. Hulton points out to me that the John White, haberdasher, of London who had close associations with Plymouth, and who died in 1584 (ibid., p. 19; *Wills proved in the Prerogative Court of Canterbury*, IV (1584–1604), 448), may provide some connexion also.

with the Roanoke voyages, though we could well do with further information on it, the sailing of the 1587 settlers from Portsmouth, and their call at the Isle of Wight before leaving,[1] might suggest that a search for John White in Hampshire would not be unfruitful. As it happens, John White of Southwick was a prominent figure in the Portsmouth district, but our John White was clearly not he.[2] However, there are two references which might prove fruitful if they could be followed up. On 12 October 1589 John Whyte and Thomas Uvedale sent a report to the privy council[3] about some disturbances between soldiers and townspeople at Portsmouth. And on 18 or 19 January 1590 the privy council instructed Francis Cotton and John White, esquires,[4] to survey and view the queen's storehouses near Portsmouth with a view to putting them in repair. It would thus appear that there was a John White, holding some official position at Portsmouth about this time, who was a surveyor by profession, as our John White almost certainly was. This evidence is, however, quite inconclusive.

Finally, it is perhaps just worth while suggesting that John White may have come of Anglo-Irish stock. A large number of members of this family were tenants of the Butlers, Earls of Ormond,[5] and a John White was acting as seneschal of the Liberty of Tipperary in 1599.[6] The Butler arms on White's coat might conceivably point the same way,[7] while the group of Irish settlers which White had with him in 1587 might also suggest that

---

[1] Cp. pp. 498–9, 516–17 below.

[2] Cp. *V.C.H. Hants.*, III, 54, 124–5, 163 [etc.]; *Cal. S.P. Dom., 1581–90*, p. 438 [21 Nov. '87]; R. East, *Extracts from Portsmouth records* (2nd ed., 1891), p. 137.

[3] Hist. MSS Comm., *Cecil MSS*, XIII, 417.

[4] *Acts of the privy council, 1589–90*, p. 314.

[5] See Index Nominum in *Calendar of Ormond deeds*, ed. E. Curtis, V (1941), VI (1943).

[6] Ibid., VI, 111. Mr Gerald Slevin of the Genealogical Office, Dublin Castle, has found no trace of White in the records there, and considers that, as only one of White's quarterings is typical of Ireland, the chances of his being of Anglo-Irish origin are not great.

[7] P. 510.

he had Irish connexions.[1] He went to settle very near to the
Butler lands in the 1590s. The seignory of 12,000 acres granted
to Hugh Cuffe on 14 November 1587 included 'Kylmore alias
the Great Woode'[2] within which White's later holding lay. By
October 1589 Cuffe had already twenty-one Englishmen on his
lands, but he later surrendered some part of his lands,[3] whether
that including White's portion or not it has proved impossible
to ascertain. At Newtown or Ballynoe in the Barony of Orrery and
Kilmore[4] White would have been a freeholder or lease-holder,
unlike his neighbour Edmund Spenser, who was an undertaker
or chief landlord of a seignory not far away at Kilcolman.

These speculations are far from exhausting the possibilities, yet
none of them leaves our feet on firm ground. All that can be
claimed is that each has some trace of plausibility about it which
may prove stimulating to future searchers. White is, perhaps,
most likely to be identified eventually as a member of one of the
London companies, but even so his place of origin may have been
far from the city.

If we cannot trace White we may record that in 1706 or 1707
Dr Hans Sloane had some contacts with his descendants, and,
some time after 1709, acquired from them a volume of drawings,[5]
bearing an inscription that they were given to 'my soon Whit'
on 11 April 1673, some ninety years after our last direct contact
with White. This might well indicate that a son of White, or
more likely his grandson, passed on the volume to his son in 1673.
But would a man called White refer to his son as 'Whit' or
'White'? It might seem unlikely, but it is not impossible.

---

[1] Pp. 519–20 below.

[2] Fiant 5066 (*16th rep. Deputy Keeper of Records, Ire.*).

[3] *Cal. S.P. Ire., 1588–92*, pp. 258, 574; Fiant 5535.

[4] For Newtown (*alias* Ballyno, Ballinoa, Ballynowe), see Fiants 3373, 5330,
5333, 5903 (*13th and 16th reps. Deputy Keeper of Records, Ire.*); Sir William Petty,
Barony Maps of Ireland (Ordnance Survey, 1908), sh. 98 (Orrery and Kilmore);
O.S. Ire., 6 in. co. Cork, sh. 2:14. The survey of 1622 (Brit. Mus., Additional
MS 4756, fo. 94 v.) does not indicate whether Newtown was within the remaining
seignory, then called Cuffes Wood.

[5] This is anticipating the discussion of the evidence on pp. 394–7 below.

A mother who had married again might well do so, however, and she might therefore be White's daughter or granddaughter. 'Whit' could also, of course, be a Christian name derived from a White surname (cp. White Kennett), in which case the name of the father or mother (or even father-in-law or mother-in-law) who made the gift is impossible to guess. It is to be hoped that Sloane somewhere recorded more about his search for White's drawings and his dealings with White's descendants.

If Hariot was to be the trained mind of the 1585 expedition, John White was to be the practised eye. Whatever else he may have been, there is little reason to doubt that he was a working surveyor, and it is probable that his interest in drawing arose incidentally from the craft of making maps and plans. His hand has not yet been traced in any English surveys of this period, but Edward Lynam had complete confidence that it would eventually be done. From measuring and plotting fields, house-plans and fortifications, it was a short step only towards more general cartography. Closely linked too with map-making was the ability to illustrate maps with drawings of plants and buildings and figures of men and beasts, both for utility, in conventional signs, and for ornament. And there were two particular reasons why the latter skill received encouragement. The first was that overseas expeditions required a pictorial record, as well as specimens, of strange peoples, plants and animals, so that the map-illustrator easily became the equivalent of the modern photographer. The growth of this practice by English explorers is obscure, but it was very well established by 1585. The second reason was that some scientific development of natural history was taking place, and one prerequisite for the accurate classification of plants and animals was the well-preserved specimen and/or the accurate drawing from life or from the specimen which was capable of reproduction by wood-cut or copper-plate engraving. Already at the opening of Elizabeth's reign John Caius (1510–73), one of the pioneers of natural history in England, was congratulated by Konrad Gesner of Zurich (1516–65), whose contribution to the dawning sciences of botany and zoology was so influential in England and Europe on the excellent quality of certain drawings he had sent him.[1]

The overseas world, with its apparently inexhaustible range of new plants and animals, provided a continuing stimulus to naturalists in England and elsewhere.[2] Each of the major figures in English natural history in the sixteenth century—William Turner (d. 1568), the pioneer English botanist, Thomas Penny (d. 1589), a scientific botanist and, in Dr Raven's opinion, the founder of entomology, Thomas Moffet (or Moufet) (1553–1604), his less able collaborator who prepared Penny's work for publication, and John Gerard (1545–1612), the most voluminous if not the most scientific English publisher of botanical information, James Garet and Hugh Morgan, leading apothecaries, Richard Garth and Walter Cope—had contacts with the pioneers of English overseas enterprise, and we find among their informants men like Drake, Cavendish, Frobisher, William Winter, Sir Robert Dudley and John White.[3]

John White was well equipped by 1585 to act as the surveyor and painter to an expedition. He could make accurate picture plans of forts and towns, he could draw maps which are in some respects superior to most others of their period,[4] he could make scientific drawings of birds, fish, animals and plants, some of which are remarkably fine,[5] and, above all, he could do water-

[1] C. E. Raven, *English naturalists from Neckam to Ray* (1947), pp. 83, 146.

[2] W. Blunt, *The art of botanical illustration* (1950), pp. 60–2; Arber, *Herbals*, pp. 69–70, 85, 105–10.

[3] Cp. Raven, *English naturalists*, pp. 168–9, 182–5, 192; T. Moffet, *Theater of insects*, trans. John Rowlands (1658), pp. 951, 953, 978, 998, 1083, 1149, *Health's improvement*, ed. C. Bennet (1655), p. 154, 'Theatrum…insectorum', Brit. Mus., Sloane MS 4014, p. 240. Of continental naturalists Charles de l'Écluse was most closely in touch with Englishmen engaged in exploration and those interested in the specimens brought home. His *Rariorum plantarum historia* (1601) and *Exoticorum libri decem* (1605) contain frequent references to his English informants (cp. pp. 329, 339–40, 345–6, 347–8, 353–4 below). For Cope see T. Platter, *Travels*, pp. 171–3.

[4] The merits and defects of the maps are discussed on pp. 460–2, 846–50.

[5] They vary in accuracy, especially the fish (difficult to draw). It is unfortunate that many of the bird and fish drawings survive only in copies (cp. pp. 447–60).

colour figure drawings of a peculiar freshness and fidelity. White normally used blacklead for the outline of his drawings, sometimes working on a ground of grey, brown or tinted wash, and added brown, red, black and blue body-colours, with gold, silver and white for touching and heightening. Pen work is generally confined to the legends on the drawings and to the maps and plans, but is occasionally used to strengthen the outlines of figure drawings. Technically and in his choice of subject-matter John White belongs to the direct line of sixteenth-century English draughtsmen of topographical and natural history subjects and to a broader European tradition of naturalistic figure-drawing deriving from Dürer. His position as artist-draughtsman to the expedition of 1585 and the colony of 1585–6 allowed him to develop further the naturalistic style which reaches its highest development in the Indian figure drawings. But when he attempted unobserved subjects like the ancient Britons, he tended to use a flamboyant style commonly employed for imaginary or theatrical figures throughout western Europe at this time.[1] It was this which tempted Binyon to say that he had been trained in 'the rhetorical school of the Italianized Flemings',[2] but these few drawings are exceptional rather than typical and tell us nothing about White except that he was versatile.

Much of the impetus to employ such men as Hariot and White in exploring and colonizing ventures came from the emergence of the geographical consultant, men like Richard Eden and the two Richard Hakluyts, who, we might say, ran clearing houses for overseas information derived from oral and literary sources, and who disposed of their information to merchants, speculators, explorers and would-be colonists. Their concern was almost wholly utilitarian, though on the one hand popular love of marvels and novelties stimulated their collecting and publishing

---

[1] I owe the technical description to Mr P. H. Hulton, but he is not responsible for the way it is expressed.

[2] Laurence Binyon, 'The drawings of John White', in *Walpole Society* [*Pubns.*], XIII (1924–5), 19–24.

activities, and on the other the growing exactness of the questions asked and answered by the naturalists, particularly the botanists, impelled them towards more scientific ways of acquiring and assembling their information. We can trace something of this process in the activities of the Hakluyts. Thus Richard Hakluyt the elder, when briefing the promoters of the North-east Passage expedition of 1580, was admirably specific and practical on the trade goods to be sought for and brought home, but he took a dilettante attitude towards natural history specimens, suggesting that seeds of strange plants be brought home, since they 'comming from another part of the world, and so far off, will delight the fancie of many, for the strangenesse and for that the same may grow and continue the delight long time'.[1] Richard Hakluyt, the younger, in listing the known products of North America for the *Divers voyages* in 1582 and helping to conduct the interrogation of witnesses, was more systematic, but still far from scientific[2] (though the newly identified instructions, discussed below, are a different matter). There is a substantial advance in method in the memoranda contributed by way of advice for the organization of the 1585 voyage—the younger Hakluyt's addendum to his *Discourse of western planting*,[3] the elder Hakluyt's 'Inducements',[4] and even the rather rough and ready 'Notes'[5], discussed above. The last of these, amongst recommendations for various specialist inquirers to go to America, included a 'good geographer to make discription of the landes discouerd, and with him an exilent paynter',[6] while the 'Inducements' in a similar, more systematic, list advised that 'A skilful painter is also to be caried with you, which the Spaniards used commonly in all their discoveries to bring the descriptions of all beasts, birds, fishes, trees, townes, &c.',[7] indicating one source for the development of the English practice. Thus the positions which Hariot and

---

[1] Taylor, *Hakluyts*, I, 151.
[2] See Quinn, *Gilbert*, II, 281–313, etc.
[3] Taylor, *Hakluyts*, II, 320–6.
[4] Ibid. 336–8.
[5] Pp. 130–9 below.
[6] P. 135.
[7] Taylor, *Hakluyts*, II, 338.

White were to occupy in the 1585 expedition were those which well-informed opinion by that time considered necessary to the effective conduct of any reconnaissance in newly explored territories, whether the objective was trade, mines, or settlement.

When completing the documentation of Sir Humphrey Gilbert's voyages in 1939 I overlooked the set of instructions (lacking one page) prepared for one of the expeditions planned by Gilbert or his associates to go to sea in 1582. They form the opening pages of a commonplace book of Sir Edward Hoby in the British Museum.[1] Professor E. G. R. Taylor recently published a most illuminating commentary on them, with special reference to the scientific and technical equipment which they advise should be carried.[2] Professor Taylor considers that William Borough is most likely to have been responsible for their compilation, though, of course, he may have had assistance from others. Because they cover the same route, and the North American mainland (though they were intended for southern New England, not modern North Carolina), they can be used in place of the lost instructions of 1585 to indicate roughly what Hariot and White were asked to do and with what equipment. Those parts which can so be used comprise, first, notes for an observer who corresponds, so far as can be ascertained (since the first page is unfortunately missing), to Hariot, and, secondly, instructions for a certain Thomas Bavin, who corresponds to White as surveyor and painter.

The observer is to make a journal in which all his observations are inserted and he is also to see that their results, so far as possible, are incorporated in the maps which his colleague was to make. Springs, islands, fishes ('bothe shell fishes and other'), 'the resemblances of all sortes of beastes & their differences either in kinde or colour with or from ours', 'the like of birdes

---

[1] Additional MS 38823, fos. 1–8. It is hoped to print them in a forthcoming volume.

[2] 'Instructions to a colonial surveyor in 1582', in *The Mariner's Mirror*, xxxvii (1951), 48–62.

Flyes', 'their manner of taking byrdes fowles Fyshes and beastes', soils, trees, fruits, gums, herbs, seed, apothecary drugs, pitch, tar and resin, 'the manner of their planting & manuring of the earthe', all sorts of minerals and sub-minerals were to be noted. Special attention was to be given to the native inhabitants, especially 'the statures Conditions apparell and manner of foode', 'the greatnes and quantetie of euery distinct Kinges Contryes people and forces', 'the dyversitie of their languages and in what places their speache beginnethe to alter…And the same man to Carry with him an englishe Dictionarie with the Englishe wordes before therin to sett downe their langage',[1] and to note their kinds of boats.

Just as it is evident that Hariot undertook most of the tasks indicated above, so did White those assigned to Bavin, except that Hariot, not White, is likely to have taken the more delicate observations by instrument, and that the two co-operated very closely on the map. Bavin was expected to equip himself with an array of instruments and materials:

A universal dial.
A cross staff.
A sailing compass.
An instrument for the variation of the compass.
An instrument for the declination of the needle.
Three watch clocks 'which dothe shewe & devide the howers by the minutes'.
Ephimerides or some other calculated tables.
A table.
A pair of writing tables.
'all his marckes written in parchment'.
Paper royal.
Quills.
Ink.
Black powder to make ink.
'A pensill with blacke leade'.
Black lead.
'all sortes of colours to drawe all thinges to life'.
A stone to grind colours.
'mouth' glue.

[1] Cp. Hariot, pp. 370, 389 below.

Gum.

Two pairs of 'brazen Compasses'.

'other Instrumentes to drawe cardes and plottes'.[1]

On the way across the Atlantic he was to observe the eclipse of the sun which it was calculated would occur at London at 4.5 a.m. on 20 June 1582, and to make an attempt to determine longitude with the help of a time-piece.[2] The eclipse was to be painted, and observations made of 'the elevacion of the pole...variacion of the Compasse & declyning of the nedle'. It is highly probable that Hariot and White were asked to do the same thing during the eclipse calculated to occur on 19 April 1585, the eleventh day out from Plymouth,[3] but no record has survived of the observations, nor are they likely to have been of any value.

In 1582 the surveyor and his associate were to go around attended by men who would carry their writing materials and their instruments so that they should never be unable to make notes, drawings or observations. From the southern tip of Florida northwards they were to make 'cardes', that is maps, composed of four sheets of paper royal according to the size of the plane table, marking them in series of letters to avoid confusion. These 'first draftes in paper' were to be 'garnished' with conventional signs, specimens of which are given, but it was stressed that Bavin must 'in the discovery drawe to lief one of each kinde of thing that is strange to vs in England' so that he can make his own signs as he goes along, 'As by the portraiture of one Cedar Tree he may drawe all the woodes of that sorte'. The latitude of every 'Notatious' place was to be entered both in the journal and on the map. A uniform scale was to be maintained at all costs. Distances of capes, headlands and hills, depth and breadth of inlets and rivers, elevations of land, with the variations in vegetation and land-use, location of springs, occurrence of shell-fish (especially

---

[1] The instruments are fully identified in Professor Taylor's paper. The equipment for drawing and painting may usefully be compared with that listed in John Bate, *The mysteries of nature and art* (1634, 2nd ed. 1635), p. 144.

[2] Taylor, loc. cit., pp. 59–61.   [3] Cp. pp. 380–1 below.

those with pearls), and the various sorts of trees, were all to be entered both in the journal and on the map.[1]

Two final instructions may be cited in full:

> Also drawe to liefe all strange birdes beastes fishes plantes hearbes Trees and fruictes and bring home of each sorte as nere as you may.
>
> Also drawe the figures & shapes of men and woemen in their apparell as also of their manner of wepons in every place as you shall finde them differing.

From what evidence we have it seems that Hariot and White did their best to follow some such programme from May 1585 to June 1586. It would appear that Hariot kept a series of note-books into which he entered information regarding a very wide range of topics, and it is probable that as White made a drawing of a particular specimen or scene, Hariot obtained a copy where it fitted in with his own material. Such a set of illustrated notes appears to lie behind Hariot's *Briefe and true report*. No trace of them appears to have survived; some of the materials collected were lost when the settlers left Roanoke Island hurriedly on 18 June 1586,[2] but it seems likely that these covered only a small part of the collections and may have been confined largely to specimens. Hariot clearly regarded his 1588 pamphlet as merely a preliminary to an elaborate illustrated publication,[3] but the notes which he wrote for De Bry[4] dealt solely with the Indians, and White's drawings engraved with them covered the same field. This is strange, since between them they had made a remarkable collection of pictures and notes on American birds and fish. It is not impossible that the reason for the non-publication of the natural history material is that the botanical notes or drawings, or both, were not regarded as sufficiently comprehensive.[5] What is stranger still is that there is no evidence of Hariot having con-tributed unpublished information from them to contemporary

---

[1] Professor Taylor informs me that the amount and range of economic information asked for is unprecedented for its period.

[2] Pp. 293, 334.

[3] P. 359.   [4] P. 430.

[5] Which he suggests on p. 359.

botanists or zoologists.[1] It was White who did a certain amount of this.[2] Hariot's collections, with probably a complete, or almost complete, set of White's drawings, simply disappeared, though there were some of his materials on the Indian languages still extant nearly a century later.[3] Similarly, his history of the voyages from 1584 to 1587 vanished also,[4] and among his surviving manuscripts there is scarcely anything about his overseas activities or interests.[5] Even so, what Hariot provided in his pamphlet is a sufficient earnest of the careful and scientific character of his work on the natural resources of the country, and in it and in his notes he gives an invaluable picture of the economy, society and culture of an Indian group of which almost nothing further is known directly, while he has left the only records of their language and made a sincere attempt to do so systematically.[6]

Much more record of White's work has survived than of Hariot's, and it is of the greatest importance and interest, but, like everything associated with White, it raises many problems of analysis. We catch a glimpse of White through Spanish eyes going about Puerto Rico drawing the local fauna and flora.[7] From then onwards he can never have been far away from Hariot until their return to England.[8] It is highly probable, in fact almost certain, that whenever he gave Hariot a drawing to insert in his collections he kept an example (probably the original) himself, so that his own portfolios grew throughout the expedition. The

---

[1] It is just possible that he was John Gerard's informant on the Milkweed (pp. 444–6). Though L'Écluse translated Hariot's tract for De Bry he makes no reference in his *Exoticorum* to materials or drawings obtained directly from Hariot or White. Instead he depended on roots and fruits sent to him by James Garet, Hugh Morgan and Richard Garth as having come from 'Wingandecaow'. The majority of such specimens as can be identified are West Indian, but could have been brought to England as the result of one of the Roanoke voyages. The herbalists were careless, however (witness Gerard and the potato), and L'Écluse would have done better had he gone direct to Hariot (cp. pp. 339–40, 353–4 below). Cope's specimens were inadequately labelled (Platter, *Travels*, pp. 171–3).

[2] Pp. 397–8. [3] P. 389. [4] P. 387.
[5] Cp. pp. 388–9. [6] Cp. pp. 337–46, 368–82, 389. [7] P. 742.
[8] They were not in the same boat crossing Pamlico Sound in July 1585 (p. 190 below).

majority of the plants, fishes and birds were captioned with Spanish or Indian names (the latter in the forms which Hariot had adopted),[1] and sometimes with information as to their size and characteristics. The Indian drawings as they were made were probably very different from any versions we have now. They were probably mainly drawings of individuals and of individual features of Indian life and agriculture.[2] They do not seem to have been too well labelled as a number of discrepancies in the descriptions[3] arose when White made copies and composites, while the more elaborate pictures of villages and ceremonies were composed from a series of drawings of details and individuals, and varied in the composition in detail according to White's purpose in making the picture.[4] Along with these went the many sheets of the maps as surveyed and the rough sketches linking together the surveyed and the roughly examined or unseen portions of the extensive area from Cape Lookout to Chesapeake Bay and behind the coast, which were gradually assimilated into his smaller scale maps.[5]

Nothing of this archetypal collection is now known to be extant, but White's graphic record of the Virginia colonies may be studied in surviving copies and derivatives of his drawings. These are described, and a tentative scheme of their relationship is put forward, in Chapter VI below.[6] It appears likely that a volume of drawings in the British Museum (formerly Sloane MS 5270),[7] by a single copyist, was acquired from White's descendants by Sir Hans Sloane sometime after 1709.[8] They are clearly not from White's hand and they contain, besides many American drawings (a number of which are not otherwise known), other material which cannot at present be linked directly with White, but they may provide us with a direct link with the archetype. White, himself, however, made a number of sets of drawings and copies of individual drawings. The most important of them were

---

[1] Pp. 406–13, 444–60. [2] Cp. no. 37 (see pp. 420–3) with the engraving.
[3] E.g. no. 36 (see pp. 319–20. [4] Cp. pp. 443–4.
[5] Cp. pp. 413, 460–2. [6] Pp. 392–8 below.
[7] Now P. & D. 199. a. 3. [8] Cp. pp. 394–7 below.

Hariot's set, of which nothing is now known;[1] that in the British Museum, without doubt from White's hand;[2] and the set (no longer extant) made by White for Theodor de Bry in 1588 or 1589, which furnished the originals for the engravings in *America*, pt. i (1590). Copies of his drawings are known to have been given by White to other contemporaries, including Richard Hakluyt, Thomas Penny the entomologist, and possibly John Gerard: a few of these have been preserved in their original form, in copies, or in printed versions.

The editor's object in these volumes has been to include such information as would enable the graphic material collected by John White to be used as a set of historical documents parallel with, and complementary to, Hariot's texts, as was originally intended by him, but which was only incompletely achieved by De Bry. There is little doubt that the result is to extend considerably the documentation of the 1585 voyage and the 1585–6 colony, although White's contribution can only be used with full effect when all the drawings have been published. There is, of course, one objection which can legitimately be brought against this use of White's drawings. If, in fact, he made five voyages to Virginia, why, it may be asked, should we imagine that he made drawings only between April 1585 and July 1586? The only answer is the empirical one that there is good positive evidence that many of these drawings were made in the period specified, while there is a reasonable presumption that others which fit in with Hariot's descriptions also belong there. Thus, if the list includes drawings which were made by White in 1584, 1587 or 1590 they are not likely to be so numerous as to invalidate the more general arguments drawn from the White material. It must not be forgotten that between April 1585 and July 1586 White was employed and paid as a surveyor and painter, which was a substantial incentive to produce a large number of drawings during this period. The Swallow-tail Butterfly[3] may represent a drawing made in 1587; all we know is that he gave Thomas

[1] Cp. p. 392 below.   [2] P. & D. 1906-5-9-1.   [3] Pp. 458–9 below.

Penny the drawing in that year, though he may have made it in 1585-6. The revisions in the De Bry map, too, may in one or two cases represent fresh data gathered in 1587.[1] But there is no other positive evidence.

It remains to estimate summarily the effects of the work of Hariot and White on European knowledge of the people, fauna, and flora of the New World. Hariot's pamphlet was the first important original English contribution to the subject, and his comments on plants used by the North Carolina Indians are frequently referred to by European botanists during the following century.[2] The information he gave on the Indians, both there and in the notes to the De Bry engravings, was more detailed and accurate than anything else on the subject to be published within the next quarter of a century, but because it was not followed up quickly by other similar sets of observations it was not perhaps very helpful in leading to a more scientific study of strange peoples, and of the North American Indians in particular. De Bry's engravings of White's drawings, even though they Europeanized the Indians' physical appearance, were the most accurate of any in his great published collections and they were repeatedly copied and re-used as the type-figures of natives of North America throughout the seventeenth century. The map of the North Carolina coastlands, as engraved by De Bry, whatever its defects in detail, was by far the best representation of this part of the eastern North American seaboard, and the only one for a long time to be derived, at least in part, from survey on the ground.[3] Its value was recognized in so far as English, French and Dutch map-makers of the earlier seventeenth century incorporated its findings in the general picture of the North American coastline. It was, however, neglected when fresh exploration of this area began after about 1650.

White's natural history drawings did not have the influence they ought to have had. The drawings of insects which he gave to Thomas Penny, and which are preserved in Sloane MS 4014,

[1] Cp. pp. 849-50 below.   [2] E.g. p. 347 below.   [3] Cp. pp. 847-8 below.

Thomas Hariot and John White

together with the information he gave with them, were generously acknowledged by Thomas Moffet when he put together Penny's collections and they lie behind a small but valuable group of engravings in the *Insectorum...theatrum* of 1634 and its translation of 1658.[1] He made, as far as can be ascertained, no contributions to the more-or-less zoological works of Edward Topsell, *The historie of foure-footid beastes* (1607)[2] and *The historie of serpents* (1608). Yet some of his bird-drawings reached Topsell, partly or wholly through the younger Richard Hakluyt, before 1614, but 'The Fowles of Heauen' was never completed and remains unprinted amongst the Ellesmere MSS.[3] There are hints in this that White's bird-drawings may have been in use by natural history collectors and observers in the Jamestown settlement.[4] Although White may have made more plant-drawings in North America than are now extant, the only one to achieve publication and description was the Milkweed (in Gerard's *Herball* (1597)).[5] The fine pictures of fish and birds and reptiles remained—except, through the copies he had, to Sir Hans Sloane—unknown, though they were not, like Hariot's notebooks and chronicle, irrecoverably lost. Had Hariot's heart been in natural history rather than in mathematics, and had White been more persistent in his distribution of the drawings, instead of being involved in the

[1] Pp. 406, 457–60.
[2] See M. St Clare Byrne, *The Elizabethan zoo* (1926); Raven, *English naturalists*, pp. 217–26.
[3] Huntington Library, Ellesmere MS 1142. See Bayard Henderson Christy, 'Topsell's "Fowles of Heauen"', in *The Auk. A quarterly Journal of Ornithology*, n.s., L (Lancaster, Pa., 1933), 275–83; J. R. Swanton, 'Newly discovered Powhatan bird names', in *Journal of the Washington Academy of Sciences*, XXIV (1934), 96–9; Elsa G. Allen, 'The history of American ornithology before Audubon', in *Trans. American Philosophical Soc.*, n.s., XLI, pt. 3 (1951), 447–8.
[4] This is a topic which is very obscure. We have no sets of drawings and natural history notes such as White and Hariot put together. Something is known (Raven, *English naturalists*, and G. R. Gunther, *Early British botanists*, passim) about the transmission of plants and botanical information, but nothing, apparently, about the study of animals and fishes. Mrs Allen (pp. 450–1) is able to add very little about birds for the early seventeenth century.
[5] P. 752; cp. pp. 444–6 below.

colony of 1587 and its disaster, the impact of the Grenville-Lane colony on European knowledge of North America and on the natural sciences might have been much more significant than it was.

The sources for the 1586 ventures cannot be said to be satisfactory although our knowledge has now been greatly strengthened by a Spanish document. Hakluyt, when he came to compile the *Principall navigations*, realized that for once he did not have a first-hand account available of the two voyages made this year, and, clearly not having Hariot's full chronicle before him,[1] he must have found he had no alternative but to compose himself such a linking narrative as would bridge the gaps between his documents on the first colony and that on White's expedition of 1587. There is no proof that he did write the brief document we have,[2] but it seems at least highly probable that he did so, and no name of a possible alternative author can be put in his place. The new information in it is slight, but is such as Hakluyt himself would have had. It is our sole authority for the sending out of Raleigh's ship which brought relief to Roanoke Island only very shortly after Lane had departed with Drake, but it merely paraphrases the information in Lane's narrative and in *A summarie and true discourse of Sir Frances Drakes West Indian voyage* on the circumstances which led to the return of the first colony. Further, it is the main English authority for the American activities of Grenville's expedition, which followed the supply ship and arrived still later. So far as it goes it provides an adequate link but it gives no details of either expedition and leaves us very much in the dark on a number of important points.

Hakluyt has now been supplemented in many respects by the deposition made by Pedro Diaz at Havana in March 1589.[3] Diaz

[1] Cp. pp. 387, 477.

[2] Document no. 64, pp. 477–80 below.

[3] Document no. 149, pp. 786–92 below, and see p. 774 below; Wright, *Further English voyages*, pp. 237–41.

was a pilot on the *Santa Maria* when she was taken by Grenville in 1585. He was kept prisoner and was brought on the 1586 expedition, of which he gives a reasonably full account which adds very substantially to our knowledge. His narrative is not, however, a substitute for a full journal of the voyage. It is the result, somewhat summarized, of an interrogation of Diaz by a Spanish official at Havana. The latter scarcely knew the questions to ask which would most interest us, and Diaz's own further statement, which he doubtless made after his return to Spain,[1] has not yet been found, if indeed it still exists. We are thus uninformed, for example, about names of ships and their commanders; Diaz was not too precise or too much concerned about dates; and, finally, he was kept on board one of Grenville's ships at Port Ferdinando, so that his information about the situation on Roanoke Island is much less detailed than we would like. Withal, Diaz was an intelligent witness, and his interrogator preserved in his report information which is sufficiently precise to be of the greatest interest both on this and on subsequent ventures.

The remaining documents on the 1586 expeditions are very miscellaneous. We have from Exeter one glimpse of an unsuccessful attempt to collect subscriptions there;[2] evidence that Raleigh's factors were using his requisitioning powers to take supplies without payment from a French ship in port[3]; and a brief note of the queen's reply,[4] probably sent with Raleigh's supply ship, to Lane for his letter of the previous autumn. Philip Wyot's diary supplies some useful evidence about Grenville's attempt to set out on 16 April and also on his return in December,[5] though we could do with more about both episodes. There are a few details about an Indian probably brought back by Grenville.[6] A number of documents from the High Court of Admiralty records provide us with a little evidence on the Bideford-Barn-

---

[1] Cp. p. 812 below.   [2] Document no. 56, p. 471 below.
[3] Document no. 61, pp. 474-5 below.
[4] Document no. 60, p. 474 below.
[5] Documents nos. 62, 70, pp. 475-6, 494 below.
[6] Document no. 71, p. 495 below.

staple participation in the voyage, while they provide details (corroborating Diaz) of French and Dutch ships taken on the outward voyage, and illustrate Grenville's determination to take prizes from friend and enemy alike.[1]

Otherwise the documents of this year contain some dedications —by Martin Basanier[2] and John Hooker[3]—which break the silence, so far as publications are concerned, about the Virginia ventures,[4] though without supplying much significant detail; the mention by Hakluyt of another, forthcoming, venture; and some advice which he gave Raleigh about expeditions subsequent to 1586;[5] while, from Antwerp, Ortelius began making inquiries about the geography of the discoveries.[6]

THE 1587 VOYAGES

The main voyage in 1587 is very much better documented than those of the previous year, since we have John White's journal of his expedition,[7] and this is rather fuller than, for example, the 1585 *Tiger* journal. It records carefully the main incidents of the voyage, but, at the same time, it has some unfortunate omissions which White, as leader of the expedition, could well have supplied. He tells us very little of how the colonists were got together and why they delayed so long before setting out. He does not make clear the names and commanders of his vessels. He gives no explanation of his long wrangle with Simon Fernandez in the course of their passage through the Caribbean. He fails to state precisely where the expedition was bound for after its intended call at Roanoke Island, and he does not convince us why the settlers insisted on his going home or, indeed, why the sailors would not bring them on to Chesapeake Bay. At the

---

[1] Documents nos. 65–6, pp. 480–8 below.
[2] Document no. 58, pp. 472–3 below.
[3] Document no. 68, pp. 489–93 below.   [4] Cp. pp. 5–6 above.
[5] Document no. 69, pp. 493–4 below.
[6] Documents nos. 57, 67, 73, pp. 472, 488, 496 below.
[7] Document no. 77, pp. 515–38 below.

same time he is clear about most of the incidents of the voyage and the journal is accompanied by a list of the colonists.[1] It is highly probable that both documents came to Hakluyt, like earlier material, direct from Raleigh as part of the documentation which it was agreed between them should be given to the Virginia ventures in the *Principall navigations*, but they could possibly have come to Hakluyt direct from White.

The only other English document so far found which throws any light on the voyage is the grant of arms made to the City of Raleigh, its governor and assistants, on 7 January.[2] If we had the agreement between Raleigh, White and the assistants on the terms on which the City of Raleigh was to be founded we should know a good deal more about what is after all the most interesting of all the sixteenth-century American colonizing ventures, but it has, unfortunately, not yet been found and is known entirely from references in the grant of arms and elsewhere.[3]

The dedications to Raleigh with which Hakluyt in this year prefaced his editions of Peter Martyr[4] and Laudonnière[5] respectively are rather more informative about the objectives of the Virginia voyages than those of the previous year, and some of the incidental information they contain is important, as, for example, that which they give on Thomas Hariot.

The most interesting new material concerns a privateering venture sent out by Sir George Carey to the West Indies, which called in at the 'Virginia' shore on its way homewards. English sources merely give us the licence for sending the ships out and very brief notes on their prize.[6] The important source is that in the Spanish archives,[7] again the report of the interrogation of a Spanish seaman, Alonso Ruiz, who was captured in the West

---

[1] Document no. 78, pp. 539–43 below.

[2] Document no. 74, pp. 506–12 below.   [3] Pp. 385, 569–76 below.

[4] See Document no. 76, pp. 513–15 below.

[5] See Document no. 81, pp 545–52 below.

[6] Documents nos. 75, 79, pp. 512, 543 below.

[7] Document no. 147, pp. 781–4 below; Wright, *Further English voyages*, pp. 233–5.

Indies and taken back to England. Unfortunately, he, or his interrogator, is by no means precise about where or in what circumstances the call at the Carolina Banks or Chesapeake Bay was made, and there are even a few tears in the document to make translation more difficult. Piecing together this evidence with a little from Darby Glande[1] we have the first clear indications of a hitherto unknown facet of the Roanoke story. Carey's ships were perhaps carrying settlers and were certainly experimenting in using the American settlement as a port of call for privateers. Somewhere in the High Court of Admiralty records there may well be materials which would give this shadowy picture substance.

FROM 1587 TO 1589

After John White's return the sources on the events of the next two years, so tragic in their implications for the colony, are meagre. Raleigh's attempt to make it possible for Grenville to sail on his third Virginia expedition failed on account of the Spanish danger.[2] We have then the short, discouraging report[3] of John White's venture in the *Brave* and the *Roe* to bring the colonists at least some token reinforcements and supplies, which ended in the vicinity of the Azores. To White's account Pedro Diaz now adds some further information, as he was with White and succeeded in escaping to tell his story[4] at Havana in March 1589 following. There is nothing further until the agreement of 7 March 1589[5] between White and the assistants of the City of Raleigh colony and a group of men, mostly London merchants, headed by Thomas Smythe, William Sanderson, and Richard Hakluyt, by which the latter underwrote the colony, agreeing to support and supply it, and recording a grant from Raleigh for the furtherance of those ends. Isolated as it is, and not followed by any rescue

[1] P. 836 below.   [2] Documents nos. 82–5, pp. 559–62 below.
[3] Document no. 86, pp. 562–9 below.
[4] Document no. 149, pp. 793–5 below; Wright, *Further English voyages*, pp. 237–41.
[5] Document no. 87, pp. 569–76 below.

venture in 1589, this document fails to explain fully why nothing was done in what was, surely, a critical time for the colonists. Hakluyt included White's account of the 1588 voyage and the agreement of March 1589 in his *Principall navigations*, not long after the agreement was made,[1] but he omitted them both in 1600, the former, no doubt, for its lack of maritime interest, and the latter because nothing effective had been done to follow it up and White had, in the meantime, written the last chapter in the story of the ventures.[2]

THE 1590 VOYAGE

John White's journal[3] of the last of the Roanoke voyages is the best of the three accounts he has left of these ventures. It is fuller than the others; there is less grumbling self-pity (though there is some); the passages in which he describes his last visit to Roanoke Island in search of the colonists have a moving simplicity; and with it we have the covering letter which he wrote to Hakluyt.[4] Now, however, we have much to add to White, mainly about the West Indian part of the venture, and we can see some of his defects as a reporter more clearly. White, we are now aware, was less than completely frank about the circumstances in which he set out in 1590, since he suppressed William Sanderson's part in the venture and gave us no clear impression of what the role of his ship, the *Moonlight*, was intended to be. The new document which has turned up[5] on this episode is not fully self-explanatory, but it shows at least that White's in this respect is not the whole story. Then, too, as regards what happened in the West Indies, we find that while the journal gives an honest story and preserves information which is of very considerable interest, it fails to make clear

[1] It was inserted out of order at pp. 815–17, as having been received, apparently, while the earlier material in this section was at the press. Hakluyt may have received both from either White or Raleigh, or, being a party, he may have had his own copy of the latter document.

[2] Documents nos. 89, 107.

[3] Document no. 89, pp. 598–622 below.

[4] Document no. 107, pp. 712–16 below.

[5] Document no. 102, pp. 704–10 below.

which ships were doing what. White confuses us among the various *Johns*, he does not give us the name of the *Conclude* and gets her captain's name wrong—though there is an excuse for this in that she was in company with the *Hopewell* only for a short time—and his topographical information is not always impeccable.[1] He also conveys the impression that the sailors in the *Hopewell* regarded him as a useless impediment to their privateering when in fact they went through the West Indies boasting to the Spaniards that they had the governor of the English North American colony on board and that the colony itself was soon to be used as a base against the Spanish Indies.[2] We may find reason also to criticize certain vague statements he made about the lost colonists. He expected to find them on Roanoke Island, yet he had already told us in the 1587 journal[3] that they had intended to move to a place 50 miles away on the mainland, the whereabouts of which he did not specify. He does not give in this 1590 journal an adequate critical discussion of what they planned,[4] and he even seems to blame Captain Spicer for being drowned as this prevented his search of Croatoan.

The journal was clearly based on that kept by White on the voyage, like those for 1587 and 1588, but rewritten at leisure. This time it is clear, however, that he sent it direct to Hakluyt at his request,[5] and that it was not intended for Raleigh and not sent by Raleigh to Hakluyt. White's covering letter to Hakluyt,[6] written on 4 February 1593 gives his version of the circumstances which led to his sailing in 1590, blaming the sailors for most of the mishaps of the voyages, and declaring his intention of giving up the search for the colony. It is not without dignity, but it confirms the impression of his less personal journals that he was a man unfitted for leadership, his *métier* clearly being painting and cartography.

[1] Cp. pp. 605–7 (text and footnotes) below.
[2] Wright, *Further English voyages*, pp. lxxix, 244, 251–2, 253–4, 256, 258; p. 799 below.
[3] P. 533 below.   [4] Pp. 613–16 below.
[5] P. 712 below.   [6] Document no. 107, pp. 712–16 below.

The 1590 Voyage

To White's letter and journal, long the only sources for the voyage, can now be added a mass of new material, which falls into two groups, the one being the Spanish documents on the passage of the English through the West Indies,[1] affording some glimpses of White and showing the English privateers as their victims saw them, the other a series of documents[2] arising from legal actions in the High Court of Admiralty. The records of the latter, though its written procedure was complex and its surviving records, voluminous though they are, jumbled and incomplete, still provide a remarkable mine of information on maritime affairs which has never been definitively explored.[3] For the Roanoke voyages between 1584 and 1589 the contribution of these records has been mainly in the form of bits and pieces which throw an incidental, rather than a direct, light on the voyages; for the 1590 voyage, however, we have almost too much material, since we are fortunate in having nearly all the documents which can assist us through the maze of procedure to a verdict—a fairly unusual circumstance in such cases.

The High Court of Admiralty cases began on the initiative of the privy council. Thomas Middleton, who with his partners James Bagge and Nicholas Glanville, owned the *Conclude*, petitioned the council that Robert Hallett was trying to defraud them of a prize taken jointly, and on 11 October 1590 the matter was referred to the judge of the admiralty,[4] Dr Julius Caesar, the case being opened on 19 October.[5] Behind Hallett were his employer, John Watts, the most active and successful London merchant[6] in what we may well call the privateering trade, and his partners.

---

[1] Wright, *Further English voyages*, pp. lxxv–ix, 244–62; Document no. 152, pp. 797–801 below.

[2] Documents nos. 90–106, pp. 623–712 below.

[3] Dr K. R. Andrew's thesis, 'The economic aspects of Elizabethan privateering' (London University, 1951) is the most effective sally so far into the Elizabethan admiralty court material, to which, and to Dr Andrews personally, I am much indebted, both as regards procedure and the documentation of the venture.

[4] Document no. 90, p. 623 below.

[5] Document no. 92, p. 624 below.

[6] Andrews, 'Elizabethan privateering', pp. 57, 122–3, 242–3.

Watts was a frequent litigant in the admiralty court and his counsel knew all the legal tricks by which a verdict might be obtained. The libel,[1] the statement of the plaintiffs' case, with the positions he claimed to be able to prove, and the verdict he desired, was answered in an allegation by the defence.[2] This was done on 23 October,[3] Hallett being produced, and four of the plaintiffs' witnesses named, together with three more on the following day.[4] The witnesses were examined during the days following on articles made out by the plaintiffs[5] and cross-examined on interrogatories set down by the defence.[6] The depositions of Henry Millett and John Tayler were made on the 26th,[7] those of Thomas Harding (or Harden), William Davell (or Cable) and John Bedford on the 27th,[8] and those of Henry Swanne and Hugh Hardinge on the 29th.[9] On 3 November the defendant Robert Hallett made his personal answer[10] to articles based on the positions set out in the libel by the plaintiffs. This was paralleled on the same day[11] by the defence bringing forward a *materia*, an additional allegation stating why the libel was legally inapplicable, and setting out articles based on it upon which witnesses could be examined. The names of six witnesses were put in, but we have not the depositions of any of them. The next stage was the intervention of the Lord High Admiral in the case. The prize had been seized under letters of reprisal and the admiralty court had the duty of appraising the prize, proving to its satisfaction that all the prize goods were intact and were all taken from

[1] P.R.O., H.C.A. 24/58, no. 126, fo. 199. For procedure I have relied on Andrews, loc. cit. pp. 380–1; A. A. Ruddock, 'The earliest records of the High Court of Admiralty, 1515–1558', in *Bulletin of the Institute of Historical Research*, XXIII (1950), 139–51; *Select pleas in the Court of Admiralty*, ed. R. G. Marsden, 2 vols. (1894, 1897).

[2] P.R.O., H.C.A. 24/58, no. 121, fo. 193.

[3] Document no. 93, pp. 624–5 below.

[4] Document no. 94, p. 625 below.

[5] Document no. 95, pp. 625–46 below. The articles have not been found.

[6] Document no. 96, pp. 647–81 below.

[7] See pp. 625–31 below.   [8] See pp. 632–40 below.

[9] See pp. 640–6 below.   [10] Document no. 98, pp. 682–7 below.

[11] Document no. 97, p. 682 below.

Spaniards and not from neutrals or natives, and that the Lord High Admiral's tenth, less the 5% of it which the judge of the admiralty had as his perquisite, together with the queen's custom, tunnage and poundage, were duly deductable. We have in this connexion the examination, on articles on behalf of the Lord High Admiral, of Abraham Cocke, Robert Hutton and Michael Geere on 10 November[1] and that of Christopher Newport, by then sufficiently recovered from his wound to give evidence, on 23 November.[2] This in turn was followed by the official inventory of the prize, the *Buen Jesus*, on 20 December,[3] and two depositions by Spanish members of the crew of the prize, on behalf of Watts, on 8 January 1591.[4]

The third and final stage was an action by John Watts and his partners against William Sanderson. The first stage had hinged on whether Middleton's ship, the *Conclude*, had taken part in the capture of the *Buen Jesus*, and if she had done so or not, whether she was formally in partnership with Watts's vessel, the *Hopewell*, or *Harry and John*, from which Hallett had come to command the prize crew which brought the *Buen Jesus* to England. At that stage a number of the plaintiffs' witnesses had come from the *Moonlight*, William Sanderson's ship, which was also present when the *Buen Jesus* was taken. Watts's action, though we do not know the precise grounds on which it was based, was begun on 11 January 1591,[5] and was in general terms directed to attacking the implicit claim that the *Moonlight* had been in formal partnership with the *Hopewell*. Sanderson's men claimed they had a partnership with the *Conclude* in the same way as the *Moonlight* had with the *Hopewell*, so that the three ships were all entitled to their shares in the prize. By attacking Sanderson Watts hoped to be able to show that there was no partnership between his ships and the *Moonlight* and that neither she nor the *Conclude* had actively

[1] Document no. 99, pp. 687–9, 691–2 below.
[2] See pp. 690–2 below, and cp. pp. 590, 619.
[3] Document no. 100, pp. 692–5 below.
[4] Document no. 101, pp. 695–703 below.
[5] Document no. 103, p. 710 below.

participated in taking the prize. Watts on 12 January[1] put in a long list of seventeen witnesses whom he wished to have examined before they went to sea. We have the interrogatories which were drawn up on Sanderson's behalf,[2] and these give us such new information as we have on the Virginia aspect of the expedition, but unfortunately we have no account of the examinations in which they were used. We do not know the detailed story of the alleged Watts-Sanderson partnership, but Watts appears to have established his claim that his ships were not in partnership with the *Moonlight* at the critical time. The case now turned merely on the parts played by the three ships in the actual capture of the prize, irrespective of previous contractual obligations; here the two depositions by Spanish members of the crew of the *Buen Jesus*, Antonio de Çamora Carreño and Francisco Gomez, made on 8 January,[3] proved decisive; they declared that the *Hopewell* was solely responsible for the capture of their ship. We may suspect, but not prove, that they were primed, and bribed, by Watts. All was now virtually over. Watts produced the inventory of the prize to have it formally passed, and the judge gave a final decision in the case.[4]

There remained only the signing of the decree. Each party normally drew up a draft decree in accordance with what they hoped the court would decide. That which the judge signed became effective, and in this case we have the signed decree[5] in Watt's favour. Watts and Hallett had won, and the *Conclude* and the *Moonlight* were excluded from any share in the prize. We may suspect, even if we cannot prove it, that Sanderson was paid off by Watts behind the scenes for his failure to fight his case with all his resources. The net result is that we have, perhaps, two-thirds of the documents in the case, and their publication below provides a good illustration of the value of the admiralty court records.

[1] Document no. 104, p. 711 below.
[2] Document no. 102, pp. 704–10 below.   [3] Pp. 695–703 below.
[4] Document no. 105, p. 711 below.
[5] Document no. 106, pp. 711–12 below.

Clearly the examinations provide the most interesting material, and through the formal framework of questioning we often see vivid patches of narrative and personal revelation. But without the contingent formal documents no convincing picture of the relevance of the depositions can be built up. The main regret we must express here is that, illuminating as the documents are on the West Indies prize-taking, they tell us so tantalizingly little about the last Roanoke voyage.

THE SPANISH DOCUMENTS

The Spanish documents presented in the final two chapters [1] below belong to rather a different category from those previously described. They do not cover the voyages entirely consecutively, since some are depositions taken a considerable time after the events, and they represent the point of view, naturally, of those who regarded the voyages in a hostile manner, as directed in greater or lesser measure against themselves. They fall into three general groups. The first comprises the dispatches now at Simancas, sent to Spain from the Spanish ambassador in France and containing reports of English activities in, or directed to, North America. The second includes documents now at Seville, Madrid, and the British Museum which supplement or (in two cases) [2] duplicate material recently printed by Miss Irene A. Wright in her *Further English voyages to Spanish America*. These first two groups are in turn supplemented in some degree from the State Papers, Foreign, especially the Spanish papers, in the Public Record Office, and by two depositions taken from Hakluyt. [3] The third group, derived from Seville, Madrid and from a nearly contemporary printed source, [4] is mainly concerned with the Spanish expedition of 1588 to Chesapeake Bay in search of the English colony, and includes other documents deriving indirectly from that voyage.

[1] Pp. 717–838.   [2] Documents nos. 147, 149, pp. 781–4, 786–95 below.

[3] Documents nos. 138–9, pp. 761–6, both from men brought by Drake from San Agustín in 1586.

[4] Oré, *Relacion* (c. 1617), see below, pp. 802–16.

The Spanish investigation of the supposedly surviving English settlement on Chesapeake Bay went on long after the lost colony on Roanoke Island disappeared. Here it is taken to 1600, but there is a further chapter to be added on continuing Spanish activity along the coast north of the Florida settlement between 1600 and 1606. This fits in best with the revived English voyages to America from 1602 onwards and will be considered subsequently in relation to them.

The extracts[1] comprising the first category of documents are already well known. Taken by Napoleon from Simancas to Paris, they remained in the Ministère des Affaires Étrangères, where they were abstracted for the *Spanish calendar*, until some time between 1931 and 1941, when they were returned to Simancas. They have now been translated direct from the Spanish and this has yielded a few additional crumbs of information.[2] One document referred to in the *Calendar* cannot now be found at Simancas.[3] Brief as they are, and often inaccurate or imprecise, they are of considerable interest as showing how much or how little the Spaniards knew of affairs in England. To begin with, Mendoza, from Paris, kept in close touch with Raleigh's preparations for the Virginia enterprises, but he gradually lost contact as Spanish agents were weeded out. Santa Cruz had his own agents in England and Ireland, and these were sometimes more effective than Mendoza's, but unfortunately we have not many reports from them.[4] In the State Papers, Foreign, there are a number of intercepted (or copied) reports of Spanish agents, and one at least is of some interest for our purposes,[5] while news and rumours from Spanish sources provide a few sidelights on Spanish policy.[6]

[1] Sixteen in all, Documents nos. 108–9, 111–16, 118, 123–4, 133–6, 146, pp. 725–6, 728–32, 743–4, 756–61, 770–1 below.

[2] Cp. pp. 725, 728, 732 below.

[3] The relation of the German captain, cp. pp. 756–60 below.

[4] E.g. Document no. 131, pp. 753–4; Cp. Wright, *Further English voyages*, p. 8.

[5] Document no. 117, pp. 731–2 below.

[6] Mainly through the Venetian agents. Documents nos. 129–30, 137, 141, 144, 151, 153, pp. 752, 761, 768, 770, 797, 801 below.

The Spanish Documents

Although the documents in the second group, those which supplement Miss Wright's selection, number nineteen in all, they cannot individually be said to be of outstanding importance. Two of them,[1] one of 1585 and one of 1590, are abbreviated English versions of Spanish correspondence seized crossing the Atlantic. One document on the 1585 ventures is very similar to one printed by Miss Wright,[2] but another, the relation of Hernando de Altamirano,[3] is a useful supplement. The remainder are chiefly important because they provide some guide to the changing policy and the administrative arrangements of the Spanish government regarding the English colony, together with additional material on Pedro Menéndez Marqués,[4] the Spanish governor of Florida, who was the main instrument in all the Spanish attempts to track down the site of the English settlement, and who had bad luck in most of his ventures. The effect of them is to provide, with Miss Wright's documents, and with a few gaps, a fairly coherent picture of Spanish policy and action from 1585 to 1590, when the Spanish effort was finally diverted. The duplication of the depositions of Alonso Ruiz and Pedro Diaz[5] was found desirable in view of the multiplicity of their links with the English documents and the possibility of annotating them more fully as a result.

Unrepresented in this second group, apart from a single letter by Pedro Menéndez Marqués,[6] is the story of the Spanish expedition in 1588 under Vicente González to search for the English settlement on, it was believed, Chesapeake Bay. The detailed account of this voyage by Juan Menéndez Marqués—and whatever report González sent to supplement it—has long been lost,[7]

[1] Documents nos. 120, 152, pp. 738–9, 797–801 below.
[2] Document no. 119, pp. 733–8 below; cp. Wright, *Further English voyages*, pp. 10–11.
[3] Document no. 121, pp. 740–3 below.
[4] Documents nos. 110, 124–8, 132–3, 140, 142–3, 148, pp. 726–7, 744–51, 754–7, 766–70, 785–6 below.
[5] Documents nos. 147, 149, pp. 781–4, 786–95; cp. Wright, *Further English voyages*, pp. 233–5, 237–41.
[6] Document no. 146, pp. 778–81 below.   [7] Cp. pp. 812, 822 below.

but we can replace it to some extent, as it was used in some detail by Luis Jerónimo de Oré in his *Relación de los martires que a avido en la provincias de la Florida.... Ponese assi mesmo la descripcion del Jacan, donde se an fortificado los Ingleses,* which was written about 1616 and published, possibly at Madrid, about 1617. This remained unknown to English and American historians until it was edited by Atanasio Lopez, 1931-3,[1] and translated and published in America in 1936 by Dr Maynard Geiger.[2] Even then it was apparently ignored by students of early English colonization. In fact it contains a succinct and apparently accurate account of the 1588 voyage, based mainly, though not solely, on Juan Menéndez Marqués. The extracts given below[3] form a useful basis for assessing a group of later documents referring to the voyage. An investigation begun in 1598 by the governor of Florida, Gonzálo Méndez de Canzo, on what was known of the territories north of Florida led to an examination of past history, and in the course of it Vicente González was asked to give an account[4] of his voyage in 1588. The result is far from satisfactory, but it adds a little to Oré. Further, Juan Menéndez Marqués, who had settled down as treasurer of the Florida colony, wrote about the 1588 voyage in 1602, 1605 and 1606,[5] consequent on these inquiries. His material is rather allusive and incomplete, but it adds something to Oré, and probably justifies the description of his original report by the latter as *tan puntual y prolija*.[6] One of Méndez de Canzo's most interesting discoveries was that among the Florida garrison was an Irishman who had served with Lane at Roanoke Island in 1585-6—the Darby Glande (or Glavin) who deserted White in 1587. His deposition,[7] first published in English in 1924,[8] is of

[1] *Relación histórica de la Florida*, 2 vols. (Madrid, 1931-3).
[2] *The martyrs of Florida, 1513-1616* (New York, 1936).
[3] Document no. 154, pp. 802-16 below.
[4] Document no. 156, pp. 822-5 below.
[5] Documents no. 155, pp. 816-21 below.
[6] Cp. p. 812 below.   [7] Document no. 158, pp. 834-8 below.
[8] Translated by Miss Katherine Reding in *Georgia Historical Quarterly*, VIII (1924), 215-28.

considerable interest, though it was not that of a very intelligent man. It inspired Méndez de Canzo with the belief that in 1600 the English were still established in force to the north and he planned[1] elaborately, and with complete futility, for their overthrow. As a whole, this last group is perhaps the most valuable of the contributions here printed from Spanish sources in its relevance to the Roanoke voyages and fills out in an adequate manner our knowledge of a series of episodes which were hitherto imperfectly known.

Rich as has been Miss Wright's harvest of the Spanish materials, especially those at Seville, and useful as the supplement here published is to the understanding of the setting of the Roanoke voyages, it is unlikely that the Spanish archives have now yielded by any means all of their secrets. There may yet be discoveries on the Roanoke voyages to be made in Spain.

THE AFTERMATH

One surprising thing about the Roanoke ventures is that apart from continued Spanish interest in them, which has been illustrated, and White's contributions of 1593, nothing has so far emerged to show continued English interest in the voyages or their resumption before 1600. The Molyneux globe of 1592 is an exception, but the documents have so far remained silent. Of course the war and the larger-scale operations against Spain and the Indies, East and West, tended to blanket the western lands, but it would not be surprising if English privateers were found, like Carey's in 1587, to have called to look for water and fuel and even, casually, to have sought the lost colonists. If so, their records have still to be disclosed. Whether there was any organized planning of further colonies before 1600 we cannot say. Certainly, in 1600 Richard Hakluyt thought that it was time there was some conscious revival of English activity in this field. His selection of documents for his third volume was deliberately directed towards

[1] Document no. 157, pp. 826–33 below.

that end, and he provides his own tail-piece to the documentation of the earlier series of voyages in a famous little passage of his dedication to Sir Robert Cecil:[1]

> Thus Sir I haue portrayed out in rude lineaments my Westerne Atlantis or America: assuring you, that if I had bene able, I would haue limned her and set her out with farre more liuely and exquisite colours: yet, as she is, I humbly desire you to receiue her with your wonted and accustomed fauour at my handes....

These volumes are a tribute to what he preserved and a commentary on his not ungracious modesty.

[1] *Principal navigations*, III (1600), sig. A 3 v., dated 1 Sept. 1600.

CHAPTER I

THE DISCOVERY OF
RALEIGH'S VIRGINIA, 1584

'There are stranger things to be seen in the world than are
between London and Stanes.'   SIR WALTER RALEIGH[1]

NARRATIVE

The early months of 1584 saw a flurry of preparations to follow
up the enterprises initiated by Sir Humphrey Gilbert. Sir George
Peckham fades out of view after January 1584.[2] Richard Hakluyt
was prepared to go himself on one enterprise or another at
the opening of the year,[3] and he was busy in the spring trying
to stimulate English merchants in Rouen to invest in a western
venture.[4] Sir John Gilbert and others had plans to follow up
Sir Humphrey's dealings in Newfoundland.[5] Above all, Christopher Carleill was still in the field, but, setting out, probably for
New England, early in the summer, he got no further than
Ireland.[6] Out of Gilbert's plans too had come in February the
patent for the north-west passage discoveries to his brother Adrian
which prefaced the Davis voyages.[7] It was his half-brother
Walter Raleigh who stepped, however, into Sir Humphrey's

---

[1] Attributed by John Aubrey, *The natural history of Wiltshire*, ed. John Britton
(Wilts. Topographical Soc., 1847), p. 64. Staines was evidently Raleigh's first
stopping-point outside London on his way to the south-west and his last on his
return (cp. 4 Oct. 1595, 'Sir Walter Rawley lay yesternight at Stanes', Hist. MSS
Comm., *De L'Isle and Dudley MSS*, II, 169).

[2] Pp. 3–5 above; Quinn, *Gilbert*, I, 90–3.

[3] 7 January 1584. Richard Hakluyt to Sir Francis Walsingham, from Paris
(Taylor, *Hakluyts*, II, 206).

[4] An interesting document (Brit. Mus., Additional MS 14027, fos. 289–90),
hitherto overlooked, provides some information on this project. It will be published in a future volume of the Society's publications.

[5] Quinn, *Gilbert*, I, 95. The precise nature of English projects regarding Newfoundland after Sir Humphrey Gilbert's death remains somewhat obscure.

[6] Ibid. pp. 94–5.   [7] Ibid. pp. 96–100.

shoes. His patent followed Gilbert's grant of 1578, due to expire on 11 June 1584, being unlimited in its rights to territories newly discovered, but excepting interference with the Newfoundland fishery.[1] When did he make his first move? At least some weeks before the issue of a privy seal warrant on 16 March which passed the great seal on 25 March.[2] It would appear that Raleigh had, under his patent, rights to control other English venturers to North America unless they could, under assignments from Gilbert, establish a foothold by 11 June. Yet Carleill had been a law to himself in 1583 and was under Walsingham's wing.[3] If, in the summer of 1584, he was going west to New England, then probably a zone had been reserved for him under an agreement which has not survived. It is tempting to assume some such agreement, as Raleigh clearly intended an expedition well to the south of 'Norumbega'. Gilbert's voyage in 1583 by the northerly route has obscured until recently his plans for approaching New England by the southerly route as well.[4] What we cannot say is how far there was at this time a clearly formulated idea in Raleigh's mind of combining exploration, colonization and the establishment of a base for shipping near enough to raid the Spanish Indies, but far enough away from Florida to be reasonably free from molestation.

We know nothing, directly, of the preparation of the 1584 expedition. Raleigh had saved his *Bark Raleigh* from the wreck of Gilbert's fortunes in 1583, but was she Amadas's ship in 1584? The other vessel was a pinnace and could have been his *Dorothy*.[5] But there is no evidence. Amadas, who commanded the expedition, was a Plymouth man who was born about 1565; Barlowe,

---

[1] P. 85 below. [2] P. 82 below.

[3] Quinn, *Gilbert*, I, 76–81, 93–5.

[4] Incomplete instructions for a voyage to be made in 1582 by the southerly route survive in a copy in Brit. Mus., Additional MS 38823, fos. 1–8, which are also to be published by the Society. See E. G. R. Taylor, 'Instructions to a colonial surveyor in 1582', in *Mariner's Mirror*, XXXVII (1951), 48–62, and pp. 51–4 above.

[5] Cp. p. 179 below.

the second captain, remains unknown except through his narrative. Simon Fernandez, the Azorean Portuguese who was the pilot, had been Walsingham's man and had made a daring reconnaissance for Gilbert to, apparently, New England in 1580. Benjamin Wood was destined for later prominence at sea. Otherwise, we know by inference that John White was on board,[1] but little can be gathered of the other few men who are named. The vessels were prepared in the Thames,[2] sailed round to a West Country port, almost certainly Plymouth, and left there on 27 April. They took the West Indies course, apparently picking up the north-east trades at the Canaries and entering the Caribbean by the Dominica passage. There are several indications[3] that they landed near the south-west tip of Puerto Rico before leaving for the Florida Channel. On 2 July they realized they were near land, on 4 July they saw it, and on 13 July, after coasting 120 miles, they found an inlet. This was evidently found by Fernandez and is, with little doubt, the inlet in the Carolina Banks below Roanoke Island, later called Port Ferdinando or Hatarask.[4] Formal possession was taken in the queen's name of the island, called Hatarask by the Indians, which lay to the south of the inlet. After two days contact was made with Indians fishing. Granganimeo, brother of the local chief Wingina, appeared the following day with many others. This was the prelude to several days' trading and was followed by a visit by Barlowe and seven others to the chief's village at the north-western end of Roanoke Island. There are indications of some cursory examination of the sounds inside the Banks and of the Banks themselves from the seaward side, since several other entrances were noticed in vague terms.[5] Nothing is said of when or in what circumstances they left, but the return voyage, ending in mid-September, was evidently easy and speedy.

[1] Cp. pp. 40, 715 below.   [2] P. 92 below.
[3] Cp. pp. 80, 93, 181 below.
[4] Pp. 95, 202, 863–4 below, and map at end.
[5] P. 114 below. This should, however, be supplemented by Hariot's notes to De Bry, pl. II, (fig. 5, pp. 413–15 below), which are, however, somewhat difficult to interpret.

The Roanoke Voyages

Such is the outline from Barlowe, recording a voyage of reconnaissance, the precise instructions for which have not survived,[1] and the exact results of which lack precision and definition in space and time. The narrative, it is true, carries us continuously from 2 to 15 July, and then, without dates, for only another week or so until the visit to Roanoke Island. Can there be anything in the tangled version given in Jamaica in 1586 by an English castaway from the 1585 expedition?[2] I give a translation of the relevant passages (somewhat varying from Miss Wright's though not clarifying all the ambiguities in an obscure text) the first of which reads:

He says that the Portuguese Hernando [Simon Fernandez] had, some eight years before, left to explore a part of Florida suitable for settlement, but could not get there until [after] he reached Puerto Rico; whence he made the voyage he had originally intended to make, arriving on the Florida coast at a headland which on the chart was at 38¼°; and the Englishman said that on the English chart it was at 36° where, he says, the vessels anchor. And from that point [westwards?] there is a large bay with some islands, and the water is fresh. This bay is four leagues long and opens into the sea; and according to the Indians is the largest along that coast and is a channel to the other sea.

If this translation does not strain the Spanish too far I take it to mean that in 1578 Fernandez set out[3] to explore the southeastern shore of North America, that he failed to get there, and that subsequently, in 1584, he went by way of Puerto Rico to an inlet at 38½° on the Spanish chart and 36° on the English—the latter could represent the 'G. de Mᵃ' (Golfo de Madre?) of Dee's chart of 1580.[4] The great bay with its islands would represent the Carolina Sounds, and the Indian story could well have been told by, or deduced from, Manteo and Wanchese. Apart from chrono-

[1] They are referred to but not quoted by Barlowe, p. 92 below.
[2] Seville, A. G. I. 2.5.1/20 (Patronato 265); Wright, *Further English voyages*, pp. 175–6.
[3] I.e. with Raleigh in the *Falcon* on Gilbert's 1578 expedition. (Quinn, *Gilbert*, I, 44–5, 236–8). The reference does not even require that he reached American waters though it may do so.
[4] See the relevant sections reproduced in Taylor, *Hakluyts*, and in Quinn, *Gilbert*.

logy this paragraph does not raise issues of great significance. It is otherwise with the next which reads:

> Deponent says that when the Portuguese [Fernandez] discovered this port he wished to land on one promontory, but the wild Indians ate thirty-eight Englishmen, and he went on to the other promontory, where there is a good port, and found the savages there gentler. He asked them if there was gold or silver and the Indians replied that there was much, and gave him four pounds of gold and a hundred [pounds] of silver, buffalo-skins [*queros de ante*] and many other valuable things. The Portuguese took with him to England two wild Indians, leaving two Englishmen as hostages that he would return later....

The prior landing which was opposed and where some Englishmen were lost cannot be fitted into Barlowe's narrative unless we presume him to be a liar. If, however, a landing was made after leaving the Roanoke Indians and there was hostility by the Indians, he would not be guilty of more than suppression of some information which did not fit in with the necessary propaganda for the 1585 expedition. The gold and silver do not figure in Barlowe's account of his commerce with the Indians—he was unsure whether Granganimeo's metal headpiece was of copper or gold [1]—though pearls and buffalo-skins do. [2] The taking of the two Indians is true, but the statement that two Englishmen were left in their place is nowhere hinted at by Barlowe, though it is not inherently impossible or even unlikely. If they were so left it would appear likely that they were not maltreated and were restored to the expedition in 1585, though it is surprising, if this was so, that no reference was made to their experiences of life in an Indian society. In sum, therefore, the Spanish document suggests that there is something of significance which occurred on the American coast but which is absent from Barlowe's discourse, even if we are left in some considerable doubt about what it was. Yet this first reconnaissance was undoubtedly a success. It paved the way for a much more ambitious venture.

[1] P. 102 below.   [2] Pp. 100–2 below.

1. 25 MARCH 1584.

LETTERS PATENT TO WALTER RALEIGH[1]

Elizabeth by the grace of God &c[2] To all people to whome thes presentes shall come greting Know yee that of our especiall grace certeyne science and meere mocyon We haue gyuen and graunted and by thes presentes for vs our heyres and successors doe geve and graunte to our trusty and welbeloved servaunte Walter Raleighe Esquier and to his heyres and assignes for ever free liberty and license from tyme to tyme and at all tymes for ever hereafter to discover search fynde out and viewe such remote heathen and barbarous landes Contries and territories not actually possessed of any Christian Prynce and[3] inhabited by Christian *Extractum.* people as to him his heyres and assignes and to every or any of them shall seme good and the same to haue holde occupy and enioye to him his heyres and assignes for ever with all preroga- taves[4] comodities iurisdiccions and[5] royalties priviledges Fraun- chises and preeminences there[6] or thereaboutes bothe by sea and lande what so ever we by our lettres patentes may grante and as we or any of our noble Progenitors haue heretofore graunted to any person or persons bodies politique or corporate And the said

---

[1] Patent Roll, 26 Eliz , pt. 1, mm. 38–40, P.R.O., C66/1237, collated with Richard Hakluyt, *Principall navigations* (1589), pp. 725–8; III (1600), 243–5 (VIII (1904), 289–96). Hakluyt heads his version, which was taken from the original patent (not extant) or a copy of it, and not from the patent roll entry: 'The letters patents, graunted by the Queenes Maiestie to Master Walter Ralegh now knight, for the discouering and planting of new lands and Countreis, to continue the space and time of 6. yeeres and no more.' Our knowledge of this grant is taken nine days further back by the discovery of the privy seal for the issue of the patent, which was dated at Westminster on 16 March 26 Elizabeth [1584], but whose text does not vary from the patent as enrolled (Chancery Warrants, series II, 26 Eliz., Mar. 1584 (*a*), P.R.O., C82/1414).

[2] Hakluyt adds 'of England, France and Ireland Queene, defender of the faith'.

[3] 'nor' (Hakluyt).

[4] This word is omitted in the prototype of the patent, that to Sir Humphrey Gilbert on 11 June 1578 (Quinn, *Gilbert*, I, 188).

[5] 'and' omitted by Hakluyt. He added in the margin, misleadingly, 'A.D. 1585' in 1589 but deleted it in 1600.

[6] 'thereto' (this and the subsequent variants being all in Hakluyt).

Walter Raleigh his heyres and assignes and all such as from tyme
to tyme by license of vs our heyres and successors shall goe or
travell thither to inhabite or remayne there to buylde and fortifye
at the discresyon of the said Walter Raleighe his heyres and
assignes the statutes or actes of Parliamente made againste fugityues
or against such as shall departe remayne or contynue out of our
Realme of England without lycense or any other Acte statute
lawe or ordinaunce[1] whatsoever to the contrary in any wise notwithstanding And we doe likewise by thes *presentes* of our grace[2]
especiall meere mocíon and *certeyne* knowledge for vs our heyres
and successors, gyve and graunte full authority liberty and power
to the said Walter Raleighe his heyres and assignes and every of
them That he and they and every or any of them shall and maye
at all and every tyme and tymes hereafter haue take and leade in
the sayde voyages to travell[3] thitherward or to inhabite there with
him or them and every or any of them such and so many of our
subiectes as shall willingly accompany him and them and them
[*sic*] and every or any of them to whome also by these *presentes*
we doe gyue full liberty Power and aucthority[4] in that behalf and
also to haue take employ[5] and vse sufficient shippyng and furniture
for theire transportacions[6] and Nauigacíons in that behalf so that
none of the same *persons* nor[7] any of them be such as hereafter
shalbe restreyned by vs our heyres or successors And further that
he the[8] said Walter Raleighe his heyres and assignes and every of
them shall haue holde occupy and enioye to him his heyres and
assignes and every of them for ever all the soyle of all such landes
Countryes and *territories* so to be discovered or[9] possessed as
aforesaid and of all Cittyes[10] Castles townes villages and places in
the same with the rightes royalties francheses and Iurisdiccíons as

[1] 'statute, act, law, or any ordinance'.   [2] 'especial grace'.
[3] 'and travaile'.
[4] 'presents, giue full libertie and authoritie'.
[5] 'and employ'.   [6] 'the transportations'.
[7] 'or'.   [8] 'that the'.
[9] 'territories, and Countreis, so to be discouered and'.
[10] 'all such Cities'.

well maryne as other within the sayd landes or Countryes or the seas therevnto adioyning to be had or vsed with full power to dispose therof and of every parte in fee simple or otherwise according to the order of the lawes of England as nere as the same conveniently may be at his and theire will and plesure to any person then beyng or that shall remayne within the allegiance of vs our heires and successors Reseruing alwayes to vs our heyres and successors for all seruices dueties and demaundes the fifte parte of all the owre of Gold and silver that from tyme to tyme and at all tymes after such discovery subduyng and possessing shal be there gotten or[1] obteyned All which landes Countreys and territories shall for ever be holden by[2] the said Walter Raleigh his heyres and assignes of vs our heyres and successors by homage and by the said paymente of the said fifte parte before reserued[3] onely for all seruices And moreover we doe by thes presentes for vs our heyres and successors geve and graunte licence to the said Walter Raleighe his heyres and assignes and every of them that he and they and every or any of them shall and may from tyme to tyme and at all times for ever hereafter for his and theire defence encounter expulse[4] repell and resiste aswell by sea as by lande and by all other wayes whatsoever all and every such person and persons what so ever as without the speciall license and likyng[5] of the said Walter Raleighe and of his heyres and assignes shall attempte to inhabite within the said Countreys or any of them or within the space of twoe hundred leagues nere to the place or places within such Countries as aforesaide of [*sic*][6] they shall not be before planted or inhabited within the lymytes aforesaid[7] with the subiectes of any Christian Prynce being in amyty with vs where the said Walter Raleighe his heyres or assignes or any of them or his or theire or any of theire Associates or Company shall within sixe yeares next ensuing make theire dwellynges or abidinges or that shall enterprise or attempte at any time hereafter

---

[1] 'and...and'.   [2] 'of'.   [3] 'part reserued'.
[4] 'and expulse'.   [5] 'especiall likïng and licence of'.
[6] 'if'.   [7] 'as aforesayd'.

vnlawfully to annoye eyther by sea or lande the said Walter Raleigh his heyres [m. 39] or assignes or any of them or his or theyre or any of theire companyes Gevyng and grauntyng by these presentes further power and authority to the sayd Walter Raleighe his heyres and assignes and every of them from tyme to tyme and at all tymes for ever hereafter to take and surprise by all manner meanes[1] whatsoever all and every those person and persons with theyre shippes vesselles or other[2] goodes and furniture which without the license of the said Walter Raleighe or his heyres or assignes as aforesaid shalbe founde traffiquinge into any harbor or harborowes Cricke or Crickes within the lymyttes aforesaid the subiectes of our Realmes and Domynyons and all other persons in amytye with vs tradyng to the Newe founde landes for fishinges as they[3] heretofore haue commonly vsed[4] or beyng dryven by force of tempest[5] or shipwracke onely excepted And those persons and every of them with theire shippes vesselles goodes and furnitures to deteyne and possesse as of good and lawfull price accordinge to the discrecyon of hym the said Walter Raleigh his heyres and assignes and every or any of them And for vynting [*sic*][6] in more perfecte league and amitye of such Countryes landes and territories so to be possessed and Inhabited as aforesaid with our Realmes of England and Ireland and the better encouragemente of men to this enterprise We doe by thes presentes graunte and declare that all such Countryes so hereafter to be possessed and inhabited as is aforesaid from thenceforthe shalbe of the allegiaunce of[7] vs our heyres and successours And we doe graunt to the sayd Walter Raleighe his heyres and assignes and to all and every of them and to all and every other person

---

[1] 'of meanes'. [2] 'and other'.

[3] 'fishing as heretofore they'.

[4] 'trading...vsed', not included in Gilbert's patent of 1578 (Quinn, *Gilbert*, I, 191). This means that Newfoundland, formally annexed by Gilbert in 1583, was excluded from the scope of Raleigh's patent. Whether this was done in the interests of the established English fishermen, or of the monopoly rights in Newfoundland which Sir John Gilbert and others may have claimed as Sir Humphrey's representatives, is not yet clear.

[5] 'of a tempest'. [6] 'vniting'. [7] 'to vs'.

and persons being of our allegiaunce whose names shalbe noted
or entred in some of our Courtes of Record within this our
Realme of England and[1] that with the assente of the said Walter
Raleighe his heyres or assignes shall in his Iorneyes for discovery
or in the Iorneys for Conquest hereafter travell to such landes
Countreys and territories as aforesaid and to theyre and every of
theyre heyres that[2] they and every or any of them being eyther
borne within our said Realme of England or Ireland or in any
other place within our allegiaunces and which hereafter shalbe
Inhabiting within any the landes Countryes and territories with
such license as aforesaid shall and maye haue and enioye[3] all the
pryvyledges of free Denizens[4] and persons natyve of England and
within our allegiaunce in such like ample manner and forme as yf
they were borne and personally resiante within our said Realme
of England any lawe custome or vsage to the Contrary notwithstanding And forasmuch as vpon the fynding out discovering or
Inhabityng of such remote landes Countryes and territories as
aforesaid it shalbe necessary for the safety of all men[5] that shall
adventure themselues in those Iorneys or voyages to determine
to lyue together in Christian peace and Civile quietnes eche with
other whereby every one maye with more plesure and profite
enioye that where vnto they shall atteyne with greate payne and
perill we for vs our heires and successors are likewise pleased and
contented and by thes presentes doe gyve and graunte to the said
Walter Raleighe his heyres and assignes for ever that he and they
and every or any of them shall and maye from tyme to tyme for
ever hereafter within the said mencioned remote landes and Countreys in the waye by the seas thither and from thence haue full
and mere power and aucthorty to correct punishe pardon governe
and rule by theire and every or any of theire good discrecions
and pollecies aswell in causes Capitall or Criminall as Ciuile both

[1] 'within our Realme of England that'. Hakluyt adds in the margin 'Note'.
[2] 'and euery of their heires, and they'.
[3] 'haue and enioye all'.
[4] Hakluyt adds in the margin 'Free Denization granted'.
[5] 'to all men'.

marine and other all such our subiect*es* as shall from tyme to
tyme hereafter adventure[1] themselues in the said Iorneys or
voyages or that shall at any tyme hereafter inhabite any such
land*es* Countryes or territories as aforesaid or that shall abide
within twoe hundred leagues of any the saide place[2] or places
where the said Walter Raleigh or[3] his heyres or assignes or any of
them or any of his or theyre Associates or Companyes shall
Inhabite within sixe yeares nexte ensuyng the date hereof according
to such statutes lawes and ordinaunces as shalbe by him the said
Walter Raleighe his heyres and assignes and every or any of them
devised or established for the better gou*er*nemente of the said
people as aforesaid So alwaies that[4] the said statutes lawes and
ordinaunces may be as nere as conueniently they may be[5]
agreable to the forme of the lawes statutes gou*er*nement or pollicy
of England and also so as they be not against the trewe Christian
faithe or Religion now pro*f*essed[6] in the Churche of England nor
in any wise to withdrawe any of the subiect*es* or people of those
land*es* or places from the allegiance of vs our heyres and successours As theyre imm*e*diate Sovereignes vnder God And furder
we doe by thes pr*e*sent*es* for vs our heyres and successors gewe
and graunt full power and authority to our trustye and welbeloved
Counsellor Sir Willi*a*m Cecill knighte Lorde Burghley our High
Tresorer of England and to the Lorde Tresorer of England of vs[7]
our heyres and successors for the time being and to the Privy
Counsell of vs our heyres and successors or any fower or more
of them for the tyme beyng That he they or any fower or more
of them shall and maye from tyme to tyme and at all tymes
hereafter vnder his or theyre handes or seales by v*e*rtue of thes
pr*e*sent*es* aucthorise and license the said Walter Raleighe his heyres
and assignes and every or any of them by him and by themselues
or by theyre or any of theyre sufficiente Attorneys Deputies
Officers mynysters factors and se*r*uaunt*es* to imbarke and trans-

---

[1] 'time aduenture'.   [2] 'of the sayde place'.   [3] Not 'or'.
[4] 'alwayes as the'.   [5] 'conueniently may bee'.
[6] 'faith, nowe professed'.   [7] 'for vs'.

porte out of our Realmes of England and Ireland or the[1] Do-mynyons therof all or any of his or there or any of there goods[2] and all or any the goodes of his and their Associates and Com-panyes and every or any of them with such other necessaries and commodities of any our Realmes as to the sayde Lorde Tresorer or foure or more of the Privy Counsell of vs our heyres or[3] successors for the tyme beyng as aforesaid shalbe from tyme to tyme by his or theyre wisedoms or discrecions thought meete and conveniente for the better Relief and supportacion of him the said Walter Raleighe his heyres and assignes and every or any of them and of his or theyre and every[4] or any of theire Associates and Companyes any acte statute lawe or thinge[5] to the Contrary in any wise notwithstandyng Provided alwayes and our will and plesure is And we doe hereby declare to all Christian kynges Prynces and states that yf the said Walter Raleigh his heyres or assignes or any of them or any other by theyre license or appoyntemente shall at any tyme or tymes hereafter robbe or spoyle by sea or by lande or doe any acte of vniuste and vnlawfull[6] hostility to any the subiectes of vs our heyres and successors[7] or to any of the subiectes of any Kinge[8] Prynce Ruler Governor or state being then in perfecte league and amytye with vs our heyres and successors And that vpon such Iniury or vpon iuste Complaynte of any such Prince Ruler Governor or [m. 40] state and theire[9] subiectes we our heyres and successors shall make open Proclamacion within any the portes of our Realme of England commodious that[10] the saide Walter Raleighe his heyres or assignes or any other to whome[11] thes our letters patentes maye extende shall within the tearmes to be lymytted by such proclamacion make full restitucion and satisfaccion of all such iniuries done so as both we and the said Prynces and others[12] so Compleyning may holde vs and

---

[1] 'or the'.   [2] 'his or their goods'.   [3] 'theyre or'.   [4] 'and'.
[5] 'or thing'.   [6] 'or vnlawfull'.   [7] 'or successors'.
[8] 'any kings, princes, rulers, Gouernours, or states'.
[9] 'or their'.   [10] 'England that'.
[11] 'heires and assignes, and adherents, or any to whom'.
[12] 'or other'.

themselues fully contented And that if the said Walter Raleigh his heyres and assignes shall not make or cause to be made satis-faccion accordingly within such tymes so to be lymytted That then yt shalbe lawful to vs our heyres and successors to put the saide Walter Raleighe his heyres assignes [1] and adherentes and all the Inhabitauntes of the said places to be discovered as aforesaid [2] or any of them out of oure allegiaunce and proteccion And that from and after such tyme of puttyng out of proteccion of the said Walter Raleigh his heyres assignes and adherentes and others so to be put out and the said places within theire habitacion pos-sessyon and rule shalbe out of our proteccion and allegiaunce [3] and free for all Princes and others to pursue with hostility as being not our Subiectes nor by vs any waye to be avouched mainteyned or defended nor to be holden as any of ours nor to our proteccion or Domynyon or alliaunce [4] any way belonging For that expresse mencion of the cleere yearly value or [5] certeinty of the pre-misses or any parte therof or of anye other gyftes or grantes by vs or any our Progenitors or predecessors to the foresaid [6] Walter Raleighe before this tyme made in thes presentes be not expressed or any other graunte ordinaunce prouision proclamacion or restraynte to the contrarye therof before this tyme made gyuen [7] ordeyned or prouyded or any other thynge cause or matter what so ever in any wise notwithstanding In witnes wherof &c [8] witnes our self at Westminster the fyve and twentith day of March [9]

> per breue de priuato sigillo

---

[1] 'and assignes'.
[2] 'as is aforesaid'.
[3] 'our allegeance and protection'.
[4] 'allegeance'. [5] 'of the'.
[6] 'the said'.
[7] 'time, giuen'.
[8] 'whereof wee haue caused these our letters to be made Patents'.
[9] Hakluyt ends, 'in the sixe and twentith yeere of our Raigne', adding in the margin 'Anno 1584'. Smith (*Works*, p. 305) comments, with what authority cannot be said: 'This Patenty got to be his assistants Sir Richard Grenvell the valiant, Master William Sanderson a great friend to all such noble and worthy actions, and divers other Gentlemen and Marchants, who with all speede provided two small Barkes'.

2. 21 JULY 1584.

SIR PHILIP SIDNEY TO SIR EDWARD STAFFORD[1]

We are haulf perswaded to enter into the iourney of Sir Humphrey Gilbert very eagerly whereunto your Ma*ster* Hackluit[2] hath serued for a very good Trumpet.[3]

A.F. ex add.
G.C.[5]
Maister Walter Raleigh his viage for the discouerie of that land which lieth betwéene Norembega and Florida.

3. THE HOLINSHED NOTICE OF THE 1584 VOYAGE[4]

In this yeare, 1584, euen at the prime of the yeare, namelie in Aprill, maister Walter Raleigh esquier, a gentleman from his infancie brought vp and trained in martiall discipline, both by land and sea,[6] and well inclined to all vertuous and honorable aduentures, hauing built a ship and a pinesse,[7] set them to the sea, furnished with all prouisions necessarie for a long viage, and

---

[1] Extract. Printed by Arthur Collins (*Letters and memorials of state*, 1 (1746), 298) from an original then, but not now, extant among the State Papers (Hist. MSS Comm., *De L'Isle and Dudley MSS*, II, xxxvi), reprinted in *Complete works of Sir Philip Sidney*, ed. A. Feuillerat, III, 145.

[2] Richard Hakluyt, the younger, then chaplain to Stafford, the English ambassador in Paris.

[3] The letter acts as a link between Sidney's dealings with Gilbert and Sir George Peckham (Quinn, *Gilbert*, I, 60 n., 63, 74, 81, 90, 93; II, 260–5, 278, 329, 376–8) and his association with Drake in 1585 (pp. 204, 250 below). It does not necessarily mean that Sidney was drawn by Hakluyt directly into Raleigh's enterprise, since he may have been connected with Carleill's and Frobisher's abortive American ventures in the same year, though these had, apparently, petered out by July (cp. Quinn, *Gilbert*, I, 90–5; Taylor, *Hakluyts*, I, 205–6, 209).

[4] R. Holinshed, *Chronicles*, III (1587), 1369. This is the first published account of the voyage.

[5] 'A.F.' was Abraham Fleming, a contributor to the second edition of the *Chronicles* (see *DNB*). 'G.C.' is less easy to identify with certainty. He could be Sir George Carey, who may have had close contacts with Raleigh on the voyages from their inception (see pp. 123, 498–9 below), but in this case his knighthood would probably have been noticed. George Carew (later earl of Totnes, and not knighted until 1586) is another possibility, though his direct connexion with the voyages is not attested. Most probable, or least unlikely, is William Camden, then a master at Westminster School and still in his collecting phase. If this is so the phrase would read '*Abraham Fleming ex additamentis Guilielmi Camdeni*'.

[6] Raleigh's early involvement in the French wars is sufficiently well attested, but we know nothing of his introduction to maritime service.

[7] Cp. p. 91, n. 6.

committed the charge of them to two gentlemen (his owne seruants)[1] the one called Philip Amadis; the other Arthur Barlow, with direction to discouer that land which lieth betwéene Norembega and Florida in the west Indies; who according to their commission, made as sufficient a discouerie thereof as so short a time would permit: for they returned in August[2] next following, and brought with them two sauage men of that countrie,[3] with sundrie other things, that did assure their maister of the goodnesse of the soile,[4] and of great commodities that would arise to the realme of England, by traffique, if that the English had anie habitation, and were planted to liue there. Wherevpon, he immediatlie prepared for a second viage, which with all expedition (nothing at all regarding the charges that it would amount vnto) did presentlie set in hand.

Philip Amadis, and Arthur Barlow.

Two sauage men and other things brought from the said land discouered.

Maister Walter Raleigh prepareth for a second viage to the said land late discouered.

4. [1584–5.]

ARTHUR BARLOWE'S DISCOURSE OF THE FIRST VOYAGE[5]

The first voyage made to the coastes of America, with two barkes,[6] wherein were Captaines Master Philip Amadas,[7] and

---

[1] This indicates that both Amadas and Barlowe were in Raleigh's service before being employed on the voyage.

[2] September, see p. 115 below.

[3] This is the first reference to Manteo and Wanchese being brought over to be published before 1600, though they were mentioned in the abortive parliamentary bill and by Harvey (pp. 116, 127, 232 below).

[4] Apart from the skins traded with the Indians (p. 101 below) we have no record of the specimens brought on this voyage. John White may have made some drawings (see p. 391 below).

[5] Hakluyt, *Principall navigations* (1589), pp. 728–33, collated with III (1600), 246–51 (VIII (1904), 297–310). It is argued above (pp. 15–17) that this report (Barlowe's authorship being admitted on p. 98) cannot have been written until some months after the return. Hakluyt evidently obtained it from Raleigh.

[6] The ship, the flagship or admiral, had Philip Amadas as captain and Simon Ferdinando (or Fernandez) as master and pilot (p. 98). She may well have been the *Bark Raleigh* of 200 tons which had been sent by Raleigh on Sir Humphrey Gilbert's 1583 voyage but had turned back (Quinn, *Gilbert*, pp. 37, 84, 378–9, 383, 396). The pinnace, commanded by Arthur Barlowe, could have been Raleigh's *Dorothy* (p. 179 below).

[7] Amadas was a member of Raleigh's household before the voyage (see above). He was over 16 at the death of his father, John Amadys of Plymouth on

The Roanoke Voyages

Master Arthur Barlowe,[1] who discouered part of the Countrey, now called Virginia, Anno 1584: Written by one of the said Captaines, and sent to sir Walter Raleigh, knight, at whose charge, and direction, the said voyage was set foorth.

The 27. day of Aprill, in the yeere of our redemption, 1584. we departed the west of England,[2] with two barkes, well furnished with men and victuals, hauing receyued our last, and perfect directions by your letters, confirming the former instructions,[3] and commandements deliuered by your selfe at our leauing the riuer of Thames.[4] And I thinke it a matter both vnnecessarie, for the manifest discouerie of the Countrey, as also for tediousnes sake, to remember vnto you the diurnall of our course, sailing thither, and returning:[5] onely I haue presumed to present vnto you this briefe discourse, by which you may iudge how profitable this land is likely to succeede, as well to your selfe, (by whose direction and charge, and by whose seruants this our discouerie hath beene performed) as also to her Highnes, and the Common wealth, in which we hope your wisedome will be satisfied, con-

27 February 1581 (*Visitations of Devon*, ed. J. L. Vivian (1895), p. 12). At some later date (after Raleigh had been knighted) he released to Raleigh his estate in the manors of Trethake, Penkelewe *alias*, Tradford *alias* Treatford, and Tolcarne. The date on the deed is imperfect, but it probably belongs between January 1585 and November 1587 (Hist. MSS Comm., *Reports on various collections* [ser. 55], IV, 90 (MSS of Dean and Chapter of Exeter) and see *William and Mary Quarterly*, 3rd ser., VI, 225–6).

[1] Of Barlowe, apart from his membership of Raleigh's household (p. 91 above), nothing has so far been discovered. There was an Anthony Barlow in command of John Watts's *Examiner* in 1590 (Andrews, 'Elizabethan privateering,' pp. 242–3), who may be the same, or a connexion.

[2] It is unlikely that this was from any other port but Plymouth.

[3] Not extant but evidently containing detailed plans for their reconnaissance.

[4] If Raleigh prepared the ships in the Thames and despatched them to Plymouth it is probable that they left him by at least the middle of April. As the privy seal for his patent was granted only on 16 March (p. 82 above) it is likely that preparations for a voyage were already well advanced by that date.

[5] It is not unlikely that the journal of the voyage was handed over to Raleigh. Barlowe's narrative was an impression of the voyage, primarily intended for propaganda purposes (pp. 15–17), though based on the ship's journal.

sidering, that as much by vs hath bene brought to light, as by those small meanes, and number of men we had, could any way haue bene expected, or hoped for.

The tenth of May, we arriued at the Canaries,[1] and the tenth of Iune in this present yeere, we were fallen with the Islands of the West Indies,[2] keeping a more southeasterly course then was needefull,[3] because we doubted that the current of the Baye of Mexico, disbogging[4] betweene the Cape of Florida, and the Hauana,[5] had bene of greater force then afterwardes we found it to be; At which Islands[6] we found the aire very vnwholsome, and our men grewe for the most part ill disposed: so that hauing refreshed our selues with sweete water, and fresh victuall, we departed the twelfth daye after our[7] arriuall there. These Islands, with the rest adioyning, are so well knowen to your selfe,[8] and to many others, as I will not trouble you, with the remembrance of them.

The second of Iuly, we found shole water, which smelt so

[1] Slow progress to the Canaries is probably explained by contrary winds. They were sighted on the sixth day out in 1585 (p. 180 below).

[2] From the Canaries to the West Indies (probably making a landfall at Dominica on the 45th day out from England) progress was a little, but not much, below average for the time of year (cp. pp. 180, 517, 600 below).

[3] In margin 'A Southerly course not greatly needful for Virginia' (Hakluyt, III (1600), 246). Barlowe's meaning is not too clear, but he is making an anticipatory reference to his course through the Caribbean, not speaking of the Atlantic passage, though 'southeasterly' does not appear to make sense. He could mean that from Puerto Rico, doubting the capacity of the current to carry him through the Bahama Channel, he steered on too easterly a course and so got involved in the Bahama group.

[4] From 'disbogue', an early and rare form of 'disembogue', to emerge from a river or strait into open sea.   [5] 'and Hauana' (Hakluyt, III (1600), 246).

[6] Apart from the Spanish reference to this expedition apparently touching at Puerto Rico, the arrangements of the rendezvous in 1585 would indicate that the call was made on the south-western shore of the island, probably at Tallaboa Bay (cp. Wright, *Further English voyages*, p. 175, and p. 181 below).

[7] 'of our' (Hakluyt, III (1600), 246).

[8] On the English evidence it would not appear that Raleigh reached the West Indies on his only voyage (that of 1578, for which see Quinn, *Gilbert*, I, 44–5; II, 237–8), but if the Spanish evidence (Wright, op. cit.) is interpreted to mean that he did (since Simon Fernandez was his pilot on that occasion) then Barlowe may mean that Raleigh had practical experience and not only book-knowledge of the West Indian islands. This is, however, highly conjectural.

sweetely,[1] and was so strong a smell, as if we had bene in the midst of some delicate garden, abounding with all kind of odoriferous flowers, by which we were assured, that the land could not be farre distant: and keeping good watch, and bearing but slacke saile, the fourth of the same moneth, we arriued vpon the coast, which we supposed to be a continent, and firme lande, and wee sailed along the same, a hundred and twentie English miles, before we could finde any entrance, or riuer[2] issuing into the Sea. The first that appeared vnto vs, we entred,[3] though not without some difficultie, and cast anker about three harquebushot within the hauens mouth, on the left hande of the same: and after thankes giuen to God for our safe arriuall thither, we manned our boates, and went to viewe the lande next adioyning, and to "take pos-

"Iuly 13. possessions[4] taken.

session of the same, in the right of the Queenes most excellent Maiestie, as rightfull Queene, and Princesse of the same: and after deliuered the same ouer to your vse, according to her Maiesties grant, and letters patents, vnder her Highnes great Seale. Which being performed, according to the ceremonies vsed in such enter-prises,[5] wee viewed the lande about vs, being whereas we first

[1] 'Wher we...sweet, and so' (Hakluyt, III (1600), 246), and, in margin: 'A sweet smell from the land'. Offshore winds at this season would be unusual in these latitudes so the phenomenon may have been caused by a small hurricane.

[2] 'The first riuer', in margin (Hakluyt, III (1600), 246). By 'English miles' he may mean land, not nautical miles. 120 miles between 2 and 13 July, with southerly following winds, is exceptionally slow progress. If, as seems likely, the inlet was that called Port Ferdinando, the first contact with the coast was made about midway between the modern Cape Lookout and Cape Hatteras along the Core Bank (cp. map at end).

[3] The inlet is, with a high degree of probability, that later called Port Fer-dinando. It was discovered by Fernandez (see pp. 202, 863-4). The landing was therefore made at the northern end of the island in the Banks called Hatarask (see p. 864). The difficult entry might have provided a warning unheeded in 1585 (cp. p. 202).

[4] 'possession' (Hakluyt, III (1600), 246). There does not appear to have been any opportunity here for the attempt to land at one headland where 'the savages ate 38 Englishmen' (Wright, op. cit., p. 175).

[5] Sir Humphrey Gilbert in 1583 had entered into possession of Newfoundland by having delivered to him '(after the custom of England) a rod & a turffe and after having the English arms, engraved on lead affixed to a pillar erected on the place' (Principal navigations, VIII (1904), 53-4; Quinn, Gilbert, II, 402-3). Some-

landed,[1] very sandie, and lowe towards the water side,[2] but so full of grapes,[3] as the very beating, and surge of the Sea ouerflowed them, of which we founde such plentie, as well there, as in all places else, both on the sande, and on the greene soile on the hils, as in the plaines, as well on euery little shrubbe, as also climing towardes the toppes of the high Cedars,[4] that I thinke in all the world the like aboundance is not to be founde: and my selfe hauing seene those partes of Europe that most abound,[5] finde such difference, as were incredible to be written.

thing similar was done by Drake in New Albion in 1579, an English sixpence being placed under the plate (see H. R. Wagner, 'The creation of rights of sovereignty by symbolic acts', in *Pacific Historical Review*, VII (1938), 297–326). Though nothing is said of it here or later some post with a suitable inscription may have been erected near the wooden slipway (for which see pp. 811, 902 below).

[1] If the arguments relating to the coastline and the location of the inlets (see especially pp. 863–4 below and map at end) are sound, the place would be some two miles east of Cedar Point on Bodie Island, nearly a mile out to sea.

[2] 'waters side' (Hakluyt, III (1600), 246): in margin 'Abundance of grapes'. It has usually been argued that Amadas and Barlowe landed on the Carolina Banks in the vicinity of Nags Head or further north (e.g. C. W. Porter, 'Fort Raleigh', in *N.C. Hist. Rev.*, XX, 25) and approached Roanoke Island from the north by way of Trinitie Harbour (see p. 415). This could be justified on grounds (*a*) of vegetation, there having been recently fairly heavy vegetation near the sea-coast with substantial remnants at Colington Island and the adjacent part of the main Bank; (*b*) of topography, the Nags Head dunes being the hills referred to by Barlowe; and (*c*) of distance (for which see below, p. 106, n. 6). The low dunes and swamps south of the present location of the Port Ferdinando inlet, together with the existence of Oregon Inlet, have turned attention from this area as it was in 1584. Then there was substantial vegetation (cp. p. 865), high dunes, called by the English Kindrickers Mounts (p. 864), and a headland, Cape Kenrick (now represented by Wimble Shoals, not many miles to the south-east. Hariot's note to De Bry (p. 415) is contemporary evidence for a northerly approach, but he was not on the expedition and his account is very hard to reconcile, in other respects, with Barlowe's. On the other hand, the reported discovery of a harbour by Fernandez and the naming of Port Ferdinando after him in 1585 (p. 202) would support the southern approach, which seems to me preferable (see map at end).

[3] If ripe the Summer Grape (*V. aestivalis*) (p. 330 below).

[4] 'tops of high Cedars' (Hakluyt, III (1600), 246): it would seem from his discussion below that Barlowe could distinguish the scarcer Red Cedar from the Swamp Cypress which could well have been taken for cedar (cp. p. 364 below).

[5] This, with the analogies below, would suggest that Barlowe had been to the Levant or possibly farther east.

The Roanoke Voyages

We passed from the Sea side,[1] towardes the toppes of those hils next adioyning, being but of meane heigth,[2] and from thence wee behelde the Sea on both sides to the North, and to the South, finding no ende any of both waies. This lande laye stretching it selfe to the West,[3] which after wee founde to be but an Island of twentie leagues[4] long, and not aboue sixe miles broade. Vnder the banke or hill, whereon we stoode, we behelde the vallies replenished with goodly Cedar trees, and hauing discharged our harquebushot, such a flocke of Cranes (the most part white)[5] arose vnder vs, with such a crye redoubled by many Ecchoes, as if an armie of men had showted all together.

This Island had many goodly woods, full of Deere, Conies, Hares,[6] and Fowle, euen in the middest of Summer, in incredible aboundance. The woodes are not such as you finde in Bohemia, Moscouia, or Hyrcania,[7] barren and fruitlesse, but the highest,

[1] In margin 'The Isle of Wokokon' (Hakluyt, III (1600), 246). This is one of the less happy examples of Hakluyt's editing practice. Barlowe makes it clear below (p. 111) that the island is not Wococon (for the location of which see p. 867 below).

[2] Kindrickers Mounts, so called by White (if the argument in n. 8, p. 610 is correct: see p. 864 below).

[3] The Banks lie approximately North–South. If he could see behind and beyond Cape Kenrick he could perhaps perceive a trend to the South-west.

[4] 'miles' (Hakluyt, III (1600), 246). Hakluyt, having put in his identification of the island as Wococon (n. 1), then proceeded to alter Barlowe's indication of its length, when, in fact, 20 leagues, or 60 miles, is a good approximation to the length of the island of Hatarask as shown by White on his maps (cp. pp. 864–5 below), and tends strongly to confirm the arguments already used to identify the place of landing. A maximum breadth of six miles is probably too great but it may at least suggest that in the process by which the Banks have been eroded on their outer and built up on their inner sides they have, on balance, been narrowed (cp. p. 844–5 below).

[5] Sandhill Cranes which do not now come so far north (cp. p. 447 below).

[6] Conies are rabbits: hares are not found. Barlowe probably distinguished the two species of rabbits found in North Carolina, the Common Cottontail (*Sylvilagus floridanus* Allen) and the more hare-like Marsh Rabbit (*Sylvilagus* (or *Lepus*) *palustris* Bachman) (*Mammals of N.C.*, no. 15). Cp. Strachey, *Hist. of travell*, pp. 124–5.

[7] 'Hercynia' (Hakluyt, III (1600), 246), a region in the Caucasus, described by Anthony Jenkinson (whom Barlowe perhaps accompanied) (cp. E. D. Morgan and C. H. Coote, *Early Voyages to Russia and Persia*, I (1886), 135).

and reddest Cedars of the world,[1] farre bettering the Cedars of the Açores, of the Indias, or of Lybanus,[2] Pynes,[3] Cypres,[4] Sassaphras,[5] the Lentisk,[6] or the tree that beareth the Masticke, the tree that beareth the rinde of blacke Sinamon, of which Master Winter brought from the Streights of Magellane,[7] and many other of excellent smell, and qualitie. We remained by the side of this Island two whole daies, before we sawe any people of the

[1] Thus indicating that he is speaking of the Red Cedar rather than the Swamp Cypress (p. 95 above).

[2] 'Indies, or Lybanus' (Hakluyt, III (1600), 246): in margin 'Goodly Cedars, Pynes, Cypres, Sassaphras'. The true Cedar is *Cedrus libani*. Barlowe's knowledge of trees may conceivably have been due to his own travels (he had probably been to the Levant (p. 95 n. 5 above) and possibly also on one of the Muscovy Company expeditions), but was probably largely literary though it has not been possible to trace his sources on European forests.

[3] The predominant tree of the coastlands, many species.

[4] See Hariot's doubts about the character of the local cypresses, p. 364.

[5] Barlowe's knowledge of sassafras is almost certainly derived from Nicholas Monardes, either in the original Spanish, or in John Frampton's translation (as *Joyfull newes out of the newe founde worlde* (1577), see below, p. 329).

[6] The Lentisk is the mastic-bearing tree (*Pistacia lentiscus*; see Charles de l'Écluse, *Rariorum plantarum historia* (Antwerp, 1601), p. 14), and its nearest equivalent on the Carolina Banks would be the Sweet Gum (*Liquidambar styraciflua*) which is probably meant here (W.C.C.; and see p. 334 below).

[7] In 1581 Charles de l'Écluse visited England and obtained specimens of the aromatic bark brought by John Winter from the Straits of Magellan in 1579. On his return to the Continent Plantin published for him an *addendum* to his Latin translations of Garcia de Orta, *Aliquot Notae in Garciae Aromatum Historiam. Eiusdem Descriptiones nonnullarum Stirpium, & aliarum exoticarum rerum, quae à Generoso viro Francesco Drake Equite Anglo, & his obseruatae sunt, qui eum in longa illa Nauigatione, que proximis annis vniuersum orbem circumiuit, comitati sunt: & quorundam peregrinorum fructuum quos Londini ab amicis accepit* (Antwerp, 1582), where *Winteranus cortex* was described and illustrated (pp. 30–2), and compared with Monardes's *Lignum aromaticum* from the West Indies (cp. *Joyfull newes*, I, 69–70). Barlowe may have had a copy with him. Hakluyt, Richard Hawkins and others were interested in the bark for its supposed medicinal qualities (cp. Quinn, *Gilbert*, II, 289, 303; R. Hawkins, *Observations*, ed. J. A. Williamson, p. 90). Winter's Bark passed into the pharmacopeia as *Cortex winteranus* (*Drimys winteri*), while Porcher (*Resources*, pp. 36–41) noted that bark from the magnolias had a similar combination of bitter and aromatic properties without astringency. This suggests that Barlowe may mean the Sweet Bay, *Magnolia virginiana* (Hariot's 'Ascopo', pp. 365–6 below), but Dr W. C. Coker thinks that, in the context, Dogwood, *Cornus florida*, is the more likely.

Countrey: the third daye we espied one small boate rowing towards vs, hauing in it three persons: this boate came to the landes side,[1] foure harquebushot from our shippes, and there two of the people remaining, the thirde came along the shoare side towards vs, and we being then all within boord, he walked vp and downe vppon the point of the lande next vnto us: then the Master, and the Pilot of the Admirall, Simon Ferdinando,[2] and the Captaine Philip Amadas, my selfe, and others, rowed to the lande, whose comming this fellowe attended, neuer making any shewe of feare, or doubt. And after he had spoken of many things not vnderstoode by vs, we brought him with his owne good liking, aboord the shippes, and gaue him a shirt, a hatte, and some other things, and made him taste of our wine, and our meate, which he liked very well: and after hauing viewed both barkes, he departed, and went to his owne boate againe, which hee had left in a little Coue, or Creeke adioyning: assoone as hee was two bowe shoote into the water, hee fell to fishing, and in lesse then halfe an howre, he had laden his boate as deepe, as it could swimme,[3] with which he came againe to the point of the lande, and there he deuided his fishe into two partes, pointing one part to the shippe, and the other to the Pinnesse: which after he had (as much as he might,) requited the former benefits receaued, he[4] departed out of our sight.

The next day there came vnto vs diuers boates, and in one of them the Kings brother,[5] accompanied with fortie or fiftie men, very handsome, and goodly people, and in their behauiour as

---

[1] 'the Island side' (Hakluyt, III (1600), 247), to the north-easterly tip of the island of Hatorask. In margin just below is added 'Conference with a Sauage'.

[2] Simon Fernandez, a Portuguese pilot from Terceira in the Azores, who had become a protestant and married in England. Engaged in piracy in 1578, he was employed by Gilbert in the same year, and performed a reconnaissance voyage for him to North America in 1580, having entered Walsingham's service (Quinn, *Gilbert*, I, 39, 41, 43, 50–2, 96, 187, 198, 211; II, 239–40, 309; Wright, *Further English voyages*, pp. 15, 175; below, especially, pp. 742, 793).

[3] In margin: 'Abundance of fish' (Hakluyt, III (1600), 247), cp. pp. 359–60 below).

[4] 'he' omitted (Hakluyt, III (1600), 247).

[5] In margin: 'The arriuall of the kings brother' (Hakluyt, III (1600), 247).

mannerly, and ciuill, as any of Europe. His name was Granganimeo,[1] and the King is called Wingina,[2] the countrey Wingandacoa,[3] (and nowe by her Maiestie, Virginia,[4]) the manner of
his comming was in this sorte: hee left his boates altogether, as the
first man did a little from the shippes by the shoare, and came
along to the place ouer against the shippes, followed with fortie
men. When hee came to the place, his seruants spread a long
matte vppon the grounde,[5] on which he sate downe, and at the
other ende of the matte, foure others of his companie did the like:
the rest of his men stoode round about him, somewhat a farre off:
when wee came to the shoare to him with our weapons, he neuer
mooued from his place, nor any of the other foure, nor neuer
mistrusted any harme to be offered from vs, but sitting still, he
beckoned vs to come and sitte by him, which we perfourmed:
and beeing sette, hee makes[6] all signes of ioy, and welcome,
striking on his head, and his breast, and afterwardes on ours, to
shewe we were all one, smiling, and making shewe the best hee
could, of all loue, and familiaritie. After hee had made a long
speech vnto us, wee presented him with diuers thinges, which hee
receaued very ioyfully, and thankefully. None of his companye
durst to[7] speake one worde all the tyme: onely the foure

[1] See pp. 265, 276 below.
[2] Wingina, a chief of the Roanoke tribe, who ruled one village on Roanoke
Island where he lived and at least one village on the mainland, Dasemunkepeuc
(cp. pp. 527–30 below).
[3] How this phrase was picked up as the name of the country is not quite clear,
but it was some time before it was spotted as misleading (cp. Raleigh on it,
pp. 116–17 below and also pp. 953–4).
[4] The name was conferred some time between the drafting of Raleigh's bill
to confirm his discoveries in December 1584 (pp. 126–9 below) and 24 March
1585 (the latest date compatible with the seal, for which see p. 147 below).
Unless inserted by Hakluyt this suggests that Barlowe's narrative was not completed until preparations for the next expedition were well advanced.
[5] Probably made of reeds like those in White's drawings, nos. 33, 37, 43
(pp. 415–17, 421, 429–30 below).
[6] 'made' (Hakluyt, III (1600), 247).
[7] 'The company durst speak' (Hakluyt, III (1600), 247). This episode is very well
told and is an excellent example of Barlowe's capacity for sympathetic and accurate
observation.

which were at the other ende, spake one in the others eare very softly.

The King is greatly obeyed, and his brothers, and children reuerenced: the King himselfe in person was at our beeing there sore wounded, in a fight which he had with the King of the next Countrey, called Wingina, and was shotte in two places through the bodye, and once cleane thorough the thigh, but yet he recouered: by reason whereof, and for that hee laye at the chiefe Towne of the Countrey, beeing six dayes iourneye off, wee sawe him not at all.[1]

After wee had presented this his brother, with such things as we thought he liked, we likewise gaue somewhat to the other[2] that sate with him on the matte: but presently he arose, and tooke all from them, and put it into his owne basket, making signes and tokens, that all things ought to be deliuered vnto him, and the rest were but his seruants, and followers. A daye or two after this, we fell to trading with them, exchanging some thinges that we had[3] for Chammoys,[4] Buffe,[5] and Deere skinnes: when we shewed him all our packet of merchandize,[6] of all things that he saw, a bright tinne dishe most pleased him, which he presently tooke

---

[1] This paragraph raises serious difficulties of interpretation. Dr Mook ('Algonkian ethnohistory', pp. 213–17) regards Wingina as head of a Secotan tribe which included all the villages from that on Roanoke Island to those on the Pamlico River. Without further evidence—and comparing what we know of Lane's experience with this chief—it is impossible to accept this interpretation. The extent of Wingina's dominion must therefore be ascribed to Indian boasting (cp. p. 870 below). We need not doubt that Wingina was recovering from his wound at another Indian village as he was frequently in alliance with other chiefs. Barlowe's naming of his opponent 'Wingina' can scarcely be other than a mistake, possibly by the printer. If we place a full stop after 'Countrey', and read 'He is called Wingina, and was shotte', we probably get the correct version.

[2] 'others' is meant, i.e. the other *weroances* or men of rank.

[3] In margin: 'Trafficke with the Sauages' and below it 'Tinne much esteemed' (Hakluyt, III (1600), 247).

[4] I.e. dressed deer-skins.

[5] The appearance of the bison east of the mountains in modern Virginia and North Carolina was occasional only, though skins may have been obtained by trade. This reference is not sufficient evidence that the Indians hunted the bison or sold its skins (cp. Swanton, *Indians*, pp. 324–8, 449; p. 357 below).

[6] Cp. the kinds of merchandise which the elder Richard Hakluyt considered it most advantageous to sell to the Indians (Taylor, *Hakluyts*, II, 332).

vp, & clapt it before his breast, & after made a hole in the brimme thereof, & hung it about his necke, making signes, that it would defende him against his enemies arrowes:[1] for those people maintaine a deadlie and terrible warre, with the people and King adioyning. We exchanged our tinne dishe for twentie skinnes, woorth twentie Crownes, or twentie Nobles: and a copper kettle for fiftie skinnes woorth fiftie Crownes. They offered vs very good[2] exchange for our hatchets, and axes, and for kniues, and would haue giuen any thing for swordes:[3] but we would not depart with any. After two or three daies, the Kings brother came aboord the shippes, and dranke wine, and ate of our meate, and of our bread, and liked exceedingly thereof: and after a few daies ouerpassed, he brought his wife with him to the shippes, his daughter, and two or three little children:[4] his wife was very well fauored, of meane stature, and very bashfull:[5] she had on her backe a long cloke of leather, with the furre side next to her bodie,[6] and before her a peece of the same:[7] about her forehead, she had a broad bande of white Corrall, and so had her husband many times:[8] in her eares she had bracelets of pearles, hanging

[1] It would appear that this was in mere imitation of the armour of the Englishmen. Hariot (p. 369 below) mentions wicker armour, but this is not corroborated, and it is doubtful if, in fact, body-armour was worn in the south-east (Swanton, *Indians*, pp. 588–9).   [2] 'vs good' (Hakluyt, III (1600), 247).

[3] These proceedings indicate that the coastal Indians were experienced traders (cp. pp. 268–70), and suggest that they were already familiar with the appearance and uses of European weapons, as they could have been from their contacts with shipwrecked Spaniards (pp. 104, 111). Trading exchanges in 1585–6 were apparently not so successful (cp. pp. 232–4 below).

[4] 'and two or three children' (Hakluyt, III (1600), 247).

[5] Cp. White, no. 50 (see pp. 439–40 below).

[6] Cp. White, no. 35 (see pp. 418–19 below).

[7] The skirt was usually a short fringed skin covering the front only: sometimes a second skin was added at the back. The breasts were normally left bare, but there is one example of the skirt being hung from the shoulders (White, no. 41, see pp. 427–8).

[8] 'a bande of white Corall' (Hakluyt, III (1600), 247) and, in margin 'White corall Perles'. The forehead decoration was often painted on (White, no. 34, see p. 417), but in this case was probably composed of shell or bone beads, not coral. For other information on the use of such materials in this area cp. Swanton, *Indians*, pp. 481–8; pp. 417, 439 below.

downe to her middle,[1] (whereof wee deliuered your Worship a litle bracelet)[2] and those were of the bignes of good pease. The rest of her women of the better sorte had pendants of copper, hanging in euery eare,[3] and some of the children of the Kings brother, and other Noble men, haue fiue or sixe in euery eare:[3] he himselfe had vpon his head a broad plate of golde, or copper, for being vnpolished we knew not what metall it should be, neither would he by any meanes suffer vs to take it off his head, but feeling it, it would bowe very easily:[4] His apparell was as his wiues, onely the women weare their haire long on both sides, and the men but on one:[5] They are of colour yellowish,[6] and their haire blacke for the most,[7] and yet we sawe children that had very fine aburne, and chestnut colour[8] haire.

[1] Ear ornaments of such elaboration are not shown in any of White's drawings though the pearl necklaces were of great length (no. 34, see p. 417). For the pearls see pp. 333–4 below.

[2] This delivery of some pearls to Raleigh and the subsequent references (cp. p. 231) suggest that he was specially fond of pearls for decoration. The National Portrait Gallery portrait, for example, shows large pearl ear-rings and a lavish use of pearl decoration on his clothes.

[3] 'in either eare' (Hakluyt, III (1600), 248). Both men and women are shown wearing ear-rings made from copper beads, but none of great size or elaboration (White, nos. 49–50, see pp. 438–9).

[4] Swanton (*Indians*, p. 501) regards this as an ornament rather than as an approach to a hat, to which he considers headbands are the closest approximation (ibid. pp. 508–10). Cp. Smith (*Works*, p. 66), who speaks of 'a broad piece of copper' worn on the head, and Spelman of 'broad plates on their heades' (ibid. p. li), and Strachey (*Hist. of travell*, p. 74), who describes 'Croisetts of bright and shyning Copper, like the new Moone', similarly used. Here, however, the Indian may be using his breast plaque, or gorget (cp. p. 439 below), to imitate an English helmet.

[5] The women's hair-style is as indicated, though the front is fringed and the back caught up (White, nos. 38, 50, see pp. 423–4, 439–40), but the men's is, characteristically, shaved at the sides, leaving a cock's comb, long, and caught up at the back (White, nos. 43, 49, see pp. 429, 438).

[6] The yellowish-brown skin-colour is well indicated in the White drawings, but is distorted to darker and more reddish shades in the reproductions in Stefan Lorant, *The new world* (see pp. 917–18 below).

[7] 'the most part' (Hakluyt, III (1600), 248).

[8] 'coloured' (Hakluyt, III (1600), 248). The hair-colour in the White drawings is invariably black, and few early descriptions mention hair of other colours,

After that these women had bene there, there came downe from all parts great store of people, bringing with them leather,[1] corrall,[2] diuers kindes of dies very excellent,[3] and exchanged with vs: but when Granganimeo, the kings brother was present, none durst to[4] trade but himselfe, except such as weare redde peeces of copper on their heades,[5] like himselfe: for that is the difference betweene the Noble men, and Gouernours of Countries, and the meaner sort.[6] And we both noted there, and you haue vnderstood since by these men, which we brought home,[7] that no people in the worlde carry more respect to their King, Nobilitie, and Gouernours, then these doe. The Kings brothers wife, when she came to vs, as she did many times, shee[8] was followed with fortie or fiftie women alwaies:[9] and when she came into the shippe, she left them all on lande, sauing her two daughters, her nurce, and one or two more. The Kings brother alwaies kept this order, as

except with the assumption that it represents admixture with the Europeans (cp. Swanton, *Indians*, pp. 219–29), but reddish hair is often found in children whose hair later becomes, to all appearances, black.

[1] Dressed deer- and other skins.

[2] Coral is taken above (p. 101, n. 8) to mean some kind of bone or shell used for decoration, possibly the *minsal* referred to below (pp. 438–9), or, if shell, probably what was later known as *peak* (conch) or *roanoke* (possibly cockle) and perhaps already used as currency. The authorities differ on the variety of the shells used and where and whether ornament or currency use predominated (cp. Swanton, *Indians*, pp. 481–5; Flannery, *Analysis*, no. 247; Frank G. Speck, 'The functions of wampum among the eastern Algonkians', *Memoirs of the American Anthropological Association*, VI, no. 1 (1919)).

[3] Cp. pp. 334–5 below.   [4] 'durst trade' (Hakluyt, III (1600), 248).

[5] I.e. the gorgets noted above, normally worn on the chest, suspended by a string round the neck.

[6] The marks on the shoulder-blade of men of rank were also distinguishing characteristics (White, no. 53, p. 443–4).

[7] The men were Manteo and Wanchese, whose names were not included in Hakluyt's 1589 version of Barlowe (p. 116 below). It would not appear probable that any of the English can have known anything of the local languages before their arrival. Therefore, all Barlowe's information not based on visual evidence must derive either from Algonquian terms picked up on the spot, or from the two Indians subsequently.

[8] 'shee' omitted (Hakluyt, III (1600), 248).

[9] This appears much too great a number to come from such small villages as that on Roanoke Island and Dasemonkepeuc on the mainland (cp. pp. 106–7, 415).

many boates as he would come withall to the shippes, so many fires would he make on the shoare a farre off, to the ende wee might vnderstand with what strength, and companie he approched.[1] Their boates are made of one tree, either of Pine, or of Pitch trees: a wood not commonly knowen to our people, nor found growing in England.[2] They haue no edge tooles to make them withall: if they haue any, they are very fewe, and those it seemes they had twentie yeeres since, which as those two men declared, was out of a wracke which happened vpon their coast of some Christian shippe, being beaten that way by some storme, and outragious weather, whereof none of the people were saued,[3] but onely the shippe, or some part of her, being cast vpon the sande, out of whose sides they drewe the nailes, and spikes,[4] and with those they made their best instruments. Their[5] manner of making their boates, is this:[6] they burne downe some great tree, or take such as are winde fallen, and putting myrrhe, and rosen[7] vpon one side thereof, they sette fire into it, and when it hath burnt it hollowe, they cutte out the coale with their shels, and euer where they would burne it deeper or wider, they laye on their gummes, which

---

[1] Fire or smoke signalling was common among the coastal Algonkian peoples though not confined to them (Swanton, *Indians*, p. 733; Flannery, *Analysis*, no. 154).

[2] In margin 'Pitch trees' (Hakluyt, III (1600), 248). The Pitch Pine (*Pinus rigida*) was not normally found on the coast, but both the Long-leaf Pine (*P. palustris*) and the Loblolly Pine (*P. taeda*) were and are known elsewhere to have been used for canoes (W.C.C.). Hariot's *rakiock* would not appear to have been either (pp. 363–4 below).

[3] If the recollections of Manteo and Wanchese were personal ones they must have been men of mature age. The year 1564–5 for the date of the wreck might make the vessel French or Spanish, and if, the latter, either a straggler from the *flota* or from Menéndez de Avilés' fleet (cp. Quinn, 'Some Spanish reactions', pp. 2–3).

[4] 'and the spikes' (Hakluyt, III (1600), 248). The normal scraping tools were shells (p. 433). Hariot did not encounter any surviving metal tools (p. 369 below).

[5] 'The' (Hakluyt, III (1600), 248).   [6] 'thus' (ibid.).

[7] 'gumme and rosen' (Hakluyt, III (1600), 248), and, in margin: 'The manner of making their boates'—the former a typical Hakluyt correction. With this description should be compared Hariot's and the engraving by De Bry (White, no. 45, pp. 432–3, 364 below). The finished boat is shown in White, no. 46 (pp. 433–5).

burneth[1] away the timber, and by this meanes they fashion very fine boates, and such as will transport twentie men. Their oares are like scoopes, and many times they sette with long pooles, as the depth serueth.[2]

The Kings brother had great liking of our armour, a sworde, and diuers other things, which we had: and offered to laye a great boxe of pearle in gage for them: but wee refused it for this time, because we would not make them knowe, that wee esteemed thereof, vntill we had vnderstoode in what places of the Countrey the pearle grewe: which nowe your Worshippe doth very well vnderstand.[3]

He was very iust of his promise: for many times wee deliuered him merchandize vppon his worde, but euer he came within the daye, and performed his promise. Hee sent vs euery daye a brase or two of fatte Buckes, Conies, Hares, Fishe, the best of the worlde. Hee sent vs diuers kindes of fruites, Melons, Walnuts, Cucumbers, Gourdes,[4] Pease,[5] and diuers rootes, and fruites very excellent good, and of their Countrey corne,[6] which is very white, faire, and well tasted, and groweth three times in fiue moneths: in Maye they sowe, in Iuly they reape, in Iune they sowe, in August they reape: in Iuly they sow, in September they reape: onely they cast the corne into the ground, breaking a little of the soft turfe with a woodden mattocke, or pickeaxe:[7] our selues prooued the

[1] 'on gummes, which burne' (Hakluyt, III (1600), 248).

[2] The paddles are illustrated in White's fishing drawing (no. 46, p. 434).

[3] Barlowe is stating that a location for a pearl fishery had been found and communicated to Raleigh (which might imply he had brought home maps), but there is no clear indication that the expedition of the following year had any such knowledge (cp. p. 333 below).

[4] There were no melons in the area at this time; they and the so-called cucumbers and the gourds were all members of the gourd family (cp. p. 340 below). For walnuts, and other nuts covered by the name, see pp. 350-1, 354-5.

[5] Beans, see p. 339 below.

[6] This, the earliest description of maize-cultivation from this area, should be compared with and Hariot's (pp. 337-8, 421-2) and those in Swanton, *Indians*, pp. 304-10.

[7] Hariot (p. 341 below) described the implements used by the men as long-handled mattocks or hoes, and the shorter ones of the women as peckers or parers. Neither type is illustrated by White.

soile, and put some of our Pease into [1] the ground, and in tenne daies they were of foureteene ynches high: they haue also Beanes very faire, of diuers colours, and wonderfull plentie: some growing naturally, and some in their gardens,[2] and so haue they both wheat and oates.[3]

The soile is the most plentifull, sweete, fruitfull, and wholsome of all the world:[4] there are aboue foureteene seuerall sweete smelling timber trees, and the most part of their vnderwoods are Bayes, and such like: they haue those Okes that we haue, but farre greater and better.[5] After they had bene diuers times aboord our shippes, my selfe, with seuen more, went twentie mile into the Riuer,[6] that runneth toward the Citie of Skicoake[7], which Riuer they call Occam: and the euening following, we came to an Island, which they call Roanoak,[8] distant from the harbour by which we entred, seuen leagues: and at the North ende thereof,

---

[1] 'in' (Hakluyt, III (1600), 248). Hariot was, in 1585–6, unable to make more systematic cultivation experiments owing to damaged seed and plants (pp. 336, 344 below).

[2] For cultivated beans see p. 339. It appears doubtful that any grew wild in this area.

[3] Here Barlowe is mistaken (cp. p. 344 below).

[4] While cleared patches of ground along the sounds were, and are, very fertile, the greater part of the mainland accessible from the sounds was swamp or swampforest.

[5] Cp. Hariot's accounts of trees below. Barlowe was evidently specially interested in trees and it is probable that he provided more detailed evidence on them than he gives here. The characteristic undergrowth of the swamp-forest vegetation has a bay-like leaf though it comprises a number of different shrubs and trees.

[6] If the identification of the landing-place, made on p. 95 above, is sound, the party—evidently using a ship's boat and not experimenting with the pinnace—apparently sailed from Port Ferdinando south-westwards into Pamlico Sound, then northwards through Croatan Sound (their Occam. See pp. 868–9), and changed course eastwards to round the northern end of Roanoke Island, making a journey of some 20 to 25 miles according to the precise course followed. Cp. Lane's estimate of distances, p. 288 below, though he probably referred to the course through Roanoke Sound. This could have been the one used here since Croatan Sound may have been too shallow.

[7] 'Skikcoak' (Hakluyt, III (1600), 248), which was an Indian village near Chesapeake Bay, possibly visited by the English in 1585–6 (p. 855 below).

[8] 'Raonoak' (Hakluyt, III (1600), 248); evidently a printer's error. The margin has 'Roanoak Island'.

was a village of nine houses, built of Cedar,[1] and fortified round about with sharpe trees, to keepe out their enemies, and the entrance into it made it like a turne pike very artificially:[2] when we came towards it, standing neere vnto the waters side,[3] the wife of Grangyno,[4] the Kings brother, came running out to meete vs very cheerefully, and friendly, her husband was not then in the village: some of her people she commanded to drawe our boate on the shoare,[5] for the beating of the billoe:[6] others shee appointed to carry vs on their backes to the dry ground, and others to bring our oares into the house, for feare of stealing. When we were come into the vtter roome, hauing fiue roomes in her house,[7] she caused vs to sitte downe by a great fire,[8] and after tooke off our clothes, and washed them, and dried them againe: some of the women pulled[9] off our stockings, and washed them, some washed our feete in warme water, and shee her selfe tooke great

---

[1] Since White left no drawing of the village this is the only description we have. It was like Pomeiooc (White, no. 33, see pp. 415–17) an enclosed village, but with fewer houses, the latter with a pole frame, possibly with bark coverings (though Secoton houses at least were mat-covered—White, nos. 37, 40, see pp. 420–3, 426).

[2] I.e. very artfully or skilfully. The village of Pomeiooc is not shown with any such entrance, the path being an open one: further, the palisade as given in the White drawing is so slight that it would not stand up to any serious assault, though as engraved by De Bry (after another version of White's drawing) the posts are much more formidable (White, no. 33, see p. 416).

[3] Apparently now submerged at North West Point (cp. p. 901).

[4] 'Granganimo' (Hakluyt, III (1600), 249): in margin 'The great kindnes of the kings brothers wife'.

[5] 'on shore' (ibid.).

[6] The strong current from Albemarle Sound was the probable reason for such precautions.

[7] Since there are no precise parallels Barlowe may be exaggerating. The long-houses shown by White (nos. 33, 37, see pp. 415–17, 420–3, 426) could have been divided into rooms by reed or bark mats or screens, but there is no other evidence that they were divided into many compartments. We may take it, however, that in this house (evidently that of the chief Wingina) there were at least two rooms and probably more (cp. Swanton, *Indians*, pp. 413–16; Beverley, *History and present state* (1947), p. 176).

[8] No internal fires, nor smoke-holes for them, appear in White's drawings, but there are Virginia examples (see Swanton, *Indians*, p. 427).

[9] 'plucked' (Hakluyt, III (1600), 249).

paines to see all thinges ordered in the best manner shee coulde, making great haste to dresse some meate for vs to eate.[1]

After we had thus dried our selues,[2] shee brought vs into the inner roome, where shee set on the boord standing along the house,[3] some wheate like furmentie,[4] sodden Venison, and roasted, fishe sodden, boyled,[5] and roasted, Melons[6] rawe, and sodden, rootes of diuers kindes, and diuers fruites: their drinke is commonly water, but while the grape lasteth, they drinke wine, and for want of caskes to keepe it[7] all the yeere after, they drinke water, but it is sodden with Ginger in it, and blacke Sinamon, and sometimes Sassaphras, and diuers other wholesome, and medicinable hearbes and trees.[8] We were entertained with all loue, and kindnes, and with as much bountie, after their manner, as they could possibly deuise. Wee found the people most gentle, louing, and faithfull, void of all guile, and treason, and such as liued after the manner of the golden age. The earth bringeth foorth all things in aboundance, as in the first creation, without toile or labour.[9] The people only care to[10] defend them selues from the cold, in their short winter, and to feede themselues with such meate as the

---

[1] This is one of the few intimate glimpses we have of domestic ceremonial hospitality for this region. For hand-washing cp. Swanton, *Indians*, p. 432.

[2] In margin 'A solemn banket' (Hakluyt, III (1600), 249).

[3] These were the benches of timber, cane or reeds which extended round the interior walls of the houses shown by White and which were mainly used for sleeping (cp. Swanton, *Indians*, p. 422; Beverley, *History and present state* (1947), p. 176).

[4] Frumenty, wheat boiled in milk and seasoned. Here maize, probably boiled with herbs for seasoning (cp. p. 339 below).

[5] Sodden, as distinct from boiled, may mean stewed, possibly with vegetables (cp. pp. 430, 437 below).

[6] Pumpkins, as above p. 105, n. 4.

[7] This is almost certainly mistaken, since the absence of deliberately fermented beverages in eastern North America was universal (Flannery, *Analysis*, no. 58), though grapes were generally eaten (Swanton, *Indians*, p. 293).

[8] The making of highly seasoned drinks of this sort is not elsewhere recorded for this area or for coastal Virginia, but it appears authentic (cp. Hariot, p. 418 below).

[9] Hakluyt omitted this sentence in 1600, apparently as not contributing anything to the narrative.

[10] 'care howe to' (Hakluyt, III (1600), 249).

soile affoordeth: their meate is very well sodden, and they make broth very sweete, and sauorie:[1] their vessels are earthen pots, very large, white, and sweete:[2] their dishes are woodden platters of sweete timber:[3] within the place where they feede, was their lodging,[4] and within that their Idoll,[5] which they worship, of which[6] they speake vncredible things. While we were at meate, there came in at the gates, two or three men with their bowes, and arrowes, from hunting, whome when we espied, we beganne to looke one to wardes another, and offered to reach our weapons: but assoone as she espied our mistrust, she was very much mooued, and caused some of her men to runne out, and take away their bowes, and arrowes, and breake them, and withall beate the poore fellowes out of the gate againe. When we departed in the euening, and would not tarry all night, she was very sorie, and gaue vs into our boate our supper halfe dressed, pots, and all, and brought vs to our boates side, in which wee laye all night, remoouing the same a pretie distance from the shoare: shee perceiuing our iealousie, was much grieued, and sent diuers men, and thirtie women, to sitte all night on the bankes side by vs, and sent vs into our boates fine mattes to couer vs[7] from the rayne, vsing very many wordes to intreate vs to rest in their houses: but because wee were fewe men, and if wee had miscarried, the voyage had beene in very great daunger, wee durst not aduenture

---

[1] Cp. pp. 338–41, 347–51, 353–5, 430, 437–8 below.

[2] White illustrates a typical cooking-vessel, and one very similar has been found in the Roanoke fort site (no. 48, see pp. 437, 907). The clays from the coastal areas produce light-coloured but not white pottery.

[3] As illustrated by White (nos. 37, 43, pp. 420, 429–30). No examples have survived.

[4] Barlowe means that in the room where he and his companions met, or in an adjoining one, the Indians slept.

[5] In margin 'Their Idole' (Hakluyt, III (1600), 249). This would mean that the idol was kept in the same building, in some further inner shrine. Such a location would be unusual (Swanton, *Indians*, p. 742), though Spelman records that Powhatan kept one of his images in his dwelling (Smith, *Works*, p. cv): an inner shrine in a temple is described fully by Beverley, *History and present state* (1947), pp. 196–8. [6] 'Whome' (Hakluyt, III (1600), 249). Cp. pp. 424–8 below.

[7] Probably of reeds (cp. Swanton, *Indians*, pp. 422, 602).

any thing, although there was no cause of doubt: for a more kinde and louing people, there can not be found in the world, as farre as we haue hitherto had triall.[1]

Beyonde this Islande, there is the maine lande, and ouer against this Islande falleth into this spatious water, the great riuer called Occam,[2] by the Inhabitants on which standeth a Towne called Pemeoke,[3] and sixe daies iourney further vpon[4] the same is situate their greatest citie, called Schycoake,[5] which this people affirme to be very great: but the Sauages were neuer at it, onely they speake of it, by the report of their Fathers, and other men, whome they haue heard affirme it, to be aboue one daies[6] iourney about.

Into this riuer falleth another great riuer, called Cipo,[7] in which there is found great store of the Muscels,[8] in which there are pearles: likewise there descendeth into this Occam, another riuer, called Nomopana,[9] on the one side whereof standeth a great Towne, called Chowanoake,[10] and the Lord of that Towne and Countrey, is called Pooneno:[11] this Pooneno is not subiect to the

[1] The most precise example in Renaissance English of the myth of the gentle savage.

[2] The word refers, not to the waters of the Sound, but to the land beyond them. Cp. pp. 868–9 below.

[3] 'Pomeiock' (Hakluyt, III (1600), 249), for the location of which see pp.871–2.

[4] 'from' (Hakluyt, III (1600), 249).

[5] 'Skicoak' (Hakluyt, III (1600), 249: in margin 'Skicoak a great towne'). It was situated, according to subsequent information, near Chesapeake Bay (see p. 855).

[6] 'houres' (Hakluyt, III (1600), 249); another typical Hakluyt correction. There were not, of course, Indian towns of any size throughout the Atlantic coastal area.

[7] Probably simply meaning 'the river' Cp. p. 869 below.

[8] 'of Muskles' (Hakluyt, III (1600), 249) cp. p. 869: a number of the fresh-water estuaries have mussels, though pearls are now uncommon (cp. pp. 260–1, 333 below).

[9] Apparently the upper portion of Albemarle Sound, rather than either the Roanoke or the Chowan River (cp. p. 868).

[10] 'Chawanook' (Hakluyt, III (1600), 249), located well up the Chowan River (see p. 857).

[11] It is not unlikely that he was the chief of the Moratuc tribe rather than of the Chowanoac, though he is not so described elsewhere He could have been chief of the Weapemeoc, although in 1586 the name of their chief was Okisco. (cp. p. 281).

King of Wingandacoa, but is a free Lorde. Beyonde this Countrey, is there another King, whome they call Menatoan,[1] and these three Kinges are in league with eache other. Towards the Sunne set,[2] foure daies iourney, is situate a Towne called Sequotan, which is the Westermost Towne of Wingandacoa,[3] neere vnto which, sixe and twentie yeeres past, there was a shippe cast away,[4] whereof some of the people were saued, and those were white people, whom the Countrey people preserued.

And after ten daies, remaining in an out Island vnhabited, called Wococan,[5] they with the helpe of some of the dwellers of Sequotan, fastened two boates of the Countrey together, and made mastes vnto them, and sailes of their shirtes, and hauing taken into them such victuals as the Countrey yeelded, they departed after they had remained in this out Island three weekes: but shortly after, it seemed they were cast away, for the boates were found vppon the coast, cast aland in another Island adioyning:[6] other then these, there was neuer any people apparelled, or white of colour, either seene, or heard of amongst these people, and these aforesaide were seene onely of the Inhabitants of Sequotan[7]: which appeared to be very true, for they wondred meruelously when

---

[1] 'Menatonon' (Hakluyt, III (1600), 249), who is clearly distinguished below (p. 259) as the chief of the Chowanoac tribe. The alliance of the chiefs of Weapemeoc and Chowanoac with Wingina was somewhat intermittent (cp. pp. 265, 276–7, 281, 284).

[2] 'the Southwest' (Hakluyt, III (1600), 249).

[3] 'the Southermost' (Hakluyt, III (1600), 249). For the location of Secoton see p. 871 below. Once again Wingina is made to appear as chief of all the villages from the Pamlico River to Roanoke Island, but again there is no corroboration from other sources (cp. pp. 100, 870).

[4] In margin: 'A ship cast away' (Hakluyt, III (1600), 249). The date on this reckoning would be 1558, and the ship most probably Spanish. It is likely to be distinct from that mentioned above, p. 104.

[5] 'Wocokon' (Hakluyt, III (1600), 249). For its location see p. 867. This is the first mention of it and the only definite statement that it was not inhabited.

[6] Either Endesokee on the south, or Croatoan on the north, most probably the latter as Manteo's mother lived there and he is likely to have contributed the story.

[7] 'Secotan' (Hakluyt, III (1600), 250).

we were amongst them,[1] at the whitenes of our skinnes, euer coueting to touch our breastes, and to view the same: besides they had our shippes in maruelous admiration, and all things els was[2] so strange vnto them, as it appeared that none of them had euer seene the like. When we discharged any peece, were it but a harquebush, they would tremble thereat for very feare, and for the strangenes of the same: for the weapons which themselues vse, are bowes and arrowes: the arrowes are but of small canes,[3] headed with a sharpe shell, or tooth of a fishe[4] sufficient enough to kill a naked man. Their swordes are[5] of wood hardened: likewise they vse wooden breastplates for their defense.[6] They haue besides a kinde of clubbe, in the ende whereof they fasten the sharpe hornes of a stagge, or other beast.[7] When they goe to warres, they carry with[8] them their Idoll, of whome they aske counsell, as the Romanes were woont of the Oracle of Apollo. They sing songs

[1] Did they visit the village of Secoton, as this suggests, or did they meet some of its people at Roanoke Island? He may, of course, be speaking generally of the Indians.

[2] 'were' (Hakluyt, III (1600), 250). For the Indian reactions—caused apparently by some belief that the white men were supernatural beings—cp. Hariot, pp. 379-80 below.

[3] In margin: 'Their weapons' (Hakluyt, III (1600), 250). The arrows are shown by White (nos. 41, 51, see pp. 427, 440-1) and described below (p. 369). The cane was *Arundinaria tecta*.

[4] This is the only reference to the points used in this area (cp. Swanton, *Indians*, pp. 572-3, 577).

[5] 'be' (Hakluyt, III (1600), 250): they are probably the same as Hariot's flat-edged truncheons (p. 369 below; cp. Swanton, *Indians*, p. 568). They are not illustrated.

[6] This specific reference to breast-plates (if they were not shields) might be held to modify what is said about the imitation by the Indians of European armour (p. 369, n. 6), though the surviving references are not conclusive (Swanton, *Indians*, pp. 588-9; Flannery, *Analysis*, nos. 144-5).

[7] Barlowe is the only writer to distinguish 'swords' from 'clubs' in this way amongst the Carolina Algonkian tribes, but this falchion club is recorded for Virginia and is considered to represent a south-eastern influence (Swanton, *Indians*, pp. 566-70; Flannery, *Analysis*, no. 136). Again the weapon is not illustrated.

[8] 'About with' (Hakluyt, III (1600), 250). This appears to be the only example for this area of an idol being carried into battle; among the south-eastern tribes it was usually an 'ark', a bundle of sanctified objects, which was so carried (cp. Swanton, *Indians*, pp. 687, 694).

as they march to wardes the battell,[1] in steede of drummes, and trumpets: their warres are very cruell, and bloodie, by reason whereof, and of their ciuill dissentions, which haue happened of late yeeres amongest them, the people are maruelously wasted, and in some places, the Countrey left desolate.[2]

Adioyning vnto this Towne aforesaide called Sequotan,[3] beginneth a Countrey called Ponouike,[4] belonging to another King, whom they call Piemacum,[5] and this King is in league with the next King, adioyning towardes the setting of the Sunne, and the Countrey Neiosioke,[6] situate vppon the side of a goodly Riuer, called Neus: these Kings haue mortall warre with Wingina, King of Wingandacoa, but about two yeeres past, there was a peace made betweene the King Piemacum, and the Lorde of Sequotan,[7] as these men which we haue brought with vs into England, haue made vs vnderstande:[8] but there remaineth a mortall malice in the Sequotanes,[9] for many iniuries and slaughters done vppon them by this Piemacum. They inuited diuers men, and thirtie women, of the best of his Countrey, to their Towne[10] to a feast: and when they were altogether merrie, and praying before their Idoll,[11]

---

[1] References to war-songs appear scarce for this area; most of the early writers on North Carolina and Virginia emphasize singing rather in connexion with other festivals (Swanton, *Indians*, p. 747; though cp. Strachey, *Hist. of travell*, pp. 85–6).

[2] This is the earliest comment on the long series of often senseless wars, which continually disrupted Indian society except in a few instances where they led to relatively stable confederations, such as that ruled by Powhatan in the early seventeenth century.

[3] 'to this countrey aforesaid called Secotan' (Hakluyt, III (1600), 250); in margin 'Or Pananuaioc'.

[4] 'Pomouik' (Hakluyt, III (1600), 250): a tribe, probably Algonkian, living apparently between the Pamlico and Neuse rivers (pp. 871–2 below).

[5] 'Piamacum' (Hakluyt, III (1600), 250): he is not elsewhere named.

[6] 'Newsiok, situate vpon a' (Hakluyt, III (1600), 250): possibly an Algonkian tribe. For their location on the Neuse River, see p. 872 below.

[7] 'Secotan' (Hakluyt, III (1600), 250): probably, though not certainly, meant to be Wingina (cp. p. 100 above).

[8] 'haue giuen vs to vnderstand' (Hakluyt, III (1600), 250).

[9] 'Secotanes' (Hakluyt, III (1600), 250).

[10] Apparently the village of Secotan.

[11] For such festivals, cp. pp. 381, 427–9 below.

which is nothing else, but a meere illusion of the Deuill: the Captaine or Lorde of the Towne came suddenly vpon them,[1] and slewe them euery one, reseruing the women, and children:[2] and these two haue oftentimes since perswaded vs to surprise Piemacum his Towne, hauing promised, and assured vs, that there will be founde in it great store of commodities. But whether their perswasion be to the ende they may be reuenged of their enemies, or for the loue they beare to vs, we leaue that to the triall hereafter.

Beyond this Island, called Croonoake, arc many Islands,[3] very plentifull of fruites and other naturall increases, together with many Townes, and villages, along the side of the continent, some bounding vpon the Islands, and some stretching vp further into the land.

When we first had sight of this Countrey, some thought the first lande we sawe, to be the continent: but after wee entred into the Hauen, wee sawe before vs another mightie long Sea: for there lieth along the coast a tracte of Islands, two hundreth miles in length, adioyning to the Ocean sea, and betweene the Islands, two or three entrances: when you are entred betweene them (these Islands being very narrowe, for the most part, as in most places sixe miles broad, in some places lesse, in fewe more,) then there appeareth another great Sea, containing in bredth in some places, fortie, and in some fiftie, in some twentie miles ouer, before you come vnto the continent: and in this inclosed Sea, there are about a hundreth Islands of diuers bignesses,[4] whereof one is sixteene miles long, at which we were, finding it to be[5] a most pleasant,

---

[1] Is this an attempt to distinguish him from Wingina? (Cp. pp. 100, 113).

[2] Cp. Strachey, *Hist. of travell*, p. 109, for the use of such treachery and for the reservation of women and children. It is not clear whether or not the latter were enslaved (cp. Swanton, *Indians*, pp. 686–91).

[3] 'Roanoak, are maine Islands' (Hakluyt, III (1600), 250), though 'maine' is here probably a misprint for 'manie'.

[4] The best general description of the Carolina Banks and the Sounds lying behind them (cp. pp. 200–2, 413–14).

[5] 'finding it a most': in margin 'Roanoak sixteen miles long' (Hakluyt, III (1600), 250), a fair approximation of its length.

and fertile ground, replenished with goodly Cedars, and diuers other sweete woods, full of Currans,[1] of flaxe,[2] and many other notable commodities, which we at that time had no leasure to view. Besides this Island, there are many, as I haue saide, some of two, of three, of foure, of fiue miles, some more, some lesse, most beautifull, and pleasant to behold, replenished with Deere, Conies, Hares,[3] and diuers beastes, and about them the goodliest and best fishe in the world, and in greatest aboundance.

Thus Sir, we haue acquainted you with the particulars of our discouerie, made this present voyage, as farre foorth, as the shortnes of the time we there continued, would affoord vs to take viewe of: and so contenting our selues with this seruice at this time, which we hope hereafter to inlarge, as occasion and assistance shall be giuen, we resolued to leaue the Countrey, and to apply our selues to returne for England, which we did accordingly, and arriued safely in the West of England, about the middest of September.[4]

And whereas we haue aboue certified you of the Countrey, taken in possession by vs, to her Maiesties vse, and so to yours, by her Maiesties grant, wee thought good for the better assurance thereof to recorde some of the particular Gentlemen, and men of accompt, who then were present, as witnesses of the same, that thereby all occasion of cauill to the title of the Countrey, in her Maiesties behalfe,[5] may be preuented, which other wise, such as like not the action may vse, and pretend, whose names are:

> Master Philip Amadas, } Captaines.
> Master Arthur Barlowe, }

---

[1] Small grapes (cp. pp. 95, 330).

[2] Cp. p. 326–7 below.

[3] On Barlowe's confusion of rabbits and hares, see p. 105 above.

[4] Hariot (p. 320 below) says they were six weeks in the country. They may have left therefore, about 23 August, and must have had a rapid passage home.

[5] This may be connected with the bill for confirming Raleigh's title (pp. 122–9 below). It certainly suggests that Barlowe's discourse was prepared at the same time as the bill.

William Greeneuille,[1]
Iohn Wood,
Iames Browewich,[2]
Henrie Greene,
Beniamin Wood,[3]   } Of the companie.[6]
Simon Ferdinando,[4]
Nicholas Petman,
Iohn Hewes,[5]

5. RALEIGH ON THE NAMING OF 'WINGANDACON'[7]

But when Francis Pisarro first discouered those landes to the South of Panama, arriuing in that Region which Atabaliba commanded (a Prince of magnificence, riches and Dominion inferiour

---

[1] Mr A. L. Rowse attempts to identify him with William Grenville of Penheale and, therefore, as a relative of Sir Richard, but admits that corroboration is lacking (*Grenville*, p. 202). A William Greynvile appears in the reversion to Grenville's estates in 1585 (R. Granville, *Hist. of the Granville family*, p. 120).

[2] Possibly identical with the 'Master Bremige' of 1585 (p. 180 below).

[3] For his career as a navigator and sea-captain, ending in disaster in the East Indies in 1598, see Foster, *England's quest of eastern trade*, pp. 138–42, and Andrews, 'Elizabethan privateering,' p. 275.

[4] See pp. 200–1, 511, 517–23, 742, 793.

[5] There was a Lieut. Hewes with Raleigh in Guiana in 1595 (Hakluyt, *Principal navigations*, X, 380).

[6] Hakluyt adds in 1600 (III, 251): 'We brought home also two of the Sauages being lustie men, whose names were Wanchese and Manteo.' Did he go back to the manuscript for this or did he add it on his own authority? He already had the names on record elsewhere (pp. 270–1, 280). John White was also, by his own reckoning (cp. pp. 40, 715), with the expedition. Lupold von Wedel reported (under 18 October 1584): 'A ship had arrived that had found a land or an island which is said to be larger than England, and which had as yet been untrodden by Christians. A certain Master or Captain Rall [Raleigh] had brought two men of this country with him, and had them about his person. We were permitted by this said Captain to see these men. They were in countenance and stature like white Moors. Their usual habit was a mantle of rudely tanned skins of wild animals, no shirts, and a pelt before their privy parts. Now, however, they were clad in brown taffeta. No one was able to understand them and they made a most childish and silly figure' (V. von Klarwill, ed., *Queen Elizabeth and some foreigners* (1928), p. 323; cp. *Trans. R. Hist. S.*, 2nd ser., IX (1895), 251).

[7] Sir Walter Raleigh, *History of the world* (1614), bk. I, ch. 8, pp. 175–6 (first numeration).

to none) some of the Spaniards vtterly ignorant of that language, demaunding by signes (as they could) the name of the Countrie, and pointing with their hand athwart a riuer, or torrent, or brooke that ran by, the Indians answered Peru which was either the name of that brooke, or of water in generall. The Spaniards thereupon conceiuing that the people had rightly vnderstood them, set it downe in the Diurnall of their enterprise and so in the first description made, and sent ouer to Charles the Emperour, all that West part of America to the South of Panama had the name of Peru, which hath continued euer since....

The same hapned among the English, which I sent vnder Sir Richard Greeneuile [1] to inhabite Virginia. For when some of my people asked the name of that Countrie, one of the Saluages answered *Wingandacon* which is to say, as you weare good clothes, or gay clothes. [2]

---

[1] He is mistaken, since the name was brought back by Amadas and Barlowe in 1584.

[2] Thomas Hariot, as the expert on the language, is likely to have been the author of this interpretation on his return in 1586. That it is possible is argued in *Handbook of American Indians*, ed. F. W. Hodge, II (1910), *s.v.*, but that it is unlikely is suggested by Professor J. A. Geary, pp. 853–4 below. Its latest use is in 1589 (p. 590 below) when it appears along with the name which supplanted it, 'Ossomocomuck' (cp. also p. 508).

CHAPTER II

PREPARATIONS FOR THE 1585 VOYAGE

Item, yf any man hath many Iourneys to take by land or by
water, let hym haue an eye rounde about hym, for Force is
lykely to exceede in all places, and Violence already shaketh
his head, and frowneth vpon Trauaylers: but warinesse and
courage, are the best spelles agaynst such Sprites and Goblins.

THOMAS PORTER, *An almanacke or prognostication
for the yeere...M.D. LXXXV.*

NARRATIVE

The preparations for the second Virginia voyage began before
Amadas and Barlowe had returned, since Richard Hakluyt, at
Raleigh's request, was busy during July and subsequent months
in writing his 'Particular discourse', or *Discourse of western
planting*,[1] as part of an elaborate plan to arouse the queen to
sponsor the occupation and settlement of the North American
coast. The argument stressed the need to embarrass Spain and to
strengthen England's position by such a venture, while it was also
directed towards solving current problems of employment, commerce and industry by the exploitation of the people and resources
of North America. By 5 October, when Hakluyt made his
presentation of the manuscript to the queen,[2] Amadas was back
with two Indians, some skins and pearls, and with a glowing
report of American potentialities in commerce, natural resources,
and strategic sites. But the queen's response was evidently slow.
Hakluyt returned to his embassy chaplaincy at Paris with a reward,
while Raleigh received sufficient encouragement to lead him to
have a bill drafted to confirm his legal title to the lands discovered
under the terms of his patent, which received its first reading in the
house of commons on 14 December. This provided an excellent

---

[1] Taylor, *Hakluyts*, II, 211–326; see pp. 4–5, 18–19 above.
[2] Parks, *Hakluyt*, p. 248.

advertisement for the project. The fact that it passed the commons four days later only after a row about some provisos, which Raleigh—and the crown—did not wish to have added to it, led it to be dropped after it had received its first reading in the lords.[1]

There is evidence for concluding that Raleigh's main propagandists in these early months were the Indians, Manteo and Wanchese, who had been brought to England in September and had rapidly learnt English. In Raleigh's household there was at this time Thomas Hariot, who had been employed to teach Raleigh mathematics and had instructed the pilots and masters of Amadas's expedition in navigation for their American voyage.[2] As he was sent out in 1585 with special responsibility for relations with the Indians it may be assumed, without direct evidence but plausibly, that he taught the two Indians English and was taught by them their Algonquian tongue.[3] They made sufficient progress to be cited in the parliamentary bill in December[4] and there is evidence that they were used to invite adventurers to go on the voyage.[5] Added to their testimony were the expedition's reports of 'singular great commodities', including, with little doubt, Arthur Barlowe's discourse.[6] The bill itself, even if it did not pass, was used as evidence of government approval for the venture,[7] and the elder Hakluyt's 'Inducements' in one or both of its surviving forms[8] was almost certainly employed as promotion propaganda. Sir Richard Grenville was brought into association with Raleigh in the project, it would appear, through his presence on the commons' committee which dealt with the bill, and Thomas Cavendish and Anthony Rowse through their membership of the house of commons.[9] Grenville evidently soon left to raise support and shipping in the west country;[10] Cavendish consulted a military expert on the organization of the venture,

---

[1] Documents nos. 6–7, pp. 122–9 below.   [2] Cp. pp. 36–7.
[3] Cp. p. 37 above.   [4] P. 127 below.
[5] Document no. 43, p. 232, below.
[6] P. 127 below.   [7] P. 232 below.
[8] Taylor, *Hakluyts*, II, 327–43: see pp. 4–5, 18–19 above.
[9] P. 123 below.   [10] Documents nos. 12, 15, pp. 146, 151 below.

and we have a rough version of the 'Notes' he compiled.[1]
Sir Francis Walsingham was clearly a prominent adventurer in
the voyage and sent a number of members of his household with
Grenville,[2] and it is possible that Sir George Carey was also
enrolled to support the venture at this time.[3]

The queen gave Raleigh a number of signs of her favour early
in the new year. She knighted him at Greenwich on Twelfth
Day,[4] and authorized him to name the newly-discovered territories
in America 'Virginia' in her honour.[5] She empowered him to
obtain gunpowder from the Tower worth over £400.[6] This
may have been a gift or it may have been part of her personal
venture in the voyage. Similarly, the queen put one of her ships,
the *Tiger*, at Raleigh's disposal,[7] though again it cannot be certainly established whether this was hired, or adventured, or lent
without charge. Most probably she acted in this case, as in so many
others, as an adventurer, making a contribution in kind which was
assessed for dividend on its assumed value, though perhaps she
was more generous to her favourite Raleigh than she was to some
other venturers with whom she associated herself.[8] Then too, the
queen placed her authority at Raleigh's disposal in having Ralph
Lane released from service in Ireland on terms advantageous to him.[9]

Among the powers which Raleigh and his friends had tried to
obtain from parliament in December were rights to bring certain
prisoners to America, and to impress other persons and also
shipping for the expedition.[10] From a draft in the state papers[11]
it appears that a commission was prepared for giving him, by

---

[1] Document no. 8, pp. 130–9: see pp. 19–22 above.

[2] Pp. 197–8, 202 below.

[3] He was a member of the house of commons, and his close later association
with the ventures (pp. 123, 498–9, 502–3, 581 below) may have begun then.

[4] Cp. p. 145 below.   [5] Fig. 2, p. 147 below.

[6] Document no. 13, p. 148 below.   [7] Pp. 178–9 below.

[8] Her investment of £120 in the *Golden Royal*, which was to have followed
Grenville, and her gift of it to Raleigh when the ship was diverted (p. 237
below), would tend to confirm these conclusions.

[9] Document no. 14, pp. 149–50 below.

[10] Pp. 125, 128–9 below.   [11] Documents no. 10, 44, pp. 144–5, 235 below.

prerogative, powers with which the commons had been unwilling to trust him in December. Authority to impound shipping, men and supplies was here limited to Devonshire, Cornwall and Bristol. In fact, signet letters were not issued for this purpose until 10 June,[1] after the first expedition had sailed, though he may, in fact, have made use of such powers before April. At least one of the members of the expedition, the Irishman, Darby Glande, claimed he had been forced to go.[2] One at least of Raleigh's ships, commanded by John Clarke, probably the *Roebuck*, was at sea in the early months of the year, searching for prizes with which to enlarge his fleet. It is not unlikely that the *Water-hound* of Brill was seized for this purpose[3] and renamed as a member of the expedition, while her master and pilot, who may have been French,[4] were taken, apparently unwillingly, on the voyage. Another French ship was also taken about this time.[5] We do not know for certain how Raleigh got together the rest of the squadron. According to Mendoza in Paris, he bought two Dutch fly-boats and two supply ships, while he was building four pinnaces, with a total fleet of sixteen vessels in prospect,[6] but this may be an exaggeration. The *Tiger* at least was fitted out on the Thames,[7] but how many more is not clear. No fewer than thirteen ships are said by Mendoza to have assembled at Plymouth.[8] In fact only seven, including two pinnaces, are known to have left there on 9 April. Of these, the *Tiger* was the queen's, the *Roebuck* and *Dorothy* and the two pinnaces Raleigh's, the *Elizabeth* owned or victualled by Cavendish, and the *Lion*[9] probably owned in part, at least, by her captain, George Raymond. The decision to send a second squadron after Grenville in June was probably taken because all the vessels could not be fitted out in good time. The *Tiger* carried 160 men,[10] and we may put the total complement at about 600, including perhaps as many as 300 soldiers and specialists of one

[1] Document no. 20, p. 156–7 below.   [2] Pp. 834–5 below.
[3] Document no. 16, pp. 151–2; cp. p. 229 below.
[4] Cp. p. 229 below.   [5] Pp. 153–5 below.
[6] P. 728 below.   [7] Pp. 139–44 below.
[8] P. 730 below.   [9] Pp. 234–42 below.   [10] P. 228 below.

sort or another.[1] Grenville's was not a large expedition, but it was adequate (especially with its intended successor) to establish a privateering and exploring base on the American shore.

6. DECEMBER 1584.
PARLIAMENTARY PROCEEDINGS ON THE BILL TO CONFIRM RALEIGH'S PATENT

(*a*) Monday morning, 14 December 1584. House of Commons. The Bill for Confirmation of Letters Patents made unto Walter Rawleigh Esquire for the discovery of Foreign Countries was read *primâ vice*.[2]

(*b*) Ibid.

A byll requyringe confirmation of the Queenes letters patentes to Mr. Water Rawley by which the Queene hathe graunted unto him all suche lande being beyonde sea out of the jurisdiction of any christian kinge which he shall at his costes discover and get, and to take suche subjectes with him to dwell ther, and they maye passe, anye statute to the contrarye notwithstandinge; the same to be helde of the Queene by homadg and a vth parte of the profyttes of the minerals of golde and silver ore are to be to her Majestye; they all to be the Queenes homadgers; none to dwell or coome there but suche as he shall licence; the Englishe mens children borne there to be denizens; he also to have auctorytye to establishe lawes there not repugnant to the doctrine established in England or lawes of the same; the Lord Treasurer and iiii[or] of the counsell to have auctorytye to give licence to him to transporte anye there which he shall think necessary, recytinge also that he hath already discovered a place called Windaganroza, desiring the confirmation thereof to him accordinge to the same letters patentes: first red.[3]

[1] P. 173 below.
[2] Sir Simonds D'Ewes, *The journals of all the parliaments during the reign of Queen Elizabeth*, ed. P. Bowes (1682), p. 339.
[3] Thomas Cromwell's diary, pp. 14-15. I am greatly indebted to Professor J. E. Neale for allowing me to use this and other of his transcripts, and for his assistance in interpreting the circumstances surrounding the introduction and passage of the bill.

Preparations for the 1585 Voyage

(c) Monday afternoon, 14 December 1584. House of Commons.

The Bill lastly[1] for Confirmation of Letters Patents made unto Mr. Walter Rawleigh was read the second time and committed unto Mr. Vice-Chamberlain,[2] Mr. Secretary,[3] Sir Philip Sidney,[4] Sir Francis Drake,[5] Sir Richard Greenfield,[6] Sir William Courtney,[7] Sir William Mohun[8] and others[9]....The Committees for

[1] This was the third of three bills discussed that afternoon and it is probable that some little time was spent on it.

[2] Sir Christopher Hatton, M.P. for Northamptonshire, not otherwise known to be associated with the Roanoke ventures, but an investor in a number of other overseas voyages (E. St John Brooks, *Sir Christopher Hatton* (1946), pp. 193–5).

[3] Sir Francis Walsingham, M.P. for Surrey, a subscriber to the 1585 venture, in which a number of members of his household took part (pp. 197–8, 202 below). He had been a consistent supporter of western ventures (see Conyers Read, *Mr secretary Walsingham* (3 vols., 1925); Quinn, *Gilbert*, passim).

[4] M.P. for Kent (Brit. Mus., Add. MS 38823, fo. 18 v.), but his name does not appear in the official *Return of members of parliament* (1878). He was interested in the Roanoke ventures, as he had been in Gilbert's, and may have subscribed to them, but he was mainly concerned in plans for Drake's voyage and for a military outpost in the Caribbean or Central America (cp. pp. 90, 204–7).

[5] M.P. for Bossiney, Cornwall. He was at this time preparing his expedition against the Spanish Indies which was intended to dovetail with the acquisition of a base on the eastern coast of North America under Raleigh's auspices (see pp. 249–52, and Corbett, *Drake*, II, 16–21).

[6] M.P. for Cornwall. For his earlier Terra Australis projects see Rowse, *Grenville*, pp. 83–112. He had not been, apparently, associated previously with Gilbert or Raleigh. It is probable that he had already been designated to command the 1585 expedition (cp. ibid. pp. 190–203).

[7] M.P., with Raleigh, for Devonshire. He is not otherwise known to be associated with the Roanoke ventures, though Rise Courtney (p. 195) may have been a relative.

[8] M.P., with Grenville, for Cornwall. He is not otherwise known to have been associated with the Roanoke ventures, but he is probably the 'William Moham Esquire' who subscribed to Gilbert's voyage in 1578 (Quinn, *Gilbert*, II, 332). He had been knighted in 1583 (Shaw, *Knights of England*, II, 82).

[9] The two M.P.s who are known to have accompanied Grenville, Anthony Rowse (East Looe, Cornwall) and Thomas Cavendish (Shaftesbury, Wilts.), were, in view of the comment below, almost certainly members. What other members (if any) accompanied Grenville is not known. Carew Raleigh (Wiltshire), certainly, and Sir George Carey (Hampshire), possibly, were subscribers to the enterprise (cp. pp. 154, 224, 499). Sidney's brother Robert (Glamorganshire) and Nicholas Gorges (Boston), a connection of Edward Gorges, may well have been. Thomas Digges (who sat with Carey for Hampshire); Fulke Greville (Heydon),

Mr. Rawleigh's Bill were appointed to meet presently in the Committee Chamber[1] of this House.[2]

(*d*) Ibid.

Mr Rawleyes byll 11°· red, argewed uppon and in fine committed.[3]

(*e*) [March 1585.] Notes on committees.

In a bill for woode destroyd by Iron mylles, no reason to comytt it to any that hath an iron myll, but it was.

Mr. Rawleys commyttes, many that were to go in that iorny, Waingandacow.[4]

(*f*) Thursday, 17 December 1584. House of Commons. The Bill for confirmation of Letters Patents granted unto Mr. Walter

Philip Sidney's partner; James Erisey (St Michael's, Cornwall), Grenville's cousin (cp. Hakluyt, *Principal navigations*, x, 98); Edward and Henry Unton (Berkshire and New Woodstock), Oxford acquaintances of Raleigh's and one of them an associate of Gilbert (Emden, *Oriel papers*, pp. 9–21; Quinn, *Gilbert*, II, 382); Humphrey Prideaux (Helston), a relative of the Prideaux who remained with Lane (pp. 177, 195, 283 below); and George Carew (St German's), previously linked with Gilbert (cp. Quinn, *Gilbert*, II, 218, 223, 332, 375), are amongst the members who might be expected to have had some interest in the venture. The best guide to the affiliations of members of this parliament is Hazel Matthews, 'The personnel of the parliament of 1584–5' (University of London, M.A. thesis, 1948).

[1] 'Possibly it was an upper room over the vestibule or lobby of the House.... But it was little used by members' (J. E. Neale, *The Elizabethan house of commons* (1949), p. 365).

[2] D'Ewes, *Journals*, p. 339.

[3] Cromwell's diary, p. 21. It adds the information that there was some appreciable debate on the bill, which was one of two dealt with that morning (though there were two other pieces of business in hand as well). The suggestion would seem to be that the committee was given an indication of the changes which some members wished to have made.

[4] Anonymous diary of this parliament, p. 35 (cited from Professor Neale's transcript). These jottings are probably by the diarist on the question of whether interested parties should be represented on committees to which bills were referred. The bill for preventing the establishment of iron mills in certain areas was debated on 2, 6 and 9 March 1585 (Cromwell's diary, pp. 45, 47, 55, 57–8) and this comment was presumably made shortly after (possibly on March 10 in reference to a bill for restraining shoemakers and tanners). The reference to Raleigh's bill infers the committee was packed with adventurers in the 1585 expedition, and it may imply that more members of the House went with Grenville than the other evidence indicates.

Rawleigh, was brought in by the Committees not altered in any word; and upon motion for ingrossing, was after some Arguments upon the Question, ordered to be ingrossed.[1]

(g) Ibid.

Mr. Rawleyes byll brought in, excepted ageynst for ii causes, specially one in respect of lybertye gyven to him to take anye person with him which ys willinge to goe; the other in that yt was made lawful to carye anye thinge over bye licence: agreed to be engrossed.[2]

(h) Friday, 18 December 1584. House of Commons.

...and the Bill for confirmation of Letters Patents made unto Walter Rawleigh Esquire, was upon the third reading after many Arguments and a Proviso added unto it, passed upon the Question.[3]

(i) Ibid.

Mr. Rawleyes byll iii⁰· red and a proviso added and the byll passed.[4]

(j) Saturday, 19 December 1584. House of Lords.

Hodie allatae sunt a Domo Communis 4 Billae:

Prima, For the Confirmation of the Queen's Majesty's Letters Patents, granted to Walter Raughleighe, Esquire, touching the Discovery and Inhabiting of certain Foreign Lands and Countries *quae 1ᵃ vice lecta est*.[5]

---

[1] D'Ewes, *Journals*, p. 340.

[2] Cromwell's diary, p. 20. The bill was the second of five discussed so that the discussion may not have gone on for long. The objection to export under licence (because it might easily be abused) was subsequently dropped. It is clear that the bill was engrossed on parchment unaltered, the officials not having yet given way to the critics.

[3] D'Ewes, *Journals*, p. 341.

[4] Cromwell's diary, p. 21. It was the second of two bills discussed, but it was followed by two important pieces of business, Hatton's message from the Queen and proceedings in Dr Parry's case, so that we cannot estimate how long the discussion took. The bill now preserved in the House of Lords is the original paper bill kept as an office copy in the House of Commons but brought up to date by the addition of the provisos and a note of the third reading.

[5] *Journals of the house of lords*, II, 74.

(*k*) Thomas Cromwell's note.

Yn this session of parliament these bylls also passed our house, which had no passadge with the Lords.

A byll of confirmation of the Queenes letters patentes to Sir Walter Rawley concerning Mingandicoza (*sic*).[1]

7. DECEMBER 1584.

BILL TO CONFIRM RALEIGH'S PATENT, AS PASSED BY THE HOUSE OF COMMONS[2]

An acte for the confermacion of the Quenes maiesties Lettres Patentes graunted to Walter Ralegh Esquire Touchinge the discoverie and Inhabitinge of certeyn Foreyne Landes & Cuntries[3]

Wheras the Queenes most exelent Maiestie of her most gracious disposicion to the Benyfite and proffite of her Realme of Englande emongeste sondrie other the singuler frewtes of her goodnes towardes the same Hath by all good meanes endeavored, that the gospell of our saviour Iesus Christe might be trewlye and syncerelie sette forth, And Ignoraunce error and supersticion Abolished within her Maiesties Domynions, And is also desirous that the knowledge of god and trewe religion might by her heighnes

---

[1] Cromwell's diary, p. 73. While there is no direct evidence why the bill was dropped in the Lords the indications are that, besides the provisos being unwelcome to Raleigh, they would be wholly unacceptable to the Queen. Professor Neale suggests strongly that the initiative in stopping the bill came from her since the restriction of the scope of royal letters patent would involve a dangerous limitation of her prerogative which she would not accept. The episode is, therefore, one of some constitutional significance. Why Raleigh should have gone to the expense of having the bill introduced is not yet clear. By its introduction he gained some contingent advantages in publicity but no sustained financial advantage. No competitive threat to his monopoly of the proposed area of settlement is known to have been contemplated at this time.

[2] House of Lords MS (see Hist. MSS Comm., *3 rep.*, app., p. 5). I am indebted to Mr M. F. Bond, Clerk of the Records, House of Lords, for permission to have this MS microfilmed. There is a copy in S.P. Domestic, Elizabeth, S.P. 12/169, 36, and a full abstract of Raleigh's patent and 'The substance of the acte of Parliament' in S.P. 12/179, 21. Neither is of any textual importance but their existence shows that the bill aroused some contemporary interest amongst officials.

[3] Crossed out: 'not before actuallie possessed or Inhabited by anye Christian Prynce or Christian peoples'.

Labors be propagatyd Amongeste foreign Nacions,[1] The people of this her heighnes Realme mainteyned and encresed And traficke to the most benefitte and Comodytie of her lovinge subiectes as otherwise shulde spende there tyme in Idellnes to the greate preiudice of the Com*m*on Welthe be trayned in vertuous and Com*m*odyous Labor,[2] And[3] beynge enformed of some greate hope of a discoverie to be hadd by her trustie and well beloued servaunte Walter Raleigh Esquier of an vnknowen Lande never hertofore possessed by anye Christian Prynce or Christian people[4] The nerenes[5] whereof and Infynite Comodities of the same mighte yelde vnto this her Realme of Englande the benefittes before remembred and manye others, Her ma*i*estie for the consideracions aforesaid hath by her heighnes Letteres Patentes vnder her greate Seale of England graunted vnto the said Walter Raleigh in manner and forme folowinge vide*l*icet....[6]

Sythence w*h*ich *Lette*rs Patent*es* made & graunted as aforesaid to the said Walter Rawleigh, There is discou*er*d by the meanes charge Labor & proc*u*rement of the said Walter Rawleigh a Land called Wyngandacoia,[7] not inhabited by anye Christian Prince or Christian people And some of the people borne in those p*a*rties brought home into this our Realme of England[8] by whose meanes & direcc*i*on & by suche of her ma*i*esties subiectes as were sent thyther by the said Walter Rawleigh singuler great comodities of that Lande are revealed & made knowen vnto vs[9] w*h*ich discoverie

---

[1] On the missionary idiom, cp. L. B. Wright, *Religion and empire* pp. 1–56.

[2] The increase of trade being expected to increase employment, cp. p. 491; Taylor, *Hakluyts*, II, 313–19.

[3] Crossed out: 'to that ende'. [4] Crossed out: 'whose'.

[5] This originally read: 'as the nerenes whereof'.

[6] The patent of 25 March 1584 is then recited (pp. 82–9 above).

[7] The earliest dated appearance of the name (for which see pp. 116–17, 853–4). Following it, crossed out, is 'beinge never heretofore'.

[8] The earliest record of the bringing of Manteo and Wanchese to England (cp. p. 116).

[9] The first information that the Indians had been taught enough English (or had taught enough Algonquian) to be able to communicate in detail with their hosts. Barlowe's narrative above (pp. 90–116) may be as early in date as this bill but is possibly later (cp. p. 16). The statement also implies that the expedition

hath byn heretofore attempted by dyuerse persons & never brought
to any suche perfection[1]

It maye therfore please the Queenes most exelent maiestie with
thassent of the Lordes spirituall & temporall And the Comons in
this presente parliament assembled And by the aucthoritie of the
same That it be enacted That the said Walter Rawleigh his heires
& assignes shall & maye by the aucthoritie of this present parliament from henceforth for ever Haue holde & enioye the saide
Land so discouerd with all realties previledges powers prehemy-
nences & authorities menconed & conteyned in the said Lettres
Patentes accordinge to the purport effect & true meanynge of the
same Letters Patentes and that the said Lettres Patentes and all and
singuler the grauntes Liberties priviledges & other thinges therin
conteyned shalbe by aucthoritie aforesaid Established approued
confirmed allowed and be effectuall vnto the said Walter Rawleigh his heires & assignes accordinge to the tenour & purport of
the said Lettres Patentes[2]

Provided allwayes that this Acte or anie thinge therein con-
tayyned shall not in any wise be intended to geve any Licence
power or Aucthority to any person or persons beinge in Prison
either vppon Execucion at the sute of any person for debte[3] or
being imprisoned or vnder Arreste for any other cause whatsoever
or the wife ward or apprentyce of any other person or persons to

---

brought home specimens of produce. Apart from a few pearls, and hides and
furs we do not know what they were (cp. pp. 100–2).

[1] Probably a reference to the unsuccessful ventures, 1578–83, under Sir Hum-
prey Gilbert's auspices, and to the failures of Sir George Peckham and Christopher
Carleill to achieve any discoveries after his death (cp. pp. 3–4 above).

[2] The patent had specified (p. 84 above) that discovery and occupation must
be effective within six years. This bill would have ensured title to Raleigh to
the lands so far discovered for ever.

[3] This originally read 'debte or for Any other cause'. It was probably inserted
at the instance of members who had seen or heard of the younger Richard
Hakluyt's suggestions for the shipping out of debtors and other offenders recently
made in his 'Discourse of western planting' (Taylor, *Hakluyts*, II, 319, 326). The
primary reason was that debt was a civil suit and if the defendants were allowed
to emigrate the plaintiffs would lose their remedy, but as drafted the clause would
forbid the transportation of criminals also.

departe this Realme[1] or to geve Any Lycence power or Aucthority to the said Walter Rawley hys heyres or assignes to enlardge any such person or to take or sende any such person or persons over Sea or [   ][2] or take any shippinge, or furnyture for shipping withowt the assent & good wylle of the person or persons[3] this Acte or any thinge therein contaygned to the contrary hereof in any wyse notwithstandinge

[*Endorsed:*] [Act for t]he confermacion [of l]ettres patentes [grau]nted to Walter [Ral]eghe esquier

Lune xiij° decembris 158'4[4] The fyrst Reading
post meridiem The secund Reading and commytted
Iouis xvij° decembris 1584 Ordered to be ingrossed[5]
Veneris xviij° decembris 1584 The thirde Readinge
and with a proviso added was passed vpon the questyon
Novembris[6] et Decembris 1584
Iudicium

---

[1] The patent had been so general in its permission to authorize emigration (p. 83–8) that this was a legitimate safeguard of the property rights of husband or master as then understood.

[2] This word cannot be read.

[3] Raleigh subsequently obtained similar powers to impress men and goods by royal prerogative (cp. pp. 144–5, 156–7).

[4] Monday was 14 December (cp. p. 123 above).

[5] A paper bill of this nature is at first sight an anomalous document to find in the House of Lords MSS. We should expect, rather, the copy ordered to be engrossed on parchment on 17 December which, after amendment and the addition of the traditional formula 'Soit baille aux Seigneurs', went to the Lords on 19 December, but this has not survived. The paper bill must, therefore, belong of right to the Commons' muniments, and is perhaps that presented to them for a first reading on 14 December, and then retained by the clerks after engrossing so that it could be used as a rough record on which to enter amendments and notes of the completion of successive stages in the bill's progress through both houses.

[6] No explanation for the mention of November can be suggested.

8. [1584-5.]

ANONYMOUS NOTES FOR THE GUIDANCE OF RALEIGH AND CAVENDISH[1]

For *Master* Rauleys[2] Viage.

In to that cuntery I would haue men geo armored of this sorte,[3] for that they ar to deall with naked men, yett will I haue furnytur to preuent the Inuasion of the Spanyardes.[4]

The Number being, 800,[5] I would haue them thus deuided. Fyrst 400. harqubusiers.[6]

[1] A rough draft, written on both sides of a double leaf of quarto paper (Essex County Record Office, County Hall, Chelmsford, MS D/DRh, M 1). It is printed in part in *English history from Essex sources*, ed. A. C. Edwards (Essex Record Office Publications, no. 17, 1952), pp. 178–9. It came with a group of military and diplomatic memoranda of the period 1580–1600, and other family and estate papers of the Rolt and Caswall families, from the library of the historian John Horace Round. Round's home was in Colchester, but his grandfather married the daughter of George Caswall (d. 1825), son of Timothy Caswall, M.P. (d. 1802) and Mary Constantia, daughter and heiress of Thomas Rolt of Sacomb Park, Herts. Whether this paper came to Round through these connexions or through his association with Colchester is not known. Mr F. G. Emmison, Essex County Archivist, and Miss Hilda E. P. Grieve, his Senior Assistant, have taken a great deal of trouble to trace back this document and to help me to get an accurate version of it. I am also indebted to Miss Norah H. Evans, and to the late Edward Lynam. Sir John Smythe, Sir Roger Williams, or Thomas Digges may have been its author (cp. pp. 19–22 above).

[2] Raleigh being knighted on 6 January 1585 (p. 145).

[3] Cp. for style Thomas Digges, *Stratioticos* (ed. 1590), p. 83, 'Finally, I would haue a Souldior....'

[4] The meaning is that they should wear armour so as to be prepared for a Spanish attack, even though they will be dealing in the main with Indians who were not so equipped. Cp. the marginal note in Sir John Smythe, *Certain discourses...of weapons* (1590, fo. 42 v.): 'Some peraduenture will say that the Spaniards without Long bowes, but with Crosbowes, Harquebuze shot, & other weapons, haue conquered a great part of the west Indies: whereunto it is to be answerd, that those Indians were simple people, that went naked, and had no vse for yron nor steele', the parallel being obviously close.

[5] Grenville is not likely to have had more than 400 soldiers with him in April 1585, and only 100 were left at Roanoke Island (cp. pp. 173, 194–7 below).

[6] Smythe was a strong advocate of the light arquebus as against the heavier caliver: 'light Harquebuses well formed of conuenient length, and ranforced... are a great deale more maniable, more fit...than our ordinarie and heauie Caliuers' (*Certain discourses*, fo. 6). The appropriate length of their barrels should be a yard, neither more nor less, and 'considering the lightnesse of their peeces

Preparations for the 1585 Voyage

Then 100. swordes and lyght moddena targetes[1]

Then 150. long bows,[2]

Then 100, Armed men with millan corsseletes lyght[3]

Then 50. Armed men with lyght Corsseletes with short weapons.[4]

Of this nomber I would dayly haue in the forte 100 in garde, and, so, nyghtly for the sentenels,[5] all the rest should labor by turns tyll the forte be Ended.

Whylst the forte is a buldyng I would haue, 200,[6] that should

they may as well and as readilie without rests at any time take their sights from point at blanke', while their effective range was 50 or 60 paces (*Instructions* (1595), pp. 143–4, 188–9). Soldiers with arquebuses are seen in several of White's drawings (cp. pp. 403–5 below).

[1] Smythe advocated swords 'of the length of a yard and not aboue' (*Instructions*, p. 186). Targets were round or oval shields, with loops at the back. Sir Roger Williams, *Briefe discourse of warre* (1590), p. 45, said 'targeters' should 'haue the corslets of reasonable proofe, and the targets light'.

[2] The proportion was high. Sir John Smythe spoke very highly of the long bow, considering that arquebusiers should be chosen 'chieflie of such as haue small skill and dexterite in the long bowe, and archerie' (*Instructions*, p. 187). He thought its great value was its flexibility in use, its users being 'readie vpon euery opportuitie, to stoupe, and take euery litle aduantage of hillocks, banckes, vines, trenches, shrubbes, or anie such like' (*Certain discourses*, fo. 19 v.). Sir Roger Williams (*Briefe discourse of warre*, p. 46) said '500 musketers are more seruiceable than 1500 bowmen', and Humphrey Barwick (*Briefe discourse of weapons* (1591?), fo 19 v.) agreed in effect. References to the use of bows in America are few (cp. pp. 369, 440–2).

[3] The men wearing armour, including light Milan corselets, were clearly pikemen, the proportion being small by European usage. Williams (op. cit., p. 44) says 'The Pike is the chiefest weapon to defend': Smythe (*Instructions*, p. 96), gives some details of its use. The pikes in White's Puerto Rico drawings would appear to be half-pikes and not the full eighteen-foot pike (see pp. 403–5 below).

[4] Men, wearing armour, including light corselets, with halberds, bills, partizans or battle-axes. Williams (p. 45) has the nearest parallel passages: 'Both bills & halbards ought to haue corslets, with light Millain murrians', with to 1000 pikes '200 short weapons, as Holberts or Bills' (p. 44). Smythe (*Instructions*, p. 194) considered 'souldiers with battleaxes or halbarders...should bee apparelled and armed in Corselets in all points and pieces of armour like vnto the piquers', their weapons 'short staued battleaxes or halbards, of not aboue 6. foot in their whole length', so as not to get mixed up with the longer pikes (p. 97).

[5] Followed by 'in' crossed out. Lane may have used some such rota system. He emphasizes the 'strong Corps of guard' he posted when on expeditions (cp. p. 266 below).

[6] '300' crossed out. The sending out of such parties may perhaps be deduced from what little we know of Grenville's activities in July and August 1585 while the fort was building (pp. 166–7 below). Lane probably also held the remainder

continually geo a discoueryng, and returne euery eyght or tenthe day, and then 200, mor to do the lyke and that Companys that Com from discouery to be iij days excempte from labor wache or ward after ther returne, so as yow shall haue ,500, men to labor for the buldyng of your forte[1]

I would not haue any Company aboue, 50, bycause the mor Commaunders the better servis, and the Companys wilbe the fayrer and better[2]

What maner of forte I woulde haue I would haue It a pentangell in this manner. with ,v, large bulwarkes[3] the Casemates of the Boulwarkes large and open, with a way out of the bulwarke and an other Into the Streat   The Collionsides or ocrechons,[4] large

of his men at the fort on Roanoke Island until the Chesapeake Bay party returned and then resumed his own journeys (pp. 257–8 below).

[1] The Roanoke Island fort was evidently run up with fair speed, but, to judge from Mr J. C. Harrington's excavations, the fortifications there were smaller and simpler than envisaged by this writer (cp. pp. 903–6 below).

[2] This does not accord with the views of either Sir John Smythe or Sir Roger Williams as expressed in their published writings. Smythe (*Certain discourses*, fos. 6–10 v.) argued against 'our trained Low Countrie Captaines' who wished to reduce 'bands' to 150–200 men under an ensign, preferring 300 or more. Later (*Instructions*, pp. 100–101) he urged still larger companies of 500 footmen. Williams (*Briefe discourse of warre*, pp. 18–19) cited with apparent approval Spanish practices of having up to 300 footmen in a company. Humphrey Barwick (*Briefe discourse concerning...weapons*, fo. 6 v.) is less partizan, saying 'as concerning great or small Bandes of footmen: my opinion is this, that it is necessarye for foote-bands or bands of horsemen, to be of diuers numbers, for sundry causes'. On Roanoke Island Lane had two captains (Stafford and Vaughan) for little over 100 men, and so the proposal for companies of 50 may have been adopted.

[3] 'large' is crossed out and re-inserted before 'bulwarkes', and 'the curtyns' is crossed out after. The pentangular fort with five bulwarks appears very similar to that depicted in Paule Ive, *The practise of fortification* (1589), p. 30. Lane had his own preferences in fortification and his designs for ramparts and bulwarks do not usually follow the text-books too closely (cp. White's drawings and the Roanoke fort reconstruction, fig. 11 at p. 905 below). Thomas Hariot was also interested in this type of fort, and worked out methods of calculating angles for the bastions, etc., of regular- and irregular-shaped fortifications (Brit. Mus., Additional MS 6788, ff. 55–65: n.d., but possibly *c.* 1595).

[4] The sides of the cullions or orechions (from Italian *orecchione*), the shoulders (or ears) of the bulwark covering the casemates (*OED* and Ive, op. cit., p. 16). I am much indebted to Dr Charles W. Porter and Mr J. C. Harrington for assistance on fortification nomenclature and practice.

and longe, The Curtyns sumwhat slant, that the yearthe may lye
the faster and the rampir of the Curtyns very braude, Euery
bulwarke shall haue bye It a caualir to beat the feald,[1] or tow wer
better, In the mydst I would haue a markitt plase large, for
assemblys, and to sytt in if neade be.[2]

[fo. 1 v.] I would haue Euery streat strayt to euery bulwarke,
and to Euery gatt and to the mydst of Euery Curtyne, so as
standyng In the market plase yow may see all the bulwarkes
Curtyns and gates .

The diche I would haue large with walles, beyound the diche
a 20 foot from the diche I would haue a wall of , 4. foot hyght
with arayll on the tope so as the tope of this wall shouldbe within
a 3 foot as hyght as the parrepett of my Curtyns or bulwarkes.
Within the diche I would haue a hyght pall[3] of xv foot hyght by
Cause It shall preuent any suddeyn Scallado,[4] for that your forte
is of yearthe, which yow know in tyme moulders.[5] This forte
with 500, men with the help and Incorragment of the Commander
wilbe fenyshed In a monthe . bysydes the howses.[6] which being
fynyshed I know no reason but it is abell long to hould a gaynst

---

[1] 'In the' crossed out. The cavalier was a platform raised above the height of
the bulwark (and usually in the form of a horseshoe) so as to command the
adjacent works and country (cp. Ive, op. cit., p. 39). No trace of any such have
been found on Roanoke Island.

[2] The page ends with the words 'from the'.

[3] A high paling, palisade or stockade. If placed in the ditch it made it difficult
to keep the latter in repair: if on the outer edge of the ditch it was liable, if high,
to interrupt the field of fire of the guns in the casemates. No evidence for a
palisade round the 1585 Roanoke fort has been found, but the 1587 enclosure
had 'a high palisado' (pp. 604, 902–7 below).

[4] Attempted assault by escalade.

[5] Cp. the 1585 Roanoke Island fort where 'Archaeological evidence shows that
some earth washed down into the bottom of the ditch very soon after the fort
was built' (J. C. Harrington, in *The Iron Worker*, xv (1951), no. 3, p. 12; and
'Report', I, 135–6).

[6] We do not know precisely how long the Roanoke fort took to build in 1585,
but Lane was installed there by 8 September at latest and possibly by 17 August
(cp. pp. 214, 255 below), so that it may have been built in less than a month. In
this project it is not specifically said that the houses were to be inside the fortifications though what is said above about the market square could imply that they
were. They were certainly outside the 1585 fort perimeter (cp. pp. 282, 902 below).

all the forces of Indda.[1] how I would haue It seated, eyther vppon rocke, marrishe, an Iland or peninsulla, if this forte wer In an Iland then would I haue on the next land to It a forte, wherby I would always be sure of a landyng assured, and of a retreat, for nothing would be so dangerus as to lande men In disorder, neyther any thing so eminent a distruction as Imbarkyn follow'd by the Enymy,[2]

What men ar nessesary to Carry. I will leaue the ministers and officers of war, which all men know what ar nessesary, but the choyse of them is a great matter, for a discreat vigelant temporat experimented and a vallient commander, acthiuethe all with honor, and the, vndiscreat rashe, vnexperimented[3] and Necligent, is the vtter ouer throw of all bothe army and honner, I leaue this to his Iugment who chuses & [pays?] the officers[4] I woulde haue, an

---

[1] For 'India'? It could be 'Iudda', Judah. Although the subject is not identical there is a considerable similarity of nomenclature in a passage in Williams (*Briefe discourse of warre*, pp. 49–50): 'The best drie ditch, is to haue the ditch 100. paces broad, and fiftie foote deepe, foure Casamats on euery side of the Bulwarks, the lowest to flanke the bottome of the ditch from one side vnto the other; the second likewise within ten foot, with broad Casamats, that the Artillerie may be raised high behind, to beate a long the ditches, as nigh to the bottome as can be deuised...also the fourth Casamat must flanke the Counterskarfe...the head ought to couer the ditch & rampier as high as the fourth Casamat....The Counterscarfe ought to haue parapets cut in them foure foote deepe...euery Curten ought to haue two Caualeres to command the field with their shootes...no drie ditch can be compared for strength vnto a wet ditch.' Smythe (*Certain discourses*, p. 11) showed himself a stickler for the observation of fortification technique even in small and temporary structures, attacking 'Sconces...without anie Bulwarks, Flankers, Trauerses, Mounts, Platformes, wet or drie Ditches in forme, with Counterscarps, or any other good form of fortification, but onelie raised and formed with earth, turfe, trench, and certen poynts, angles, and indents'. On the whole, the evidence suggests (pp. 904–6 below) that the engineer of the 1585 expedition agreed with him.

[2] In the 'Discourse' the younger Hakluyt stressed the importance of fortifying against the Spaniards and urged the bringing out of men able to fortify and fight (Taylor, *Hakluyts*, II, 240, 248, 274, 323, 326), while the elder's 'Inducements' (ibid., pp. 334, 337) stressed similar points. For the position of the site chosen in 1585 see Harrington, 'Report', I, 142–3; pp. 905–6 below.

[3] Sir Roger Williams (*Briefe discourse of warre*) uses 'experimented' for 'experienced'.

[4] This sentence is inserted in the margin: 'pays' is a mere guess as the word is illegible. Cp. Digges, *Stratioticos*, p. 92, on the captain of a company: 'he ought first to make choyse of sufficient, expert, honest payneful Officers, A skilful

Ingenyr and Cu*n*ynge treuese M*aster*[1] whos Iugment wer abell
to know the plases of Best aduantages to buylde on, he to bulde,
wit*h* Iugment that his forte be not to byge, that his men may not
be abell to defend It,[2] nor to littell for that is mor dangerus, and
an ould maxime a monxt the men of war that nothi*n*g that is
littell Is abell to hould longe. for diuers reasons I could allege.[3]

[fo. 2] Then I would haue a phisitien as well for the healthe of
the souldier as to discouer the simpels of earbs plantes trees roothes,
and stons,[4] [a] good geographer to make discription of the landes
discouerd, and wit*h* hym an exilent paynter,[5] potticaris[6] and
Surgiantes[7] for low sycniss[8] and woundes.

Lieutenant, a diligent Serieant, vigilent Corporals, a godly Priest, a trustie Clearke
or Register, a prouident Harbinger, a cunning Surgeon, with necessarie prouisions, and two or three good Drummes.' And also (ibid., p. 144): 'The General
ought also not onely to haue expert Engineers, and menne of excellent knowledge
in the arte of Fortification both of Fortes and Campes, conducting of Mines,
planting of Batteries, &c., but also to haue therein himselfe exquisite knowledge.'

[1] The engineer and traverse-master were evidently to be separate officials, but
none are found named as such in the 1585 expedition.

[2] 'as beas in a monkes whoude' (as bees in a monk's hood), crossed out. It
was considerations such as this which led the 1586 settlers to level the fort defences.
Mr Harrington does not consider that they would, in any case, have been needed
if only Indians were in view as possible enemies and not Spaniards also (*North
Carolina Hist. Rev.*, XXVI, 142), though I am not convinced that this was so.

[3] The page ends with an isolated 'but'.

[4] The younger Hakluyt stressed the need for a physician to go with the settlers
(Taylor, *Hakluyts*, II, 325). There was one with Lane as late as 8 September 1585
(p. 213 below), but it is uncertain that he remained with the colonists.

[5] 'An exilent' is crossed out before 'geographer'. An expert so named is not
suggested elsewhere. 'A skilful painter is also to be caried', says the elder Hakluyt
(Taylor, *Hakluyts*, II, 338). The surveyor and painter planned for in the 1582
instructions (Brit. Mus., Add. MS 38823, see pp. 51-4 above) had comparable
tasks assigned to them.

[6] The younger Hakluyt mentions an apothecary and it was he, not the physician,
who was to send 'into the Realme by seede and roote herbes and plantes of rare
excellencie' (Taylor, *Hakluyts*, II, 325). Lane speaks of 'our Appotycaryes' on
12 August 1585, but it is unlikely (in view of Hariot's vagueness about medicinal
plants) that any remained over the winter (cp. p. 334 below).

[7] The younger Hakluyt considered a surgeon desirable (Taylor, *Hakluyts*, II,
325), but we hear of none before the drowning of Hance, apparently ship's
surgeon of the *Moonlight*, in 1590 (p. 612 below). He could have been the Hance
Walters of the 1585 settlement (p. 197).   [8] Fevers.

An alcamist is not Impertinent, to trye the mettaylls [1] that maybe discouerd and an perfett lapidary [2] not to be forgotten. Masons, Carpenters. makers. of mudwals,[3] su[m] of ye myners of Cornwell,[4] Sume exelent husband men, with all thinges appertayninge to husbandry, and all maner of Sead Corne [5]. for all other [Sienus?] [6] nessessaty will not spare them . at home, .

What manner of geouernement is to be vsed and what offics to geouerne.

The generall, to Commaund absolutly within the forte and without all matters marshall, to geue all offices In the geouernement, to punnyshe any man by his Commandment but not to prosead to deathe of any man but by order of law. To haue autoryty to pardon all offences sauing Treason to hir Maiestie and the Cuntrye.[7]

Tow Iustis one cauled hight Iuge. who shall sett vppon all

---

[1] 'yearthe' crossed and 'mettaylls' substituted.

[2] Both Hakluyts urged bringing out 'Mynerall men' and 'Men skilful in all Minerall causes' (Taylor, *Hakluyts*, II, 323, 336). Lane's expert was 'Master Yougham' (the Dougham or Doughan Gannes, or Joachim Ganz, of the 1585 list, cp. p. 196 below), and he may have had others. But there is no suggestion of a lapidary elsewhere.

[3] Masons, carpenters and many other building craftsmen appear in the Hakluyt prescriptions (Taylor, *Hakluyts*, II, 323, 337), but not mud-wall makers.

[4] A usual excuse for impressing miners was to do military fortification work (cp. the 100 that Raleigh had to supply in 1586 for the Netherlands (Edwards, *Ralegh*, II, 33; *Acts of the privy council, 1586–7*, p. 102)).

[5] For detailed recommendations regarding agricultural specialists and seeds and plants see Taylor, *Hakluyts*, II, 320–1, 336–8.

[6] Badly written, this approximation to 'sinews' may not be correctly read, but it makes some kind of sense.

[7] Since the Drake-Doughty affair there was a sincere determination to avoid both division of authority and arbitrary action by the commander in overseas expeditions. The younger Hakluyt stressed the need to have both a coherent scheme of law enforcement and a legal code. Lane several times emphasized the severity of the discipline he enforced (pp. 228, 271 below). Smythe (*Certain discourses*, sig. *** 4v) emphasized the importance of 'discipline Militarie', while Williams (*Briefe discourse of warre*, p. 8) asked 'What makes the Spaniards discipline to be so famous as it is?' 'Their good order', he replied, 'otherwise it is well known, the Nation is the besest and cowardlie sort of people of most others.'

matters In Law and haue autoryty to make an end definitiue of all Causes,[1] and from whos Iugment no appelation, nor no Contradiction no not at the Counsell tabell, for wher appeals ar contrauersis neuer sease.[2]

For the Collonell, the sergant maior, the marshall and Captens[3] all know ther offices. and what by duty they ar to do,

The hyght Tresorir shall once euery year yeald vp his account vnto the geouerneur and Counsell. he shall reseaue all appertaynynge vnto the Prince, and shall geue all officers appertaynyng to a hyght treserer which is petty treserers audites, Customers Conptrulers searchers & suche lyke.[4]

The Admirall[5] shall once euery . 3 . monthes be accountabell

[1] It is not unlikely that the inclusion of a high marshal, Thomas Cavendish, in an expedition as small as Grenville's was an attempt to meet the requirements here set out. In Spanish practice, in the absence of the captain general 'the high Marshal or master of the Camp general commandeth all' (Williams, *Briefe discourse of warre*, p. 15). The high marshal in the 1585 expedition was, in fact, soon at loggerheads with the general (cp. p. 210 below). Cp. Digges, *Stratioticos*, pp. 117–19, on the Lord High Marshal: 'To him apperteyneth the true administration of Iustice, the hearing and determining of controuersies, and the punishing of disorders.' And (ibid., p. 111): 'I holde it more conuenient, that all matters concerning life, be heard by the high Marshal.'

[2] The requirement that the general should consult his council was fundamental to any control of his actions and the holding of him to his instructions. Grenville did not take easily to limitations on his authority (cp. p. 210–11, 228–9 below) but in the West India expedition of 1585–6 Drake was scrupulous to consult his council at every stage. Smythe (*Certain discourses*, sig. ✶✶ 4v) considered this essential in military operations of any kind.

[3] This is the sequence of officers below the general, high marshal and lieutenant-general in a military force. Sir John Smythe (*Certain discourses*) has a section on 'The sufficiencie of Coronells', and another on captains. Lane says (pp. 283, 286–7) that he had a colonel, serjeant-major and provost marshal (and deputy provost), but gives none of their names. The captains were Stafford and Vaughan. This was rather an elaborate establishment for such a small force.

[4] Sir Roger Williams (*Briefe discourse of warre*, pp. 15–16) says that in the Spanish service treasurer at wars was an office of honour whose holder (though he had no concern with military discipline) was directly responsible to the captain general, and controlled the auditor, mustermaster and commissary, presenting his accounts to the general. Francis Brooke, who returned with Grenville, was treasurer in 1585. He left his under-treasurer (unnamed) with Lane (pp. 210, 214, 290 below).

[5] Philip Amadas was admiral of Virginia and probably ranked second to Grenville on the naval side (cp. p. 179 below). We find him leading an

vnto the hyght Tresorir of all suche parte as shall appertayne to the P*ri*nce whiche shalbe the fyfte p*ar*te of all acquisted.

When the generall shall send out any Company of discouery ther shalbe ouer, 200, wh*i*ch is iiij Companys, and w*i*th them shall euer geo Sume great officer and a Tresorir to reseaue the fyft for the Q*ueens* Ma*i*estie,[1] That the chefe officer shall aunswer for his Compa*n*yes and Euery particuler Capten In his Company for Com*m*yttyng any of thes disorders[2]

[fo. 2 v.] First that no Souldier[3] do violat any woman, 2 That no Souldier do take any mans goodes forcibly from hym.[4] 3 That no Indian be forced to labor vnwillyngly. 4. That no Souldier shall defraud Her Ma*i*este of her fyfte. 5 That no Souldier abbandon his ensegne w*i*thout leaue, of his Capten, 6 That non shall stryke or mysuse any Indian . 7 That non shall Enter any Indians howse w*i*thout his leaue, 8 That non shall stryke w*i*thin the forte nor fytt w*i*thin a myll of It. 9 That non offer to draw

expedition to Weapemeoc (p. 192) and assisting in planning fortifications (p. 612). He may, indeed, have doubled the role of admiral and colonel in such a small establishment as was left on Roanoke Island. As such he could have been the leader of the Chesapeake Bay expedition, since Lane refers to 'the Colonel of the Chesepians' (pp. 194, 286–7). The writer, envisaging the admiral as having some financial responsibility, is probably thinking ahead to the development of an admiralty jurisdiction when the colony should become stable.

[1] This is the fifth part of the ore of gold and silver reserved to the queen in Raleigh's patent (p. 84 above). The small scale of the settlement of 1585–6 made this advice irrelevant.

[2] Both Hakluyts had urged (Taylor, *Hakluyts*, II, 318, 334) the treatment of the Indians 'with all humanitie, curtesie, and freedome', so as to win them from paganism, make them into allies against Spain, and teach them commerce and civility. The items relating to the Indians here are original, though doubtless adapted, like the more purely military ones, from existing military codes of conduct, e.g. the almost contemporary *Lawes and ordinances set downe by Robert Earle of Leycester,...in the Lowe Countries*, London [1586], reprinted in C. G. Cruickshank, *Elizabeth's army* (1946), pp. 144–51. For the treatment of Indians, 1585–6, cp. pp. 275–88, 368–82 below.

[3] 'Comyte' crossed out. Cp. 'Offences to be punished with pane of Death in euery Camp or Armie'; 'Whosoeuer shall forcibly abuse any woman.' (Digges, *Stratioticos* (1590), pp. 122–4) According to Hariot (p. 370 below) the Indian women did not attract Lane's men sexually.

[4] Grenville showed himself ready to proceed very severely against Indian pilfering (p. 191 below).

any weapon vppon any Conseler or his Capt*ain*, 10 That no. Souldier sleep in sentenell or abbandon his sentenell or garde[1]

To the fyrst deathe, To the second a dubbell restutution, if the souldier be not abell, to haue a years Imprisonme*nt* the whype and bannisheme*nt* or condemd to the gallys for vij years. and the p*ar*ty to haue his restutition of the . *Prince*, To the ,3.[2] iij monthes Imprisonment , to the .4. deathe or a p*er*petuall Condemnation to the gallys or myns. to the 5 deathe or vij yeres Slauery[3] to the 6 , to haue xx blows with a cuggell In the p*re*sentz of the Indian strucken. To the .7. vj monthes imprisonment or slauery To the .8. lose of hand. To the .9. & 10th p*re*sent deathe wit*h*out remission.[4]

[*Endorsed across fold*:] Notes geuen to M*aste*r Candishe.[5]

9. THE LEGAL CONSEQUENCES OF AN INCIDENT ON THE THAMES EARLY IN 1585

(*a*) Februarii 8° die.[6] A warr*ant* for Iohn Stile against Hugh Tucker, act*ion* 100. lib.[7]

(*b*) Maii 1585 9° die.[8] A decree for Iohn Stile to call Iohn Powell and others to be witnesses in a cause betwene he and Tucker.

---

[1] '9. That non offer to' is crossed out and the tenth item entered in the margin.

[2] 'that vj' crossed out.

[3] Crossed out: 'iij monthes Imprissonme*nt* .to the sixte, 6. monthes Slauery', which, though not clear, suggest that the writer on reconsideration was inclined to stiffen his proposed penalties substantially.

[4] The penalties are savage, though not more so than those normal in criminal and military practice at the time. We learn of one man being hanged on Roanoke Island (p. 790), but there is no evidence on what grounds.

[5] For Thomas Cavendish see pp. 174, 179, 182, 230. The 1585 Virginia expedition was the only one in which he was associated with Raleigh and this (together with the internal circumstantial evidence in the 'Notes') clinches the association of the document with the 1585 expedition. As for dating, the limits are October 1584 and March 1585, with December 1584 and January 1585 as the most likely months, since it was in them that the organization of the expedition was decided (cp. p. 19).

[6] Dr Julius Caesar's list of decrees and warrants, Brit. Mus., Lansdowne MS 133, fo. 10, giving the earliest date so far met with.

[7] Showing Stile to be taking an action for damages of £100 against Tucker.

[8] Brit. Mus., Lansdowne MS 133, fo. 13 v.

(c) 10 June 1585. Examination of John Pavie, citizen of London.[1]

'That about the monethe of Januarye or Februarye laste to his nowe remembrance this examinate comminge vppe the River of Thames with his master master Powell Surveyor of Thordenance[2] in a double whery of foure oares belonginge to Sir Walter Rawleighe beinge rowed by John Stile and two or three other watermen and stered by Captayne Hamedes a gentleman of the said Sir Walter Rawleighes,[3] they overtooke the articulate Hughe Tucker as this examinate then herde him caled and another waterman rowinge vpppe with a faire winde towardes London, and comminge nere them the said Captayne Hamedes stered the boate wherein he and this examinate were, somewhat thwarte the said Tuckers boate, wherewith the same Tucker vttered vile and vnreverente speeches agaynst the said Hamedes with whiche vile speeches the said Hamedes being moved made towardes the said Tucker once or twise and not being able to come soe nere him as he woulde he tooke the helme staffe and threwe yt at the said Tucker,[4] Wherevppon the same Tucker tooke vppe a stretcher and flonge yt at the said Hamedes, and therewith strake the said John Stile on the head with suche violence that he fell downe on his face in the boate soe as this examinate sittinge nexte vnto the said Stile thoughte he had byn stricken deade, and got him by the heade and lifted him vppe agayne and revived him. And sayethe that with the blowe his heade was grevouslye broken and blede

---

[1] Extracts, P.R.O., High Court of Admiralty, Instance and Prize, Examinations, H.C.A. 13/25. The libel on which the questions asked of Powell were based is dated 26 April 1585 (H.C.A. 24/53, no. 153).

[2] John Powell (see P.R.O. 30/26/96, 1; Signet Office Docquet Book, Ind. 6800, fo. 19 v.). His presence, and that of Pavie, would suggest that they had been to visit the *Tiger* and others of Raleigh's ships in the vicinity of Greenwich, in connexion with the supply of gunpowder (see p. 148 below).

[3] Captain Philip Amadas, already described as a member of Raleigh's household (p. 91). As admiral of Virginia he was second in command on the naval side in the 1585 expedition, apparently sailing in the *Tiger* (cp. p. 159 below).

[4] This incident, with the references below (pp. 143-4) suggest that Amadas was distinguished by a hot temper.

abundantlye, and was soe wounded that he was not able to rowe.'
He also said 'that John Stile at the tyme of his hurte was hired by
Sir Walter Rawleighe knighte to goe to the seas in his then
appoynted viadge. But what wages he was to haue, for that viadge,
or what he loste by reason thereof he knowethe not'.[1]

(*d*) 18 November 1586. Examination of Nicholas Faunte,
citizen of London, gentleman.[2]

'That the said Hughe Tucker and his fellowe rowinge with a
payre of oares tooke this *examinate* m*aste*r Hamdon [*recte*
Holmden] & M*aste*r Cordell into his boate at Grenewich stayres
a yeare paste or somewhat more betwixte fyve and six of the
Clocke at night to bringe them to London.

And being vppon the thames over agaynst Deptforde they
overtooke a longe boate havinge foure oares and a Stereman &
the said Tucker and his fellowe laboringe to owt goo them, the
waterman in the said longe boate or some other of the companye
thereof as yt seemed being offended thereat furthwith assayled the
saide Tucker and his company severall tymes and soughte by all
meanes they coulde to hinder or stay them whereby this *examinate*
and his companye dowted some yll meaninge to be in them for
that their boate was noe ordenary wherie but rowed with foure
oares,[3] and they themselves in the boate assayled them in such
sorte and soe often as they did. Wherevppon the said Tucker and
his fellowe gettinge before them and kepeinge theire course
towardes London one of the company in the longe boate threwe

---

[1] The libel (H.C.A. 24/53, no. 153) says: 'Quod tempore predicto Iohn Stiles
conductus et saliaratus fuit per egregium virum Walterum Raleighe militum ad
navigandum in navi quadam appellata The Tyger of the Queenes maiestie in
partes transmarinas.'

[2] H.C.A. 13/26.

[3] The four-oared, or double, wherry was evidently a sufficiently unusual boat
to arouse comment on the Thames. It seems highly probable that it was being
employed specifically for the exploration of the shallow sounds of the newly
discovered Virginia. Lane there used one which could carry fifteen to twenty men
(pp. 256, 264 below). The younger Hakluyt had advocated the carrying of specially
designed boats (Taylor, *Hakluyts*, II, 322), but not of this type. In the latest statement of the plaintiff's case (26 January 1587, H.C.A. 24/54, no. 70) the wherry
appears as a 'Boate or Bardge of Sir Walter Rauleighes'.

the helme staffe at this ex*amina*te and his companye which missed them verey narrowly and the said Tucker p*er*ceavinge the same tokke vp his stretcher and threwe yt at the said longe boate beinge in the nighte time and somewhat darcke.'[1]

In his re-examination Nicholas Faunte stated that he was born at Canterbury and now serves at Court. He said that the other boate had a rudder, and that 'the longe boate first crossed the water and began to molest the said Tucker and his passengers'.

(*e*) 19 January 1587. Examination of Edward Holmden, citizen of London, grocer.[2]

He had been a passenger in the boat with Hugh Tucker 'aboute a yeare paste'. The other boat followed Tucker and came up against his boat. Tucker put them off and, presently, the other boat came up again and struck Tucker's boat amidships, and struck an oar into the stern of Tucker's boat. This was done wilfully, as they might have passed safely.[3] The other boat had a 'helme and a rudder'. 19 January 1586.

(*f*) 18 November 1686. Examination of Thomas Cordell, citizen of London, gentleman.[4]

He had been a passenger in the boat with Tucker 'more than a yere past'. He 'saw a pinnace with foure oares and a man at the helme crossing the water from Deptford, and [it] rowed soe nere the said Tuckers boate as they came foule of his oares thre

---

[1] The allegations on behalf of Tucker (21 January 1586, H.C.A. 24/53, no. 134) maintain that he was repeatedly attacked from the other boat before throwing the stretcher.

[2] H.C.A. 13/26. Edward Holmden (or Holmeden), an important London merchant, was actively engaged in the Levant trade and had also some privateering interests (see K. R. Andrews, 'Elizabethan privateering', p. 124).

[3] Additional positions, made by Stile on 26 January 1587 (H.C.A. 24/54, no. 70), deny that Tucker was provoked. Thomas Rice and John Paine, apparently oarsmen in the wherry, are said to have given their testimony before a public notary that Tucker called Amadas (Hamedes) a knave and rascal before casting a stretcher at him.

[4] H.C.A. 13/26. Thomas Cordell, mercer, another leading merchant, with whom Holmden was often associated. He also was concerned in the Italy and Levant trades, but had extensive privateering interests (Andrews, 'Elizabethan privateering', pp. 124, 233).

sondry tymes'. Tucker landed his passengers at Billingsgate. Cordell believed the other boat to be 'a pinnace of Sir Walter Rawleighes shipps as he thinketh'.

(g) 4 May 1585. Examination of John Evans, waterman.[1]

John Evans says that he knows that John Stile was hurt 'some what after' Christmas Day. After Stile was hurt he was with him at 'the Cardinalls hat on the bancke side', and as they were there Hugh Tucker came in and, seeing Stile with a 'kercher' on his head, asked him how he did, and Stile said 'not well'. Tucker said he was as sorry for it as for his own brother, and prayed him to be contented and he would make him amends for the harm he had done him. Stile said he could not end the matter himself 'because he was in service with Captayne Hamedes and the cause towched him and therefore advised the said Tucker to kepe him furthe of the waye leste his Captayne shoulde mete with him,[2] vntill he herde more from him and soe they departed'. He also says that for some weeks after John Stile did not follow his labour, but lay 'at expenses' and had a surgeon coming to dress his head. Stile was, he says, a waterman and a fisherman, but, at the time, 'he was in wages vnder Sir Walter Rawleighe and then rowinge in one of his boates...and was appoynted to goe forthe on the viadge with Captayne Hamedes'.[3]

(h) 4 May 1585. Examination of Edward Johnson, waterman.[4]

Edward Johnson says he knew that, since Christmas last, John Stile had been struck by Hugh Tucker with a stretcher as he was coming 'from Grenewiche with Captain Hamedes towardes London'. He was at the Cardinal's Hat with John Stile and others when Hugh Tucker came in. He corroborates John Evans and says that Stile told Tucker 'he was sure if his Captayne met with

---

[1] H.C.A. 13/25.

[2] This indicates that the meeting at the Cardinal's Hat in Bankside took place shortly after the incident and before Amadas had set out for Plymouth (cp. p. 121).

[3] Thames watermen thus provided one source from which the crews of the 1585 expedition were drawn.

[4] H.C.A. 13/25.

him he woulde laye him in prison'. Stile went to his bed for at
least a week. 'And knowethe that he was appoynted at that
presente to goe with Captayne Hamedes the said hurte was the
onlye stay and losse of his said viadge.'

(i) 4 May 1585. Examination of Thomas Wilkinson, waterman.[1]

Thomas Wilkinson says that he and John Doode met Hughe
Tucker in the Temple Lane and, hearing before that he and John
Stile had fallen out upon the Thames in Limehouse Reche and
some harm done between them, he asked Hugh Tucker if he and
John Stile had ended their controversy. Hugh Tucker said he
would never be friends with Stile and, that things fell out so as
they did, he cared not a straw if he had killed the said Stile.

Thomas Wilkinson says he knew that John Stile was a waterman
and a fisherman and thereby getteth his living, and by no other
trade, but 'aboute the tyme that he had geven his worde to
Sir Walter Rawleighe to goe on a viage with his shippes to the
partes of beyonde the sea'. He had heard that Stile, by the loss
he received from Tucker, had lost his voyage, but does not know
what loss of wages he sustained.[2]

10. [*c.* JANUARY 1585.]

DRAFT COMMISSION TO SIR WALTER RALEIGH TO TAKE UP SHIPPING AND MARINERS[3]

Elizabeth by the grace of God Quene of England fraunce and
Irland defendour of thee faith etc. To all Iustices of peace Mayors

[1] Ibid. Corroborated (on same day) about the meeting with Tucker in Temple
Lane by John Doode, waterman.

[2] The decree has not been found, and so the result of the case is not yet known.
A provisional discussion of the case appears in Quinn, 'Preparations for
the 1585 Virginia voyage', in *William and Mary Quarterly*, 3rd ser., VI (1949),
224-8. Apart from Mendoza's references we know nothing of the fitting-out of
the vessels in the Thames. How many vessels were there is not clear, nor how
many were being fitted out in the West Country (possibly at Bideford for a
rendezvous at Plymouth). From December onwards, Sir Richard Grenville was
concerned in this task.

[3] State Papers, Domestic, Elizabeth, S.P. 12/185/59. The powers which
Raleigh was thus offered by prerogative were amongst those which had led to

shirifs baillifz Constables and all other our officers Ministers and subiectz to whom thies our [lettres] shall cum and to euery of them greting Whereas for our speciall service we haue appointid and by thies *presentes* we do appoint and authorize our trusty and welbilouid servaunt Sir Walter Raleigh knight to take vp and imprest in our name. in any our portz havons crekes or other places within our Counties of Devon Cornewall & at Bristowe such shipping Maisters of Ships Maryners souldyours and all other prouisions and munitions whatsoeuer as he shall see to be mete and requisite for this service

We will and commaund youe and euery of youe not only to suffer the sayd sir Walter Raleigh and such other person or persons as shalbe deputid by his for this purpos bringing with them this our commission or testimony vnder his hand and seale of their deputation not only to execute the same in all these thinges before mentioned but also to help and assist the sayd Sir Walter and his deputes in the doing therof to the Vttermost of your power Not failing herof as ye tender our pleasure and the furtherance of our service and will answer for the contrary at your vttermoost perill. Geven vnder our Signet at

[*Endorsed:*] *Memorandum* of a commission for master Rawley to imprest mariners and shipping

the withdrawal of the bill for the confirmation of his title to Virginia. Raleigh was knighted by the queen at Greenwich on Sunday, 6 January 1585 (Twelfth Day) (W. A. Shaw, *Knights of England*, II, 83), so that the reference to him as 'master' in the endorsement might suggest the draft was made soon after. If so, why the commission was not issued is unknown, though allegations that he used powers of impressment such as it conferred were made (pp. 151, 834-5 below). The draft may, however, have been made in June not January (cp. no. 20, pp. 156-7 below).

11. 2 FEBRUARY 1585.
     GEORGE WAPULL[1]

2 Febr' [Tuesday]

George Wapull[2]

by assent of a court holden this day There is gyven to him
to further him in his voiage which he proposeth into
Norembegue — x s. Yf he goo not in y^t voiage he is to
restore ye mony[3]

12. [BEFORE 25 MARCH 1585.]
     A POSSIBLE RECRUIT FOR GRENVILLE[4]

Paymentes.... And to Master Middelton[5] his sonne to brynge
hym to Plymmouth to Sir Richard Greynfild:—iis vid.

[1] Extract, *Records of the court of the Stationers Company, 1576–1602*, ed. W.W.
Greg and E. Boswell (Bibliographical Society, 1930), p. 17.

[2] He had been clerk of the company from 1571 to 1575.

[3] There is no evidence either that he accompanied Grenville or repaid the
money. The company's register contains a briefer, undated, entry of the transaction:

'Item gyven by order of a full Courte of Assistantes to George Wapull towards
his voyage vnto Norembegue x^s/' (*A transcript of the registers of the Company of
Stationers of London, 1554–1640*, ed. E. Arber, I, 509).

[4] Barnstaple Borough Records, Receivers' Accounts, 1584–5 (in North Devon
Athenaeum, Barnstaple). There is no date but the item following is for bringing
a man to Plymouth to Drake, which would fit in with the spring of 1585. I am
indebted for the transcript to Dr Joyce Youings. (Cp. J. R. Chanter and T. Wainwright, *Barnstaple records*, II (1900), 128.)

[5] This may well be Thomas Middleton, grocer of London (1550–1631, see
DNB), who in 1589 made a gift for the use of the poor of Barnstaple (Chanter
and Wainwright, I, 48–9). If so, the link with Grenville is significant of the
contacts he and Raleigh had with the city of London merchants at this time, of
which other evidence is lacking (cp. pp. 155, 232–3, 544–5, 576–8).

Fig. 2. Sir Walter Raleigh's seal as Lord and Governor of Virginia (British Museum, *Catalogue of British seal-dies in the British Museum* (1952), no. 347). This is the first evidence of the queen's authority to Raleigh to call the American territories 'Virginia', and was issued before 25 March 1585. 'Amore et virtute' was his personal motto, cp. p. 319 below.

The inscription reads 'Propria Tnsihnia [for Insignia] Walteri Ralegh Militis Domini & Gubernatoris Virginiae'. Raleigh was knighted on 6 January 1585 (cp. p. 145) while the date '1584' indicates that it cannot be later than 24 March 1585.

13. 2 FEBRUARY 1585.

SIGNET LETTER TO THE EARL OF WARWICK FOR RALEIGH[1]

By the Quene

Elizabeth R*egina*

Right trusty and right welbilouid Cousin and Counseller[2] we grete you well. Our will and pleasur is that of such oure store as remaineth in thoffice of our Ordenance ye deliure to our trusty and welbilouid Servant Sir Walter Rawlegh knight or to such as he shall appoint for the purpos, Foure lastes of corne pouldre put in double cask[3] to be vsed and imployid in such sorte as we haue appointid him.[4] Wherof we will you not to faill. And these our L*ett*res shalbe your sufficient warrant and dischardg in this behalf Geven vnder our Signet at our Manour of Grenewich the second day of February in the xxvij[th] yere of our reign /

To our Right trusty and said right welbilouid Cousin and Counseler the Erle of Warwike M*aster* of our Ordenaunce.

[*Signet seal.*]   Examinatur p*er* Yetsweirt

[1] Original, signed, Brit. Mus., Additional MS 5752, fo. 39.

[2] Ambrose Dudley, earl of Warwick (1528?–1590), had been master of the ordnance in the Tower of London since 1560.

[3] While proof is lacking, it may be assumed with reasonable certainty that this gunpowder was intended for the use of the ships which were then preparing in the Thames for the Virginia voyage. Since it was usual for such warrants to specify the price to be paid for powder delivered by the master of the ordnance, it is probable that this represents a gift by the queen to Raleigh or, more probably, was part of her adventure in the voyage. An almost contemporary privy seal (P.R.O., Exchequer of Receipt, Warrants for Issues, E. 404/126, 30 July 1586) for the issue of the same quantity of powder, gives the price as 10*d.* a pound, and four lasts (making the last 2400 lb.) £400, with the double cask charged £4. 16*s.* 'Corn' had reference to the grain of the powder (cp. Sir John Smythe (*Certain discourses* (1590), fo. 18): 'If the powder also with the which they are charged bee not well corned, and with sufficient quantitie of saltpeter, and kept very drie, it furreth the peeces').

[4] The visit of John Powell, Warwick's surveyor, to the ships which Raleigh was preparing down the river may well be associated with the delivery of the powder (p. 140 above).

14. 8 FEBRUARY 1585.

SIGNET LETTER TO SIR JOHN PERROT FOR RALPH LANE[1]

By the Queene

Right trustie and welbeloved wee greet youe well. Whereas before your departure hence it was ordred here emongste other thinges for the establishment of the Province of Monster in that our Realme, That twentie horsemen and Fourtie Footemen shoulde be appoynted for Kerry and Clanmoresse[2] and our servant Raphe Lane one of Quirries the of our great Stable[3] to haue the Government thereof, and of the sayd horsemen & footemen: We lett you weete that as oure pleasure ys, that our said appoyntment shall stand for our saide Servante. So forasmutche as wee have occasion to imploye him presently in other our service of importance Wee are pleased for his better encoragement therevnto that he duringe the tyme, that he shalbe thus imploied shall enioye that his Government & supplye the same by his sufficient & able substitute or Liefetenaunte And also haue full allowance & payment of his owne enterteynment appoyntyd vnto hym for the saide chardge, Withoute checke or abatement from the feaste of S[t] Michaell the Archangell laste paste[4] Wherefore our wish ys that you doe gyve order that this oure pleasure may take full effect to the benefite of our said Servante, and not to be discontinewed, nor the saide Horsemen and Footemen to be dischardged vnlesse youe receave Commaundement thereof from vs by our lettres vnder our hande & signett And theise our Lettres shalbe vnto youe aswell our Deputie chiefe Governour there for the tyme beinge for the doinge therof, as our Treasurer at Warres there that nowe ys[5]

---

[1] Copy. State Papers, Ireland, S.P. 63/114, 71 (see *Cal. S.P., Ire., 1574–85*, p. 551).   [2] Clanmaurice, a barony now in co. Kerry.

[3] The office of equerry of the great stable was a minor post in the royal household under the master of the horse.

[4] This amounted to an indirect subsidy to the expedition which Raleigh was preparing.

[5] For Lane's Irish service see *Cal. S.P., Ire., 1574–85*, pp. 423, 494, 497, 505. It would appear that he had taken up his appointment in Kerry at Michaelmas

and that hereafter for the time shalbe for the payment of our said servantes interteynment sufficient warrant & dischardge. Gyven vnder our Signett at our Mannour of Greenewiche the eight daye of Februarie 1584 in the xxvijth yeare of our Reign.

This coppie agreeth with the originall

Examinatur R Yetswart

[*Endorsed:*] The coppye of her Maiesties Warrant for the gouerne-ment of Kerrye and Clanmoresse, with ye chardge of xx^{tie} horse, and -40- footemen, to haue beine deliuered to Rafe Lane, one of hcr Maiesties Equiers: the same directed to sir Iohn Perrot knight, the Deputye of Irelande,¹ or to any other supplying the sayde place of Deputy, there: Bering date At Grenewich the -8th- daye of Februarii 1584.²

Graciousely giuen him by her Maiestie in consideration of his redye vndertakinge ye Voyage to Virginia for sir Walter Raughley, at her Maiesties commaundement.³

1584, and there he had incurred the hostility of Sir Henry Wallop, vice-treasurer of Ireland and treasurer-at-war there, who wrote on 21 May 1585 (after Lane had sailed with Grenville) that Kerry was too large for Mr Lane; he expected to have the best and greatest things there in the way of land, and to have the letting and setting of all the rest (Ibid., p. 563). It is not improbable, however, that Lane was already in England by February 1585.

¹ Perrot had been sworn in as deputy of Ireland on 21 June 1584. That he objected to this grant to Lane may be judged from these notes in his letter book:

'A lettre to the Quenes Maiestie concerning Mr Raphe Lane. [to be one of the esquires of her great stable, have government of 20 horse and 40 foot for Kerry and Clanmorris from Michaelmas. His objections]. 31 May 1585....

A lettre to the Lords of the Council 31 May 1585

Concerning Raphe Lanes two petitions.' (*Analecta Hibernica*, no. 12 (1943), pp. 19, 22.) For the arrangements made in Ireland in his absence see *Cal. S.P., Ire., 1574–85*, p. 572.

² The abstract in the Signet Office Docquet Book (Ind. 6800, fo. 7) is evidently of an earlier form of the warrant since it is 'Dated at Somerset house the vth of feb.' The charge of 6s. 8d. was made for its issue.

³ The endorsement implies that Lane was instructed by the queen to go with Grenville, but it may have been at his own request, since he was on bad terms with his superiors in Ireland. Incidentally, if the endorsement is of the same date as the warrant (or near it), the mention of 'Virginia' is the earliest we have of the name, though Raleigh's seal (p. 147 above) was made before 25 March.

15. 16 MARCH 1585.

SIR RICHARD GRENVILLE APPOINTS TRUSTEES DURING HIS ABSENCE[1]

'This indenture made the syxtenthe daye of March in the seven and twentith yere of the Raigne of our Soveraigne Lady Elziabeth' between Sir Richard Greynvill of Stowe in the county of Cornwall, knight, and Sir Walter Rawley, Sir Arthur Basset, Sir Francis Godolphin, Henry Killigrew, Richard Bellew, John Heale and Christopher Harrys esquires, Thomas Dorton[2] and John Facie gentlemen, giving, granting and enfeoffing them with his possessions to the use of his wife and his heirs, provided that if at any time he demands the sum of £50,000 of the trustees in the parish church of Kilkehampton and is not paid the grant is to be void.

[*Witnessed:*]	Tho. Roscarrock	Degorie Tremayne
	Phyllph Cole	Degorie Ned[ ]
	A. Arundell	Josh Deg. Greynvill
	Thom C.	Geo. Greynevill

16. FOREIGN SEAMEN IMPRESSED FOR THE VOYAGE[3]

First that a Shipp of the Briell named the waterhounde, returninge from Nantes, laden with wine, was mett and inter-

---

[1] Brief abstract from Roger Granville, *History of the Granville family* (Exeter, 1895), pp. 124–7, the location of the deed not being stated. Mr A. L. Rowse, following Granville, gave its date as 16 March 1586, and associated it with the voyage of that year. He gives a full summary (*Grenville*, pp. 232–3). Grenville had already written to Walsingham from 'Stowe this xx^th of February 1584[-5]', the letter including the phrase 'I being nowe prepared to comitte myself to the pleasure of god on the seas' (S.P. Dom., Eliz., S.P. 12/176, 58; see Rowse, *Grenville*, pp. 176–7, 203). By making this transfer to foeffees Grenville was taking normal and reasonable precautions against the chances of being lost at sea. It is significant of the closeness of their association that Raleigh should have been named first.

[2] This should be 'Docton' (cp. Roger Granville, *History of Bideford* (1883), p. 36; Chanter and Wainwright, *Barnstaple records*, II, 243; R. Pearse Chope, *The book of Hartland* (1940), pp. 142–3).

[3] 2 March 1589, extract from 'Articles of Complaintes made by sondrye Inhabitauntes of the vnited Provinces....' State Papers Foreign, Holland and

cepted on her voyage in the yeare 1585 by a shipp of Sir Walter
Rawleys, and sent into Plymouth, takinge the master and pilott[1]
of the said shipp, and kept them .33. weekes & more as Captiues
in the Iorney to Wigantekoy, so that the poore men were vtterly
restrayned from suyinge of their owne. Yet vppon their arrivall
and great suites made in their behalf. and to the end her Maiesty
shold not comme to the knowledge therof, the said Estates (vpon
firme promesse that the said Sir Walter Rawley shold always
shewe himself a wellwiller vnto them and their Inhabitauntes)
weare contented at his request to leaue him freely bothe shipp and
goodes. although they themselues did paye for the same vnto the
honours[2] the valewe of more then a thousand pound sterlinge in
readye money.[3] / which favour to requite / a shipp of his called
the Roebucke of late hath taken and brought to Plymouth another
shipp of holland, named the Angell Gabriell, cominge out of

Flanders, S.P. 84/31, 104. On 27 February Joachim Ortell, the Dutch ambassador,
wrote to Walsingham that he had seen Burghley the previous morning about the
ship taken by Raleigh's people (S.P. 84/31, 74). He followed this by presenting
the series of 'Articles' on 2 March from which the extract above is taken, and
asking that Raleigh, together with the captain and five principal men of the
Roebuck should be called before the council to answer his charges. He presented
a further series of complaints on 13 March (S.P. 84/31, 135) which gave more
details about the *Angel Gabriel*. The vessel was taken in January 1589, partly
despoiled of goods worth £1000 sterling, and brought 'out of hir Course to
Plimouth where falcely pretendinge the same ship to have serued hir Maiesties
enimes and the goodes to be Spaniardes, they have vnladen the goodes of the
same ship and now practise to sende out the same ship in this presente iorney
thereby to spoile the owner and merchauntes bothe of theire ship and goodes'.
Petition was made that Raleigh should be placed under bond to re-deliver the
vessel and her cargo to the owners. The intended voyage mentioned is unlikely
to have been a further Virginia expedition which proved abortive, but rather the
Portugal voyage of April 1589. On 5 July the States' deputies requested the privy
council to require Raleigh and his servants to answer certain articles, desiring that
his men be imprisoned until they give surety to answer the Dutch complaints (S.P.
84/31, 131). The 1585 seizure may have been by the *Roebuck* also (cp. pp. 153-5).
   [1] It is not clear whether they were Dutch or French.   [2] 'Owners'.
   [3] Raleigh got away with the piracy in 1585 in return for his good offices at
Court—a bargain which might be considered a corrupt one. The Dutch revealed
the arrangement when, in 1589, they again had cause for complaint (see Quinn,
'Preparations', in *William and Mary Quarterly*, 3rd ser., VI, 235).

Spaine of the burthen of .340. Tonnes, richely laden with diuers goodes and marchandises.

17. SEIZURE OF A FRENCH SHIP BY ONE OF RALEIGH'S[1]

(a) 8 June 1586. Deposition of Roberte Tillier of Blamford [Blandford] in Dorset, soldier, examined on articles on behalf of Julian le Clercke, Giles Ravenell, Reginald le Cog and other merchants of Vittry and Paris.[2]

'To the first article he confesseth he knoweth Iohn Challice[3] Edwarde Roche and Iohn Lynnix also when he was livinge and that they with others aboute a yeare paste beinge in a shippe of Sir Walter Rawleighes wherof Iohn Clarcke was Captaine,[4] did apprehende and take at the seas a french shippe laden with Lynnen clothe and some wheate as this *examinate* hath herde. For shortly after the taking of the said shippe and goodes this *examinate* cominge owt of Flannders arrived in Purbecke and was intertayned by Captayne Challice to serve him,[5] and the nexte day after this *examinates* cominge vnto him the said frenche shippe then beinge in theire possession was delivered vppe at Waymouth to the owners vse. . . .'[6]

'To the iiij[th] he sayeth the said Captayne Clercke Challice

---

[1] The following extracts illustrate well the indirect, circumstantial evidence which is often provided by the records of the High Court of Admiralty, but which can nevertheless throw a good deal of light on what went on behind the scenes, if it is carefully—and cautiously—interpreted.

[2] H.C.A. 13/26.

[3] A notorious pirate, who had deserted Gilbert's expedition in 1578. He was later in 1585 to set out on a voyage of privateering (or piracy) to Barbary (Quinn, *Gilbert*, passim; C. L'Estrange Ewen, *The Golden Chalice* (Paignton, privately printed, 1939)).

[4] John Clarke is described in Lane's letter of 8 September 1585 (p. 210 below) as captain of the flyboat, the *Roebuck*, in the Virginia voyage. The French ship must therefore have been taken some time before the departure of the expedition from Plymouth on 9 April (p. 178 below). Clarke went privateering again in 1586, in command of the *Golden Noble* (Andrews, 'Elizabethan privateering', p. 246).

[5] It would appear that Clarke had handed over the prize to Challice while he took his own ship back to Plymouth, while Tillier may have sailed with Challice on his Barbary voyage.

[6] The subsequent proceedings being to recover the cargo or its value.

and theire consortes broughte the said French shippe to the Isle of Wight and Portlande and thereaboutes as he thinkethe....'

Two persons of 'the Vise' [Devizes] came to Challice before the delivery of the French ship and bargained with Edward Roche for cloth. He does not know their names, 'But sayethe that Roberte Davys beinge purser of the Flyboate[1] was acquaynted with them and knoweth their names'.

(*b*) 12 October 1586. Deposition of Gregory Sugar in the same case.[2]

1. He was on board the French ship with Challice and Roche, which was taken with linen cloth, 'and certayne Lynnen cloth was delivered vppe into the handes of morgan moone and hugh Randulphe maior of Waymouth to the vse of Sir Walter Rawliegh as yt was reported in Portlande....'[3]

3. John Challice sold to one Martin Parker of London some linen cloth 'in Sir George Caryes house in the Isle of Wighte in his stewardes chamber'. He, Gregory Sugar, was sent with Parker to 'master Somers at Thorney in the Wighte agente of Sir George Caryes' to deliver part of the money, and part was delivered to Challice 'in Sir George his Castle in Master Blandes chamber the Steward in presence of the said Martyn Parker and Blande also....'[4]

---

[1] Robert Davis of Bristol had been master of the *Bark Raleigh* in the Gilbert expedition of 1583 and this is probably the same man, while his ship, being described as a fly-boat, was apparently the *Roebuck*, and this provides sufficient circumstantial evidence that this ship, before meeting its consorts at Plymouth, had been out taking prizes in the Channel. It appears not unlikely, therefore, that she took the *Waterhound* as well (pp. 153–4 above). It is not improbable also that it was for the return of the French ship (which he did not know at that time had been taken by one of Raleigh's own vessels) the French ambassador, Castelnau de la Mauvissière, thanked Raleigh on 2/12 July 1585. The ship, a Breton vessel, had been stayed, he said, in May at Poole by Raleigh 'in his late voyage' (S.P. 78/14, 37; *Cal. S.P. foreign, 1584–5*, p. 576).   [2] H.C.A. 13/26.

[3] This suggests at least that Raleigh profited from the prize even though the ship was returned.

[4] This provides a link between Challice (or Callice), Sir George Carey (cp. p. 123), and Raleigh in privateering business. Carey's headquarters were at Carisbrooke Castle. He was not only 'governor' of the Isle of Wight (a title he invented), but, amongst other things, vice-admiral for Hampshire and the island (*V.C.H., Hants.*, v, 224, 240, 378; cp. pp. 224, 499, 512, 516–17, 543, 784).

8–9. He heard Martin Parker say to Challice 'that he retayned to master Customer Smith of London and dwelled at the signe of the thre Doves in newegate marckett, and desired him that yf he came on the quoaste with eany good prizes, to send him worde, and he would repayre vnto him and bringe ready gould and pay him on the hatches for what soever he delte for that as he sayde he did yt for his master....'[1]

18.   7 APRIL 1585.

Howe carefull I haue bin to aduertise Sir Walter Rawley from tyme to tyme, and to send him discourses both in printe and written hand concerninge his voyage[3] I had rather you shold vnderstand of him then of my selfe.... Paris....

[*Postscript:*] The rumor of Sir Walter Rawles fleet, and especially the preparation of Sir francis Drake doth soe much vexe the Spaniard and his fautors as nothing can doe more:[4] and therefore I cold wish that although Sir Frances Drakes iourney be stayed yet the rumor of his setting forward might be continued.[5] They haue sent some to enquire of that action in conning manner of my lorde himselfe[6] as he told me.

[1] This again provides a link between the privateers and a most influential London merchant, Thomas Smythe, who was later to lend money to Raleigh and Sanderson (p. 544). As an indication of how privateering cargoes were dispersed the extract is of considerable interest. A full treatment of this subject is given by Andrews, 'Elizabethan privateering', pp. 62–107.

[2] Extracts. P.R.O., S.P., Dom., Eliz., Additional, S.P. 15/29, 9 (printed in Taylor, *Hakluyts*, II, 343–5). Hakluyt had returned to Paris by the middle of October 1584, after the delivery of his 'Discourse' to the Queen. This is the first evidence of his activity in 1585 (Parks, *Hakluyt*, p. 248). It is not known whether he was using New or Old Style dating.

[3] None of these can now be identified, but Hakluyt was busy collecting both French and Spanish evidence on America.

[4] See the reports from Bernardino de Mendoza, Spanish ambassador in Paris, pp. 728–32 below.   [5] Drake's departure was, in fact, delayed until September.

[6] Sir Edward Stafford, English ambassador in Paris, to whom Hakluyt was acting as chaplain. The Spanish inquiries indicate that Mendoza considered his own sources of information were inadequate (cp. Quinn, 'Some Spanish reactions...', *T.R. Hist. S.*, 5th ser., I, 9).

19. [1585.]

CHARLES THYNNE TO SIR FRANCIS WALSINGHAM[1]

He offers his duty to Walsingham and says that he has discussed the matter with Master Hakluyt.[2] The Jesuit, who is the Spanish Ambassador's confessor, 'understanding that I appertaned unto Sir Walter Ralegh somwhat nere[3]...marvelled that whereas the King of Spain was shortly to take possession of England, Sir Walter Ralegh...doth neverthelesse undertake voyages to seek to hinder the Spaniards'.

20. 10 JUNE 1585.

SIGNET LETTER FOR SIR WALTER RALEIGH

(a)[4] A Commission to Sir Walter Rawley and to such persons as he shall apoint vnder his hand and seale to take vp in any portes Creekes havens or other places in the Counties of Devon and Cornwall and at Bristoll such shippes & shipping, Masters of Shippes marriners and Souldiors & all other provisions and munitions as the said Sir Walter Rawley shall see meet & requisite for

---

[1] Abstract. S.P. Foreign, France, S.P. 78/14, 120, undated (see *Cal. S.P. foreign, 1585–6*, p. 261), apparently from Paris.

[2] It is probably closely associated with the previous item in time and content, the approach to Stafford being linked with an attempt to make contact with Raleigh. Hakluyt left for England in May and was in Bristol on 24 May (Parks, *Hakluyt*, p. 248).

[3] Charles Thynne of Cheddar was one of the younger sons of John Thynne (died 1580) whose widow had married Carew Raleigh, Sir Walter's elder brother (Sir Richard Colt Hoare, *Modern Wiltshire*, I (ii. Hundred of Heytesbury, pp. 60–1); *DNB*). Hakluyt had been responsible for Charles Thynne coming to France to study and, on 30 December 1586, recommended him to Raleigh for 'the great service that he might doe his countrie being therewithal furnished eyther in the enterprise of your Indies, or in any other place of warrelike service' (Taylor, *Hakluyts*, II, 356). His association with Raleigh was a long one, and he visited him early on the morning of his execution, 29 October 1618 (P.R.O., S.P. 14/103, 74; see *William and Mary Quarterly*, 3rd ser., IX (1952), 537–8).

[4] Signet Office Docquet Book, Ind. 6800, fo. 24, clearly the final form of the commission of which the draft may go back to January (no. 10, pp. 144–5 above). It was issued to cover the diversion by Raleigh of his second Virginia squadron to Newfoundland under the Queen's orders (cp. pp. 234–42 below).

her Ma*iestes* service. Dated at Greenwich the xth of Iune 1585—
nil.[1]

(*b*) June. [*Lord Burghley's note:*[2]] Sir Walter Raleigh had
Authority to take up Men, and Shipping for his Voyage.

The like to Sir Francis Drake.

---

[1] The last word means that no fee was paid to the clerk, i.e. that authority for
issue of the letters came from the queen herself.

[2] From Lord Burghley's 'Memoria Mortuorum', in William Murdin, *A collection of state papers...1571 to 1596...left by William Cecill Lord Burghley* (1759),
p. 782.

CHAPTER III

THE 1585 VIRGINIA VOYAGE

Moreouer, discoueries this yeere attempted, are like to prove
but badly: and the trauellers to sustaine great labour and
trouble therein, and to returne with but smal gaine or much
losse.   EVAN LLOYD, *An almanacke and prognostication
for this present yeare...1585*

As shippes in ports desir'd are drownd,
As fruit, once ripe, then falles to ground,
As flies that seek for flames, are brought
To cinders by the flames they sought:
So fond Desire when it attaines,
The life expires, the woe remaines.
A poesie to prove affection is not love.[1]

NARRATIVE

On 9 April Grenville left Plymouth with seven vessels. The
flagship or 'admiral' was the *Tiger*, a galleass of the queen's,
of 160 tons,[2] Sir Richard Grenville, general of the expedition,
captain, Simon Fernandez, chief pilot of the fleet,[3] master. Her
complement was some 160, about half being sailors. The *Roebuck*,
flyboat of 140 tons, bearing the name of Raleigh's device, John
Clarke captain,[4] was probably vice-admiral. The *Lion*, or *Red
Lion*, of Chichester, 100 tons, was commanded[5] by George
Raymond. The *Elizabeth*, 50 tons, had Thomas Cavendish, high
marshal of the expedition,[6] as captain. The *Dorothy*, 50 tons, may

---

[1] *The poems of Sir Walter Ralegh*, ed. A. M. C. Latham (1929), p. 41. The first
line might seem to be an echo of the striking of the *Tiger* at Wococon.
[2] The journal puts her tonnage at 140 and another official source at 200
(pp. 178–9 below).
[3] So described by Lane, p. 201 below.
[4] Cp. pp. 153, 178–9, 210.
[5] Cp. pp. 234–42 below.
[6] So described by Lane, p. 210 below.

have been commanded by Arthur Barlowe [1]. The two pinnaces were attached as tenders to the *Tiger* and to either the *Roebuck* or the *Lion*. The total number on board was about 600,[2] of which nearly half were seamen and the remainder soldiers and specialists, leaving some 300 to 400 available to establish the North American colony.

The organization of the expedition was somewhat elaborate.[3] The general (who was also admiral) had next to him the high marshal and then the lieutenant, Ralph Lane, who sailed on the *Tiger*, and the treasurer, Francis Brooke. Captain Philip Amadas, 'admiral of Virginia' designate, was possibly vice-admiral, and would thus be second to Grenville on the maritime side,[4] with the chief pilot next in the hierarchy. These, together with the ships' captains, Captains Boniten and Aubry, John Arundell, John Stukely, Edward Gorges, Masters Bremige and Vincent, and the fourteen captains and gentlemen who remained in Virginia, are likely to have made up the council [5] which Grenville was expected to consult about major alterations in the plan of campaign.

After leaving Plymouth there is word of an encounter with a Spanish Newfoundlander, whose crew is said to have been killed and which was sent back prize to Ireland, but this lacks corroboration,[6] though it may be the basis for rumours that Grenville had himself returned.[7] Then 'in the Bay of Portingal' a storm sank the *Tiger*'s pinnace and scattered the squadron,[8] the admiral keeping on her way, making the Canaries on 14 April and Dominica on 7 May—a rapid passage.

The *Tiger* passed by St Croix along the southern coast of Puerto Rico to a small island called Cotesa or Cottea,[9] south-east of

---

[1] His presence is only mentioned in the Holinshed account (p. 175 below).

[2] Document no. 21, p. 173.

[3] The organization of other contemporary expeditions may be compared in C. G. Cruickshank, *Elizabeth's army*, pp. 34–47; cp. pp. 19–22 above.

[4] Cp. pp. 140, 165, 190–2, 194 below.

[5] Mentioned only in general terms, p. 180 below.

[6] P. 731 below.

[7] Cp. pp. 731–2 below.

[8] Cp. pp. 175, 182; Wright, *Further English voyages*, p. 175.

[9] Cp. pp. 180, 182, 403, 519 below.

Guayanilla Point, landed her men on 10 May for refreshment and moved on the following day into the Bay of Mosquetal or Las Boquillas, now Tallaboa Bay,[1] which was evidently the rendezvous agreed as the result of the visit by Amadas and Barlowe in 1584. There an elaborate encampment was begun,[2] defended on the shore and northern boundaries by lines of earthworks, the eastern limit also being fortified, leaving a swamp to the north-east and a stream to the west as natural defences. The reason may have been to establish a base at which a holding party could perhaps be left for Drake to take over later in the year.[3] Perhaps, however, one reason for making it so strong was that the Spaniards had strengthened their position in the neighbourhood, having now a garrison in San German.[4] The men had to be rested, the ships watered, and, especially, a new pinnace built for the *Tiger*, necessary for prize-taking and for the exploration of the North Carolina sounds alike. A forge was set up to make nails, and on low four-wheeled trucks trees cut in the neighbouring woods were hauled to the camp for her timbers. Just as Lane had made rapid, if rather elaborate, defences so the ship's carpenters made speedy headway with the pinnace, launching and rigging her within ten days. She appears to have been a stout little craft though perhaps not distinguished for her sailing qualities.[5] The arrival of Cavendish in the *Elizabeth*,[6] on the 19th, after a scare that she was a Spaniard, was clearly a great relief to Grenville, since he now had over 200 men.

The Spanish authorities on Puerto Rico were not passive while this was going on. The governor, Diego Menéndez de Valdés, claimed that he received news at San Juan de Puerto Rico of the *Tiger's* approach to the southern shore as early as 10/20 May.[7] He ordered his lieutenant at San German, who had 40 men, to keep

[1] Cp. pp. 175, 181, 403, 733, 740 below and Wright, *Further English voyages*, p. 9.
[2] It is shown in detail in John White's drawing (no. 2, see pp. 403–4 below).
[3] Cp. pp. 204, 250 below.
[4] Wright, *Further English voyages*, p. 9.
[5] Cp. p. 256 below.
[6] Cp. pp. 182–3 below and Wright, *Further English voyages*, p. 12.
[7] Cp. p. 733 below; Wright, p. 9.

watch on the English who had, he assumed, only landed to water. On 16 May a patrol of eight Spanish horsemen made their appearance at the encampment, but soon disappeared when challenged by ten of Lane's arquebusiers. On 22 May a further party of twenty horse appeared, probably led by the commander of the local garrison. This time Grenville sent out two horsemen of his own and some footmen to arrange a parley. Two men from each side exchanged formal courtesies, the English declaring they were anxious to trade and to purchase food. A rendezvous for an exchange was arranged two days ahead. The lieutenant was now in a position to send a full report to the governor, which reached him on 25 May/5 June. He at once sent off thirty-five arquebusiers to assist the lieutenant in harrying the English if they emerged from the encampment. These reinforcements were only one day's march from San Juan when they were met by news that the Englishmen had quitted their fort. Grenville, after launching his pinnace on the 23rd, had gone to the rendezvous the next day, but the Spaniards did not appear. He thereupon fired the woods and returned to the camp, where the huts were burnt and, it is likely, the embankments thrown down. In a prominent place a post was erected, carved with an inscription announcing the safe arrival and departure of the *Tiger* and *Elizabeth* as a guide to the missing vessels of the squadron should they arrive later. The Spaniards, however, uprooted the post soon after and, with some difficulty, had its inscription translated and forwarded to Spain.[1]

The reason for Grenville's desertion of the encampment was probably the likelihood of a Spanish attack, but he did not, at once, leave the coast. Lying in wait for prizes in the Mona Channel, a small frigate was taken, but she proved to be empty. A more valuable prize was made the same night, a large frigate, belonging to Lorenzo de Vallejo, which had come from Spain with the *flota* carrying cloth and other merchandise. She had put into Santo Domingo and was making her way, with cargo and passengers, to San Juan, when she was taken without a struggle. Grenville put

[1] Cp. pp. 183, 734 below, and Wright, *Further English voyages*, pp. 9–12, 15–16.

prize crews on board and retired to a nearby anchorage, having, apparently, sent word ashore to San German that he again wished to trade. Lane was persuaded to take the smaller prize, with some Spanish prisoners, to bring salt from what was apparently Salinas Bay near Cape Rojo. Finding two salt-mounds ready he enclosed them with entrenchments and began removing them,[1] but a Spanish force came up. This Lane believed to be commanded by the governor himself and to consist of 40 horse and 300 foot, but it was only the San German garrison under the lieutenant and, in any case, they did not attempt Lane's defences. Lane, on rejoining the *Tiger*, protested—violently it would seem—at having been placed in jeopardy with a handful of men,[2] and began a series of quarrels with Grenville which wrecked the harmony of the expedition. Meanwhile, the *Tiger*, the *Elizabeth*, the pinnace and the larger prize had been trading with the Spaniards in the vicinity of Guanica or Guayanilla. Neither the English nor the Spanish documents are quite clear how this was arranged, but it appears that Grenville offered one of the frigates for sale, attempted to ransom his prisoners (getting 'good round summes' he said, but nothing at all, one of the released Spaniards claimed), acquiring livestock— hogs, sows, young cattle, mares and horses—to stock the colony, and foodstuffs and probably plants of sugar-canes, bananas, and other fruits which it was intended to grow there. The governor, hearing of such exchanges, sent orders that they were to cease, but again Grenville had moved before his instructions had taken effect.[3] The squadron—now of five vessels—sailed on 29 May for the north coast of Hispaniola.

According to the Spaniards they put in at Puerto de Plata and then moved on to the Bahia Isabela, the harbour immediately to the westwards. After two days at Isabela[4] the 'Gouernour'

---

[1] Pp. 184–5 below, and White's drawing which shows that he was with Lane (no. 3, see pp. 404–5 below).

[2] Document no. 43 (*a*), pp. 228–9 below.

[3] Pp. 735–6, 740–2 below; Wright, *Further English voyages*, pp. 10–12, 16.

[4] For its location see p. 185 below.

(*alcalde*?) of the town and the warden of the fort of Puerto de Plata, Captain Rengifo de Angulo,[1] made friendly overtures to Grenville, promising to come to visit him. The English ships were now in an area which had a long record of illicit trade with the French and it is likely that Grenville had contacts with local merchants.[2] On 5 June Grenville and his company were invited on shore where an elaborate entertainment was prepared for them. Feasting was followed by a bull fight, and sport by commerce. On the 6th horses and mares (with saddles and bits), cows and bulls, sheep and swine were purchased for the colony, together with hides, sugar, ginger, tobacco and pearls, most of which were evidently for the English market. It is likely that Grenville disposed of most of his captured cloth. The English had already been observed on Puerto Rico collecting banana plants and other fruit trees along the shore and they continued to do so in Hispaniola,[3] John White also recording a number of plants and animals on paper.[4]

Whatever Grenville's views on the missing vessels were—and we do not know precisely how stores and men had been distributed between them—it is clear that he did not regard their absence as sufficient check to make him abandon the projected colony. His men were well and his new supplies of livestock, plants and food improved the prospects of the settlement though the delays had sacrificed valuable planting time. From Hispaniola on 7 June he sailed north-westwards, being nearly lost when he visited a small island next day to take seals. The following day they failed to find salt on one of the Caicos Islands and entered the Bahamas, landing at Guanima, apparently Eleuthera, on the 12th and at Ciguateo (Great Abaco) on the 15th. Then, sailing through Providence North West Channel, they sighted the American mainland on 20 June between 27° and 30° N.[5] On the 23rd they encountered the

---

[1] Who seems to be identified as such in Wright, *Further English voyages*, p. 16.
[2] Cp. pp. 185, 501, 521, 739, 743, 758-9 below.
[3] Cp. p. 743 below, Wright, *Further English voyages*, pp. 11, 16.
[4] Nos. 4–14, see pp. 405–8 below.
[5] P. 188 below; Wright, *Further English voyages*, p. 15.

shoals off a headland which they believed to be, and probably was, Cape Fear, and, rounding them with some difficulty, they anchored the next day in a harbour which is likely to have been that of Beaufort, North Carolina, where they caught many fish. They were now clearly probing the coast closely, and they came on the 26th to an inlet through the Carolina Banks, called Wococon, which is about the middle of the present Portsmouth Island.[1]

There, Lane tells us, all their ships went aground on the shallow bar,[2] but were evidently floated off without too much difficulty. However, the *Tiger* had been lying off-shore and when an attempt was made on the 29th to bring her into the harbour serious disaster nearly occurred. She struck, according to the author of the *Tiger* journal, through Fernandez's carelessness, and for two hours a struggle went on to prevent her from breaking up. Finally, she was beached. The damage she sustained was a severe blow to the intended colony since all her corn, salt, meal, rice, biscuit and other provisions were destroyed or damaged by the salt water.[3] This was a first and salutary example of the dangers which threatened shipping along this most risky stretch of coast.

At this point we must take up the obscure tale of the four missing vessels. One of them,[4] probably the *Lion*, with a pinnace, was involved in a fight with a French ship off Point Negril at the western end of Jamaica. Although the English are said to have won, the precise outcome is uncertain since the French vessel does not appear to have been captured. Later the same ship seems to have been forced ashore by a storm on the uninhabited north shore of the island. She was apparently eased off but by then her company was suffering from hunger, and the captain set some

[1] Cp. pp. 189, 867 and map at end.

[2] Document no. 26, p. 201 below.

[3] Cp. pp. 177, 189, 201; Hariot also gave some indications of the effect of this loss, p. 344 below.

[4] This discussion is based on the document already discussed in part (Francisco Marqués de Villalobos to Philip II, 27 June 1586 and its enclosures (Wright, *Further English voyages*, pp. 174–6), which have been compared with photographs of the originals, A.G.I. 2.5.1/20 (Patronato 265, 44)).

twenty of the soldiers on shore to fend for themselves and set sail after Grenville. The Englishmen split into two parties, one under Captain John Copeltope (Copleston?),[1] which disappeared into the interior. In the other there were apparently eleven men, nine of whom died of hunger, the remaining two being rescued by the Spaniards. One of them, Edward (or Edwards)[2] was ultimately interrogated by the abbot Francisco Marqués de Villalobos at Santiago de la Vega in 1586. A deposition was eventually drawn up under difficulties, since Edward would admit to little Spanish, and the Spaniards had almost no English. It is not surprising therefore if the document, as translated by Miss Wright, sets a number of problems of interpretation. The next piece of information is that Raymond, with the *Lion* and possibly the *Dorothy*, set thirty-two men on shore on the island of Croatoan, immediately north of Wococon inlet, about 17 June. Grenville's Captains Aubry

[1] A Devon name (J. L. Vivian, *Visitations of Devon*, p. 224; cp. Granville, *Hist. of Bideford*, p. 36; Chanter and Wainwright, *Barnstaple records*, I, 18).

[2] He is called 'Eduarte' in the letter but in one of the enclosures the following occurs: 'Respondido se llama Duardos y su padre se llama tanbien Duardos y su madre dorotea.' The first would suggest a Christian name. It was not unusual in Spanish records to find Englishmen referred to in this way, e.g. in the process in October 1586 of the Inquisition in the Canary Islands against three Englishmen they are referred to throughout as Edward (Duarte, Eduarte), Francis and Thomas (W. de Gray Birch, *Catalogue of a collection of original manuscripts belonging to the Holy Office of the Inquisition in the Canary Islands*, I (1903), 267–8). The second reference would, however, suggest a surname like Edwards or even Ward. The man has not been further identified. One paragraph which Miss Wright translates: 'The general in command of these four ships was Sir Richard Grenville. His second in command was depondent, called Don Armedes Eduarte. He is a gentleman, a good clerk and accountant', must however be queried. The Spanish reads: 'el general que uenia en estas quatro naos se llamaua Don Ricardus granfield y el almyrante que uenia ansimismo se llamaua don armedes Eduarte ques el que haze esta declaraçion es cauallero y buen escriuano y contador dize que....' This, literally means: 'The general who came in these four ships is called Don Richard Grenville and the admiral Don Armedes [Amadas]. Edward [or Edwards] who is he that makes this declaration is a gentleman, a good scrivener and accountant. He says that....' Don Armedes is clearly Philip Amadas, but Miss Wright attempts to identify him with the prisoner by joining the two names together. There is, however, no doubt about this version. Amadas was with Grenville on 11 July (p. 190 below). In any event, his father's name was John and his mother's Jane (J. L. Vivian, *Visitations of Devon* (1895), p. 12).

and Boniten found two of them there on 6 July and brought them to Wococon two days later.[1] On the 11th Captain Clarke, elsewhere identified as the commander of the fly-boat (i.e. the *Roebuck*),[2] and Captain Amadas were amongst those who accompanied Grenville on an expedition across Pamlico Sound. It would appear, then, that some of the missing ships had been located between 8 and 11 July and contact had been made with them. None of this is told explicitly in the *Tiger* journal and so it must remain conjectural in detail but the Holinshed story of the reunion of the ships[3] is borne out by the indications, cited above, from the journal. What may well have happened is that the other vessels, including possibly the one that had been at Jamaica, were awaiting the *Tiger* at the harbour, Port Ferdinando, discovered in 1584. When contact was made with Raymond's men on 6 July, Grenville could have sent to the more northerly harbour, and thus enabled men to come down to accompany him on his shore expedition. This, though it makes a reasonable story, must be regarded as only a very tentative reconstruction.

From 11 July the activities of the expedition can be traced more specifically. On that day Grenville set out with the pinnace[4] and three boats, with perhaps sixty men, to make a journey across Pamlico Sound to explore the mainland.[5] He first visited the enclosed Indian village of Pomeiooc which White sketched[6] on the 12th, while some of the party evidently went to visit Lake Paquippe (Mattamuskeet) nearby. The following day the boats followed the shore into the Pungo River estuary where they found a second Indian village, Aquascogoc, and on the 15th rowed up the Pamlico River to Secoton, the seat of an Indian tribe of this name. There White made a number of drawings[7] and the party

---

[1] Pp. 189–90 below.　　　　　[2] Cp. p. 210 below.
[3] P. 176 below.
[4] Pp. 190–1 below. Lane's comment that the pinnace drew too much water for that shallow sound and was too heavy to stir for an oar (p. 256 below) probably represents his conclusion from this expedition.
[5] His approximate route is shown on the map at the end of the book.
[6] No. 33 (see pp. 415–17 below).　　　[7] Nos. 37–44 (see pp. 420–32 below).

was well entertained. The next day the party set out on its return. One boat, under Amadas, was sent back to Aquascogoc to recover a silver cup taken by an Indian and, failing to do so, burnt the deserted village and its cornfield. The other boats evidently explored the estuary of the Neuse River, where they heard of a village called Nesioke, and Core Sound, which they learnt went to another village, Warreā.[1] On the 18th they got back to Wococon.[2]

At Wococon, meantime, the *Tiger* had apparently been caulked and refloated, so that the vessels were able to sail northwards on 21 July to the harbour of Port Ferdinando or Hatarask which they entered on 27 July, having evidently made a slow and cautious passage northwards. If all the ships were reunited, they would now have made nine sail.

Already on 3 July, word had been sent to the Indian chief Wingina at Roanoke Island, and it is probable that John Arundell, who set out on the 6th with Manteo for the mainland, followed up these preliminaries by a more thorough examination of Roanoke Island and its surroundings. Possible relics of his discoveries are the notes on the sketch-map[3] about oak-galls and silk-grass at Roanoke Island. By the 29th Grangamineo had come with Manteo to Port Ferdinando and it is probable that discussions were then begun with the Indians about the location of the English fort and settlement, though it is not known precisely when the decision was taken to locate it at the north-western end of Roanoke Island or, indeed, on what terms. On 2 August Amadas, possibly with the new pinnace, was sent with another party to explore Albemarle Sound. He may have spent anything up to a month with the Weapemeoc tribe and their neighbours.

On 5 August John Arundell with one of the smaller vessels was despatched to England in order to speed the sending out of supplies to replace those destroyed on the *Tiger* and also, apparently, to bring additional armaments.[4] By 12 August other vessels were

---

[1] Document no. 30, pp. 315–17 below. [2] Cp. p. 191 below.
[3] P. 215 below.
[4] Cp. p. 192 below and Wright, *Further English voyages*, p. 15.

getting ready to depart and Lane, at Port Ferdinando, wrote at least three letters home.[1] They are largely vehicles for his controversy with Grenville but they contain some information on what had been done. It had been decided that Grenville should return and that Lane with a limited number of men should remain in the settlement. This decision probably arose partly from failure to find an adequate harbour from which raids on the Indies could be maintained, and partly from a genuine shortage of stores. Lane expected to live off the country. About this he was optimistic. The specimens with which Grenville was returning—the result probably of trade as well as collection—would demonstrate the fertility of Virginia. The climate was excellent, though the Indians were wild and his men not too tame.[2] Only on the harbours was he somewhat pessimistic. He denounced Wococon and gave some details of Trinity Harbour, some 25 miles north of Port Ferdinando, but reserved his limited praise for the last.

Although we are told nothing of it, the fort must now have been well under way.[3] It is probable that a slipway had already been built at the harbour[4] and that equipment and stores were being transported by water through Roanoke Sound. It is likely that only finishing touches remained to be put to the fort and houses when the *Tiger* sailed on 25 August. Within a very short time Lane was writing from 'the new Fort in Virginia'. By the time he wrote to the elder Hakluyt and to Walsingham (3 and 8 September),[5] the expedition sent up Albemarle Sound had returned, bringing news of a variety of maize which produced sugar from the stalk, grapes, several drugs, flax, including a silky kind, and medicinal earth, as well as reports of a thickly inhabited territory—apparently that on the northern bank of the Sound and possibly also the eastern bank of the Chowan River.

---

[1] Documents nos. 25–7, pp. 197–206 below.   [2] Cp. p. 204 below.

[3] It was probably built well within the month suggested in the 'Notes', but it was not so large or elaborate (cp. pp. 210, 903–10 below).

[4] Cp. pp. 811, 902 below.

[5] Documents nos. 28–9, pp. 207–14 below. It is likely that the date on the former should also be 8 September.

The sketch-map sums up the topography of the discovery so far.[1] At that time the fly-boat was still with him. It must have left, with all remaining vessels except the pinnace, a few days afterwards.

Arundell may have got home late in September,[2] but the *Tiger*, sailing alone, was more fortunately delayed. Off Bermuda she came up with the flagship of the Santo Domingo squadron,[3] a straggler from the *flota*, the *Santa Maria* of San Vicente, variously said to be of 300 to 400 tons, Alonzo Cornieles,[4] captain. The *Tiger* opened fire and after a short engagement Grenville put off in an improvised boat (his own having been left with the settlers) which sank just as he boarded.[5] The Spaniard surrendered and at once Grenville took over the ship's manifest which, according to a Portuguese merchant, Enrique Lopez, who was on board, had no less than 40,000 ducats worth of gold, silver and pearls listed. This, Lopez says, was all handed to him, and more treasure was got from the passengers as well. Grenville denied that there was any treasure registered at all, and said that what was taken from private persons was embezzled by the crew.[6] He does not say anything about pearls.[7] Lopez, however, appears to speak with some authority, since he gives precise figures for the major items in the remaining cargo—8000 *arrobas* (202,880 lb.) of sugar, 1000 *quintales* (100,500 lb.) of ginger, 7000 hides, and other merchandise. Among the latter Mendoza said later there was cochineal and ivory.[8] Lopez put the value at another 80,000 ducats making 120,000 ducats

---

[1] Document no. 30, pp. 215–17 below.

[2] As he may have come direct to the Court at Richmond, where he was on 14 October (p. 192 below), he may have landed as late as 8 or 9 October.

[3] Cp. pp. 177, 192–3, 219 and Wright, *Further English voyages*, pp. 12–15. The latter is the most important account.

[4] I have compared Miss Wright's translation with a copy of Navarrete's transcript in Colleccíon Navarrete xxv, no. 53 (Museo Naval, Madrid) and have noted a few differences. Here she reads 'Corniele', and Navarrete 'Cornieles'.

[5] Cp. p. 193. Miss Wright gives his boarding party as numbering 30 (Navarrete reads 36), so that it must have been of some size.

[6] Document no. 34, p. 220.   [7] Cp. pp. 231, 757 below.

[8] P. 757 below.

registered in all. Grenville admitted to ginger and sugar with a total value of 40,000 to 50,000 ducats,[1] but we have a note of at least nine tusks of ivory that were divided between Raleigh, his brother Carew, his half-brother Adrian Gilbert and Grenville.[2]

Once the prize was mastered twenty of her men were transferred to the *Tiger* and Grenville took her over with a prize crew. The two vessels sailed together from about 31 August[3] until 10 September, when they were separated in a gale. The *Tiger* sailed on, reaching Falmouth on 6 October,[4] but the prize, lacking food and water, made for the Azores. Arriving at Flores early in October, Grenville landed the remaining Spaniards from the prize and took in supplies. Then, sailing home, he arrived at Plymouth on 18 October.[5] Raleigh either met him there or arrived within a few days, and preceded him to London.[6] On the 29th Grenville wrote to Walsingham[7] indicating that he would shortly follow, the implication being that the prize goods were under control.

We may ask was Grenville misleading his associates when he put the value of prize goods on the *Santa Maria* at about a third of the value that the Spaniards did? It is not certain that he was, but it appears likely on what evidence we have, as Lopez had no obvious reason to exaggerate. If so the transaction may perhaps show Grenville in something of that unfavourable light in which Lane painted him,[8] it being usual to deceive the state but not one's partners about prize profits. However, Grenville gives us some indications of the total investment in the voyage by saying that

---

[1] P. 220 below. [2] Cp. pp. 224–5 below.

[3] The Spanish account (Wright, *Further English voyages*, p. 13) says the ship was taken on 4 September, New Style, but as this would be 25 August, Old Style, the day the *Tiger* left Port Ferdinando, it must be mistaken.

[4] P. 193 below.

[5] Idem. [6] Cp. pp. 178, 217, 219, 744 below.

[7] Document no. 34, pp. 218–21 below.

[8] It may be significant that Walsingham is not found associated in any way with subsequent ventures. His own servants, Fernandez, Russell and Atkinson, are all cited by Lane against Grenville (pp. 197–8, 201–2 below), while Walsingham may have believed, on the strength of reports like Document no. 40 (p. 276 below), that Grenville had misled him about the value of the prize.

the approximate £15,000 at which he valued the prize would provide a dividend for the investors.[1] There were other profits too, goods traded in the West Indies, commodities brought from Virginia if they were saleable, the proceeds of the two prizes taken off Puerto Rico, against which has to be set the problematical loss of one or more vessels. Certainly, rumours about the value of the *Santa Maria* circulated widely, her value being boosted to at least a million ducats.[2] This overshadowed concern with the colony, though it showed that privateering could be used to pay for colonization.[3] We know almost nothing of how the establishment of the first English colony in America was regarded by those who were in the venture or on its fringes.

The English castaway examined in Jamaica in 1586[4] told his Spanish interrogators of his departure from England with Grenville in 1585 and added enough details to make his story tally with what we know of the expedition. But two items do not fit. The first is the date at which he said they left (1 June for 9 April), and the second is the port from which they set sail (Falmouth— 'ffall.morth'—for Plymouth). One or other could have been a mistake on the part of the Spaniards, but both could have been slips by someone who was aware reinforcements were being prepared to follow up Grenville in June, more especially if he had been put on shore from a ship commanded by a man who had had close contacts with the appointed commander of this second expedition and knew of his proposed date of departure. These conditions would be fulfilled if the ship was the *Lion* and her commander George Raymond. But even if this seems over-ingenious, there is now no doubt that Bernard Drake was preparing a ship, the *Golden Royal* of Topsham, of 110 tons, at

---

[1] We may assume he meant a profit of at least 50%, which was regarded as modest (cp. Edwards, *Ralegh*, II, 43–5). Cp. pp. 221, 598 below.

[2] Cp. Documents nos. 35, 36, 40, 123, pp. 221–3, 226, 743–4 below.

[3] Cp. D. B. Quinn, 'The failure of Raleigh's American colonies', in Cronne, Moody and Quinn, *Essays...in honour of J. E. Todd*, pp. 74–7.

[4] Wright, *Further English voyages*, pp. 174–5; A.G.I. 2.5.1/20/(Patronato 265, no. 44).

Exmouth to head a further squadron for the Virginia voyage.[1] He was acting under Raleigh's orders, and was apparently ready to sail by the beginning of June. At this point news arrived of the Spanish embargo on English shipping, and the Queen instructed Raleigh to send at once to Newfoundland to tell English fishermen there not to take their catch to Spain and also to seize what Spaniards he could find. He had no choice but to divert his second Virginia squadron for this task, but he had perhaps to use formal powers of impressment to get some of the adventurers, including Amyas Preston, Drake's partner in the *Golden Royal*, to go.

Bernard Drake was given a commission dated 20 June and sailed by the end of the month. On the way out a Portuguese prize— a Brazilman—was taken and Preston was sent back in command. Bernard Drake performed his mission speedily, rounding up seventeen fishing vessels as prizes. Not only so but, off Newfoundland, he met Captain George Raymond with the *Lion* and possibly the *Dorothy*. Whether this was wholly coincidence it is impossible to say. Probably it was, but they might well have concerted an attack on the Newfoundland fishing fleets (using Virginia as a base) before Raymond left England in April. In any event, they entered into partnership and made for the Azores, where they took three more Brazilmen and a French ship from Guinea. On the way to England, one ship, Raleigh's *Job* of 70 tons, Andrew Fulforde captain, and a Portuguese prize—a fishing vessel, the *Lion* of Viana—put into Breton ports under stress of weather and were held there.[2] The *Job's* cargo was sixteen tons of 'Cedar wodde'. This suggests timber cut in America rather than taken at sea. Might it perhaps have been obtained at Croatoan Island and transhipped from the *Lion*? Bernard Drake and George

---

[1] A summarized version of the materials from the High Court of Admiralty are given as Document no. 44, pp. 234–42. Her port and tonnage come from P.R.O., H.C.A. 25/1, pkt. 4, 8 March 1586 (when, accompanied by the pinnace *Good Companion*, she was set out by Philip Drake, with Hugh Drake as Captain).

[2] Petition of Andrew Fulforde and Thomas Raynsforde to the privy council [1586] (S.P. 12/185, 60). Fulforde appears to have commanded Raleigh's company in Munster in 1589 (*Cal. S.P., Ireland, 1588–92*, p. 171).

The 1585 Voyage

Raymond did well, financially, out of the expedition. So apparently did Raleigh though we cannot say how much he made. The profits, added to Grenville's, must have helped to float the 1586 ventures. The plan for a second Virginia enterprise in 1585 has hitherto been unknown, but it reinforces the other evidence that the American fort was primarily intended as a privateering base.

21. [9 APRIL 1585.]
SIR RICHARD GRENVILLE LEAVES PLYMOUTH[1]

Christoofer Brokyng. 1584.[2]

Sir Richard Grendfelde knighte dep*a*rted from Plymouthe[3] with vi shippes and barkes[4] for Wingane Dehoy wher he caried vi hundred men or therabowts.[5]

22. THE HOLINSHED ACCOUNT OF THE 1585 EXPEDITION[6]

In this yeare 1585, euen in Aprill, at the pleasant prime, sir Walter Raleigh knight, being incouraged by the reports of his men of the

Abr. Fl. ex chirographo D.G. militis.[7]

---

[1] Plymouth City Records, Black Book, fo. 7 (see Rowse, *Grenville*, p. 204). I am indebted to Colin Campbell, Esq., O.B.E., Town Clerk of Plymouth, for having this item checked for me.

[2] Christopher Brooking was mayor of Plymouth between 17 September 1584 and 17 September 1585 (Worth, *Calendar of the Plymouth municipal records*, pp. 18–19).

[3] 'Here, mostly, haue the troops of aduenturers, made their *Rendez vous* for attempting new discoueries or inhabitances: as, Tho. Stukeligh for Florida, Sir Humfrey Gilbert for Newfound land, Sir Rich. Greynuile for Virginia' (Richard Carew, *The survey of Cornwall* (1602), pp. 14–15).

[4] The journal of the voyage (p. 178 below) says seven, and the Holinshed account eight (p. 174). Usage varied in regard to the inclusion or exclusion of pinnaces, of which there were two, and which were frequently towed, or carried, by the larger ships.

[5] This is the most probable estimate of the total personnel of the expedition. Some 300 seamen would have been necessary to man the vessels listed in the journal, 108 colonists were left to establish the colony, while 200 would appear to be a reasonable estimate for the number of soldiers and gunners carried by Grenville in addition, though numbers could have been larger by another 100 (p. 159, and, for Spanish estimates, pp. 728, 734, 739, 753, Wright, p. 16).

[6] Holinshed, *Chronicles*, III (1587), 1401–2.

[7] As we have already seen (p. 90 above) 'Abr. Fl.' was Abraham Fleming (*c.* 1552?–1607), who was actively concerned in the preparation of this edition

173

Sir Walter Raleighs chargeable voiage³ to the foresaid land latelie discouered, and by the quéenes maiestie named Virginia.

Sir Richard Gréenefield lieutenant to sir Walter Raleigh for this voiage.

Gentlemen that associated sir Richard Gréenefield.

goodnesse of the soile and the fertilitie of the countrie, which they had discouered this yeare last past,[1] and now by her maiestie called Virginia, with knightlie courage counteruaileable to his double desire of honour, by vndertaking hard aduenturs, furnished to his great charges eight[2] sailes of all sortes, and immediatlie set them to the sea, ordeining sir Richard Gréenefield his kinsman[4] (a gentleman of verie good estimation both for his parentage and sundrie good vertues, who for loue he bare vnto sir Walter Raleigh, togither with a disposition that he had to attempt honorable actions worthie of honour, was willing to hazard himselfe in this voiage) his lieutenant, inioining him either to tarrie himselfe, or to leaue some gentleman of good worth with a competent number of soldiers[5] in the countrie of Virginia, to begin an English colonie there. Who with the ships aforesaid, hauing in his companie sir Iohn Arundell,[6] Thomas Candish, Rafe Lane, Edward Gorges,[7]

(*DNB*), but the rest of the note offers some difficulty. All that can be suggested is 'ex chirographo *Domini Gréenefield*' militis'. It would not have been surprising that Grenville should have set down (subsequent to his provisional report to Walsingham, pp. 218–21 below) his own views of the voyage, especially in view of the controversies it engendered (pp. 210–14). Fleming is clearly relying on something different from the *Tiger* journal; at the same time there are so many slips from precise accuracy that the narrative reads rather like one based on hasty notes of a verbal account or possibly of a hurried run through a written document.

[1] The 1584 voyage (above pp. 90–117). 'This yeare last past' suggests that Fleming wrote before 25 March 1586.

[2] The Spanish report (p. 730 below) said that thirteen ships were being prepared, the journal that seven set sail, and the Plymouth record six (pp. 173, 178).

[3] This is possibly the origin of the persistent myth that Raleigh went himself to Virginia (cp. pp. 389, 398), though it was clearly not so intended by the compiler.

[4] There was a double connexion, the more recent by the marriage of Raleigh's mother's sister to Grenville's uncle (Rowse, *Grenville*, p. 193). See his own reference to Raleigh as 'cousin' (Document no. 34, p. 219 below).

[5] The only specific acknowledgement that the colony was a military one (cp. pp. 19–22). The reference to Grenville's discretion about remaining in Virginia himself or returning is important. If his purpose was to set up a privateering base as well as establish a settlement (cp. *William and Mary Q.*, 3rd ser., VI, 222–3; *T.R.H.S.*, 5th ser., I, 8–9) then his return indicated that the prospects did not appear too good.

[6] Knighted by the queen on his return (p. 192 below).

[7] Named otherwise only in Lane's letter (p. 210 below) and in the list of the sea captains, 5 January 1586 (Corbett, *Spanish war*, p. 293). Edward Gorges

The 1585 Voyage

Iohn Stuklie,[1] Edward Stafford, Philip Amadis, Arthur Barlow,[2] Thomas Heriot, and diuerse other gentlemen with a competent number of souldiers, departed from London in Aprill[3] aforesaid. But after they had sailed certeine numbers of leagues at the sea, by force and violence of fowle weather they were separated one from another;[4] so that sir Richard Gréenefield being singled from his fleet, all alone arriued in the Iland of Hispaniola[5] in the west Indies, about the middest of Iune following,[6] where he determined resolutelie to remaine, vntill he had built a bote (for he had lost his owne bote in the tempests aforesaid.)[7]

Sir Richard Gréenefield singled from his companie by fowle weather. arriueth in Hispaniola.

Wherevpon immediatlie after his landing, finding a place to his liking, he esconsed himselfe in despite of the Spaniards, who by all possible means did there best indeuour by proffering of sundrie skirmishes, to inforce him to retire to his ship: but he nothing appalled with their brags kept his ground.[8] Twelue daies after his arriuall there, after Thomas Candish arriued at the same place,[9]

The valiant-nesse of sir Richard Gréenefield against the Spaniards.

was either Sir Edward Gorges of London (d. 1625), soldier, and brother of Sir Arthur Gorges, or his cousin, Sir Edward Gorges of Wraxall, elder brother of Sir Ferdinando Gorges (cp. R. A. Preston, *Gorges of Plymouth Fort* (Toronto, 1953), 18, 20–1, 139, 363–4, 448–9, who favours the former).

[1] The only contemporary source which gives Stukely's christian name (cp. pp. 230–1).

[2] The only mention that the author of the 1584 narrative took part in the 1585 expedition. It is scarcely sufficient authority for certainty, since Fleming may have confused his presence on the earlier voyage with this, but, if he took part, in what capacity did he serve? Or did he write the *Tiger* journal and so forget to list himself? (See p. 178 below.)

[3] The expedition had set out, in part, from London, but before April (cp. p. 730): Plymouth was the final port of departure.

[4] For what is known of the separation and its effects see pp. 180–3, 189–90 below and Wright, *Further English voyages*, pp. 174–6.

[5] The *Tiger* arrived alone at San Juan de Puerto Rico not Hispaniola (p. 181).

[6] 11/21 or 12/22 May (cp. pp. 181, 183 below and Wright, *Further English voyages*, p. 12).

[7] The only specific reference in the English accounts to the loss of the *Tiger's* pinnace: the replacement was built at Tallaboa Bay, Puerto Rico (pp. 181–3, 404).

[8] Compare the English and Spanish accounts, pp. 182–3, 734 and Wright, *Further English voyages*, pp. 9–12.

[9] The *Elizabeth* arrived on the eighth or ninth day after the *Tiger* (cp. pp. 182–3; Wright, p. 12).

where sir Richard Gréenfield was ensconsing of himselfe, to the great reioising both of themselues & their companies. The Spaniards finding it too hard for them (notwithstanding their multitudes) to remooue these few resolute Englishmen by violence, came to a parlée, and in the same concluded an amitie, that the one nation might in safetie traffike with the other.[1] Now when sir Richard Gréenefield had taried in that Iland almost a moneth,[2] and had built his bote, reuittled himselfe, and laden his ships with horsses, mares, kine, sheep, swine, &c:[3] to transport with him to Virginia (bicause these sorts of cattell heretofore were not to be found in that countrie) he departed thense; and in his waie he made discouerie of manie Ilands and hauens vpon the continent adioining, and arriued safelie in the new discouered countrie (where he met with the rest of his fléet that attended his comming thither)[4] about the middest of Iulie[5] next insuing, not without great danger of shipwracke. For at the verie entrance into the harborough, his ship strake on the ground, and did beat so manie strokes vpon the sands, that if God had not miraculouslie deliuered him, there had

A parlée tending to the concluding of an amitie betwéene the English and Spanish.

What kind of cattel for vittelling sir Richard Gréenefield transported to Virginia.

Sir Richard Gréenefield méeteth with the rest of his fléet an is in danger of shipwracke.

[1] The journal says that the Spaniards failed to keep their appointment by 23 May (p. 183), but the Spanish accounts (pp. 735, 742; Wright, *Further English voyages*, pp. 9–12, 15–16) make it clear that commerce was being carried on between 24 and 29 May, so that it may well be that this version records an *entente* which neither side wished to acknowledge openly. Note especially Grenville's alleged attempt to sell back his prizes (Wright, pp. 10, 12) which might not have been too well regarded in England, had it been revealed. On the other hand, since this account conflates Grenville's disparate experiences on Puerto Rico and on Hispaniola the reference may well be to the latter, where there was an agreement (cp. pp. 185–7).

[2] Grenville did not remain at either island so long, his Hispaniola visit lasting from 30 May to 7 June. Sighting Dominica on 7 May he apparently cleared from the Bahamas on 16 June (p. 188).

[3] Compare what is known elsewhere of the collection of livestock, pp. 187, 742, 747; Wright, *Further English voyages*, pp. 10–12.

[4] This clearly suggests that *Roebuck, Lion, Dorothy,* and even possibly the second pinnace, had reached the Banks before the *Tiger* and her consorts. The junction of the two parts of the expedition must have taken place between 8 and 11 July (cp. pp. 189–90). But the *Lion* had already departed.

[5] Fleming puts the events at Wococon in the last week in June, after—instead of before—the reunion of Grenville with his remaining ships (cp. pp. 189–90 below).

beene no waie to auoid present death.[1] In this danger his ship was so brused, that the saltwater came so aboundantlie into hir, that the most part of his corne, salt, meale, rice, bisket, & other prouisions that he should haue left with them that remained behind him in the countrie was spoiled.[2]

After he had remained there certeine daies, according to his commission from sir Walter Raleigh, he began to establish a colonie,[3] appointing maister Rafe Lane (a gentleman of good account) generall[4] of those English which were to remaine there, being in all to the number of an hundred and seauen persons,[5] amongst whom diuerse gentlemen remained; namelie, Philip Amadis, Edward Stafford, Meruin,[6] Kendall, Prideaux, Acton, Heriot, and others. When he had taken sufficient order for the establishing of master Lane and his companie aforesaid, leauing with them as much of all prouisions as his plentie would giue him leaue, he weighed anchor for England.[7] But in his returne, not hauing sailed manie leagues from the coast of Virginia, he descried a tall ship of foure hundred tuns or thereabouts,[8] making the same course that he did, vnto whome he gaue chase, and in few houres by goodnesse of saile ouertooke, and by violence wan, richlie laden with sugar, hides, spices, and some quantitie of gold, siluer, and pearle:[9] she was the viceadmerall of the fleet of Sancto Domingo

Sir Richard Gréenefield establisheth an English colonie in Virginia by commission.

Sir Richard Gréenefield descrieth a Spanish ship, chaseth and surpriseth hir.

---

[1] This account of the grounding of the *Tiger* at Wococon on 29 June has an echo of Lane's letter of 12 August (cp. p. 201 below).

[2] This makes more specific than other references (pp. 189, 201, 314) the loss which the Roanoke Island settlers suffered by damage to their supplies on this occasion.

[3] The selection of a site on Roanoke Island probably did not take place until the beginning of August (cp. pp. 167, 198).

[4] For Grenville's lieutenant-general this is an appropriate enough title, but 'governor' is used by Lane (p. 204).

[5] The number given below (pp. 194–7), if Lane is included.

[6] Maruyn, cp. p. 194 below.

[7] The *Tiger* sailed on 25 August, but some other vessels several weeks later (cp. pp. 192, 210–14).

[8] The *Tiger* journal gives the *Santa Maria* as of 300 tons (cp. p. 300).

[9] Grenville stressed that her lading was ginger and sugar (p. 220), but both English and Spanish accounts add other commodities and all mention the bullion and pearls (cp. pp. 221–3, 226, 231, 743–4, 757; Wright, *Further English voyages*, pp. 13–14).

that yere for Spaine. After this good fortune, hauing a merie gale,

An other voiage resolued vpon by sir Walter Raleigh for the supplie of those that were left in Virginia.

not manie daies after he arriued at Plimmouth in October next insuing;[1] where sir Walter Raleigh méeting with him,[2] did presentlie resolue vpon another voiage, to supplie Rafe Lane, and his companie that were left with him in Virginia, the next spring following: which accordinglie was performed with all expedition.[3]

23. THE *TIGER* JOURNAL OF THE 1585 VOYAGE[4]

The voyage made by Sir Richard Greenuile, for Sir Walter Ralegh, to Virginia, in the yeere, 1585.

The 19. day of Maye,[5] in the yeere aboue saide, wee departed from Plymmouth, our fleete consisting of the number of seuen sailes, to wit, the Tyger, of the burden of seuen score tunnes:[6] a Flie boate

---

[1] 18 October (p. 193).

[2] This is the only specific mention of Raleigh being at Plymouth to meet Grenville, though there is contributory evidence (pp. 217, 219). He could have learnt something of Grenville's plans and his approximate time of arrival from Arundell (cp. p. 192).

[3] If this account was written up before 25 March 1586, which is possible, though not certain (cp. p. 24), it is likely that Raleigh's supply ship got away before that date, though Grenville was not yet ready to sail (pp. 465–6). In any event, no revision of the narrative after the return of the supply ship (or of Grenville in December) was attempted.

[4] Richard Hakluyt, *Principall navigations* (1589), pp. 733–6, collated with III (1600), 251–3 (VIII (1904), 310–17). This was evidently prepared from a journal kept on the *Tiger* by an anonymous member of her company. We can only say of him that he was a member of Grenville's faction in the quarrel with Lane and Fernandez (cp. pp. 188–9). If Arthur Barlowe was on the expedition (cp. p. 175 above), the absence of his name in it might suggest that he may have been the author, though in general it lacks his felicity of language.

[5] Corrected to '9. day of April' (III (1600), 251). The mistaken date was that on which Cavendish in the *Elizabeth* joined the *Tiger* off Puerto Rico. Some (we cannot say how many) of the ships sailed round from London, but Grenville joined at Plymouth, probably adding one or more vessels to the squadron (cp. pp. 121, 141, 151, 175).

[6] The *Tiger* was a royal vessel, adventured or hired by the queen. She was classed as a 'great ship' and rated officially as either 160 or 200 tons. In 1576 her armament had consisted of 6 demi-culverins, 6 sakers and 1 minion (i.e. her 'battery' was 13), which corresponds well enough with Mendoza's estimate in

called the Roe Bucke, of the like burden:[1] the Lyon of a hundred tunnes, or thereabouts:[2] the Elizabeth, of fiftie tunnes,[3] and the Dorothie, a small barke,[4] whereunto were also adioyned for speedie seruices, 2. small Pinnesses.[5] The principall Gentlemen of our companie, were, Master Ralfe Lane,[6] Master Thomas Candishe,[7]

1585 (p. 728 below). Her complement is given variously after her return as 80 (or 88) mariners, 12 gunners and 8 (or 20) soldiers, 100 to 120 in all (Michael Lewis, 'Armada guns, II', in *Mariner's Mirror*, XXVIII (1942), 147; Corbett, *Spanish War*, p. 271, *Drake*, I (2nd ed.), 372; Hist. MSS Comm., *Foljambe MSS*, p. 108; cp. S.P. 12/216, 2, 28, where in 1588 she is shown, under Raleigh's command, to have had only 90 men). She is shown in White's drawing no. 2 (see pp. 403-4). Lane gives her complement as 120 or 160 (pp. 205, 228), while a Spanish report on her heavy armament (her 'two tiers of guns on each side and other firearms (*artificios de fuego*)', cp. Wright, *Further English voyages*, p. 15), might suggest that, as with the ships which went with Drake later in the year (Lewis, op. cit., p. 117), her normal gun-power had been increased. The *Tiger* was 'admiral' or flagship of the expedition, carrying Grenville as general of the expedition (and captain of the flagship), Lane as lieutenant-general on the military side, and probably Amadas as admiral on the naval side, while Fernandez combined the posts of chief pilot of the fleet and master of the flagship (cp. pp. 165, 194, 201, 255 below).

[1] She may have been a Dutch fly-boat which Raleigh had bought fairly recently (p. 728), but if so she had been tried out in a little Channel piracy not long before (pp. 153-5). Her captain was John Clarke and she was possibly vice-admiral of the squadron.

[2] The *Lion* (or *Red Lion*) of Chichester, George Raymond captain (pp. 234-42). She may have been the vessel which left part of her complement on Jamaica (Wright, *Further English voyages*, pp. 174-6; p. 165 above).

[3] Her captain was Thomas Cavendish, who was also high marshal of the expedition (pp. 210-11): we are told that he fitted her out, so she may have been his own ship (p. 230 below).

[4] She was probably identical with the 'fine pinnesse also called the Dorothie, which was sir Walter Raleghs' (Hakluyt, *Principal navigations*, XI (1904), 203; Brit. Mus., Lansdowne MS 100, fo. 23), which went with Cumberland in 1586.

[5] These would probably be undecked pinnaces of 20-30 tons, which could be carried on deck if need be: the *Tiger's* was lost (p. 175); the second probably acted as tender for the vice-admiral—either the *Roebuck* or the *Lion*.

[6] Pp. 149-50 above; *DNB*. Lane's career had been mainly as a soldier, but he had bought a share in *The Carick Sidney* as early as 1570 (Hist. MSS Comm., *De L'Isle and Dudley MSS*, I, 411-12), and set out several ships privateering in 1572 (Andrews, 'Elizabethan privateering', pp. 29-30).

[7] Pp. 122, 139, 174, 182, 230; *DNB*.

Master Iohn Arundell,[1] Master Raimund,[2] Master Stukely,[3] Master Bremige,[4] Master Vincent,[5] and Master Iohn Clarke,[6] and diuers others, whereof some were Captaines, and other some Assistants for counsell, and good directions in the voyage.[7]

The 14. day of Aprill, we fell with Lançacota, and Forte Ventura,[8] Isles of the Canaries, and from thence we continued our course for Dominica, one of the Antiles of the West India, wherewith we fell the 7. day of Maye,[9] and the 10. day following, we came to an anker at Cotesa, a little Island situate neere to the Island of S. Iohn,[10] where wee landed, and refreshed our selues all that day.

[1] John Arundell of Tolverne, Cornwall, born 1550 (J. L. Vivian, *Visitations of Cornwall*, p. 6). Mr Rowse identifies him as John Arundell of Trerice (*Grenville*, pp. 27, 69), and writes to me: 'I am not convinced that it is one of the Tolverne branch'.

[2] 'Raymund' (Hakluyt, III (1600), 251): George Raymond of Chichester, captain of the *Lion* (pp. 234, 236–7), whose career as a privateer captain and promoter can be traced in Corbett, *Spanish war*, pp. 141, 162, 181, 292, 299; Andrews, 'Elizabethan privateering', pp. 262, 272; Purchas, *Pilgrims*, XVI, 145. He commanded the *Penelope* in Lancaster's 1591 voyage and was lost (Foster, *Lancaster*, passim; Hakluyt, *Principal navigations*, VI (1904), 387 seq., VII, 30, 194 seq.).

[3] 'Stukeley' (Hakluyt, III (1600), 251): John Stukely (p. 175 above), whom Mr Rowse thinks may have been a brother of Grenville's brother-in-law Thomas Stukely (*Grenville*, pp. 205, 270). He was father of Sir Lewis Stukely (p. 230–1 below).

[4] Probably the James Browewich (or Bromwich?) of the 1584 expedition (p. 116 above).

[5] Not identified. He might be the Vincent, one of 'his bravest men', reported lost by Raleigh in Guiana in 1595 (Hist. MSS Comm., *De L'Isle and Dudley MSS*, II, 163).

[6] John Clarke, apparently captain of the *Roebuck* (p. 153).

[7] The chief officers, together with a number of assistants, often twelve, made up the council of war, which the general was expected to consult and by which he was in some measure bound.

[8] 'Lancerota and Forteventura' (Hakluyt, III (1600), 251): nothing is said of the storm which had scattered the squadron before the *Tiger* got alone to the Canaries.

[9] For the comparative length of the crossing, cp. pp. 517, 600. John White made profile sketches of Dominica and St Croix, probably on this occasion (see p. 403, no. 1, below). For the landfalls see *West Indies Pilot*, II (8th ed., 1931), 141–9 (St Croix), 232–9 (Dominica).

[10] John White's 'Cottea' of 1587 (p. 519 below). It has not been identified by name, but is one of a number of small islands south-east of Guayanilla Point (U.S. Coast and Geodetic Survey Chart 902; *West Indies Pilot*, II, 56).

The 1585 Voyage

The 15.[1] day of Maye, we came to an anker, in the Baye of Muskito, in the Island of S. Iohn,[2] within a Fawlcon shot of the shoare: where our Generall Sir Richard Greenuill, and the most part of our companie landed,[3] and began to fortifie, very neere to the sea side: the riuer ranne by the one side of our forte, and the other two sides were enuironed with woods.[4]

The 13. day we began to builde a new pinnesse within the Fort,[5] with the timber that we then felled in the countrey, some part whereof we fet[6] three myle vp in the land, and brought it to our Fort vpon trucks, the Spaniards not daring to make or offer resistance.[7]

[1] Corrected to '12' (Hakluyt, III (1600), 251): 'They land vpon the Iland of S. Iohn de porto Rico', in margin. It will be noted that they considered the date of their arrival to be 11 May (p. 183).

[2] The site was known to the Spaniards as Mosquetal (p. 740) or, less precisely, as Gaudianilla or Guardianilla (cp. pp. 733-4, 747 and Wright, *Further English voyages*, p. 11). The camp was at Tallaboa Bay, three miles east of Guayanilla Point (which marks the entrance to the deep-water Guayanilla Harbour (18° N., 67° 13′ W.)). The bay has a number of islands offshore and offers a fairly sheltered anchorage, with good holding grounds to small vessels with local knowledge (*West Indies Pilot*, II, 53-6). Inland, to the north-west was the town of San German, which apparently gave its name to what is now Sucia Bay, immediately to the east of Cape Rojo. In 1582 San German and 'Guardianilla' were described as being in the hands of French corsairs who were terrorizing the western part of the island (Germán Latorre, *Relaciones geográficas de Indias* (Bibl. Col. Americana, III (Seville, 1919), pp. 39-40). This was evidently the rendezvous chosen in 1584 (cp. pp. 79-81, 93), but by 1585 the Spaniards had succeeded in garrisoning San German (p. 734).

[3] Lane says they put 120 men on shore (p. 205 below): the Spanish figures were very much higher (cp. pp. 734, 739; Wright, *Further English voyages*, pp. 9, 12, 16).

[4] The completed encampment is shown in great detail in John White's drawing (no. 2, see pp. 403-4 below). If the argument above is correct, the river would be the Tallaboa River.

[5] This was to replace the *Tiger's* pinnace lost on the way out (pp. 175, 179): it was considered essential to have one to explore the Carolina Sounds in case no other small vessels of the squadron rejoined Grenville. The other objective was to get fresh water (pp. 403-4).

[6] Fetched. The White drawing shows this being done while the boat is taking shape on the sand (p. 404). The Spaniards noted that the English had a forge with them for making nails (p. 740; Wright, *Further English voyages*, p. 9).

[7] The Spaniards thought the English intended a permanent establishment (p. 734; Wright, *Further English voyages*, p. 9). Grenville may have wished to

The 16. day, there appeared vnto vs out of the woods 8. horsemen of the Spaniards, about a quarter of a myle from our Fort, staying about halfe an hower in viewing our forces: but as soone as they saw x. of our shot marching towards them, they presently retyred into the woodes.[1]

The 19. day, Master Candish, who had bene sepcrated from our fleete in a storme in the Bay of Portingal arriued at Cotesa, within the sight of the Tiger:[2] we thinking him a farre off to haue ben either a Spaniard or French man of warre thought it good to waigh ankers, and to goe roome with him, which the Tyger did, and discerned him at last to be one of our Consorts, for ioy of whose comming our ships[3] discharged their ordinance, and saluted him, according to the manner of the Seas.

The 22. day, 20. other Spanishe horsemen shewed them selues to vs vpon the other side of the riuer: who being seene, our General dispatched 20. footemen towards them, and two horsemen of ours, mounted vpon Spanish horses, which wee before had taken in the time of our being on the Iland:[4] they shewed to our men a flagge of truce, and made signes to haue a parle with vs: whereupon two of our men went halfe of the way vpon the sands, and two of theirs came and met them: the two Spaniards offred very great salutations to our men, but began according to their Spanish proud humors, to expostulate with them, about their arriual, and forti-

experiment with such a fortification in view of Drake's (and Sidney's) plans for obtaining footholds in the Caribbean, but he is not likely to have meant it to be held until Drake arrived. On the other hand it seems probable that he found Spanish military activity in the area round about much greater than he had anticipated.

[1] This was evidently a patrol from San German: its report got back to the governor, Diego Menéndez de Váldes, at Puerto Rico, on 25 May/4 June, who thereupon sent reinforcements to San German (Wright, *Further English voyages*, p. 9).

[2] The *Elizabeth's* arrival (cp. p. 175) shows that the *Tiger* was at the general rendezvous: the latter was kept sufficiently manned to be able to put to sea at short notice.

[3] There is no reason to believe that there was more than one vessel there already, the *Tiger*: the writer is including the *Elizabeth* in his statement.

[4] Shown in right centre on White's drawing (see p. 404).

fying in their countrie, who notwithstanding by our mens discrete answers were so cooled, that wheras they were told, that our principal intention was onely to furnish our selues with water, and victuals, and other necessaries wherof we stood in neede, which we craued might be yelded vs with faire, and friendly means, otherwise our resolution was to practise force, and to releeue our selues by the sworde: the Spaniards in conclusion, seeing our men so resolute, yelded to our requestes with large promises of all curtesie, and great fauor, and so our men and theirs departed.[1]

The 23. day our pinnesse was finished, and lanched,[2] which being done, our Generall with his Captaines, and Gentlemen, marched vp into the Country about the space of 4. myles,[3] where in a plaine marsh, they stayed expecting the comming of the Spanyards according to their promise, to furnish vs with victuals: who keeping their old custome for periurie and breache of promise came not,[4] whereupon our General fired the woods thereabout, and so retired to our Fort, which the same day was fired also, and each man came aboord to be ready to set saile the next morning.[5]

The 29. day[6] we set saile from Saint Iohns, being many of vs

[1] The Spanish contingent was headed by the lieutenant in charge at San German, but it is implied (p. 734 below) that his sole purpose was to obtain intelligence of the English plans.

[2] This vessel was large enough to be considered by the Spaniards as a ship (p. 736), and is apparently that shown in White's map (fig. 7 and p. 467). Lane later considered her draught rather too great for safe navigation of Pamlico Sound (p. 256 below). As shown (incomplete) (White, no. 2, p. 404) she was undecked.

[3] Probably in the direction of San German.

[4] Yet the Spanish intelligence was good enough to be able to send off a report at once when Grenville deserted his encampment (Wright, *Further English voyages*, p. 9).

[5] The Spaniards soon after inspected the deserted site but say nothing of its firing (p. 734): they found cut into the bole of a tree an inscription intended to guide other vessels which came to the rendezvous, which reads (after double translation): 'On May 11th we reached this place with the *Tiger* and on the 19th the *Elizabeth* came up and we are about to leave on the 23rd in good health, glory be to God. 1585.' (Wright, *Further English voyages*, p, 12; p. 734 below).

[6] 'The 29. day' is evidently a mistake. The writer meant '23': Hakluyt or his printer altered it, not realizing that what happened was that the two vessels moved

stoong before vpon shoare with the Muskitoes:[1] but the same night wee tooke a Spanish Frigat, which was forsaken by the Spanyards vpon the sight of vs,[2] and the next day in the morning very early, wee tooke another Frigat, with good and rich fraight,[3] and diuers Spaniards of accompt in her, which afterwards we ransomed for good round summes, and landed them in Saint Iohns.[4]

The 26. day our Lieutenant Master Ralfe Lane, went in one of the Frigats which we had taken, to Roxo bay vpon the Southwest side of Saint Iohns, to fetch salt,[5] being thither conducted by a Spanish Pilot:[6] as soone as he arriued there, he landed with his

---

west to San German Bay, made contact with the civilian inhabitants and attempted, apparently with some success, to buy livestock from them for the Virginia settlement (cp. pp. 735, 742; Wright, *Further English voyages*, p. 11).

[1] Cp. the passage in Moffet, *Insectorum...theatrum* (1634), p. 84 (translated in *Theater* (1658), p. 955): 'The Gnats in America, especially those they call *Yetin*, do so slash and cut, that they will pierce through very thick cloathing. So that it is excellent sport to behold how ridiculously the barbarous people when they are bitten will frig and frisk, and flap with their hands their thighs, buttocks, shoulder, arms, sides, even as a carter doth his horses.' Moffet may have derived something of this picture from White's experiences in the West Indies and North America (cp. pp. 403–8 below).

[2] This was on the night of the 23rd, when one of the ships was patrolling in the Mona Channel near the small island of Mona. The bark was on its way from Santo Domingo to Puerto Rico (pp. 734–5; Wright, *Further English voyages*, p. 9). There is an unconfirmed suggestion that she was French (Wright, op. cit. p. 16).

[3] 24 May. She was coming from Santo Domingo with a substantial cargo of cloth (recently brought out by the fleet from Spain) for the town of Puerto Rico (pp. 735, 740; Wright, *Further English voyages*, pp. 9–10, 16).

[4] The account of one of the prisoners, Don Fernando de Altamirano, is given below (pp. 740–3). He alleges that Grenville found it impossible to raise livestock locally as ransoms and finally released his prisoners without penalty on the 28th. This version must, however, be taken with caution.

[5] Cape Rojo is the more easterly of the capes at the south-western tip of Puerto Rico, and Rojo Bay is either Salinas Bay between it and Pt. Aguila or Boqueron Bay to the north of it, the former being the more probable (cp. *West Indies Pilot*, II (1931), 48–50). In 1582 Cape Rojo was said to be the best source of salt on the island (Latore, op. cit. pp. 49–50).

[6] Lane alleges that Grenville told him he need not fear any Spanish resistance (p. 229). The pilot was probably from the smaller prize and she was almost certainly the vessel shown in White's drawing (no. 3, see p. 404–5) just offshore from the salt-hills.

men, to the number of 20. and intrenched him selfe vpon the sandes immediatly, compassing one of their salt hils within the trench:[1] who being seene of the Spanyards, there came downe towards him two or three troopes of horsemen, and footemen, who gaue him the looking, and gazing on, but durst not come neere him to offer any resistance,[2] so that Master Lane mauger their troopes, caried their salt aboord and laded his Frigat, and so returned againe to our fleete the 29. day, which road at Saint Germans Bay. The same day we all departed, and the next day arriued in the Iland of Hispaniola.[3]

Iune.

The 1. day of Iune we ankered at Isabella,[4] in the North side of Hispaniola.

The 3. day of Iune, the Gouernor of Isabella, and Captaine of the Port de Plata, beeing certifyed by the reports of sundry Spanyards, who had bene wel intertained aboord our shippes by our General, that in our fleete were many braue, and gallant Gentlemen, who greatly desired to see the Gouernor aforesaid, he

[1] Lane himself admits to having had 25 soldiers and 6 Spanish prisoners (p. 229). His elaborate entrenchments are shown by White, who also includes two tall mounds of salt, evidently gathered from local salt-pans, within the entrenchment.

[2] Lane mistakenly believed the force to have been led by Diego Menéndez de Valdés, governor of the island (cp. Wright, *Further English voyages*, pp. 9–10), with 40 horse and 300 foot (cf. p. 734 below). It was probably the San German garrison. Lane afterwards blames Grenville for putting him in danger and this was the cause of one of their quarrels (cp. pp. 228–9). However, it is conceivable that Lane was right and that Grenville had arranged the operation to draw off the San German garrison in order that he might have an opportunity to trade with the townspeople.

[3] If the smaller prize was not French it is possible that a French prize was taken during the crossing (29–30 May) of the Mona Channel (cp. Wright, *Further English voyages*, p. 16).

[4] 'on' (Hakluyt, III (1660), 252). This is not the modern Isabela on Puerto de Sagua la Grande, but Isabela, on Colombus' Rio de Isabela, the Bahia Isabela being the harbour to the westward of Puerto de Plata in lat. 19° 49′ N., long. 70° 41′ W. (cp. *West Indies Pilot*, III (3rd edn., 1933), 281–4). There they had tried to get horses, dogs, cattle and sheep (pp. 736, 742, 747; Wright, *Further English voyages*, p. 11). French merchants had a substantial hold on illegal trade from this coast (p. 739 below), and it is not unlikely that Simon Fernandez's friend Alanson (p. 521) lived there, this providing one reason for the call.

thereupon sent gentle commendations to our Generall, promising within few daies to come to him in person, which he performed accordingly.

The 5. day the foresaid gouernor, accompanied with a lusty Frier, & 20. other Spaniards, with their seruants, & Negroes, came downe to the sea side, where our ships road at anker, who being seene, our General manned immediatly the most part of his boats with the chiefe men of our fleete, euery man appointed, and furnished in the best sort: at the landing of our Generall, the Spanishe Gouernor[1] receiued him very curteously, and the Spanish Gentlemen saluted our English Gentlemen, and their inferiour sort did also salute our Souldiers and Sea men, liking our men, and likewise their qualities, although at the first, they seemed to stand in feare of vs, and of so many of our boats, whereof they desired that all might not land their men, yet in the end, the curtesies that passed on both sides were so great, that all feare and mistrust on the Spanyardes part was abandoned.

In the meane time while our English Generall and the Spanish Gouernor discoursed betwixt them of diuers matters, as of the state of the Country, the multitude of the Townes and people, and the commodities of the Iland, our men prouided two banquetting houses couered with greene boughs, the one for the gentlemen, the other for the seruants, and a sumptuous banquet was brought in serued by vs all in Plate, with the sound of trumpets, and consort of musick, wherewith the Spanyards were more than delighted. Which banquet being ended, the Spanyardes in recompense of our curtesie, caused a great heard of white buls, and kyne, to be brought together from the Mounteines, and appointed for euery Gentlemen and Captaine that woulde ride, a horse ready sadled, and then singled out three of the best of them to be hunted by horsemen after their manner, so that the pastime grew very plesant for the space of three houres, wherein all three of the beasts were killed, whereof

---

[1] The governor of Isabela and captain of Puerto de Plata was, apparently, Rengifo de Angulo, and the place of meeting is described as four leagues below (i.e. east of Puerto de Plata (Wright, *Further English voyages*, p. 16)).

one tooke the sea, and there was slaine with a musket. After this sport, many rare presents and gifts were giuen and bestowed on both partes,[1] and the next day wee plaied the Marchants in bargaining with them by way of trucke and exchange for diuers of their commodities, as horses, mares, kyne, buls, goates, swine, sheepe, bul hydes, sugar, ginger, pearle, tabacco, and such like commodities of the Iland.[2]

The 7. day we departed with great good will from the Spanyardes from the Island of Hispaniola: but the wiser sort do impute this greate shew of friendship, and curtesie vsed towardes vs by the Spanyards rather to the force that we were of, and the vigilancie, and watchfulnes that was amongst vs, then to any harty good will, or sure freindly intertainment: for doubtlesse if they had bene stronger than wee,[3] we might haue looked for no better curtesie at their handes, then Master Iohn Hawkins receiued at saint Iohn de Vllua,[4] or Iohn Oxnam neere the streights of Dariene,[5] and diuers others of our Countrymen in other places.

The 8. day we ankred at a small Iland to take Seales which in that place wee vnderstood to haue bene in great quantitie,[6] where the

[1] Nothing of these dealings had crept into any of the Spanish accounts so far seen, apart from a hint in the abstract of the intercepted letter from Diego Osorio (p. 739).

[2] It will be noted that, while the livestock (cp. pp. 735–6, 742, 747 and Wright, *Further English voyages*, pp. 10–12, 16) and sugar (so far as it consisted of rooted cane (p. 336)) were (with the banana plants, etc. (p. 742)) designed for the use of the Virginia colonists, the hides, ginger, pearls and tobacco were acquired for sale in England and must have contributed towards the profits of the venture. Were these bought with the cloth seized on their recent prize?

[3] How far this represents the writer's feelings and how far it was a politic cloak for this narrative of commercial diplomacy, now that hostilities were becoming open, it is not possible to say. It was clearly inserted after the event, possibly by Hakluyt.

[4] San Juan de Ulua, 1568.

[5] John Oxenham, 1576–7 (Williamson, *Age of Drake* (2nd ed., 1946), pp. 133–44).

[6] If Grenville, with the *Tiger*, the *Elizabeth*, his pinnace and two prizes, sailed north from Puerto de la Isabela, the island was probably an outlying member of the Turks and Caicos group. The West Indian Monk Seal, *Monachus tropicalis*, was not rare at this time (according to Mr F. C. Fraser, Brit. Mus. (N. H.)).

Generall and certaine others with him in the pinnesse, were in very great danger to haue bene all cast away, but by the helpe of God they escaped the hazard, and returned aboord the Admirall[1] in safetie.

The 9. day we arriued and landed in the Isle of Caycos, in which Islande we searched for salt pondes,[2] vpon the aduertisment, and information of a Portingall: who in deede abused our General and vs, deseruing a halter for his hire, if it had so pleased vs.[3]

The 12. we ankered at Guanema, and landed.[4]

The 15. and 16. we ankered and landed at Sygateo.[5]

The 20. we fell with the mayne of Florida.[6]

The 23. wee were in great danger of a Wracke on a breache called the Cape of Feare.[7]

The 24. we came to anker in a harbor where we caught in one tyde so much fishe as woulde haue yelded vs xx. pounds in London: this was our first landing in Florida.[8]

[1] The *Tiger*. This may be one of the three places where Lane says (p. 212) the expedition was nearly destroyed by Grenville's carelessness.

[2] In margin: 'They land on Iles of Caicos' (Hakluyt, III (1600), 253). If they sailed through the Silver Bank Passage the island is likely to have been either East Caicos or Grand Caicos.

[3] The Portuguese is likely to have been Fernandez, whom the writer blames also for the grounding of the *Tiger* (p. 189 below), but a Spanish account (p. 742) mentions another Portuguese with the squadron. This is a further example of the friction generated on the voyage (cp. pp. 197-8, 210-14).

[4] 'Guanima', in margin (Hakluyt, III (1600), 253). Thereafter the *Tiger's* course can be traced through the Bahamas with rather more certainty from White's map (fig. 6, p. 460). Guanima appears on this north of Moyagora (probably Mariguana) and apparently represents a combination of Cat Island and Eleuthera. In the Diogo Homem map of 1568 (Wright, *English voyages to the Caribbean, 1527-68*) 'Guainima' most probably represents Cat Island.

[5] 'Cyguateo', in margin (Hakluyt, III (1600), 253). White's 'Cigatao' is apparently Great Abaco, though Diogo Homem's 'Gatao' is probably Eleuthera.

[6] White's map suggests that the *Tiger* sailed through Providence N.W. Channel, in which case they may have sighted the mainland coast about lat. 27° N.

[7] Cape Feare was identified, at least in De Bry's version of White's map, with what is now Cape Lookout (p. 868), though White himself distinguishes two capes, each with its dependent shoals, but does not name them (fig. 7, p. 461). Possible interpretations therefore exist for either present-day Cape Fear or Cape Lookout: my own preference would lie towards the former in this case.

[8] If the assumption above is correct, Beaufort Harbour is the most likely location (though the White maps give several inlets in the Banks north of Cape

The 1585 Voyage

The 26. we came to anker at Wocokon.[1]

The 29. wee waighed anker to bring the Tyger into the harbour, where through the vnskilfulnesse of the Master whose name was Fernando, the Admirall strooke on grounde, and sunke.[2]

Iuly.

The 3. we sent word of our ariuing at Wococon, to Wingino at Roanocke.[3]

The 6. *Master* Iohn Arundell was sent to the mayne, and Manteio with him:[4] and Captayne Aubry,[5] and Captaine Boniten the same day were sent to Croatoan, where they found two of our men left there, with 30. other by Captaine Reymond, some 20. daies before.

Lookout and south of the next anchorage). Any suggestion that White drew here from life his man and woman of Florida is completely mistaken (nos. III, 1–2, see p. 462 below). It should be remembered that the whole of the east coast, as far north as the Hudson at least, could be described as Florida.

[1] The inlet at the southern end of an island in the Banks of that name which, it is argued on p. 867, was made up of parts of the present Portsmouth and Ocracoke Islands. For its shoals see the sketch-map (fig. 3, p. 215).

[2] The *Tiger* got completely out of control and struck repeatedly on the shoal. Eventually she was mastered (probably taken off under tow) and safely beached (cp. p. 201). The blame assigned to Fernandez by the writer (and apparently by Grenville as well as his friends) was not shared by Lane (pp. 201–2).

[3] 'Wingina at Roanak' (Hakluyt, III (1600), 253). It is probable that a boat, or the new pinnace, was sent through the inlet to sail across Pamlico Sound to the northern end of Roanoke Island (some 90–100 miles sailing). This is in places a difficult course. She must, at least, have been piloted by someone who had been out in 1584.

[4] 'Arundel'; 'Manteo' (Hakluyt, III (1600), 253). Possibly to the mainland across Pamlico Sound (Secoton?), though Manteo (now first named in the 1589 texts) had been born on Croatoan Island (cp. p. 616); no indication is possible of what vessel they may have used. However, a second pinnace may by now have been available.

[5] Captain Aubrey (possibly a connexion of William Aubrey (1529–95), a friend of John Dee), and Captain Bonython (as this is the usual form of his name as found in Cornwall), were quite possibly captains of the two Spanish prizes. Croatoan, being the island immediately to the north of Wococon, could be approached by sea and it is likely that they took their vessels outside Cape Hatteras to the Chacandepeco inlet north of the cape where there was an Indian settlement (cp. p. 866). The sketch-map would suggest that among their discoveries was a root used for red dye (cp. pp. 215–16).

The 8. Captaine Aubry, and Captaine Boniten returned with two of our men found by them to vs at Wocokon.[1]

The 11. day the Generall accompanied in his Tilt boate[2] with Master Iohn Arundell,[3] Master Stukelye,[4] and diuers other Gentelmen, Master Lane, Master Candish, Master Harriot,[5] and 20. others in the new pinnesse,[6] Captaine Amadas, Captaine Clarke,[7] with tenne others in a ship boate, Francis Brooke,[8] and Iohn White[9] in another ship boate, passed ouer the water from Ococon[10] to the mayne land victualled for eight dayes, in which voyage we

[1] Captain George Raymond had thus arrived with the *Lion* near Cape Hatteras about 16 June. He may have already left some men on Jamaica (cp. pp. 164–5). He sailed to Newfoundland and is likely to have taken in supplies there before he made contact with the *Golden Royal* (cp. pp. 236, 238). It seems likely that the other men left on Croatoan were found later.

[2] A Thames boat with an awning over the bows to shelter passengers. She could have been the double wherry (cp. pp. 141, 256, 264).

[3] Arundell's expedition, begun on the 6th, cannot have taken him far, if he was ready to set out again with Grenville five days later.

[4] 'Stukely' (Hakluyt, III (1600), 253); see pp. 230–1.

[5] 'Hariot' (Hakluyt, III (1600), 253). This is the first glimpse of him in action and it is worth noting that he was not here working in partnership with White.

[6] The first mention of her use, though it is suggested above that she may have been sent to Roanoke Island on the 3rd. She appears under sail in the direction of Pamlico River on White's map (fig. 7, p. 461).

[7] If John Clarke was captain of the *Roebuck* (pp. 153, 210), then at some time since Grenville's arrival at Wococon on 26 June (and probably after the return of Aubry and Boniten on 8 July) he had been joined by some or all of the vessels with which he had long parted company: the *Roebuck*, the *Dorothy* and the second small pinnace.

[8] The earliest reference to the expedition's high treasurer (cp. pp. 210, 742). He has not been positively identified, but he may be the Captain Francis Brooke, gentleman, of London, who commanded the privateer *Eleanour* of London in 1590 and, probably, the *William Bonaventure* of Southampton in 1591 (Andrews, 'Elizabethan privateering', pp. 282, 290).

[9] This is the only certain reference to John White's presence in Virginia in 1585 (cp. pp. 196–7), but the fact that he is named along with the high treasurer, Francis Brooke, indicates that he was not a humble craftsman but an official of some standing in the hierarchy. Of his drawings nos. 33–8, see pp. 415–24, are probably, and nos. 39–44, pp. 424–32, possibly, the fruits of this expedition.

[10] 'Wococon' (Hakluyt, III (1600), 253). For the probable route taken by the expedition see map at end, and also the sketch map recording the results of their discoveries (fig. 4, p. 215).

first discouered the townes of Pomioke, Aquascogoc and Secota, and also the great lake called by the Sauages Paquype,[1] with diuers other places, and so returned with that discouery to our Fleete.

The 12. we came to the Towne of Pomeioke.[2]

The 13. we passed by water to Aquascococke.[3]

The 15. we came to Secotan and were well intertayned there of the Sauages.[4]

The 16. we returned thence, and one of our boates with the Admirall was sent to Aquascococke to demaund a siluer cup which one of the Sauages had stolen from vs, and not receiuing it according to his promise, we burnt, and spoyled their corne, and Towne, all the people beeing fledde.[5]

The 18. we returned from the discouery of Secotan, and the same day came aboord our fleete ryding at Wocokon.[6]

The 21. our fleete ankering at Wokocon, we wayed anker for Hatoraske.

---

[1] 'Pomeiok'; 'Secotan'; 'Paquipe' (Hakluyt, III (1600), 253). The lake, now Lake Mattamuskeet, is roughly indicated—and rather exaggerated in size—in the sketch-map, lying between Pomeiooc and Secoton.

[2] This was some 30 miles from their starting point and is indicated as an enclosed village on the sketch-map: White may have made his drawings of the village and its people at this time (nos. 33–6; see pp. 415–20 below).

[3] 'Aquascogok' (Hakluyt, III (1600), 253). Not named on the sketch-map. White's drawings relating to the village present some difficulties (cp. pp. 439, 444).

[4] Secoton, the chief village of the Secotan tribe, is shown on the sketch-map as unenclosed. White's drawings of the village and its inhabitants were probably made on this occasion (nos. 37–41; see pp. 420–32). Soundings of the Pamlico River shown on the sketch-map give a depth of 3 fathoms.

[5] Philip Amadas, as admiral, was sent back with his boat to undertake these punitive operations, the first we hear of, against the Indians. On later occasions they were again to desert their villages rather than stay to fight (cp. pp. 206–7, 530). Grenville, with the remaining boats, if we can judge from the sketch-map, continued the exploration by identifying at least the mouths of the Neuse River and Core Sound (see pp. 215–16). They may have sailed some little way up the former.

[6] 'Wococon' (Hakluyt, III (1600), 253). This means that they came back to find the *Tiger* caulked and refloated and, with her consorts, anchored well off the treacherous shoals.

The 27. our fleete ankered at Hatoraske, and there we rested.[1]
The 29. Grangino, brother to King Wingino,[2] came aboord the Admirall, and Manteo with him.

August.

The 2. The Admirall was sent to Weapemeoke.[3]
The 5. Master Iohn Arundell was sent for England.[4]
The 25. our Generall wayed anker, and set saile for England.[5]
About the 31.[6] he tooke a Spanish ship of 300. tunne richly

---

[1] By 'Hatoraske' he means the inlet at the northern end of the island of Hatarask, which Lane called Port Ferdinando from its discovery by Simon Fernandez (pp. 201–2). If the discussion above (p. 95) is sound the discovery of this inlet was made in 1584. It is likely that the construction of a slipway was soon begun (cp. pp. 186, 202, 811, 902).

[2] 'Wingina' (Hakluyt, III (1600), 253). Granganimeo (see pp. 98–107) had probably come to invite Grenville to establish his settlement near the Indian village at the north-west end of Roanoke Island, and it was probably on this occasion that final decisions were taken on where the settlement should be and how many men were to stay in it. Manteo was needed as interpreter.

[3] Philip Amadas was being sent to explore Albemarle Sound, and since the pinnace could be taken it is possible that he went in her, though if there was not a second pinnace available one would be needed to begin shifting men and gear to Roanoke Island from Port Ferdinando. Amadas returned before 8 September (cp. pp. 207, 213, 216–17 below).

[4] He was probably sent in command of the fastest-sailing seaworthy vessel, possibly one of the prizes. His despatch was necessary to inform Raleigh that Grenville had arrived safely; to make it clear that the settlers would be poorly supplied on account of the accident to the *Tiger* and so would need supplies soon (cp. pp. 203, 344; Wright, *Further English voyages*, p. 15); and probably also to say that, in view of the absence of an adequate harbour for a privateering base, Grenville would not himself remain (cp. pp. 25–6, 168). We do not know when he arrived, but, as 'John Arondell, of Tolverne (at Richmond)' he was knighted on Thursday, 14 October (W. A. Shaw, *Knights of England*, II, 84), having by then, no doubt, delivered his report of the voyage to the queen (cp. pp. 174, 180 above).

[5] The laconic passing over of three important weeks is unfortunate. During this time the essential tasks of transferring the settlers to the Island and getting the houses and fort started were carried out. Lane was at Port Ferdinando writing letters on 12 August (pp. 197–206) but he evidently moved to his new headquarters on 17 August (p. 255). Grenville had probably to delay some days longer than he intended (cp. p. 203): he left the *Roebuck* at least behind him, and she could not have sailed before 10 September (pp. 210–14).

[6] Enrique Lopez (Wright, *Further English voyages*, p. 13) gives the date as 25 August/4 September which must be wrong.

loaden, boording her with a boate made with boards of chests, which fell a sunder, and sunke at the shippes side, assoone as euer hee and his men were out of it.[1]

September.

The 10. of September, by foule weather the Generall then shipped in the prise lost sight of the Tyger.[2]

October.

The sixt the Tyger fell with the landes ende, and the same day came to an anker[3] at Falmouth.

The 18. the Generall came with the prise to Plymmouth,[4] and was courteously receiued by diuerse of his worshipfull friends.[5]

---

[1] Lopez merely says that after the *Santa Maria de San Vicente* had surrendered, Grenville boarded from a boat with 30 (or 36) men, but it is highly probable that he left his ship's boats or boat with the colonists and had to improvise by constructing one hastily in this way. The index to the *Principall navigations* (1589) included this incident as 'His [Grenville's] valiant boording, & taking of a rich Spanish ship, with a little cocke boate'.

[2] Lopez (Wright, *Further English voyages*, p. 14) says that Grenville came on board with thirty-six men and transferred twenty Spaniards to the *Tiger*, along with most of the foodstuffs from the *Santa Maria*. The ships sailed in consort from near Bermuda to within some 1200 miles of the Azores, but were separated in a storm.

[3] 'to anker' (Hakluyt, III (1600) 253).

[4] He had reached Flores on 2/12 October (Wright, *Further English voyages*, p. 14) and had coerced the islanders into giving him supplies before he released his remaining twenty-two prisoners.

[5] The writer had probably remained on the *Tiger*, and it is probable that she came on to Plymouth to welcome the prize on her arrival (since all the *Tiger's* crew were entitled to shares in her). Raleigh was at Plymouth, but we do not know which of Grenville's other associates were there (cp. pp. 217–19). She then went to be 'well-repaired'. By 30 December she had been stripped of her guns and recommended for rearmament, while on 18 March 1586 she was still 'in the West Country', probably completing her refit at Plymouth (Lewis, 'Armada guns', in *Mariner's Mirror*, XXVII, 116–17; Corbett, *Spanish war*, pp. 229, 271, 300, 313). She was not therefore available for Grenville's 1586 expedition.

24. THE NAMES OF LANE'S COLONISTS[1]

The names of all those as well Gentlemen as others, that remained one whole yeere in Virginia, vnder the Gouernement of Master Ralfe Lane.

Master Philip Amades,[2]	Master Thomas Haruie.[8]
Admirall of the countrie.	Master Snelling.
Master Hariot.[3]	Master Anthony Russe.[9]
Master Acton.[4]	Master Allyne.[10]
Master Edward Stafford.[5]	Master Michel Polyson.[11]
Thomas Luddington.	Iohn Cage.
Master Maruyn.	Thomas Parre.
Master Gardyner.[6]	William Randes.
Captaine Vaughan.[7]	Geffery Churchman.

[1] Richard Hakluyt, *Principall navigations* (1589), pp. 736–7, collated with III (1600), 254 (VIII (1900), 317–18): the order was changed by the printer in 1600.

[2] 'Amadas' (Hakluyt, III (1600), 254). Of him after this date we only hear specifically that he had some part in making the entrenchments for the Roanoke Island fort. It is suggested, however, that it may be to him that Lane refers when he speaks of 'the colonel of the Chesepians' (p. 287 below).

[3] We must imply Thomas Hariot's position from his book (cp. pp. 318, 321).

[4] Was he the John Acton knighted at Cadiz in 1596 (Hakluyt, *Principal navigations*, IV (1904), 259)?

[5] Captain Edward Stafford was probably commander of one of Lane's companies (cp. pp. 283, 288). He has so far defied identification though he was probably some relative of Sir Edward Stafford (1552?–1605), ambassador at Paris. In 1589 he was serving under Raleigh in Devonshire (Lodge, *Illus. of English history* (3rd ser.), III (separate list of Talbot papers, p. 61)).

[6] 'Gardiner' (Hakluyt, III (1600), 254).

[7] He may have been the commander of Lane's second company (cp. pp. 132, 137, 286). He is probably the John Vaughan noted in the list of captains of 5 January 1586 as absent (Corbett, *Spanish war*, p. 293).

[8] Grocer and citizen of London, cape merchant of the expedition (pp. 232–4 below).

[9] Anthony Rowse, 'the friend and later an executor of Drake's' (Rowse, *Grenville*, p. 205; pp. 119, 123 above).

[10] A Thomas Allen, esq., afterwards settled on Raleigh's lands in White's Island, co. Cork, but the name is, of course, a common one (*Cal. S.P., Ire., 1588–92*, p. 171; Quinn, *Raleigh*, p. 143).

[11] 'Polison' (Hakluyt, III (1600), 254).

Master Kendall.[1]

Master Prideox.[2]

Robert Holecroft.

Rise Courtney.

Master Hugh Rogers.

Thomas Foxe,

Edward Nugen.[3]

Darby Glande.[4]

Edward Kelle.[5]

Iohn Gostigo.[6]

Erasmus Clefs.[7]

Edward Ketcheman.

Iohn Linsey.

Thomas Rottenbury.

Roger Deane.

Iohn Harris.

William Farthowe.[8]

Iohn Taylor.

Philppe Robyns.

Thomas Phillippes.[9]

Valentine Beale.

Iames Skinner.

George Eseuen.

Iohn Chaundeler.[10]

Philip Blunt.

Richard Poore.

Robert Yong.

Marmaduke Constable.

Thomas Hesket.[11]

William Wasse.

Iohn Feuer.

Daniel.[12]

---

[1] Of Pelyn near Lostwithiel? (cp. J. L. Vivian, *Visitations of Cornwall*, p. 259).

[2] Grenville had been associated shortly before he sailed with a Richard Prideaux (Rowse, *Grenville*, p. 177). Mr Rowse describes Master Prideaux as 'one of the Prideaux of Padstow' (p. 205). There were four branches of the Prideaux family in Devonshire which had sons of suitable ages (J. L. Vivian, *Visitations of Devon*, pp. 617, 619, 621, 624, cp. his *Visitations of Cornwall*, p. 611).

[3] Lane's 'Irishman seruing me, one Nugent' (p. 287), who probably had been in Kerry with him.

[4] Precedes 'Nugen' (Hakluyt, III (1600), 254). For his statement see pp. 834–8 below. He was an Irishman who deserted from White's expedition in 1587 (pp. 519–20). His name may have been Glany or Glavin (cp. pp. 519, 834).

[5] 'Kelley' (Hakluyt, III (1600), 254). He is likely to be the man of this name who served on the *Moonlight* in 1590 and was drowned at Port Ferdinando (p. 612 below). He was probably Irish.

[6] He too was possibly Irish (Costigan).

[7] He was possibly German (and if so probably a miner), or Dutch.

[8] 'Farthow' (Hakluyt, III (1600), 254).

[9] 'Philips' (Hakluyt, III (1600), 254); he was possibly Welsh.

[10] 'Chandeler' (Hakluyt, III (1600), 254).

[11] There was a Thomas Hackett in Raleigh's company in Munster in 1589 who may have been the same man (*Cal. S.P., Ire., 1588–92*, p. 172; Quinn, *Raleigh*, p. 143).

[12] Possibly, like the Saxon of the same name lost in 1583 (Quinn, *Gilbert*, pp. 87, 408, 414, 417), a miner; and conceivably Daniel Höchstetter, the younger, who was concerned with the Keswick copper mines and was still alive in 1604 (cp. W. G. Collingwood, *Elizabethan Keswick*, p. 201).

Frauncis Norris.	Thomas Taylor.
Mathewe Lyne.	Richard Humfrey.
Edward Kettell.	Iohn Wright.[3]
Thomas Wisse.	Gabriell North.
Robert Biscombe.	Bennet Chappell.
William Backhouse.	Richard Sare.
William White.	Iames Lasie.[4]
Henry Potkin.	Smolkin.
Dennis Barnes.	Thomas Smart.
Ioseph Borges.	Robert
Doughan Gannes.[1]	Iohn Euans.[5]
William Tenche.	Roger Large.
Randall Latham.	Humfrey Garden.
Thomas Hulme.	Frauncis Whitton.
Walter Myll.[2]	Rowland Griffyn.[6]
Richard Gilbert.	William Millard.
Steuen Pomarie.	Iohn Twyt.[7]

[1] 'Dougham Gannes' (Hakluyt, III (1600), 254), Lane's mineral expert, 'Master Youghan' or 'Yougham' (pp. 274, 331–2 below). He can be identified as the Jochim Gaunse (Joachim Ganz) who was associated in 1581 with George Nedham in the smelting of copper by improved methods at the Keswick works of the Mines Royal Company, and who shortly afterwards put forward plans for 'makeing of Copper, vitriall, and coppris, and Smeltinge of Copper and Leade ures' (S.P. 12/142, 88–9; G. Grant Francis, *The smelting of copper in the Swansea district* (2nd ed., 1881), pp. 25–34 (although there is no positive evidence that Ganz was associated with the Neath smelting works of the Mines Royal); *Elizabethan Keswick*, ed. W. G. Collingwood (1912), p. 202). He was probably Jeochim Gaunz, the Jew, born in Prague, but living in Blackfriars, London, who was examined at Bristol in September 1589 on charges of blasphemy by denying the divinity of Christ (S.P. 12/226, 40). If this is so he may have been the son of David Ganz, astronomer and historian, b. in Westphalia 1541, d. at Prague 1613 (see I. Abrahams, 'Joachim Gaunse: a mining incident in the reign of Queen Elizabeth', in *Trans. Jewish Historical Society*, IV (1903), 83–103).

[2] 'Mill' (Hakluyt, III (1600), 254).

[3] Of the same name as, and probably identical with, a man who accompanied White in 1587 (cp. p. 541 below).

[4] 'Lacie' (Hakluyt, III (1600), 254): he is evidently the man who returned with White in 1587 and remained in Virginia (p. 541). He may have been Irish.

[5] Possibly Welsh.　　　　　　　　　[6] Probably Welsh.

[7] 'Twit' (Hakluyt, III (1600), 254). As John White remained in Virginia, which is almost certain (p. 41 above), this may have been he, although Twit and

Iohn Brocke.	Edwarde Seklemore.[4]
Bennet Harrye.[1]	Iohn Anwike.
Iames Steuenson.	Christopher Marshall.
Charles Steuenson	Dauid Williams.
Christopher Lowde.	Nicholas Swabber.
Ieremie Man.	Edward Chipping.
Iames Mason.[2]	Syluester Beching.
Dauid Salter.	Vincent Cheyne.
Richard Ireland.	Haunce Walters.[5]
Thomas Bookener.	Edward Barecombe.
William Philippes.[3]	Thomas Skeuelabs.
Randall Mayne.	William Walters.

25. 12 AUGUST 1585.

RALPH LANE TO SIR FRANCIS WALSINGHAM[6]

R*ight* honorable, The bearer hereof M*aste*r Attekynson yo*ur*
ho*nours* s*er*vante[7] hathe carryed him selfe soo honestely, and soo
industryously in all occasyones and acciones of thys voyeage, that
I canne not lesse doo hauynge sume prynsypalle chardege in yᵉ
same to note him by thys my bolde l*et*tre to your ho*nour*, for one
moost worthye of grete accompte emongest vs, and w*ith* yo*ur*
ho*nour*, not to bee yᵉ lesse reckenned of in thys behalfe, hauynge
doonne your ho*nour* by suche hys honeste demeano*ur*s as myche
honour as eny s*er*vante canne doo to soo honorable a m*aste*r :/

Tuite are surnames in their own right. Other alternatives are that he is mistakenly put down as William White (above), that he compiled the list himself
and omitted his own name, or that he was simply omitted by a printer's error.

  [1] 'Harrie' (Hakluyt, III (1600), 254).

  [2] There was a James Masone, settled with his family on Raleigh's estates in
co. Waterford in 1589, who may have been the same (*Cal. S.P., Ire., 1588–92*,
p. 170; Quinn, *Raleigh*, p. 143).

  [3] 'Philips' (Hakluyt, III (1600), 254): possibly Welsh.

  [4] 'Seclemore' (Hakluyt, III (1600), 254).

  [5] 'Hance' (Hakluyt, III (1600), 254): just possibly 'Hance the Surgion' of the
Moonlight in 1590, who was drowned at Port Ferdinando (p. 612 below).

  [6] Holograph. State Papers Colonial, C.O. 1/1, 4.

  [7] Atkinson has not been identified. It was apparently by him or by Russell
that the letters of this date were carried to England.

I haue also wrytten to your honour, by your servante Master Russelle to a lyke effecte, Who notwithstandynge ye generales dysplesure towardes him; and his complayentes, wyll neuerthelesse I am persuaded cleare him selfe very well to your honour of Euery chardege or ymputacione whatsoeuer:[1] And euen soo sir, humbly comyttyng your honour to ye mercyes of ye Allmyghty, For thys tyme I take my leaue of ye same.

From the Porte FerdyNando, in Verginia,[2] ye 12th of Auguste:

<u>1585</u>   Your honours, humble and most assured,

Rafe Lane

[*Addressed:*] To ye Right honorable Sir Frances Wallsyngham Knight, prynsypall Secrettary to her maiesty and one of her highness most honorable pryvy Counselle: thys bee deliuered at ye courte, of ENglande./

[*Endorsed:*] 1585 12 Aug.

Master Rafe Lane. from Virginia

Virginia[3]

---

[1] He was probably the Rowland Russell, who offered his continuing services to Walsingham in humble terms in 1581 (S.P. 15/27, 58, *Cal. S.P. Dom., Add., 1580–1625*, p. 52). The editors of the *Calendars* cannot make up their minds whether he is the Gregory (or Rowland) Russell (or Rossel), who was serving John Gilpin, secretary of the Merchant Adventurers at Antwerp (ibid. p. 21; *Cal. S.P., For., 1579–80*, pp. 264, 266, *1581–2*, p. 644). Walsingham thus contributed at least three members of his household, apart from his own investment, to the expedition. It may have some significance on the origin of the quarrel that two at least, Russell and Fernandez, were Walsingham's men. It may, too, be the case that, as we hear no more of his participation in the Virginia venture after 1585, Walsingham accepted Lane's and his servants' view of Grenville's incapacity for leadership. Mr Rowse takes this second paragraph to refer to Atkinson, not Russell (*Grenville*, pp. 223–4), but, while it is not impossible that Lane meant this, it appears unlikely. The testimonial (for this is what it would have amounted to) sent by Russell is apparently not extant.

[2] This and the letters following are the earliest letters sent from an English North American settlement. At this date—the seventeenth day after his arrival—Lane was probably in some temporary lodging on shore on Hatarask Island supervising the unloading of materials for the Roanoke Island fort.

[3] 'from Virginia' and 'Virginia' are in a different hand from the rest of the endorsement.

The 1585 Voyage

26. 12 AUGUST 1585.

RALPH LANE TO SIR FRANCIS WALSINGHAM[1]

Right honorable, With humble Remembrance of all dewetye and most hartye affeccione vnto you, accordynge as I acknowledge my selfe to haue moost good cause: The Generalles returne in hys owene personne into Englande dothe presently[2] cutte me of from vsinge[3] cyrcumstances in reporte of ye partycularityes of thys countreye in thys my lettre vnto your honor: / Only thys yt maye plese you by mee in generally to vnderstande, that thys our presente arryvalle into thes partes, thoughe late in ye yeare, (and that whoolly thoroughe ye defalte of him y^t intendethe to accuse others)[4] hathe neuerthelesse dyscouerdde vnto vs soo many, soo rare, and soo singulare commodytyes (by ye vnyuersalle opynyone bothe of our Appotycaryes[5] and all our merchantes[6] here) of thys her Maiestes newe kingedom of Verginia, As all ye kingedomes and states of Chrystendom theyere commodytyes ioyegned in one together, doo not yealde ether more good, or more plentyfulle whatsooeuer for publyck vse ys needefull, or pleasinge for delyghte.[7] They partycularytyes whereof I leaue to ye generalles reporte,[8]

[1] Holograph. State Papers Colonial, C.O. 1/1, 3. Lane may have sent other letters, including possibly the lost letter to Queen Elizabeth (p. 474), by John Arundell on the 5th (p. 192). The letters of 12 August were in all probability taken by the *Tiger* on 25 August, but in the care of Atkinson and Russell.

[2] The *Tiger* evidently intended to clear for England earlier than she did.

[3] Followed by an illegible word crossed out.

[4] The first charge by Lane against Grenville and his party: from the *Tiger* journal it is clear that Simon Fernandez was one of those likely to be accused by Grenville (p. 189).

[5] It is not known that any apothecary remained with Lane, though there had been suggestions that one should be sent (pp. 135, 213, 334).

[6] If Thomas Harvey was one of them he changed his tune later (pp. 232–4 below). It is probable that during Grenville's stay brisk bartering was carried on with the Indians (on the lines described by Barlowe for 1584, pp. 100–1), if only to provide an adequate range of specimens to bring home.

[7] For such a brief experience of America, Lane is certainly giving way to hyperbole!

[8] We have from Grenville, directly, only a very general statement (pp. 218–19): a more elaborate report probably lies behind the Holinshed account (pp. 173–8).

As also to yᵉ iudgementes of all your honores, your selfes, and yᵗ vppon yᵉ vyewe, of a grete amasse of good thynges yᵗ hee bryngethe hys shippe presently frayegheted with*all*; to avoyde all suspycyone of fraude:¹ / Theye thynges yᵗ wee haue had tyme as yeate to see, and to sende, are but suche as are fyrst cum*m*en to hande *with* very smalle s*e*rche, and w*h*ich² doo presente them selfes vpp*on* the vpp*er* face of yᵉ Earthe: They barreneste, and moost suncken plattes whereof, doo neu*er*thelesse, euery where yealde sumwhat yᵗ ether for knowen V*er*tue ys of pryce in Chrystendom, or sumwhat at leeste to yᵉ smelle plesinge; Not hauynge as yeate founde on all *our* s*e*rche one stynckinge weede³ growynge in thys lande; (A matter in all *our* opynyones here very straunge) / Into yᵉ bowelles of yᵉ Earthe as yeate we haue not s*e*rched:⁴ And therefore not meanynge to adu*er*tyse your ho*nor*, of eny thinge yᵗ myne owene eyes haue not seene, I leaue to certefye your ho*nor* of what lyckelyhuddes founde, or what yᵉ sauuages reporte of better⁵ matters: / The mayene Terrytory As yt ys Vaste [fo. 1 v.] and huge, and replenysshed as beefores*aid*, Soo also all yᵉ entryes into yᵉ same are soo by Nature fortefyed to yᵉ sea warde, by reason of a shoelle⁶ and moost daungerouse coaste aboue 150 leagues⁷ lyinge all alonge thys her ma*ie*stes domynyone allready dyscou*er*dde, That yt ys not w*ith* grete Shippinge at eny hande to bee d*e*lte *with* all:⁸ / There bee only in all iij Entryes, and Portes; The one w*h*ich

¹ We have no full account of the specimens he brought. Those mentioned on pp. 207, 215–17, were probably included.

² 'growe' crossed out.

³ 'In' crossed out.

⁴ Mineral and mining experts were suggested for the expedition (p. 136), and at least one was left with Lane (p. 274). Their achievements as recorded by Hariot (pp. 327, 332–3 below) are not impressive.

⁵ 'suche' crossed out.

⁶ Shoaly: an earlier use of the word than is recorded in *OED*.

⁷ 120 leagues (360 miles) would be a rough approximation of the Cape Fear—Cape Henry coastline.

⁸ This was probably to tell Walsingham that the coast, as so far discovered, could not be used to provide harbourage or bases for privateering (cp. p. 22).

wee haue named TryNytye harboroughe,[1] The other Ococan,[2] in yᵉ Entry whereof[3] all our Fleete strucke agrounde,[4] and yᵉ Tyger[5] lyinge beatynge vppon yᵉ shoalle for yᵉ space of ij houres by yᵉ dyalle,[6] wee were all in extreeme hasarde of beyng casteawaye, but in yᵉ ende by yᵉ mere worck of god flottynge of wee ranne her agrounde harde to yᵉ shoare, and soo with grete spoyelle of[7] our prouysyones, saued our selfes and ye Noble shippe also,[8] with her backe whoolle, which all they marryners aborde thoughte coolde not possybelly but haue beene brooken in sunder; hauynge abydden by iuste talle[9] aboue ,89, strockes agrounde:[10] The iijᵈᵉ Entry and beste harboroughe[11] of all yᵉ reste, ys the Porte which is called FerdyNando Dyscouerdde by yᵉ master and Pylotte maggiore[12] of

[1] From the not too precise evidence available Trinity Harbour has been located on the map some 25 miles north of Port Ferdinando, where Lane was writing (p. 863 below). If this was so it indicates that exploring parties had pushed northwards along the coast—it is presumably the most northerly of the inlets in the September 1585 sketch-map (p. 215). It is suggested that the name was probably given because the inlet was found on one of the Sundays after Trinity (either 1 or 8 August) following the *Tiger's* arrival at Port Ferdinando, if it had not already been discovered in 1584.

[2] Wococon (cp. pp. 111, 867), believed to have been the inlet which would now lie about half-way along Portsmouth Island.   [3] 'wee were wrekte' crossed out.

[4] This is the only indication that other vessels went aground as well as the *Tiger*: but presumably they were floated off with the tide.

[5] Three words (illegible) crossed out. This is the fullest account of the *Tiger's* stranding on 29 July, but cp. p. 189.

[6] A time-piece, probably a spring-clock like those described by Professor E. G. R. Taylor, in *Mariner's Mirror*, xxxvii, 59.

[7] 'all' crossed out. Cp. pp. 203, 344.

[8] 'Withoute' crossed out.   [9] Tally or count.

[10] Crossed out: 'Thys Porte in yᵉ Carte ys by yᵉ Spanyardes called Sᵗ Marryes baye'. This is of interest, as Lane evidently had a Spanish map at hand and as virtually nothing else is known of the cartographic equipment of the expedition. It is not possible to indicate precisely which map this was, but most Spanish maps contained (in one form or another) this name for Chesapeake Bay. It may be noted that on the sketch-map (p. 215), which was completed a few weeks after Lane's letter, there is the same equation of Wococon with the Spanish 'Bahia de Santa Maria'—evidently from the same map.

[11] Lane crossed this word through lightly and began another with 'E' (entrance?), but changed his mind a second time.

[12] Pilot-major, chief pilot. It is suggested above that the evidence points strongly to the discovery having been made in 1584 (p. 95).

o*ur* Fleete yo*ur* ho*nors* s*e*rvante Symon FerdyNando[1] who trewly hathe carryed him selfe bothe wi*th* greate skylle, and grete gou*er*nem*en*t all thys voyeage, notwi*th*standy*ng* thys grete crosse to vs all; As ye whoolle gynge[2] of m*as*te*r*es and marryn*er*s wyll wi*th* one voyce affyrme: / The ij harboroghes aboue mensyoned (Whereof Trynyty harboroughe ys one, and[3] only of viij foote, Vppo*n* the barre at hyghe wat*er*) are as you may Iudge: / Thys other called ye FerdyNando hathe a barre also, but at xij foote vppo*n* the same at hyghe wat*er*: and ye barre very shorte, bey*ng* wi*th*in iij, iiij, and v, fathom wat*er*: Soo as thys Porte at y*e* poynte of y*e* lande bey*ng* fortefyed wi*th* a skonse, yt ys not to bee ent*er*dde by all ye force y*t* Spayne canne make, wee hauyng y*e* fauure of God.[4] / The clymate ys soo whoollesom, yeate somewhat tendy*ng* to heate,[5] As y*t* wee haue not had one sycke synce wee [fo. 2] ent*er*dde into ye countrey; but sundry y*t* came sycke, are recou*er*d of longe dyseases especially of Reumes.[6]

My selfe haue vnd*er*taken wi*th* y*e* fauoure of God, and in hys feare, wi*th* a good compagnye moore aswell of gentlemen as others,

[1] Fernandez had already been described in 1582 as 'mr. Secretary Walsinghams man' (Quinn, *Gilbert*, II, 309). He may not have remained in Walsingham's service after 1585.

[2] Gang, or company. Compare the unfavourable view taken of Fernandez by the author of the *Tiger* journal (p. 189).

[3] 'but' crossed out.

[4] Lane considers Port Ferdinando as a single inlet, when in fact it was a double one dividing round a small island (and with the northern channel named, it is not known when, Port Lane). The point of land is, it is argued above, that where Amadas and Barlowe landed and took possession in 1584 (p. 94 above), and where a slipway was constructed (possibly at the time Lane was writing). It was at the northern tip of the island of Hatarask (p. 864). A sconce is a small fort or earthwork, usually used as a lookout or a link in a chain of communications (cp. pp. 262-3), but none was, in fact, built here. The emphasis on the need for defence against Spanish attacks is good evidence for the intention to use Virginia as a privateering base (pp. 22, 173), but the failure of the Spaniards in 1588 to find the fort justified the decision to conceal it on Roanoke Island (pp. 812-13).

[5] The area lies between the July isotherms of 70° and 80° F. with local temperatures often exceeding 90°, whereas Lane was used to averages of 60-65° in the same month in England.

[6] Rheums were colds, catarrh, bronchitis, pulmonary tuberculosis (occasionally also rheumatic pains), which would often be helped by the dry weather.

to remayene here,[1] ye returne of a newe supply. As resolute rather to loose our lyfes then to deferre a possessione to her Maieste, our Countrey, and that our moost Noble Patrone Sir Water Rawelley, of soo noble a kingedome, as by hys moost woorthy endeuoure and ynfynytte chardege, as also of your honor and ye reste of ye mooste honorable aduenturerres, our honorable entry ys made into (by ye mercy of God)[2] to ye conqueste of: And for myne owne parte doo finde my selfe better contented to lyue with fysshe for my dayely foode, and water for my dayelye dryncke,[3] in ye prosecucione of suche one Accione, then oute of ye same to lyue in ye greateste plenty y^t ye Courte coolde gyue mee: Comforted cheefely hereunto with an assuerance of her Maiestes gretenes hereby to growe by ye Addycione of suche a kingedom as thys ys to y^e[4] reste of hir Domynyones, by meane whereof lykewyse ye Churche of Chryste thoroughe Chrystendom, may by ye mercy of God in shorte tyme finde a relyfe and freedom from ye seruytude, and tyrannye y^t by Spayene (beynge ye swoorde of y^t Antychryste of Rome and hys secte) ye same hathe of longe tyme beene moost myserabelly oppressed with;[5] / Not doutyng in ye mercy of God, to bee[6] suffycently provyded for by hime, and most assuered by fayethe in Chryste y^t rather then hee wyll sufferre hys ennemyes ye Papystes to tryumphe ouer ye ouerthrowe, ether of thys most Chrystyan Accione or of vs hys poore seruantes in yt thoroughe famyne or other wante,[7] beyng in a vaste Countrey yett vn-manuredde, (thoughe most apte for yt) that hee wyll commaunde

---

[1] Grenville's decision to return was probably taken in the last few days of July or at the beginning of August (cp. pp. 192, 199), and, it is argued, was due primarily to the failure to find an adequate harbour (pp. 25–6, 168). It is probable that of those who remained the gentlemen were volunteers.

[2] Grenville also refers to Walsingham as an adventurer in the expedition (p. 220), but we have no specific information regarding the others (cp. pp. 123–4, 283).

[3] Not to be taken too literally, but as an oblique reference to the lack of stores (cp. pp. 201, 274, 344).

[4] Written 'y^e to'.

[5] The familiar motif (cp. pp. 206, 490) is here combined with a militant Protestantism.

[6] 'preserued' crossed out.   [7] 'y^t he' crossed out.

even yᵉ Ravennes to feede vs, As hee did by hys seruante yᵉ Prophett Abacuc,[1] and yᵗ only for hys mercyes sake: To yᵉ which I moost hartely comytt your honor, and with my humble commendaciones to my lady your Wyffe, for thys tyme I take my leaue of yᵉ same: / From yᵉ Porte FerdyNando, in Verginia:[2] the 12ᵗʰ of Auguste: 1585

Your honors humble and most assuered duryng lyfe:

Rafe Lane: ///

[*Addressed:*] To yᵉ Right honorable Sir Frances Wallsingham, Knight, Prynsypalle Secrettary to her Maieste, and one of her highness, moost honorable pryvy Counselle: thys bee deliuered att yᵉ Courte of ENgland.

[*Endorsed:*] 12 August 1585. From Master Ralphe Lane. Virginia.[3]

27. 12 AUGUST 1585.

RALPH LANE TO SIR PHILIP SIDNEY[4]

My moost Noble Generalle.[5] Albeyt in yᵉ myddest of infynytt busynesses, As hauyng, emungst sauuages, yᵉ chardege of wylde menn of myne owene nacione,[6] Whose vnrulynes ys suche as not to gyue leasure to yᵉ goouernour to bee all most at eny tyme from

---

[1] Habakkuk.

[2] This is the least legible and coherent of Lane's surviving letters, probably reflecting the circumstances in which it was written.

[3] 'Virginia' is in a different hand from the rest of the endorsement.

[4] Holograph. State Papers Colonial, C.O. 1/1, 5.

[5] This title is a courtesy one derived from Sidney's projected post as commander of the land forces (lieutenant-general) in the earlier plans for Drake's West Indian expedition. According to Fulke Greville (*Life of Sidney* (1907), p. 109) his object was to 'invade possess, & inhabite some well chosen havens in Peru, Mexico, or both' (cp. pp. 206–7 below). Sir Sidney Lee (*DNB*, s.n.) says of him: 'He recommended in February 1585 the appointment of Ralph Lane as the first governor, and some of the letters which Lane wrote to Sidney the former incorporated in his account of Virginia.' There is no warrant for the first statement (see pp. 149–50 above), and the second is also misleading, since Lane did not include any reference to Sidney in his Virginia narrative (pp. 255–94 below) and this letter is, so far as is known, the only one from Lane to Sidney extant.

[6] He had commended them previously as 'a good compagnye' (p. 202) though he and others were to revise this opinion somewhat before the end.

them. Neuerthelesse I wolde not omytte, to wryte thes fewe lynes
of dewety, and affeccione vnto you; In yᵉ which I am to leaue you
to yᵉ letre which I wrotte to your most honorable father in lawe
Master Secrettary,¹ touchyng yᵉ aduertysementes of² thys her
Maiestes newe kingedom³ of Verginia, and yᵉ singularityes thereof,
and to aduertyese you alltogether (but bryefely) of⁴ sume such
matter as in our⁵ coursse hytherwardes wee haue found worthye of
your partycpacione: Which in fewe wordes ys thys, that yf her
maieste shall at eny tyme finde her selfe burthened with yᵉ King
of Spayene, wee haue by our dwellyng vppon yᵉ Ilande of Sᵗ Ihon
and Hyspagniola for yᵉ space of 5, weekes, soo dyscoueredde yᵉ
forces thereof with yᵉ infynytt ryches of yᵉ same, As that I find yt
an attempt most honorable and fesible, and proffytable, and only
fytte for your selfe to bee cheeffe commaunder in.⁶ / Thys entry
wolde soo gaulle yᵉ king of Spayene, as yt wolde dyuerte hys forces
yᵗ hee troublethe these partes of Chrystendom with, into thos partes
where hee⁷ canne not gretely annoye vs with⁸ them. And how
gretely a small force woulde garboyelle⁹ hym here, when ij of hys
most rychest and strongest Ilandes Sᵗ Iohn, and Hyspagnyola, tooke
suche allarmes of vs not only landyng but dwellyng vpon them
with only 120, menn,¹⁰ I referre yt to your Iudgement. [fo. 1 v.]
To conclude, findynge by myne owene vyewe, hys forces at Lande
to bee soo meane, and hys terror made soo grete emongeste vs in
ENgland, consyderyng that the reputacione thereof dothe all-
togeather growe from yᵉ mynes of hys threasor¹¹ and yᵉ same in

---

¹ Sidney had married, in 1583, Frances, daughter of Sir Francis Walsingham:
the letter referred to being no. 26 above.

² 'this Co' crossed out.

³ Technically a dominion, not a kingdom.

⁴ 'suche' crossed out.   ⁵ 'voyage' crossed out.

⁶ This letter was intended as encouragement to Sidney to pursue his West
Indian project.

⁷ 'coulde' crossed out.   ⁸ 'the same' crossed out.

⁹ Garboil, confuse or disturb.

¹⁰ Compare the numbers which the Spaniards believed had landed on Puerto
Rico (pp. 734, 739 above).

¹¹ 'which y' crossed out.

places which wee see here are soo easye bothe to bee taken and kepte by¹ eny small force sent by hyr Maieste, I colde not but wryte these ylle fasshyoned lynes vnto you, and to exhorte you my Noble Generalle by occasyone not to refuse yᵉ good oportunyty of suche a seruyce, to yᵉ churche of Chryste, of greate² releyffe from many callamytyes that thys threasor in Spanyardes handes, dothe inflycte vnto ye members thereof,³ veary honorable and proffytable for her maieste and our countrey, and moost commendable and fytte for yourselfe to bee yᵉ Enterpryser of: / And euen soo for thys tyme ceasyng further to trouble you, with my humble commendacyones to my lady your wyffe, I commytt you, my Noble Generalle, to yᵉ mercie of ye Allmyghty.

From yᵉ Porte FerdyNando in Verginia, yᵉ 12ᵗʰ of Auguste: 1585

Your poore soldyoure,

and assured at Commandement,

Rafe Lane

[*Addressed:*] To my moost honorable Frende, Sir Phyllyppe Sydney Knight thys bee delyuered at yᵉ Courte of ENglande.⁴

[*Endorsed:*] 12 August 1585

From master Ralphe Lane to Sir Phillippe Sydneye⁵

---

¹ 'her Maieste' crossed out.   ² Word (illegible) crossed out.

³ This familiar reference to the corrupting influence of Spanish treasure shows that Lane's indoctrination was complete.

⁴ Paper seal (bearded man's head?).

⁵ About 7 September following, Sidney appeared at Plymouth and asked Drake, then about to sail, to take him, though he was believed to have withdrawn from the expedition. Drake reacted by sending the news to court, and leaving the queen to recall him. Corbett (*Drake and the Tudor navy*, II, 15–19) has an ingenious, but untenable, explanation. According to him, Lane dated his letter New Style, which would be 2 August Old Style, and so caught Arundell's ship which left on 5 August. This, in turn, reached England by the end of the month. When Sidney received his letter from Lane he at once dashed down to Plymouth to join Drake (cp. pp. 250–1 below). A more recent biographer (Alfred H. Bill, *Astrophel or the life and death of the renowned Sir Philip Sidney*, pp. 276–9) suggests he went to Plymouth either as a joke or else to put pressure on Elizabeth to make him governor of Flushing. Fulke Greville, who accompanied him to Plymouth, insists that Sidney's intention to sail was genuine, and not the result of a change of mind after withdrawal (*Life of Sidney* (1907), pp. 70–8). After Drake had gone,

28. 3 SEPTEMBER 1585.

RALPH LANE TO RICHARD HAKLUYT THE ELDER, AND
MASTER H—— OF THE MIDDLE TEMPLE[1]

An extract of M*aster* Lanes letter, to M*aster* Richard Hakluyt
Esquire, and another gentleman of the middle Temple, from
Virginia:[2]

In the meane while you shall vnderstand that since sir Rich*ard*
Greenuils departure from vs,[3] as also before, we haue discouered
the maine[4] to bee the goodliest soile vnder the cope of heauen, so
abounding with sweete trees, that bring such sundry rich and most
pleasant gummes,[5] grapes of such greatnes, yet wild, as France,
Spaine nor Italy[6] hath[7] no greater, so many sortes of Apothecarie
drugs,[8] such seuerall kindes of flaxe,[9] and one kind like silke, the
same gathered of a grasse, as common there as grasse is here.[10] And
now within these few dayes we haue found here a Guinie wheate,[11]

perhaps influenced by Lane's letter, he planned a 'hazardous enterprize of Planting
upon the Main of America...with a design to possess Nombre de Dios, or some
other haven near unto it' (ibid. p. 117).
   [1] Richard Hakluyt, *Principall navigations* (1589), p. 793, collated with III (1600),
254–5 (VIII (1904), 319–20). The only other known connexion of the elder
Hakluyt with the enterprise was his 'Inducements' (in Taylor, *Hakluyts*, II,
327–41).
   [2] Richard Hakluyt, the younger, evidently received this letter from his elder
cousin only when the printing of his first edition was well advanced, and so he
adds 'the right place whereof is next before the Account of master Lane. Pagina
737', and there 'Master Ralph Lane's letter' went in 1600.
   [3] On the previous 25 August (p. 192).
   [4] Apparently as the result of the return of the expedition led by Philip Amadas
to Weapemeoc on 2 August (p. 192). This would imply that the information
included on the sketch-map (pp. 215–17 below) was available by the time this
letter was written.
   [5] See pp. 328, 334.
   [6] Specially noted on the sketch-map (in Weapemeoc) (pp. 215, 217).
   [7] 'haue' (Hakluyt, III (1600), 254).
   [8] Not, unfortunately, specified (cp. p. 334).
   [9] Cp. pp. 326–7 below.
   [10] Noted on the sketch-map as being found on the islets south-west of Roanoke
Island (pp. 215–16 and cp. pp. 325–6).
   [11] 'Maiz or or [*sic*] Guinie wheate' (Hakluyt, III (1600), 254); a good example
of Hakluyt's care in editing, and also of his willingness, where he thought it

whose eare yeeldeth corne for bread, 400. vpon one eare, and the Cane maketh very good and perfect suger,[1] also Terra Samia, otherwise Terra sigillata.[2] Besides that, it is the goodliest and most pleasing territorie of the world (for the soile is of an huge vnknowen greatnesse,[3] and very wel peopled and towned, though sauagelie) and the climate so wholesome, that we haue not had one sicke, since we touched land here.[4] To conclude, if Virginia had but Horses and Kine in some reasonable proportion, I dare assure my selfe being inhabited with English, no realme[5] in Christendome were comparable to it. For this alreadie we find, that what commodities soeuer Spaine, France, Italy, or the East parts do yeeld vnto vs in wines of all sortes, in oiles, in flaxe, in rosens, pitch,

helpful, to alter his text. Lane did not know the word 'maize' (cp. p. 213 below), but his identification of it with an African grain was not shared by contemporary naturalists, who usually ascribed its origin to Asia (especially the Near East, hence 'Turkey wheat') and America, or either. Thus John Gerard (*Herball* (1597), pp. 74–7) says: 'In England it is called Turky corne and Turkey wheate: the inhabitants of America and the Islandes adioining, as also the east and west Indies, do call it Maizium and Maizum and Mais.... These kinds of Graine were first brought into Spaine, and thence into other prouinces of Europe, out of Asia which is in the Turkes Dominions, as also out of America and the Ilands adioyning from the east and west Indies, and Virginia or Norembega, where they vse to sowe or set it, and to make bread of it, where it groweth much higher than in other countries.' It may be noted that in Thomas Johnson's edition of Gerard (1633) the passage is changed to deny an American origin for maize. (John J. Finan, 'Maize in the great herbals', in *Annals of the Missouri Botanic Garden*, xxxv (1948), 167–9; Agnes Arber, *The Gramineae* (1934), pp. 29–33.) The term 'Guinea wheat' remained in use in England, but for sorghum, not maize (for sorghum, see Arber, op. cit. pp. 16–24), and this may suggest the origin of Lane's mistake.   [1] Cp. p. 213 below.

[2] Samian Earth, or Sealed Earth (correctly Lemnian earth, i.e. from Lemnos, not Samos), was fine, red clay, used in medicine. It got its name of Terra Sigillata from being sold in lumps to which was affixed an official Turkish seal as proof of its authenticity (cp. Hariot, p. 328 below; John Smith, *Works*, p. 49; Strachey, *Hist. of travell*, p. 39; J. T. Bent, *Early voyages and travels in the Levant* (1893), pp. 282–5).

[3] 'the continent is of an huge and vnknowen greatnesse' (Hakluyt, III (1600), 254).

[4] 'that wee had not one sicke since we touched the land here' (Hakluyt, III (1600), 254). For other evidence on the health of the settlers see pp. 208–9, 384.

[5] In margin: 'The rich and manifold commodities of Virginia' (Hakluyt, III (1600), 255).

frankensence, currans, sugers, & such like,[1] these parts do abound with yᵉ growth of them all, but being Sauages that possesse the land, they know no vse of the same.[2] And sundry other rich commodities, that no parts of the world, be they West or East Indies, haue, here we finde great abundance of.[3] The people naturally most[4] curteous, & very desirous to haue clothes, but especially of course cloth rather then silke,[5] course canuas they also like wel of,[6] but copper carieth yᵉ price of all, so it be made red.[7] Thus good *Master* Hakluyt and master H.[8] I haue ioyned you both in one

[1] As for oil (e.g. walnut-oil), resin, pitch, and currants, Lane's estimate was superficially adequate, though only the timber products were worth commercial exploitation (cp. pp. 328–30, 363–6). But the flax was doubtful (cp. pp. 326–7) and sugar more so (p. 336), while frankincense was apparently a confusion with the Sweet Gum (pp. 97, 334).

[2] The implication may be that English settlers could exploit these natural products without disturbing the native Indian society.

[3] Hariot again was to stress 'secret' commodities (cp. pp. 336–7).

[4] 'are most' (Hakluyt, III (1600), 255): in margin: 'Commodities fit to carie to Virginia' (Hakluyt, III (1600), 255).

[5] They wanted clothes, but of course woollen cloth rather than silk. This was excellent news for both Hakluyts as they had stressed the need to find new markets for woollen cloth (Taylor, *Hakluyts*, II, 235, 313–14, 327, 331–2, 343). In fact, the Indians regarded European clothes merely as novelties and had little use for English woollens except as blankets.

[6] Some of the more astute Indians may have recognized that canvas could usefully replace the bark and fibre mats with which their houses were covered. It was not a suitable object for barter in quantity, however, as it was rather expensive and had largely to be imported into England.

[7] For the primary importance of copper as a medium of exchange and adornment see pp. 101–3, 268–9, 273–4, 332–3: it was not substantially in use for making tools (cp. pp. 274, 366).

[8] Richard Hakluyt the elder was admitted to the Middle Temple in 1550, but between that date and April 1585 there were no fewer than eighty-eight other men whose surnames began with 'H', none of whom has an obvious dual association with Lane and with the elder Hakluyt. One which is possible—though it is only a guess in the dark—is Sir Edward Hoby (the omission of the title might be the fault of the younger Hakluyt). He had already had some dealings with Sir Humphrey Gilbert (Hist. MSS Comm., *Cecil MSS*, III, 72–4; and the instructions for the 1582 voyage in his commonplace-book, Brit. Mus. Additional MS 38823, fos. 1–11, which also reveals an interest in Raleigh's Guiana voyage; Quinn, *Gilbert*, II, 335–8), and he had been admitted to the Middle Temple on 24 January 1584 (*Register of admissions to the Middle Temple*, ed. H. A. C. Sturgess, I; *Middle Temple records. Minutes of parliament*, I, 265).

letter of remembrance, as two that I loue dearely well, and commending me most hartily to you both, I commit you to ye tuition of the almighty. From the new Fort[1] in Virginia, this 3.[2] September 1585.

Your most assured friend, Rafe[3] Lane.

29. 8 SEPTEMBER 1585.

RALPH LANE TO SIR FRANCIS WALSINGHAM[4]

Right Honorable,

Sythence *Sir Richard* Greenefecldc, by ye tyme of ye arryvalle of thys my *lettre* ys to delyu*er* vnto your ho*nor*[5] as also to *Sir* Wa*lter* Rawlley o*ur* lorde,[6] sundry complayntes, against sundry gentlemen, of thys se*ruyce*; and p*artyc*ularely against o*ur* hyghe M*ars*shell M*aste*r Candysshe,[7] M*aste*r Edw*ard* Gorge[8] M*aste*r Frances brooke o*ur* Threasu*rer*,[9] and Capt*ain* Clerck, capt*ain* of ye flee boate,[10] I thoughte good thus muche to adue*rtyse* your ho*nor*

---

[1] This is the earliest reference to the fort on Roanoke Island (cp. pp. 903–10). On 12 August its construction was not even mentioned (pp. 168, 197–206). The light sandy soil would offer few difficulties in the way of roughing out the earthworks in a few days (cp. the rapidity of Lane's building in the West Indies, pp. 181, 185, 403–5), though considerable time could have been taken in perfecting them and in building inside the entrenchments.

[2] 'this third of' (Hakluyt, III (1600), 255). Since the following letter is dated 8 September (p. 214 below) it is very possible that Hakluyt misread the date of his original in this case and that it should be 8 September, especially as the other letter refers to a report about 'Gynneye wheate' which reached Lane on 5 September.

[3] In 1600 the Christian name becomes 'Ralph'.

[4] Holograph. State Papers Colonial, C.O. 1/1, 6.

[5] Since Grenville did not reach Plymouth until 18 October (p. 193), it is possible that this letter reached Walsingham before he made his report.

[6] Here he may be consciously stressing the mutual dependence of Grenville and himself on Raleigh.

[7] Thomas Cavendish is only here described as high marshal (elsewhere he appears as captain of the *Elizabeth*, pp. 182–3). The fact that he and Grenville should have fallen out was possibly a result of inadequate definition of the respective limits of their authority (cp. pp. 136–7 above).

[8] See p. 175 above.

[9] He is only here described as high treasurer (cp. pp. 190, 742); his undertreasurer remained with Lane (p. 290 below).

[10] Captain John Clarke is mentioned above (p. 180), but only here as captain of the fly-boat, the *Roebuck* (cp. p. 153 above). The identification of this ship

and that moost trewly concernynge them: That yt ys not possyble for men to beehaue them selfes moore fayethefully, and moore Industryousely in an Accione, (the same by yᵉ generalles only grete defalte hauynge beene made bothe moost payenefulle and moost perellouse) then euery of thes gentlemen, but especially *Master* Candysshe *our high* Marsshall, and *Master Frances* broke *our* Threasurer haue donne and that euen since yᵉ fyrste to yᵉ laste:[1] / Contrarywyse how *Sir Richard* Greenefeelde Generalle, hathe demeaned him selfe, from yᵉ fyrst daye of hys entry into gouernement at Plymmouth,[2] vntyll the daye of hys departure from hence ouer yᵉ barre in yᵉ Porte Ferdinando,[3] farre otherwyse then my hoope of him, thoughe very agreeable to yᵉ expectaciones, and predycciones of sundry wyse and godly personnes of hys owene Countreye,[4] that knewe hym better then my selfe, and partycularely how tyrannouse an Execucione withoute eny occasyone of my parte offered, hee not only purposed, but even propounded yᵉ same, to haue broughte mee, by indyrecte meanes, and moost vntrewe surmyses, to yᵉ questione for my lyfe, and that only for an aduyse, in a publycke consultacione by mee gyuen, which yf yt had beene executed had beene for yᵉ grete good of vs all, but moost cheefely of him selfe,[5] I am therefore to referre your honor to an ample dyscourse of the[6] whoolle voyeage in a booke to[7] *Sir Walter*

has an important bearing on what vessels reached Port Ferdinando. The letters were most probably being sent on board Clarke's ship.

[1] Compare the testimonials given by Lane to Fernandez, Atkinson and Russell (pp. 197–8, 201–2 above).

[2] This confirms the assumption above that Grenville took over command of the expedition at Plymouth after some of the ships had arrived there from the Thames (cp. pp. 151, 175 above).   [3] 25 August (p. 192 above).

[4] I.e. West Country men. Mr A. L. Rowse writes to me: 'I think his critics were to be found chiefly in Plymouth.'

[5] Lane is saying that, after giving certain advice (what it was we cannot guess unless it was to hurry through the West Indies to Virginia (cp. pp. 180, 188 above)), in open council, Grenville threatened to put him on trial for his life. Though this may have been only an instance of Grenville's hot temper, it is not unlikely that Grenville assumed too many of the prerogatives of justice to please Cavendish as high marshal (cp. pp. 136–7 above).

[6] He appears to have written 'yᵉ' and then altered it to 'the' or *vice versa*.

[7] 'your' crossed out.

Rawley dedycated of ye[1] same, wherein hys vsed manner of
[fo. I v.] proceedynge towardes all men in y⁰ Accione in generally,
and partycularely towardes my selfe (y⁰ same to bee approoued
by y⁰ testymonyes and deposycyones of Master Canndysshe,
Master Edward Gorge, and Captain Clercke) ys playenely and trewly
sette doune;[2] which gentlemen hee aparte and together at dyuers
tymes sounded, by all meanes to haue drawen theyere [con]sentes[3]
to have ioyegned with him vppon a mmost vntrewe surmyse
of hys owne,[4] to haue broughte my hedde in questione: Soo as
for myne owene parte I haue had soo muche experyence of hys
gouernement, as I am humbelly to desyre your honor and y⁰ reste
of my honorablest frendes, to gyue mee theyere fauoures to bee
freedde from y⁰ place where sir Richard Greenefeelde ys to carry
eny authorytye in chyeffe.[5] Assueringe you sir, with all y⁰ y⁰
Lorde hathe myraculosely bleste thys accione, that in y⁰ tyme of
hys beeynge emongest vs, euen thoroughe hys intollerable pryede,
and vnsaciable ambycione, hyt hathe not at iij seueralle tymes taken
a fynalle ouerthrowe,[6] y⁰ which had bene gretely to haue beene
pyttyed, not only in respecte of y⁰ losse of soo many subiectes,
but cheefely for y⁰ ruyne of soo honorable an Accione, which the
Lord to hys glory dothe dayely blesse here with[7] a dayely dyscouerye
of sumwhat rare growynge y⁰ Chrystendom wantethe, (as even

[1] Followed by 'whoolle voyage' and part of another word crossed out.
[2] Lane's discourse has not survived. If it reached Raleigh he may never have
passed it on to Walsingham. Lane is requesting Walsingham not only to insist
on seeing it, but to gather corroborative evidence from Cavendish, Gorges and
Clarke.
[3] Part of this word is torn off.
[4] He probably means that Grenville tried to induce them to put their names
to some statement which favoured himself, or, possibly, merely attempted to get
verbal assurances that they would uphold him.
[5] After his return to England in 1586 there is no indication that Lane ever did
serve under Grenville: at the same time he did not let any hint of his disagreement
slip into his account of the colony's fortunes (pp. 255-94 below). It must be
remembered, however, that this narrative was an edited one (cp. p. 29 above).
[6] Two of these occasions were probably the salt-taking episode at Cape Rojo
(pp. 184-5, 228-9) and the grounding of the *Tiger* (for which Grenville's
partisans blamed Fernandez (p. 189)).
[7] 'sume' crossed out.

iij dayes before ye date hereof[1] a kinde of Gynneye wheate[2] founde here growynge and vsualle, y[t] yealdethe bothe corne, and suger, whereof *our* Physycyan here hath sente an assaye to *our* Lord *Sir* W*alter* Rawlleye)[3] or elles of sume fertylle and plesante prouynces in y[e] mayene fytte to bee cyvylly, and Chrystyanly inhabyted, as at the presente yt ys inhabyted only *with* sauages, but most [fo. 2] populousely, specially, towardes y[e] weste; where there are towene[s] of theyere fasshyone, scytuated vpon moost delycate plattes of grounde, dystant y[e] one from y[e] other not aboue 3 Englysshe myelles:[4] Soo as vppon one of theyere holly dayes there hathe beene of my compagnye in y[e] mayene that hathe seene aboue 700[5] personnes, yonge and [olde to]gether[6] on a playene.[7] I meane *with* y[e] fauoure of y[e] Allmyghtye to vysytte y[t]

---

[1] I.e. on 5 September.

[2] In the letter to the elder Richard Hakluyt (pp. 207–8 above) he already refers to Guinea wheat (maize) whose stalk yields sugar, but this letter is dated 3 September by the younger Hakluyt, so that the suggestion that he, or his printer, mistook '8' for '3' is strengthened.

[3] Probably a simple saturation test would have given sufficient indication of the sweetness of the cane. According to Strachey (*Hist. of travell*, p. 119) the Jamestown Indians sucked green corn stalks for the sugar they contained (cp. Swanton, *Indians*, p. 352). Nearer the equator some sugar may have been made from maize stems before the Europeans arrived (A. Arber, *The Gramineae*, p. 54; cp. Porcher, *Resources*, p. 639). It seems likely that the physician accompanied his 'assaye' home on the *Roebuck* as there is no evidence of any medical man or apothecary having remained with Lane, (cp. pp. 199, 334). For the proposals to bring out a physician see p. 135 above.

[4] This almost certainly represents the findings of the expedition which Amadas led to Weapemeoc on 2 August, and whose geographical discoveries appear on the sketch-map below (pp. 215–17, though only two, unnamed, village sites are indicated). The relative density of population on this fertile shore can be judged roughly by the number of villages on the map at end.

[5] The top of the first figure is rubbed along the fold. It could be '9' but '7' is more probable.

[6] The words supplied have been rubbed along the fold.

[7] This was the green corn festival celebrated in August, and this reference should be added to those in Flannery (*Analysis*, pp. 133–4). For the nature of the festival, cp. Swanton (*Indians*, p. 775). A similar ceremony is illustrated by White for Secoton (no. 37, see pp. 420–1 below). The figure of 700 is one of the few items on population (cp. pp. 259, 265) and it probably represents the approximate adult population of the Weapemeoc tribe. As villages ranged from nine to thirty households (cp. pp. 107–369), a conservative estimate

prouynce and [1] summe parte of y^e wynter to passe there, beynge 140
myelles wi*th*in y$^{e\,2}$ mayene; [3] In y^e meane whylle and durynge lyfe,
I am to praye to y^e Allmyghty to blesse you and yo*urs*: / From
the Newe Forte in Verginia, the 8th daye of September: 1585 [4]
Yo*ur* hono*urs* and most assuered durynge lyfe
Rafe Lane

Postscript—Si*r* the bearer hereof o*ur* Threas*ur*er M*aste*r brooke
shall d*e*lyuer to yo*ur* hono*r* a trewe copye of ye whoolle dyscoursse
of ye voyeage, dyrected to Si*r* W*alte*r Rawlley: and subscrybed,
and to bee co*n*fyrmed wi*th* sundry credyble deposyciones: [5] /
[*Addressed:*] To the R*igh*t honorable Si*r* F*rances* Wallsingham, K*nigh*t,
prynsypalle Secrettary to ye Q*ueenes* Maieste, and one [of] her hi*gh*-
ness moost honorable pryvy Counselle, thys bee del*yuered* at Courte.
[*Endorsed:*] 1585. 8th September 1585. M*aste*r Rafe Lane. Virginia. [6]

of five to the household would give a village range from 45 to 150 people. If the
assignment of eight villages to this tribe (pp. 858–61) is correct, the population
would range from 350 to 2000, with an average of 1175, which fits in well enough
with Lane's statement. Dr Mook takes 800 as a probable figure, out of a total of
5000 for the Carolina Algonkian tribes as a whole ('The aboriginal population
of tidewater Virginia', in *American Anthropologist*, new ser., XLVI (1944), 206).

[1] 'to wynter' crossed out. [2] 'lande' crossed out.

[3] It was not more than 70 miles from where Lane was writing to the head of
Weapemeoc Sound, but it was possible for exploring parties which followed the
open river estuaries up to the narrowing of their streams from Powell Point
westwards to cover at least 150 miles. He may, however, have had the Chesapeake
Bay expedition in prospect and it is not unlikely that it did make a base (at
Chesepiuc?) for the winter (cp. pp. 257–8). Lane was not, however, reliable on
distances (cp. pp. 256–7). Apart from his list of Weapemeoc villages (p. 258) his
references to the tribe are largely incidental to his account of visits to the
Chowanoac and Moratuc tribes (pp. 267, 272, 279, 281).

[4] The Hakluyt letter (pp. 207–10 above), and the sketch-map (pp. 215–17) with
the discourse (and letter no doubt) for Raleigh would have been sent down to
reach Port Ferdinando not earlier than 9 September. We may assume that the
Roebuck, if we are right in interpreting the reference to her captain as implying
that she was still there (pp. 210–11), left about, or shortly after, this date. Nothing
has so far been learnt of her arrival. A similar argument would place the *Elizabeth*,
under her captain Thomas Cavendish, at Port Ferdinando at the same time
(p. 210).

[5] It remains somewhat obscure (cp. p. 212 above) whether the depositions
were attached or were to be added in England.

[6] The second date and 'Virginia' appear to be in a later hand.

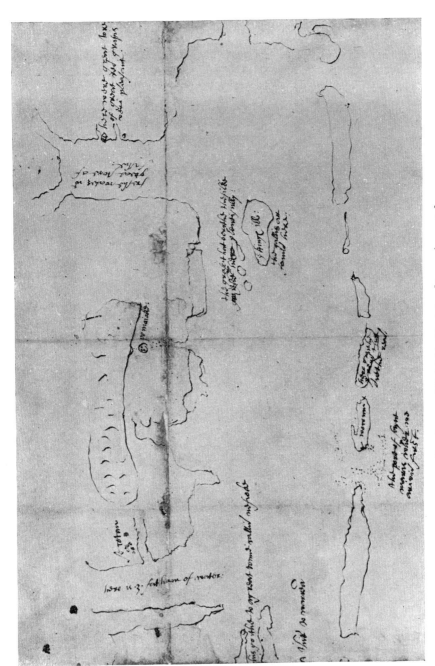

3. Sketch-map of Raleigh's Virginia. [September 1585].

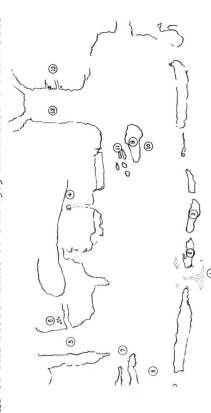

Fig. 4. Key to the notes on the 1585 sketch map (fig 3).

[1] the port of saynt maris wher we arivid first:[2]
[2] wococan[3]
[3] here groith y^e roots that diethe read:[4]
[4] pomaioke:[5]
[5] here is .3. fatham of water:[6]
[6] secotan[7]
[7] [t]his goithe to a great toune callid nesioke[8]

[8] [   ] this to warrea[9]
[9] ye kinges ill:[10]
[10] the gallis are found here:[11]
[11] the grase that berither the silke groithe here plentifully:[12]
[12] freshe water with great store of fishe:[13]
[13] here were great store of great red grapis veri pleasant:[14]

[Endorsed:]   A discription of the land of virginia[15]

[Footnotes appear on pp. 216-17.]

NOTES TO DOCUMENT 30

[1] P.R.O., Maps and Plans G. 584 (fig. 3). Formerly C.O. 1/5, 42 (II), there was no justification for linking it with a letter from John Smith to Francis Bacon, Lord Verulam, in 1618, as a contemporary map of English discoveries. Alexander Brown accepted it as such and printed a version in *Genesis of the United States*, I, 596. A reasonable assumption is that it was sent by Lane to Walsingham with no. 29 above, and that it remained among his papers with nos. 25–27, 29 and 34 until the State Papers were redistributed in the nineteenth century.

[2] This is the Spanish name for Chesapeake Bay (cp. pp. 502–3 below), and it suggests that Grenville had with him a Spanish map. Lane had made a similar reference (p. 201 above). It was here the *Tiger* went aground (cp. pp. 189, 201).

[3] This island is in a position corresponding to its location on White's maps, cp. pp. 460–2, 867 below.

[4] Probably here Dogwood, *Cornus florida*, which still grows near Cape Hatteras: 'from the bark of the fibrous roots the Indians extracted a scarlet color...soluble in water alone' (Porcher, *Resources*, pp. 64–5). Aubry and Boniten went to Croatoan Island on 6 July, returning on the 8th, and they may have brought the roots back with them.

[5] The pinnace and three boats sailed from Wococon on 11 July, reaching Pomeiooc on the 12th (p. 191 above). The ring around the village site indicates that it was palisaded as it appears in White's drawing (no. 33, see pp. 415–17 below), which was probably made by him on this occasion. The rough markings behind the village represent the Lake Paquippe which was exaggerated on White's map (cp. p. 191 above, and pp. 461, 870 below).

[6] It was apparently on 15 July that Grenville and his party ascended the Pamlico River. They would naturally take soundings such as this as they went.

[7] The party spent 15–16 July in the village. Its location here is probably the correct one, that on White's maps being confused (cp. pp. 461, 871). The village is shown unenclosed as in White's drawing (no. 37 see pp. 420–3 below). A substantial number of other drawings (nos. 38–44, see pp. 423–32 below) were also made (or probably made) by him on this visit. They were hospitably entertained.

[8] The boats turned back down the Pamlico River on the 16th, detaching that under Amadas to return to Aquascogoc (p. 191 above), the others continuing to explore rather cursorily the river estuaries to the south of them. Manteo is likely to have been their informant about Nesioke (cp. Barlowe, p. 113 above), which appears in White's maps as Newasiwac. This visit was probably the only basis for White's mapping of the Neuse River estuary.

[9] This records the entry of the boats into Core Sound as their last place of call before returning to Wococon on the 18th. Warreā is probably Cwarreuuoc of the White-de Bry map (pp. 462, 872 below) or another village of the Coree tribe, also Hakluyt's Waren (p. 765 below).

[10] Roanoke Island, the 'king' being Wingina, and word of their arrival having been sent to him on 3 July (p. 189 above).

[11] These are quite likely to have been oak-galls useful in tanning. If not, it might be suggested that they were specimens of American Centaury, *Sabbatia angularis*, or even White's Rosegentian, *Sabbatia stellaris* (cp. p. 447 below), since the

English Lesser Centaury was known as Gall for its bitterness and was prized for its medicinal uses (cp. Porcher, *Resources*, pp. 554–7), though such an interpretation would be highly speculative. It is worth making only as oaks were so abundant that the noting of oak-galls here would not appear specially intelligent.

¹² For these small islands in Croatan Sound see pp. 862–3 below. Lane had already mentioned silk-grass to the elder Hakluyt (p. 207 above), but there were several plants so described (cp. pp. 325–6 below). Here a yucca, Bear Grass, *Yucca filamentosa* (the most likely), Spanish Bayonet, *Y. gloriosa*, or Spanish Dagger, *Y. aloifolia*, all yielding fibre, is meant (cp. J. K. Small, *Manual of the south-eastern flora*, pp. 302–4).

¹³ Amadas had been sent up Albemarle Sound to Weapemeoc on 2 August (p. 192 above), and had, by the implications of Lane's letter, returned by 8 September (p. 212–14 above). The sketch-map shows that besides discovering fish he had outlined fully the shape of the Sound with the two main inlets to it, the Roanoke and Chowan Rivers, at its western end. He may even have penetrated into Chawanoac territory, but this is not proved from this map.

¹⁴ De Bry marks grapes in a similar place (p. 413 below). These were either the small sweet Summer Grapes, ripening in July and August, or the large sweet Muscadine Grapes, which come in in September (cp. p. 330). Lane had already mentioned them in his letter to Hakluyt (p. 207 above). The two estuaries entering the Sound on the north are possibly the Perquimans and Little Rivers, though the two villages marked are not easy to identify from the other maps (cp. pp. 461, 860–1 below). They are unnamed, but distinguished by circles, presumably to indicate that they were palisaded villages like Pomeiooc. There is no indication elsewhere that the Weapemeoc tribe adopted this practice.

¹⁵ This is the earliest English map of North America made from direct observation and has some connexions with De Bry's engraving (p. 413 below). Its watermark (entwined columns) is one appropriate to the year 1585. (Cp. C.M. Briquet, *Les filigranes* (2nd ed. 1923), nos. 4432–4437: French paper in use *c.* 1580–90.)

---

31. [*c.* SEPTEMBER 1585.]

SIR WALTER RALEIGH AT PLYMOUTH¹

1584–5. John Trelawnye....²

Item paid to M*aster* Hawkins³ for S*ir* Walter
Rawleghes diett   iiij li.

¹ Plymouth City Records, Receiver's Accounts, 1584–5, in 'Widey Court Book', fo. 61. I am indebted to Colin Campbell, Esq., O.B.E., Town Clerk of Plymouth for having this item checked for me.

² Mayor 17 September 1584–17 September 1585. Although these entries refer to dates before 17 September it is probable that Raleigh stayed some time in Plymouth awaiting Grenville's return (cp. pp. 193, 219). He may have come on hearing of Arundell's arrival (cp. p. 192).

³ William Hawkins, the elder brother of Sir John.

Item paid to Martin White[1] for Sir Walter
Rawleghes diett as by a bille appearethe   viijli. xjs. iiijd.

32. 7 OCTOBER 1585.

COMMISSIONERS OF THE MUSTERS IN DEVON TO THE PRIVY COUNCIL[2]

The have deferred the musters since 'somme of the Captanes are nowe absent'[3] and 'besydes the vnseasonable time of the yeare'.

33. $\frac{14}{24}$ OCTOBER 1585.

NEWS FROM COLOGNE[4]

Some English ships are said to have left England six or seven months ago, and to have built a fort in Florida in the Indies.[5] Consequently, all English ships and subjects in Spain and Portugal have been detained[6]....Cologne, Oct. 24, 1585.

34. 29 OCTOBER 1585.

SIR RICHARD GRENVILLE TO SIR FRANCIS WALSINGHAM[7]

Remembringe my dutie to your honor, Beinge by the hande of god delyvered from the daungers on the seas, and aryved in Ing-

---

[1] Raleigh's factor at Plymouth (cp. pp. 44, 475).

[2] Brief abstract. S.P., Domestic, Elizabeth, S.P. 12/183, 5, from Arthur Basset, Robert Denys, Sir John Gilberte, and John Chechester.

[3] With Grenville on the Virginia voyage and with Drake in the West Indies venture.

[4] Extract. *Fugger news-letters*, 2nd ser., ed. V. von Klarwill, p. 96. The letters were copied from originals addressed to Count Philip Edward Fugger, in the Nationalbibliothek, Vienna, but were translated by L. S. R. Byrne and published in England without a previous German edition.

[5] The translation reads 'in India'.

[6] The Spanish embargo on English commerce in May 1585 was not directly connected with the Roanoke voyages (cp. A. F. Pollard, *Political history of England, 1547-1603*, pp. 389-91), but it is interesting that it was thought to have been so.

[7] Holograph. State Papers Colonial, C.O. 1/1, 7. It was written by Grenville on the twelfth day after his arrival at Plymouth in the *Santa Maria* (p. 193), after he had seen Raleigh (p. 219), and after, in all likelihood, the *Tiger* had come up from Falmouth where she had arrived on 6 October (p. 193).

londe I may not forgette to acquainte your honor with the successe
of my voiadge, wherin I am perswaded that god hath bene the
rather favorable vnto me for that your honour hathe bene an
adventurer therin[1]/ I haue god be thanked performed the action
wherunto I was directed as fullye as the tyme wherin I haue bene
absente from hense and all possibilities wolde permitte me.[2] I haue
possessed and peopled the same to her Maiesties vse, And planted it
with suche cattell & beastes as are fitte and necessary for manuringe
the Countrey[3] and in tyme to geve reliefe with victuall, as also
with such fruites and plantes as by my travaile by the waie thether-
wardes I mighte procure[4]/ And as the Countrey of hit selfe, as
never bene labored with mannes hande, so I hope that hit being
once by our industrie manured will prove moste fertill

The Comodites that are founde there are suche as my cousen
Raleighe hathe advertized yo[u] of,[5] your honor shall herafter haue
the reporte of suche as I haue broughte with me[6]/

In my waie homewardes I was encountred by a spanishe shippe
whome assaultinge me and offeringe me violence god be thanked
with defence and safetie of my selfe and all my companye after
some fighte I overcame[7] and brought into Inglonde with me her

[1] A piece of flattery which would later have seemed blasphemous, but would
not appear so to the godly Walsingham.

[2] Some detail on why he had returned would have been welcome (cp. p. 168).

[3] A good deal is known of the animals collected in the West Indies (p. 187),
but almost nothing of their fate on American soil (apart from some accidental
traces in 1587 (p. 782)).

[4] Again we have a fair amount of detail on what was brought to Virginia,
but, apart from the failure to grow sugar-canes (p. 336), little is known of their
fate. This part of the letter is a formal report, probably intended to forestall
Lane's allegations on his defects as a leader.

[5] Raleigh had probably returned to court by the time this letter was written.

[6] Neither reports nor much information on specimens brought home (cp.
pp. 187, 339–40, 353–4; Platter, *Travels*, pp. 171–3) have survived.

[7] Enrique Lopez tells (Wright, *Further English voyages*, pp. 12–15) how the
Santa Maria de San Vicente, flagship of the Santo Domingo squadron of the fleet,
on 4 September (25 August by English reckoning (cp. p. 192)), was overhauled
by the *Tiger*, to whom she fired a friendly salute only to be fired on in earnest.
After a chase, and some casualties and damage, she surrendered (for Grenville's
boarding see p. 193 above).

ladinge is gynger & Suger,[1] And whereas by the ignoraunce of such as haue come before me a large reporte hathe bene made of great quantitie of pearle and mettall of golde and sylver, I do assure your honour that [we] haue founde but lytell nether dothe ony suche quantitie passe from St Domingo from whence they came vnto Spayne, That which was heere belonged only to pryvate persons who were passengers into Spaine from St Domingo, And the same when the Shippe yelded was imbesiled by the company.[2] The whole estimate of the shippe by the Confession of the Spanierdes and viewe of their bookes amountethe only to 40000 or 50000 Ducates[3] The same beinge sufficiente to awnswer the charges of eache adventurer, wherein I am gladde that my happe is to yealde your honor the retorne of your adventure with some gagne[4]/ the acounte wherof with other relacions of the whole course of the voiadge at my repaire to the Courte which god

[1] According to Lopez her register showed 120,000 ducats' worth of sugar and other merchandise (including ivory, etc. (pp. 169–70, 222, 224–5, 757)).

[2] Again according to Lopez, Grenville himself insisted that the 40,000 ducats' worth of gold, silver and pearls entered in the register be handed to him, while he supervised and took away more in the possession of individual passengers. There were many rumours about the treasure on board (cp. p. 226), and John Stukely handed down one story about Queen Elizabeth's acquisition of some pearls (p. 231). No doubt the crew took what they could as pillage: Lopez says that the twenty-two Spaniards released at Flores were stripped and searched before being released.

[3] The Spanish account would place the registered value of the cargo as 160,000 ducats (together with unregistered luggage and cargo). A precise exchange value for the ducat at this time is not easy to obtain, but the question was answered for Cadiz about this time (for 1583–4), and the figures of 5s. 10d. and 6s. 2d. given (H.C.A. 13/25, exam. S. Lucke, 19 October 1585, A. Bowen, 21 January 1586), so that 6s. may be taken as an approximation. This would give a value of £48,000 for the registered cargo apart from the hull and tackle of the ship, as against Grenville's £12,000–£15,000.

[4] A substantial part of Dr K. R. Andrews's 'The economic aspects of Elizabethan privateering' is devoted to showing how the spoils of privateering were divided. If we take, as a round figure, £50,000 as the proceeds, after pillage, of the three West Indian prizes and the *Santa Maria* (profits of trade in the West Indies, together with saleable imports from Virginia (if any) would probably not be included), the division of the proceeds would be:

(1) Custom   £2500 (in cash).

(2) Tenth to Lord High Admiral   £5000 (in kind).

willinge shalbe shortlye I will my self imparte vnto you[1] And so restinge alwaies moste bownde to your honour I humbly take my leave

Plymouth this 29 of October 1585.

Your honours alwaies at

Your comaundement

[unsigned][2]

[*Addressed:*] To the Righte honorable Sir Frauncys Walsingham knighte principall Secretary to the Queenes Maiestie

[*Endorsed:*]   1585

29 Oct.

Sir Ric: Grenvile

35. 30 OCTOBER.

9 NOVEMBER.

NEWS FROM LONDON[3]

A ship of the Indian fleet belonging to Richard Grenfield has come in here.[4] She is richly laden with sugar, ginger, hides,

---

(3) Crew   *circa* £14,000.
(4) Owners   „   £14,000.
(5) Victuallers   „   £14,000.

On Dr Andrews's average figures (pp. 62–74) it would have cost about £3000 (and not more than £4000) to keep the seven vessels at sea for six months. If only one pinnace was lost the capital loss would not exceed £200 out of an investment of some £2000. The hired ships would have had to be 'made good' at an unknown cost. Wages and stores for Lane's men might range in cost from £3000 to £5000. The total investment would thus be within the limits £8000 to £11,000. The adventurers, then (if owners and victuallers formed a single syndicate, as seems likely), may have had a profit approaching £20,000, though if the net yield was less and the losses of shipping greater this figure could have been substantially reduced. Grenville, in this letter, was undoubtedly trying to minimize receipts (cp. pp. 597–8).

[1] No accounts have been found. It is possible (see pp. 25–6, 174) that a narrative of the voyage by Grenville lies at the back of the Holinshed version (pp. 173–8 above).   [2] In spite of his neglect to sign it the letter is in Grenville's hand.

[3] Extract. *Fugger news-letters*, 2nd ser., ed. V. von Klarwill, p. 96 (see p. 218 above). It is not clear whether one of the Fugger correspondents in England would use Old or New Style dating, but the latter seems likely.

[4] 'Here' probably means simply England.

gold, silver and cochineal,[1] and is worth a million.[2] .... London,
Nov. 9, 1585.

36. 15 NOVEMBER 1585.

JOHN STUBBE TO LORD WILLOUGHBY DE ERESBY[3]

'I thought to have writte nothing of "Windangancoyn" voiage
because I supposed others wold advertise your lordship of Sir
Richard Greenefields retorn[4] and of the variable speeches given
forth touching the fraught and commodities he hath brought
home.[5] Neverthelesse happenyng upon a letter of Mr. Rafe Lane
sent to hir Majestie,[6] I thought not unfitt to send to you, that you
might in those northest countries know also what is don in the
Southwest. The speech is diverse touching the commodities and
value of that voiage, this letter promeseth well. *Exitus acta probat.*
And yet in the meen whyle been ther endevours honorable and
praiseworthy to themselves and the land.[7] The letter seems un-

---

[1] Compare other accounts of the lading of the *Santa Maria de San Vicente*,
pp. 220, 743–4, 757, and Wright, *Further English voyages*, pp. 12–15.

[2] He probably means 1,000,000 ducats, about £300,000, which is substantially
above Spanish and English estimates (cp. pp. 220, 226).

[3] Extract. Hist. MSS Comm., *Ancaster MSS* [66] (1907), pp. 16–17. Peregrine
Bertie, Lord Willoughby de Eresby (1555–1601), had been sent on a diplomatic
mission to Frederik II of Denmark. His interest in the Virginia voyages is not
otherwise indicated, but it is possible that he was a subscriber to the 1585 expedition. John Stubbs or Stubbe (1543?–1591) was the puritan gentleman of Norfolk
who in 1579 had his right hand struck off—hence his description of himself as
scaeva, left-handed—for his *The discoverie of a gaping gulf*, attacking the marriage
treaty with Anjou. He was, in 1585, a member of Lord Willoughby's household.

[4] On 18 October in the prize, the *Santa Maria*, at Plymouth (above p. 193).

[5] This reference is valuable, as it is the only indication that the debate about
the value or otherwise of Virginia products (cp. pp. 273, 320–4 below) had begun
as early as November 1585.

[6] The letter from Lane to the queen from Virginia does not now appear to
be extant, though a note of her reply exists (p. 474 below). The group of letters
dated 12 August (pp. 197–206 above) would appear to have reached Falmouth on
the *Tiger* on 6 October (p. 193 above), but the date of arrival of the *Roebuck*,
which apparently carried the letters written in September (pp. 207–14 above), is
not known. This letter could have come still earlier with Arundell (cp. p. 199).

[7] Stubbe is, it may be noted, willing to praise the voyage as an honourable
achievement irrespective of its material returns.

perfect,[1] which yet I wrote out as I found it knowing your Lordship can better perfect it then I.' Barbican, London, 'From your lordship's own howse'. Jhohn Stubbe, *scaeva*.

37. $\dfrac{18}{28}$ NOVEMBER 1585.

NEWS FROM COLOGNE[2]

The English warships have brought in many ships from Spain and Portugal which were fishing off Terra Nova.[3] They are said also to have brought in some ships from San Domingo and to have sunk the flagship.[4]...Cologne, Nov. 28, 1585.

38. 'SPOYLE AND RICHES OF MOST FORCE WITH THE COMMON SOULDIOR'[5]

We finde it in daily experience that all discourse of magnanimitie, of Nationall Vertue, of Religion, of Libertie, and whatsoeuer else hath beene wont to moue and incourage vertuous men, hath no force at all with the common-Souldier, in comparison of spoile and riches, The rich ships are boorded vpon all disaduantages, the rich Townes are furiosly assaulted, and the plentifull Countries willingly inuaded. Our *English* Nations haue attempted many places in the *Indies*, and runne vpon the *Spaniards* head-long, in hope of their Royalls of plate, and Pistolets, which had they beene put to it vpon the like disaduantages in *Ireland*, or in any poore Countrie, they would haue turned their Peeces and Pikes against their Commanders, contesting that they had beene brought without reason to the Butcherie and slaughter. It is true that the warre is made willingly, and for the most part with good successe,

[1] Stubbe may well have made his copy from the original as Lane's imperfections as a letter-writer are well illustrated above (pp. 197–214).

[2] Extract. *Fugger news-letters*, 2nd ser., ed. V. von Klarwill, p. 98 (see p. 218 above).

[3] As the result of Bernard Drake's Newfoundland expedition (Quinn, *Gilbert*, I, 95; pp. 234–42 below).

[4] Echoes mainly of Grenville's captures (cp. pp. 184, 192–3).

[5] Sir Walter Raleigh, *History of the world*, bk. 4, ch. 2, sect. 4, p. 178 (second numeration).

that is ordained against the richest Nations; for as the needie are alwaies aduenturous, so plentie is wont to shunne perill, and men that haue well to liue, doe rather studie how to liue well, I meane wealthily, than care to die (as they call it) honourably. *Car où il ny' a rien a gaigner, que des coups volontiers il ny' va pas; No man makes hast to the market, where there is nothing to be bought but blowes.*

39. 9 DECEMBER 1585.

ADRIAN GILBERT TO DR JULIUS CAESAR[1]

Sir wheras you are informed by a french man that there are fyve olofantes tethe claymed by one master Pryor[2] & that ys stayed in master Customers smyths[3] handes I am herby vpon my Credyt to aduertyse you vnder my hand that the teth came with Sir Rychard Greynvyle[4] & that I had the same of my brother Sir Walter Raleigh. Which when soever you shall appoynt I will vpon my othe veryfy before you / & besydes those that I have there were .4. more one Sir Walter Raleigh had, & one Carrew Raleighe & the other .2. Sir Rychard Greynfyle had. / & this you shalbe satysfyeth by the othe of a dosen honest persons that knewe the same. / but good Sir these frenchemen are very forward to procure falshode agaynst me / I wold to god I cold fynd somwhat of theirs, for at nans[5] I lost a barke with 300 li. woorthe of kersyes & have out of your

---

[1] Brit. Mus., Lansdowne MS 145, fo. 235 (Caesar papers). Dr Julius Caesar (1558–1636), was judge of the High Court of Admiralty.

[2] Prior may be the Jeffery Prior, described on 25 October 1584 as 'a lewde vnthankefull frenche varlete' (Francis Hawley to Caesar, from Corfe Castle. Ibid. fo. 366). [3] For Thomas Smythe, see pp. 544, 569–75 below.

[4] Mendoza also mentions ivory on the *Santa Maria* (p. 757). Ivory frequently figures in cargoes from the Spanish West Indies as a re-export, brought originally by slavers from West Africa. If Gilbert's story is correct, it would seem that Grenville handed over the lading of his prizes to Raleigh who subsequently redistributed it. The assignment of shares to his half-brother, Adrian Gilbert, and to his elder brother, Carew Raleigh, by Raleigh may well be evidence that they had both invested in the 1585 expedition (cp. p. 471). But the ivory may possibly have come from Bernard Drake's prize which was on its way from Guinea (cp. p. 238 below).

[5] Nantes. Grenville appears to have shared Adrian Gilbert's antipathy to the French (cp. p. 743 below).

cort in Doctor lewse ¹ his tyme a suffycient warrant for the recovery therof, wherin I hope to fynde yo*u* my favorable good Frynd as occasio*n* shall se*r*ve / So with harty Comendations I most humbly take my leave. / this .9ᵗʰ. of December.

Yo*u*rs to Comavnd
Adryan Gylbarte

[*Addressed:*] To the Ryghte Worshipfull m*aste*r Doctor Seasor Iudge of the Admyralty yeve these.
[*Endorsed:*] 9°. Dece*m*bris 1585.
M*aste*r Adrian Gilbert about 5. Elephants teeth.²

40. 20 DECEMBER 1585.

[WILLIAM HERLE?] TO QUEEN ELIZABETH³

Yf yo*u*r ma*i*estie do plant sufficient Colonies, vnder discreete gouerno*u*rs in the aptest places of *Terra Virginea,*⁴ yow may increase yo*u*r nauie by shipping made there,⁵ and be neere vppon euerie euent, to possesse king Phillippes pursse,⁶ W*h*ich is the sure waie, to ruine att one instant, both him, and all the vsurers depending of him, that ar and haue bin the only nursses of vniust warres in Christendom, by the space of manie yeres.

For the substanciall ground worke, and effecting wherof Sir Francis Drakes enterprise, will shake euen the kinges state there,

---

¹ Dr David Lewis (1520?–1584), Caesar's predecessor as judge of the admiralty.
² The endorsement is, apparently, in Caesar's hand. The case of the elephants' teeth does not appear to have gone to the admiralty court for settlement.
³ Extract. P.R.O., State Papers, Foreign, Holland and Flanders, S.P. 84/5, 133 (calendared in *Cal. S.P. For., Sept. 1585–May 1586,* p. 230, where the tentative identification of the author is given).
⁴ From this it would appear that the writer was, with the younger Richard Hakluyt (Taylor, *Hakluyts,* II, 313–19), a protagonist of the view that the state, and not private persons, should undertake the establishment of the American settlements.
⁵ Both Hakluyts strongly urged that the Virginia settlements would provide a source for naval stores and shipping (Taylor, *Hakluyts,* II, 270–3, 331).
⁶ This view fits in with other proposals that the colony should be used as a base against the Spanish Indies and the treasure fleets (p. 22, above, and Quinn, 'Preparations for the 1585 Virginia voyage', in *William and Mary Quarterly,* 3rd ser., VI, 211–24).

and enriche yo*ur* ma*i*estie notably sondrie waies, and yo*ur* whole realme, in traffick and com*m*oditie.

By le*tt*res from Siuile[1] of late is signifyed, that the shipp taken by S*ir* Richard Greenefeild: had vj C.M. duckattes[2] by register, besydes that com*m*only they bring asmuch vnregistred, w*h*ich is no treasure for priuate persones to vsurpe,[3] seing your ma*i*estie hath neede thereof, for the peace of the land, and must be chargeable for the same, when it com*m*es to a rekoning.[4]...London the 20ᵗʰ of December 1585.[5]

41. MARTIN LAURENTSON, A DANISH MEMBER OF GRENVILLE'S EXPEDITION

(*a*) 27 August 1584. Letters of credence for Martin Laurentson from Frederik II of Denmark to Queen Elizabeth.[6]

The bearer of these presents, our subject Martinus Laurentius [Martin Laurentson], has in all humility made known unto us, that he intends to devote his attention to the art of naval warfare, in the study of which he finds especial pleasure. To this end he has requested from us a letter of recommendation to your majesty. For him, we affectionately request your majesty to think fit to place him in the charge of some skilled and practised officer of your navy, a captain or lieutenant, whence he may be enabled to learn that art thoroughly and completely. In this matter your majesty

---

[1] Seville.

[2] 600,000 ducats (about £180,000) (cp. pp. 220, 222 above).

[3] The writer, if he is not betraying some animosity towards Grenville or Raleigh, cannot have known that the Queen was an investor in the voyage and was experienced in getting more than her due return on her investments. As no record of the disposition of the profits exists (though Grenville (p. 220 above) was at pains to minimize their extent), we cannot say to what extent she profited in this instance.

[4] I.e. when open war became inevitable.   [5] Unsigned.

[6] Latin. Extract, translated, of the entry preserved in the Rigsarkivet, Copenhagen. I am indebted for this item to Hr. Axel Linvald of the Rigsarkivet, who informs me that the letter is referred to in H. D. Lind, *Fra Kong Frederik den Andens Tid. Bidrag til Den dansk-norske Sømagts Historie, 1559–88* (Copenhagen, 1902), p. 319, though without further information on Laurentson.

will oblige us greatly, and perform an action of singular gracious-
ness for our subject. We, in our turn, offer to your majesty, with
all due affection, that zeal and duty which is proper to our goodwill.

(*b*) 30 January 1586. Martin Laurentson to Sir Francis Wal-
    singham.[1]

To the most excellent noble and mighty Sir Francis Walsingham,
knight, secretary of state to her majesty: may happiness be yours
for all time.

I cannot believe, most noble sir, that your excellency has forgotten that I, in accordance with your injunctions,[2] performed
loyal service for the most noble lord, Gualtherus Raleh [Sir Walter
Raleigh], in the voyage to Vingandicon; but that on my return
I sought by petition from her royal highness[3] that her majesty
might, in her turn, commend me to the illustrious and mighty lord
and reverend prince, Frederik, king of Denmark and Norway, and
my most gentle master (for it was by him that I was commended
to her majesty the queen), and that she, from the generosity of her
highness, might aid my poverty; whereby alone I shall depart
hence with greater safety from the worrying extortions and demands of those to whom I am here bound for my living,[4] and
return to my most gentle monarch a more welcome subject.

In this matter I respectfully ask your lordship's favour, that she
[the queen], as she has great power in her wealth and resources,
may aid my straitened circumstances, and (which is most important) vouchsafe me a reply. I, in my turn, although I cannot
do more,[5] shall declare your kindness towards me before all; and

---

[1] Latin, translated. P.R.O., State Papers, Foreign, Denmark, S.P. 75/1, 79,
fos. 191–2 (see *Cal. S.P. For.*, *Sept. 1585–May 1586*, p. 337). I am indebted to
Mr W. R. Smyth, Department of Classics, University College, Swansea, for
translations of this and of the item above.

[2] This letter provides another instance of Walsingham's help in providing
personnel for Grenville's expedition in 1585 (cp. pp. 197–8 above).

[3] This petition to Queen Elizabeth has not been traced.

[4] It might appear from this that Laurentson had been proceeded against for debt.

[5] 'cum aliud non possim', i.e. that he cannot return in kind any help given
to him.

I shall pray to the great and good God to preserve your lordship secure for all time, for the propagation of the faith and as the glory and mainstay of the common weal.

Your lordship's humble servant,

Martinus Laur:

[*Endorsed:*]   Marten Lawrence   30 Ianuarie 1585.[1]

42.   REMINISCENCES OF THE 1585 EXPEDITION
      7 JANUARY 1592. BY RALPH LANE.[2]

(*a*) And yet neuertheles my selfe was (by tymes) one whole yere and a halfe[3] vnder all the intemperate clymates, for heate and sicknes within tenne degrees of the lyne,[4] bothe at Sea and lande, bearinge the seconde place vnder *Sir* Richard Grinvile, where hauinge beine permitted by him to sett downe a discipline[5] which was severly executed first at sea, and then afterwarde by me in lyke sorte continued at lande, neither at sea nor at lande we loste by sicknes aboue fowre *per*sons of eight score,[6] in one small barcque of her ma*ies*ties called the Tygre. Wherein I appeale to the attesta-ci*on* of *Sir* Walter Raghley, whoe receiued *par*ticuler informaci*on*

---

[1] Nothing further is known of the writer.

[2] Extract. 'The particularities of the speciall duetye belonginge to the Muster ma*ster* generall...', addressed by Ralph Lane to Lord Burghley on 7 January 1591[-2], Brit. Mus., Lansdowne MS 69, fos. 28–32 (the extract is from fos. 29–29 v.). This is in the hand of a copyist, and is followed by an addendum (fos. 34–34 v.), in Lane's own hand, dated 15 February 1591[-2]. The extract was printed, incorrectly, in *Archaeologia Americana*, IV (1860), 27. Lane is stressing the need for strict disciplinary measures to avoid sickness among soldiers engaged on land or at sea.

[3] Lane left England on 9 April 1585 and returned on 27 July 1586.

[4] This statement is, as it stands, absurd. The expedition in 1585 may have swung as far south as lat. 10° N., but Lane's year in America was spent almost wholly between the 35th and 36th parallels.

[5] The suggestion that the disciplinary code was drawn up as the result of sug-gestions by the Hakluyts and in the anonymous 'Notes' is made above, pp. 136–9.

[6] 160 is presumably the total personnel of the *Tiger* on her outward voyage, (though on p. 205 he says 120), but the four deaths which Hariot records (p. 384) took place among the 108 colonists at Roanoke Island, after the *Tiger* had returned to England. Lane is unlikely to have known anything of mortality on board, after she sailed from America. He is not here speaking in precise terms.

of the same by Sir Richard Greinuile himselfe, though he tooke the matter vppon the rare effect, absolutelye to himselfe./ My exceptione vnto him for which, and for his engaginge of me with my onely squadre of .xxv. Souldiours and sixe Spanishe prisoners, with mattockes, and Spades,[1] (at Cape Rosso[2] against the gouernour there Diego Melindes[3] with fortye horse & -300- foote) to lade salte, where he toulde me I shoulde fynde none to resiste, but findinge the contrary, my tellinge him of it bred the grete vnkindnes afterwardes one his parte towardes me./[4]

(b)[5] I haue heard of a pilot of Newhauen[6] that was with the Englishmen in Virginia 24.[7] years agoe, that, being come thither, there died 36. of them in three months.[8] Neuertheless, Virginia is taken to be in the 36. 37. and 38. degrees of latitude, which is a good temperate country. Which considering, I yet beleeue (as I haue already said before) that such mortality commeth by the bad fare.

[1] They can be seen at work in White's drawing (no. 3, see pp. 404–5 below). The journal of the voyage gives the number of Lane's soldiers as 20 (above p. 185).

[2] Cape Rojo.

[3] Diego Menéndez de Valdés (cp. Wright, *Further English voyages*, p. 9).

[4] Compare Lane's other grievances against Grenville (pp. 210–12 above).

[5] Marc Lescarbot, *Nova Francia: or the description of that part of New France, which is one continent with Virginia*, translated by P. Erondelle (1609), p. 51; ed. H. P. Biggar (1928), p. 54. The passage does not appear in *Histoire de la Nouvelle France* (Paris, 1609), p. 541, despite a chapter heading (p. 525) mentioning the incident. The translator must have received from Richard Hakluyt (cp. Biggar, p. vii) either a manuscript, a set of unrevised sheets or a variant issue containing the passage. The French text appeared in the second edition (1611), p. 499 (cp. the critical edition, by W. L. Grant and H. P. Biggar, II (Champlain Soc., VII, 1911), 278, 526).   [6] 'Havre de Grace' (*Hist. de la Nouvelle France* (1611), p. 499).

[7] Lescarbot was writing in 1608 (Biggar, p. x), and strictly should mean 1584. We know so little of the personnel of the 1584 expedition that it is possible that a French pilot was carried, but 1585 is a more probable date. The pilot may even have been he of the Dutch-owned *Waterhound*, who was carried off by Grenville (above, pp. 151–2).

[8] The only indication of any deaths on the 1584 voyage is an obscure reference to the killing of 38 Englishmen by the Indians (Wright, *Further English voyages*, p. 175; cp. p. 81 above). For the 1585–6 colony we have the testimony of both Hariot (p. 384 below) and Lane (p. 228) that only 4 out of 108 settlers died. But the three months could well comprise the period from 24 June to 12 September when all, or some, of Grenville's ships were there, and 36 deaths out of a complement of about 600 (p. 159 above) are not improbable.

(c) [1] The *Sharke*. . . is the most revenous Fish knowne in the Sea; for he swalloweth all that he findeth. . . . It hath chanced that a yonker casting himselfe into the Sea to swimme, hath had his legge bitten off aboue the knee by one of them. And I haue beene enformed, that in the *Tyger*, when Sir *Richard Greenfild* went to people *Virginia*, a *Sharke* cut off the legge of one of the companie, sitting in the Chaines, and washing himselfe.

(d) Thomas Cavendish. [2]

The worshipful and worthy gentleman Master Thomas Candish of Suffolke [3] hauing in the yeere 1585. Furnished out a ship [4] wherein he went as Captaine with sir Richard Greeneuill to Virginia, [5] in which course he passed by the Canaries, and so to the Isles of Dominica, Hispaniola, Saint Iohn de Porto ricco, the Lucaios, [6] and Florida in the west Indies, thus fleshed and somewhat hardened vnto the Sea, immediatly after his comming home [7] began to take in hand a voyage into the South sea.

(e) An allegation that Raleigh cheated John Stukely. [8]

Hitherto I haue prooued hee was angry, both with your Maiesty, & with my selfe, and therefore his testimony ought not to be of

[1] *The observations of Sir Richard Hawkins knight, in his voiage into the South Sea. Anno Domini 1593* (1622), p. 43 (reprinted in *The Hawkins voyages*, ed. by C. R. Markham (Hakluyt Society, 1st ser., LVII (1877), pp. 150–1; and *The observations*, ed. by J. A. Williamson (1933), p. 47).

[2] Extract from N.H.'s narrative of the circumnavigation, in Hakluyt, *Principall navigations* (1589), p. 809 (for which Francis Pretty's narrative was substituted in 1599). [3] See pp. 123, 139, 174, 179, 182–3 above.

[4] The *Elizabeth* (p. 183 above). The mode of expression would suggest that he was the victualler of the vessel not the owner.

[5] He was also high marshal of the expedition (above p. 210).

[6] The Bahamas.

[7] The date or circumstances of the return of his ship are not known. On 5 January 1586 he was included in the list of sea captains available for the royal service (Corbett, *Spanish war*, pp. 291–9, no. 28).

[8] Extract. *To the kings most excellent majestie. The humble petition and information of Sir Lewis Stucley, Knight, vice-admirall of Devon, touching his owne behaviour in the charge committed unto him, for the bringing up of Sir Walter Raleigh, and the scandalous aspersions cast upon him for the same* (1618), pp. 7–9. For Stukely's relations with Raleigh after his last return from Guiana see V. T. Harlow, *Ralegh's last voyage*, pp. 88–91, 98.

any force against me. It followeth next to proue, that his protestations and oathes, concerning others were false, both before he came to the Scaffold, and vpon the Scaffold. Before, against Queene Elizabeth, of infinite famous memory, who aduanced him with great fauour from the dust. For one day my selfe vpbrayding him with the notorious extreame iniury he did my father,[1] in deceiuing him of a great aduenture which my sayd father had in the Tyger, when hee went to the West Indies with my Vncle Sir Richard Greenuill; which was by his owne confession worth fifty thousand pound:[2] which came all to his hands, my fathers portion at the least being tenne thousand pound that hee might lawfully clayme:[3] Hee answered That the Queene howsoeuer she seemed a great good mistresse vnto him in the eyes of the world, yet was so vniust and tyrannous vnto him, that she layde the enuie as well of this, as of many other her oppressions vpon him: and that shee tooke all the pearle in a Cabinet vnto her selfe, without euer giuing him so much as one pearle.[4] This hee swore to me, and to Captaine Pennington,[5] he did so basely and barbarouslie raile vpon that our most excellent Queene oftentimes, as hee can attest, that no man hath cause to beleeue his oth against others, that would breake his oath of Allegeance to so excellent a mistresse, that had raysed him from such meannesse to such greatnesse, as we of his countrey did well know.

[1] John Stukely (above, pp. 175, 180).

[2] Grenville's own estimate of the value of the *Santa Maria's* cargo was about one-third of this amount (above, p. 220).

[3] No reliance at all need be placed on this claim. While little is known of the finance of the 1585 expedition, the accounting for the shares of the crew and the lord admiral would ensure that no adventurer netted 20% of the gross proceeds (cp. pp. 220-1).

[4] Grenville denied that there were any pearls listed in the manifest (p. 220 above), but other accounts indicate that he was misleading Walsingham or had been unable to prevent the crew embezzling the lot (pp. 220, 757). While there is no corroboration that the Queen acquired a cabinet of pearls under circumstances which irked Raleigh, it is not unlikely that she insisted on an especially high return on her own adventure in the voyage.

[5] John Pennington, commanding the *Star*, was vice-admiral of Raleigh's Guiana expedition of 1617 (Edwards, *Ralegh*, I, 600; II, 353).

43. 20 FEBRUARY 1591.

THE CASE OF THE CAPE MERCHANT, THOMAS HARVEY[1]

...this defendant sayth that before his marriadge with the saide Anne [Middleton] ther was by Aucthority of parliament in the 27th yeare of her Maiestyes Reygne as he remembrethe a voyadge entended & appoynted to be made into the West Indians as well to descrye & fynde out the Commodytyes of the same Country hertofore not certeynly knowne which might have beene very profitable to the whole Common wealth of our land[2] yf the Report had beene true which was geven out by twoe straungers Inhabitauntes of the same foreyne Nation[3] as to have barteryed & vsed trafficke with those Country men by interchaunge of mar-

---

[1] Extract from the answer, 20 February 1591, of Thomas Harvey to the chancery bill of 4 February 1591, P.R.O., C. 2, Eliz., S. 16/48 (2/13/314). Harvey's name appears above in the list of Lane's colony in 1585 (p. 194). He was a member of the Grocers' Company and a citizen of London, who, on 7 November 1586, after his return from Virginia, married Anne, widow of William Middleton and mother of the dramatist Thomas Middleton. She had inherited certain property for the use of her children, but her new husband was unable to remain solvent, so, giving her a power of attorney, he departed for the Netherlands as a soldier late in 1588. On his return he was imprisoned for debt and, he alleged, his wife would not maintain him, even in prison. He made her a further power of attorney before leaving on the Portugal voyage in 1589, and thereafter returned to the Netherlands. His wife continued to refuse him money, so about September 1590 he received his captain's permission to come to England. In London he evidently attempted to collect rents from his wife's tenants, an effort to reach an accommodation with her having brought him the threat of arrest. Her tenants—at her instigation, he alleged—began proceedings in chancery to restrain him from interfering with their rents. His answer makes a long plea of his wife's unhelpfulness and alleges he is unable to follow a trade in London as he is in danger of arrest. A certificate for his arrest for debt in 1593 appears to be the last that is heard of him. See Mildred G. Christian, 'A sidelight on the family history of Thomas Middleton', in *Studies in Philology*, XLIV (1947), 490–7, where the case was first brought to light. I am obliged to Professor F. J. Fisher for a number of suggestions.

[2] The bill (pp. 122–9 above) was not passed. Harvey's reference suggests that the introduction of the bill may have been influenced in some degree by the publicity which could thus be based upon the venture as one approved by parliament as well as crown.

[3] Manteo and Wanchese, as referred to in the bill (p. 127 above). Their direct use as propagandists is not elsewhere indicated.

chandise or otherwise.[1] of which sayd voyadge and adventure this defendant was ordeyned Cape Marchaunt[2] by reason of which office and place & for the bettre furnishinge of himself in the sayd voyadge he did not only disburse & bestowe the greatest parte of his owne wealth which he had vppon the same but also borowed diuers sommes of money of others for his better expedicion therin[3] but the successe of the same voiadge not fallinge out so prosperous as was expected[4] And the said Thomas Harvie beinge there landed and after for sake of the generall[5] also Continued ther by the space of one whole yeare & more in very miserable Case[6] and spent or lost what soeuer he embarked & shipped in the same trafficke of marchandise[7] or otherwise by occasion of which evill successe and

[1] Cp. Barlowe (pp. 100–1).

[2] There is no reason to doubt Harvey's statement that he was the cape or chief merchant of the expedition. As such he would have acted as chief factor and have been responsible for the barter and purchase of commodities and livestock in the West Indies for the use of the colony and for sale in England (see p. 187 above). In America he would have organized the barter which supplied some part of the cargo which Grenville and the other vessels took home in 1585 (see pp. 200, 212–13), as well as remaining to conduct similar exchanges under Lane. It is likely that he was the keeper of the store at the Roanoke Island fort (pp. 282, 290 below).

[3] Harvey could have borrowed money towards (*a*) fitting himself out for the voyage, (*b*) adventuring in the expedition in money or goods, and (*c*) financing trading on his own account, whether with the Spaniards in the West Indies, with the Indians from Roanoke Island, or with Lane's men who were apparently paid wages (see p. 290 below) and had, therefore, some purchasing power. (Such private trading was usual for a cape merchant.) How much he borrowed and lost is not known.

[4] It may be noted that Lane on 12 August 1585 quoted the opinion of the merchants of the expedition as being favourable, at least as regards the natural produce of the area (p. 199 above).

[5] Sir Richard Grenville. The reference may imply that he was one of Grenville's adherents and therefore an opponent of Lane's in the controversies noted above (pp. 188–9, 210–12).

[6] He probably landed on 27 or 28 July 1586 (cp. pp. 294, 303 below).

[7] It is not unlikely that he had to dissipate a high proportion of the colony's stocks in the purchase of food (cp. pp. 276, 279–80, 282), while he was also faced for a time with an Indian boycott (p. 282). This may have affected his commission. He may also have had to contribute his private stocks for the use of the colony when supplies ran short. In neither case should the result have been absolute loss, since he would have a claim on the adventurers' account when he returned. Lane, however, was also in the end convinced that commerce could not be more than a subsidiary asset to a colony (p. 273 below).

233

losse this defendant Confesseth that he became poore and vnable to paye his creditors at his returne from thence and the said Thomas Harvie further sayth that of his poore estate and small ability & of the hope which he had to recouer some of his losses[1] he before the sayd marriadge, made the sayd Anne and some of her friendes one whom she relyed acquainted withall.[2] . . .

44. THE GOLDEN ROYAL AND THE 1585 VENTURES[3]

(*a*) 7 June 1586. Libel[4] on behalf of Amyas Preston against John Drake, executor of Sir Bernard Drake, deceased. Preston claims ownership of eight parts of the ship, the *Golden Royall*.

(*b*) 12 November 1586. Decree,[5] signed by Dr Julius Caesar, judge of the admiralty, in Preston *v.* Drake. Preston's claim to have owned eight parts of the *Golden Royall* is proved, and Drake is to give bond to satisfy him.

(*c*) 21 October 1588. Libel[6] on behalf of Amyas Preston against John Drake. Amyas Preston was principal victualler of the *Golden Riall*, to the amount of £300, in 1585. He and Bernard Drake had agreed to consort together to share in all

---

[1] He here implies either that he did not get a speedy settlement of his claims on Raleigh and the other adventurers or that he did not obtain any at all.

[2] Whatever mistake Anne Middleton made in accepting Harvey's stories before marrying him, she showed determination and resource in keeping her property out of his clutches. It may be that his stories of his losses (and of their cause) were exaggerated, but there is little doubt that he was one of those ex-colonists whose adverse propaganda affected later attempts to obtain subscribers and colonists for the Virginia ventures (cp. pp. 320–4, 497–8).

[3] The documents in the High Court of Admiralty records on Bernard Drake's voyage to Newfoundland in 1585 reveal an unexpected connexion at several points with the Virginia ventures of that year. Here no detail is given on the Newfoundland expedition, but brief abstracts and summaries of those documents which throw some light, direct or indirect, on the projected expedition by the *Golden Royal* to Virginia and, after her diversion to Newfoundland, her association with one of the vessels which did accompany Grenville in April, the *Red Lion* of Chichester under Captain George Raymond (Riman, Ryman, Reyman, Rayman) of Chichester. Dr K. R. Andrews drew my attention to Raymond's identity and found several of the documents.

[4] P.R.O., H.C.A. 24/54, no. 205.

[5] Ibid. no. 131.   [6] H.C.A. 24/56, no. 85.

prizes proportionately, according to their adventures. The expedition brought in prizes worth £20,000, of which Preston claims £2000 as his share 'accordinge to his adventure'.[1]

(*d*) Allegation[2] by John Drake, in reply to the libel by Amyas Preston. He says that the consortship between his father, Bernard Drake, and Preston covered the months of February to May, inclusive, in the twenty-seventh year of the queen's reign [1585] and was for the purpose of making an expedition to foreign parts, commonly called 'Wingan de Coy', and not to 'the new found land', for taking Spanish ships and those of the subjects of the king of Spain. If Preston expended the money he alleges in victualling the said ship it was for the voyage to Wingan de Coy and not for that to Newfoundland. Bernard Drake prepared his expedition to Wingan de Coy by authority of a licence from the queen and in virtue of her commission. He was compelled to abandon the pretended expedition to Wingan de Coy on the queen's orders. By her commission of 20 June (27 Elizabeth)[3] he was empowered to make an expedition to Newfoundland, and the 'golden ryall' was prepared at Exmouth between June and September for that purpose. Both Bernard Drake and Amyas Preston were pressed for that expedition. The queen authorized Sir Walter Raleigh and Sir John Gilbert to order the division and distribution of the ships and goods taken prize by Bernard Drake and this was done.

(*e*) 24 October 1588. Deposition of John Staple[4] of Culleton, Devon, yeoman. He was servant to Bernard Drake when he bought the *Golden Riall* from Master Ivory of Chard, Master Tucker of Exmester, Jeffrey Caswell of Exmouth and Master Alexander Ivery of London, and was sent by him to Exmouth to see what furniture was needed for the ship. Amyas Preston was chief victualler and spent up to £200 to his knowledge, and more

[1] At this rate the total amount adventured in the expedition would have been £3000, or, if allowance is made for tenths and customs, some £3500.

[2] Ibid. no. 49.   [3] P.R.O., S.P. 12/179, 21–2.

[4] H.C.A. 13/27.

besides. He brought a Brazilman back as prize to Exmouth. (The schedule attached is signed by Staple and by Dr Julius Caesar. It itemizes food and equipment supplied by Preston for the *Golden Riall* amounting to £113. 19s. 8d., including: 'Item payed for xvj mens vitalls from the xiij of aprill[1] vnto the xxix of Iune at iij[2] the meale which comes to xxx^{li}', and adds £65 as 'payed for part of the ship', making £178. 19d. 8d. in all).

(*f*) 24 October 1588. Deposition of Gilbert Turner[3] of Crickett in Somerset, servant to Christopher Preston. He was given charge of a Brazilman brought to Apsham while Amyas Preston went to court with letters. Sir John Gilbert and John Drake took over the ship and its contents, 'by the meanes of the said Sir Walter Rauleigh', and kept them from Preston. Bernard Drake later brought two other sugarmen to Exmouth, and another to Chichester, which were worth £9000 to £10,000.

(*g*) 8 November 1588. Deposition of John Marshall[4] of the Middle Temple, citizen of London, and born in Tucgrayes in Devon, aged 36. Bernard Drake endorsed a bill for £160 expended by Amyas Preston in victualling the *Golden Riall* and more later (about £60). Marshall verified with Drake that Preston's share in the victualling came to £220. He himself was part-victualler of the vessel. Arbitrators later awarded Preston £220, but he only received £10. He says 'That the said shipp the Golden Riall beinge so victualed and sent to sea did with the healpe of the Red Lion of Chichester[5] surprise and take foure shippes laden with sugers some gould & silver and other commodities, and also xvj sayle of Portingalles laden with fishe in the Newe

---

[1] Grenville had left Plymouth on 9 April (p. 178 above). Victualling of the *Golden Royal* at Exmouth would appear to have been begun almost immediately after his departure.

[2] Andrews ('Elizabethan privateering', pp. 67–73) reckons £3 a ton as a fair average price for a privateer, which would make £330 and would show Preston's own share to have been small. Of her victualling costs (£350–£400), however, his share was considerable.

[3] H.C.A. 13/27.   [4] Ibid.

[5] The vessel which the *Tiger* journal calls the *Lion* of 100 tons (p. 179 above).

founde lande whereof the first foure and ix or xij of the Newe
founde lande men were brought into this Realme beinge all
lawfull prize excepte for some smale quantity of sugers and[1] one
of the shippes which was claymed by Englishemen'. The same
ship took one prize when she was alone, which was sent to England
under Preston. He says the prizes were worth £60,000 and that
'the greatest parte of the said goodes came to the handes of the
said Barnard Drake For her maiestye having Cxx^li adventure in
the said viadge by meanes made passed over her interest to
Sir Water Rawly,[2] and by him a co[mmi]ssion was made to the
said Barnard Drake or his sonne Hugh as he remembrethe and by
that meanes the said Drake defeated the other Adventurers of
theire partes in the said shippes and goodes.'

(h) 25 November 1588. Deposition of Nicholas Hooddey (or
Hoddy),[3] citizen of London, gentleman, testifies to an arbitration
made between Amyas Preston and the Drakes, when Preston was
awarded £240, with which he was not satisfied.

(i) 2 December 1588. Deposition of Robert Bragge,[4] citizen of
London, merchant, who says he was of the company of the
Golden Riall. Amyas Preston's adventure was worth about £160
in victuals, while his father also paid for part of the ship. He
knows Sir Bernard Drake wrote to Sir Walter Raleigh by Master

---

[1] Probably for 'on' or 'in'.

[2] This would appear to mean that the queen had invested £120 in the *Golden
Royal's* expedition (with how many consorts we do not know) to Virginia, and
that when she obliged Raleigh to divert it to Newfoundland she made over her
investment to him as, we might say, a consolation prize. As the Newfoundland
expedition proved so profitable Raleigh must have earned a handsome profit at
the queen's expense. On what little is known of the queen's investment in
Grenville's squadron see Quinn, 'Preparations for the 1585 Virginia voyage', in
William and Mary Quarterly, 3rd ser., VI, 232–3, and pp. 148, 178, 231 above. A letter
from the privy council to Sir John Gilbert, 10 October 1585 (S.P. 12/183, 13),
recites that 'yt was of late thoughte meete by her maiesty to direct Sir Walter
Rawleghe knight to set fourth certen shipps to the seas out of the west partes of this
realm for th'intercepting of such of the K. of Spaynes subiectes as should repare
to the fishing at newfoundland.'   [3] H.C.A. 13/27.

[4] Ibid. Later associated with privateering (Andrews, in *William and Mary
Quarterly*, XI, 35).

Preston to pay him £160 out of the prize he took home, and that the rest would be satisfied on his [Drake's] return. Further, 'he knoweth that the said shipp the Golden Riall beinge soe furnished to sea did apprehend and take in consorte with Captaine Ryman and other shipps[1] foure spanishe and portingall shipps comming from Brasile laden with suger in[2] Fernambucke and other goodes. And also a Rocheller comminge from Guiny havinge wines and some goulde. Which he knoweth to be trew for that he was presente at the takinge of the said shippes.' Part of the goods in the ship of Frances Roch were Englishmen's. The ships taken were worth upwards of £10,000.

(*j*) 30 November 1588. Deposition of Henry Browne[3] of Loder, Dorset, soldier, who says that there was a consortship between Amyas Preston and Bernard Drake that all prizes taken by the *Golden Riall* should be shared according to the rate of their adventures. 'Master Drake and Amias Preston with this examinate and company beinge victualled and furnished as aforesaid did proceede with the said shipp the Golden Riall on the viadge aforesaid and first they apprehended a Brasill man laden with sugers wherewith Master Preston was sente for Englande, and then the said Drake with the said shipp and company proceeded to the Newe found [land] where they tooke xvij portingall shipps laden with fishe which they sente home and then meeting with Captaine Riman in the bay of Bulls[4] they consorted together[5] and sayled to the Isles of Surreyes[6] Where they took thre Brasill men and an Indian man laden with sugers wynes oliphantes teth[7] and some

---

[1] They may have included another vessel or vessels of Grenville's squadron since the *Dorothy* and one pinnace remain unaccounted for (cp. pp. 165, 169).

[2] For 'of'?   [3] Ibid. Did he go to Virginia in 1587 (p. 542)?

[4] Newfoundland, now Bay Bulls, lat. 47° 10′ N., long. 52° 46′ W. The name is first found on Thomas Hood's chart of the North Atlantic (n.d. but *c.* 1590, Brit. Mus., Additional MS 17938 B), cp. Harrisse, *Découverte et évolution cartographique de Terre-Neuve*, pp. 294, 304, 306, 308, 312–13, 340, 366.

[5] This means that Drake and Raymond made a formal agreement to co-operate in prize-taking and to share the proceeds.

[6] Azores.

[7] An alternative source of the ivory noted above (pp. 224–5).

goulde which were brought into Portesmouth or Chichester and Exmouth of this ex*amin*ates knowledge beinge presente at the takinge of all the said prizes.' The ships were worth upwards of £20,000. Further, 'he knoweth that m*aster* Bernard Drake and Captaine Riman had the disposinge of the goodes in the thre Brasill men and one Indian man of this ex*amin*ates knowledge and of p*art*e of the fish also.'[1]

(k) 15 February 1588[-89]. Personal answer of Amyas Preston,[2] 'that he made the consorteshippe articulate in the monethes and yeares articulate, and that never the lesse that iorney beinge disappointed he entered into a second consortshippe withe the said Barnarde Drake suche as is deduced in his libell....That the money by him layd out was secondly for the viadge and purpose mentioned in this res*p*ondentes Libell and soe aggreed to be taken, and not for the cause and viadge expressed in this article onely....Yet soe as her m*aiest*es pleasure was, that the consorte-shippe shoulde continewe and every adventurer shoulde receave accordinge to the rate of his adventure as it was first aggreed'. The commission here mentioned did not import 'any dissolucon of the consorteshippe afores*aid*, or hindered any p*artic*ion to be made of prizes taken accordinge to the said consortshippe....That her m*ai*estie meaninge that the consorteshippe aforesaide should not be hindered by color of her Com*m*ission appointed the p*er*sons

[1] On 7 December 1585 George Rayman, citizen of Chichester, gentleman, was awarded 60,000 fish (remaining in the hands of Amyas Preston, and thus showing that he was associating with Drake and Raymond after their return) and 16 tuns of oil as lawful prize in the High Court of Admiralty, together with 1000 chests of sugar on 8 December (H.C.A. 24/54, nos. 122-4). 100 chests of sugar taken by Bernard Drake were appraised on 16 April at £380 (ibid., no. 248), at which rate Raymond's sugar would be worth £3800. How much, if any, of this went towards the expenses of Grenville's squadron (of which Raymond's ship had been part) is not known. Preston was included in a Dorset commission and Bernard Drake in a Somerset one to value prize-goods brought home from the New-foundland voyage (H.C.A. 14/23, 164 (*bis*), 165, 19 October 1585).

[2] H.C.A. 13/101, the questions he answered being based on John Drake's allegations, (*d*) above. Preston maintains that he had a second consortship with Bernard Drake for the Newfoundland voyage, superseding his earlier one for the abortive Virginia expedition.

articulate, to see that distribucion shoulde be made accordinge to the same, and accordinge to every mans adventure.' He believes 'that Bernard Drake reteined the whole prices or the greter parte, the persons articulate orderinge that the same shoulde be disposed accordinge to the consorteshippe and not otherwise....That parte of the prises were taken by Sir Water Rawley and Sir Iohn Gilberte to which vse this respondente was not made privey but the greatest parte remayned withe Barnarde Drake to the vse of ye consortes aforesayde and by right of the sayd consortshipp and not by other authoritie otherwisc then by ways of assistance.' Signed 'per me Amyas Preston'.

(*l*) 16 February 1588[–89]. Personal answer of John Drake[1] 'that in Iune the xxvijth of her maiestes Raigne according to her maiestes commission in that behaulfe to the articulate Barnard Drake geiven and graunted the said Barnard did prepare and furnish the shipp articulate in Warlike sort to take anie of the kinge of Spaines or of his subiectes shippes and goodes'. He believes 'that the said master Amias Preston did bestowe some chardges towardes the furnishing and victualling of the ship called the golden riall for an adventure to be made by her to Quinvandequoie[2] and the said Amias Preston being a Captaine named and appoyncted therein for that viadge did laye oute aboute the Chardges of furnishing and victualling the said ship and other necessaries towardes the said viadge as this respondent beleeveth the somme of j C^{li} and not aboue and the said ship so furnished as afore with the captaines and men therein was after-wardes chardged and prest by vertue of her maiestes Commission aforesaid to alter their iorney and adventure before appoincted to Quinvandequoie and to goe to the New found land there to ayde

---

[1] Ibid. John Drake maintains, against Preston, that there was no second consort-ship, and that his father, Bernard Drake, was impressed to go to Newfoundland under the queen's orders, the subsequent disposition of the spoil being her responsibility, not his father's.

[2] A unique variant for 'Wingandacoia', probably due to the clerk, since Drake's version (in (*d*) above) is 'Wingan de Coy'.

her maiestes subiectes and their shippes and goodes and to seaze vppon the kinge of Spaines shippes or subiectes to her maiestes accompte and vse.' He believes 'that the said shipp the Golden Riall being readie prepared as ys aforesaid in Exmouth Havon in Devon was there as before prest & chardged to chandge her Course and make her adventure to the Newe founde landes to the purposes and end aforesaid and the said shipp accordinglie to her maiestes Commission with the Captaines and soldiers therein did sett furth from the said havon vnto the seas in anno Regni domine Regine xxvij° towardes the newe founde landes there to do according to her maiestes Commission.'[1]

He answers 'that the articulate ship called the Golden Riall being consorted with other ships by vertue of her maiestes Commission aforesaid did take first one ship laden with Brazill Farnando Bucke and sugers and assone as the said ship was taken the articulate Amias Preston was appoincted Captaine of the said prize and to bringe her home which he did accordinglie and afterwardes the said Golden Riall proceeded on her viadge and being consorted with one other shipp called the Lion by vertue of her maiestes said Commission did take three other shippes laden with Brasills sugers and other merchandises'. Further, 'he beleveth the said shippes were taken as lawfull prizes to her maiestie were lawfull prizes to her maiestie and were taken to her vse and disposition.' He believes 'that the said foure shippes and merchandize in the said foure shippes were worth 8 M[li] and not aboue....Bernard and also Hugh Drake his sonne after they had taken the said shippes and goodes did bringe them into the western partes according to her maiestes Commission and afterwardes by vertue of her maiestes graunte and Commission the articulate Barnard and also Hugh Drake his sonne did receave and

---

[1] Preston appears to have got his decree for £220, not against John Drake, but against Raleigh and Sir John Gilbert. When they did not pay him he took the matter to the privy council, who commanded Gilbert, in July 1589, four years after the event, to produce the accounts of the disposal of the prizes (*A.P.C.*, *1588–9*, pp. 283–4, 412–13; Ralegh, *The discoverie of Guiana*, ed. V. T. Harlow (1928), p. xxviii).

dispose to their owne vse one of the said shippes lyeng at Exmouth and were and ys by vertue of her maiestes graunte and Commission to haue and receyve the other twoe shipps and goodes therein'. He believes 'the said spanishe shipp and goodes which by her maiestes graunte and commission came to the articulate Barnard and Hugh was worthe xviij C^{li} and not aboue.... Amias Preston by order from the articulate Barnard receyved iij^{xx} ^{li}...otherwise the said Barnard by anie Convention agreement societie or contracte between him and the articulate Amias Preston did make noo division nor contribucion but hath and did soe refuse to doe.

CHAPTER IV

THE FIRST COLONY:
LANE AND DRAKE,
1585-6

Then homeward as their course did lie,
At sundry Isles they put a shore:
Their former wantes for to supply,
With victuales and fresh water store.
   At Florida they did ariue:
   Saint Augustine for to atchiue.

These townesmen trusting in their strength,
Then fiercely set against the Drake:
Yet he and's men preuaile at length,
When they were faine theyr towne forsake,
   Which when he had possest with fame:
   Vpon humble sute release the same.

This towne they wan most valiantly,
As they did all the rest before:
The Lord was still their victory,
Whose name be praysed euermore.
   And yeeld to Drake his due and right:
   Let fame extoll this noble knight....

After he had such valours wonne,
And ouercame the enemie:
To merry England he would returne,
The pleasants land in Christiantie.
   At Portesmouth then by Gods good grace:
   With all his fleete riude in short space.

THOMAS GREEPE, *The true and perfecte newes of the woorthy and valiaunt exploytes, performed and doone by that valiant knight Syr Frauncis Drake* (1587), sigs. C 1 v.–C 2 v.

NARRATIVE

We have no adequate account of the progress of the first colony under Lane after the departure of the last of Grenville's vessels in September 1585, until Lane provides us from March 1586 onwards with the materials for a story which carries us down to Drake's visit in June 1586. We should like to have some clear account of conditions at the fort and the houses near it, of the day-to-day relations between Lane's men and Wingina's village nearby, and of how White and Hariot proceeded with their task of surveying the ground and investigating the fauna and flora of the surrounding territory.[1] Lane begins his account by telling us that no effective exploration of the sounds and mainland south of Roanoke Island was carried out. His statement is not pellucidly clear and does not exclude some minor visits to the inner shore of Pamlico Sound, but it is unlikely that his men got as far as Secoton and it is certainly highly improbable that they went any further south. This may well mean, for one thing, that White's map[2] was constructed for this region largely, if not wholly, on the results of the expedition headed by Grenville in July 1585, which were roughly embodied in the sketch-map already considered.[3] Lane's excuse was that the pinnace was not suitable for traversing the sounds and that, in any case, winter was coming on.[4] So far as we can judge also, though it is a matter purely of inference, Lane relied for his knowledge of Albemarle Sound and probably the Chowan River on the information brought back by Amadas about the beginning of September,[5] until he was ready to make his own investigations the following spring. It is just possible that he visited the Weapemeoc tribe during the autumn, but he is very unlikely, if he did so, to have penetrated into the territory of the Chowanoac people.

What Lane did do in the autumn was to arrange for a party of

[1] Cp. pp. 54–6, 315–17, 901–10. [2] Figs. 6–8, pp. 460–2, 847–50.
[3] Pp. 215–17 above. [4] Pp. 256–7 below.
[5] Cp. pp. 207–17 above.

his men to explore to the northward and, apparently, to winter there. He is likely to have heard quite early of the Indian tribes on Chesapeake Bay and to have determined to explore the coastal area in this direction, since the desirability of finding a really good harbour must have been present in his thoughts from a very early stage, the reports that he had sent to Walsingham about those already found having been unflattering.[1] It is most exasperating that we have no detailed knowledge of the progress of this party. It was organized under a colonel[2] who might have been any one of Lane's leading assistants, Hariot, Amadas, Stafford or Vaughan being least unlikely, though it may well have been none of them. It certainly included either Hariot or White, or both, as the map[3] indicates that some detailed survey work was done, including marking a shoal near the head of Currituck Sound, noting a final breach in the Banks, and tracing the coastline round Cape Henry to a fair depiction of Lynnhaven Bay, and a more conjectural drawing of the land and water distributions to the west and north. Lane says the Chesepian tribe had its centre some fifteen miles from the water[4] and, if so, this must have been at Skicóak rather than at the village of Chesepiuc situated near Lynnhaven Bay.

At some place in this district, we are not told where, the exploring party set up a camp and settled down for some little time.[5] To their camp came members of what was later to be known as the Powhatan Confederacy—Virginia Algonkians, and also, it would appear, Iroquois.[6] The evidence on the map does not suggest that they touched at the Eastern Shore or that they entered the James or York Rivers, though they learnt something of the layout of the land around them. Very conjecturally, we may suggest that they went north about October and returned about February. Perhaps the winter was cool enough for them to remain in their camp over a good part of that time, and it is possible that this accounts for some part of the obscurity in which the episode

---

[1] Cp. pp. 200–2 above.
[2] Pp. 286–7 below.
[3] Fig. 7, pp. 461, 854–6.
[4] P. 257 below.
[5] P. 258.
[6] Cp. pp. 257–8, 855–7 below.

is wrapped. On the other hand, there are many indications[1] that this area was deliberately not described, as it was to be kept a secret from the Spaniards and from other Englishmen. There is no doubt at all that White's colony in 1587 set out to settle there and failed to do so only by accident. Lane, therefore, is either being deliberately reticent or else his narrative, in this form, has been censored; of course, he may be leaving the description of the Chesapeake to the leader of the party that explored it, this report being lost or having been suppressed. This is, indeed, as far as we can go in legitimate speculation about what is, perhaps, the most interesting chapter in the history of the first colony—the first English entry into what was to become the colony and state of Virginia.

The history of the explorations which Lane gives in detail is primarily that of the Chowan and Roanoke Rivers. His first move, in March, was to the Chowan River, when he brought his pinnace at least to the head of Albemarle Sound, going further, most probably, by boat.[2] At Chawanoac he became involved in what might easily have become a fatal tussle with the Indians. Wingina (now calling himself Pemisapan) had turned against the English[3]— partly from greed for their possessions, partly because they were pressing him to give them supplies of maize which he could not spare, and partly, there is some evidence to suggest, because Lane reacted with violence to his people on every provocation, however slight.[4] He had tried to arrange, therefore, a great alliance of neighbouring tribes which would descend on the English and wipe them out. Lane, provided with some dubious information by Wingina, managed to forestall the opposition; when he got to Chawanoac he found a great assembly in progress, with representatives of the Weapemeoc and Moratuc tribes, as well as the Iroquoian Mangoaks, conferring with Menatonon, the Chawanoac

[1] Cp. pp. 257–8 below.
[2] Cp. pp. 259, 264 below.
[3] Pp. 265–6. Lane treats it as a purely irrational shift.
[4] Cp. pp. 259, 265, 271, 286–8 below.

chief, about the project of allying with Wingina. Instead of being intimidated or overwhelmed he boldly entered the village, seized Menatonon, who was crippled, and managed to dominate the whole assembly.[1] Keeping the chief handcuffed for two days, he set out to glean from him as much information as possible about the interior—particularly with regard to harbours, inland water-channels, and sources of minerals and pearls. Menatonon proved very responsive and provided much valuable information. In the first place he indicated that three days' journey by canoe upstream and four days' marching overland to the northwards would bring them to a bay, where there was an island with an Indian chief who did an extensive business in pearls.[2] This sounded to Lane like the deep-water harbour he desired and he determined to follow it up by the suggested route, in co-operation with an expedition by sea.[3] Secondly, Menatonon provided the news that up the Roanoke River (River of Moratuc) there were ample supplies of a mineral (gold or copper) at a place called Chaunis Temoatan, which was also near a salt sea.[4] The lure of gold and of a passage to an inland sea was irresistible. Taking Skiko, Menatonon's son, as a hostage and sending him down to Roanoke Island in the pinnace, Lane, with several Indians, including Manteo, and some forty men in his double wherry and the other boat called a 'light horseman' set out to ascend the Roanoke River.[5]

Meantime, however, Wingina had learnt of their plans and had sent messengers ahead of them to warn the people of the Moratuc and Mangoak tribes that he meant them harm. These consequently kept completely out of Lane's sight so that he was unable to get any food from them, and after three days' rowing his supplies were exhausted, so that he was reduced to eating sassafras leaves and cooked dog, and had to return. Speedily running down on the current, he found the Weapemeoc villages also deserted, but got

[1] Cp. pp. 259, 264–5 below. Lane nowhere gives us a clear, straightforward account of this dramatic episode, but alludes to it only in passing.

[2] Pp. 259–61 below. For the island see the map at end, and p. 854.

[3] Pp. 261–3 below.   [4] Pp. 263–6 below.   [5] Pp. 264, 266 below.

enough fish in the weirs to bring him to Roanoke Island again on Easter Monday, 4 April.[1] The survival of the English Wingina found almost magical; he became more friendly and agreed to plant some corn for them and to give them more ground to work themselves; but until the crop was harvested a wearing time of waiting when food was short was now in prospect. Lane expected supplies by Easter, but they did not come; and by June he was becoming somewhat desperate.

Wingina turned hostile again after the death of one of his elders, Ensenore, who had been friendly with the English, late in April.[2] True, Menatonon sent pearls, induced Okisko, the Weapemeoc chief, to submit to Lane as the queen's vassal, and negotiated for his son's release;[3] but Wingina began a subtler campaign. He left the island, deserting the village there, for Dasemunkepeuc on the mainland; he ceased supplying the colony with fish and dried roots.[4] In consequence Lane was forced to disperse his men, some being sent to the vicinity of Cape Hatteras, others to Port Ferdinando, partly to fend for themselves, partly to be on the lookout for shipping.[5] This left his base weak. Meantime, Wingina was working to unite the Moratuc, Mangoak and Chesepiuc Indians against Lane, and to seduce the Weapemeoc tribe from its dual allegiance to Lane and to Menatonon, with the object of assembling them all in June to attack and overwhelm the settlement.[6] Skiko, Lane's prisoner, and some other friendly Indians managed to pick up enough information on these plans to warn him of what Wingina planned to do, so, ten days ahead of the rendezvous of the tribes on 10 June, Lane struck, entered Dasemunkepeuc on a pretext, attacked Wingina and his chief supporters and killed the chief,[7] presumably then dispersing or dominating the rest of the tribe, and letting news of his actions be spread so that no Indians appeared on the 10th. If he could

---

[1] Pp. 270–2 below. [2] Cp. pp. 274–5 below.
[3] P. 279 below. [4] P. 284 below.
[5] P. 283 below. [6] Pp. 281–6 below.
[7] Pp. 286–8 below, the most exciting incident of Lane's narrative.

hold out into July he would be able to reap a corn harvest and would be safe, so far as food supplies were concerned, for over a year, even if no reinforcements came.[1]

Should supplies and additional settlers arrive he had his plans cut and dried. He would have taken 200 men up the Chowan River and struck overland to the bay with the island and the pearl-fishery, leaving small fortified posts in his rear, while by sea he would have sent round a bark and two pinnaces to find the bay from that side. When the two expeditions had linked up he would first have constructed his base on the deep-water bay, and then have moved the remaining members of the settlement from Roanoke Island. He would keep open his line of communications with the Chowan river by means of his chain of posts so that he would have easy access to the land of the Mangoaks, the Roanoke River, and the hoped-for mine at Chaunis Temoatan.[2] This was a feasible programme if Grenville had arrived on time. Raleigh's supply ship was on its way and Grenville was at sea,[3] but it was Drake who appeared first and who altered so drastically Lane's, Grenville's and Raleigh's plans.

Drake's West Indian expedition of 1585-6 is the first major move in the sea-war with Spain which become open and unashamed for the first time in 1585. The character of the blows which Drake struck at Santo Domingo and Cartagena and the disturbance arising from his actions, which spread so rapidly throughout the Spanish overseas dominions, have not, perhaps, been fully realized until the recent publication by Miss Wright of a magnificently vivid and complete set of documents from Spain.[4] Drake's actions drove the Spaniards to consider as urgent the thorough revision of the defences of their American possessions, if they were to preserve them at all. It obliged them to lay the foundations of an effective

---

[1] Pp. 279–80 below.
[2] Pp. 272–5 below. This constitutes the main part of Lane's apologia, and was accepted by Raleigh as being, in most respects, a practicable programme since it was in fact prescribed for the settlers of 1587 (pp. 497–8, 523 below).
[3] Pp. 465–7 below.
[4] Occupying the greater part of her *Further English voyages* (1951).

ocean-going fleet. It impelled them to decide on 'the enterprise of England', by the success of which the pirates and heretics might be finally eliminated.[1] On the English side there were discussions going on during the early months of 1585 on the co-ordination of a series of blows at Spain, the establishment of a shore base on the North American coast which would shelter privateers as well as nourish a colony, the destruction of the Spanish fishing fleet at Newfoundland, and finally, and most important of all, Drake's expedition which had been long in preparation. These, though part of a single design, were kept flexible and separate, capable of readjustment to meet local circumstances, but calculated, between them, to begin the overthrow of the Spanish empire.

What exactly did Drake intend when his fleet left Plymouth on 14 September? Clearly all the main steps he took—a major naval demonstration off the Spanish coast, an attack on Santiago in the Cape Verdes, the looting of Santo Domingo and of Cartagena—were parts of his intended plan. But there were other objectives. One alternative provided that he should occupy Havana with a garrison in March 1586 and return to England by June.[2] Lane clearly expected in August 1585[3] that Sir Philip Sidney would be going with, or following Drake, to take command of English forces to be left at Havana and possibly other places in the West Indies. This was evidently still in Drake's programme as a possible contingency when he sailed, but the curious incidents at Plymouth, when Sidney tried to thrust himself on the expedition and Drake had to repel him,[4] probably mean that this part of the project had been relegated from a high to a low priority. There now seems ample proof that the key project which Drake left England

---

[1] For some remarks in this context see Quinn, 'Some Spanish reactions to Elizabethan colonial enterprises', in *Trans. R. Hist. Soc.*, 5th ser., I, 8–13.

[2] Brit. Mus., Lansdowne MS 100, fos. 98–9.

[3] Document no. 27, pp. 204–6 above.

[4] Cp. Fulke Greville, *Life of the renowned Sir Philip Sidney* (1907), p. 109; Corbett, *Drake*, II, 16–21; Emma Denkinger, *Sidney*, pp. 276–80; Mona Wilson, *Sidney* (1929), pp. 229–35. The explanations in secondary works are not, for the most part, satisfactory.

determined to attempt was the holding of Cartagena as a preliminary to the crossing of the Isthmus and the garrisoning of Panama.[1] For this he had much equipment, but it does not necessarily follow that he himself would have remained with the forces he expected to establish at these two keystones of the Spanish imperial system. A speedy return to England with plans for a Pacific squadron and an Atlantic fleet to keep the seas open would appear to have been his probable intention. Can we assume he had planned to co-ordinate his actions with those of Grenville? We know that Drake was well informed of what Grenville hoped to do,[2] and, since some of his vessels were bound to return to England by the Florida Channel, it is highly probable that he promised before leaving England that he would see, if possible, that the Spanish hold on Florida was broken so as to eliminate any threat it could offer to the English settlement further north. Whether he promised to call at the Virginia settlement to test the value of its harbour and its use as a supply base we cannot say. What is now clear is that, when he had been forced to leave Cartagena and to relinquish his plans for the Isthmus crossing, he began to think of aiding the Virginia settlement in some substantial way, and this before he had decided whether or not he would attempt Havana.

He carried with him from England parts of boats and small ships, shoes and clothing and other equipment for the Isthmus venture.[3] At Santo Domingo and Cartagena he had also been collecting men —galley slaves (mainly Moors, but including some Europeans), a few soldiers (again mainly Moors), negro domestic slaves to whom he promised their freedom, and a substantial number of South American Indians (about 300, including women),[4] all of

---

[1] Wright, *Further English voyages*, p. 44. [2] Ibid. pp. 172–3; p. 299 below.
[3] Wright, *Further English voyages*, pp. 44, 52, 195.
[4] Ibid., pp. 35, 54, 159, 168, 212. An early report to reach England said he had rescued no less than 1200 English, French, Flemings and Dutch from the galleys at Santo Domingo and took, besides, 800 people of the country with him (Nicholas Clever to Nicholas Turner, 26 May 1586, S.P. 12/189, 42, see *Cal. S.P. Colonial, 1675–6, and addenda 1574–1674,* pp. 28–9), the numbers being, of course, exaggerated.

whom, being acclimatized, he reckoned would help him to cross the Isthmus. Whether these motley passengers were responsible for the outbreaks of sickness among his own men we cannot say, nor can we tell how many of them succumbed, but he had not set any of them on shore when he turned back from Cartagena, decided not to attempt Havana, and made for Florida and Virginia. By that time it was clear that he planned to leave all of them, except the Moors and European galley slaves, at the Virginia settlement.[1]

The governor of Florida, Pedro Menéndez Marqués, had some advance warning of Drake's approach, but he had not the men to defend San Agustín very effectively. His wooden fort, scarcely completed when Drake arrived, was situated where it could most inconvenience the invaders and could act as an effective outpost for the unwalled town.[2] When Drake appeared on 27 May he was able to land unopposed on the sandy neck which faced the fort across the channel, and at once began putting up his batteries and preparing small vessels and boats for an attack on the fort. He flushed his quarry too soon, however, as the reconnaissance parties which went ashore at night made the commander of the fort decide to withdraw before he was surrounded. He could not protect both the fort and the non-combatants, since he feared to trust the latter to the Indians, so with his eighty soldiers he slipped away to the town and took all the people there into hiding with him. There had been some firing from the fort and a few small skirmishes in the bushes, but no fighting to speak of, so that all Drake could do was to destroy the fort and town, which he did as systematically as possible, even to cutting down the fruit trees. Having won this easy but not definitive victory (since the Spaniards had escaped him) he held a council to make a final decision on his next moves; this council agreed to attack Santa Elena, where Gutierre de Miranda

[1] Cp. p. 253, notes 7–8.
[2] For the assault on San Agustín cp. Documents nos. 6–7, pp. 295–9, 303–6 below, and Wright, *Further English voyages*, pp. 163–5, 180–9, 202–7, which between them provide for the first time a full account; however, a few puzzling features still exist. The topography is clearly shown in the plan in Bigges (conveniently reproduced in Wright at p. 166).

had fifty men, and then go on to Virginia, where it was expected to find the settlers in about 36° N. lat.[1] The fleet moved on, but the attack on Santa Elena was not made. Drake's pilots did not, as the Spaniards feared, know the difficult entry,[2] and so he anchored some little way to the north at Oristan,[3] taking in water and firewood, and obtaining a mast for one of his vessels. He again sailed north and on 8 June he was sighted by Captain Stafford's party on Croatoan Island near Cape Hatteras,[4] though at first it was not known whether he was friend or foe.[5] On the 9th contact was made, when he saw the signal fires and sent a boat on shore to pick up a pilot who brought him to Port Ferdinando on the 10th, his larger ships having to anchor well off shore,[6] thus demonstrating the inadequacy of the harbour.

By the time he wrote to Lane offering his assistance, Drake knew something of the situation of the colonists, and on the 11th they met. Drake had much to offer—his motley crew of passengers, the small boats he had seized at San Agustín, the furniture, the hardware (down to the locks on the doors) and other small articles which he had stripped so thoroughly from San Agustín for the benefit of the settlement.[7] He did not have much food to spare, since he had been dissatisfied with what San Agustín had yielded.[8] Lane, clearly disappointed that it was Drake and not Grenville, cannot have been too enthusiastic about these proffered gifts. His wants, however, were clear—a vessel (or vessels) to carry him along the coast to look for a better harbour and then home to make arrangements to come back in strength, boats, seamen, and arms. All of these Drake offered—the 70-ton *Francis*, two pinnaces, four boats, two experienced sailing-masters, and crews, weapons, tools, clothing, but only food for 100 men for four months, which Drake

---

[1] P. 299 below.
[2] P. 300 below; cp. Wright, *Further English voyages*, pp. 191, 204–5.
[3] Ibid., p. 191. This may have been the entry to Charleston Harbour.
[4] Cp. pp. 288, 300 below. Lane's dates may be a day too early (p. 288, n. 2).
[5] P. 288 below.   [6] Pp. 289, 300–1 below.
[7] Cp. Wright, *Further English voyages*, pp. 181–9, 204.
[8] P. 306 below.

must have been hard-pressed to spare.[1] The transfer of men and stores was almost completed on the 12th, and some of Lane's men were on board the *Francis* when a great hurricane blew up on the 13th. The larger ships broke their anchors or had to run clear, many pinnaces and boats were wrecked, and the *Francis* disappeared, though Drake was able to assemble most of his ships on the 16th.[2] He was still willing to help Lane, but now he could only offer the *Bark Bonner* (170 tons), which Lane considered too large for coastal exploration. In any case he had lost some of his men. So, calling such of his associates as he could together, he decided to abandon the settlement and return to England.[3] It was a reasonable decision, but more courage and fortitude might well have led Lane and his men to stay on. Had they done so supplies and reinforcements would soon have come. But having decided against the gamble of remaining Lane had to hurry away. The boats' crews sent (in rough water) to take the settlers' goods from Roanoke were impatient, pitching books, maps and papers, as well as pearls, into the water, and refusing to wait for three men who were up-country, probably with Menatonon.[4] On the 18th (or 19th) they sailed away, arriving at Portsmouth on 28 July[5] and finding, apparently, the *Francis* come home before them.

The mystery of Drake's dealings with the Roanoke settlement lies in the question, what did he do with his passengers? He had perhaps 300 South American Indians and 100 negro slaves to dispose of as a free labour for the Roanoke settlers. Were some of them lost in the storm? Were they all set on shore, with the pots and pans of San Agustín, to make what sort of life they could for themselves? If so, did Raleigh's ship and Grenville's expedition find any trace of them? If not, did they die or were they killed on the way to England, or were they landed at Portsmouth? The only trace we find of the passengers is of negotiations to send home some 100 ex-galley slaves to the Turkish dominions, which was

---

[1] Cp. pp. 289–91, 301 below.
[2] Cp. pp. 291–2, 302 below.
[3] Pp. 292–3 below.
[4] Cp. pp. 209, 307 below.
[5] Pp. 294, 303 below.

probably done.[1] But the Indians and negroes may well be reckoned a 'lost colony'. If they were lost in what is now North Carolina, when free coloured labour was Drake's intended gift to the English colonies there, it is a curious and ironic commentary on the later history of this and other plantation colonies.

45. 17 AUGUST 1585–18 JUNE 1586.

RALPH LANE'S DISCOURSE ON THE FIRST COLONY[2]

An account of the particularities of the imployments of the English men left in Virginia by Sir Richard Greeneuill vnder the charge of Master Ralfe Lane Generall of the same, from the 17. of August, 1585. vntill the 18. of Iune 1586.[3] at which time they departed the Countrie: sent and directed to Sir Walter Ralegh.[4]

That I may proceed with order in this discourse, I thinke it requisite to deuide it into two partes. The first shall declare the particularities of such partes of the Country within the mayne, as our weake number, and supply of things necessary[5] did inable vs to enter into the discouery thereof.[6]

The second part, shall set downe the reasons generally mouing

2 parts of this discourse.

---

[1] *Acts of the privy council, 1586–7*, pp. 205–6; Wright, *Further English voyages* p. 212; Corbett, *Spanish war*, pp. 21, 95.

[2] Hakluyt, *Principall navigations* (1589), pp. 737–47, collated with III (1600), 255–64 (VIII (1904), 320–45).

[3] These dates represent the limits of Lane's command at the fort on Roanoke Island. The first of them fits in well enough with what can be deduced from his letters (pp. 197–214), and it may also very well mark the date of Grenville's departure from the site of the colony for Port Ferdinando, preparatory to his sailing on 25 August.

[4] This report could have been made at any time after Lane's arrival at Portsmouth on 27 July 1586, but it is not likely to have been long delayed. It probably followed a verbal report to Raleigh, and was designed to give explanations of Lane's activities rather than a narrative of them, the papers he had written having mostly been lost at the departure from Roanoke Island (p. 293 below). Raleigh probably gave it to Hakluyt for publication, but it is not improbable that certain details were omitted from the original version (cp. pp. 29–31, 245–6).

[5] Lane is excusing, on account of lack of men and supplies, what Raleigh may have been expected to consider an inadequate achievement.

[6] 'of' (Hakluyt, III (1600), 255).

vs to resolue on our departure at the instant with the General Sir Frauncis Drake, and our common request for passage with him, when the barkes, pinnesses, and boates with the Masters and Mariners ment by him to bee left in the Countrie for the supply of such, as for a further time ment to haue stayed there, were caried away with tempest, and foule weather:[1] In the beginning whereof shalbe declared the conspiracie of Pemisapan, with the Sauages of the mayne to haue cutt vs off, &c.

The first part declaring the particularities of the Countrey of Virginia.

First therefore touching the particularities of the Countrey, you shal vnderstand our[2] discouery of the same hath bene extended from the Iland of Roanoak, (the same hauing bene the place of our settlement or inhabitation) into the South, into the North, into the Northwest, and into the West.

The vttermost place to the Southward of any discouerie was Secotan, being by estimation foure score miles distant from Roanoak.[3] The passage from thence was thorowe a broad sound within the mayne, the same being without kenning of land, and yet full of flats and shoales:[4] we had but one boate with foure oares[5] to passe through the same, which boat could not carry aboue fifteene men with their furniture, baggage, and victuall for seuen dayes at the most: and as for our Pinnesse, besides that she drewe too deepe water for that shalow sound, she would not stirre for an oare:[6] for these and other reasons (winter also being at hand)

---

[1] This was also intended to justify Lane's actions, since Raleigh had embarked expensively on the supply expeditions of 1586 (cp. pp. 465–6, 477).

[2] 'that our' (Hakluyt, III (1600), 255).   [3] About 100 miles (see map at end).

[4] The soundings on U.S. Coast and Geodetic Survey Charts, nos. 1229, 1232, 1231 and 537 fully bear out this statement.

[5] The double wherry described above, p. 141, and see pp. 264, 271 below.

[6] Grenville had sailed the pinnace, built on Puerto Rico (pp. 181, 183), to Secoton and elsewhere, so that Lane is probably exaggerating her unsuitability, though her failure to respond to oars, probably through having been too sturdily built, could be a substantial handicap on a protracted expedition in the treacherous Sound waters.

we thought good wholly to leaue the discouery of those partes vntill our stronger supplie.[1]

To the Northwarde our furthest discouerie was to the Chesepians,[2] distant from Roanoak about 130. miles, the passage to it was very shalow and most dangerous, by reason of the breadth of the sound, and the little succour that vpon any flawe was there to be had.

But the Territorie and soyle of the Chesepians (being distant fifteene miles from the shoare) was for pleasantnes of seate, for temperature of Climate, for fertilitie of soyle, and for the commoditie of the Sea, besides multitude of beares (being an excellent good victual, with great woods of Sassafras, and Wall nut trees) is not to be excelled by any other whatsoeuer.[4] *The excellency of the seate of Chesepiok.[3]*

There be sundry Kings, whom they call Weroances,[5] and Countries of great fertilitie adioyning to the same, as the Mandoages,[6] Tripanicks, and Opossians,[7] which all came to visit the

---

[1] It would thus appear that no exploration of this region, other than that undertaken by Grenville, was attempted, though Lane's statement does not rule out altogether some further preliminary reconnaissance in the period after Grenville's departure and before the winter of 1585-6.

[2] 'Chesepians, distant' (Hakluyt, III (1600), 255). The Chesapeake expedition was probably that designed by Lane for the winter (pp. 213-14 above), and it is probable that it did pass the winter at or near Chesepiuc (see the map at end). But the precise route taken is not known though conjectural routes are indicated on the map (cp. p. 856). The distance was nearer 100 miles than 130.

[3] 'Chesepiook' (Hakluyt, III (1600), 255). Hakluyt's interest in this area is shown in this comment, as previously in his letter to Raleigh (pp. 493-4), and it probably contributed somewhat to the attempted diversion of the 1587 colony to the Bay (pp. 497-8 below).

[4] Lane's brief notes (abbreviated possibly in order to maintain some degree of secrecy or else because the leader of the party had made, or was expected to make, his own report) should be used with George Percy's account (1607, in Smith, *Works*, pp. lxi–iii) and with White's maps (figs. 6-8, pp. 460-2, 854-6). The interior of the southern shore of Chesapeake Bay, westwards from Lynnhaven Bay, is very well wooded, but it is much broken up by swamps and waterways.

[5] Usually used for the chief men of a tribe and not the chief alone (cp. pp. 281, 370 below).

[6] Probably an Iroquoian tribe, either Nottoway or Meherrin (cp. pp. 264-75).

[7] Probably Algonkian tribes: Nansemond and Warrasqueoc being suggested below (pp. 855-6).

Colonie of the English, which I had for a time appointed to be resident there.[1]

To the Northwest the farthest place of our discouerie was to Choanoke distant from Roanoak about 130. miles.[2] Our passage thither lyeth through a broad sound, but all fresh water, and the chanell of a great depth, nauigable for good shipping,[3] but out of the chanell full of shoales.

The Townes about the waters side situated by the way, are these following: Pysshokonnok, The womans Towne, Chipanum, Weopomiok, Muscamunge, and Mattaquen:[4] all these being vnder the iurisdiction of the king of Weopomiok,[5] called Okisco:[6] from Muscamunge we enter into the Riuer, and jurisdiction of Choanoke:[7] There the Riuer beginneth to straighten vntill it come to Choanoke, and then groweth to be as narrowe as the Thames betweene Westminster, and Lambeth.

Betweene Muscamunge and Choanoke vpon the left hand as we passe thither, is a goodly high land, and there is a Towne which

[1] The absence of specific information on the organization and activity of this expedition is the most serious gap in our knowledge of the first colony. Its leader was evidently the 'Colonel of the Chesepians' referred to below (pp. 286–7).

[2] 'Chawanook' (Hakluyt, III (1600), 255). The distance to the presumed site of the village of Chawanoac was less than 100 miles (cp. p. 857 and map at end).

[3] From White's map (no. 110, fig. 7, p. 461) and p. 264, we learn that the pinnace was taken to the head of Albemarle Sound and that the rest of the journey up the Chowan River was made by boat. The strong downstream current from the Roanoke and Chowan Rivers keeps a deep channel clear (for soundings see U.S. Coast and Geodetic Chart 1228). This expedition was apparently Lane's first after the end of winter, in March 1586, and probably followed the return of the Chesapeake Bay expedition to Roanoke Island.

[4] 'Passaquenoke The womans Towne, Chepanoc, Weapomeiok, Muscamunge, and Metackwem' (Hakluyt, III (1600), 256), all villages of the Weapemeoc tribe on or near the northern shore of Albemarle Sound, except possibly Metackwem which may have stood on the peninsula between the Roanoke and Chowan Rivers and may have been a Chawanoac village (cp. p. 858). Hakluyt apparently altered the spellings of the names under the influence of White's maps (nos. 109–10, figs. 6–7, pp. 460–1).

[5] 'Weapomeiok' (Hakluyt, III (1600), 256).

[6] Cp. pp. 279, 281, 284, 892–3.

[7] 'Chawanook' (Hakluyt, III (1600), 256), and below. For location of the tribe and village see p. 857.

we called the blinde Towne, but the Sauages called it Ooanoke,[1] and hath a very goodly corne field belonging vnto it: it is subiect to Choanoke.

Choanoke it selfe is the greatest Prouince and Seigniorie lying upon that Riuer, and the very Towne it selfe is able to put 700. fighting men into the fielde, besides the forces of the Prouince it selfe.[2] *The Towne of Choanoak able to make 700. men of warre.*

The King of the sayd Prouince is called Menatonon, a man impotent in his lims, but otherwise for a Sauage, a very graue and wise man, and of very[3] singular good discourse in matters concerning the state, not onely of his owne Countrey, and the disposition of his owne men, but also of his neighbours round about him as wel farre as neere, and of the commodities that eche Countrey yeeldeth. When I had him prisoner with me, for two dayes that we were together, he gaue mee more vnderstanding and light of the Countrey then I had receiued by all the searches and saluages that before I or any of my companie had had conference with: it was in March last past 1586.[4] Amongst other things he tolde me, that going three dayes iourney in a canoa vp his Riuer of Choanoke, and then descending to the land, you are within foure dayes iourney to passe ouer land Northeast to a certaine Kings countrey, whose Prouince lyeth vpon the Sea, but his place of greatest strength is an Iland situate as he described vnto me in a Bay, the water round about the Iland very deepe.[5] *An Iland in a Bay.*

[1] 'Ohanoak' (Hakluyt, III (1600), 256), on the west bank of the Chowan River (cp. p. 858).

[2] This would mean that the village had a total population of some 2000, which is far too high. His earlier use of the figure (p. 213 above) would appear to be for the adult population of the Weapemeoc tribe and as such is reasonable. (Dr Maurice A. Mook ('The aboriginal population of tidewater Virginia', in *American Anthropologist*, n.s., XLVI, 206) takes 1500 as a working estimate for the Chawanoac tribe.) [3] 'a very' (Hakluyt, III (1600), 256).

[4] Lane's failure to provide a narrative sketch for this expedition leaves us in some doubt at this point as to the circumstances, but the story can be pieced together from pp. 264–6 below.

[5] It is assumed, in view of what is said below (pp. 262–3), that it is a route to Chesapeake Bay which is being outlined, though Lane was not clear that this was so. Such a route is indicated on the map at the end. The times required

Pearles in exceeding quantitie. Out of this Bay hee signified vnto mee, that this King had so great quantitie of Pearle, and doeth so ordinarily take the same, as that not onely his owne skins that he weareth, and the better sort of his gentlemen and followers, are full set with the sayd Pearle, but also his beds, and houses are garnished with them, and that hee hath such quantitie of them, that it is a wonder to see.[1]

He shewed me that the sayd King was with him at Choanoak two yeeres before, and brought him certaine Pearle, but the same of the worst sort, yet was he faine to buy them of him for copper at a deere rate, as he thought:[2] He gaue me a rope of the same Pearle, but they were blacke, and naught, yet many of them were very great, and a fewe amongst a number very orient and round, all which I lost with other things of mine, comming aborde Sir Francis Drake his Fleete:[3] yet he tolde me that the sayd King had great store of Pearle that were white, great, and round, and that his blacke Pearle his men did take out of shalowe water, but the white Pearle his men fished for in very deepe water.[4]

It seemed to mee by his speech, that the sayde king had traffike

for the journey up-stream and overland are somewhat exaggerated. We have nowhere a clear indication of what tribe on the Chesapeake is meant, but it is probable that it is the Kecoughtan, which occupied the peninsula on the north bank of the James River at its mouth. The tribal village was located between the present town of Hampton and Old Point Comfort, so that the island may well have been Old Point Comfort (cp. Smith, *Works*, pp. 9–10; Mook, 'The ethnological significance of Tindall's map of Virginia, 1608', in *William and Mary Quarterly*, 2nd ser., XXIII (1943), 384–7, and p. 854 below). The chief who visited Chawanoac in 1583 may have been he whom Powhatan killed about 1596 or 1597 (Strachey, *Hist. of travell*, p. 68; Speck, *Powhatan tribes*, p. 293).

[1] While there is a fair amount of evidence from the Jamestown colony that pearls were used for decoration by the Powhatan tribes, they were not so prominent as with the Carolina Algonkians, though John Smith refers to the 'plentie of good Oysters' he obtained at Kecoughtan (*Works*, II, 449).

[2] This reference to Indian trade is interesting, as it would suggest that Menatonon obtained his copper from a western (Iroquoian?) rather than a northern source (cp. p. 269).

[3] Cp. pp. 293, 334 below.

[4] This is possibly an attempt to distinguish between mussel and oyster pearl-fishing, though much of the blackening, (cp. pp. 261, 333) was due to the Indian practice of cooking the shell-fish in the shell.

with white men that had clothes as we haue, for these white Pearle,[1] and that was the reason that he would not depart with other then with blacke Pearles, to those of the same Countrey.

The king of Choanoak[2] promised to giue me guides to goe ouer land into that kings Countrey whensoeuer I would: but he aduised me to take good store of men with mee, and good store of victuall, for he sayd, that king would be loth to suffer any strangers to enter into his Countrey, and especially to meddle with the fishing for any Pearle there, and that hee was able to make a great many of men into the fielde, which he sayd would fight very well.[3]

Hereupon I resolued with my selfe, that if your supplie had come before the end of April,[4] and that you had sent any store of boats or men, to haue had them made in any reasonable time, with a sufficient number of men, and victuals to haue found vs vntill the new corne were come in, I woulde haue sent a small Barke with two Pinnesses about by Sea to the Northwarde to haue found out the Bay he spake of, and to haue sounded the barre if there were any, which shoulde haue ridden there in the sayd Bay about that Iland,[5] while I with all the small boats I could make, and with two

---

[1] This may reflect some echo of Spanish contacts with the Chesapeake Bay Indians between 1559 and 1572 (see the references in Quinn, 'Some Spanish reactions', *T.R. Hist. Soc.*, 5th ser., I, 4, 15; Luis Gerónimo de Oré, *Relación histórica de la Florida*, ed. A. Lopez, I (1931), 63–70; *Monumenta antiquae Floridae, 1566–72*, ed. F. Zubillaga (*Monumenta Historica Societatis Iesu*, LXIX (Rome, 1946)), especially pp. 51, 527–8; F. Zubillaga, *La Florida: la misión jesuitica* (1943); C. M. Lewis and A. J. Loomie, *The Spanish Jesuit mission in Virginia, 1570–1572* (1953)).

[2] 'Chawanooke' (Hakluyt, III (1600), 256), and below.

[3] The Kecoughtan tribe early in the seventeenth century had declined, becoming one of the weakest in the Powhatan group (Smith, *Works*, I, 345).

[4] Lane expected relief by Easter (April 3) but reckoned it might well be some weeks late. It would be mid-July before the corn harvest was ready.

[5] There is a certain failure on Lane's part here to correlate the reports of Chesapeake Bay, brought by the exploring party which wintered there, with Menatonon's explanation of the overland route. This may have been because the exploring party reached Chesapeake Bay overland and Lane could not be certain that both sets of reports related to the same harbours (cp. alternative routes sketched on map at end).

hundreth men[1] would haue gone vp to the head of the Riuer of Choanoak, with the guides that Menatonon would haue giuen,[2] which I would haue bene assured should haue bene of his best men, (for I had his best beloued sonne prisoner with me) who also should haue kept me companie in an handlocke[3] with the rest foote by foote all the voyage ouer land.

My meaning was further at the head of the Riuer in the place of my descent where I would haue left my boates to haue raysed a sconse with a small trench, and a pallisado vpon the top of it, in the which, and in the garde of my boates I would haue left fiue and twentie, or thirtie men,[4] with the rest would I haue marched with as much victuall as euery man could haue carried, with their furniture, mattocks, spades and axes,[5] two dayes iourney. In the ende of my marche vpon some conuenient plot would I haue raised another sconse according to the former, where I would haue left 15. or 20. And if it would haue fallen out conueniently, in the way I woulde haue raised my sayd sconse vpon some corne fielde, that my companie might haue liued vpon it.[6]

[1] Lane expected a substantial reinforcement, since he was reckoning to have 100 additional men to spare (in spite of having to leave a garrison on Roanoke Island for the time being) and to send a further expedition by sea. The size of Grenville's expedition suggests that he could have left sufficient men to do all that Lane proposed (cp. p. 479).

[2] 'haue giuen me, which' (Hakluyt, III (1600), 256): in margin 'An enterprise of speciall importance'. The latter insertion shows that while Hakluyt took up the Chesapeake Bay project at once after Lane's return (cp. pp. 493–4), he was still concerned to stress its importance in 1600.

[3] See pp. 285, 287 below for his continued restraint of Skiko after the return to Roanoke Island.

[4] This is apparently the kind of light fortification which Lane had proposed to erect at Port Ferdinando (where he was probably overruled by Grenville, p. 202 above). Even his temporary trenches in sand were inclined to be over-elaborate (cp. White, no. 3, see pp. 404–5) and a small palisaded fort of this character would have taken more time than he reckoned to build. For some discussion and criticism of sconces see Humphrey Barwick, *Breefe discourse* (c. 1591), fo. 27 v. and Sir John Smythe, *Certain discourses* (1590), pp. 11, 13; p. 134 above.

[5] The tools being required for clearing a passage and for the entrenchments and fortification at each stage.

[6] A corn field implied a village, and the leaving of small outposts of this sort, liable to become involved with superior numbers of Indians, does not appear

Ralph Lane

And so I would haue holden this course of insconsing euery two *Whether Master Ralph Lane meant to remooue.* dayes march, vntill I had bene arriued at the Bay or Porte he spake of:[1] which finding to be worth the possession, I would there haue raised a mayne forte, both for the defence of the harboroughs, and our shipping also, and would haue reduced our whole habitation from Roanoak and from the harborough and port there (which by proofe is very naught) vnto this other before mentioned,[2] from whence, in the foure dayes march before specified, could I at all times returne with my companie backe vnto my boats ryding vnder my sconse, very neere whereunto directly from the West runneth a most notable Riuer, and in all those partes most famous, called the Riuer of Morotico.[3] This Riuer openeth into the broad sound of Weopomiok: And whereas the Riuer of Choanoak, and all the other sounds, and Bayes, salt and fresh, shewe no currant in the world in calme weather, but are mooued altogether with the winde: This Riuer of Morotico hath so violent a currant from the West and Southwest, that it made me almost of opinion that with oares it would scarse be nauigable:[4] it passeth with many creeks and turnings, and for the space of thirtie miles rowing, and more, it is as broad as the Thames betwixt Greenwich,

very sound strategy. Lane may have worked out this plan on the basis of Irish experience, where English punitive forces often found themselves unable to maintain themselves in hostile territory and had difficulty in securing a line of retreat.

[1] The whole scheme was over-elaborate, especially as (if the interpretation of Menatonon's direction, above, is correct) the overland journey, though through difficult country, would not have exceeded 50 miles, and would probably have taken less than the estimated four days. Was it this journey that White's colony in 1587 contemplated making? Cp. pp. 533–4, 613 below.

[2] The plan for the 1587 expedition was to do just this (p. 502 below). Hakluyt's influence in continually stressing the Chesapeake Bay venture was probably a factor in the settlement of the 1607 colony on the James River, even though nothing came of the 1586 and 1587 ventures.

[3] 'Moratoc' (Hakluyt, III (1600), 257), and below. Lane is getting both his bearings and his distances confused, since the Roanoke River entered the head of Albemarle Sound from the west some 40 miles south of the place of which he was speaking (cp. map, at end).

[4] The Roanoke River, rising in the Blue Ridge Mountains, does carry down appreciably more water than the Chowan. The downstream current did, therefore, indicate that it would better repay exploration than the more mature Chowan.

and the Ile of dogges,[1] in some place more, and in some lesse: the currant runneth as strong being entred so high into the Riuer, as at London bridge vpon a vale water.[2]

And for that not onely Menatonon, but also the Sauages of Morotico themselues[3] doe report strange things of the head of that Riuer, and that from Morotico it selfe, which is a principall Towne vpon that Riuer, it is thirtie dayes as some of them say, and some say fourtie dayes voyage to the head thereof, which head they say springeth out of a maine rocke in that abundance, that forthwith it maketh a most violent streame: and further, that this huge rocke standeth nere[4] vnto a Sea, that many times in stormes (the winde comming outwardly from ye Sea) the waues thereof are beaten into the said fresh streame, so that the fresh water for a certaine space, groweth salt and brackish:[5]

I tooke a resolution with my selfe, hauing dismissed Menatonon vpon a ransome agreed for, and sent his sonne into the Pinnesse to Roanoak,[6] to enter presently so farre into that Riuer with two double whirries, and fourtie persons one or other,[7] as I could have victuall to carrie vs, vntill we could meete with more either of the

---

[1] The Isle of Dogs lies between Blackwall Reach and Limehouse Reach on the Thames.   [2] Ebb-tide.

[3] Lane's contacts (and his 'league' with the Moratoc tribe (p. 266 below)) were made at the great Indian assembly at Chawanoac in March, but when he actually entered the Roanoke River they avoided him.

[4] 'so neare' (Hakluyt, III (1600), 257).

[5] This tale may owe something to information about the river's sources in the Alleghenies, but mention of salt water may link up with the salt-panning explanation of the 'mining' technique discussed below and thus imply some knowledge of the Mississippi basin. The Indian chief, whom Francis Yeardley found at Roanoke Island in 1653, told him a not dissimilar story (A. S. Salley, *Narratives of early Carolina, 1650–1708* (1911), pp. 25–6).

[6] This might suggest that the pinnace was brought as far up the Chowan as the village of Chawanoac, but it is more likely that Lane did not risk her beyond the head of Albemarle Sound (cp. p. 461).

[7] Note the inconsistency with Lane's statement above (p. 256) that he had only one four-oared boat which could take only fifteen men and their equipment. One of those used was a double wherry, the other a 'light horseman' (p. 271 below). Lane may have rested at the head of Albemarle Sound but within a very short time, with such provisions as he had, he pushed on up the Roanoke (Moratuc) River.

Moratiks,[1] or of the Mangoaks,[2] which is another kinde of Sauages, dwelling more to the Westwarde of the sayd Riuer: but the hope of recouering more victuall from the Sauages made me and my company as narowly to escape staruing in that discouerie before our returne, as euer men did that missed the same.

For Pemisapan, who had changed his name of Wingina vpon the death of his brother Granganimo,[3] had giuen both the Choanists & Mangoaks word of my purpose touching them, I hauing bin inforced to make him priuie to ye same, to be serued by him of a guide to the Mangoaks, and yet he did neuer rest to solicite continually my going vpon them, certifying me of a generall assembly euen at that time made by Menatonon at Choanoak of all his Weroances, & allyes to the number of 3000. bowes[4] preparing to come vpon vs at Roanoak, and that the Mangoaks also were ioyned in the same confederacie, who were able of themselues to bring as many more to the enterprise: And true it was, that at that time the assembly was holden at Choanoak about vs, as I found at my comming thither, which being vnlooked for did so dismay them, as it made vs haue the better hand at them. But this confederacie against vs of the Choanists and Mangoaks was altogether and wholly procured by Pemisapan himselfe, as Menatonon confessed vnto me, who sent them continuall worde

Wingina changeth his name

---

[1] 'Moratoks' (Hakluyt, III (1600), 257).

[2] The Mangoak tribe, apparently Iroquoian, was located behind the Moratuc and Chawanoac peoples, between the Roanoke and Chowan Rivers (cp. p. 857).

[3] No precise analogy to this name-changing has been found—unless Wingina was merely taking a new 'war-name' in anticipation of his victory over the English—but it may be a variation of the practice of the Creeks and certain other south-eastern tribes who 'adopted the names of their children, sometimes in succession as the elder children died' (Swanton, *Indians*, pp. 671–4).

[4] Presumably the Moratuc and Weapemeoc tribes as well as his own. The alliance with the latter is somewhat surprising and does not accord too well with other references (cp. pp. 278, 281), though there were some trading contacts between the Algonkian tribes and non-Algonkian peoples of the interior (pp. 257, 268–70). The figure of 3000 fighting men implies a total population of at least 10,000, which other sources would suggest was substantially too high. Mook would put the total Carolina Algonkian population at 5000 (*American Anthropologist*, n.s., XLVI, 206, cp. pp. 213, 259).

that our purpose was fully bent to destroy them: on the other side he tolde me that they had the like meaning towards vs.[1]

Hee in like sort hauing sent worde to the Mangoaks of mine intention to passe vp into their Riuer, and to kill them (as he sayd) both they and the Moratiks, with whome before we were entred into a league, and they had euer dealt kindely with vs, abandoned their Townes along the Riuer,[2] and retyred themselues with their *★Crenepoes,[3] and their corne within the mayne: insomuch as hauing passed three dayes voyage vp the Riuer, we could not meete a man, nor finde a graine of corne in any their Townes: whereupon considering with my selfe, that wee had but two dayes victuall left, and that wee were then 160. miles from home,[4] besides casualtie of contrarie windes or stormes, and suspecting treason of our owne Sauages in the discouerie of our voyage intended, though we had no intention to be hurtfull to any of them, otherwise then for our copper to haue had corne of them:[5] I at night vpon the corps of garde, before the putting foorth of centinels,[6] aduertised the whole

★Their women (margin note)

---

[1] The paragraph is a typical example of Lane's lack of lucidity in composition. Having given us a version of his visit to Chawanoac in March 1586, he now reverts to the background of that expedition, namely to Wingina's stimulation of a great Indian assembly of a hostile character to receive him. He still leaves untold the circumstances in which he braved this assembly, took Menatonon prisoner, ransomed him (p. 259, 264) and, finally, convinced him of his peaceful intentions.

[2] This was a surprise to Lane since he had made friends with the Moratuc representatives he met at Chawanoac.

[3] 'Crenepos' (Hakluyt, III (1600), 257): the word means 'women', but its etymology is not clear (cp. pp. 886–7).

[4] As it was some 60 miles from Roanoke Island to the head of Albemarle Sound this would bring Lane some 100 miles up the Roanoke River in three days' rowing against a strong current. This distance has been marked out on the map (at end), but Lane usually tended to exaggerate distances and he may not have gone so far. He probably got as far as the modern Hamilton in Martin Co. and not so far as Halifax in the county of that name.

[5] This shows that late in March 1586 Lane still had copper which he had not been able to exchange at Roanoke Island for corn (cp. pp. 280, 282). Thus one subsidiary object in his spring expeditions was to try to collect some surplus corn from other Indian tribes.

[6] This was part of the strict discipline on which Lane prided himself (p. 228), the desirability of which had been impressed on Raleigh and Cavendish before the expedition left England (p. 131 above).

companie of the case wee stoode in for victuall, and of mine opinion that we were betrayed by our owne Sauages,[1] and of purpose drawen foorth by them, vpon vaine hope to be in the ende starued, seeing all the Countrey fledde before vs, and therefore while we had those two dayes victuall left, I thought it good for vs to make our returne homewarde, and that it were necessarie for vs to get the other side of the sound of Weopomiok[2] in time, where we might be relieued vpon the weares of Chypanum, and the womans Towne,[3] although the people were fled.

Thus much I signified vnto them, as the safest way: neuerthelesse, I did referre it to the greatest number of voyces, whether we should aduenture the spending of our whole victuall in some further viewe of that most goodly Riuer in hope to meete with some better hap, or otherwise to retyre our selues backe againe.: And for that they might be the better aduised, I willed them to deliberate all night vpon the matter, and in the morning at our going aborde to set our course according to the desires of the greatest part. Their resolution fully and wholly was (and not three found to be of the contrary opinion) that whiles there was left one halfe pinte of corne for a man, that we[4] should not leaue the search of that Riuer, and that there were in the companie two mastiues,[5] vpon the pottage of which with sassafras leaues (if the worst fell out) the companie would make shift to liue two dayes, which time would bring them downe the currant to the mouth of the Riuer, and to the entrie of the sound, and in two dayes more at the farthest they

---

[1] I.e. those of Roanoke Island.

[2] 'Weapomeiok' (Hakluyt, III (1600), 258), that is Albemarle Sound, on the north side of which the Weapemeoc tribe lived.

[3] Pasquenoke (see p. 258 above), which with Chepanoc, was a Weapemeoc village. The reason for the name is not known as the word gives no clue (p. 861), but it may be it was so named on account of the survival of matriarchal customs. Dr Flannery (*Analysis*, nos. 239–40) points out that there are examples of women inheriting office (including chieftaincy) among the southern coastal Algonkians.

[4] 'left but one...for a man, wee' (Hakluyt, III (1600), 258).

[5] Bull-mastiffs brought from England as Hakluyt had proposed (Taylor, *Hakluyts*, II, 321). They were valuable fighting and watch dogs. For their use in New England by Martin Pring in 1603, and the Indians' fear of them, see Purchas, *Pilgrims*, XVIII (1906), 325, 328.

hoped to crosse the sounde and to bee relieued by the weares,[1] which two dayes they would fast rather then be drawen backe a foote till they had seene the Mangoaks, either as friends or foes. This resolution of theirs did not a little please mee, since it came of themselues, although for mistrust of that which afterwards did happen, I pretended to haue bene rather of the contrary opinion.

And that which made me most desirous to haue some doings with the Mangoaks either in friendship or otherwise to haue had one or two of them prisoners,[2] was, for y[t] it is a thing most notorious to all y[e] countrey, that there is a Prouince to the which the sayd Mangoaks haue recourse and traffike vp that Riuer of Moratico,[3] *A maruellous Mineral in the countrey of Chaunis Temoatan.* which hath a marueilous and most strange Minerall. This Mine is so notorious amongst them, as not onely to the Sauages dwelling vp the sayde riuer, and also to the Sauages of Choanoke, and all them to the westward, but also to all them of the mayne: the countries name is of fame, and is called Chaunis Temoatan.[4]

The mineral they say is Wassador, which is copper, but they call by the name of Wassador euery mettall whatsoeuer:[5] they say it is of the couler of our copper, but our copper is better then theirs: and the reason is for that it is redder and harder, whereas that of Chaunis Temoatan is very soft, and pale: they say that they take the sayd mettall out of a riuer that falleth very swift from hie rocks, and hyls, and they take it in shallowe water: the manner is

[1] The fish-weirs of the Weapemeoc villages.
[2] Lane reckoned that by this time he had passed through the Moratuc country into that of the Mangoaks.
[3] 'Moratoc' (Hakluyt, III (1600), 258).
[4] If there was a place of this name it is quite impossible to suggest a location for it, unless it was some salt-making village across the Appalachians as W. W. Tooker maintained ('Discovery of Chaunis Temoatan', in *American Antiquarian*, XVII (1895), 9), and cp. pp. 270, 273, 340, 859 below. Hakluyt suggested, on the strength of reports by prisoners taken by Drake at San Agustín in 1586 (p. 763 below), that there was gold and copper in 'the mountains of Apalatci', that the 'hils of Chaunis Temoatam' might be there.
[5] Professor Geary suggests 'small reddish masses' as a possible meaning (p. 898), and this is borne out by Hariot's recollection of what the Indians told him of 'a great melting of red metall' (p. 388).

this. They take a great bowle by their discription as great as one of our targets,[1] and wrap a skinne ouer the hollowe part thereof, leauing one part open to receiue in the minerall: that done, they watch the comming downe of the currant, and the change of the couler of the water, and then suddenly chop downe the said bowle with the skin, and receiue into the same as much oare as will come in, which is euer as much as their bowle wil hold, which presently they cast into a fire, and forthwith it melteth, and doeth yeelde in 5. partes, at the first melting, two parts of metall for three partes of oare.[2] Of this metall the Mangoaks haue so great store, by report of all the sauages adioyning, that they beautifie their houses with

---

[1] A shield. Tooker (op. cit. pp. 9–11) records vessels of this size associated with salt-spring workings on the Ohio R.

[2] Discussion of the Indian sources of copper and their use has involved a good deal of confusion. No copper ore was smelted in any part of North America before the Europeans arrived. Native copper in a pure state was obtained (a) from the extensive lodes in the region of Lake Superior 'in beds of conglomerate and amygdaloid', (b) from small exposed lodes in various parts of the Appalachian chain (notably the Blue Ridge Mountains where the Roanoke River rises and where lodes of 1 lb. or more have been found), (c) in the widely dispersed glacial drift from Lake Superior throughout the Mississippi valley, (d) possibly from alluvial deposits deriving from eastern mountains. The Indians in the east obtained their copper mainly from (a), where it was quarried and from which it was dispersed through the interior by recognized trade routes. They may have quarried occasional lodes from (b), but this is not certain. They collected a certain amount from (b), (c), and probably (d), in places sufficient for gorgets and other large pieces, and in other places adequate only for beads. There is some evidence that they washed alluvium for free copper nodules, and they may (though there is no corroborative evidence) have put some of their finds in fire to detach the nodules from their stony matrix. This last is Dr T. A. Rickard's suggested explanation ('The use of native copper by the indigenes of North America', in *Journal of the Royal Anthropological Institution*, LXIV (1934), 265–87, especially p. 267) of this passage which he calls 'an untechnical and hearsay description of alluvial mining' (cp. also pp. 388, 820–1 below). This is not a sufficient comment, however, as it has been suggested that what Lane is describing is salt gathering and boiling (cp. p. 268, n. 4, above, and Swanton, *Indians*, pp. 492–3). Swanton ingeniously attempts to identify salt-making tribes of Kentucky as distributors of Lake Superior copper across the mountains, thus leading Indians further east to confuse the processes by which each was obtained, but this is unconvincing. The salt-boiling process is well attested (see Swanton, *Indians*, pp. 300–1) and could easily be confused with alluvial mining, but the latter need not be ruled out of account here solely for this reason.

great plates of the same:[1] and this to be true, I receiued by report of all the country, and particularly by yong Skiko, the King of Choanokes[2] sonne my prisoner, who also himselfe had bene prisoner with the Mangoaks,[3] and set downe all the particularities to mee before mentioned: but hee had not bene at Chawnis Temoatan himselfe: for he sayd, it was twentie dayes iourney ouerlande from the Mangoaks,[4] to the saide minerall country, and that they passed through certaine other territories betweene them and the Mangoaks, before they came to the said country.

Vpon reporte of the premisses, which I was very inquisitiue in all places where I came to take very particular information of, by all the sauages that dwelt towards those parts, and especially of Menatonon himselfe, who in euery thing did very particularly informe mee, and promised mee guides of his owne men, who shoulde passe ouer with mee, euen to the sayde country of Chaunis Temoatan, (for ouer lande from Choanok to the Mangoaks is but one dayes iourney from sunne rysing to sunne setting, whereas by water it is 7. daies with the soonest:)[5] These things I say, made me verie desirous by all meanes possible to recouer the Mangoaks, to get some of that their copper for an assay, and therefore I willingly yeelded to their resolution: But it fell out very contrarie to all expectation, and likelyhood: for after two dayes trauell, and our whole victual spent, lying on shoare all night, wee could neuer see man, onely fires wee might perceiue made alongst the shoare where we were to passe, and vp into the countrie vntill the very last day. In the euening whereof, about three of the clocke we heard certaine sauages call as we thought, Manteo, who was also at that

[1] There is no indication that early travellers noted any special profusion of copper among the Mangoak and other Iroquoian tribes of this area, though as distributors of copper they might well have had more than their eastern neighbours.

[2] 'Chawanooks' (Hakluyt, III (1600), 258).

[3] An indication, perhaps, that peace, rather than war, was exceptional as between the Mangoaks and the coastal Algonkian tribes (cp. pp. 278, 281).

[4] This would place it well into the mountains at least (cp. p. 268, n. 4 above).

[5] This was the clearest indication in locating the territory of the Mangoak tribe on the map (cp. p. 857).

time with mee in boate,[1] whereof we all being verie glad, hoping of some friendly conference with them, and making him to answere them, they presently began a song, as we thought in token of our welcome to them: but Manteo presently betooke him to his peece, and tolde mee that they ment to fight with vs:[2] which word was not so soone spoken by him, and the light horseman[3] ready to put to shoare, but there lighted a vollie of their arrowes amongst them in the boate, but did no hurt God be thanked to any man. Immediatly, the other boate lying ready with their shot to skoure the place for our hand weapons to land vpon, which was presently done, although the lande was very high and steepe, the Sauages forthwith quitted the shoare, and betooke themselues to flight: we landed, and hauing fayre and easily followed for a smal time after them, who had wooded themselues we know not where: the sunne drawing then towards the setting, and being then assured that the next day, if wee would pursue them, though wee might happen to meete with them, yet we should bee assured to meete with none of their victuall, which we then had good cause to thinke of, therefore choosing for the companie a conuenient grounde in safetie to lodge in for the night, making a strong corps of garde, and putting out good centinels,[4] I determined the next morning before the rising of the sunne to be going backe againe, if possibly wee might recouer the mouth of the riuer into the

A conflict begun by ye Sauages.

---

[1] 'in the boat' (Hakluyt, III (1600), 259). Manteo, who was evidently Lane's chief interpreter, was accompanied by three Indians from Roanoke Island (p. 277).

[2] The 'song' being evidently a war chant.

[3] Lane's boat was a double wherry, but the second boat (cp. p. 264 above), a 'light horseman', although it could be described as a long, light wherry, probably differed in some respects in design and accommodation. We find Richard Hawkins using a light horseman in 1594 (*Observations*, ed. Williamson, p. 19) and Weymouth in 1605 (James Rosier, *A true relation of the most prosperous voyage made...by Captaine George Waymouth*, sigs. B 4v., C 4v., D 1 (repr. in *Early English and French voyages, 1534–1608*, ed. H. S. Burrage, pp. 370, 378–9)), and on one occasion Raleigh 'came out of Falmouth Harbor in a Lighte horseman' (H.C.A. 23/30, dep. of A. Leedes, 28 June 1592). They could be carried in sections on shipboard (*The strange adventures of Andrew Battell*, ed. E. G. Ravenstein (1901), pp. 2–5).

[4] Cp. p. 228 above.

broade sownde, which at my first motion I found my whole companie ready to assent vnto: for they were nowe come to their dogs porredge, that they had bespoken for themselues, if that befell them which did,[1] and I before did mistrust we should hardly escape. The ende was, we came the next day by night to the riuers mouth within 4. or 5. miles of the same, hauing rowed in one day

The great current of the Riuer of Morottico.[3]

downe the currant, as much as in 4. dayes we had done against the same: we lodged vpon an Islande,[2] where wee had nothing in the worlde to eate but pottage of sassafras leaues, the like whereof for a meate was neuer vsed before as I thinke.[4] The broad sownde[5] wee had to passe, the next day all fresh and fasting: that day the winde blewe so strongly,[6] and the billow so great, that there was no possibilitie of passage without sinking of our boates. This was upon Easter eue,[7] which was fasted very trulie. Vpon Easter day in the morning the wind comming very calme, wee entred the sownde, and by 4. of the clocke we were at Chipanum,[8] wher all the Sauages that wee had left there were fled, but their wears[9] did yeelde vs some fish, as God was pleased not utterly to suffer vs to be lost: for some of our companie of the light horsemen[10] were far spent. The next morning we arriued at our home Roanoake.[11]

I haue set downe this voyage somewhat particularly, to the ende it may appeare vnto you (as true it is) that there wanted no great good will from the most to the least amongst vs, to have perfited

---

[1] See Hariot's reference to this incident, p. 357 below.

[2] Sans Souci Island, around which the Roanoke River divides before flowing into Albemarle Sound.

[3] 'Morattico' (Hakluyt, III (1600), 259).

[4] He is probably correct since the tough, aromatic leaves of the sassafras tree would not suggest an edible vegetable.

[5] Albemarle Sound.

[6] From the east or north-east.   [7] Saturday, 2 April 1586.

[8] 'Chipanum, whence' (ibid.). A Weapemeoc village: a run of 35–40 miles (cp. p. 861).

[9] Not elsewhere mentioned but probably similar to those at Roanoke Island (cp. pp. 414, 433–5).

[10] A misprint for 'the light horseman', i.e. the boat thus called.

[11] 'Roanoak' (Hakluyt, III (1600), 259).

this discouerie of the mine:[1] for that the discouery of a good mine, by the goodnesse of God, or a passage to the Southsea, or someway to it,[2] and nothing els can bring this country in request to be inhabited by our nation. And with the discouery of any[3] of the two aboue shewed, it willbe the most sweete, and healthfullest climate, and therewithall the most fertile soyle, being manured in the world: and then will Sassafras, and many other rootes & gummes there found make good Marchandise and lading for shipping, which otherwise of themselues will not bee worth the fetching.[4]

Prouided also, that there be found out a better harborough then yet there is, which must bee to the Northward, if any there be, which was mine intention to haue spent this summer[5] in the search of, and of the mine of Chawnis Temoatan: the one I would haue done, if the barks that I should haue had of *Sir* Francis Drake, by his honorable curtesie, had not bene driuen away by storme:[6] the other if your supply of more men, and some other necessaries had come to vs in any conuenient sufficiencie.[7] For this riuer of Moratico promiseth great things, and by the opinion of *Master*

---

[1] Lane is here recording the relative keenness of his men to take risks for the discovery of treasure (cp. the quotation from Raleigh, pp. 223–4 above), contrasting with their lack of enthusiasm for agriculture or commerce.

[2] For the expectations that there might be passages through North America to the Pacific in temperate latitudes see Sir Humphrey Gilbert's map of 1583 (Quinn, *Gilbert*, pp. 67–71, 374: the map is now in the Philadelphia Public Library). Clearly the discovery of such a passage to the Pacific would be of the utmost economic and strategic importance.

[3] 'either' (Hakluyt, III (1600), 259).

[4] In his view that commerce could only be a subsidiary factor in the maintenance of a colony Lane was probably correct. Hakluyt had, indeed, so regarded it, but he placed his main emphasis on plantation agriculture, which Lane does not even mention. Even if that is taken into account the scale of investment was so small and its continuity so uncertain that a verdict such as Lane's would not appear unreasonable (cp. Taylor, *Hakluyts*, II, passim; Quinn, *Raleigh*, pp. 89–91, 97, 106, 126–8, 'The failure of Raleigh's American colonies', pp. 70–9, 84–5; pp. 497–8 below).

[5] That of 1586, indicating that Lane was writing very soon after his return (cp. pp. 29, 294).

[6] Cp. pp. 291–2 below.   [7] Cp. p. 261.

Harriots[1] the heade of it by the description of the country, either riseth from the bay of Mexico, or els from very neere vnto the same, that openeth out into the South sea.

And touching the Minerall, thus doth Master Yougham[2] affirme, that though it be but copper, seeing the Sauages are able to melt it, it is one of the richest Minerals in the worlde.

Wherefore a good harborough founde to the Northward, as before is sayd, and from thence foure dayes ouerland, to the riuer of Choanoak sconses being raysed, from whence againe ouerlande through the prouince of Choanoak one dayes voyage to the first towne of the Mangoaks vp the riuer of Moratico by the way, as also vpon the sayd riuer for the defence of our boats like sconses being set, in this course of proceeding you shall cleare your selfe from all those dangers and broad shallowe sownds before mentioned, and gayne within foure dayes trauell into the heart of the mayne 200. myles at the least,[3] and so passe your discouerie into that most

---

[1] 'Hariots' (Hakluyt, III (1600), 259). This reference does not necessarily mean that Hariot accompanied Lane on the Roanoke River expedition, though it does not exclude the possibility that he had done so. Lane is rather speaking of Hariot as the geographer who knew the literature and the maps. He may even be referring to Hariot's reaction to his reading of the narrative of the Espejo journey after his return to England (see pp. 549–51 below).

[2] 'Youghan' (Hakluyt, III (1600), 259), the mineral man, Lane's mining prospector, is identified above as Joachim Ganz (p. 196). The evidence (p. 269 above) is all against any smelting of copper, though elsewhere it was shaped by hot working or by cold working and annealing. What the expert meant is that the more nearly pure the copper was the easier it would be to melt, so that, if the Indians could melt it, it must be pure (cp. pp. 332–3). The finding of lumps of copper which had been melted and also part of a goldsmith's crucible on the site of the Fort (pp. 907–9 below) may link up with Ganz's experiments.

[3] Lane is here giving his plan (pp. 261–4) in reverse. If the fort is on Chesapeake Bay, then the route already marked by 'sconses' back to the Chowan River could be taken, and an overland route to the Roanoke River (cp. p. 263) worked out, so that the journey further up-stream, though requiring to be marked by additional 'sconses', would be greatly shortened, thus bringing Chaunis Temoatan within manageable distance of the port and avoiding sailing through the treacherous Carolina Sounds. On what Lane knew and surmised, his calculations were reasonable (cp. map at end). It is not unlikely that the southward probing expeditions from Jamestown into the Chowanoac country in the early days of the Virginia colony were influenced by Lane's programme (cp. p. 852 below).

notable,[1] and to the likeliest partes of the mayne, with farre greater felicitie then otherwise can bee performed.

Thus sir, I haue though simply, yet truely set downe vnto you, what my labour with the rest of the gentlemen, and poore men of our company, (not without both payne, and perill which the lorde in his mercy many wayes deliuered vs from) could yeelde vnto you, which might haue bene performed in some more perfection, if the lorde had bene pleased that onely that which you had prouided for vs had at the first bene left with vs,[2] or that he had not in his eternall prouidence now at the last set some other course in these things, then the wisedome of man could looke into, which truely the carying away, by a most strange, & vnlooked for storme all[3] our prouision, with barks, master, Marryners, and sundrie also of mine owne company, all hauing bene so curteously supplyed by the Generall *Sir* Francis Drake,[4] the same hauing bene most sufficient to haue performed the greatest part of the premisses, must euer make me to thinke, the hand of God only, (for some his good purpose to my selfe yet vnknowne), to haue bene in the matter.[5]

The second part[6] touching the conspiracy of Pemisapan, the
    discouerie of the same, and at the last, of our request to depart
    with *Sir* Francis Drake for England.

Ensenore a sauage father[7] to Pemisapan being the only frend to our nation that we had amongst them, and about the king, dyed

---

[1] 'notable countrey' (Hakluyt, III (1600), 260).

[2] A reference to the loss of much of the stores of the colony when the *Tiger* grounded (pp. 189, 201, 203, 344), which may also hide a further complaint (cp. pp. 211–12) to Raleigh against Grenville, that even so he did not leave as much as he might have done.   [3] 'of all' (Hakluyt, III (1600) 260).

[4] Cp. pp. 289–92 below.

[5] Lane here, as elsewhere (cp. pp. 203–4), finds signs of God's providence in his misfortunes.

[6] The second part, like the first, is mainly an apologia by Lane for his failure to achieve more than he did. Hariot was not so shamefaced about a not inconsiderable achievement.

[7] A foster-father, stepfather or, even, father-in-law?

the 20. of April, 1586. hee alone, had before opposed himselfe in their consultations against al matters proposed against vs, which both the king, and all the rest of them after Grangemoes death, were very willing to haue preferred.[1] And he was not onely by the meere prouidence of God during his life, a meane to saue vs from hurt, as poysonings[2] and such like, but also to doe vs very great good, and singulerly in this.

The king was aduised and of himselfe disposed, as a ready meane to have assuredly brought vs to ruine in the moneth of March, 1586,[3] himselfe also with all his Sauages to haue runne away from vs, and to haue left his ground in the Island vnsowed,[4] which if he had done, there had bene no possibilitie in common reason, (but by the immediate hande of God) that we could haue bene preserued from staruing out of hand.[5] For at that time wee had no weares for fishe,[6] neither could our men skill of the making of them, neither had wee one grayne of corne for seede to put into the ground.

In mine absence on my voyage that I had made against the Chaonists, and Mangoaks,[7] they had raised a bruite among them-

---

[1] The influence which Granganimeo and Ensenore are alleged to have exercised as 'weroances' in Wingina's councils would suggest that the latter's authority was not absolute (cp. pp. 281, 370).

[2] Of which allegation we have no corroborative evidence.

[3] This plan emerged when Lane visited the Chowan River, but was not, apparently, suspected before the expedition left Roanoke Island (cp. p. 259 above).

[4] Wingina on leaving Roanoke Island could presumably get sufficient corn grown on the mainland, where Lane's men might not be able to find the corn-patches.

[5] It is difficult to see how Lane could have come to this conclusion at that time, since he still expected a relief to arrive by Easter (cp. p. 261).

[6] In margin: 'This skill of making weares would be learned' (Hakluyt, III (1600), 260). Does Hakluyt not mean 'should'? The art of setting fish-traps would require rather a specialized craftsmanship, but the complete lack of confidence which Lane had in his men's skill is surprising, seeing that there were presumably some craftsmen amongst them (cp. pp. 365, 384).

[7] The Chowanoac tribe. Lane speaks as if he had deliberately gone on a warlike expedition, while his references above would suggest that the threat of hostilities had arisen incidentally.

selues, that I and my company were part slayne, and part starued by the Chaonists, and Mangoaks. One part of this tale was too true, that I and mine were like to be starued,[1] but the other false.

Neuerthelesse vntill my returne, it tooke such effect in Pemisapans breast, and in those against vs, that they grew not onely into contempt of vs, but also (contrary to their former reuerend opinion in shew, of the almightie God of heauen, and Iesus Christ, whome wee serue and worship, whome before they woulde acknowledge and confesse the onely God:)[2] nowe they began to blaspheme, and flatly to say, that our Lord God was not God, since hee suffered vs to sustaine much hunger, and also to be killed of the Renapoaks, for so they call by that generall name, all the inhabitants of the whole mayne,[3] of what prouince soeuer. Insomuch as olde Ensenore, neither any of his fellowes, coulde for his sake haue no more credite for vs: and it came so farre that the King was resolued to haue presently gone away as is aforesaid.

But euen in the beginning of this bruite I returned, which when hee sawe contrarie to his expectation, and the aduertisement that he had receiued: that not only my selfe,[4] and my company were al safe, but also by report of his owne 3. sauages, which had bene with mee besides Manteo in that voyage, that is to say, Tetepano, his sisters husband Eracano,[5] and Cossine, that the Chaonists,[6] and Mangoaks, (whose name, and multitude besides their valour is terrible to al the rest of the prouinces)[7] durst not for the most part of them abide vs, and that those that did abide vs were killed,[8] and

---

[1] Cp. pp. 267–8, 272 above.

[2] Cp. Hariot's account of the willingness of the Indians to listen to Christian teaching, pp. 376–80 below.

[3] Meaning 'the true men' (p. 895 below).

[4] Either on Easter Sunday or Monday, 3 or 4 April (p. 261 above).

[5] Wingina's brother-in-law, or step-brother, not Tetepano's. This provides the only specific reference to the presence of these Indians (cp. pp. 270–1).

[6] 'Chanoists' (Hakluyt, III (1600), 260), probably a misprint for 'Choanists'.

[7] It is not clear why Lane should (except for effect) so closely associate the Chowanoac and Mangoak tribes (cp. p. 278).

[8] There is no certain indication above (p. 271) that there was any serious fighting.

that we had taken Menatonon prisoner, and brought his sonne that he best loued to Roanoak with me,[1] it did not a little asswage all deuises against vs: on the other side, it made Ensenors[2] opinions to be receiued againe with greater respects. For hee had often before tolde them, and then renewed those his former speeches, both to the king and the rest, that wee were the seruants of God, and that wee were not subiect to be destroyed by them: but contrariwise, that they amongst them that sought our destruction, should finde their owne, and not be able to worke ours, and that we being dead men were able to doe them more hurt, then now we coulde do being aliue:[3] an opinion very confidently at this day holden by the wisest amongst them, and of their olde men, as also, that they haue bene in the night, beeing 100. myles from any of vs in the ayre shot at, and stroken by some men of ours,[4] that by sicknesse had dyed among them:[5] and many of them holde opinion, that wee be dead men returned into the worlde againe, and that we doe not remayne dead but for a certaine time, and that then we returne againe.[6]

All these speeches then againe grew in ful credite with them, the King and all touching vs, when hee saw the small troupe returned againe, and in that sort from those whose very names were terrible vnto them:[7] but that which made vp the matter on our side for that time, was an accident, yea rather, (as all the rest was) the good prouidence of the Almightie for the sauing of vs, which was this.

---

[1] Skiko (pp. 262, 270, 285, 287–8). He was not brought by Lane, but sent from the head of Albemarle Sound in the pinnace (p. 264 above).

[2] 'Ensenores' (Hakluyt, III (1600), 260).

[3] This demonstrates the Indian belief that the white men were reincarnated spirits (cp. pp. 379–80), and also probably explains why their religious teaching was so readily acceptable.

[4] Cp. Hariot (pp. 377–80 below) on Indian conceptions of disease.

[5] Hariot said only four died from sickness (p. 384 below).

[6] Cp. pp. 374, 379–80 below.

[7] He would appear to mean the members of the Mangoak tribe, but this is scarcely consistent with the statements above (p. 281) that this tribe was at times allied to the coastal Algonkian tribes.

Ralph Lane

Within certaine dayes after my returne from the said iourney,[1] Menatonon sent a messengere to visite his sonne the prisoner with me, and sent me certaine pearle for a present, or rather as Pemisapan told me, for the ransome of his sonne,[2] and therefore I refused them: but the greatest cause of his sending then, was to signifie vnto me, that hee had commaunded Okisko king of Weopomiok, to yelde himselfe seruant, and homager, to the great Weroanza of England,[3] and after her to Sir Walter Ralegh: to perfourme which commandement receiued from Menatonon, the sayd Okisko ioyntly with this Menatonons messenger, sent foure and twentie of his principallest men to Roanoak to Pemisapan, to signifie that they were readie to perfourme the same, and so had sent those his men to let me knowe, that from that time forwarde hee, and his successours were to acknowledge her Maiestie their onely Soueraigne, and next vnto her, as is aforesayde.[4]

All which being done, and acknowledged by them all, in the presence of Pemisapan his father,[5] and all his Sauages in counsel then with him, it did for the time, thorowly (as it seemed) change him in disposition toward vs: Insomuch as forthwith Ensenore wan this resolution of him, that out of hand he should goe about, & withall, to cause his men to set vp weares forthwith for vs: both which he, at that present went in hand withal & did so labour the expedition of it, that in the end of April, he had sowed a good quantitie of ground, so much as had bene sufficient, to haue

[1] After Easter.

[2] Skiko. Lane can have been holding Skiko only because he wished to have security for Menatonon's goodwill towards the dual projects of the overland journey to Chesapeake Bay and the inland search for Chaunis Temoatan.

[3] Queen Elizabeth. The holding of chiefly (or other) office by a woman was not unfamiliar among the coastal Algonkian peoples (Flannery, *Analysis*, pp. 115–16).

[4] This episode throws some light on the hierarchical character of Indian chieftaincy in this area. Okisco was in some manner subordinate to Menatonon, and was therefore obliged to enter into a form of submission to the English on his orders. It is curious that these overtures should have been made through Wingina, who with his advisers was acting as something more than an interpreter, but no useful explanation can be suggested.

[5] Ensenore.

279

fed our whole company (God blessing the grouth) and that by the belly for a whole yere: besides that he gaue vs a certaine plot of grounde for our selues to sowe.[1] All which put vs in marueilous comfort, if we could passe from Aprill, vntill the beginning of Iuly,

(which was to haue bene the beginning of their haruest,)[2] that then a newe supplie out of Englande or els our owne store would well inough maintayne vs: All our feare was of the two moneths betwixt, in which meane space, if the Sauages should not helpe vs with Cassada,[3] and Chyna,[4] and that our weares should fayle vs, (as often they did) wee might very well starue, notwithstanding the growing corne, like the staruing horse in the stable, with the growing grasse, as the prouerbe is, which we very hardlye had escaped but onely by the hand of God, as it pleased him to try vs. For within few dayes after, as before is sayde Ensenore our friende dyed, who was no sooner dead,[5] but certaine of our great enemies about Pemisapan, as Osocan[6] a Weroance, Tanaquiny and Wanchese[7] most principally, were in hand again to put their old practises in vre[8] against vs, which were readily imbraced, & al their former deuises against vs renewed, & new brought in question.

[1] The weirs and the allocated plots both inside and outside the Indian cornfields were presumably all on Roanoke Island. We do not hear from Hariot how the colonists took to the unaccustomed agricultural labour, or what, besides corn, they planted in the land handed over to them. This inference shows clearly that there had been no purchase or appropriation of land by the English on Roanoke Island and that they held their position, formally at least, by the tolerance of the Indians. Wingina's capacity to sow extra corn-patches indicates that he had, or could buy, seed from reserves held by him or his neighbours (cp. pp. 282–3).

[2] Cp. pp. 388, 422.

[3] 'Cassaui' (Hakluyt, III (1600), 261), meaning food prepared from the Arrow-arum or Golden-club (cp. p. 349 below).

[4] Food prepared from the roots of the Woody Smilaxes (cp. pp. 348–9 below). These two items of food represented part of the dried winter store conserved by the Indians but used up by April.

[5] 20 April (p. 276 above).   [6] 'Osacan' (Hakluyt, III (1600), 261).

[7] Wanchese had been in England with Manteo (p. 116 above). What turned him against the English is nowhere indicated, but it may merely have been the favour shown to Manteo.

[8] The meaning is 'into effect'.

But that of staruing vs, by their forbearing to sowe, was broken by Ensenore in his life, by hauing made the king all at one instant to sowe his grounde not onely in the Islande but also at Addesmocopeia[1] in the mayne, within two leagues ouer against vs. Neuerthelesse there wanted no store of mischeuous practises among them, and of all they resolued principally of this following.

First that Okisko, king of Weopomiok, with the Mandoages, should bee moued, and with great quantitie of copper intertayned to the number of seuen, or 800. bowes[2] to the enterprise[3] the matter thus to be ordred. They of Weopomiok should be inuited to a certaine kind of moneths minde[4] which they do vse to solemnise in their Sauage maner for any great personage dead, and should haue bene for Ensenore. At this instant also should the Mandoaks, who were a great people[5] with the Chesepians, and their friends to the number of 700. of them[6] be armed at a day appoynted to the mayne of Addesmocopeio, and there lying close at the signe of fyers, which should interchangeably be made on both sides, when Pemisapan *with* his troup aboue named should haue executed me, and some of our Weroances (as they called all our principall officers,)[7] the mayne forces of the rest should haue come ouer into the Iland where they ment to haue dispatched the rest of the company, whome they did imagine to finde both dismayed and

*The con-
spiracie of
Pemisapan.*

[1] 'Dasemonquepeio' (Hakluyt, III (1600), 261), as also below. For the corn-patches attached to this village see pp. 530–1 below.

[2] 'to enterprise' (Hakluyt, III (1600), 261). Wingina was now rich enough in copper, obtained in exchange from the English, to contemplate retaining mercenaries with it.

[3] For another estimate of the strength of the Weapemeoc tribe see p. 213.

[4] The celebration of a monthly mass for the repose of the souls of the dead in the Roman Catholic church. No such similar ceremony is suggested from other sources as typical of coastal Algonkian tribal practice.

[5] No estimates of the strength of this tribe (apparently Iroquoian) are given elsewhere.

[6] This is the sole estimate of the war-strength of the Chesepian tribe with its associates (the Tripanicks and Opossians?), and it is also the only indication that there was any close association between the Virginia and Carolina Algonkian tribes (cp. pp. 245, 257–8). Lane may have been exaggerating his peril by reference to almost all the tribes of which he knew.

[7] An indication of the meaning of 'weroance' (cp. pp. 370, 899).

dispersed abroade in the Islande seeking of crabs, and fish to liue withall.[1] The manner of their enterprise was this.

Tarraquine and Andacon two principall men about Pemisapan, and very lustie fellowes with twentie more appointed to them had the charge of my person to see an order taken for the same, which they ment should in this sort haue bene executed. In the dead time of the night they would haue beset my house, and put fire in the reedes, that the same was couered with:[2] meaning (as it was likelye) that my selfe woulde haue come running out of a sudden amazed in my shirt without armes, vpon the instant whereof they woulde haue knocked out my braynes.[3]

The same order was giuen to certaine of his fellowes, for Master Herriots:[4] so for all the rest of our better sort, all our houses at one instant being set on fire as afore is sayde, and that as well for them of the forte, as for vs at the towne.[5] Now to the end that we might be the fewer in number together, and so be the more easilie dealt withall (for in deede ten of vs with our armes prepared, were a terrour to a hundred of the best sort of them,) they agreed and did immediatly put it in practise, that they should not for any copper, sell vs any victuals whatsoeuer:[6] besides that in the night they should send to haue our weares robbed, and also to cause them to be broken and once being broken neuer to be repayred

The margin note: The suffi-ciencye of our men to deale against the Sauages, 10. to 100.

---

[1] Cp. p. 283 below.

[2] In margin: 'The forme of the treason' (Hakluyt, III (1600), 262). The passage adds something to what is otherwise known of the settlement. The individual houses of the leading members of the expedition were outside the fort ditch, probably between it and the village, and some, at least, were thatched cottages (cp. p. 902).

[3] In view of Lane's insistence on maintaining sentinels it sounds somewhat unwise of him to have left the houses unguarded (cp. p. 266).

[4] 'Heriots' (Hakluyt, III (1600), 262). The possession of a separate cottage by Hariot indicates that he enjoyed some considerable status amongst the settlers.

[5] The only indication that there were, apparently, sufficient cottages for them to be laid out in a street or streets. It is possible that there was even a trading-store outside the fort to which the Indians could come (cp. p. 290).

[6] This indicates once again that the Indians were not entirely without reserves of food (cp. p. 280). Wingina was now sufficiently well supplied with copper that he could afford abstinence in the expectation of getting a larger quantity when the English had been overwhelmed.

againe by them.[1] By this meanes the King stood assured, that I must bee enforced for lacke of sustenance, there to disband my company into sundry places to liue vpon shell fishe, for so the Sauages themselues doe, going to Ottorasko,[2] Croatoan, and other places fishing and hunting, while their grownds be in sowing, and their corne growing, which fayled not his expectation. For the famine grewe so extreeme among vs, our weares fayling vs of fish, that I was enforced to send captaine Stafford with 20. with him to Croatoan my lord Admirals Island to serue two turnes in one, that is to say to feede himselfe, and his company, and also to keepe watch, if any shipping came vpon the coast to warne vs of the same.[3] I sent master Pridiox with the Pynnesse to Otterasco, and ten with him, with the Prouost Marshal to liue there,[4] and also to wayte for shipping: also I sent euery weeke 16. or 20. of the rest of the companie to the mayne ouer against vs,[5] to liue of Casada,[6] and oysters.[7]

The sauages liue by fishing, and hunting, till haruest.

[1] Cp. pp. 276, 384 for the inability of the English to make the weirs.

[2] 'Hatorask' (Hakluyt, III (1600), 262), and also below, the island lying south of Port Ferdinando, with Croatoan southward again from it. All early authorities are agreed that such a reversion to a primitive gathering economy was forced on the Algonkian tribes during the late spring and early summer, but it is clear in this instance that it was the result of insufficient food storage and not the absence of a food-reserve of any sort (cp. pp. 280–1).

[3] Stafford (for whom see pp. 194, 288) was probably posted near modern Cape Hatteras where there were probably already high forested dunes which would be valuable as look-out posts. He may have resided near or even with the Croatoan Indians (pp. 526, 866). It is probable that he had the double wherry with him so that he could get word of reinforcements to Roanoke Island quickly. The naming of Croatoan after Charles Howard, Lord Effingham, is not elsewhere indicated. The earl of Lincoln died in February 1585, but Howard did not apparently take up his duties as Lord High Admiral until May (*DNB*). The name may have been given after Lane's return. Taken with Raleigh's letter of 1602 (Edwards, *Ralegh*, II, 252), it indicates that he was a subscriber to the expedition.

[4] For Prideaux see p. 195 above: we are nowhere told the provost marshal's name. They were probably based at Port Ferdinando with a look-out on the high ground of Kenricks Mounts near Cape Kenrick (cp. pp. 864–5). The implication is that the pinnace was normally kept at Roanoke Island, presumably at the creek to the east of the fort (cp. p. 615).

[5] Along the shore to the south-west between Dasemunkepeuc and Pomeiooc (pp. 869–70).   [6] See p. 349, n. 4, below.

[7] Cp. pp. 361, 368.

In the meane while Pemisapan went of purpose to Addesmoco-peio for 3. causes, the one, to see his grounds there broken vp, and sowed for a second croppe:[1] the other to withdrawe himselfe[2] from my dayly sending to him for supply of victuall for my company, for hee was afrayde to denye me any thing, neither durst he in my presence but by colour, and with excuses, which I was content to accept for the time, meaning in the ende as I had reason, to giue him the iumpe once for all: but in the meane whiles, as I had euer done before, I and mine bare all wrongs, and accepted of all excuses.

My purpose was to haue relyed my selfe with Menatonon, and the Chaonists, who in truth as they are more valiant people and in greater number then the rest, so are they more faithfull in their promises, and since my late being there, had giuen many tokens of earnest desire they had to ioyne in perfect league with vs, and therefore were greatly offended with Pemisapan and Weopomiok for making him beleeue such tales of vs.

The third cause of his going to Addesmacopeio was to dispatch his messengers to Weopomiok, and to the Mandoages, as afore-said, al which he did with great impresse of copper in hand, making large promises to them of greater spoyle.

The answere within fewe dayes after, came from Weopomiok, which was deuided into two parts. First for the King Okisko, who denyed to be of y[e] partie for himselfe, or any of his especial fol-lowers, and therefore did immediatly retyre himselfe with his force into the mayne: the other was concerning the rest of the sayd prouince who accepted of it:[3] and in like sort the Mandoags receiued the imprest.[4]

[1] For the corn-sowing sequence see pp. 388, 421.

[2] It would appear that the Indians simply abandoned the village on the Island for the time being.

[3] Once again we are handicapped by insufficiently detailed knowledge of the Indian polity. Lane appears to mean that Okisko, in view of his engagements to Menatonon and to Lane, led away his own immediate entourage in order to allow the subordinate chieftains of the Weapemeoc villages to associate with Wingina in return for receiving his bribe of copper.

[4] The advance payment of copper. We hear no more of the alleged participa-tion of the Chesapeake tribe (cp. p. 281, n. 6, above).

The day of their assembly aforesayd at Roanoak, was appointed the 10. of Iuly:[1] all which the premises were discouered by Skyco, the king Menatonon his sonne my prisoner, who hauing once attempted to run away, I laid him in the bylboes,[2] threatning to cut off his head, whome I remitted at Pemisapans request:[3] whereupon he being perswaded that he was our enemie to the death, he did not only feede him with himselfe, but also made him acquainted with all his practises. On the other side, the yong man finding himself as well vsed at my hand, as I had meanes to shew, and that all my companie made much of him, he flatly discouered all vnto me,[4] which also afterwards was reuealed vnto me by one of Pemisapans owne men, y⁰ night before he was slaine.[5]

These mischiefes being al instantly vpon mee, and my companie to be put in execution,[6] stood mee in hand to study how to preuent them,[7] and also to saue all others, which were at that time as aforesaid so farre from me: whereupon I sent to Pemisapan to put suspition out of his heade, that I ment presently to goe to Croatoan, for that I had heard of the ariual of our fleete, (though I in trueth had neither heard nor hoped for so good aduenture,) and that I meant to come by him, to borrow of his men to fish for my company, and to hunt for me at Croatoan, as also to buy some foure dayes prouision to serue for my voyage.

---

[1] Corrected to 'Iune' (Hakluyt, III (1600), 262).

[2] A long iron bar fastened by a lock to the floor, along which ran sliding leg-irons. This probably formed part of the gaol which Lane must have had (since he had both a provost marshal and a deputy, pp. 283, 287) inside the fort enclosure. Cp. Barnabe Rich, *A path-way to military practise* (1587), sig. E 3 v.: 'The Prouost is to haue the charge of the Marshal sea hée must be prouided of Fetters, Giues, hand-lockes and all manner of Irons, for the safe keeping of such prisoners as shall bée committed to his kéepinge.'

[3] This probably occurred during the brief period of rapprochement with Wingina during April.

[4] Skiko was evidently allowed to visit Wingina's camp on parole by this time.

[5] We are not told the name of this Indian who was, it would seem, executed for treachery by Wingina.

[6] 'execution, it stood' (Hakluyt, III (1600), 262).

[7] Meaning 'forestall'.

He sent mee word that he would himselfe come ouer to Roanoak, but from day to day hee deferred, only to bring the Weopomioks with him, and the Mandoags, whose time appoynted was within 8. dayes after. It was the last of May, 1586. when all his owne sauages began to make their assembly at Roanoak, at his commandement sent abroad vnto them,[1] and I resolued not to stay longer vpon his comming ouer, since he ment to come with so good company, but thought good to go, and visite him with such as I had, which I resolued to do the next day: but that night I ment by the way to giue them in the Island a Canuisado,[2] and at the instant to sease vpon all the Canoas about the Island to keepe him from aduertisements.

But the towne tooke the allarum, before I ment it to them: the occasion was this. I had sent the Master of the light horsemen[3] with a few with him, to gather vp all the Canoas in the setting of the sunne, & to take as many as were going from vs to Adesmocopeio, but to suffer any that came from thence to land: he met *The slaughter,* with a Canoa, going from the shoare, and ouerthrew the Canoa, *and surprise of* and cut off 2. sauages heads: this was not done so secretly but hee *the Sauages.* was discouered from the shoare, wherupon the cry arose: for in trueth they, priuie to their owne villanous purposes against us, held as good espial vpon vs, both day and night, as we did vpon them.

The allarum giuen, they tooke themselues to their bowes, and we to our armes: some three or foure of them at the first were slayne with our shot, the rest fled into yᵉ woods: The next morning with the light horseman, & one Canoa, taking 25. with the Colonel

---

[1] This assembly on 31 May being forced on Wingina in view of Lane's tactics.

[2] Usually 'camisado', a night attack, so called because the attackers allowed their shirt-tails to hang out behind so that they would not be fired on by their own men.

[3] Corrected to 'light horseman' (Hakluyt, III (1600), 262, cp. pp. 271–2 above). This was probably the largest boat Lane still kept at the Island. The master is nowhere named, but could well have been Captain Vaughan (cp. p. 194 above).

of the Chesepians,[1] and the Serieant maior,[2] I went to Adesmoco-peio, and being landed sent Pemisapan word by one of his owne sauages that met me at the shore, that I was going to Croatoan, and ment to take him in the way to complaine vnto him of Osocon, who the night past was conueying away my prisoner, whom I had there present tied in an handlocke:[3] hereupon the king did abide my comming to him, and finding my selfe amidst 7. or 8. of his principal Weroances, & followers, (not regarding any of the common sort) I gaue the watchword agreed vpon, (which was Christ our victory,) and immediatly those his chiefe men, and himselfe, had by the mercie of God for our deliuerance, that which they had purposed for vs. The king himselfe being shot thorow by the Colonell with a pistoll lying on the ground for dead, & I looking as watchfully for the sauing of Manteos friends,[4] as others were busie that none of the rest should escape, suddenly he started vp, and ran away as though he had not bene touched, insomuch as he ouerran all the companie, being by the way shot thwart the but-tocks by mine Irish boy[5] with my Petronell.[6] In the end an Irish man seruing me, one Nugent[7] and the deputie prouost vndertooke

---

[1] Not identified, but conceivably either Philip Amadas or Thomas Hariot (cp. pp. 194, 245). As commander of the Chesapeake Bay expedition with the title of colonel, the assumption would be that he was second-in-command of the force.

[2] Again not named. Lane's fondness for rank must have led to his men having rather too many officers. The serjeant-major was responsible for drawing up soldiers in battle-order and in a large expedition was one of the senior officers (C. G. Cruickshank, *Elizabeth's army*, p. 37; cp. p. 137 above). Thirty-three men had already been sent to Croatoan and Hatarask, so that Lane's party of twenty-eight would leave about forty at the fort.

[3] Osocan evidently tried to remove Skiko, but not, it is implied, with his consent. Why Lane should have alternately allowed the latter to go on parole and then at other times kept him handcuffed is not explained, but it may have been a ruse to suggest that Skiko was still hostile to Lane.

[4] Evidently a faction inside the tribe friendly to the English or possibly members of the Croatoan tribe (cp. p. 526 below).

[5] One of the small Irish group with Lane but not identifiable by name (cp. p. 195 above).

[6] A heavy cavalry pistol carried in the belt. Sir John Smythe (*Certain discourses* (1590), fo. 47) shows that petronels could be wheel-locks, flintlocks or matchlocks.

[7] Edward Nugent (p. 195 above).

him, and following him in the woods ouertooke him, and I in some doubt least we had lost both the king, and my man by our owne negligence to haue bene intercepted by the Sauages, we met him returning out of the woods with Pemisapans head in his hand.

This fell out the first of Iune, 1586.[1] and the 8.[2] of the same came aduertisement to me from captaine Stafford, lying at my lord Admirals Island, that he had discouered a great Fleete of 23. sailes: but whether they were friends or foes, he could not yet discerne, he aduised me to stand vpon as good gard as I could.

The 9. of the said moneth, he himselfe came vnto me, hauing that night before, and that same day trauelled by land 20. miles, and I must truly report of him from the first to the last, he was the gentleman that neuer spared labour or perill either by land or water, faire weather or fowle, to performe any seruice committed vnto him.[3]

---

[1] We are left with no indication of what happened after Wingina's death. Did Lane receive the submission of the remaining 'weroances'? Did he release Skiko? (The three men left behind (p. 307 below) may have been taking Skiko home.) What became of the Indian forces from the Weapemeoc and Mangoak tribes which were due to reach Roanoke Island by 10 June?

[2] My impression is that Lane is one day out in his calculations, though he may be reckoning from midnight to midnight and Drake from noon to noon. There appears less reason to doubt the Drake narrative (p. 300) that the signal fires, apparently in the vicinity of modern Cape Hatteras, were seen on the 9th. Drake's ships were probably sighted on the 8th by Stafford's men and the news conveyed to the fort, a distance of some 60 miles, by the double wherry which can scarcely have arrived until well into the 9th. Stafford's first impression was, probably, that it was a Spanish fleet: its size at that time cannot be accurately checked.

[3] How did Stafford come? The Drake narrative (p. 300) would make it appear that one of Stafford's men was picked up near the modern Cape Hatteras on the 9th and acted as a pilot to bring Drake to Port Ferdinando. Stafford may have gone too and could have landed near there before daybreak on the 10th and set out for the fort. How, and why, he walked is not clear. Either he was set down by boat at the southern end of Roanoke Island and walked to the fort, or else he made his way along what is now Bodie Island from Port Lane and signalled from the vicinity of Nags Head for a boat. Drake could easily have spared him a boat or pinnace while Lane's pinnace was probably still at Port Ferdinando (cp. p. 283). It will be noted that Drake's letters to Lane were not written until he arrived at Port Ferdinando.

Ralph Lane

He brought me a letter from the Generall sir Francis Drake, with *A letter from sir Francis Drake.* a most bountifull and honourable offer for the supplie of our necessities to the performance of the action, we were entered into, and that not onely of victuals, munition and clothing, but also of barkes, pinnaces and boates, they also by him to be victualled, manned, and furnished to my contentation.[1]

The 10. day he arriued in the road of our bad harborough, and comming there to an anker, the 11. day I came to him, whom I found in deeds most honourably to performe that which in writing and message he had most curteously offered, he hauing aforehand propounded the matter to all the captains of his Fleete,[2] and got their liking and consent thereto.

With such thanks vnto him and his captaines for his care both of vs and of our action, not as the matter deserued, but as I could both for my companie and my selfe, I (being aforehand) prepared what I would desire, craued at his hands that it would please him to take _1_ with him into England a number of weake, and vnfit men for my good action,[3] which I would deliuer to him, and in place of them to supply me of his company, with oare men, artificers, and others.[4]

That he would leaue vs so much shipping and victuall, as about _2_ August then next followyng, would cary me and all my companie into England, when we had discouered somwhat that for lacke of needfull prouision in time left with vs as yet remained vndone.

[1] The evidence that Drake had for some weeks been collecting materials and boats likely to be useful to the colony is clearly set out in Wright, *Further English voyages* (see pp. 251–3 above). It is unfortunate that we have not the precise terms of Drake's offer, since in it he would have referred to the Indians and negroes who were intended as a reinforcement to the colony's labour force. Drake is likely to have expected to find Grenville there with a substantial force and fleet, capable of carrying out some of the longer-term plans against the Spanish Indies (cp. pp. 249–51).

[2] Drake having previously consulted his council about calling on the colonists (p. 299, cp. p. 136).

[3] Either men physically weakened by disease or lack of adequate food (cp. pp. 301, 303, 310), or men poorly adapted to pioneering conditions (cp. pp. 322–4).

[4] Lane's men appear to have been predominantly soldiers, so that he needed men used to boats and the sea as well as craftsmen for fortification, making of fish-traps, etc. (cp. pp. 135–6, 276, 384).

3   That it would please him withall to leaue some sufficient masters not onely to cary vs into England, when time should be, but also to search the coast for some better harborow[1] if there were any, and especially to helpe vs to some small boats and oare men.

4   Also for a supplie of calieuers,[2] handweapons, match and lead, tooles, apparell,[3] and such like.

He hauing receiued these my requests according to his vsuall commendable maner of gouernement (as it was told me) calling his captaines to counsell, the resolution was that I should send such of my officers of my companie, as I vsed in such matters, with their notes to goe aboord with him, which were the master of the victuals, the keeper of the store, and the Vicetreasurer,[4] to whom he appointed foorthwith for me the Francis, being a very proper barke of 70. tunnes,[5] and tooke present order for bringing of victuall aboord her for 100. men for foure moneths[6] withall my other demaunds whatsoeuer, to the vttermost.

And further appointed for me two fine pinnaces,[7] and 4. small

[1] Lane possibly hoped to rush through his expedition from the Chowan River overland to Chesapeake Bay while the rest of the settlers were brought round by sea, so that a thorough reconnaissance at least could be made, even if resources did not permit of a permanent establishment.

[2] A light arquebus which could be fired from the shoulder (cp. p. 130 above).

[3] Note Hariot's mention of the lack of clothing (p. 384). Either the stores had been inadequate in this respect or else some substantial part of their stock had been bartered with the Indians. Drake carried a plentiful supply of shoes and garments (p. 251 above).

[4] We have not the names of any of these officials. Their existence suggests that inside the fort ditch there was, besides a gaol (p. 285 above), a granary or other food repository, a storehouse for reserves of equipment and possibly also of goods acquired by barter from the Indians, and a treasury, since it is probable that to maintain morale military wages were paid regularly and could be used to purchase some articles of consumption. The cape merchant, Thomas Harvey (pp. 232–4), may well have been keeper of the store. The high treasurer, Francis Brooke, had returned in September 1585 (pp. 210–11 above).

[5] Thomas Moone, her captain, had been killed at Cartagena (Hakluyt, *Principal navigations*, x, 98, 124, 134; Corbett, *Spanish war*, p. xii).

[6] Drake's food allocation was food for 100 men for a month's exploration, plus enough to bring them home, together with food for the crews (p. 301 below). Considering that he was short of food himself this can only be regarded as generous.

[7] 'And further, he appointed for me two pinnesses' (Hakluyt, III (1600), 264): the Drake account says one pinnace and certain boats (p. 301).

boats, and that which was to performe all his former liberalitie towards vs, was that he had gotten the full assents of two of as sufficient experimented masters as were any in his fleete, by iudgement of them that knewe them, with very sufficient gings to tarie with mee, and to employ themselues most earnestly in the action, as I should appoynt them, vntill the terme which I promised of our returne into England agayne. The names of one of those masters was Abraham Kendall,[1] the other Griffith Herne.[2]

While these things were in hand, the prouision aforesayd being brought, and in bringing a boord, my sayd masters being also gone aboord, my sayd barkes hauing accepted of their charge, and mine owne officers with others in like sort of my company with them, all which was dispatched by the said Generall the 12. of the said moneth: the 13. of the same there arose such an vnwonted storme, and continued foure dayes[3] that had like to have driuen all on shore, if the Lord had not held his holy hand ouer them, and the generall very prouidently foreseene the worst himselfe, then about my dispatch putting himselfe aboord: but in the ende hauing driuen sundry of the Fleete to put to sea the[4] Francis also with all my prouisions, my two masters, and my company aboord, shee was seene to be free from the same, and to put cleare to sea.[5]

---

[1] A veteran navigator, he had probably commanded the *Bark Dennis* with Frobisher in 1578 (*Principal navigations*, VII, 322, and for his later career see VI, 390, 402, X, 205, 241; Foster, *Lancaster*, pp. 4, 16; K. R. Andrews, 'New light on Hakluyt', in *Mariner's Mirror*, XXXVII, 307); he died on the same day as Drake, leaving a reputation for mathematical skill (Taylor, 'Instructions to a colonial surveyor', in *Mariner's Mirror*, XXXVII, 62). He may have been a relative of the Master Kendal who was with Lane (p. 195 above).

[2] Hearne or Heron? He has not so far been identified elsewhere.

[3] Three days is mentioned as its length below p. 302. The length of duration of a storm of hurricane strength, as also the fall of hailstones (p. 308), was somewhat unusual. But electrical storms at this season were frequent (cp. pp. 767, 781).

[4] Several vessels are said to have snapped their cables and been swept out to sea, while pinnaces and boats were wrecked (p. 302).

[5] While the *Francis* was genuinely driven to sea, her failure to put back once the storm was over may have been due to the unwillingness of her company to stay away from home any longer and also possibly risk loss in the distribution of prize money on the return of the main fleet.

This storme hauing continued from the 13. to the 16. of the moneth, and thus my barke put away as aforesayd, the Generall comming a shore, made a new proffer to[1] me, which was a shippe of 170. tunnes, called the Barke Bonner,[2] with a sufficient master and guide to tarie with mee the time appointed, and victualled sufficiently to carie mee and my companie into England with all prouisions as before: but hee tolde mee that he would not for any thing vndertake to haue her brought into our harbour,[3] and therefore hee was to leaue her in the roade, and to leaue the care of the rest vnto my selfe, and aduised me to consider with my companie of our case, and to deliuer presently vnto him in writing, what I would require him to doe for vs:[4] which being within his power, hee did assure me as well for his Captaines, as for himselfe should be most willingly performed.

Hereupon calling such Captaines and Gentlemen of my companie as then were at hand, who were all as priuie as my selfe to the Generals offer,[5] their whole request was to mee, that considering the case that we stood in, the weaknesse of our companie, the small number of the same, the carying away of our first appointed barke, with those two especiall masters, with our principall prouisions in the same, by the very hand of God as it seemed, stretched out to take vs from thence:[6] considering also, that his second offer, though most honourable of his part, yet of ours not to be taken, insomuch as there was no possibility for her with any safetie to be brought into the harbour: Seeing furthermore, our hope for supplie

---

[1] 'vnto' (Hakluyt, III (1600), 264).

[2] George Fortescue had been captain (though he may by this time have died): she was elsewhere rated at 150 tons (*Principal navigations*, x, 98, 134; Corbett, *Spanish war*, p. xii).

[3] Cp. pp. 200-2 above.

[4] He had previously offered either to leave them shipping or to take them home (pp. 301-2 below). Now he wished for tangible evidence of their desires, which suggests that he wished to keep himself right with Raleigh and his associates at his return.

[5] We do not know how many men Lane had lost with the *Francis*.

[6] Lane may be credited with being one of those who had recourse to a providential explanation (cp. pp. 203-4).

with sir Richard Greenuill, so vndoubtedly promised vs before Easter, not yet come, neither then likely to come this yeere[1] considering the doings in England for Flaunders, and also for America,[2] that therefore I would resolue my selfe, with my companie to goe into England in that Fleete, and accordingly to make request to the Generall in all our names, that he would bee pleased to giue vs present passage with him. Which request of ours by my selfe deliuered vnto him, hee most readily assented vnto, and so hee sending immediately his pinnaces vnto our Island for the fetching away of[3] fewe that there were left with our baggage, the weather was so boysterous, and the pinnaces so often on ground, that the most of all wee had, with all our Cardes, Bookes and writings, were by the Saylers cast ouer boord,[4] the greater number of the Fleete being much agrieued with their long and daungerous abode in that miserable road.[5]

From whence the Generall in the name of the Almightie, waying his ankers (hauing bestowed vs among his Fleete) for the reliefe of whom hee had in that storme sustained more perill of wracke then in all his former most honourable actions against the Spaniards,

[1] Grenville was by this time well on his way, while Raleigh's supply ship was ahead of him (cp. pp. 479–80).

[2] How recent was Drake's news from home? According to the Spaniards (Wright, *Further English voyages*, pp. 313–14) he had for some time been apprehensive of a Spanish attack on England before his return. The Netherlands alone would not be a serious distraction from western expeditions though it might affect them in some degree. What the American plan was, except possibly that Drake expected a force to follow his track so as to occupy parts of the West Indies (cp. pp. 250–1), cannot be indicated.　　[3] 'of a' (Hakluyt, III (1600), 264).

[4] How far Lane had time to dismantle the fort is not clear. It seems likely that charts and maps, as well as pictures and specimens collected by Hariot and White, were lost in whole or in part, as also whatever journals Lane kept himself. Hariot directly and indirectly refers to this unfortunate event (pp. 334, 359) which has undoubtedly deprived us of material that had some chance of survival. He and Lane were especially disappointed to have lost their collection of pearls (pp. 260, 334). Amongst the residue left behind were three of Lane's party—the first lost, or deserted, colonists (p. 307 below). It is not unlikely that they had been sent after 1 June to conduct Skiko home to Chowanoac.

[5] They were in their tenth month out from England when six months was reckoned a long voyage, and with probably a good deal of sickness still on board.

with praises vnto God for all, set saile the 19. of Iune, 1586. and arriued in Portesmouth, the 27. of Iulie the same yeere.[1]

46. MAY–JUNE 1586.

SIR FRANCIS DRAKE'S EXPEDITION: HIS VISIT TO
FLORIDA AND VIRGINIA[2]

After three dayes spent in watering our ships,[3] we departed now the second time from this Cape of S. Anthonie the thirteenth of

---

[1] Drake's chronicler gives 18 June and 27 July respectively (pp. 302–3; cp. p. 288, n. 2, above).

[2] Extract from the Field edition of Walter Bigges [and probably Lieut. Crofts], *A summarie and true discourse of Sir Frances Drakes West Indian voyage*, collated with the first (Latin) edition and those of Ward, Ponsonby and Hakluyt below. The Latin and French editions appeared at Leyden in 1588, published by Fr. de Raphelegien, (a) *Expeditio Francisci Draki equitis Angli in Indias occidentales A. M.D. LXXXV* (a second issue (b) has a variant vignette), and (c) *Le voyage de messire Francois Drake chevalier, aux Indes Occidentales*. These may have been followed by (d) *Relation oder Besscheibũg der Rheiss und Schiffahrt ausz Engellandt*, [Cologne], 1589. The first English issues (e) and (f) are usually understood to be those by Richard Field, dated 1589, with a dedication by Walter Cates to the earl of Essex, and the four engraved town-plans from the Latin edition with English letterpress. The Brit. Mus. copy of (e), G. 6510, has had its title-page and town-plans removed to G. 6509, which from the line of errata on p. 52 is of the second issue (which is also distinguished by the words 'with geographicall mappes' on the title-page). Roger Ward's edition (1589) (g), is completely reset, but with the same contents and the information on the title-page that the town-plans were engraved by Baptista Boazio—the Brit. Mus. copy, C. 32. f. 25, lacks the town-plans. A note at A2 v. suggests that Ward's was intended to appear before July 1588: 'The Reader must vnderstand that this Discourse was dedicated and intended to haue beene Imprinted somewhat before the coming of the Spanish fleet vpon our coast of England: but by casualtie the same was forgotten and slackened for a time of some better leasure.' William Ponsonby's edition (i), 1596, is now represented only by a copy in John Rylands Library, Manchester, Hakluyt following with (j) *Principal navigations*, III (1600), 534–48 (cp. p. 296, suggesting he used Ward). A second Latin edition (h) had appeared in *Narrationes duae admodum memorabiles* (Noribergae, MDXC). For Boazio's general map see p. 311 below. I am indebted for much of this information to Dr Lawrence C. Wroth's annotated copy of J. C. Wheat's unpublished 'Trial bibliography of the editions of W. Bigges' narrative of Sir Francis Drake's West Indian voyage of 1585–1586' (for which see F. K. Walter and V. Doneghy, *Jesuit relations and other Americana in the library of James F. Bell* (Minneapolis, 1950), p. 220). Miss Norah H. Evans collated the first Latin and English editions for me.

[3] 'watering our ships', not in Latin.

May,[1] and proceeding about the Cape of Florida, we neuer touched anie where, but coasting alongst Florida, and keeping the shore still in sight, the eight and twentieth[2] of May early in the morning, we descried on the shore[3] a place built like a Beacon, which was in deede a scaffold vpon foure long mastes, raised on ende for men to discouer to the seaward,[4] being in the latitude of thirtie degrees, or verie neare thereunto.[5] Our Pinnaces manned, and comming to the shore, we marched vp alongst the riuer side, to see what place the enemy held there: for none amongst vs had any knowledge thereof at all.[6]

Here the General tooke occasion to march with the companies him selfe in person, the Lieutenant generall hauing the Vantgard,[7] and going a mile vp or somewhat more by the riuer side, we might discerne on the other side of the riuer ouer against vs, a fort, which newly had bene built by the Spaniards,[8] and some mile or there about aboue the fort, was a litle towne or village without walles,

---

[1] On 27 April Drake had failed to find fresh water at Cape San Antonio at the south-west tip of Cuba. He had sailed round to the north coast, hoping to make Matanzas, but after struggling for some days against contrary winds returned to Cape San Antonio where this time sufficient water was found to enable the fleet to clear for Florida (cp. Wright, *Further English voyages*, pp. 167–9, 171–4, 176–7).

[2] 27 May (p. 303 below), confirmed by the governor of Florida, Pedro Menéndez Marqués (Wright, *Further English voyages*, p. 163).

[3] 'in the distance towards the north', Latin, translated.

[4] 'for men...seawards', not in Latin. The look-out post was shown on the plan in Bigges (Wright, *Further English voyages*, p. 166) near the sand-spit at the southern side of St Augustine Inlet (C).

[5] Lat. 29° 54′ N.

[6] The Spaniards, however, understood that Drake had with him a Portuguese pilot who was an expert on the Florida coast (Wright, *Further English voyages*, p. 185, and, for references to Portuguese with Drake, pp. 173, 227).

[7] In the Latin the sentence (in translation) begins: 'Our general ordered the lieutenant to the vanguard'. The lieutenant general was Christopher Carleill.

[8] The problem of the approach to the fort and town is stated below (pp. 303–4). The English had access to the land on either side of the inlet, but when they reached the inner channel the newly-built fort faced them on the western side across the water, while the town was some distance to the south on the same side (cp. Wright, *Further English voyages*, p. 164). Only small vessels could pass the inlet and they, in turn, were covered by the fort at the bar of the inner channel before they could reach the town.

built of woodden houses:[1] we forthwith prepared to haue ordinance for the batterie, and one peece was a litle before the euening planted, and the first shot being made by the Lieutenant generall him selfe at their Ensigne, strake through the Ensigne, as we afterwards vnderstood by a French man,[2] which came vnto vs from them. One shot more was then made, which strake the foote of the fort wall, which was all massiue timber of great trees like mastes. The Lieutenant generall was determined to passe the riuer this night with foure companies, and there to lodge him selfe intrenched as neare the fort, as that he might play with his muskets and smallest shot vpon anie that should appeare: and so afterwards to bring and plant the batterie with him, but the helpe of marriners for that sudden to make trenches could not be had, which was the cause that this determination was remitted vntill the next night.

In the night the Lieutenant general tooke a litle rowing Skiffe, and halfe a dosen well armed, as Captaine Morgan, and Captaine Sampson,[3] with some others besides the rowers, and went to viewe what gard the enemie kept, as also to take knowledge of the ground. And albeit he went as couertly as might be, yet the enemy taking the Alarum, grew fearefull that the whole Force was approching to the assault, and therefore with all speede abandoned the place after the shooting of some of their peeces.[4] They thus gone, and

[1] 'as this Plot [i.e. the plan] here doth plainlie shew'; added in Ward's edition (g) and retained by Hakluyt.

[2] 'who had been detained in prison', Latin (the parallel phrase in brackets after 'Phipher' below being omitted). For Nicholas Burgoignon see pp. 304, 763–6 below.

[3] Captain Matthew Morgan and Captain John Sampson, field corporals of the expedition (cp. Hakluyt, *Principal navigations*, x, 98, 100, 104, 106, 119). This was on the night of the 28th (p. 304 below). The Latin text (in translation) continues: 'with four others and went to view'.

[4] The Spanish accounts gloss over this affair (Wright, *Further English voyages*, pp. 163, 165, 181, 182–4), all stressing the length and strength of the resistance and the effects of the counter-fire from the fort (ignored in the English versions), except at one place (p. 165) where the Florida officials give away the panic in which the fort was abandoned when they say they left everything, even the pay-chest, behind. The governor stressed that he had only eighty effectives and decided not to resist, apart from a rear-guard, but to accompany the women and children into hiding, thus abandoning both fort and town (pp. 163–4).

he being returned vnto vs againe, but nothing knowing of their
flight from their fort, forthwith came a French man being a
Phipher (who had bene prisoner with them) in a litle boate, playing
on his phiph the tune of the Prince of Orenge his song,[1] and being
called vnto by the gard, he tolde them before he put foote out of
the boate, what he was him selfe, and howe the Spaniards were
gone from the fort, offering either to remaine in hands there, or
else to returne to the place with them that would go.

Vpon this intelligence the Generall, the Lieutenant generall,
with some of the Captaines in one Skiffe, and the Vizeadmirall
with some others in his Skiffe,[2] and two or three Pinnaces furnished
of souldiers with them, put presently ouer towards the fort, giuing
order for the rest of the Pinnaces to follow. And in our approch,
some of the enemie bolder then the rest, hauing stayed behind their
companie, shot off two peeces of ordinance at vs: but on shore[3]
we went, and entred the place without finding any man there.[4]

When the day appeared, we found it built all of timber, the
walles being none other then[5] whole masts or bodies of trees set
vpright and close together in maner of a pale, without anie ditch
as yet made, but who intended[6] with some more time, for they
had not as yet finished all their worke, hauing begun the same some

---

[1] Hakluyt has in the margin 'Nicholas Borgoignon' (see pp. 763–6 below),
but it is said below (p. 304) that he was accompanied by a Dutchman. Burgoignon
was probably a survivor of the San Mateo fight of 1580, the latest French intervention in Florida (*T.R.H.S.*, 5th ser., I, 7, 11). The tune was that of 'Wilhelmus
van Nassouwe' (1569, attributed to Sainte Aldegonde, see C. V. Wedgwood,
William the silent (1944), p. 116).

[2] Drake, Carleill, etc., in one, Captain Martin Frobisher with his lieutenant,
Waterhouse, from the *Primrose*, in the other (cp. p. 304, which says only twenty
men altogether went over, but this is not likely to be correct). According to some
of the Spanish accounts the pinnaces took down their masts (Wright, *Further
English voyages*, pp. 182–4).

[3] 'on hard' (Ponsonby edition, p. 45).

[4] The *Primrose* account says that it was some Indians who fired from the woods
and Waterhouse, following them, was killed (p. 304 below; cp. Wright, *Further
English voyages*, p. 199, which confirms it).

[5] 'but' (Hakluyt).

[6] 'but was intended' (Ponsonby edition, p. 45).

three or fower moneths before:[1] so as to say the truth, they had no reason to keepe it, being subiect both to fier and easie assault.

The platforme whereon the ordinance lay was whole bodies of long pine trees, whereof there is great plentie, layed a crosse one on another, and some litle earth amongst. There was in it thirteene or fourteene great peeces of brasse ordinance, and a chest vnbroken vp, hauing in it the value of some two thousand pounds sterling, by estimation of the kings treasure,[2] to pay the souldiers of that place, who were a hundred and fiftie men.

The fort thus wonne, which they called S. Iohns[3] fort, and the day opened, we assayed to go to the towne, but could not by reason of some riuers and broken ground which was betweene the two places: and therefore enforced[4] to imbarke againe into our Pinnaces, we went thither vpon the great maine riuer, which is called as also the towne by the name of S. Augustine.

At our approching to land, there was some that began to shewe them selues, and to bestowe some fewe shot vpon vs, but presently withdrewe them selues. And in their running thus away, the Sergeant maior[5] finding one of their horses readie sadled and bridled, tooke the same to follow the chase, and so ouergoing all his companie, was (by one layed behind a bush) shot through the head, and falling downe therewith, was by the same and two or three more, stabbed in three or foure places of his bodie with swords and daggers, before anie could come neere to his reskue. His death was much lamented, being in verie deede an honest wise Gentle-

[1] Only after news of Drake's attack on Santo Domingo in January had reached San Agustín (Wright, *Further English voyages*, p. 164).

[2] About 5000–6000 ducats (Wright, *Further English voyages*, pp. 181, 188, but cp. p. 165), which at 6s. to the ducat (p. 220 above) would be worth about £1500. It may not have been found until the 30th (p. 304 below).

[3] Ward's edition has 'S. Iohn fort'. San Juan de Pinos (cp. Wright, *Further English voyages*, p. 202, with the plan at p. 166 (1)).

[4] 'being enforced' (Hakluyt). The plan shows two streams on the west bank of the St Augustine River between the fort and the town.

[5] Anthony Powell (cp. Hakluyt, *Principal navigations*, X, 98, 112, 120; pp. 304, 804 below).

man, and a souldier of good experience, and of as great courage as anie man might be.

In this place called S. Augustine, we vnderstood the King did keepe as is before said, one hundred and fiftie souldiers, and at an other place some dozen leagues beyond to the Northwardes, called S. Helena, he did there likewise kepe an hundred and fiftie more,[1] seruing there for no other purpose, then to keepe all other nations from inhabiting any part of all that coast,[2] the gouernement whereof was committed to one Pedro Melendez Marquesse, nephew to that Melendez the Admiral, who had ouerthrown Maister Iohn Hawkins in the Bay of Mexico some fifteene or sixteene yeares agoe.[3] This Gouernour had charge of both the places, but was at this time in this place, and one of the first that left the same.

Here it was resolued in full assemblie of Captaines, to vndertake the enterprise of S. Helena, and from thence to seeke out the inhabitation of our English countrey men in Virginia,[4] distant from thence some sixe degrees Northward.

[1] Fort San Marcos at Santa Elena, lat. 32° 20′ N., more like 60 leagues away, where Gutierre de Miranda was commander (Wright, *Further English voyages*, pp. 186-8, 202; p. 723 below).

[2] 'all foreigners, as English and French', Latin. See Quinn, in *T.R.Hist.S.*, 5th ser., I, 1–13.

[3] Hakluyt has put 'seuenteen or eighteene', and the Latin text (in translation) adds: 'contrary to his pledged word'. The reference is to San Juan de Ulua in 1568, but is a quite mistaken one, since it was Don Martin Enrique (with Francisco de Lujan as general and Juan de Ubilla as admiral) who had tricked Hawkins there (Williamson, *Hawkins of Plymouth*, pp. 137–41). Pedro Menéndez de Avilés, *adelantado* of Florida, had served as general (*anglice* admiral) of the *flota* but never against Hawkins. For his nephew Pedro Menéndez Marqués, see below pp. 719–24, and Wright, *Further English voyages*, passim.

[4] 'a certain tract of that region inhabited by our English and called "La Virginia" after our queen' (Latin, translated). The addition of the latitude, which was correct enough disclosed the position of the English settlement which even in 1589 was probably scarcely politic (cp. pp. 7–8). This was knowledge added after the event, since the Spaniards appear to have been right that Drake was not too sure where the English were located (Wright, *Further English voyages*, pp. 181, 187–8, 191). The decision to call at the Virginia colony was, as the account says, taken finally at this council, but it had been in Drake's mind for some time (ibid. p. 214) and his actions at San Agustín bore out the Spanish suspicions that

When we came thwart of S. Helena,[1] the shols appearing daungerous, and we hauing no Pilot to vndertake the entrie,[2] it was thought meetest to go hence alongst. For the Admirall had bene the same night in foure fadome and halfe[3] three leagues from the shore: and yet we vnderstood, that[4] by the helpe of a knowen Pilot, there may and doth go in ships of greater burthen and draught then anie we had in our Fleete.

We passed thus alongst the coast hard abord the shore, which is shallow for a league or two from the shore, and the same is lowe and broken land[5] for the most part.

The ninth of Iune[6] vpon sight of one speciall great fire (which are verie ordinarie all alongst this coast, euen from the Cape Florida[7] hither) the Generall sent his Skiffe[8] to the shore, where they found some of our English countrey men (that had bene sent thither the yeare before by Sir Walter Raleigh)[9] & brought one[10] aboord, by whose direction we proceeded along to the place, which they make their Port.[11] But some of our ships being of great draught

he intended to go there (ibid. pp. 185, 189, 204, 206, 230–1). The account's omission of the English actions after the capture of the fort and town is partly supplied on pp. 304–5 below.

[1] 'Santa Helena' added in margin by Hakluyt.

[2] The Spaniards believed him to have an expert pilot (Wright, *Further English voyages*, p. 185), but they reported that in fact he had put in at a harbour (Cruz = Savannah River? Ibid. pp. 190–1) some seven leagues south of Santa Elena, tried to probe the entrance and fired to attract attention, but then cleared out to sea and passed the entrance to Santa Elena at night (ibid. pp. 191, 203, 204–6).

[3] 'and a halfe' (Ward and Hakluyt). The *Elizabeth Bonaventure*, the flagship or admiral, was of 600 tons burden (Corbett, *Spanish war*, p. xii).

[4] 'vnderstood by' (Hakluyt): the informant was probably the Frenchman Burgoignon (pp. 763–6 below).

[5] 'insulis plusculis distinctae', Latin version.

[6] Stafford, according to Lane, had sighted Drake's fleet on the 8th (p. 288 above).

[7] 'Cape of Florida' (Hakluyt): for the spontaneous fires see pp. 610, 613 below.

[8] 'his skiff with some companions' (Latin, translated).

[9] There is no reference to Raleigh in the Latin text which reads: 'qui in regione illa aliquot Anglos offenderunt'. Stafford's men were on Croatoan Island in the vicinity of the modern Cape Hatteras (cp. p. 283).

[10] 'them' (Hakluyt).

[11] Port Ferdinando (cp. p. 283 above). From 'Port' to the end of the pamphlet the Latin text is much briefer, and the English version offers the first

vnable to enter, we ankered all[1] without the harbour in a wild road at sea, about two miles from shore.

From whence the General wrote letters to Maister Rafe Lane, being Gouernour of those English in Virginia, and then at his fort about six leagues from the rode in an Island, which they call Roanoac,[2] wherein specially he shewed how readie he was to supply his necessities and wants, which he vnderstood of, by those he had first talked withall.

The morrowe after[3] Maister Lane him selfe and some of his companie comming vnto him, with the consent of his Captaines, he gaue them the choise of two offers, that is to say: Either he would leaue a ship, a Pinnace, and certaine boates with sufficient Maisters and mariners, together furnished with a moneths victuall to stay and make farther discouerie of the country and coastes, and so much victuall likewise that[4] might be sufficient for the bringing of them all (being an hundred and three persons)[5] into England if they thought good after such time, with anie other thing they would desire, & that he might be able to spare.

Or else if they thought they had made sufficient discouerie

published account, in any detail, of the taking off of Lane's men. The Latin reads, in translation:

'Since our ships were unable to enter this, they cast anchor outside it. There on the day after we had made the port such a fierce storm struck them that the greater part were forced to weigh anchor and spread sail: of these some returned to the rest of the fleet, others went straight back to England. Here our general offered to provide Ralph Lane [printed 'Laue'], general of all the English captains who were in Virginia, and his men, with all the main necessities and to leave them one of the larger of his own vessels, a fast-sailing ship, in which he could return to England if within a month his men, at that time numbering 150 [cp. above], were not reinforced. But they were so hard-pressed and broken by the scarcity of all things, that they wanted nothing more than to return to their native country with us as soon as possible. Accordingly they were soon taken on to our ships and sailed thence with us. At length we all arrived together at Portsmouth on the 27 July 1586 alive and well.'

[1] 'enter, anchored without' (Hakluyt).
[2] The name is added in the margin by Hakluyt.
[3] 11 June, according to Lane (p. 289 above), with whose account this tallies closely. Lane had already received a letter from Drake by Stafford.
[4] 'as might be' (Hakluyt).
[5] For the numbers, cp. pp. 194–7, 228, 384.

alreadie, and did desire to returne into England, he would giue them passage.[1] But they as it seemed, being desirous to stay, accepted verie thankefully, and with great gladnesse that which was offred first. Whereupon the ship being appointed and receaued into charge, by some of their owne companie sent into her by Maister Lane, before they had received from the rest of the Fleete, the prouision appointed the*m*, there arose a great storme (which they sayde was extraordinarie and verie straunge) that lasted three dayes together,[2] and put all our Fleete in great daunger, to be driuen from their ankoring vpon the coast. For we brake manie Cables, and lost manie Ankers. And some of our Fleete which had lost all (of which number was the ship appointed for Maister Lane and his companie[3]) were driuen to put to sea in great danger, in auoiding the coast, and could neuer see vs againe vntill we met in England. Manie also of our small Pinnaces and boates were lost in this storme.

Notwithstanding after all this, the Generall offered them (with consent of his Captaines)[4] another ship with some prouision, although not such a one for their turnes, as might haue bene spared them before, this being vnable to be brought into their harbour.[5] Or else if they would, to giue them passage into England, although he knewe we should performe it with greater difficultie then he might haue done before.

But Maister Lane with those of the chiefest of his companie which he had then with him, considering what should be best for them to doe, made request vnto the Generall vnder their handes, that they might haue passage for England: the which being graunted, and the rest sent for out of the countrey and shipped, we departed from that coast the eighteenth of Iune.[6]

---

[1] Lane does not indicate this alternative (pp. 289–91).

[2] From 13 to 16 (or 14 to 17) June; evidently a hurricane slowly moving northwards. Few continue inshore north of Cape Hatteras.

[3] The *Francis* (p. 291 above). Hakluyt follows with 'was'.

[4] As always, this account is careful to stress that Drake never took a decision without consulting his council. [5] The *Bark Bonner* (p. 292 above).

[6] 19 June, Lane says (p. 294). It was the summary as it appeared in the Latin edition (above) which influenced the more general accounts in the chronicles

And so God be thanked, both they and we in good safetie arriued at Portesmouth the eight and twentieth of Iuly 1586.[1] to the great glorie of God, and to no small honour to our Prince, our countrey, and our selues....[2]

47. [1586.]

THE *PRIMROSE* JOURNAL OF DRAKE'S VOYAGE. FLORIDA AND VIRGINIA[3]

The discourse and description of the voyage of Sir Frawncis Drake & *Master* captaine Frobisher, set forward the 14 daie of September. 1585/....

The 23 [4] of Maie wee put of into the sea for the Cape of florida, and the xxv^th daie wee gott sight therof & sealinge alonge the coast, the 27 daie[5] wee fell with a Towne called *Saint Awgustine*, There wee went on shore in the morninge, but coulde not enter the Towne for they had warninge of *our* com*m*inge, and made a castle of pur[pose] for there defence against vs in suche order that wee must winne the castle before wee coulde get the Towne, and *our*

of the end of Lane's colony, e.g. Emanuel van Meteren, *Historia belgica* [1598] (as *L'histoire des Pays-Bays* (1618), fo. 283 v.), and William Camden, *Annales* (1615), pp. 387–8 (4th ed. trans. 1688, p. 324). The latter says: 'Hereupon Lane and those who were planted there, being in great Penury and want, and out of all Hope of Provisions out of England, their Number also much diminished [cp. pp. 301, 384], with one voice besought Drake that he would carry them back again into their own Countrey, which he readily and willingly did. And these men who were thus brought back were the first that I know of that brought into England that Indian plant which they call Tabacca and Nicotia, or Tobacco which they used against Crudities [contra cruditates]', continuing with his diatribe against tobacco whereby, he says, the English 'seem as it were to be degenerated into the nature of Barbarians'. He is wrong about the introduction of tobacco (pp. 344–6).

[1] Lane gives 27 July (p. 294; cp. p. 312).

[2] The account concludes with some mention of the financial and material results of the voyage, noting (Field, p. 52) that 'In the fort of S. Augustine were fourteene peeces', and mentioning the principal men who died.

[3] Extracts from Brit. Mus., Royal MS 7. c. xvi, fos. 166–73, printed with modernized spelling in Corbett, *Spanish war* (1898), pp. 1–26, and referred to by him as 'the *Primrose* log', since the only thing he knew of its author was that he served under Frobisher in the vice-admiral, a vessel of 200 tons (Corbett, p. xii).

[4] fo. 172.   [5] Cp. p. 295 above.

s[hips] could not come neere the Towne to batter hit, the water w[as] shallow excepte it weare a v or 6 miles from hit, Yet there wa[s] a goodlie Riuer runninge close by the towne into the countrie.[1]

The 28 daie[2] wee tooke ordinawnce on shore to batter the Castle which stoode on the one side of the river & wee were on the other yet when wee had shott ij peeces at them, like fainte harted Cowardes they ranne awaie, This was abowte midnight, Then came over the river to vs a frenche man & a dutcheman who tolde vs they were all fledd,[3]

Then the Admyrall & Vizadmirall[4] went over with xx^{ti} men & Entringe there Castle fownde there woordes trew, Then on the other side where our men laie the savages & others came owte of the woodes & with a verie strawnge crie, assawlted our men,[5]

But they weare soone driven backe and our men followinge them into the woodes by mischawnce on master Waterhouse the Captaines lieftenaunte[6] Of our shipp was slaine,

The 29 daie of Maie wee entered the Towne & the Spaniardes gave vs 3 or 4 small shott & Ranne awaie & in followinge of them Captaine Powell was slaine by a horsman & ij footmen spaniardes[7]

The 30 daie after wee had taken the spoile of this Towne wee set it on fire & soe wente to the Castle where wee rested 3 daies[8]

In this Castle wee fownde a Cheste with the kinges Treasure,[9]

---

[1] Cp. p. 295 above, and plan in Wright, *Further English voyages*, p. 166.

[2] Cp. pp. 295–6 above.

[3] The Frenchman was Nicholas Burgoignon (pp. 296–7, 763–6). The Spaniards add a Fleming (the Dutchman?) and a Spaniard (Morales?) (Wright, *Further English voyages*, pp. 182, 186).

[4] Sir Francis Drake and Captain Martin Frobisher.   [5] Cp. Ibid. p. 199.

[6] Crossed out 'viz. vnto Frobisher vizadmiral', showing Waterhouse to have been Frobisher's lieutenant on the *Primrose*. Corbett considered this to be one of the earliest appearances of the office of naval lieutenant (p. 24).

[7] Cp. pp. 298–9 above and Wright, *Further English voyages*, p. 187.

[8] The destruction of the town is not mentioned above (p. 299), but bulks large in the Spanish accounts. The church, and every house, the orchards, the very maize-fields, were destroyed and everything portable was taken away, tools and furniture (down to the locks on the doors), money (estimated at 3000–5000 ducats) belonging to private persons, launches and all kinds of small craft (Wright, *Further English voyages*, pp. 164, 181, 183–5, 188–9, 204).

[9] Cp. pp. 298, 310 above.

and hard by the Castle wee fownde a small Carvell with certaine treasure in her and some letters from the kinge of Spaine,

For Shee was newlie come thence and further Wee fownde a lit[tle] Childe in her which the Spaniardes had lefte behinde them for has[te] Wee sent them the childe and they tooke her but woulde not c[ome] to vs for anie thinge wee coulde doe,[1]

There was 9 of the savages set vp a flagge of Truce abo[ut] ij miles from the Towne, which our men fownde and carried them another,[2]

The seconde daie of Iune wee set fire on the Castle, w[ee then the] same night set saile from Thence,[3]

Also In that nighte wee set fire on the Carvell [which wee] had taken by the Matacosse laden with salte[4] / and tooke t[he other] Carvell along with vs,

This Towne Saint Awgustine / standeth in florydaie [where is] as goodlie a soyle as maie bee, with so greate abundance [of] sweete woodes &c' as is woonderfull with goodlie meadowes, [and] store of fisshe Oysters & mussels with deere & goodlie feeldes of Corne after there manner,[5]

There was abowte 250 howses[6] in this Towne, but wee left not one of them standinge,

---

[1] Nothing of this is known from any Spanish document so far published.

[2] Menéndez Marqués was in a difficult position. The 150 to 200 non-combatants were at the mercy of a large number of only nominally friendly Indians who had assembled, so that he feared to defend the fort and leave them to take a chance. This instance shows that the English were anxious to mobilize the Indians against the Spaniards—as the latter feared—and with some hope of success (cp. Wright, *Further English voyages*, pp. 183–4, 187). Juan de Posada, noting that Drake did no damage to this Indian village, considered the inhabitants were too good Catholics to be influenced by English flattery.

[3] For the dates compare Wright, *Further English voyages*, pp. 188 (3/13 June), 190 (2/12 June).

[4] Matanzas, Cuba (see Corbett, *Spanish war*, p. 24). She had probably become unseaworthy. Drake had taken the opportunity of careening one of his ships (Wright, *Further English voyages*, pp. 181–2).

[5] This is only the second direct description of this area by an Englishman, the first being John Sparke's of 1565 (Hakluyt, *Principal navigations*, X, 51–62). Spanish opinions of Florida in 1586 ranged from the completely unfavourable (Wright, *Further English voyages*, p. 187) to the entirely favourable (ibid. pp. 189, 191).   [6] Probably an overestimate.

Wee fownde 40 pipes of meale in this place & muche ba[rley] but wee fownde neither wine nor Oyle nor anie other vict[ual] to make accompte of[1]

Wee had in this towne xij greate peeces of Brasse Ordinawnce[2]

This Towne had v weekes warninge before, of our comminge, and had builded this castle onlie for vs keepinge 90 sowldiers there in garrison, And There wee vnderstoode that the Hyabans[3] had burn[ed] there towne themselves, and had gotten 1200 men to helpe the[m] thinkinge that we woulde come to them,[4]

The wilde people at first comminge of our men died verie fast and saide amongest themselues, It was the Inglisshe God that made them die so faste/[5]

There ar divers kinges emongest them, and these kinges ar distaunte on from an other & they haue manie wifes, They tolde our men of one kinge not far from thence that had 140 wives,

Oure men killed the kinge of that place wee were In[6] for that

---

[1] The Spanish women and children had, doubtless, been supplied with a certain amount of food to take with them, but Menéndez Marqués carried nothing away from the fort and was soon on very short rations. Posada's arrival from Spain (on 9/19 July) saved much hardship (Wright, *Further English voyages*, pp. 203–5). The surviving evidence stresses the poverty in which the Spanish garrison and settlers were kept.

[2] The final reckoning was fourteen pieces (Hakluyt, x, 134).

[3] Habitants. There is no suggestion in the Spanish texts that the burning of the town was due to anyone except the English.

[4] The meaning is not too clear, but it apparently implies that the Spaniards had enrolled 1200 Indians to meet an English assault.

[5] They were possibly given measles or small-pox by the English (cp. Hariot, p. 378 below).

[6] Cp. p. 301. These relations must refer not to their contact with the Indians near San Agustín but with those much further along the coast. According to the Spanish reports the English ships kept well off-shore, but put in first (on 7/17 June) in search of Santa Elena, seven leagues to the south, at Cruz harbour (apparently the Savannah River) and then, passing the Spanish post at night, at Oristan, three leagues to the north (pp. 191, 203–5). Orista or Oristan was a name for the whole province north of the Savannah River in modern South Carolina, where the coast was occupied by the Cusabo tribe (Swanton, *Indians*, pp. 18, 128, map at p. 34). The Spaniards believed Drake had given the Indians presents and that he had got water and firewood, but evidently their relations were not wholly friendly.

hee with hys people in on nighte had determined to murther all the Inglishmen / And an Indian did Bewraie the[ir] cowncell, Soe wee gave the kinge that for his paines which hee woulde haue geeven vs,

The haue a churche with 3 Images in hit,[1] And the[y] speake with the Divell once everie yeere vppon an highe Mowntaine,[2]

Also they ar cladd in Skins and they haue a Copper myne emongest them,[3] And for the tagge of a pointe, a bell a cownter, a pinne or suche like, They will geeve you anie thinge they haue/[4]

Then wee sailed alonge the coast of this lande vntill wee Came to the place where those men did lyve that Sir Walter Raleghe had sente thither to Inhabit the yeere before[5]

Those gentlemen[6] and others, as soone as they s[aw vs, thin]kinge wee had bin a new supplie[7] [came from the] shore & tarried certaine daies, & a[fterwards we brought]e thense all those men with vs, except iij [who had gone furt]her into the countrie and the winde gre[we so that] wee coulde not staie for them/[8]

[The 13th][9] of Iune iiij of our Shippes[10] weare forced to [put to sea] the weather was so sore & the Storme so [great th]at our Ankers woulde not holde, and no shipp [of them all] but eyther

---

[1] Cp. the Algonkian temples, pp. 373, 424-7, below.

[2] He probably refers to some religious ceremony held in the mountains.

[3] Unlikely (cp. p. 269 above).

[4] Cp. the bartering habits of the Algonkian peoples further north (pp. 98-101, 103). From Lane's experience they soon appear to have learnt the techniques of harder bargaining. These small scraps of ethnological material do not appear to have been used by Swanton. For the use of counters (jettons) cp. p. 908 below.

[5] Cp. pp. 251-3.

[6] From here the MS is damaged in both margins. The gaps can be filled from pp. 292-4, 300-3, above or by conjecture. For the most part Corbett (*Spanish war*, pp. 26-7) is followed. These two words, survive as catchwords only.

[7] It does not appear from Lane's account that Stafford, after his very earliest view of Drake, can have thought so, as he waited and got a letter from him before going to tell Lane (pp. 288-9).

[8] This is the only reference to the deserting of three of the settlers—the first 'lost colonists'—by Lane and Drake, cp. pp. 293, 302 above.

[9] Corbett (*Spanish war*, p. 27) gives the 10th but see p. 292.

[10] The other accounts do not give a number, but merely mention the *Francis* by name.

brake or lost ther Ankers, And o*u*r [ship th]e Prymrose Brake an Anker of 250 li. waighte [All the] Time wee weare in thys countrie, We had thunder [lightning] and raigne with hailstones as Bigge as hennes egges [There were] greate Spow*tes* at the seas as thoughe heaven & [earth] woulde haue mett/[1]

[This c]owntrie is Indifferent frewtfull[2] and hathe good [store of] fisshe w*i*th land Turtles[3] & nice Frew*tes* & saxafrage[4] [which are] the best thing*es* in all the lande that wee know of: [the rest] after the reporte of the people woulde bee to longe[5] [Let th]is suffice/

[The 18th][6] daie of Iune 1586 wee set saile directinge o*u*r course [to Ne]wfownd Lande[7] & so homewardes/

Henrey[8]

[1] This implies at least one, and probably more, hurricanes, with a number of minor thunderstorms.

[2] This a modest but fairly warm commendation.

[3] See p. 362 below.   [4] Sassafras (see p. 329).

[5] Badly as some of Lane's men spoke of Virginia on their return, their first reports when they were taken off were evidently not too unfavourable (cp. p. 324).

[6] This is either the 18th or 19th (cp. pp. 294, 302). It is possible that the majority of the vessels sailed on the first day and the remainder the day after.

[7] Drake would expect to get fish and water at Newfoundland. This homeward route was often taken by privateers from the West Indies (cp. p. 767).

[8] This name is near the centre of the page at the bottom and may possibly read 'O Henrey'. It is in the same hand as the journal and is likely to be the signature of the author. Though the bottom right hand corner is torn away, it is unlikely that 'Henrey' is a christian name of which the surname is missing as there is nearly an inch between the 'y' and the edge of the tear. Corbett did not note this name.

48. [1586?]

A FRENCH ACCOUNT OF DRAKE'S VOYAGE[1]

They took six or seven score bronze pieces,[2] as well in the city as in the galleys,[3] remaining at Cartagena all through Lent,[4] and departing only on the last Thursday.[5] Leaving it, they passed by the island of Cayamans, which is not inhabited. There are on this island great serpents called 'cayamans', like large lizards, which are edible.[6] From there they came to anchor off the island of Cuba at Cape San Antonio.[7] They saw no one there, took on water, and

---

[1] Extract, translated. The 'Voiage du sieur Drach' is printed in *Mémoire du voyage en Russie fait en 1586 par Johan Sauvage suivi de l'expédition de Fr. Drake en Amérique à la meme époque. Publiés...d'après les manuscrits de la Bibliothèque impériale*, ed. Louis Lacour (Paris, 1855). The MS used by Lacour is now Bibliothèque Nationale, MS français, ancien fonds, 704. The brief account of Drake's voyage is followed by a newsletter, dated at London, 15 July 1587, on Drake's Cadiz exploit. It may have been sent to France with it. A copy of the Drake narrative, collated herewith, is in Archives de la ministère des affaires étrangères, MS 24270 (Correspondence politique d'Angleterre, tome 22), fos. 421–4, and has some slight variations. The narrative is difficult to evaluate. It has some small independent value, and might be thought to represent a summary report drawn up by a French agent in England, on the basis of a version of the Bigges [etc.] narrative, with some additional oral evidence, rather than an original narrative written by a Frenchman who had accompanied Drake.

[2] 63, according to the English (Bigges, in Hakluyt, *Principal navigations*, x, 134).

[3] For the two galleys and their tender, see Wright, *Further English voyages*, pp. xliv–v, 52, 58–9).

[4] They arrived on Ash Wednesday (N.S.), 9/19 February (Wright, *Further English voyages*, pp. xlvii, 41, etc.; cp. *Primrose* journal, in Corbett, *Spanish war*, p. 18, which gives 11/21 February).

[5] They left on Thursday, 31 March/10 April, but this was Holy Thursday only by the English (O.S.) reckoning (cp. Wright, *Further English voyages*, pp. lvii, 135, 145, 159; Bigges, in Hakluyt, x, 127). This was Drake's first departure, as he reappeared on 4/14 April (Wright, op. cit.), and left finally either on Thursday, 14/24 April, as the Spaniards say, or on 18/28 April by an English account (Wright, op. cit. pp. lvii, 136, 145, 160; *Primrose* journal, in Corbett, op. cit. p. 22).

[6] For Cayman Island and its 'serpents', which they saw 22–24 April (O.S.) cp. *Primrose* journal (Corbett, *Spanish war*, pp. 22–3).

[7] On 27 April/7 May they arrived for the first time at Cape San Antonio but found no water, put to sea and eventually, after fourteen days of contrary winds, put back and this time found water, leaving on 13/23 May (Bigges, in Hakluyt, *Principal navigations*, x, 127–8; pp. 294–5 above).

The said town was besieged for a single day. They have there, both in the town and in the fort, about six score men. It is at least 800 leagues from Cartagena to San Agustín. The governor of San Agustín and of Fort San Juan is Don Petro Melando, marquis.[14]

then set their sails to the wind and passed by La Havenna,[1] which is in the said island of Cuba. They did not wish to stay as they were short of men, and came directly to the coast of Florida, whence, having coasted for two days,[2] they arrived at the river of Matanes,[3] and took the town of San Agustín, which is on the said river, and also Fort San Juan.[4] The town and fort were besieged and at last the Spaniards quitted them.[5]

The English set fire to everything and took fourteen bronze pieces and one of iron.[6] They found within the town the king's chest, in which there were about five thousand ducats:[7] the rest [of the loot] might be worth five or six thousand ducats.[8]

From San Agustín they went to Norambega,[9] distant some three hundred and fifty leagues,[10] where they took away Master Lames, who was in great want of provisions.[11] They remained there eighteen days because of a storm which separated them.[12]

They were five weeks coming from Norambega to Porthmuitz.[13]

The ships' lading was of hides, wine and pieces of cannon only, and they were but half laden.[15]

---

[1] On Drake's brief appearance off Havana on 20/30 May see Wright, *Further English voyages*, pp. 168–72, 176–8. Drake made no attempt to besiege the port and the two shots fired by its guns were to prevent his pinnaces catching a merchant vessel.   [2] 25–27 May (O.S.) (p. 303 above).

[3] The Matanzas Inlet is somewhat to the south of San Agustín, which is, itself, on the St John's river.

[4] For the fort, San Juan de Pinos, see pp. 297–8 above and the engraving from Bigges (reproduced in Wright, *Further English voyages*, p. 166).

[5] Cp. pp. 296, 304 above.

[6] Confirmed in Bigges (Hakluyt, *Principal navigations*, x, 134).

[7] This is near enough to the English estimate of £2000 (p. 298 above).

[8] No similar estimate has been found elsewhere.

[9] Neither of the English accounts use the name for a zone so far south, though the Spaniards may have tended to do so (cp. pp. 729, 731 below).

[10] The sailing distance was not over 600 miles.

[11] Ralph Lane. For the condition of his men cp. pp. 301, 303, 324.

[12] This sentence is omitted by Lacour. They were eleven or twelve days off the Carolina Banks (cp. pp. 288–94, 300–2 above).

[13] Portsmouth.

[14] Pedro Menéndez Marqués. The form might seem to have been derived from Bigges (p. 299 above).

[15] This is a useful sidelight which does not appear elsewhere.

The whole is estimated at only five to six hundred thousand crowns,[1] but it is certain that they have destroyed to the value of two to three millions in gold.[3]

This Lames had been left there when Frobisher[2] made a voyage to there a year and a half before.

49. [1588.]

LETTERPRESS FOR BAPTISTA BOAZIO'S MAP OF DRAKE'S WEST INDIAN VOYAGE[4]

MAY.

The 13. of May we departed the second time from the Cape Saint Antony, and proceeding about the Cape of Florida, wee neuer touched any where, but kept the coast alongst.

The 28. of May earely in the morning we describe the Riuer of Saynt Augustine in Florida, in 36. degrees of Latitude, wher some small Spanish Garrison was planted, of some 150. men, or thereabouts: Here we spent two dayes in taking the fort and spoiling

---

[1] £166,000–£200,000 (cp. p. 473, for exchange values): Bigges gives £60,000 (Hakluyt, *Principal navigations*, X, 133).

[2] Lacour, p. 28, has 'Forbigno', but the other version has the word corrected in, possibly, a later hand. Grenville is meant. The settlers had been there a year only.

[3] In gold crowns (*écus d'or*). This estimate also has not been encountered elsewhere.

[4] Extract from a brief account of the voyage which was set up in six columns either for use as a broadside (as in the Society of Antiquaries' set), or to be pasted below the general map of Drake's voyage by Baptista Boazio. The map is found with the attachment in only one copy of Bigges (Brit. Mus., G. 6509), and once separately—the map formerly owned by the duke of Leeds which was bought by the John Carter Brown Library in 1947. A copy of Hakluyt's *Principall navigations* (1589), now in the New York Public Library, has a loose set of the printed matter inserted. My authority is Wheat and Wroth (see p. 294 above). The four town-plans were clearly done for the Latin edition, but it has been thought that the map was a venture independent of the English versions of Bigges. John White's close association with all five, noted below (pp. 406–7, 411–13), would suggest that the engravings were planned as a single series, but the map was (for strategic reasons?) withheld from the Leyden publisher. It may well have been intended to appear with the plans in the English edition but as this was delayed the map is likely to have been issued separately in advance with this letterpress, only some copies being added in due course to the second and third English issues (pp. 34, 294 above).

the Town, and so departed agayn keeping as nigh the shore as might be, to haue a sight it myght be of our English men planted in Virginia.

IVNE.

The 9. of Iune in com*m*yng alongst the coast, we discouered some par[t] of Virginia, and found some of our English men, and the next day spake wyth more of them, & so afterwards with them al.[1]

The 18. of Iune we departed from the coast of Virginia, and so betweene Virginia and the first sight of England, we were in sayling one whole moneth, or thereabouts.[2]

IVLY.

The 22. of Iuly we fell in sight of the Sorlinges, or the Ilandes of Syly, being the westermost part of all England.

The 22. of Iuly 1586.[3] God be thanked we arriued all in good safety at Portesmouth.

50.   1586.

JOHN HOOKER ON THE RESULTS OF DRAKE'S VOYAGE[4]

1584-[5][5]

In September yn this mayors yere Sir Francys Drake toke shipping at Plymmouthe and sayled to hispaniola: where [he] most valyantly toke the townes of S^t domingo and of Carthegena & the countrie there about & returned with great spoyles & ryches and honor:

1585-[6]

Sir Francis drake returned from hispaniola with great ryches and honor which so inflamed the whole countrie with a desyre to

---

[1] Cp. the dates pp. 288, 302-3.   [2] Cp. pp. 294, 303, 308.

[3] The 27th and 28th are given elsewhere (pp. 294, 303).

[4] Exeter City Library, Exeter City MSS, Book no. 51, extracts. (See W. J. Harte, *Extracts from the common place book of John Hooker, relating to the City of Exeter, 1485-1590* [1926], p. 39.) I am indebted to Miss Norah Evans for transcripts of these entries.

[5] The mayoral year beginning 29 September.

adventure vnto the seas yn hope of the lyke good successe that a greate nomber prepared shipps marynors & soylders & travelled every place at the seas where any proffite might be had. Some yn to Indians.[1] some to wyndganne do Coye[2] some seeking a waye to China by the northe pole.[3] and some to fynde that which was not loste whereby many were vndonne and theym selffes yn the ende never the better even as is the common sayenge male partum in peius delabitur/.

[1] I.e. the West Indies.
[2] Or 'wyndganne do Coyr', for Wingandacoia.
[3] I.e. the North-west Passage ventures of Adrian Gilbert and John Davis in which the Exeter Merchant Adventurers were investors.

CHAPTER V

THE FIRST COLONY: THOMAS HARIOT

Three sea marriadges

Three new Marriadges here are made
one of the staffe & sea astrolabe
card & compasse is another
one is sister thothers a brother.

Of the Sunne & starre is another
Which now agree like sister & brother.

And the carde & compasse which now of late
will now agree like master & mate.

If you voyage well in this your iourney
They will be the Kinge of Spaynes Atomy
To bringe you to siluer & Indian gold
which will kepe you in age from hunger & cold
God spare you well & send you fayre wether
And that agayne we may meet to gether.

THOMAS HARIOT[1]

FOREWORD

Thomas Hariot's *Briefe and true report* has two aspects. It is the propagandist tract to discourage adverse rumours about Raleigh's Virginia and to set out the facts which would encourage settlers to go there.[2] This governs its form and limits its contents. But it is also a record of the first colony, and it makes, with John White's drawings, and the notes which Hariot wrote to accompany those which Theodor de Bry engraved, a most valuable and intimate record of the doings of that colony. The presenting of Hariot's texts with some account of White's drawings is intended to provide, so far as is possible in print, a full record of a great collaboration, but it is no substitute for reading the texts and notes alongside the drawings and engravings themselves.[3]

[1] Rough notes for some verses. Brit. Mus., Add. MS 6788, fo. 490.
[2] Cp. pp. 319–25, 382–7.
[3] Stefan Lorant's *The new world* (1946), provides part of the material for doing so. The edition now in preparation (cp. pp. 917–18) will do so fully.

Lane has already told of some of the incidents of the colony, but one example may show his limitations. In his narrative Wingina (Pemisapan) is shown as the savage whose actions are unpredictable, but Hariot makes him live, as a man near whom he had resided and with whom he had talked.[1] He shows him participating with his people in the Englishmen's worship, being sick and asking the help of their god, pleading with them to bring rain when the corn withered and treating them like men who had some greater magic than any he could himself command. Hariot illustrates very well his wonderment and the divisions in his mind, as well as the savage inconstancy of his actions. And White portrays him for us[2] dressed for a ceremonial occasion or for war, formidable with his bow, his paint, his animal's tail, credulous in his appearance. It is also not at all unlikely that he is also shown dancing,[3] dressed in little but a breech-cloth, and waving his gourd rattle. White, too, draws one of his wives for us,[4] perhaps the same one that befriended Barlowe and his men in 1584.[5]

Throughout the *Report* and the other White-Hariot materials the emphasis is on the Indians, their villages—brought vividly to life—their domestic habits, their crafts, their ceremonies and their religious beliefs. In regard to the latter, Hariot has more of significance to say than has perhaps previously been realized.[6] He is, of course, in the *Report* largely concerned with their crops, and from it, with the pictures and notes, we carry away the fullest impressions of the details of the agriculture of these coastal Algonkian people. Then, too, Hariot gives us more detail than any other early writer on the vegetable foods the Indians collected, though here we are handicapped by the loss of his notes on their words[7] and probably the loss also of a series of White's drawings

[1] Pp. 377–9. [2] No. 49, see pp. 438–9 below.
[3] No. 41, see p. 427 below. The second figure on the bottom left of the picture (*b*) has similar, but not identical, markings on his back to those (no. 53) Wingina bore, but the identification is by no means certain.
[4] No. 50, see p. 439 below, though there is an element of doubt here too.
[5] See pp. 107–10 above. [6] Cp. pp. 372–81 below.
[7] Cp. pp. 356, 358, 360, 366, 389 below.

of plants.[1] Though progress has been made in identifications some things still remain obscure. Of Indian dress and crafts, and the materials they used for them, the *Report* has less to tell than the drawings and their notes. What Hariot did not give us is a full description of their political and social life. He contributes to our knowledge in these respects, but once again we have lost the full discussion which his chronicle may well have contained.

In all his dealings with the Indians Hariot is optimistic but not credulous. He sees them clearly as primitives whose culture is worthy of respect within its own limitations,[2] but who have the potentiality to appreciate European civilisation and religion. It is the remarkable naturalism of White's drawings, combined with the sympathetic detachment of Hariot's observations, which makes the collaboration of the two men so noteworthy. Had they had leisure and opportunity to sit down and write the great illustrated works on Raleigh's Virginia which Hariot envisaged,[3] how revealing they would have been. As it is, we know the Indians of the Carolina sounds as well in some respects as we know the contemporaries of the Tudor Englishmen who drew and described them.

If the achievement of the *Report* and the associated drawings is most obviously remarkable for the light they throw on native society, their contribution to natural history is also outstanding. Apart from a few gleanings out of Florida by the French and the Spaniards,[4] the plants and animal life of temperate North America had not yet been described by any European, except quite incidentally. In the *Report*, though much abbreviated, there was some systematic account of trees and plants, of birds and fish and animals. Hariot had clearly much more material than he was able to use, even if some had been lost at the departure from Roanoke Island,[5] and his activity, and that of his assistants, in getting drawings, specimens, Indian names and descriptions during the eleven

[1] Only two now survive, nos. 54–5, see pp. 444–7 below.
[2] Cp. especially pp. 368–72. [3] Pp. 359, 387 below.
[4] Notably the discovery of sassafras, cp. p. 329 below.
[5] Pp. 260, 334, 379.

months that he spent in America is evident from what survives. The fifty-five drawings by, or after, White of plants, birds, fish, turtles and insects,[1] constitute a remarkable tribute to the industry and single-mindedness not only of the artist who drew them but of Hariot, who arranged for them to be drawn and who made, it is clear, his own collection to which they constituted merely the illustrations. Through Hariot and White we are able, uniquely, to see natural conditions in a part of North America before they were disturbed by white settlement.

The third great contribution was in cartography. The maps present many problems and not all are yet capable of solution.[2] But Hariot and White did a remarkable piece of work in this respect also. The first sketch-map of 1585 gives a rough-and-ready glimpse of the coastal topography, but how much more detailed work over a very much wider area lies behind the general maps of Raleigh's Virginia? Though the precise area surveyed in detail on the ground remains in some doubt, it is still true that the close and intelligent adherence of Hariot and White to their task of revealing the topography of the country and its difficult coastline led to their producing cartographic work which was incomparably the best yet done on any part of North America by any Europeans.

The contribution of Hariot and White then to the story of the year spent under Lane in Raleigh's Virginia is very substantial. Possibly even greater is their contribution to knowledge, the opening up—even though by a small sample—of a remarkable continent to inquiring European eyes.

51. FEBRUARY 1588.

THOMAS HARIOT, *A BRIEFE AND TRUE REPORT*[3]

[A1]   A briefe and true report of the new found land of Virginia: of the commodities there found and to be raysed, as well mar-

---

[1] Nos. 54–108, pp. 444–60 below.   [2] Cp. pp. 460–2, 847–50.

[3] For this edition the first quarto edition has been collated—minor variations in spelling and punctuation being ignored—with those in De Bry, *America*, pt. i

chantable, as others for victuall, building and other necessarie vses for those that are and shalbe the planters there; and of the nature and manners of the naturall inhabitants: Discouered by the English Colony there seated by Sir Richard Greinuile Knight in the yeere 1585. which remained vnder the gouernment of Rafe Lane Esquier, one of her Maiesties Equieres, during the space of twelue monethes: at the speciall charge and direction of the Honourable Sir Walter Raleigh Knight, Lord Warden of the stanneries; who therein hath beene fauoured and authorised by her Maiestie and her letters patents:

Directed to the Aduenturers, Fauourers, and Welwillers of the action, for the inhabiting and planting there:

By Thomas Hariot; seruant to the abouenamed Sir Walter, a member of the Colony, and there imployed in discouering.[1]

Imprinted at London 1588.[2]

(1590) (a faithful reprint); in Hakluyt, *Principall navigations* (1589), pp. 748–64 (with some editing), and *Principal navigations*, III (1600), 266–80 (VIII (1904), 348–86) (with further revision). Of the first edition the following copies survive (all except the last have been seen either in the original or in facsimile): (*a*) British Museum (repr. by Henry Stevens (London, 1900)); (*b*) Bodleian Library; (*c*) Henry E. Huntington Library (facsimile, ed. Luther S. Livingston (New York, 1903)); (*d*) William L. Clements Library (facsimile, ed., with valuable introduction, by the late Randolph G. Adams (Ann Arbor, Michigan, 1931)); (*e*) New York Public Library (imperfect, the first signature having been supplied in facsimile); (*f*) Leyden University Library (particulars of which were kindly supplied by Dr A. Kessen). No additional copies have been found to add to R. G. Adams' list (in (*d*) above), and I am grateful to Dr W. A. Jackson, Houghton Library, Harvard University, for checking this with his records. The surviving copies provide no variants, and none of them contains any early notes or indications of ownership.
    [1] Followed by an ornament, identified (by R. G. Adams) as used by Robert Robinson, who is, therefore, presumed to have been the printer. There is no entry in the Stationers' Register. It is probable that the pamphlet was commissioned by Raleigh. On the question of the delay in its publication, which weakened its value as an instrument of propaganda to attract new settlers, see pp. 38, 548.
    [2] Hakluyt abbreviates the title to 'A briefe and true report of the new found land of Virginia: of the commodities there found and to be raysed, as well marchantable, as others: Written by Thomas Harriott [1600, Heriot], seruant to

'A briefe and true report'

[A2]¹   Rafe Lane one of her Majesties Equieres,² and Gouernour of the Colony of Virginia aboue mentioned for the time there resident.

To the gentle Reader wisheth all happines in the Lord.

Albeit (Gentle Reader) the credite of the reports in this treatise contained, can little be furthered by the testimonie of one as my selfe, through affection iudged partiall, though without desert: Neuerthelesse, for somuch as I haue bene requested by some my particular friends,³ who conceiue more rightly of me, to deliuer freely my knowledge of the same; not onely for the satisfying of them, but also for the true enformation of anie other whosoeuer, that comes not with a preiudicate minde to the reading thereof: Thus much vpon my credit I am to affirme: that things vniuersally are so truely set downe in this treatise by the authour therof, an Actor in the Colony, or a man no lesse for his honesty [A2 v.] then learning commendable: as that I dare boldly auouch it may very well passe with the credit of trueth euen amongst the most true relations of this age. Which as for mine owne part I am readie any way with my word to acknowledge, so also (of the certaintie thereof assured by mine owne experience) with

Sir Walter Raleigh [1600, Ralegh], a member of the Colonie and there imployed in discouering a full tweluemoneth.' De Bry's title-page is:

'A briefe and true report of the new found land of Virginia, of the commodities and of the nature and maners of the naturall inhabitants. Discouered by the English Colony there seated by Sir Richard Greinuile Knight In the yeere 1585. Which Remained Vnder the gouernement of twelue monthes, At the speciall charge and direction of the Honourable Sir Walter Raleigh Knight lord Warden of the stanneries Who therein hath beene fauoured and authorised by her Maiestie and her letters patents: This fore booke Is made in English By Thomas Hariot seruant to the abouenamed Sir Walter, a member of the Colony, and there imployed in discouering.'

¹ A1 v. has a woodcut of Raleigh's achievement, with the motto 'Amore et virtute'.

² Equerry of the Great Stable. In 1600 'Equieres' was mistakenly altered to 'Esquiers', probably by the printer.

³ Lane may mean those of his companions in the 1585–6 colony who had still retained their enthusiasm for America, or, alternatively, those who were sponsoring the pamphlet as propaganda for a further expedition. The latter is the more probable.

this my publique assertion, I doe affirme the same. Farewell in the Lorde.[1]

[A3] To the Aduenturers, Fauourers, and Welwillers of the enterprise for the inhabiting and planting in Virginia.[2]

Since the first vndertaking by Sir Walter Raleigh to deale in the action of discouering of that Countrey which is now called and known by the name of Virginia, many voyages hauing bin thither made at sundrie times to his great charge;[3] as first in the yere 1584, and afterwardes in the yeeres 1585, 1586, and now of late this last yeere of 1587:[4] There haue bin diuers and variable reportes, with some slaunderous and shamefull speeches bruited abroade by many that returned from thence. Especially of that discouery which was made by the Colony transported by Sir Richard Greinuile in the yeare 1585,[5] being of all the others[6] the most principal, and as yet of most effect, the time of their abode in the countrey beeing a whole yeare, when as in the other voyage before they staied but six weekes,[7] and the others after were

---

[1] Lane presumably wrote this letter (or allowed Hariot to put his name to it) in February 1588. During the months from December 1587 to April 1588 he was employed in reviewing the county militia in East Anglia (Hist. MSS Comm., *Foljambe MSS*, pp. 28–9, 34). A decoration follows the letter. De Bry omits Lane's letter and inserts his own epistles (pp. 399–402 below).

[2] The heading indicates clearly the purpose of the pamphlet, the encouragement of past investors and settlers and the attraction of new. Grenville's preparations for the projected 1588 voyage must have been well under way by the time this was published but there was time for additional settlers to join him as he was not ready by 31 March (pp. 560–1).

[3] For what is known about the financing see pp. 220–1, 473, 544, 576–8.

[4] 'yeere 1587' (Hakluyt (1589), p. 749; III (1600), 266).

[5] By October 1586 there was already a bad press for Virginia (cp. p. 492 below), but Hariot's is the main evidence that Lane's men, returning in 1586, systematically ran down the colonizing project. Only three joined White in 1587 (and one deserted), cp. pp. 519, 541.

[6] 'all others' (Hakluyt (1589), p. 749; III (1600), 266).

[7] Barlowe does not, himself, say how long he stayed, so this is a small piece of additional evidence on the 1584 expedition. Reckoning from his formal occupation of the land on 13 July this would give a departure date around 24 August (cp. pp. 94, 115 above).

onelie for supply and transportation, nothing more being discouered then had been before.[1] Which reports have not done a
litle wrong to ma[A3 v.]ny that otherwise would haue also
fauoured & aduentured in the action, to the honour and benefite
of our nation, besides the particular profite and credite which
would redound to them selues the dealers therein, as I hope by
the sequele of euents to the shame of those that haue auouched
the contrary, shalbe manifest: if you the aduenturers, fauourers
and welwillers do but either encrease in number, or in opinion
continue, or hauing bin doubtfull renewe your good liking and
furtherance to deale therein according to the worthinesse thereof
alreadye found and as you shall vnderstand hereafter to be requisite.
Touching which woorthines through cause of the diuersitie of
relations and reportes, manye of your opinions coulde not bee
firme, nor the mindes of some that are well disposed, bee setled
in any certaintie.

I haue therefore thought it good, beeing one that haue beene
in the discouerie, and in dealing with the naturall inhabitantes
specially imploied;[2] and hauing therefore seene and knowne more
then the ordinarie: to impart so much vnto you of the fruites of
our labours, as that you may knowe how iniuriously the enterprise is slaundered. And that in publik manner at this present,
chiefelie for two respectes.

First, that some of you which are yet ignorant or doubtfull of
the state thereof, may see that there is sufficient cause why the
chiefe enterpriser[3] with the fauour of her Maiestie, notwithstanding suche reportes; hath not onelie since continued the action
by sending into the countrey againe, and replanting this last yeere

---

[1] This was true, so far as we know, of the visit by Raleigh's ship in 1586, and
of White's 1587, expedition, but Grenville in 1586 at least did some exploration
(cp. p. 469 above).
[2] Hariot's special responsibility for dealing with the Indians may have been
due, *inter alia*, to his having acquired some knowledge of the language from
Manteo and Wanchese (to whom he may well have taught English) in the months
after their arrival in England (cp. pp. 37, 368).
[3] Raleigh.

a new Colony;[1] but is also readie according as the times and meanes will affoorde, to follow and prosecute the same.[2]

[A4] Secondly, that you seeing and knowing the continuance of the action by the view hereof you may generally know & learne what the countrey is; & therevpon consider how your dealing therein, if it proceede, may returne you profit and gaine; bee it either by inhabiting & planting or otherwise in furthering thereof.

And least that the substance of my relation should be doubtful vnto you, as of others by reason of their diuersitie; I will first open the cause in a few wordes, wherefore they are so different,[3] referring my selfe to your fauourable constructions, and to be adiudged of as by good consideration you shall finde cause.

Of our companie that returned some for their misdemeanour and ill dealing in the countrey, haue beene there worthily punished, who by reason of their badde natures, haue maliciously not onelie spoken ill of their Gouernours, but for their sakes slaundered the countrie it selfe.[4] The like also haue those done which were of their consort.

Some being ignorant of the state thereof, notwithstanding since their returne amongest their friendes and acquaintance and also others, especially if they were in companie where they might not be gainesaide; woulde seeme to knowe so much as no men more, and make no men so great trauailers as themselues. They stood so much as it maie seeme vpon their credite and reputation that

[1] For what is known of his share in the financing and dispatch of the third colony see pp. 497–8 below.

[2] Hariot was not, in print, committing Raleigh too far to a further expedition.

[3] I.e. because of the divergence between Hariot's account and other versions current.

[4] It is clear that we know very little of Lane's relations with his men in the later stages, at least, of the colony's residence on Roanoke. He subsequently stressed his strict discipline there (p. 228), and the punishments to which Hariot refers were probably inflicted by him for indiscipline. Hariot is thus, apparently, charging the men who had fallen foul of Lane (and their supporters) of malicious attacks on him and on Virginia since their return. Thomas Harvey (pp. 232–4 above) was probably one of them.

hauing been a twelue moneth in the countrey, it woulde haue beene a great disgrace vnto them as they thought, if they coulde not haue saide much whether it were true or false. Of which some haue spoken of more then euer they saw or otherwise knew to bee there;[1] othersome haue not bin ashamed to make absolute deniall of that which although not by them, yet by others [A 4 v.] is most certainely and there plentifully knowne. And othersome make difficulties of those things they haue no skill of.

The cause of their ignorance was, in that they were of that many that were neuer out of the Iland where wee were seated, or not farre, or at the leastwise in few places els, during the time of our aboade in the countrey:[2] or of that many that after gold and siluer was not so soone found, as it was by them looked for, had little or no care of any other thing but to pamper their bellies;[3] or of that many which had litle vnderstanding, lesse discretion, and more tongue then was needfull or requisite.

Some also were of a nice bringing vp, only in cities or townes, or such as neuer (as I may say) had seene the world before. Because there were not to bee found any English cities, nor such faire houses, nor at their owne wish any of their olde accustomed daintie food, nor any soft beds of downe or feathers, the countrey was to them miserable, & their reports thereof according.[4]

[1] Once again we know little of the circumstances, but Darby Glande at least, one of those who returned, was not above telling rather tall stories in 1600 (pp. 834–8) and may well have begun telling them in 1586.

[2] Lane had nothing to complain of as to the keenness of the party which accompanied him up the Chowan and Roanoke Rivers, rather the contrary (pp. 270–2). We know nothing of the behaviour of the personnel of the expedition to Chesapeake Bay.

[3] Reading between the lines of Lane's account (especially pp. 272–3 above) it is not hard to see that he could sympathize in some degree with them, though his military training led him to maintain discipline, and the prospect of a move to Chesapeake Bay kept him reasonably optimistic.

[4] This is apparently a reflection on the gentlemen of the party, but again we cannot particularize. Lane, in his account, praised only Captain Stafford by name (p. 288), but the presence of married settlers of the 1587 colony bears witness to the belief that too many rootless young men of family were taken on the earlier occasion.

The Roanoke Voyages

Because my purpose was but in briefe to open the cause of the varietie of such speeches; the particularities of them, and of many enuious, malicious, and slaunderous reports and devices els, by our owne countreymen besides; as trifles that are not worthy of wise men to bee thought vpon, I meane not to trouble you withall: but will passe to the commodities, the substance of that which I haue to make relation of vnto you.[1]

The treatise whereof, for your more readie view & easier vnderstanding, I will diuide into three speciall parts. In the first I will make declaration of such commodities there alreadie found or to be raised, which will not onely serue the ordinary turnes of you which are and shall bee the planters and inhabitants, but such an ouerplus suffi [B 1] ciently to bee yelded, or by men of skill to bee prouided, as by way of trafficke and exchaunge with our owne nation of England, will enrich your selues the prouiders: those that shal deal with you; the enterprisers in general, and greatly profit our owne countrey men, to supply them with most things which heretofore they haue bene faine to prouide, either of strangers or of our enemies:[2] which commodities for distinction sake I call Merchantable.

In the second, I will set downe all the commodities which wee know the countrey by our experience doeth yeld of it selfe for victuall, and sustenance of mans life; such as is[3] vsually fed vpon by the inhabitants of the countrey,[4] as also by vs during the time we were there.[5]

---

[1] This paragraph, and the appropriate section following, is directed not only to intending settlers but to the mercantile subscribers at home. Both the Hakluyts had stressed the need for substantial exports from the colonies of native and introduced vegetable products (Taylor, *Hakluyts*, II, 321, 323, 331-8).

[2] Principally those Mediterranean products which either involved a loss in exchange or were by this time scarce or unobtainable in England on account of the stoppage of trade with Spain and Portugal (cp. ibid., 316-17, 327, 331-8).

[3] 'are' (Hakluyt, III (1600), 267).

[4] 'countreys' (Hakluyt (1589), p. 750).

[5] Hariot is concerned not only to show that future colonies can be self-supporting in food but that the 1585-6 colony was not removed by Drake because its members were starving (cp. pp. 301, 303, 310).

'A briefe and true report'

In the last part I will make mention generally of such other commodities besides, as I am able to remember, and as I shall thinke behoofull[1] for those that shall inhabite, and plant there to knowe of, which specially concerne building, as also some other necessary vses:[2] with a briefe description of the nature and maners of the people of the countrey.[3]

The first part of Merchantable commodities.

Silke of grasse, or grasse Silke. There is a kind of grasse in the countrey vppon the blades whereof there groweth very good silke in forme of a thin glittering skin to bee stript of.[4] It groweth two foot and an halfe high or better: the blades are about two foot in length, and half inch[5] broad. The like groweth in Persia, which is in the selfe same climate as Virginia, of which very many of the [B1 v.] silke works that come from thence into Europe are made. Hereof if it be planted and ordered as in Persia, it

[1] 'behoouefull' (Hakluyt (1589), p. 750; III (1600), 267).

[2] Desirable to counteract impressions easily conveyed by those who had returned (and largely true of the immediate surroundings of Roanoke Island) that there were only sandy beaches and swamps, with little possibility of settlement.

[3] Again desirable to counteract tales of the ferocity and treachery of the Indians. Lane's account was not so reassuring (cp. pp. 265–72, 275–88 above), but it had not yet been published.

[4] This discovery was made early, as the September 1585 sketch-map (fig. 3, pp. 215–17 above) indicates that silk-grass was found on the small islets in Croatan Sound between Roanoke Island and the mainland. Though other kinds of silk-grass were found (cp. pp. 444–6 below) this is clearly a Yucca, various species of which are known as Bear Grass, Spanish Bayonets, Adam's Needle and Bog Grass. Kearney ('Ecology', pp. 270–1) found *Yucca aloifolia* and *Y. gloriosa* on Ocracoke Island, but *Y. filamentosa* appears the most likely species in this instance, although the leaves are wider than Hariot indicates (W. C. C.; F. G. Speck, *The Rappahannock Indians of Virginia* (Indian Notes and Monographs, v, no. 3), pp. 61–2; Swanton, *Indians*, p. 247; A. C. Whitford, 'Textile fibers used in eastern aboriginal North America', in *Anthropological Papers of the American Museum of Natural History*, XXXVIII (New York, 1941), 1–22)). William Byrd (*Histories of the dividing line* (1929), p. 72) records that in 1728 at Currituck Inlet 'We also found some few Plants of the Spired Leaf Silk grass, which is likewise an Evergreen, bearing on a lofty Stemm a large Cluster of Flowers of a Pale Yellow'.

[5] 'halfe inche' (Hakluyt (1589), p. 750).

cannot in reason be otherwise, but that there will rise in shorte time great profite to the dealers therein, seeing there is so great vse and vent thereof as well in our countrey as els where. And by the meanes of sowing & planting it in good ground, it will be farre greater, better, and more plentifull then it is. Although notwithstanding there is great store thereof in many places of the countrey growing naturally and wilde, Which also by proofe here in England, in making a piece of silke Grogran,[1] we found to be excellent good.

Worme Silke. In many of our iourneys we found silke wormes fayre and great; as bigge as our ordinary walnuts.[2] Although it hath not beene our happe to haue found such plentie, as elswhere to be in the countrey we haue heard of, yet seeing that the countrey doth naturally breede and nourish them, there is no doubt but if art be added in planting of mulbery[3] trees, and others fitte for them in commodious places, for their feeding and nourishing, and some of them carefully gathered and husbanded in that sort as by men of skill is knowne to be necessarie: there will rise as great profite in time to the Virginians, as thereof doth now to the Persians, Turkes, Italians and Spaniards.

Flaxe and Hempe. The trueth is that of Hempe and Flaxe there is no great store in any one place together,[4] by reason it is not planted but as the soile doth yeeld it of it[5] selfe: and howsoeuer the leafe, and stemme or stalke doe differ from ours; the stuffe by the

[1] The specimens were probably brought by Grenville in 1585. Grosgrain is a coarse fabric of silk alone, mohair and wool, or these mixed with silk, and often thickened with gum.

[2] While the Silkworm is not native to North America, Hariot might easily have mistaken the larvae of the Tent Caterpillar, or those of the Fall Web-worm, together with their webs, for silkworms (W. L. H.).

[3] The White Mulberry (*Morus alba*) was introduced by the Spaniards, but it is perhaps surprising that Hariot didnot identify with it the Red Mulberry (*M. rubra*) which is indigenous (W. L. H.).

[4] Hariot is here making a statement with something less than the emphasis of certainty. It might be that he is referring to a Wild Flax (*Carthartolinium*), but its yellow flowers would have been unfamiliar to him (W. C. C.). Cp. Strachey, *Hist. of travell*, p. 75.

[5] 'yeeld of it' (Hakluyt (1589), p. 750; III (1600), 268).

iudgement[1] of men of skill is altogether as good as ours. And if not, as further proofe should finde otherwise, we haue that experience of the soile, as that there cannot bee shewed anie [B2] reason to the contrary, but that it will grow there excellent well,[2] and by planting will be yeelded plentifully: seeing there is so much ground whereof some may well be applyed to such purposes. What benefite heereof may growe in cordage and linnens who can not easily vnderstand?[3]

Allum. There is a veine of earth along the sea coast for the space of fourtie or fiftie miles, whereof by the iudgement of some that haue made triall heere in England, is made good Allum,[4] of that kind which is called Roche allum.[5] The richnesse of such a commoditie is so well knowne that I need not to saye any thing thereof. The same earth doth also yeeld White Copresse,[6] Nitrum,[7] and Alumen plumeum,[8] but nothing so plentifully as the common Allum, which be also of price, and profitable.

[1] 'by iudgement' (ibid.).

[2] Here Hariot is correct since flax and hemp could have been grown in the more fertile parts of the coastlands.

[3] The search for alternative sources of naval stores was a secondary incentive in the commercial development of North American colonies (cp. Taylor, *Hakluyts*, II, 230, 271, 317, 328).

[4] It is difficult to give an explanation. There is, of course, no alum in the coastal clays. Mr Harry T. Davis suggested that it might be a plumy substance sometimes found in clays and representing the breaking down of iron pyrites, but this is unlikely to be an adequate description.

[5] 'roche-alum', the compacted crystalline form of alum (double sulphate of aluminium and potassium), which when reduced from rock was solidified in 'roching casks' (see Charles Singer, *The earliest chemical industry* (1948), pp. 94, 223, 226, 282). Apart from some more or less consolidated shell-rock it is hard to know what substance would have given Hariot this idea.

[6] 'white copperas' was, correctly, protosulphate of zinc, but 'copperas' was iron sulphate, which the 'mineral man' of the expedition may well have identified, while 'white copperas' would not have been found.

[7] 'Nitrum' was potassium nitrate, but at this date many other substances were known as 'nitre'. Thus Thomas Chaloner (*On the most rare vertue of nitre* (1584)) identified as 'nitre' crude sodium carbonate (Singer, op. cit. pp. 185, 223). It is highly improbable that potassium nitrate was identified in this case.

[8] 'Alumen plumeum' was the plume or feather alum, or *Alume scissile*, which split up after reduction into fine white fibres or filaments, or was a natural hair

Wapeih,[1] a kinde of earth so called by the naturall inhabitants, very like to terra Sigillata:[2] and hauing beene refined, it hath beene found by some of our Phisitions and Chirurgeons to bee of the same kinde of vertue and more effectuall.[3] The inhabitants vse it very much for the cure of sores and woundes:[4] there is in diuers places great plentie, and in some places of a blewe sort.

Pitch, Tarre, Rozen and Turpentine. There are those kindes of trees which yeelde them abundantly and great store.[5] In the very same Iland where we were seated, being fifteene miles of length,

salt (two parts of sulphate of iron to one part of sulphate of aluminium) from which alum could be made. It was also confused with asbestos (Singer, op. cit., pp. 113, 233-43). All the mineral substances which Hariot believed had been found were in great demand in England, especially alum, used as a mordant for dyes and acids, for dressing leather, and as a drug. Burghley was closely associated with the comparatively unsuccessful experiments in making alum in Hampshire and Dorset, which had temporarily broken down by 1581 (Singer, op. cit., pp. 182-3, and R. B. Turton, *The alum farm* (1938)). Copperas (for dyeing and many other industrial uses) and nitre (for the infant gunpowder industry) were also in demand (see J. U. Nef, 'The progress of technology and the growth of large scale industry in Great Britain, 1540-1640', in *Economic History Review*, 1st ser., v (1934-5), 3-24). The German 'mineral men' usually employed as prospectors were notoriously unreliable, and could 'find' almost any mineral for which they were asked.

[1] The Indian word (p. 898 below) seems to suggest a whitish clay.

[2] The term normally used for Lemnian earth. Lane speaks above (p. 208) of Samian earth (*Terra Samia*). Kaolin and other earths were extensively used for their real and presumed medicinal properties in Europe. Kaolin was to be found in a pure form in the Upper Cretaceous formation, possibly reached by Lane on the Roanoke River (pp. 331-2; Richards, in *Trans. A.P.S.*, n.s., xl, 52), but there were many other clays which might have come to Hariot's notice. Clay-eating by the Indians is noted in Virginia (Purchas, *Pilgrims*, xix (1906), 92; Flannery, *Analysis*, no. 59).

[3] Does Hariot mean that he had with him at Roanoke at least a physician and a surgeon? Certainly there were both on the vessels which went out in 1585 (pp. 199, 213, 334), but it is unlikely that any stayed. Hariot must, therefore, refer to experiments made before the vessels returned in 1585, or to the bringing of samples to England for testing.

[4] This is the only reference found to the external medicinal use of clay by the Indians of this region.

[5] By far the greater number of trees in the coastal area are coniferous, mainly pine, and North Carolina's nickname, 'The Turpentine State', was originally derived from the intensive exploitation of these trees in her coastal lands.

and fiue or sixe miles in breadth, there are few trees els but of the same kind, the whole Iland[1] being full.

Sassafras,[2] called by the inhabitants Winauk,[3] a kinde of wood of most pleasant and sweete smel; and of most rare vertues in phisick for the cure of many diseases. It is found by experience to bee far better and of more vses then the wood which is called Guaiacum, or Lignum vitae.[4] For [B2 v.] the description, the maner of vsing, and the manifold vertues therof, I refer you to the booke of Monardes, translated and entituled in English, The joyfull newes from the West Indies.[5]

Cedar,[6] a very sweet wood & fine timber; wherof if nests of chests be there made, or timber therof fitted for sweet & fine bedsteads, tables, deskes, lutes, virginalles & many things else, (of

---

[1] Roanoke Island. He somewhat exaggerates its length, and (rather more) its breadth.

[2] *Sassafras officinale* (or *albidum* or *variifolium*), a slender, aromatic tree, which on the western side of Roanoke Island reaches 20–40 ft. high. The root-bark and bark make a tea, the root yields an oil, the stem a pith. All have been used medicinally, with doubtful efficacy. Discovered by the French in Florida, 1562–5, it was exploited by the Spaniards, and described by Nicholas Monardes in 1571 and 1574 (as translated by John Frampton in 1577 in the *Joyfull newes out of the newe founde worlde*, ed. Sir S. Gaselee, 1925, I, 99–120), who specified its main uses, amongst others the treatment of syphilis (see Charles Manning & Merrill Moore, 'Sassafras and syphilis', in *New England Quarterly*, IX (1936), 473–5) and malaria (Childs, *Malaria and colonization*, pp. 82–91), on account of which it was known as 'the ague tree' and for which it was long prized. Charles de l'Écluse received specimens of it from Richard Garth, Hugh Morgan, and James Garet, some of which, at least, came from Virginia (*Exoticorum* (1605), p. 322), adding: 'in Wingandecao, ab Anglis, qui eam occuparant, Virginia dicta, nasci intellexi, & inde, virgulta eius arboris in Angliam esse delata'.

[3] The word, apparently, means 'sticky' (p. 899 below).

[4] Guaiacum (*lignum vitae*) from Santo Domingo is described by Monardes (op. cit. I, 33). An infusion of the wood was believed to have value in the treatment of syphilis and other diseases (cp. p. 366).

[5] Nicholas Monardes, *Ioyful newes out of the newe founde worlde...Englished by Ihon Frampton, marchaunt* (1577), from *La historia medicinal de las cosas que se traen de nuestras Indias Occidentales que se siruen en medicina*, Seville, 1574; 2nd ed., with additions, 1580. L'Écluse published Latin translations in Antwerp. This volume was almost certainly brought by Hariot to America, in one or other edition. It was the only book available in English which gave any help in identifying North American species of medicinal plants.

[6] Cp. pp. 95, 97, 172, 364.

which there hath beene proofe made already),[1] to make vp fraite with other principal commodities will yeeld profite.

Wine: There are two kinds of grapes that the soile doth yeeld naturally: the one is small and sowre of the ordinarie bignesse as ours in England: the other farre greater & of himselfe lushious sweet.[2] When they are planted and husbanded as they ought, a principall commoditie of wines by them may be raised.

Oyle: There are two sortes of Walnuttes, both holding oyle, but the one farre more plentifull then the other.[3] When there are milles & other deuices for the purpose, a commodity of them may be raised because there are infinite store. There are also three seuerall kindes of Berries in the forme of Oke akornes, which also by the experience and vse of the inhabitantes, wee find to yeelde very good and sweete oyle.[4] Furthermore the Beares[5] of the countrey are commonly very fatte, and in some places there are many: their fatnesse because it is so liquid, may well be termed oyle, and hath many speciall vses.

Furres: All along the Sea coast there are great store of Otters,[6] which beyng taken by weares and other engines made for the purpose, wil yeelde good profite. Wee hope also of Marterne furres, and make no doubt by the relation of the people but that in some places [B3] of the countrey there are store, although

---

[1] Indicating that experiments in using 'cedar' for fine joinery work had already been made (cp. pp. 364, 495).

[2] The species found in the coastal lands are the small, sweet Summer Grape (*Vitis aestivalis*), ripe in July and August; the large, sweet Muscadine (*V. rotundiflora*, of which the white mutation, the Scuppernong, is still found on Colington Island), ripe in September; the sweet Fox Grape (*V. labruska*), ripe in October and November; and the small Sour Grape (*V. cordifolia*), ripe in November (W. L. H.; W. C. C.; Kearney, 'Ecology', p. 271). The fourth and the second are those probably meant by Hariot. The sketch-map of September 1585 and De Bry's engraving of the arrival of the Englishmen both show grapes as the principal product of Weapemeoc (pp. 215–17, 413, and cp. pp. 95, 352).

[3] For Hariot's more specific references see p. 351 below.

[4] Similarly, he is more specific on acorns below, pp. 354–5.

[5] Bears, too, appear below, p. 356.

[6] The form occurring in North Carolina is the Carolina Otter, *Lutra canadensis lataxina* Rhoads (*Mammals of N.C.*, pt. 8).

there were but two skinnes that came to our handes.[1] Luzarnes[2] also we haue understanding of, although for the time we saw none.

Deare Skinnes[3] dressed after the maner of Chamoes or vndressed are to be had of the naturall inhabitants thousands yeerely by way of trafficke for trifles:[4] and no more wast or spoyle of Deare then is and hath beene ordinarily in time before.

Ciuet cattes:[5] In our trauailes, there was founde one to haue beene killed by a saluage or inhabitant: and in another place the smell where one or more had lately beene before: whereby we gather besides then by the relation of the people that there are some in the countrey: good profite will rise by them.

Iron: In two places of the countrey specially, one about fourescore and the other six score miles from the Fort or place where we dwelt:[6] we found neere the water side the ground to be rockie, which by the triall of a minerall man,[7] was found to holde yron richly. It is founde in many places of the country else.[8]

---

[1] Possibly skins of the South-eastern Mink, *Mustela vison mink* (*Mammals of N.C.*, pt. 7), though the skins which the Spaniards described as 'Marten' farther south were apparently Muskrat (Swanton, *Indians*, p. 440). If Hariot meant this, however, it is surprising that he did not see more, as the Muskrat, *Ondatra zibethica* Linn. (*Mammals of N.C.*, pt. 13), is still common in the marshes north of Pamlico Sound

[2] American Wild-cat, or Bay Lynx, *Lynx rufus* Guldenstat (*Mammals of N.C.*, pt. 8).   [3] 'Deers skinnes' (Hakluyt, III (1600), 269).

[4] The Indian skill in skin-dressing is remarked on elsewhere (pp. 423, 439): some of the southern techniques are described in Swanton, *Indians*, pp. 442–8.

[5] The Southern Skunk or Polecat, *Mephitis elongata* Bangs (*Mammals of N.C.*, pt. 7), which frequents the coast as far north as Albemarle Sound, but civet, valuable for compounding perfumes, could not, of course, be obtained from it.

[6] The farthest distances penetrated from Roanoke were about 100 miles. The Roanoke River expedition was probably the most extended, and 120 miles would not be an unreasonable estimate of Lane's farthest point from Roanoke, nor would 80 miles be for the Chowan River trip, while both the visits to the Chesapeake and the Pamlico River approximated between 80 and 100 miles. The two former expeditions are most likely to be those referred to here.

[7] Almost certainly Joachim Ganz (cp. p. 196).

[8] There are frequent traces and some deposits of 'bog ore' in the swamp forests and marshes, while there is iron sulphide (marcasite) in the Tuscaloosa formation (Upper Cretaceous) outcropping at the crossing of the Roanoke River

I knowe nothing to the contrarie, but that it maie bee allowed for a good merchantable commoditie, considering there the small charge for the labour and feeding of men: the infinite store of wood: the want of wood and deerenesse thereof in England: & the necessity of ballasting of shippes.

Copper: A hundred and fiftie miles into the maine in two townes we founde with the inhabitaunts diuers small plates of copper, that had beene made as we vnderstood, by the inhabitantes that dwell farther into the countrey,[1] where as they say are moun-

---

by the Atlantic Coast Lines Railroad, at about the upper limit of Lane's exploration of the river (cp. p. 266). More obviously, the explorers would have seen the ilmenite (iron-titanium oxide) of the Yorktown (Miocene) formation on the banks of the Chowan River, where it occurs in the Colerain bluffs on the right bank, and where some outcrops are 'slightly consolidated' (cp. H. G. Richards, 'The geology of the coastal plain of North Carolina', in *Trans. American Phil. Soc.*, n.s., XL (1950), 2, 4, 25, 51; L. J. Cappon, 'Iron-making—a forgotten industry of North Carolina', in *North Carolina Historical Review*, IX (1932), 331). Iron ores, more easily identifiable by the 'mineral man' than the minerals noted above (p. 327), were an important objective in English plans for North America as, in combination with plentiful timber, they offered a means of supplying pig-iron for the growing English industry without the depletion of woodlands which was causing such acute concern at the time.

[1] Lane's story of alleged copper (or gold) deposits in the interior is discussed above (p. 269). It is worth noting Hariot's much greater caution (though cp. p. 388 below). The plates of copper were apparently obtained at Chawanoac and were said to have been made of copper from Chaunis Temoatan (pp. 269–70 above) by the Mangoak tribe. It is likely that this tribe traded in Lake Superior copper but it is possible that there was some commerce in copper (and copper goods) obtained in the western parts of North Carolina and Virginia. Exposed native copper lodes or nodules are on record from Guilford, Gabarrus, Person, Rowan, Jackson, Ashe, Lower Mecklenberg, and Stokes counties in western and north-western North Carolina (F. A. Genth, *Minerals of N.C.*, p. 14; Rickard in *Jnl Royal Anthropological Inst.*, LXIV, p. 270). Genth notes one lump of copper about two inches in size, 'much resembling that from the Cliff mine, Lake Superior', said to have been found in Stokes county, and (in 1891) in the State Museum at Raleigh, which was probably Indian and may have been a local product. In 1950 Mr J. C. Harrington found on Roanoke Island two chunks of pure copper (of 12 and 21½ oz. respectively), one from the topsoil inside the fort and the other from the bottom of the ditch round the fort. Both were of a rough, spongy appearance but had been melted. They could have been contemporaneous with the Roanoke voyages (pp. 907–8 below). Comparative analyses have provided data which it is claimed will serve to distinguish European copper of the sixteenth century from that of North America. The former is smelted copper of

taines and [B 3 v.] Riuers that yeelde also whyte graynes of Mettall, which is to be deemed Siluer. For confirmation whereof at the time of our first arriuall in the Countrey, I sawe with some others with mee, two small peeces of siluer grosly beaten about the weight of a Testrone, hangyng in the eares of a *Wiroans* or chiefe Lord that dwelt about fourescore myles from vs; of whom thorowe inquiry, by the number of dayes and the way, I learned that it had come to his handes from the same place or neere, where I after vnderstood the copper was made and the white graines of mettall founde.[1] The aforesaide copper wee also founde by triall to holde siluer.[2]

Pearle: Sometimes in feeding on muscles wee found some pearle; but it was our hap to meet with ragges, or of a pide colour; not hauing yet discouered those places where wee heard of better and more plentie.[3] One of our companie; a man of skill in such matters, had gathered together from among the sauage people aboute fiue thousande:[4] of which number he chose so many as made a fayre chaine, which for their likenesse and

[1] 97·42 to 97·93% purity with lead, nickel, arsenic and antimony; the latter was 99·90 to 99·96% pure with traces of silver and iron (Rickard, op. cit., p. 271). On this basis it should, when analyses have been made, be possible to determine whether the Roanoke Island specimens are of European or native origin. Hariot retained some recollections of Indians 'smelting' copper (Document no. 52, p. 388 below). A recent general survey (P. S. Martin, G. I. Quimby and D. Collier, *Indians before Columbus* (Chicago, 1947), pp. 70–2) says categorically that the Indians had no knowledge of stamping—the crushing of copper-bearing rocks into tiny particles so that grains of copper can be separated from rock by washing.

[1] Natural silver is rare in eastern North America. Small nodules were occasionally picked up and made into beads. There is no evidence of quarrying for natural silver or of systematic attempts to win it from alluvial deposits. Natural silver is on record from at least three of the western counties of North Carolina (*Minerals of N.C.*, pp. 13–14; Swanton, *Indians*, p. 244; Willoughby, in *American Anthropologist*, n.s., IX, 73). Any record of extensive use of silver in the south-east would point to pillaging of wrecked cargoes of Spanish-American silver.

[2] It is unlikely that a normal sample of native copper would have revealed in analysis the small trace of silver it contained, but the mineral men were credulous.

[3] See below p. 361.

[4] In margin: 'Fiue thousand pearles gathered' (Hakluyt, III (1600), 269). We do not know the name of the pearl-gatherer. Perhaps he was the lapidary Raleigh had been advised to send (p. 136 above).

vniformitie in roundnesse, orientnesse, and pidenesse of many excellent colours, with equalitie in greatnesse, were very fayre and rare; and had therefore beene presented to her Maiestie, had wee not by casualtie, and through extremity of a storme, lost them with many things els in comming away from the countrey.[1]

Sweet Gummes of diuers kinds, and many other Apothecary drugges,[2] of which we will make speciall mention, when we shall receiue it from such men of skill in that kynd, that in taking reasonable paines [B4] shall discouer them more particularly then wee haue done; and than now I can make relation of, for want of the examples I had prouided and gathered, and are nowe lost, with other things by casualtie before mentioned.[3]

Dyes of diuers kindes: There is Shoemake well knowen, and vsed in England for blacke;[4] the seede of an hearbe called *Wasewówr*,[5] little small rootes called *Cháppacor*,[6] and the barke of

---

[1] Lane records also the loss of a rope of pearls he had from Menatonon. The occasion was 17 June 1586, when Drake's sailors tipped much of the baggage accumulated at Roanoke Island into the water (p. 260).

[2] Hariot is undoubtedly weak on the medicinal plants found. The apothecaries, physicians, and surgeons who were with Grenville's fleet (pp. 199, 213, 328 above) are likely to have returned with him. Sweet gum (American storax) was certainly obtained from the Liquidambar tree (p. 97 above), but probably other trees yielded promising gums also. The aromatic bark of the Sweet Bay is noted by Hariot below (p. 365), as well as the China root (pp. 348–9).

[3] This was on 17 June 1586 also, but specimens of many medicinal, or supposedly medicinal, plants had already been sent back in 1585 (cp. pp. 200, 207). It is not known how, and when, specimens, some of which were passed on to L'Écluse, came into the hands of London apothecaries like James Garet (cp. pp. 48, 55).

[4] Black dye was obtained from the leaves of (a) Dwarf Sumach (*Rhus copallina*), and (b) Smooth Sumach (*R. glabra*), both of which were common on dry open soil (the berries also giving a red dye) (W. C. C.). *R. radicans* was also noticed on Ocracoke Island by Kearney ('Ecology', p. 316).

[5] 'Wasebur' (Hakluyt (1589), p. 752; III (1600), 269); meaning, probably, 'shiny seeds' (p. 898). It is difficult to tie this down at all precisely. The least unlikely plant is the Pokeweed (*Phytolacca americana*) which is found in North Carolina, the purplish dye from which was used in the south-east (Porcher, *Resources*, p. 405; Wells, *Natural gardens*, p. 362).

[6] 'Chappacor' (Hakluyt, as above), meaning merely 'roots' (p. 886). Dr W. C. Coker suggests New Jersey Tea (*Ceanothus americana*), whose roots yield red dye, but I have no record of its growing on the Carolina Banks. It will be noted that

the tree called by the inhabitaunts *Tangómockomindge*:[1] which Dies are for diuers sortes of red: their goodnesse for our English clothes remayne yet to be proued. The inhabitants vse them onely for the dying of hayre,[2] and colouring of their faces,[3] and Mantles made of Deare skinnes;[4] and also for the dying of Rushes[5] to make artificiall workes withall in their Mattes[6] and Baskettes;[7] hauing no other thing besides that they account of, apt to vse them for. If they will not proue merchantable there is no doubt but the Planters there shall finde apt vses for them, as also for other colours which wee knowe to be there.

Oade; a thing of so great vent and vse[8] amongst English Diers, which can not be yeelded sufficiently in our owne countrey for spare of ground, may be planted in Virginia, there being ground enough. The grouth thereof need not to be doubted, when as in

in the 1585 sketch-map 'ye roots that diethe read' are marked on Croatoan Island (now either the northern end of the modern Ocracoke Islands or the southern end of Hatteras Island (pp. 215–16 above)). Here the source is Dogwood (*Cornus florida* and other spp.), from the bark of whose roots red dye was obtained (Porcher, *Resources*, pp. 64–6). The same may well be true of Hariot's '*Cháppacor*'.

[1] 'Tangomockonomindge' (Hakluyt, as above; this being the altered form used by Hariot in his *Corrigenda*). The Indian word (pp. 896–7) is probably the shorter form, meaning 'little bear shrub' and would suggest a small bush rather than a tree. One of the alternatives suggested above may well be correct. The main source of red dye was the Pocone root (*Sanguinaria canadensis*), but this was traded in from the uplands.

[2] Hair-dyeing is not otherwise noted for this area.

[3] For face-colouring see p. 441.

[4] Deer-skin mantles, dyed black or red, are not otherwise noted for this area (for the mantles see p. 368).

[5] The 'rushes' were normally the split canes of *Arundinaria tecta* (cp. Swanton, *Indians*, pp. 602–8, and p. 365 below), but might be the Soft Rush (*Juncus effusus*) which could be used for mats (see Porcher, *Resources*, pp. 616, 682–3).

[6] For mats see pp. 99, 109, 415–17, 421, 429–30. This is the only clear evidence in this area of their being dyed, though dyeing was common elsewhere.

[7] One of the very few references to baskets amongst the south-eastern Algonkians, and the only one among the North Carolina group to their being dyed (cp. Swanton, *Indians*, p. 603). F. G. Speck (*The Rappahannock Indians of Virginia* (1925), pp. 60–3) gives some information on materials used in modern times.

[8] 'Woad: a thing of so great vent and vses' (Hakluyt (1589), p. 752; III (1600), 269).

the Ilands of the Asores it groweth plentifully, which is[1] in the same climate. So likewise of Madder.[2]

We caryed thither Suger canes to plant, which beeing not so well preserued as was requisit, & besides the time of the yere being past for their setting when we arriued, wee could not make that proofe of them as wee desired.[3] [B4 v.] Notwithstanding, seeing that they grow in the same climate, in the South part of Spaine and in Barbary, our hope in reason may yet continue. So likewise for Orenges and Lemmons. There may be planted also Quinses.[4] Whereby may grow in reasonable time if the action be diligently prosecuted, no small commodities in Sugers, Suckets, and Marmalades.

Many other commodities by planting may there also bee raised, which I leaue to your discret and gentle considerations:[5] and many also bee there,[6] which yet we haue not discouered. Two more commodities of great value, one of certaintie, and the other in

---

[1] 'Açores it groweth plentifully, which are' (Hakluyt, III (1600), 269).

[2] Woad (*Isatis tinctoria*) was still the principal source of the blue pigment and dye used extensively in the cloth industry, with alum as an unnecessary mordant; Madder (especially *Rubia tinctoria* from the Levant) was a source, with alum as a necessary mordant, of madder-red dye (C. Singer, *Earliest chemical industry*, pp. 264–6). At a time when much effort was being made to expand the production of finished cloth the discovery of suitable locations for growing these specialized crops appeared of considerable importance. In 1585 the elder Hakluyt recommended the bringing out of seeds or plants of woad as a quick crop 'of great gaine to this clothing realme', as well as the acquisition of 'Anile', Indigo (*Indigofera tinctoria*, and *I. anil*), for the same purpose (cp. Taylor, *Hakluyts*, II, 335).

[3] The roots were obtained in the West Indies (pp. 187, 408 above) and probably kept alive in 'drifats' (cp. Taylor, *Hakluyts*, I, 121), specially prepared frames, possibly with glazed lids. The temperature would have been adequate, but neither the light sandy soil nor the exposed situation of Roanoke Island would have suited sugar-canes, so that the experiment must, in any event, have been fruitless (W. L. H.).

[4] Hariot assumed, as did the Hakluyts (Taylor, *Hakluyts*, I, 119; II, 321, 336), that the cultivation limits in eastern North America were identical with those in Europe. In fact, effective outdoor cultivation of citrus fruits is not possible north of Cape Fear, except as a rather rare horticultural feat (W. L. H.).

[5] The Hakluyts had suggested many other crops which might be tried (especially Taylor, *Hakluyts*, II, 320–1, 333–8).

[6] 'also may be' (in Hariot's *Corrigenda* and Hakluyt (1589), p. 752; III (1600), 270).

hope, not to be planted, but there to be raised & in short time to be prouided and prepared, I might haue specified.[1] So likewise of those commodities already set downe I might haue said more; as of the particular places where they are founde and best to be planted and prepared: by what meanes and in what reasonable space of time they might be raised to profit and in what proportion; but because others then welwillers might be therewithall acquainted, not to the good of the action, I haue wittingly omitted them: knowing that to those that are well disposed I haue vttered, according to my promise and purpose, for this part sufficient.[2]

[C1] The second part of suche commodities as Virginia is knowne to yeelde for victuall and sustenance of mans life, vsually fed vpon by the naturall inhabitants: as also by vs, during the time of our aboade.[3] And first of such as are sowed and husbanded.

Pagatowr,[4] a kinde of graine so called by the inhabitants; the same in the West Indies is called Mayze: English men call it

---

[1] These two mystery commodities (cp. pp. 364, 549) were evidently natural local products. It is possible that Hariot had encountered the Indian medicinal use of the Yaupon (*Ilex vomitoria*), which within a century was to be the most famous product of the Carolinas (cp. [J. Peachie], *Some observations made upon the herb Cassiny imported from Carolina: shewing its admirable virtues in curing the small pox* (London, 1695); Lawson, *A new voyage to Carolina* (1709), p. 90; Porcher, *Resources*, pp. 431–3; A. H. G. Alston and R. E. Schultes, 'Studies of early specimens and reports of *Ilex vomitoria*', in *Rhodora*, LIII (1951), 273–9). Another, though less likely, candidate is the 'Wysauke' (Milkweed), drawn by White and later described by Gerard (see no. 54, pp. 444–6 below), also credited with substantial medicinal value.

[2] This is a somewhat disingenuous explanation. If Hariot was writing in the expectation that White's colony was to be firmly established and Raleigh's rights to the coastline thereby safeguarded (though cp. p. 38 above), little harm could have been done to the enterprise by such detail as Hariot stated he was in a position to give. The requirement of secrecy is more likely to have been made by Raleigh, who may well have found it advantageous in dealing with potential subscribers to have a number of tempting mysteries to disclose as the fish rose to the bait.

[3] As a consequence of the loss of their supplies (cp. pp. 201, 203).

[4] The Indian word for 'things put in a kettle to boil' (p. 893 below), could—but probably did not—cover other things than Maize, Indian Corn (*Zea mays*), on which so much of the Indian polity depended. For the literature see E. E. Edwards and W. D. Rasmussen, *A bibliography on the agriculture of the American Indians* (1942), pp. 45–54.

Guinny wheate or Turkie wheate,[1] according to the names of the countreys from whence the like hath beene brought. The graine is about the bignesse of our ordinary English peaze and not much different in forme and shape: but of diuers colours: some white, some red, some yellow, and some blew.[2] All of them yeelde a very white and sweet flowre: being vsed according to his kinde it maketh a very good bread.[3] Wee made of the same in the countrey some mault, whereof was bruwed as good Ale as was to bee desired. So likewise by the helpe of hops therof may bee made as good Beere.[4] It is a graine of marueillous great increase; of a thousand, fifteene hundred and some two thousand fold. There are three sortes, of which two are ripe in eleuen and twelue weekes at the most: sometimes in ten, after the time they are set, and are then of height in stalke about sixe or seuen foote. The other sort is ripe in foureteene, and is about ten foote high, of the stalkes some beare foure heads, some three, some one, and some two: euery head conteining fiue, sixe, or seuen hundred graines within a few more or lesse. Of these graines besides bread, the inhabitants make victuall, ey [C 1 v.] ther by parching them, or

[1] The name Guinea Wheat is common to Lane and Hariot (pp. 207-8 above). No illustration of Maize had yet been published in England, although there had been a number in continental herbals. The fullest description available in English to Hariot—the note in Frampton's *Monardes* being brief—was in Henry Lyte's version of Dodoens, *A niewe herball* (1578), pp. 463-4, of which there was a new edition in 1586 (cp. Finan, in *Annals of the Missouri Botanic Garden*, xxxv, 167).

[2] What Hariot says here is almost all that is known about the early varieties (though cultivation details appear on pp. 341-2 and the sowing sequence in White's drawing, no. 37, see p. 421). A copy of one drawing of White's (not yet reproduced) shows the multi-coloured kernels (no. 82, see p. 452 below). Finan (*Annals of the Missouri Botanic Garden*, xxxv, 169) analysed thirty herbals, 1539-1686, recording various coloured kernels with the following frequencies: yellow (25), white (23), red (19), purple (16), brown (11), black (9), blue (6). L'Écluse (*Rariorum plantarum historia* (1601), sig. SS 6) describes 'Panici Americani Spica grandis', brought home (from Virginia?) by an English captain and given to him by James Garet in 1592.

[3] The bread is yellow and is still eaten in the southern states.

[4] The making of malt, ale and beer in this way is quite practicable. It is probable that the brewing of ale was of great value to Lane in maintaining the morale of the settlement, in view of the probable absence of wine, spirits and beer after the loss of much of the settlement's provisions.

seething them whole vntill they be broken; or boyling the floure with water into a pappe.[1]

Okíndgíer, called by vs Beanes, because in greatnesse & partly in shape they are like to the Beanes in England; sauing that they are flatter, of more diuers colours, and some pide. The leafe also of the stemme is much different.[2] In taste they are altogether as good as our English peaze.

Wickonzówr, called by vs Peaze, in respect of the beanes, for distinction sake, because they are much lesse; although in forme they litle differ:[3] but in goodnesse of taste much,[4] & are far better then our English peaze. Both the beanes and peaze are ripe in tenne weekes after they are set. They make them victuall either by boyling them all to pieces into a broth, or boiling them whole vntill they bee soft and beginne to breake as is vsed in England, eyther by themselues, or mixtly together: Sometimes they mingle of the wheate with them. Sometime also beeing whole sodden, they bruse or pound[5] them in a morter, & thereof make loaues or lumps of dowishe bread, which they vse to eat for varietie.[6]

[1] Corn, roasted, boiled and taken as gruel, thus made an essential basis for most Indian dishes, but it was commonly cooked with meat, fish, and cultivated and wild vegetables (cp. p. 430).

[2] The common Kidney or Haricot Bean (*Phaseolus vulgaris*) was universally cultivated by the Indians (Yanovsky, *Food plants of the North American Indians,* p. 38; cp. Smith, *Works,* pp. cxi–xii, 62; Strachey, *Hist. of travell,* p. 119; Swanton, *Indians,* p. 302). There is, surprisingly, no trace of the cultivation of leguminous plants in White's drawings. The Indian name appears to derive from the pod (p. 892). Mr A. H. G. Alston identified L'Écluse's 'Lobus ex Wingandecaow' (*Exoticorum,* pp. 61–2) as the Locust Bean of the West Indies. The other American bean given him by James Garet has not been identified (ibid. p. 64; cp. Gerard, *Herball,* p. 1040).

[3] C. C. Willoughby ('The Virginia Indians in the seventeenth century', in *American Anthropologist,* n.s., ix (1907), 83) believed this to be the smaller variety of the Kidney Bean (*Phaseolus nanus*) and this appears probable (cp. Yanovsky, *Food plants,* p. 38). Dr W. C. Coker suggested that it might possibly be the round 'bean' of *Apios tuberosa* (see p. 346 below), but this does not appear to have been cultivated.

[4] 'much like' (Hakluyt (1589), p. 753; iii (1600), 270).

[5] 'punne' (Hakluyt, as above).

[6] Hariot's description of the variety of Indian cooking is of value, since otherwise it might appear that an *olla podrida* was virtually their only dish. His interest

Macócqwer, according to their seuerall formes, called by vs Pompions, Mellions, and Gourdes,[1] because they are of the like formes as those kinds in England. In Virginia such of seuerall formes are of one taste and very good, and do also spring from one seed. There are of two sorts; one is ripe in the space of a moneth, and the other in two monethes.

There is an hearbe which in Dutch is called *Melden*. Some of those that I describe it vnto take it to be a kinde of Orage; it groweth about foure or fiue foote high:[2] of the seede thereof they make a thicke broth, and pottage [C2] of a very good taste: of the stalke by burning into ashes they make a kinde of salt earth, where-withall many vse sometimes to season their broths; other salte they knowe not.[3] Wee our selues vsed the leaues also for pot-hearbes.

arises, no doubt, from the prominent part peas and beans played in the contemporary English diet.

[1] 'Macocquer, according to their seueral formes, called by vs Pompions, Melons, and Gourdes' (Hakluyt (1589), p. 753; III (1600), 270). The melon should not appear among the pumpkins, squashes and gourds but was a later introduction. All the rest had come from the south. The most clearly identified is the Bottle Gourd (*Lagenaria siceraria*), illustrated by White (no. 34, see p. 417 below; F. G. Speck, *Gourds of the southeastern Indians* (Boston, 1941), pp. 19-20), while the Common White Bush Scallop Squash (*Cucurbita pepo*) is also probable (Speck, p. 21). Willoughby (op. cit., p. 83) suggested that the pumpkin was most likely *Cucurbita maxima*, but the identification of particular varieties is doubtfully based in most instances. It is only in De Bry's engraving of White's Secoton drawing that we have a picture of the cultivation of the plants (no. 37, see p. 423 below). L'Écluse illustrates 'Macocquer Virginiensium' (*Exoticorum*, p. 23) by a gourd (with seeds) given to him by James Garet in 1591. It was, he says, brought 'ex Wingandecaow Provincia', and he adds (from De Bry, cp. p. 429 below) a description of the use of gourd rattles by the Indians. Mr A. H. G. Alston identified it as a West Indian calabash (Calabash Tree, *Crescentia cujete* Linn.) It and other West Indian specimens thus mistakenly assigned may very well have been acquired on one of the outward voyages to Roanoke Island and brought to England unlabelled, so that it was easy to confuse their place of origin.

[2] *Melde* is Dutch for members of the spinach and beet family. It is clearly a member of the genus *Atriplex*, known as Oraches or Salt-bushes (J. K. Small, *Manual of the south-eastern flora* (1933), p. 466; Swanton, *Indians*, pp. 244, 270), possibly *A. hastata*.

[3] It is of interest that knowledge of salt-getting had not yet reached this southern Algonkian group. There is the possibility that rumours of salt-making in the Mississippi Valley had crossed the mountains, but this is far from certain (cp. Swanton, *Indians*, pp. 242-3, and p. 268-9 above).

There is also another great hearbe, in forme of a Marigolde, about sixe foot in height, the head with the floure is a spanne in breadth. Some take it to be Planta Solis:[1] of the seeds heereof they make both a kinde of bread and broth.

All the aforesayd commodities for victuall are set or sowed, sometimes in groundes apart and seuerally by themselues, but for the most part together in one ground mixtly: the manner thereof, with the dressing and preparing of the ground, because I will note vnto you the fertilitie of the soile; I thinke good briefly to describe.

The ground they neuer fatten with mucke, dounge, or any other thing, neither plow nor digge it as we in England, but onely prepare it in sort as followeth. A few daies before they sowe or set, the men with wooden instruments, made almost in forme of mattockes or hoes with long handles; the women with short peckers or parers,[2] because they vse them sitting, of a foote long and about fiue inches in breadth: doe onely breake the vpper part of the ground to rayse vp the weedes, grasse, & olde stubbes of corne stalks with their rootes. The which after a day or twoes[3] drying in the Sunne, being scrapte vp into many small heapes, to saue them labour for carrying them away; they burne into ashes. (And whereas some may thinke that they vse the ashes for to better the ground, I say that then they would either disperse the ashes abroade, which wee obserued they do not, except the heapes bee too great: or else would [C2 v.] take speciall care to set

---

[1] Sunflower (*Helianthus*, eighteen species now in N.C. (Wells, *Natural gardens*, p. 439)). The Indians dried the seeds and ground them for flour. When crushed the seeds were also boiled but usually for the oil which was skimmed off (Swanton, *Indians*, pp. 244, 269; Fernald and Kinsey, *Edible plants*, pp. 356–7). Sunflowers appear in the White drawings only in De Bry's engravings of Pomeiooc and Secoton (nos. 33, 37, see pp. 416, 422 below), but they are mentioned by Monardes (*Joyfull newes*, II, 23). White's sunflowers have been identified as the cultivated variety *Helianthus annuus*, var. *macrocarpus* (D.C.) Ckll. (C. B. Heiser, 'The sunflower among the North American Indians', in *Proc. American Phil. Soc.*, XCV (1951), 432, 435). Specimens described by R. Dodoens (*Florum...historia* (1568)) and by Monardes were believed to come from Peru. They must have been brought from Mexico or Florida.

[2] No drawings or full descriptions of these important artifacts have survived.

[3] 'two dayes' (Hakluyt, III (1600), 271).

their corne where the ashes lie, which also wee finde they are carelesse of.) And this is all the husbanding of their ground that they vse.[1]

Then their setting or sowing is after this maner. First for their corne, beginning in one corner of the plot, with a pecker they make a hole, wherein they put foure graines, with that care[2] they touch not one another (about an inch asunder) and couer them with the moulde againe: and so through out the whole plot, making such holes and vsing them after such maner: but with this regard, that they bee made in rankes, euery ranke differing from other halfe a fadome or a yarde, and the holes also in euery ranke, as much. By this meanes there is a yard spare ground betwene euery hole: where according to discretion here and there, they set as many Beanes and Peaze; in diuers places also among the seedes of *Macócqwer, Melden* and Planta solis.[3]

The ground being thus set according to the rate by vs experimented, an English Acre conteining fourtie pearches in length, and foure in breadth, doeth there yeeld in croppe or ofcome of corne, beanes, and peaze, at the least two hundred London bushelles, besides the *Macócqwer, Melden,* and Planta solis: When as in England fourtie bushelles of our wheate yeelded out of such an acre is thought to be much.[4]

[1] The information that the corn grounds were often cleared by burning but not with the idea of manuring them is not given elsewhere than in Hariot. In the production process the men appear to have played a rather larger part than usual, not only in preparing the ground, but in sowing the seed, which was normally a woman's task (Flannery, *Analysis*, p. 105). The descriptions of corn culture amongst all the south-eastern Algonkian peoples are very similar (cp. Smith, *Works*, pp. cxi–xii, 62; Strachey, *History of travell*, pp. 118–19; Beverley, *Hist. and present state* (1947), pp. 143–4), although they have never been fully analysed (but see Swanton, *Indians*, pp. 306–10).

[2] 'care that' (Hakluyt, as above).

[3] White's Secoton drawing (no. 37, see pp. 420–1) does not indicate any mixture of other plants with the corn, nor indeed does De Bry's engraving (see pp. 422–3), as the pumpkins, etc., sunflowers, and tobacco are in separate patches. The practice may have varied from place to place. Hariot's is the only indication of the cultivation of 'Melden' with the other vegetables.

[4] Hariot is here mistaken in his optimism, since the U.S. Census 1950 gave North Carolina's average yield in that year as 28·5 bushels per acre. His contribu-

I thought also good to note this vnto you, y^t you which shall inhabite and plant there, maie know how specially that countrey corne is there to be preferred before ours: Besides the manifold waies in applying it to victuall, the increase is so much that small labour and paines is needful in respect that must[1] be vsed for ours. For this I can assure you that according to the rate we haue made proofe of, one man may prepare and husband so much grounde [C3] (hauing once borne corne before) with lesse then foure and twentie houres labour, as shall yeeld him victuall in a large proportion for a tweluemoneth, if hee haue nothing else, but that which the same ground will yeelde, and of that kinde onelie which I haue before spoken of: the saide ground being also but of fiue and twentie yards square. And if neede require, but that there is ground enough, there might be raised out of one and the selfsame ground two haruestes or ofcomes; for they sowe or set and may at anie time when they thinke good from the middest of March vntill the end of Iune: so that they also set when they haue eaten of their first croppe.[2] In some places of the countrey notwithstanding they haue two haruests, as we haue heard, out of one and the same ground.[3]

tion to the rather meagre evidence on English wheat-yields is, however, interesting and bears out the contention (not universally accepted) that yields of 40 to 48 bushels on good enclosed land, well cultivated, were possible at this time but were (except in rare circumstances) a maximum (see Robert Trow-Smith, *English husbandry* (1951), pp. 105-6, and discussion in *The Times Literary Supplement*, 27 April, 25 May, 1, 8 and 15 June 1951). It may be noted that in taking the London bushel of 8 gallons and the acre of 40 by 4 perches Hariot is giving the nearest approach to standard measures at a time when these varied greatly from place to place.

[1] 'of that which must' (Hakluyt, as above).

[2] Hariot is correct in most of what he says about the advantages of maize culture, but he underestimated (*a*) the amount of clearing necessary for large-scale cultivation, (*b*) the high proportion of marginal or unsuitable ground in the coastlands, and (*c*) the high wastage of unmanured ground, together with the difficulty of maintaining sufficient livestock to supply animal manure. The relatively small and mobile Indian population obscured the effects of these limiting conditions.

[3] Double cropping so far north does not seem to be corroborated by other early reports.

343

For English corne neuerthelesse whether to vse or not to vse it, you that inhabite maie doe as you shall haue farther cause to thinke best. Of the grouth you need not to doubt: for barlie, oates and peaze, we haue seene proof of, not beeing purposely sowen but fallen casually in the worst sort of ground, and yet to be as faire as any we have euer seene here in England. But of wheat, because it was musty and had taken salt water we could make no triall: and of rye we had none.[1] Thus much haue I digressed and I hope not vnnecessarily: nowe will I returne againe to my course and intreate of that which yet remaineth apperteining to this Chapter.

There is an herbe which is sowed apart by it selfe & is called by the inhabitants *vppówoc*:[2] In the West Indies it hath diuers names, according to the seuerall places & countreys where it groweth and is vsed: The Spaniardes generally call it Tobacco.[3] The leaues thereof being dried and brought into pouder, they use to take the fume [C 3 v.] or smoke thereof by sucking it thorough pipes made of claie, into their stomacke and heade; from whence it purgeth superfluous fleame & other grosse humors, openeth all the pores & passages of the body: by which meanes the vse thereof, not only preserueth the body from obstructions; but also if any be, so that they haue not beene of too long continuance, in short time breaketh them: wherby their bodies are notably

---

[1] The plans for testing European seeds fully were upset both by the late arrival in 1585 and by the loss and damage to supplies (the cause of the wheat going musty) when the *Tiger* struck (pp. 177, 203 above). Insufficient attention was, however, given to testing, for example, peas, if Hariot had to depend on observation of the growth of casual droppings. Wheat, oats and barley would grow in this area while neither soil nor climate was very suitable: peas would flourish.

[2] 'Vppowoc' (Hakluyt (1589), p. 754; III (1600), 271). The separate planting of tobacco is shown in De Bry's engraving of White's Secoton drawing (no. 37, see p. 422 below).

[3] Hakluyt, III (1600), 271, adds 'Tabacco' in margin. It is now generally accepted that the tobacco cultivated in eastern North America was *Nicotiana rustica*, in a number of varieties (see especially George A. West, *Tobacco, pipes and smoking customs of the American Indians* (Milwaukee, 1934, 2 parts), pp. 59–66; and for the literature J. E. Brooks, *Tobacco* (New York, 1937–52, 5 vols.); S. A. Dickson, 'Panacea or Precious Bane', in *Bull. N.Y. Publ. Library*, LVII–VIII (1953–4)).

preserued in health, & know not many greeuous diseases where-
withall wee in England are oftentimes afflicted.[1]

This *Vppówoc* is of so precious estimation amongest them, that
they thinke their gods are maruelously delighted therwith: Wherupon sometime they make hallowed fires & cast some of the
pouder therein for a sacrifice: being in a storme vppon the waters,
to pacifie their gods, they cast some vp into the aire and into the
water: so a weare for fish being newly set vp, they cast some
therein and into the aire: also after an escape of danger, they cast
some into the aire likewise:[2] but all done with strange gestures,
stamping, sometime dauncing, clapping of hands, holding vp of
hands, & staring vp into the heauens, vttering therewithal and
chattering strange words & noises.

We our selues during the time we were there vsed to suck it
after their maner, as also since our returne,[3] & haue found manie

[1] See West, *Tobacco*, pp. 47–51. The earliest English work on tobacco,
A[nthony] C[hute], *Tabaco* (London, Adam Islip, 1595) (see R. J. Kane, 'Anthony
Chute, Thomas Nashe and the first English work on Tobacco', in *Rev. Eng. Stud.*,
VII, 151–9), makes no reference to Hariot, Raleigh or Virginia, but (p. 19) states:
'I think that there is nothing that harmes a man inwardly from his girdle vpward,
but may be taken away with a moderate vse of Tabacco.'
The earliest English illustration of the tobacco plant is in John Frampton's
edition of Monardes in 1577 (*Joyfull newes*, ed. Gaselee, I, 46, see above p. 329).
The second was apparently that of De Bry (see below, p. 422); the third, in A. C.,
Tabaco (1595), p. 35; and the fourth in Gerard's *Herball* (1597), p. 285. It is
probable that White made a detailed drawing of the plant but, if so, it has not
survived, unless Gerard's is taken from it.
[2] Tobacco offerings were general among the coastal Algonkian peoples
(Flannery, *Analysis*, p. 140): Hariot's description is especially useful for his discussion of the use of tobacco in a dry state (West, *Tobacco*, pp. 66–7).
[3] That the colonists of 1585–6—and Sir Walter Raleigh—introduced smoking
into England is one of those myths which it appears almost impossible to kill.
There is no doubt that Raleigh and the colonists alike did much to popularize
what was already an established custom. Hariot himself was a heavy smoker,
as repeated memoranda on the purchase of tobacco among his papers at Petworth
House and in the British Museum confirm, while Raleigh learnt to cure tobacco
expertly (see Raven, *English naturalists*, p. 270). What the colonists apparently
introduced was the smoking pipe used on Roanoke Island as a model for English
pipe-makers. L'Écluse added an important note to his reprint of Monardes in
1605 (*Exoticorum*, p. 310): 'Detecta ab Anglis duce Richardo Grenfeldio anno
á Christi nativitate M.D.LXXXV. Wingandecaow (quam ipsi Virginiam nuncu-

rare and wonderfull experiments of the vertues thereof; of which the relation woulde require a volume by it selfe: the vse of it by so manie of late men & women of great calling as else and some learned Phisitions also, is sufficient witnes.[1]

And these are all the commodities for sustenance of life that I know and can remember they vse to husband: all else that followe, are founde growing naturally or wilde.

[C4] Of Rootes.

Openauk[2] are a kind of roots of round forme, some of the bignes of walnuts, some far greater, which are found in moist &

pârunt) novi orbis Provinciâ, triginta sex gradibus ab Aequatore Septentrionem versus distante: Compererunt incolas frequenter uti tubulis quibusdam ex argilla factis, ad foliorum Tabaci magnâ abundantiâ apud eos nascentis, incensorum fumum hauriendum, sive verius sorbendum, valetudinis conservanda gratiâ. Angli inde reduces similes attulerunt tubos ad Tabaci fumum excipiendum; inde Tabaci usus per universam Angliam adeó invaluit, praesertim apud aulicos, ut multos similes tubos fieri curârint, ad Tabaci fumum sorbendum.' This is rendered by J.R. (*Panacea; or the universal medicine* (1659), pp. 62-3, which includes a translation of Gilles Everaerts, *De herba Panacea* (Antwerp, 1587) itself based on Monardes): 'That in the year 1585 Wingandecaow (which is now called Virginy) being discovered to the English (to their Captain Richard Grenfield, and is a Province of the new world, and is thirty-six degrees from the Aequator toward the North Pole) they found that the Inhabitans did frequently use some Pipes made of Clay, to draw forth the fume of Tobacco leaves set on fire, which grew among them in great quantity or rather to drink it down, to preserve their health. The English returning from thence brought like Pipes with them, to drink the smoak of Tobacco; and since that time, the use of drinking Tobacco hath so much prevailed all England over, especially among the Courtiers, that they have caused many such like Pipes to be made to drink Tobacco with.' Mr J. C. Harrington recently found at the bottom of the fort ditch on Roanoke Island an Indian pipe (possibly contemporaneous with the colony) made of clay, which closely resembles some very early English examples (cp. pp. 430, 907 below).

[1] It could be argued that Hariot's discussion of tobacco was designed to promote its use in England and so to make it a valuable export from the Virginia colony. If so, he anticipated what occurred under the Virginia Company, when it became a staple without which the colony might have failed to survive.

[2] Although the Indian word was a general one meaning 'roots' (p. 893 below), it is now generally agreed that what Hariot is describing is the Ground-nut, Indian Potato or Marsh Potato (*Apios tuberosa* or *Glycine apios*) which grows in low ground in thickets or along streams in the North Carolina and Virginia coastlands. For the generality of its use among the Indians see Fernald and Kinsey, *Edible plants*, pp. 252-5; Yanovsky, *Food plants*, p. 37; Swanton, *Indians*, pp. 296, 362.

marish grounds growing many together one by another in ropes, as though they were fastnened with a string. Being boiled or sodden they are very good meate.[1]

Okeepenauk[2] are also of round shape, found in dry grounds: some

[1] Hakluyt, III (1600), 272, added the sentence: 'Monardes called these roots, Beades or Pater nostri of Santa Helena', with the marginal reference: 'Monardes parte 2. lib. 1 cap. 4' (*Joyfull newes* (1577), ed. S. Gaselee, I, 126–7). The reference is to roots found at Santa Elena and sent home by a Spanish soldier. It would appear to be a correct identification, so that Hakluyt is in no way responsible for the other, almost ineradicable, myth that Raleigh brought (*sic*) the potato (*Solanum tuberosum*) from Virginia. The name 'Virginia Potato' for the latter was invented by John Gerard (*Herball* (1597), pp. 335, 781), who, with a woodcut, described 'Potatoes of Virginia' and went on to say: 'It groweth naturally in America, where it was first discouered, as reporteth C. Clusius [Charles de l'Écluse, who had received a drawing of *S. tuberosum* on 26 Jan. 1588], since which time I have receiued rootes hereof from Virginia, otherwise called Norembega, which growe and prosper in my garden as in theire owne native countrie.' Dr R. S. Salaman, whose *History and social influence of the potato* contains a most illuminating discussion of the whole problem, makes the ingenious suggestion (pp. 83, 149) that Gerard knew Hariot to have described specimens of similar roots, and that among specimens given him were examples of the common potato picked up in the cook-house of Drake's ship on which Hariot returned from Virginia in 1586. This, however, will not do. Gerard claims to have received the potato after hearing of it from L'Écluse, long after Hariot's return, nor was L'Écluse himself confused since, in his *Rariorum plantarum historia* (Antwerp, 1601), bk. IV, p. lxxix (see Salaman, op. cit., pp. 83, 91), he says, quite legitimately: 'it likewise appears that the root which the Virginians call *Openauk* is not wholly dissimilar.' Gerard was his own deceiver (cp. his *Catalogus* (1596), ed. B. D. Jackson (1876), p. 45), but it was Gaspard Bauhin (*Prodromos* (Frankfort-on-Main, 1620), p. 90; see Salaman, op. cit., pp. 83, 92) who added Hariot to Gerard: 'They [potatoes] were brought first from the Isle of Virginia to England. ...The tubers of this plant are described under the name of *Openauck*...'. The name 'Thomas Henreiotus.' (Thomas Hariot) was given as the authority in J. Bauhin and J. H. Cherler *Historia plantarum universalis*, III (Lyons, 1651), 622 (see Salaman, p. 96). Before the end of the seventeenth century the legend had been fixed (see R. B. Gunther, *Early British botanists* (1922), pp. 18, 321). Robert Morison, *Plantarum historia universalis*, III (Oxford, 1699), 522 says: 'From Virginia called *Openhauch* or *Apenauk*, it was brought into England and whence, it was scattered over Europe', though he was the first to note that subsequent search of Virginia had not disclosed it (Salaman, op. cit. p. 98).

[2] Again the Indian word is not helpful (p. 892 below). The identification remains somewhat uncertain but it is highly probable that Man-of-the-earth, Wild Potato Vine (*Ipomea pandurata*) is normally meant. This vine has a yam-like tap-root often weighing 15–30 lb., and was found in dry or light alluvial soils (Fernald and Kinsey, *Edible plants*, p. 326; Swanton, *Indians*, p. 270). A coastal

are of the bignes of a mans head. They are to be eaten as they are taken out of the ground, for by reason of their drinesse they will neither roste nor seeth. Their tast is not so good as of the former roots, notwithstanding for want of bread & sometimes for varietie the inhabitants vse to eate them with fish or flesh, and in my iudgement they doe as well as the houshold bread made of rie heare in England.

Kaishucpenauk[1] a white kind of roots about the bignes of hen egs[2] & neere of that forme: their tast was not so good to our seeming as of the other, and therfore their place and manner of growing not so much cared for by vs: the inhabitants notwithstanding vsed to boile & eate many.

Tsinaw[3] a kind of roote much like vnto y^t which in England is called the China root brought from the East Indies.[4] And we

habitat for it in North Carolina has not, however, been confirmed. Salaman (*History and social influence of the potato*, p. 83) is mistaken in thinking *Okeepenauk* can certainly be identified as the 'tuckahoe' fungus.

[1] 'Kaishucpenauk' (Hakluyt (1589), p. 755; III (1600), 272), the word possibly meaning 'easily-dug tubers' (p. 888). It is probable that this comprises several members of the water-plantain family, especially the Common Arrow-head or Duck Potato (*Sagittaria latifolia* Willd., and also *S. cuneata*), found on pond and river margins and in marshes (W. C. C.; Yanovsky, *Food plants*, p. 7; Fernald and Kinsey, *Edible plants*, pp. 86–9; Wells, *Natural gardens*, p. 284; Porcher, *Resources*, p. 615); cp. Salaman, op. cit., pp. 82–3, and Swanton, *Indians*, p. 270, where unlikely identifications are suggested.

[2] 'hennes egges' (Hakluyt, III (1600), 272).

[3] Professor James A. Geary shows (p. 898 below) that this is merely an Indian attempt to reproduce 'China'. The probable explanation is that during the 1584 voyage one of the Indian captives, Manteo or Wanchese, heard the word used of a root, and reproduced it later for Hariot in a way which he did not recognize. The plant is one of the Woody Smilaxes (*Smilax lancelata* or *S. laurifolia* are the most likely) on which the historical references and description are fully given by W. C. Coker, 'The Woody Smilaxes of the United States', in *Jnl. Elisha Mitchell Scientific Society*, LX, 27–69.

[4] Of *Smilax China* William Mount had already written in 1582, commending 'The diet roote Chinea whereof we haue none growing in Englande for the Great pockes, allso for all diseases proceadinge from a moyste brayne and the lyuer obstructed' (Gunther, *Early British botanists*, p. 258). American 'China' had already been described in Monardes (*Joyfull newes*, I, 34–7). L'Écluse (*Exoticorum* (1605), p. 83) illustrates a root which he says he received from James Garet in 1590 'é Wingandecaow, sive Virginiam relatam cum hac inscriptione, *Chinae species*' (cp. the name *Smilax pseudochina* Linn.). He also refers to this passage by Hariot.

know not anie thing to the contrary but that it maie be of the same kinde. These roots grow manie together in great clusters and do bring foorth a brier stalke, but the leafe in shape farre vnlike: which beeing supported by the trees it groweth neerest vnto, will reach or climbe to the top of the highest. From these roots while they be new or fresh beeing chopt into small pieces & stampt, is strained with water a iuice that maketh bread, & also being boiled, a very good spoonemeate in maner of a gelly, and is much better in tast, if it bee tempered with oyle.[1] [C4 v.] This *Tsinaw* is not of that sort which by some was caused to be brought into England for the China roote,[2] for it was discouered since, and is in vse as is afore said: but that which was brought hither is not yet knowne, neither by vs nor by the inhabitants to serue for any vse or purpose, although the rootes in shape are very like.

Coscúshaw,[3] some of our company tooke to bee that kinde of root which the Spaniards in the West Indies call *Cassauy*,[4] whereupon also many called it by that name: it groweth in very muddie pooles and moist groundes. Being dressed according to the countrey maner, it maketh a good bread, and also a good sponemeate, and is vsed very much by the inhabitants. The iuice of this

---

[1] The use of the roots to make a reddish flour, a jelly and a drink like sarsaparilla was widespread in the south-east, but did not, apparently, extend north of North Carolina (Swanton, *Indians*, pp. 270, 276; Fernald and Kinsey, *Edible plants*, pp. 140–3; Porcher, *Resources*, pp. 616–18). The object in breaking up and soaking the roots was to get rid of the fibre.

[2] Brought home from America, in all probability, either in 1584 (cp. p. 348 above) or in the autumn of 1585, but not identifiable on the purely negative particulars given.

[3] 'Coscushaw' (Hakluyt (1589), p. 755; III (1600), 272), probably meaning 'enclosed like an ear'—i.e. the flower (p. 886). A member of the arum family, all of which have a strong peppery taste removable by drying, but are not highly poisonous. The two species used were the Arrow-arum (*Peltranda virginica*) and the Golden-club (*Orontium aquaticum*), both found on pond margins and swamps on the coastal plain (W. C. C.; Yanovsky, *Food plants*, pp. 10–11; Fernald and Kinsey, *Edible plants*, pp. 111–21; Swanton, *Indians*, p. 271; Wells, *Natural gardens*, pp. 285–6).

[4] Cassava made in the Caribbean from the pressed root of *Manihot utilissima*. Monardes (*Joyfull newes*, II, 34–5) had described it (Frampton Englishing it as 'Casany'). So had Sir Humphrey Gilbert in 1577 (Quinn, *Gilbert*, I, 178–9). For Lane's name 'Cassava' for the arum-root flour see pp. 280, 283 above.

root is poison,[1] and therefore heede must be taken before any thing be made therewithall: Either the rootes must bee first sliced and dried in the Sunne, or by the fire, and then being pounded into floure wil make good bread: or els while they are greene they are to bee pared, cut into[2] pieces, and stampt; loues of the same to be laid neere or ouer the fire vntill it be soure, and then being well pounded againe, bread, or spone meate very good in taste, and holesome may be made thereof.

Habascon[3] is a root of hoat taste almost of the forme and bignesse of a Parseneepe, of it selfe it is no victuall, but onely a helpe beeing boiled together with other meates.

There are also Leekes, differing little from ours in England that grow in many places of the countrey, of which, when we came in places where they were, wee gathered and eate many, but the naturall inhabitants neuer.[4]

[D 1] Of Fruites.

Chestnuts,[5] there are in diuers places great store: some they vse to eate rawe, some they stampe and boile to make spoonemeate, and with some being sodden they make such a manner of dowe bread as they vse of their beanes before mentioned.

[1] 'The iuice of Coscushaw is poison': in margin (Hakluyt, III (1600), 272).

[2] 'in' (Hakluyt, as above).

[3] Neither the name (though it may mean 'spicy' (p. 887)) nor the description is very helpful. It may well be the Cow-parsnip (*Heracleum lanatum*), which was used by the Indians as a salt-substitute, but it is not likely to have been found in any quantity near the coast (W. C. C.; Wells, *Natural gardens*, p. 376; Fernald and Kinsey, *Edible plants*, pp. 297–300). Swanton (*Indians*, pp. 270, 276) prefers to suggest the Angelico (or Nondo) (*Ligusticum aetaeifolium*), but this is also scarce near the coast.

[4] One of many species of wild onions (*Allium*). *A. tricoccum*, the only one having broad leaves, is likely, but a definite habitat for it in the North Carolina coastlands has not been confirmed (W. C. C.; Fernald and Kinsey, *Edible plants*, pp. 126–30).

[5] The characteristic tree of this family found on or near the coast is the small Coastal Chinquapin (*Castanea Ashei* Sudw.), neither the common American Chestnut (*C. dentata*) nor the Chinaquapin (*C. pumila*) being normally found near the Carolina Sounds though they may well have been met with on the Roanoke River and Chowan River expeditions (cp. Coker and Totten, *Trees of N.C.*, pp. 102–6). The chinquapin nut was extensively used by the Indians (Fernald and Kinsey, *Edible plants*, pp. 158–9).

Walnuts:[1] There are two kindes of Walnuts, and of them infinit store: In many places where [are] very[2] great woods for many miles together the third part of trees are walnut-trees. The one kind is of the same taste and forme or litle differing from ours of England, but that they are harder and thicker shelled: the other is greater, and hath a verye ragged and harde shell: but the kernell great, verie oylie and sweete. Besides their eating of them after our ordinarie maner, they breake them with stones and pound them in morters[3] with water to make a milk which they vse to put into some sorts of their spoonmeate; also among their sodde wheat, peaze, beanes and pompions which maketh them haue a farre more pleasant taste.[4]

Medlars[5] a kinde of verie good fruit, so called by vs chieflie for these respectes: first in that they are not good vntill they be rotten: then in that they open at the head as our medlars, and are about the same bignesse: otherwise in taste and colour they are farre different: for they are as red as cheries and very sweet: but whereas the cherie is sharpe sweet, they are lushious sweet.

Metaquesúnnauk,[6] a kinde of pleasaunt fruite almost of the shape

---

[1] Hariot probably uses 'walnut' to include the hickories. In that case his smooth nut is probably the Pig-nut Hickory (*Carya glabra*), as the White Walnut is not found near the coast. The dark, ragged-shelled sort might have been the Black Walnut (*Juglans nigra*), because, though unusual near the coast, it tended to seed round Indian settlements: otherwise the dark sort is one, or more, of the Shell-bark Hickories (*Carya ovata* (Mill.) Koch and *Carya carolinae-septentrionalis* (Ashe) Engl. & Graetor are the more probable) (W. C. C.; W. L. H.; Coker and Totten, *Trees of N.C.*, pp. 102–6).

[2] 'where are very' (Hakluyt (1589), p. 755; III (1600), 273).

[3] These invaluable artifacts—hammer-stones and flat or hollowed stones for mortars—had to be traded from the interior (cp. p. 367).

[4] They were a main source of vegetable fat and hair oil amongst the coastal Indians (Fernald and Kinsey, *Edible plants*, pp. 147–51).

[5] 'Medlars we have none', says Lawson (*New voyage* (1709), p. 111), having already described (pp. 102–3) the Persimmon or American Date-plum (*Diospyros virginiana*) of which 'The Fruit is rotten, when ripe'. This is what Hariot means. (W. C. C.; Swanton, *Indians*, p. 272; Porcher, *Resources*, pp. 423–7.)

[6] 'Mutaquesunnauk' (Hakluyt (1589), p. 756; III (1600), 273), possibly meaning 'eaten uncooked' (pp. 891–2); the Prickly Pear (*Opuntia,* several spp.; *O. pes-corvi* Le Conte, noted on Ocracoke Island by Kearney ('Ecology', p. 317), see Wells, *Natural gardens,* p. 365). There are few references in the early narratives to its appearance east of the Mississippi (Swanton, *Indians,* p. 272; cp. Strachey, *Hist. of Travell,* p. 120).

& bignesse of English peares, but that they are of a perfect red colour as well within as without. They grow on a plant whose leaues are verie thicke and full of prickles as sharpe as needles. Some that haue bin in the Indies, where they haue seen that kind of red die of great [D 1 v.] price, which is called Cochinile, to grow, doe describe his plant right like vnto this of *Metaquesúnnauk* but whether it be the true cochinile or a bastard or wilde kinde, it cannot yet be certified, seeing that also as I heard, Cochinile is not of the fruite but found on the leaues of the plant; which leaues for such matter we haue not so specially obserued.[1]

Grapes[2] there are of two sorts which I mentioned in the marchantable commodities.

Straberies[3] there are as good & as great as those which we haue in our English gardens.

[1] Hakluyt adds in the margin in 1600: 'There are iii kinds of Tunas whereof that which beareth no fruit bringeth forth the Cochinillo.' He, and his cousin, had long been gathering information and rumours about cochineal: 'A singuler commoditie for dyenge of englishe clothe' as it was described in 1585 (Taylor, *Hakluyts*, II, 232, see also pp. 323, 332, 502; *Principal navigations*, VII, 247; IX, 358, 360, 363–7). By 1600 he knew it to be associated with a cactus. Samuel Champlain was the first non-Spaniard to sketch the plant in Mexico ('Brief narrative, 1599–1601', in *Works* (Champlain Soc., n.s., 1922), I (i), 43; I (ii), pl. XXXI), but his illustration bears no resemblance to the Nopal Cactus (*Nopalea coccinellifera* Salm-Dyck of Mexico and Central America), host of the parasitic scale-insect the crushed body of which is cochineal. The natural monopoly was well-maintained by the Spaniards who kept the outside world largely ignorant of the true nature of the product (see Raymond L. Lee, 'Cochineal production and trade in New Spain', in *The Americas* (1947–8), pp. 458–63, and 'American cochineal in European commerce, 1526–1625', in *Journal of Modern History*, XXIII (1951), 205–24). Hariot was, in some respects, on the right track, but a long way from Mexico! Porcher, in 1869, could still write of the Prickly Pear: 'Its cultivation has been recommended on account of the cochineal insect, which is said to feed on it' (*Resources*, p. 20).

[2] See p. 330 above. Lawson (*New voyage* (1709), p. 102) speaks most highly of the winter Fox-grapes: 'These refuse no Ground, swampy or Dry but grow plentifully on the Sand-Hills along the Sea-Coast, and elsewhere and are great bearers.'

[3] Virginia Strawberry (*Fragaria virginiana* Duchesne, also *F. vesca*). In North Carolina they are unlikely to be found near the coast (W. C. C.; Wells, *Natural gardens*, p. 347, cp Lawson, *New voyage* (1709), p. 111; Porcher, *Resources*, p. 173). As they were found in quantity near the southern shore of Chesapeake Bay in 1607 (Smith, *Works*, p. lxiii), it is possible that Hariot is referring to that area in particular, which would indicate that he was a member of the expedition which wintered there in 1585–6, but this, in turn, might imply that he had not returned

'A briefe and true report'

Mulberies,[1] Applecrabs,[2] Hurts or Hurtleberies,[3] such as wee haue in England.

Sacquenúmmener[4] a kinde of berries almost like vnto capres but somewhat greater which grow together in clusters vpon a plant or herbe that is found in shalow waters: being boiled eight or nine houres according to their kind, are very good meat and holesome, otherwise if they be eaten they will make a man for the time franticke or extremely sicke.

There is a kinde of reed which beareth a seed almost like vnto our rie or wheat, & being boiled is good meate.[5]

In our trauailes in some places wee found wilde peaze like vnto ours in England but that they were lesse,[6] which are also good meate.[7]

from there until the strawberries were ripe, unless he brought some plants with him (cp. p. 245).

[1] The Red Mulberry (*Morus rubra*) is abundant near the coast (W. C. C.; Coker and Totten, *Trees of N.C.*, pp. 162–3; Fernald and Kinsey, *Edible plants*, pp. 163–4). Cp. p. 326 above.

[2] Crab-apple (*Pyrus angustifolia*), the only species on the coast (W. C. C.; Fernald and Kinsey, *Edible plants*, p. 229).

[3] The Black Huckleberry (*Gaylussacia* spp.), Squaw Huckleberry (*Polycodium* spp.), and Blueberry or Cranberry (*Vaccinium* spp.) are probably intended (W. C. C.; Porcher, *Resources*, p. 421).

[4] 'Sacquenummener' (Hakluyt (1589), p. 756; III (1600), 273). They have not been identified. Dr W. C. Coker suggests as a possibility the Pepper-vine (*Ampelopsis arborea* and *A. cordata*) which, however, grows on the edge of, and not in, the water. Swanton (*Indians*, pp. 272, 276) suggests they may well be the berries of the Arrow-arum or Virginia Wake-robin (*Peltranda virginica*), the root of which was known as *Coscushaw* (p. 349, n. 3 above; cp. Smith, *Works*, p. 58; Strachey, *Hist. of travell*, p. 120).

[5] Wild Rice (*Zizania aquatica*) was widely used by the Indians (Fernald and Kinsey, *Edible plants*, pp. 102–5; Porcher, *Resources*, pp. 677–8), but it is scarce in North Carolina and is therefore only possible, not probable, here. Alternatively the seed of some form of salt-water marsh grass or of cane may be meant (cp. Swanton, *Indians*, pp. 272, 276; J. Bartram, 'Diary of a journey through the Carolinas, Georgia, and Florida, 1765–66', ed. F. Harper, in *Trans. Amer. Phil. Soc.*, n.s., XXXIII (1942), 53, comparing *Spartina alterniflora* with Wild Rice; Smith, *Works*, p. 58; Strachey, *Hist. of travell*, p. 120).

[6] Few wild peas in this area are of a size worth eating. It is just possible that the Beach Pea (*Lathyrus japonicus* or *maritimus*) is meant (W. C. C.; Fernald and Kinsey, *Edible plants*, pp. 251–2).

[7] L'Écluse describes and illustrates (*Exoticorum*, pp. 30–1, 70–1) two fruits which came, he believed, from Virginia. Mr A. H. G. Alston identifies the

Of a kinde of fruite or berrie in forme of Acornes.

There is a kind of berrie or acorne, of which there are fiue sorts that grow on seueral kinds of trees;[1] the one is called *Sagatémener*, the second *Osámener*, the third *Pummuckóner*. These kind of acorns they vse to drie vpon hurdles made of reeds[2] with fire vnderneath almost after the maner as we dry malt in England. When they are [D2] to be vsed they first water them vntil they be soft & then being sod they make a good victual, either to eate so simply, or els being also pounded, to make loaues or lumpes of bread. These be also the three kinds of which, I said before, the inhabitants vsed to make sweet oyle.

Another sort is called *Sapúmmener*, which being boiled or parched doth eate and taste like vnto chestnuts. They sometime also make bread of this sort.

second, 'Lobus ἐχινώδης' (sent by James Garet or Hugh Morgan), as the Nickar Nut, *Caesalpina bonduc* (Linn.) Roxb., of the West Indies (cp. p. 340, n. 1 above); but the first 'Fructus reticulato corio constans' (sent by Richard Garth 'pro officulo magni cujusdam fructus in Wingandecaow sive Virginia nascentis, ut adscriptum erat') appears to be more like a mango than a North American fruit.

[1] These nuts were not necessarily from the oak alone and may include the Chinquapin (already covered, however, with some probability, p. 350 n. 5 above), and the Hazel-nut, but probably neither Walnut nor Hickory (p. 351 n. 1). Yet it is possible to suggest sufficient varieties of acorns from oaks with a considerable variety of foliage. The Live Oak (*Quercus virginianus*) is the commonest on Roanoke Island and the Carolina Banks (Kearney, 'Ecology', p. 272, found it the sole representative on Ocracoke Island): its acorns vary from sweetish to rather bitter. The Post Oaks (*Q. margaretta* and *Q. stellata*), the White Oak (*Q. alba*) and the Basket Oak (*Q. michauxii*) yield reasonably sweet acorns. L'Écluse (*Exoticorum*, p. 43) notes a large specimen said to have been brought from Virginia, which he regards as Hariot's 'Mangummenauck'. Mr A. H. G. Alston regards the calix he illustrates as that from *Q. michauxii* (cp. C. S. Sargent, *The silva of North America*, VIII (1895), 68, where the edibility of the acorn is stressed), leaving *Sapúmmener* as possibly the acorn of the Swamp Chestnut Oak (*Q. prunus*) or a chinquapin. The Willow and Water Oaks (*Q. phellos* and *Q. nigra*), common on the coastlands, have both bitter acorns (W. C. C.; Coker and Totten, *Trees of N.C.*, pp. 107–50). The Indian names do not help greatly (pp. 893–5 below): all are printed by Hakluyt without accents.

[2] The hurdle was doubtless similar to that used for grilling fish (White, no. 47, see pp. 435–7 below), but with much less space between the slats.

The fifth sort is called *Mangúmmenauk*, and is the acorne of their kinde of oake, the which beeing dried after the maner of the first sortes, and afterward watered they boile them, & their seruants or sometime the chiefe themselues, either for variety or for want of bread, doe eate them with their fish or flesh.[1]

Of Beastes.

Deare,[2] in some places there are great store: neere vnto the Sea coast they are of the ordinarie bignes as[3] ours in England, & some lesse: but further vp into the countrey where there is better feed[4] they are greater: they differ from ours onely in this, their tailes are longer and the snags of their hornes looke backward.

Conies, Those that we haue seen & al that we can heare of are of a grey colour like vnto hares:[5] in some places there are such plentie that all the people of some townes make them mantles of the furre or flue of the skinnes of those they[6] vsually take.

Saquénuckot & *Maquówoc*; two kinds of small beastes greater then conies[7] which are very good meat. We neuer tooke any of

---

[1] The Indian uses, especially for vegetable fats, are discussed in Fernald and Kinsey, *Edible plants*, pp. 159–61, and H. B. Battle, 'The domestic use of oil among the southern aborigines', in *American Anthropologist*, n.s., XXIV (1922), 171–82.

[2] Virginia White-tailed Deer (*Odocoileus virginianus*) (*Mammals of N.C.*, pt. 16).

[3] 'of' (Hakluyt, III (1600), 273).

[4] 'food' (Hakluyt (1589), p. 756; III (1600), 273). Hariot's statement may be correct, but it is possible that he had heard of the Elk (*Cervus canadensis*), which may then have ranged as far south as North Carolina (*Mammals of N.C.*, pt. 16).

[5] The two species common on and near the coast are the Marsh Rabbit (*Sylvilagus palustris*), probably the 'hare' of Barlowe (p. 115 above), and the Common Cottontail (*S. floridanus*) (*Mammals of N.C.*, pt. 15).

[6] 'which they' (Hakluyt, III (1600), 273). For the rabbit-skin mantles cp. White, no. 44 (see p. 431 below).

[7] Having already eliminated the Otter and the Marten (p. 430 above) these two must belong to the following group: Musk Rat (*Ondatra zibethica*), Mink (*Mustela vison*), Common Raccoon (*Procyon lotor*), Beaver (*Castor canadensis*), Common Opossum (*Didelphys virginianus*), all of which are found in the coastlands (*Mammals of N.C.*, pts. 1, 7, 6, 9, 13,). The first two appear slightly more probable (cp. p. 331 above), but the last three are recorded by Lawson as having been eaten in North Carolina (see Swanton, *Indians*, p. 277).

them our selues but sometime eate of such as the inhabitants had taken & brought vnto vs.

Squirels, which are of a grey colour,[1] we haue take*n* and eate*n*. [D 2 v.] Beares[2] which are all of[3] blacke colour. The beares of this countrey are good meat; the inhabitants in time of winter do vse to take & eate manie, so also sometime did wee. They are taken commonlie in this sort. In some Ilands or places where they are, being hunted for, as soone as they haue spiall of a man they presently run awaie, & then being chased they clime and get vp the next tree they can, from whence with arrowes they are shot downe starke dead, or with those wounds that they may after easily be killed;[4] we sometime shotte them downe with our calleuers.

I haue the names of eight & twenty seuerall sortes of beasts which I haue heard of to be here and there dispersed in the countrie, especially in the maine: of which there are only twelue kinds that we haue yet discouered,[5] & of those that be good meat we

[1] Grey Squirrel (*Sciurus carolinensis*). The Fox Squirrel (*S. niger*) and the Common Flying Squirrel (*Glaucomys volans*) are also found in the coastal areas (*Mammals of N.C.*, pt. 10).

[2] Black Bear (*Ursus americanus*), see p. 330 above, which remained plentiful in the Great Dismal Swamp, north of Albemarle Sound, until recent years.

[3] 'are of' (Hakluyt, III (1600), 274).

[4] Swanton comments (*Indians*, pp. 321-4) on the few descriptions of bear-hunting that have survived in the south-east. Hariot's appears to be the only one among the early narratives of hunting the bear in the open, the others being of the taking of bears from their winter quarters. There is no record of the bear ceremonials, if any, used by the North Carolina Algonkians (cp. Flannery, *Analysis*, nos. 282-4).

[5] The list is now lost (cp. pp. 358, 360, 366): to the six just mentioned, of which he gives the Indian names for two only, are to be added his otter, marten, 'ciuet cattes' (pp. 330-1 above), 'Luzarnes', 'Lyon', bison, and wolf (or dog) (below, p. 357), so making thirteen. Sixteen more, if there were no duplicates among the Indian names (or misunderstandings), would comprise virtually all the larger mammals of the area. An Algonkian Indian burial, likely to be of the sixteenth or seventeenth century, found on the bank of the Chowan River (Bertie co., east of Colerain) in July 1948, produced a group of 27 drilled animal teeth which had apparently formed a necklace. They comprised 18 Grey Wolf (*Canis lupus lycaon* Schreber), 3 Coyote (*Canis latrans*, not found east of the Alleghenies and therefore acquired by trade), 2 Raccoon, 2 Bear, 1 Puma

know only them before mentioned. The inhabitants sometime kill the Lyon,[1] and eat him: and we somtime as they came to our hands of[2] their Wolues or woluish Dogges,[3] which I haue not set downe for good meat, least that some would vnderstand my iudgement therein to be more simple then needeth, although I could alleage the difference in taste of those kindes from ours, which by some of our company haue beene experimented in both.[4]

(*Felis concolor cougar*) and 1 Red Fox (*Vulpes fulvus*, frequently thought to have been introduced from Europe). Together they indicate most of the larger animals killed by the Indians. I am indebted to Mr Harry T. Davis for the information about this find.

To the animals mentioned by Hariot by name it is possible to add another. The Bison was known in central North Carolina at this time and it is possible that the coastal Indians had some buffalo-skins acquired by trade. Lawson (*A new voyage* (1709), p. 115) says: 'He seldom appears amongst the English Inhabitants...yet I have known some killed in the Hilly Part of Cape-Fair River.' (See Douglas L. Rights, 'The buffalo in North Carolina', in *North Carolina Hist. Rev.*, IX (1932), 242–9; William Byrd, *Histories of the dividing line* (1929), pp. 168–9; and p. 100 above.)

[1] American Panther, Cougar, or Puma (*Felis concolor cougar*), now extinct in this area (*Mammals of N.C.*, pt. 8).

[2] Hariot's meaning is not quite clear, but it is probable that his 'of' is superfluous, and that he is proceeding directly from his discussion of lion-eating by the Indians to that of dog-eating by the settlers. Opinions vary as to how far the domesticated dogs (little is known of their species) were used for hunting in the south-east (Swanton, *Indians*, pp. 324, 344–6). White's drawing of Pomeiooc (no. 33, see p. 415 below) gives the only early picture of one of these dogs. The scale is very small, but it is clearly a medium-sized animal with a pointed nose and is, apparently, short-haired (cp. Smith, *Works*, p. 60; Strachey, *Hist. of travell*, pp. 125–6).

[3] Hariot does not say, specifically, that the Indians ate their dogs but the eating of them by the settlers would strongly suggest that they did. If so, Dr Flannery (*Analysis*, pp. 32–4) might wish to alter her diagnosis of dog-eating as a specifically northern coastal Algonkian trait.

[4] The reference is, of course, to the eating of the two English bull-mastiffs, by Lane's men when on their Roanoke River expedition (pp. 267, 272 above).

Of Foule.

Turkie cockes and Turkie hennes:[1] Stockdoues:[2] Partridges: Cranes:[3] Hernes:[4] & in Winter great store of Swannes[5] & Geese.[6] Of al sorts of fowle I haue the names in the countrie language of fourescore and sixe[7] of which number besides those that be named, we haue taken, eaten, & haue the pictures as they were there drawne with the names of the inhabitaunts of seuerall strange sorts of [D3] water foule eight,[8] and seuenteene kinds more of land foul,[9]

[1] The absence of any illustration of the Turkey, *Meleagris galloparvo*, from the surviving White drawings is curious. Le Moyne was the first to illustrate it (*America*, pt. ii, pl. 5; Lorant, *New world*, p. 45; E. G. Allen, 'The history of American ornithology before Audubon', in *Trans. American Phil. Soc.*, n.s., xLII, 441; A. H. Wright, 'Early records of the wild turkey', in *The Auk*, XXXI, 334, 463; XXXII, 61, 207, 348).

[2] Eastern Mourning Dove, *Zenaidura macrona carolinensis* Linn. (*Birds of N.C.*, no. 94). This is not illustrated by White. The Mourning Dove first appeared in U. Aldrovandi, *Ornithologia*, (1599) (cp. Allen, op. cit. p. 405).

[3] The Florida sub-species of the Sandhill Crane, *Megalornis mexicana*, now only an occasional visitor to the North Carolina coastlands from the south. For the White drawing (reproduced in Allen, op. cit. as fig. 17, pp. 445–6) see pp. 96, 447 below.

[4] The regular summer visitors to the coast, none of them illustrated by White, are now the Louisiana Heron, *Hydranassa tricolor ruficollis* Gosse; the Little Blue Heron, *Florida caerulea caerulea* Linn.; the Eastern Green Heron, *Butorides virescens virescens* Linn.; the Black-crowned Night Heron, *Nycticorax hoactli* Gmelin; and the Yellow-crowned Night Heron, *Nyctanassa violacea violacea* Linn. (*Birds of N.C.*, nos. 23–7).

[5] Formerly the Trumpeter Swan appears to have been common (see the White drawing discussed on p. 448 below), but now it is the Whistling Swan, *Cygnus columbianus* Ord (*Birds of N.C.*, no. 35), which gathers in large flocks on the sounds and in Chesapeake Bay in winter.

[6] None of the geese is illustrated by White. The present-day winter visitors are the Common Canada Goose, *Branta canadensis canadensis* Linn.; American Brant, *Branta bernicla hrota* Muller; and the Greater Snow Goose, *Chen hyperborea atlantica* Pallas (*Birds of N.C.*, nos. 26, 38, 42).

[7] This list is now, of course, lost, but twenty-one Indian bird-names are preserved in White's pictures and possibly a few more, indirectly, in Topsell's list (cp. pp. 448–53 below).

[8] Nine are preserved in the copies of White drawings nos. 56–64, see pp. 447–8 below.

[9] Here there are nineteen White drawings but four lack the Indian names, nos. 65–83, see pp. 449–53 below.

although wee haue seene and eaten of many more, which for want of leasure there for the purpose coulde not bee pictured: and after wee are better furnished and stored vpon further discouery, with their strange beastes, fishe, trees, plants, and hearbes, they shalbe also published.[1]

There are also Parats,[2] Faulcons,[3] & Marlin haukes,[4] which although with vs they bee not vsed for meate, yet for other causes I thought good to mention.

Of Fishe.

For foure monethes of the yeere, February, March, Aprill and May, there are plentie of Sturgeons.[5] And also in the same monethes of Herrings,[6] some of the ordinary bignesse as ours in England, but the most part farre greater, of eighteene, twentie inches, and some two foote in length and better; both these kindes of fishe in those monethes are most plentifull, and in best season, which wee found to bee most delicate and pleasaunt meate.

[1] This promise of publication shows that Hariot contemplated not only a chronicle (see p. 387), but an illustrated account of his survey of American natural history. It was only his notes dealing with the Indians which were, in fact, published by De Bry (cp. pp. 413–44).

[2] The Carolina Paroquet, *Conuropsis carolinensis carolinensis*, is not, unforfunately, illustrated by White. It was formerly common in summer, but is believed to have become extinct in Florida since 1904 (*Birds of N.C.*, no. 176; A. H. Wright, 'Early records of the Carolina Paroquet', in *The Auk*, XXIX (1910–11), 343–63; Byrd, *Histories of the dividing line*, p. 94).

[3] The Duck Hawk, *Falco peregrinus anatum* Bonaparte (*Birds of N.C.*, no. 90). It is almost identical with the European Peregrine Falcon. It was noted, with the Pigeon Hawk following, by Strachey, *Hist. of travell*, p. 126; Allen, in *Trans. American Phil. Soc.*, n.s., XLI, 450.

[4] Eastern Pigeon Hawk, or American Merlin, *Falco columbarius columbarius* Linn. (*Birds of N.C.*, no. 91). Neither hawk is illustrated by White.

[5] White drew the sturgeon, no. 84 (see p. 453 below).

[6] The Sea Herring is not significant off North Carolina, but several species of the Alewife or River Herring contribute extensively to the fisheries in the Sounds and rivers. They are the Hickory Shad, *Pomolobus mediocris* Mitchill; Branch Herring (this is apparently the one illustrated by White, no. 85, see p. 453 below); Glut Herring, *Pomolobus aestivalis* Mitchill; and Shad, *Alosa sapidissima* Wilson, the most important food fish (*Fishes of N.C.*, nos. 107–10). The fish in the Indian canoe in the fishing scene, no. 46 (see p. 434) may well be shad.

There are also Troutes:[1] Porpoises:[2] Rayes:[3] Oldwiues:[4] Mullets:[5] Plaice:[6] and very many other sortes of excellent good fish, which we haue taken & eaten, whose names I know not but in the countrey language;[7] we haue of twelue sorts more the pictures[8] as they were drawn in the countrey with their names.[9]

The inhabitants vse to take the*m* two maner of wayes,[10] the one is by a kinde of wear made of reedes which in that countrey are very strong.[11] The other way, which is more strange, is with poles made sharpe at one ende, by shooting them into the fish after the maner as Irishmen cast dartes; either as they are rowing in their boats or els as [D 3 v.] they are wading in the shallowes for the purpose.[12]

[1] Brook Trout, *Salvelinus fontinalis* Mitchill (C. M. Breder, *Field book of marine fishes of the Atlantic coast* (1929), p. 74).

[2] By porpoises he is most likely to have meant the Bottle-nosed Dolphin, *Tursiops truncatus* Montagu (*Mammals of N.C.*, pt. 17).

[3] Eleven species of Rays and Skate are found off North Carolina (*Fishes of N.C.*, pp. 40–8). A sting-ray and a skate were included in White's fishing scene, no. 46 (see pp. 433–4): none is illustrated separately.

[4] The Sheepshead Bream (no. 86 (see p. 453 below).

[5] The Striped (Grey) Mullet was illustrated by White, no. 87 (see p. 454 below).

[6] Eleven species of Flounders and Soles are found off North Carolina (*Fishes of N.C.*, pp. 385–98): the Summer Flounder (Plaice), *Paralichthys dentatus* Linn. (ibid., no. 332); the Southern Flounder (apparently that illustrated by White, no. 88 (see p. 454 below)); and the Winter Flounder (Common Flat-fish), *Pseudopleuronectes americanus* Walbaum (ibid., no. 336) are the most common.

[7] No general list has survived (see pp. 356, 358 above).

[8] 'the pictures of twelue sorts more' (Hakluyt, III (1600), 274).

[9] There are nine additional fish-drawings by White with Indian names, nos. 89–95, 97–8 (see pp. 454–5 below), and three included in this group which have not Indian names, nos. 96–7, 100 (see pp. 455–6).

[10] Hakluyt added in the margin (III (1600), 274): 'In the gulfe of Califormia [California] they vse the like fishing.' This information was obtained by him either from some member of Drake's expedition of 1577–80 or from a Spanish source.

[11] The fish-weirs made of cane stakes (*Arundinaria tecta*) are shown in White's drawing no. 46 (see pp. 433–5, and cp. p. 365).

[12] The long throwing darts were the characteristic weapon of the Irish kern, who made up the native light infantry in Ireland. Hariot may have seen them in Ireland before he wrote this tract (but in that case he must have spent some time

There are also in many places plentie of these kindes which follow.
Sea crabbes, such as we haue in England.[1]

Oysters, some very great, and some small; some rounde and
some of a long shape: They are founde both in salt water and
brackish, and those that we had out of salt water are far better
than the other, as in our owne countrey.[2]

Also Muscles:[3] Scalopes:[4] Periwinkles:[5] and Creuises.[6]

Seékanauk, a kinde of crustie shel fishe[7] which is good meate

there between July 1586 and February 1588, which is not unlikely, since he had
settled at Molana Abbey by May 1589), or else he obtained the comparison from
Lane or some of his Irish followers (cp. pp. 195, 287). The Indians are shown using
them in White's drawing no. 46. The Indians of Eastern Shore Virginia, Strachey
and Smith tell us, used 'staves, like vnto iauelins, headed with bone; with these
they dart fish, swymming in the water'. These were evidently the same (Smith,
Works, p. 69; Strachey, *Hist. of travell*, p. 82; cp. Swanton, *Indians*, pp. 337–9;
Flannery, *Analysis*, no. 24; pp. 333–5). They were not unlike the 'harping yron'
or 'fisgig' used on Drake's voyage of 1585–6 and by Davis in 1585 (p. 411 below;
Principal navigations, VII, 282–3), except that the latter had metal, and much more
substantial, heads. 10 ft. long light fishing darts (distinct from glaives, broad,
leaf-bladed fish-spears) were used in the Fens until the present century (J. W. Day,
'Fen tigers', in *Country Life*, Christmas 1952, pp. 48–9).

[1] White includes only the King-crab in his fishing scene, no. 46 (see p. 434
below), together with two West Indian hermit crabs, a West Indian land-crab
being added in De Bry's engraving (p. 434). For the crabs of this coast see Harden
Taylor [etc.], *Survey of marine fisheries of North Carolina* (1951), pp. 205–18.

[2] Oysters (*Ostrea virginica*) made up a substantial part of the Indians' food.
They yield fair pearls but not frequently. Hariot may here be including the
smaller clams with oysters.

[3] The fresh-water Mussel, *Unio complanatus*, was said by Barlowe (p. 110 above)
to produce good pearls (cp. Strachey, *Hist. of travell*, p. 128). Nowadays the shells
of this mussel on the Atlantic slope are thin and do not produce good quality
nacre, still less pearls (cp. R. E. Coker, 'The natural history and propagation of
fresh-water mussels', in *Bulletin of U.S. Bureau of Fisheries*, XXXVII (1922) [67th
Congr., 2nd Sess. Ho. Doc. 140]). Hariot would probably include the sea
Mussel, *Mytilus edulis*, also.

[4] For scallops (clams, etc.) of this coast see Harden Taylor, op. cit. pp. 169–78.

[5] Periwinkle, *Littorina littoralis*. That housing a hermit-crab in White's fishing
drawing is a West Indian specimen (no. 46, see p. 434 below).

[6] This probably includes the fresh-water Crayfish, *Astacus fluviatilis*. As
'Creuices', however, Hariot would include, according to the contemporary
meaning of the word, lobsters as well.

[7] This is the first description of the King-crab, *Limulus polyphemus*, as White's,
in the fishing scene, no. 46 (see pp. 433–4 below), is the first drawing.

about a foote in breadth, hauing a crustie tayle,[1] many legges like a crab; and her eyes in her backe. They are found in shallowes of salt waters, and sometime on the shoare.

There are many Tortoyses both of lande and sea kinde,[2] their backes & bellies are shelled very thicke; their head, feete, and taile, which are in appearance, seeme ougly as though they were members of a serpent or venemous:[3] but notwithstanding they are very good meate, as also their egges. Some haue bene founde of a yard in bredth and better.

And thus haue I made relation of all sortes of victuall that we fed vpon for the time we were in Virginia, as also the inhabitants themselues,[4] as farre foorth as I knowe and can remember or that are specially worthy to bee remembred.

[D4] The third and last part of such other thinges as is behoofull[5] for those which shall plant and inhabit to know of; with a description of the nature and manners of the people of the countrey.

---

[1] The long sword-shaped tail-spine which was used by the Indians to tip their fish-spears in this area (cp. p. 435, n. 1 below). Lescarbot (*Histoire de la Nouvelle France*, III (Champlain Soc. XI, 1914), 191, 407) and Champlain (*Works* (Champlain Soc. n.s. I, III, 1922 seq.), I (i), 358; III, pl. X) noted arrowheads made from the tail of a crab called by the Indians *sicnau* or *sigenoc*, which is apparently the same.

[2] Land Turtles identified up to 1926 in those parts of North Carolina which Hariot saw, comprise: (1) Snapping Turtle (*Chelydra serpentina*); (2) Mud Turtle (*Kinosternon subrubrum*); (3) Musk Turtle (*Sternotherus odoratus*); (4) Box Turtle (*Terrapene carolina carolina*), White's drawing being no. 102, see p. 456; (5) Painted Terrapin (*Chrysemys picta*); (6) Chicken Turtle (*Dierochelys reticularia*); (7) Florida Terrapin (*Pseudemys concinna*); (8) Yellow-bellied Terrapin (*P. scripta*); (9) Diamond-backed Terrapin (*Malaclemys terrapin*), White's drawing being no. 103, see p. 457. To them it may be possible to add a few species from Chesapeake Bay. The Sea Turtles found off the Carolina Banks are (1) Leather-back Turtle (*Dermochelys coricea*); (2) Atlantic Loggerhead Sea Turtle (*Caretta caretta caretta*), White's drawing being no. 101, see p. 456; (3) Kemp's Loggerhead (*C. kempi*); (4) Green Sea Turtle (*Chelonia mydas*) (*Amphibians and reptiles of N.C.*, pp. 89–92).

[3] 'or venimous beasts;' (Hakluyt (1589), p. 757; III (1600), 274). Hariot's meaning is that they have the appearance of some kinds of snakes.

[4] Swanton (*Indians*, pp. 244–310) gives a full account of the food resources of the south-eastern Indians. From his tables (pp. 293–5) a substantial list of possible additions could be made to the products mentioned by Hariot.

[5] 'things as are behouefull' (Hakluyt (1589), p. 758; III (1600), 275), i.e. such things as are fitting or suitable for those who shall plant.

Of commodities for building and other necessary vses.[1]

Those other things which I am more to make rehearsall of, are such as concerne building, and other mechanicall necessarie vses, as diuers sortes of trees for house & shiptimber,[2] and other vses els: Also lime, stone, and brick, least that being not mentioned some might haue bene doubted of, or by some that are malicious reported the contrary.[3]

Okes,[4] there are as faire, straight, tall, and as good timber as any can be, and also great store, and in some places very great.

Walnut trees,[5] as I haue saide before very many, some haue bene seen excellent faire timber of foure & fiue fadome, & aboue fourescore foote streight without bough.

Firre trees[6] fit for masts of ships, some very tall & great.

Rakíock,[7] a kinde of trees so called that are sweet wood of which the inhabitants that were neere vnto vs doe commonly make their

[1] In this section Hariot is attempting to complete the task of making his treatise serve at the same time as an incentive to new settlers and as a practical guide to those who had already committed themselves to go to America.

[2] It would thus seem that there was some expectation of building shipping on the spot. Small boats and pinnaces suited to the local conditions could most economically have been made in America from the beginning, but, in view of the fear of exhausting home timber supplies current at the time, the creation of a major shipbuilding industry there, capable of relieving pressure on that of England, had been strongly advocated by both Hakluyts (cp. Taylor, *Hakluyts,* II, 317, 322, 331, 337, 340). For the later development of shipbuilding and its effects in denuding the Carolina Banks of trees see *Coastal plain of N.C.,* ed. W. B. Clark (etc.) (Geol. Survey, N.C., III), pp. 31–3; *North Carolina Hist. Rev.,* VI (1929), 398–400; Porcher, *Resources,* p. 348.

[3] 'malitious the contrary reported' (Hakluyt (1589), p. 758; III (1600), 275). This further reply to hostile propaganda (cp. pp. 320–5) has reference to the fact that the only obvious building material was timber. Hariot hoped to counter this view as a misapprehension (cp. pp. 366–8).

[4] See p. 354 above for the principal species of oaks found on or near the coast.

[5] See p. 351 above.

[6] The Loblolly Pine (*Pinus taeda*), Longleaf Pine (*P. palustris*) and Pocoson Pine (*P. serotina*), are the most prominent 'firs' amongst the coastal trees. See also pp. 97, 104.

[7] The Indian word appears to mean 'soft wood'. This is either the Tulip Tree (*Liriodendron tulipifera*) or the White Cypress, a variety of the Swamp Cypress (*Taxodium distichum*), the latter being more durable, the former the more likely

boats or Canoes of the forme of trowes; onely with the helpe of fire, hatchets of stones, and shels; we haue knowen some so great being made in that sort of one tree that they haue carried well xx. men at once, besides much baggage: the timber being great, tal, streight, soft, light, & yet tough enough I thinke (besides other vses) to be fit also for masts of ships.

Cedar,[1] a sweete wood good for seelings, Chests, Boxes, [D4v.] Bedsteedes, Lutes, Virginals, and many things els,[2] as I haue also said before. Some of our company which haue wandered in some places where I haue not bene, haue made certaine affirmation of Cyprus[3] which for such and other excellent vses is also a wood of price and no small estimation.

Maple, and also Wich-hazle,[4] whereof the inhabitants vse to make their bowes.

Holly[5] a necessary thing for the making of birdlime.

to be that shown in De Bry's engraving after White (no. 45, see pp. 432–3 below; also W. C. C.; *Trees of N.C.*, pp. 41–4, 179–80; Porcher, *Resources*, p. 588; Hawks, *Hist. of N.C.*, I, 175; Lawson, *A new voyage* (1709), pp. 96–7). It will be noted above (p. 104) that Barlowe referred to coniferous trees as being used. While it is probable that a number of different trees were utilized the Tulip Tree was both the largest and most easily worked, although it tends to rot and to water-log rather quickly (though cp. Lawson, pp. 93–4). 　 [1] Cp. pp. 329–30 above.
[2] Porcher, *Resources*, pp. 588–9, says the wood is 'aromatic, light, soft, bearing exposure to water and weather and suitable for all kinds of cabinet work'. For the gift of a bed made from cedar, probably from North Carolina, see p. 495. Raleigh's ship, the *Job* was carrying 'Of Cedar wodde xvj tonnes' from Newfoundland or Virginia in 1585 (p. 172 above).
[3] Cp. Barlowe above, p. 95. Hariot's doubt about the identification may have been due to the fact that the Swamp Cypress (*Taxodium distichum*) and Pond Cypress (*T. ascendens*) are not evergreens like the true cypresses (*Cupressus* spp.) which are not found in eastern North America (W. C. C.; *Trees of N.C.*, pp. 41–4).
[4] The Carolina Red Maple (*Acer rubrum*, var. *tridens* Wood) is common in eastern North Carolina, but Witch-hazel (*Hamamelis virginiana*) occurs only as a rather small shrub near the coast (W. C. C.; *Trees of N.C.*, pp. 278–9, 186–7). Swanton (*Indians*, pp. 571–82) collects the references to Indian arrows, showing Witch-hazel to have been a common material, but no other reference to Red Maple being used for this purpose has been found. For the bows see White's drawings nos. 51, 53 (pp. 440–4 below).
[5] The characteristic member of the holly family found on the Carolina Banks is the Yaupon (*Ilex vomitoria*) (but see p. 337 above). The American Holly (*I. opaca*) and, on the mainland, Dahoon Holly (*I. cassine*) also occur. The

Willowes[1] good for the making of weares and weeles to take fish after the English manner,[2] although the inhabitants vse onely reedes,[3] which because they are so strong as also flexible, doe serue for that turne very well and sufficiently.

Beech[4] and Ashe,[5] good for caske, hoopes:[6] and if neede require, plowe work,[7] as also for many things els.

Elme.[8]

Sassafras trees.[9]

Ascopo a kinde of tree very like vnto Lawrell,[10] the barke is hoat[11]

reference to birdlime (not apparently used by the Indians, cp. Swanton, *Indians*, pp. 329–31) suggests that one, or both, of the latter was meant (W. C. C.; *Trees of N.C.*, pp. 265–71; Kearney, 'Ecology', pp. 270–1).

[1] Black Willow (*Salix nigra* and *S. longpipes*) and Harbison's Willow (*S. Harbisonii*) are found in the coastal plain and in the swamps (*Trees of N.C.*, pp. 64–70).

[2] There do not appear to be many contemporary references to English weirs and weels (traps) made from osiers or willow. Mr Clive Gammon has kindly brought the following references to my attention. W. Camden (*Britannia*, trs. P. Holland, Scotland, pp. 17–18) notes how in Galloway they 'take in Weeles and Weere nets…eeles'. Leonard Mascall (*A booke of fishing with hooke and line, and all other instruments thereunto belonging* (1590)) has a woodcut showing an 'otter weele', a trap made from hooped osiers. *A iewell for gentry* (*c.* 1630, 'A briefe Treatise of Fishing', pp. 3–6) describes various fixed and movable nets requiring hoops, etc. of wood. *Barker's delight* (1653) says that they have in Shropshire 'a little weele made of wicker to carry their fish so that they will bring home all their fish alive'. Cp. also pp. 276, 384.

[3] The reed was the Cane (*Arundinaria macrosperma*, being the large variety and *A. tecta* the small), which is the characteristic plant of the swamp forests and bogs (W. C. C.; Wells, *Natural gardens*, pp. 60–1; Porcher, *Resources*, pp. 682–3). For the fish-weirs made by the Indians see White, no. 46 (pp. 433–5 below); Flannery, *Analysis*, pp. 17, 178; Swanton, *Indians*, pp. 333–5; Beverley, *History and present state* (1947), p. 148—a good description; p. 360 above.

[4] Beech (*Fagus grandifolia*) (*Trees of N.C.*, p. 101).

[5] The Water Ash (*Fraxinus americana*) is the species most usual near the coast (W. C. C.; *Trees of N.C.*, pp. 358–62).

[6] Hakluyt corrects to 'caske hoopes' (1589), p. 758, and 'caske-hoopes', III (1600), 275.

[7] For making the wooden parts of ploughs, for which timber from these trees was used in England.

[8] White Elm (*Ulmus americanus*), though it is not found right on the coast (W. C. C.; *Trees of N.C.*, pp. 154–6).　　　　[9] See p. 329.

[10] For the word see p. 885 below. It is to be identified with the Sweet Bay (*Magnolia virginiana*), and cp. Porcher, *Resources*, pp. 36–41.

[11] Corrected to 'hot', Hakluyt (1589), p. 758; III (1600), 275.

in taste and spicie, it is very like to that tree which Monardus
describeth to be Cassia Lignea of the West Indies.[1]

There are many other strange trees whose names I know not
but in the Virginian language,[2] of which I am not nowe able,
neither is it so conuenient for the present to trouble you with
particular relation: seeing that for timber and other necessary
vses, I haue named sufficient. And of many of the rest but that
they may be applied to good vse, I know no cause to doubt.

Now for Stone, Bricke and Lime, thus it is. Neere vnto the
Sea coast where wee dwelt, there are no kinde of stones to bee
found (except a fewe small pebbles about foure miles off)[3] but
such as haue bene brought from far [E1] ther out of the maine.
In some of our voiages wee haue seene diuers hard raggie stones,
great pebbles,[4] and a kinde of gray stone like vnto marble, of
which the inhabitants make their hatchets to cleeue wood.[5] Vpon
inquirie wee heard that a little further vp into the Countrey were
of all sortes verie many, although of Quarries they are ignorant,
neither haue they vse of any store whereupon they should haue

---

[1] 'Monardes' (idem). *Joyfull newes*, ed. Gaselee, I, 28–33, deals mainly with
the infusion made from *Lignum vitae* which was used as a specific against syphilis.
It had been known in England since at least 1568 (Raven, *English naturalists*,
p. 126). This provides clear evidence that Hariot used Monardes (cp. pp. 329,
347–8). It is highly probable that he had a copy of *Joyfull newes* with him at
Roanoke Island.   [2] We have lost all these names.

[3] I.e. four miles from the site of the fort and settlement on Roanoke Island.
These are most likely to have been carried by the current from Albemarle Sound
and deposited on or near Colington Island.

[4] Consolidated rock is rare throughout the coastal plain, beyond which Lane
and Hariot did not penetrate. It is possible, but unlikely, that some traces of the
Trent 'limestone' (Miocene), a consolidated shell-rock now used as building
stone, was seen during Grenville's expedition in 1585 (cp. Richards, in *Trans.
Amer. Phil. Soc.*, n.s., XL, 19, 51). Glacial erratics and an occasional boulder
carried down by the Roanoke River complete the possible local resources, unless
semi-consolidated shell formations (coquina) are included.

[5] The only stone artifact so far found at the fort site by Mr Harrington is a
crude stone axe which apparently antedates the English settlement ('Report'
(1950), p. 7; p. 908 below). Little is known, from examples, of the axes of this
region (cp. Swanton, *Indians*, pp. 544–5). It is not even certain whether it was the
ready-made axe or the stone which was imported from the interior. The absence
of stone pipes and arrow-heads may be noted as showing the scarcity of stone.

occasion to seeke any. For if euerie housholde baue[1] one or two to cracke Nuttes,[2] grinde shelles,[3] whet copper,[4] and sometimes other stones for hatchets, they haue enough: neither vse they any digging, but onely for graues about three foote deepe:[5] and therefore no marualle that they know neither Quarries, nor lime stones, which both may bee in places neerer then they wot of.[6]

In the meane time vntill there be discouery of sufficient store in some place or other conuenient, the want of you which are and shalbe the planters therein[7] may be as well supplied by Bricke: for the making whereof in diuers places of the countrey there is clay both excellent good, and plentie;[8] and also by lime made of Oister shels, and of others burnt,[9] after the maner as they vse in

[1] 'baue' corrected to 'haue' in De Bry (1590), as by Hakluyt.

[2] The mortar-stones, traded from the interior, were among the most important possessions of a household. On them corn was ground and paint prepared—apart from the uses mentioned by Hariot (Swanton, *Indians*, pp. 243, 548).

[3] Sharp-edged shells were used as knives and scrapers (cp. pp. 432–3 below).

[4] The whetting of copper would suggest that it was used for tools and weapons, and that it was annealed to make it hard enough for such purposes (cp. p. 274). Other references are to its use for ornaments (e.g. pp. 438, 440–1), and it may be that the English taught the Indians to develop their use of copper in this way.

[5] Inhumation was the common method of burial, with the preservation of the bones of chiefs in special ossuaries, both among the North Carolina and Virginia Algonkians (cp. Swanton, *Indians*, pp. 718–19; Smith, *Works*, p. 75). Hariot is the only early writer to mention the depth of the graves. There has not been so far any systematic excavation of burial-places in the North Carolina coastlands, but a casual burial on the Chowan River is mentioned above (pp. 356–7, and cp. p. 901 below).

[6] This sounds improbable unless the Trent limestone of the Neuse River is meant (cp. p. 366).

[7] This makes a more direct appeal than heretofore to intending planters. It is remarkable that Hariot in this section should stress the circumstances in and near Roanoke Island rather than those of the Chesapeake Bay (cp. pp. 457–8, 503–4).

[8] There were many types of suitable clay available and it is probable that brick was made during the 1585–6 settlement, but the evidence is not conclusive (cp. pp. 902, 904, 908 below).

[9] For mortar and plaster. The local source of supply down to the middle of the nineteenth century at least was the deep middens, mainly of oyster-shells, left by the Indians (cp. Hawks, *Hist. of N.C.*, 1 (1857), 177; Talcott Williams, 'The surroundings and site of Raleigh's colony', in American Hist. Ass., *Annual rep. 1895*, p. 54).

the Iles of Tenet and Shepy,[1] and also in diuers other places of England: Which kinde of lime is well knowne to bee as good as any other. And of Oister shels there is plentie enough: for besides diuers other particular places where are abundance, there is one shallowe sounde along the coast, where for the space of many miles together in length, and two or three miles in breadth, the grounde is nothing els beeing but halfe a foote or a foote vnder water for the most part.[2]

Thus much can I say furthermore of stones, that about 120. miles from our fort neere the water in the side [E1 v.] of a hill was found by a Gentleman of our company, a great veine of hard ragge stones, which I thought good to remember vnto you.[3]

Of the nature and manners of the people.

It resteth I speake a word or two of the naturall inhabitants, their natures and maners,[4] leauing large discourse thereof vntil time more conuenient hereafter:[5] nowe onely so farre foorth, as that you may know, how that they in respect of troubling our inhabiting and planting, are not to be feared,[6] but that they shall haue cause both to feare and loue vs, that shall inhabite with them.

They are a people clothed with loose mantles made of Deere skins,[7] & aprons of the same rounde about their middles;[8] all els

---

[1] Thanet and Sheppey, both in Kent.

[2] This is clearly a natural deposit. There are shell-beds in many parts of the sounds, and at various depths, but the extent appears exaggerated.

[3] Cp. p. 366 n. 4 above.

[4] It is suggested above (p. 37) that Hariot was probably put to learn the Indian language and to teach English to the two men taken in 1584. His special assignment in 1585-6 was Indian affairs (p. 321) and this probably involved doing some interpreting.

[5] The only opportunity he had was in the notes to De Bry's engravings of White's drawings (pp. 413-44 below) which he wrote in Latin. In their English version, at least, they are somewhat colourless and display a certain unsureness of touch, though they are useful on artifacts and customs.

[6] Part of his reassurance campaign (cp. pp. 319-25 above).

[7] White, nos. 35, 41-3 (see pp. 418-19, 427, 429-30 below). Cp. no. 44, p. 431.

[8] We can distinguish in White (a) an apron-skirt of fringed skin covering from waist to knees and used by women and men, nos. 34, 37, 41-2, 49-51, 53 (see

naked; of such a difference of statures onely as wee in England, hauing no edge tooles or weapons of yron or steele to offend vs withall, neither knowe they how to make any:[1] those weapons y[t] they haue, are onlie bowes made of Witch hazle,[2] & arrowes of reeds,[3] flat edged truncheons also of wood about a yard long,[4] neither haue they any thing to defend themselues but targets made of barks,[5] and some armours made of stickes wickered together with thread.[6]

Their townes are but small, & neere the sea coast but fewe, some containing but 10. or 12. houses: some 20. the greatest that we haue seene haue[7] bene but of 30. houses:[8] if they be walled it is only done with barks of trees made fast to stakes,[9] or els with poles onely fixed vpright and close one by another.[10]

pp. 417, 427, 429, 438–40, 443), (*b*) the same, with one in front and one in the rear, nos. 36, 38, 43 (see pp. 420, 423, 430), (*c*) a woman's garment, a skin hung like a dress from both shoulders and reaching the knees, no. 41 (see p. 427), (*d*) a breech-cloth of skin, very brief, and tucked into girdle, with animal head overhanging, used by men and by women, nos. 41–2, 46, 48, 52 (see pp. 427, 429, 434, 442–3). For a general description see H. W. Krieger, 'American Indian costume', in Smithsonian Institution, *Annual rep. for 1928* (1929), p. 631.

[1] Cp. p. 104 above, showing their capacity to learn to use metal for tools.

[2] Cp. pp. 36, 440; Swanton, *Indians*, pp. 571–82.

[3] Cp. pp. 36, 442. White's arrow, no. 41 (see p. 427), appears to have two half-feathers with foreshaft (cp. Flannery, *Analysis*, no. 128).

[4] Cp. pp. 112, 526, 528. These are nowhere illustrated.

[5] Cp. p. 112. These also are not illustrated (cp. Flannery, *Analysis*, no. 142; Swanton, *Indians*, pp. 587–8).

[6] Hakluyt adds: 'Iaques Cartier, voyage 2. chap. 8' (III (1600), 275; VIII (1904), 374), cp. III, 257 (VIII, 237)). This is the most southerly record of any such thing (cp. Flannery, *Analysis*, no. 144, where it is ascribed to probable Iroquoian influence; Swanton, *Indians*, pp. 588–9; p. 112 above). It is nowhere illustrated, and it may even have been an imitation of the Englishmen's armour (cp. pp. 101, 105 above).

[7] 'hath' (Hakluyt (1589), p. 759, and subsequently).

[8] Cp. Secoton (White, no. 37 (see pp. 420–3)) and Pomeiooc (no. 33 (see pp. 415–17). It seems likely that Chawanoac was the largest town of the Carolina Algonkians (p. 259), but Hariot may have seen larger on Chesapeake Bay, e.g. Skicóac (cp. p. 110).

[9] Not illustrated, but possibly Roanoke village (p. 107) was enclosed in this way (cp. Swanton, *Indians*, p. 438).

[10] White, no. 33 (see pp. 415–16).

[E2]   Their houses are made of small poles made fast at the tops in rounde forme after the maner as is vsed in many arbories in our gardens of England,[1] in most townes couered with barkes, and in some with artificiall mattes made of long rushes, from the tops of the houses downe to the ground.[2] The length of them is commonly double to the breadth, in some places they are but 12. and 16. yardes long, and in other some we haue seene of foure and twentie.[3]

   In some places of the countrey one onely towne belongeth to the gouernment of a *Wiróans* or chiefe Lorde; in other some two or three, in some sixe, eight, & more; the greatest *Wiróans* that yet we had dealing with had but eighteene townes in his gouernment, and able to make not aboue seuen or eight hundred fighting men at the most.[4] The language of euery gouernment is different from any other, and the further they are distant the greater is the difference.[5]

---

[1] The interior construction is shown, probably correctly, in White, no. 40 (see pp. 425–7), the space between the ties being about 12 ft. square. The external appearance is shown in nos. 33, 37 (see pp. 415–17, 420–2).

[2] The bark was most probably cypress, though cedar and pine were used (Swanton, *Indians*, p. 421), the mats were of cane, rushes or skins (cp. p. 416; Swanton, *Indians*, pp. 421–2). They were probably about 2 to 3 ft. wide (cp. no. 37, p. 421).

[3] This gives an area ranging from 36 ft. by 18 ft. to 72 ft. by 36 ft., the only details to survive of the size of the Algonkian long house in its southern form. Though nothing is said of height, if the proportions of the temple in no. 37 and in no. 40 (De Bry) (see pp. 422, 426) are correct the height would be in the region of 60 ft. for a length of 60 ft. and a breadth of 36 ft. This seems too high. The proportions of the largest house in Pomeiooc are roughly 30:15:25 for length, breadth and height, while Strachey (*Hist. of travell*, p. 83) speaks of a temple 100 ft. long and 20 ft. broad (cp. Speck, *Powhatan tribes*, pp. 293–4, who considers the long house the characteristic feature of coastal Algonkian life, and Flannery, *Analysis*, no. 117, who regards it as also having affinities with the southeast). The roof structure of the Pomeiooc 'temple' (no. 33) is more like that of the southern round house, but Swanton (*Indians*, p. 413), following Hariot, is probably mistaken in thinking it circular in plan (see pp. 415–17).

[4] Cp. Swanton's definition, p. 642, though it must be pointed out that 'weroance' is used of the chief's advisers of rank as well (cp. p. 281 above). Menatonon of Chawanoac is probably the chief referred to (cp. p. 259 above), unless Hariot is referring to one on Chesapeake Bay. This is the only reference to so wide a range as 1 to 18 in the number of villages ruled by a single chief (cp. pp. 258, 854–72).

[5] Hariot's interest in language is discussed, pp. 375, 389. This indication is, however, the only definite reference to dialectal differences between the

Their maner of warres amongst themselues is either by sudden surprising one an other most commonly about the dawning of the day, or moone light, or els by ambushes, or some suttle deuises. Set battles are very rare, except it fall out where there are many trees, where eyther part may haue some hope of defence, after the deliuerie of euery arrow, in leaping behind some or other.[1]

If there fall out any warres betweene vs & them, what their fight is likely to bee, we hauing aduantages against them so many maner of waies, as by our discipline, our strange weapons and deuises else, especially by ordinance great and small, it may be easily imagined;[2] by the experience we haue had in some places, the turning vp of their heeles against vs in running away was their best defence.[3] [E2 v.] In respect of vs they are a people poore, and for want of skill and iudgement in the knowledge and vse of our things, doe esteeme our trifles before thinges of greater value: Notwithstanding in their proper manner considering the want of such meanes as we haue, they seeme very ingenious; For although they haue no such tooles, nor any such craftes, sciences[4] and artes as wee; yet in those things they doe, they shewe excellencie of wit.[5]

Carolina Algonkian tribes. Although the Carolina and Virginia Algonquian language was the same, Professor Geary has noticed indications of several dialects (cp. pp. 877–80 below; Strachey, *Hist. of travell*, pp. 209–10). Did Hariot, for example, distinguish for some such reason between place-name endings 'oc', 'oac', 'ec'? His last statement indicates contacts (direct?) with Iroquoian- or Soiuan-speaking peoples, which is quite possible (cp. pp. 257–8 above).

[1] Cp. Swanton, *Indians*, pp. 686–91.

[2] Hakluyt (1589), p. 759 (III (1600), 276; VIII (1904), 375), omits 'by' before 'ordinance' and places 'bee' after and not before 'easily'.

[3] The danger for settlers lay in the capacity of the Indians to deliver surprise attacks. So long as Lane maintained discipline and the initiative he was supreme: the 1586 holding party was not so skilful or fortunate and its fate illustrated the perils scattered civilian settlers would run (cp. pp. 528–9).

[4] Hakluyt has 'Science'.

[5] Cp. pp. 98–9, 108; though Manteo at least gave a remarkable illustration of the capacity of some of them to master English speech and concepts (cp. pp. 116, 232, 531). Hariot's appreciation of the potential adaptative power of the Indian is shrewd, but it did not take into account the difficulties of reconciling settlers with him.

And by howe much they vpon due consideration shall finde
our manner of knowledges and craftes to exceede theirs in perfection, and speed for doing or execution, by so much the more
is it probable that they shoulde desire our friendships & loue, and
haue the greater respect for pleasing and obeying vs. Whereby
may bee hoped if meanes of good gouernment bee vsed, that they
may in short time be brought to ciuilitie, and the imbracing of
true religion.[1]

Some religion they haue alreadie, which although it be farre
from the truth, yet beyng as it is, there is hope it may bee the
easier and sooner reformed.

They beleeue that there are many Gods which they call
Montóac,[2] but of different sortes and degrees; one onely chiefe
and great God, which hath bene from all eternitie. Who as they
affirme when hee purposed to make the worlde, made first other
goddes of a principall order to bee as meanes and instruments to
be vsed in the creation and gouernment to follow; and after the
Sunne, Moone, and Starres as pettie gods,[3] and the instruments
of the other order more principall. First they say were made
waters, out of which by the gods was made all diuersitie of
creatures that are visible or inuisible.[4]

[1] The sequence is thus education, friendship, obedience, civilization, Christianity,
which if so followed was not precisely the orthodox one (cp. pp. 126–7).

[2] 'Mantoac' (Hakluyt (1589), p. 760; III (1600), 276; VIII (1904), 376). 'The
ordinary term for spirit or supernatural being in the Algonquian languages is *manito*',
says Dr Flannery (*Analysis*, p. 155), and from it this derives, she instances the
concept of a supreme being as basic to all Algonkian ideas of the supernatural
(pp. 152–6), with other spiritual powers regarded as inferior if not subordinate
(but cp. p. 890 below).

[3] Flannery, *Analysis*, no. 310 (sun); no. 312 (moon), solar worship being
strongest in the south-east, but the concept of the sun being normally kept
distinct from that of the supreme being by the coastal Algonkians (cp. Swanton,
Indians, pp. 742–82).

[4] This is evidently a version of the myth of origin from the underground, often
by way of a lake, mixed in Hariot's mind with the book of Genesis (cp. Flannery,
Analysis, no. 313) and Strachey's 'godlike hare' that 'made the water, and the
fish therein, and the land' (*Hist. of travell*, pp. 102–3, and Swanton, *Indians*,
p. 749).

[E3]   For mankinde they say a woman was made first,[1] which by the working of one of the goddes, conceiued and brought foorth children: And in such sort they say they had their beginning. But how many yeeres or ages haue passed since, they say they can make no relation, hauing no letters nor other such meanes as we to keepe recordes of the particularities of times past, but onely tradition from father to sonne.

They thinke that all the gods are of humane shape, & therefore they represent them by images in the formes of men, which they call *Kewasówak* one alone is called *Kewás*;[2] them they place in houses appropriate or temples, which they call *Machicómuck*;[3] Where they worship, praie, sing, and make manie times offerings vnto them. In some *Machicómuck*; we haue seene but on *Kewás*, in some two, and in other some three; The common sort thinke them to be also gods.

They beleeue also the immortalitie of the soule, that after this life as soone as the soule is departed from the bodie, according to the workes it hath done, it is eyther carried to heauen the habitacle of gods, there to enioy perpetuall blisse and happinesse, or els to a great pitte or hole, which they thinke to bee in the furthest partes of their part of the worlde toward the sunne set, there to burne continually:[4] the place they call *Popogusso*.

[1] The myth of the woman who fell from the sky (Flannery, *Analysis*, no. 314), an Iroquoian myth taken over by some coastal Algonkian peoples, but not otherwise indicated so far south.   [2] White, no. 39 (see pp. 424–5).

[3] White, no. 40 (see pp. 425–7), but this is primarily an ossuary. In Pomeiooc (no. 33, see pp. 415–17) there is little doubt that the largest building was the temple (cp. the references in Swanton, *Indians*, pp. 742–6; and for burial customs in general see D. I. Bushnell, 'Native cemeteries and forms of burial east of the Mississippi', in Bureau of American Ethnology, *Bulletin*, no. 71 (1920); T. D. Stewart, 'The finding of an Indian ossuary in Virginia', in *Jnl of Washington Acad. of Sciences*, XXX (1940), 356–60).

[4] Differential treatment in after-life according to conduct on earth is emphasized by many coastal Algonkian peoples, although as a pre-Christian example of separation of good from bad this appears unique (Flannery, *Analysis*, no. 322, and cp. Lawson, cited in Swanton, *Indians*, p. 752). Professor Geary inclines to think this (and a few other instances) suggests Christian influence, possibly through the Spanish mission on Chesapeake Bay, 1570–2.

For the confirmation of this opinion, they tolde mee two stories of two men that had been lately dead and reuiued againe, the one happened but few yeres before our comming into the countrey of a wicked man which hauing beene dead and buried, the next day the earth of the graue being seene to moue, was taken vp againe; Who made declaration where his soule had beene, that [E 3 v.] is to saie, very neere entring into *Popogusso*, had not one of the gods saued him and gaue him leaue to returne againe, and teach his friends what they should doe to auoid that terrible place of torment.[1]

The other happened in the same yeere wee were there, but in a towne that was three score miles from vs, and it was tolde mee for straunge newes that one beeing dead, buried and taken vp againe as the first, shewed that although his bodie had lien dead in the graue, yet his soule was aliue, & had trauailed farre in a long broade waie, on both sides whereof grewe most delicate and pleasaunt trees, bearing more rare and excellent fruites, then euer hee had seene before or was able to expresse, and at length came to most braue and faire houses, neere which hee met his father, that had beene dead before, who gaue him great charge to goe backe againe and shew his friendes what good they were to doe to enioy the pleasures of that place, which when he had done he should after come againe.[2]

What subtilty soeuer be in the *Wiroances* and Priestes, this opinion worketh so much in manie of the common and simple sort of people that it maketh them haue great respect to their Gouernours, and also great care what they do, to auoid torment after death, and to enioy blisse;[3] although notwithstanding there

---

[1] This appears to be connected with belief in the transmigration of souls (see Flannery, *Analysis*, no. 324, citing instances where bad men were said to get another chance by rebirth), but it has no precise parallel.

[2] This is again without precise parallel.

[3] This runs counter to Strachey's picture of Virginia Algonkian beliefs where it is said that only chiefs (and elders?) and priests had an after-life, that they enjoyed this spirit life without discomfort and were eventually reborn to earth (*Hist. of travell*, pp. 96–103). Here again there is a possibility of contamination either from previous missionary activity, or from unconscious bias on the part

is punishment ordained for malefactours, as stealers, whore-moongers, and other sortes of wicked doers; some punished with death, some with forfeitures, some with beating, according to the greatnes of the factes.[1]

And this is the summe of their religio*n*, which I learned by hauing special familiarity with some of their priestes. Wherein they were not so sure grounded, nor gaue such credite to their traditions and stories, but through [E4] conuersing with vs they were brought into great doubts of their owne, and no small admiration of ours, with earnest desire in many, to learne more then we had meanes for want of perfect vtterance in their language to expresse.[2]

Most things they sawe with vs, as Mathematicall instruments,[3] sea compasses, the vertue of the loadstone in drawing yron, a perspectiue glasse whereby was shewed manie strange sightes,[4]

of the observer. It is clear, however, that Hariot's data on Indian beliefs has not hitherto been subjected to a sufficiently close analysis.

[1] What little evidence there is of Virginia Algonkian justice is mainly of the infliction of punishments (including torture) by Powhatan (cp. Swanton, *Indians*, p. 730). Flannery (*Analysis*) gives examples of punishment for theft (no. 259), and adultery (nos. 265–8), but not for Carolina Algonkians, although compensation for crimes, including murder, by shell money and other property is known later for this region (nos. 248, 261). Hariot had evidently some respect for the systematic administration of justice by the Indians he encountered.

[2] Hariot's only specific admission that he could speak (however imperfectly) the Algonquian tongues (cp. pp. 37, 370 above).

[3] See, for those likely to have been taken on the voyage, pp. 52–3 above and E. G. R. Taylor, 'Instructions to a colonial surveyor in 1582', in *Mariner's Mirror*, XXXVII, 48–62, especially pp. 58–9.

[4] This was either a form of telescope—at least it lay on the way to the construction of one as it involved a combination of lenses—or a magnifying glass which could be used with a concave mirror. Thus, William Bourne writes: 'In what order to make a Glass, that yow may looke thorow, that shall forther your sighte, and to haue a small thynge to seme bigg, which ys very necessary for Perspectiue: And yt may bee so made, that yow may discerne a small thynge, a greate distance, and specyally by the ayde of other Glasses' ('The property or Qualytyes of Glaces', Brit. Mus., Lansdowne MS 121, fo. 99, in J. O. Halliwell [-Phillipps], *Rara mathematica* (1839), pp. 32–47). Dr John W. Shirley kindly gave me this reference. (Cp. E. G. R. Taylor, *Ideas on the shape, size and movements of the earth* (Hist. Assoc. Pamphlet, no. 126, 1943), p. 13. Professor Taylor has come in recent years more firmly to the opinion that it must have been a telescope).

burning glasses, wildefire woorkes,[1] gunnes, bookes, writing and reading, spring clocks that seeme to goe of themselues,[2] and manie other thinges that wee had, were so straunge vnto them, and so farre exceeded their capacities to comprehend the reason and meanes how they should be made and done, that they thought they were rather the works of gods then of men, or at the leastwise they had bin giuen and taught vs of the gods. Which made manie of them to haue such opinion of vs, as that if they knew not the trueth of god and religion already, it was rather to be had from vs, whom God so specially loued then from a people that were so simple, as they found themselues to be in comparison of vs. Whereupon greater credite was giuen vnto that we spake of concerning such matters.

Manie times and in euery towne where I came, according as I was able, I made declaration of the contentes of the Bible; that therein was set foorth the true and onelie GOD, and his mightie woorkes, that therein was contayned the true doctrine of saluation through Christ, with manie particularities of Miracles and chiefe poyntes of religion, as I was able then to vtter, and thought fitte for the time.[3] And although I told them the booke materially &

---

[1] Hakluyt has 'wilde firewoorkes' which may represent a slight change of meaning. Wildfire in the Middle Ages was an inflammable compound, easy to ignite and hard to extinguish and used in warfare. We hear of 'a wildfire arrow' being fired in 1586 (p. 529 below). But by 1585 fireworks as decorative illuminants and projectiles were popular at court and Hariot is probably noting the use of some of these (cp. A. St H. Brock, *History of fireworks* (1949), pp. 29–38; Cyprian Lucar, *Lucar appendix* (1588), pp. 4, 64–98; John Bate, *The mysteries of nature and art* (2nd ed., 1635), pp. 125–32. For the effects on the Indians of Smith's use of rockets at Kecoughtan in 1608 see *Works*, II, 421).

[2] For the types of clocks proposed for use in 1582, see Taylor, 'Instructions' op. cit., p. 59. There are several ship-clocks of this period in the British Museum.

[3] This is a sincere account of attempted missionary activity—the earliest by an Englishman in North America of which there is record—and serves to balance his later reputation as an 'atheist'. We have now (in E. A. Strathmann, *Sir Walter Ralegh. A study in Elizabethan scepticism* (1951), pp. 42–6) a balanced presentation of the evidence which strongly suggests that Hariot, like Raleigh, combined a sceptical temper with Anglican orthodoxy. Incidentally, the passage provides good negative evidence for the absence of a chaplain with the colony (cp. pp. 127, 531), though Hariot was in a favourable position for missionary activity through his ability to speak to the Indians in their own language.

of it self was not of anie such vertue, as I thought they did conceiue, [E4 v.] but onely the doctrine therein contained; yet
would many be glad to touch it, to embrace it, to kisse it, to hold
it to their brests and heades, and stroke ouer all their bodie with
it; to shew their hungrie desire of that knowledge which was
spoken of.

The *Wiroans* with whom we dwelt called *Wingina*, and many
of his people would be glad many times to be with vs at our
praiers, and many times call vpon vs both in his owne towne, as
also in others whither he sometimes accompanied vs,[1] to pray and
sing Psalmes; hoping thereby to bee partaker of the same effectes
which wee by that meanes also expected.

Twise this *Wiroans* was so grieuously sicke that he was like to
die, and as hee lay languishing, doubting of anie helpe by his
owne priestes, and thinking he was in such daunger for offending
vs and thereby our god, sent for some of vs to praie and bee a
meanes to our God that it would please him either that he might
liue, or after death dwell with him in blisse, so likewise were the
requestes of manie others in the like case.[2]

On a time also when their corne began to wither by reason of
a drougth which happened extraordinarily, fearing that it had
come to passe by reason that in some thing they had displeased vs,
many would come to vs & desire vs to pray to our God of
England, that he would preserue their corne, promising that when
it was ripe we also should be partakers of the fruite.[3]

[1] This throws a rather more intimate light on Wingina than anything in Lane
(cp. pp. 266–7, 275–88 above). His own village was that on Roanoke Island. We
do not hear elsewhere that he accompanied the English on some of their journeys
(this must have been before March 1586, cp. p. 276). The love of the Indians for
ceremonies of a religious, magic or therapeutic nature is sufficient explanation for
Wingina's interest in Christian observances.
[2] Praying accorded with the Indian methods of treating diseases by the repeti-
tion of magical formulae, although to them they often added physical treatment
(cp. Swanton, *Indians*, pp. 782–91).
[3] This must have taken place during the early summer of 1586 and may, in
part, explain the transition from hostility to temporary friendliness which enabled
the settlers to get crops planted (cp. pp. 276, 279–80).

There could at no time happen any strange sicknesse, losses, hurtes, or any other crosse vnto them, but that they would impute to vs the cause or meanes therof for offending or not pleasing vs.

One other rare and strange accident, leauing others, will I mention before I ende, which moued the whole [F1] countrey that either knew or hearde of vs, to haue vs in wonderfull admiration.

There was no towne where wee had any subtile deuise practised against vs, we leauing it vnpunished or not reuenged (because we sought by all meanes possible to win them by gentlenesse)[1] but that within a few dayes after our departure from euerie such towne, the people began to die very fast, and many in short space; in some townes about twentie, in some fourtie, in some sixtie, &[2] in one sixe score, which in trueth was very manie in respect of their numbers. This happened in no place that wee coulde learne but where we had bene where they vsed some practise against vs, and after such time; The disease also was so strange, that they neither knew what it was, nor how to cure it; the like by report of the oldest men in the countrey neuer happened before, time out of minde. A thing specially obserued by vs, as also by the naturall inhabitants themselues.

Insomuch that when some of the inhabitantes which were our friends & especially the *Wiroans Wingina*[3] had obserued such effects in foure or fiue towns to follow their wicked practises, they were perswaded that it was the worke of our God through our

---

[1] It is perhaps unfortunate that we have not more examples of this, since the picture conveyed above by Lane was that he attempted to discipline them as he did his own men (pp. 259, 265–6, 277–8, 285–8 and cp. pp. 228, 266).

[2] 'in some sixtie, &', omitted by Hakluyt. For comparable results of Drake's Indian contacts in Florida see p. 306 above. The disease was most likely to have been measles or possibly smallpox (cp. Swanton, *Indians*, pp. 789–91; W. C. Macleod, *The American Indian frontier*, p. 41), though it could have been the common cold. Malaria was possibly brought out by Lane's men, but there does not seem any clear evidence that it was given to the Indians. Cp. Childs, *Malaria*, p. 27. The lethal effects of measles or colds would be quite inexplicable to the English, but they are likely to have recognized smallpox or malaria.

[3] Again note Hariot's friendly and interested attitude in contrast to Lane's hostility (cp. pp. 275–88). Reading between Hariot's lines it is evident that Lane did not explain fully the reasons for the final breach with the Roanoke Indians.

meanes, and that wee by him might kil and slaie whom wee
would without weapons and not come neere them.

And thereupon when it had happened that they had vnderstanding that any of their enemies had abused vs in our iourneyes,
hearing that wee had wrought no reuenge with our weapons, &
fearing vpon some cause the matter should so rest: did come and
intreate vs that we woulde bee a meanes to our God that they as
others that had dealt ill with vs might in like sort die; alleaging
how much it would be for our credite and profite, [F1 v.] as
also theirs; and hoping furthermore that we would do so much
at their requests in respect of the friendship we professe them.

Whose entreaties although wee shewed that they were vngodlie,
affirming that our God would not subiect himself to any such
praiers and requestes of men: that in deede all thinges haue beene
and were to be done according to his good pleasure as he had
ordained: and that we to shew our selues his true seruants ought
rather to make petition for the contrarie, that they with them
might liue together with vs, bee made partakers of his trueth &
serue him in righteousnes; but notwithstanding in such sort, that
wee referre that as all other things, to bee done according to his
diuine will & pleasure, and as by his wisedome he had ordained
to be best.

Yet because the effect fell out so suddenly and shortly after
according to their desires, they thought neuerthelesse it came to
passe by our meanes, and that we in vsing such speeches vnto
them did but dissemble the matter, and therefore came vnto vs
to giue vs thankes in their manner that although wee satisfied
them not in promise, yet in deedes and effect we had fulfilled their
desires.

This maruelous accident in all the countrie wrought so strange
opinions of vs, that some people could not tel whether to thinke
vs gods or men, and the rather because that all the space of their
sicknesse, there was no man of ours knowne to die, or that was
specially sicke: they noted also that we had no women amongst
vs, neither that we did care for any of theirs.

Some therefore were of opinion that wee were not borne of women, and therefore not mortall, but that wee were men of an old generation many yeeres past then ri [F2] sen againe to immortalitie.[1]

Some woulde likewise seeme to prophesie that there were more of our generation yet to come, to kill theirs and take their places, as some thought the purpose was by that which was already done.

Those that were immediatly to come after vs they imagined to be in the aire, yet inuisible & without bodies, & that they by our intreaty & for the loue of vs did make the people to die in that sort as they did by shooting inuisible bullets into them.

To confirme this opinion, their phisitions to excuse their ignorance in curing the disease, would not be ashamed to say, but earnestly make the simple people beleeue, that the strings of blood that they sucked out of the sicke bodies, were the strings where-withall the inuisible bullets were tied and cast.[2]

Some also thought that we shot them our selues out of our pieces from the place where we dwelt, and killed the people in any such towne[3] that had offended vs as we listed, howe farre distant from vs soeuer it were.

And other some saide that it was the speciall woorke of God for our sakes, as wee our selues haue cause in some sorte to thinke no lesse, whatsoeuer some doe or may imagine to the contrarie, specially some Astrologers knowing of the Eclipse of the Sunne which wee saw the same yeere before in our voyage thytherward, which vnto them appeared very terrible.[4] And also of a Comet

[1] It is difficult to say whether the Indians regarded the English as supernatural beings or as men returned from the dead. While belief in transmigration was common, it did not exclude the possibility of return as grown men (cp. Swanton, *Indians*, p. 749). Compare Margaret Mead (*Male and female* (1950), p. 388): 'American Indians are on the whole very little interested in immortality,' and the personalized dead play a slight rôle.'

[2] Sucking appears to have played a more significant part in Carolina Algonkian medicine than, for example, among the Virginia Algonkians where it was preliminary to herbal treatment (cp. Swanton, *Indians*, pp. 783–4).

[3] 'such', omitted by Hakluyt, III (1600), 279 (VIII, 382).

[4] Of the eclipse of the sun forecast for 19 April 1585 (p. 53 above), when the approximate position of the *Tiger* would be lat. 20° N., long. 30° W., Mr D. H. Sadler, Superintendent of H.M. Nautical Almanac Office, writes: 'The path of

which beganne to appeare but a fewe daies before the beginning of the said sicknesse.[1] But to conclude[2] them from being the speciall causes of so speciall an accident, there are farther reasons then I thinke fit at this present to be alleadged.

These their opinions I have set downe the more at [F2 v.] large, that it may appeare vnto you that there is good hope they may be brought through discreet dealing and gouernement to the imbracing of the trueth, and consequently to honour, obey, feare and loue vs.

And although some of our companie towardes the ende of the yeare, shewed themselues too fierce, in slaying some of the people, in some towns, vpon causes that on our part, might easily enough haue bene borne withall: yet notwithstanding because it was on their part iustly deserued,[3] the alteration of their opinions generally & for the most part concerning vs is the lesse to bee doubted.

totality or annularity passed from the middle of the Pacific Ocean, across North America and then across most of the North Atlantic Ocean, passing north of Newfoundland to about position N. 45°, W. 20°. At a position N. 20°, W. 30° a partial eclipse would have been seen about sunset, but only the beginning would have been visible since the Sun would set about the time of greatest phase which at this point would be roughly one-quarter of the Sun obscured. If the ship were further to the north and west more of the eclipse would have been visible.'

[1] Dr J. G. Porter of H.M. Nautical Almanac Office writes: 'There was only one comet recorded in 1585, and it appeared for about a month (mid-October to mid-November) in the northern hemisphere. It is presumably the one noted in Carolina. The comet was recorded by Tycho Brahe at Urianborg and his positions show an apparent path from Cerus northward into Aries. It would then be almost at opposition at this period, and so visible all night. Perihelion passage occurred on 8 October when the comet's longitude would be 9°; the Earth is at longitude 20° in mid-October. The orbit is best represented as a parabola.' Swanton records various Creek myths, which indicate observation of comets and eclipses, but little else has been found suggesting a capacity to forecast eclipses, though this is not necessarily implied by Hariot.

[2] Hakluyt altered this to 'exclude' ((1589), p. 762; III (1600), 279 (VIII, 382)). The alteration is made in manuscript in the Brit. Mus. and Bodleian copies of the 1588 edition.

[3] This clearly shows how Hariot differed from Lane in his dealings with Wingina. It might be possible to read into this the occurrence of some incidents which shook the faith of the Indians in the English and led to their subsequent plots, but Hariot may even be implying that Lane's presumption of a conspiracy and his acts forestalling it were unnecessary.

And whatsoeuer els they may be, by carefulnesse of our selues neede nothing at all to be feared.[1]

The best neuerthelesse in this in all actions besides is to be endeauoured and hoped, & of the worst that may happen notice to bee taken with consideration, and as much as may be eschewed.[2]

The conclusion.

Now I haue as I hope made relation not of so fewe and smal things but that the countrey of men that are indifferent & wel disposed maie be sufficiently liked: If there were no more knowen then I haue mentioned, which doubtlesse and in great reason is nothing to that which remaineth to bee discouered, neither the soile, nor commodities. As we haue reason so to gather by the difference we found in our trauails; for although all which I haue before spoken of, haue bene discouered & experimented not far from the sea coast where was our abode & most of our trauailing: yet somtimes as we made our iourneies farther into the maine and countrey; we found the soyle to bee fatter; the trees greater and to growe [F3] thinner; the grounde more firme and deeper mould; more and larger champions; finer grasse and as good as euer we saw any in England; in some places rockie and farre more high and hillie ground; more plentie of their fruites; more abundance of beastes; the more inhabited with people, and of greater pollicie & larger dominions, with greater townes and houses.[3]

---

[1] The Indians destroyed the 1586 settlement, while there is no evidence that they sheltered the 1587 settlers.

[2] This paragraph is omitted by Hakluyt (1589), p. 762; III (1600), 279 (VIII, 383), most probably because it made no contribution to Hariot's argument.

[3] This is a reasonable statement of the position as it was known to Hariot. The sandy islands, shallow sounds, swamps and swamp-forests of the North Carolina coastlands, promising as they were in some respects in Hariot's eyes, were less favourable than the parts of the coastal plain reached at the limit of the explorations into the interior and, probably, than the environs of Chesapeake Bay. But Hariot was substituting for Lane's 'good mine' or transcontinental passage (p. 273) the attraction of a more or less civilized and civilizable Indian polity behind the coastlands, as well as better lands for settlement. Though the land existed, there was no equivalent of the Mexican empire.

'A briefe and true report'

Why may wee not then looke for in good hope from the inner parts of more and greater plentie, as well of other things, as of those which wee haue already discouered? Vnto the Spaniardes happened the like in discouering the maine of the West Indies. The maine also of this countrey of Virginia, extending some wayes so many hundreds of leagues, as otherwise then by the relation of the inhabitants wee haue most certaine knowledge of, where yet no Christian Prince hath any possession or dealing, cannot but yeeld many kinds of excellent commodities, which we in our discouerie haue not yet seene.

What hope there is els to be gathered of the nature of the climate, being answerable to the Iland of Iapan, the land of China, Persia, Iury, the Ilandes of Cyprus and Candy, the South parts of Greece, Italy, and Spaine, and of many other notable and famous countreis, because I meane not to be tedious,[1] I leaue to your owne consideration.

Whereby also the excellent temperature of the ayre there at all seasons, much warmer then in England, and neuer so violently[2] hot, as sometimes is vnder & between the Tropikes, or nere them; cannot bee vnknowne[3] vnto you without further relation.

For the holsomnesse thereof I neede to say but thus much: that for all the want of prouision, as first of English victuall, excepting for twentie daies,[4] wee liued onely by drinking water[5] and by the victuall of the countrey, of [F3 v.] which some sorts were very straunge vnto vs, and might haue bene thought to haue altered

---

[1] The illusion that lands in the same latitudes had necessarily identical climates and produced identical crops has already been encountered, and it is implied throughout the writings of both the Hakluyts (cp. p. 336 above).

[2] 'vehemently' (Hakluyt (1589), p. 763; III (1600), 279).

[3] Corrected to 'knowen' (ibid.).

[4] In consequence of the *Tiger's* lading being almost wholly spoiled. We are given no indication whether the twenty days dated from that event on 29 June or from the establishment of the settlers on Roanoke Island on, or about, 17 August, but it was probably the latter (cp. pp. 189, 255 above).

[5] He reported (p. 338) that malt had been made from maize, and ale brewed, while he expected that, with the addition of hops, beer could be made also.

our temperatures in such sort, as to haue brought vs into some greeuous and dangerous diseases: Secondly the want of English meanes for the taking of beastes, fishe, and foule,[1] which by the helpe only of the inhabitants and their meanes, coulde not bee so suddenly and easily prouided for vs,[2] nor in so great number & quantities, nor of that choise as otherwise might haue bene to our better satisfaction and contentment. Some want also wee had of clothes.[3] Furthermore, in all our trauailes, which were most speciall[4] and often in the time of winter,[5] our lodging was in the open aire vpon the grounde. And yet I say for all this, there were but foure of our whole company (being one hundreth and eight) that died all the yeere and that but at the latter ende thereof and vpon none of the aforesaide causes. For all foure especially three were feeble, weake, and sickly persons before euer they came thither, and those that knew them much marueyled that they liued so long beeing in that case, or had aduentured to trauaile.[6]

---

[1] Cp. pp. 276, 365 above. Hakluyt (III (1600), 280) adds in margin: 'This want is hereafter to be supplied', showing that as late as 1600 he still considered the reinforcement of the colony (presumed to be surviving in Virginia since 1587) a practical proposition.

[2] He seems to point here to some slowness in organizing Indian supplies to the settlers at the beginning of the settlement in August and September, rather than to the hardships of the following winter. This may have been due to the ineffectiveness of the cape merchant (pp. 232–4 above) or to the low value the Indians set on labour in exchange for English goods.

[3] Possibly due to faulty stocking by the cape merchant. Drake had a surplus when he arrived in 1586 (cp. p. 251 above).

[4] 'specially' (Hakluyt, III (1600), 280).

[5] 'the Winter' (Hakluyt (1589), p. 763; III (1600), 280).

[6] For the names and number of settlers see pp. 194–7 above. The loss of four only by illness was a remarkable achievement. Lane said this covered also the rest of the company that sailed out in the *Tiger* (p. 228 above). Hariot did not mention those killed. Diaz (Wright, *Further English voyages*, p. 239; p. 790 below) says four were killed and one, apparently, hanged, while three were abandoned (p. 307 above). It would certainly seem unlikely that the settlers brought with them malaria or other fever either from England or from the West Indies. The maintenance of good health by colonists not fully acclimatized, and subsisting almost wholly on a non-European diet was unusual. Cp. Childs, *Malaria and Colonization in the Carolina Low Countries*, p. 36 n.; S. E. Morison, *Columbus*, p. 434.

Seeing therefore the ayre there is so temperate and holsome, the soyle so fertile, and yeelding such commodities as I haue before mentioned, the voyage also thither to and fro being sufficiently experimented, to bee perfourmed thrice[1] a yeere with ease and at any season thereof: And the dealing of Sir Water Raleigh[2] so liberall in large giuing and graunting lande there, as is alreadie knowen, with many helpes and furtherances els: (The least that hee hath graunted hath beene fiue hundred acres to a man onely for the aduenture of his person)[3] I hope there remaine no cause wherby the action should be misliked.

[F4] If that those which shall thither trauaile to inhabite and plant bee but reasonably prouided for the first yere, as those are which were transported the last,[4] and beeing there doe vse but that diligence and care as is[5] requisit, and as they may with ease: There is no doubt but for the time following they may haue

---

[1] Altered, more realistically, to 'twice' by Hakluyt ((1589), p. 763; III (1600), 280). The meaning is that after sufficient experience has been gained in making the voyage it will be possible to make it twice, or three times, a year. Hariot was being somewhat optimistic in expressing the belief that it would soon be possible to make it at any season.

[2] 'Sir Walter Ralegh' (Hakluyt (1589), p. 763; III (1600), 280).

[3] As we do not know many of the details of Raleigh's agreement with the City of Raleigh settlers on 7 January 1587 (pp. 506–12, 516, 571–2), this information is of great value. There are no suggestions of land-appropriation and division in Lane's colony. For White's colony the arrangements of 1587 (intended to be implemented on the shores of Chesapeake Bay) provided for land-division and consequently for the establishment of a self-perpetuating community of farmers (cp. p. 498). The offer was less generous than that made by Sir George Peckham for his projected voyage of 1584, when an adventurer in person was offered 2000 acres and double that if he wintered in the colony (Quinn, *Gilbert*, II, 477–80). The smaller figure was more realistic. Hariot, however, was aiming at attracting subscribers and planters for the 1588 or subsequent expeditions (cp. pp. 38, 320, 548) and the terms he suggested may not be precisely those offered in 1587. Raleigh's liberality in other respects probably included assistance with shipping and stores for the first year and possibly a lump sum, as in 1589 (pp. 574–5 below), for special expenses in developing the community.

[4] The 1587 settlers did not consider themselves adequately provided for, which was the reason they sent White back in August to expedite supplies (cp. pp. 533–5 below).

[5] 'that is' (Hakluyt, III (1600), 280).

victuals that is[1] excellent good and plentie enough;[2] some more Englishe sortes of cattaile also hereafter, as some haue bene before, and are there yet remayning, may and shall bee God willing thither transported:[3] So likewise our kinde of fruites, rootes, and hearbes, may bee there planted and sowed, as some haue bene alreadie, and proue wel:[4] And in short time also they may raise of[5] those sortes of commodities which I haue spoken of as shall both enrich them selues, as also others that shall deale with them.[6]

And this is all the fruites[7] of our labours, that I haue thought necessary to aduertise you of at this present: what els concerneth the nature and manners of the inhabitants of Virginia: The number with the particularities of the voyages thither made; and of the actions of such as haue bene by Sir Water Raleigh therein and there imployed, many worthy to bee remembred; as of the first discouerers of the Countrey: of our Generall for the time Sir Richard Greinuile; and after his departure, of our Gouernour

[1] 'are' (Hakluyt (1589), p. 763; III (1600), 280).

[2] Hariot is saying, in effect, that sufficient stores were supplied in 1587 and would be sent in 1588 to ensure adequate supplies until the first harvest could be obtained in the summer following. This indicates a determination to be independent of the Indians for foodstuffs from the beginning, and would be an obvious lesson to be learnt from Lane's experiences.

[3] I.e. livestock in general. In 'Englishe sortes' Hariot probably includes animals brought from the West Indies in 1585, some of which he may have reckoned were still alive (cp. Wright, *Further English voyages*, p. 234; p. 782 below), and also whatever English beasts the 1587 expedition had taken with them, the implication, in view of what White says of his failure to get stock in the West Indies (pp. 519, 521–2 below), being that in 1587 some animals were brought all the way from England, and that it was intended to ship more in 1588 either from England or the West Indies or both.

[4] Though the experiments he cites above (pp. 336, 344) were far from conclusive.   [5] 'so much of' (Hakluyt, III (1600), 280).

[6] Hariot's object would then (judging by his conclusions above) appear to be to indicate that, besides subsistence, the settlers could hope for profits in commerce mainly from cultivating crops which would yield an economic surplus in line with the Hakluyts' views (cp. p. 324 above). (Can he have had in his mind tobacco as one of them?) They would profit in some measure from the collection of natural products and, to a still lesser degree, from trade with the Indians. The emphasis from the views of 1585, through those of Lane in 1586, to Hariot's in 1588 shows a gradual shift (cp. pp. 100, 127, 273, 324).

[7] Singular in both editions of Hakluyt.

there Master Rafe Lane; with diuers other directed and imployed vnder theyr gouernement: Of the Captaynes and Masters of the voyages made since for transportation; of the Gouernour and assistants of those alreadie transported, as of many persons, accidents, and thinges els, I haue ready in a discourse by it self in maner of a Chronicle[1] according [F4 v.] to the course of times and[2] when time shall bee thought conuenient shall be also published.[3]

Thus referring my relation to your fauourable constructions, expecting good successe of the action, from him which is to be acknowledged the authur and gouernour not onely of this but of all things els, I take my leaue of you, this moneth of February. 1588.[4]

---

[1] I.e. in chronological sequence.   [2] 'which' (Hakluyt, III (1600), 280).

[3] This is the first and only reference to Hariot's chronicle, which has entirely disappeared, along with almost every scrap of his other papers on North America (cp. pp. 54–5, 359, 388–9). Dr John W. Shirley of State College, Raleigh, N.C., in the course of his research on Hariot, is among the latest and most thorough inquirers who have failed to find any trace of it. It may be noted, however, in the first place, that Hakluyt is very unlikely to have seen it at any time before 1600 or he would not have left so weak and bald an account of the 1586 expedition on record (cp. pp. 477–80 below), and, in the second, that as Hariot is likely to have acted as archivist for the records of the Virginia ventures for Raleigh while he was in his service, it is not unlikely that the material which Hakluyt obtained on the 1584 and 1585 expeditions (i.e. nos. 4, 23–4, 28, 45 above) and possibly that on those of 1587 and 1588 came to him by way of Hariot with Raleigh's approval. No useful conjectures can yet be made on why the narrative was not published (if indeed it was completed as Hariot claimed) or how it disappeared, apart from suggesting that when Hariot moved over to the service of the earl of Northumberland about 1594 it, with the rest of the Virginia papers, remained with Raleigh and perished in the general loss of his muniments.

[4] De Bry in 1590 and Hakluyt in 1589 retain 1588, but Hakluyt in 1600 gives '1587'. Hariot clearly means 1588 by our reckoning (cp. p. 320 above, where he speaks of 'the last yeere of 1587'), but Hakluyt's alteration of the date in 1600 to accord with the English reckoning, at the same time that he was printing new documents using the calendar year, underlines his inconsistency in this respect (cp. pp. 598–9). Nevertheless, Hakluyt probably remembered that some version of Hariot's treatise was already in existence by October 1587, or possibly even by May, as he referred to it in his dedication of his Laudonnière translation (p. 548).

The date is followed by 'Faults escaped', which have been incorporated in the text (as they were by De Bry in 1590 and by Hakluyt in 1589)—'The rest if any be the discreete Reader may easily amend'. It is perhaps surprising it did not conclude with the publication of the terms offered to adventurers in the Virginia enterprise.

52. 1609.

THOMAS HARIOT RECOLLECTS INDIAN TALK OF METAL-WORKING[1]

To the Right Honourable, the Right Worshipfull Counsellors, and others the cheerefull aduenturors for the aduancement of that Christian and noble plantation in Virginia....

But what neede I to stand vpon forren testimonies, since Master Thomas Heriot, a man of much iudgement in these causes, signified vnto you all, at your late solemne meeting at the house of the right honourable the Earle of Exeter,[2] how to the Southwest of our old fort in Virginia, the Indians often informed him, that there was a great melting of red metall, reporting the manner in working of the same.[3] Besides, our own Indians haue lately reuealed either this or another rich mine of copper or gold in a towne called Ritanoe, neere certaine mountaines lying West of Roanoac....[4] From my lodging in the Colledge of Westminster this 15. of Aprill, 1609....

RICHARD HAKLUYT

53. JOHN AUBREY ON THOMAS HARIOT[5]

Mr. Thomas Harriot:—Memorandum:—Sir Robert Moray (from Francis Stuart), declared at the Royal Society—'twas when the comet appeared before the Dutch warre—that Sir Francis had heard Mr. Harriott say that he had seen nine cometes, and had predicted seaven of them, but did not tell them how. 'Tis very strange: excogitent astronomi.

---

[1] Extract from Hakluyt's dedication of his translation of the Gentleman of Elvas' *Relaçam* (Evora, 1557) of De Soto's expedition as *Virginia richly valued* (1609), sig. A 3 r. (reprinted in Taylor, *Hakluyts*, II, 499–503).

[2] This meeting at the house of Thomas Cecil, earl of Exeter, was apparently that of the adventurers of the Virginia Company of London which decided, in February 1609, to petition the king for a new charter (cp. C. M. Andrews, *Colonial period in American history*, I, 102–3; W. F. Craven, *The southern colonies in the seventeenth century*, pp. 82–3).

[3] Cp. pp. 269, 274, 332–3 above.　　　　[4] See Strachey, *Hist. of travell*, p. 25.

[5] Extract from John Aubrey, *Brief lives*, ed. Andrew Clark, I (1898), 285, from Bodleian Lib., Aubrey MS 8, fo. 12; 6, fo. 35.

Mr. Hariot went with Sir Walter Ralegh into Virginia, and haz writt the Description of Virginia, which is printed.[1]

Dr. Pell[2] tells me that he finds amongst his papers (which are now, 1684, in Dr. Busby's[3] hands), an alphabet[4] that he had contrived for the American language, like Devills.[5]

54. THOMAS HARIOT'S NOTES ON CORPORATIONS FOR TRADE AND FOR PLANTATIONS[6]

There is great difference betwixte a corporation priveleged for only trade; & a corporation priveledged for planting & trade; & a corporation priveleedged only for planting.

Of the first we haue examples of many corporations of[7] Societyes. The Moscouy Company, Turky, Barbary, Guinny, Spagnishe, & others: which are knowne well in there gouernement.

Of the other two we haue yet noe especiall example that haue[8] proued well. Sir Humfry Gilbert[9] for planting[10] & trading in Norumbega & Sir Walter Raleigh for Virginia.[11]

---

[1] Aubrey notes below (ibid., p. 287) the English edition of *A briefe and true report* (1588) from the printed Bodleian catalogue of 1674.

[2] John Pell (1611–85), mathematician.

[3] Richard Busby (1606–95), headmaster of Westminster School. If Busby retained those of Hariot's papers which referred to the Virginia expedition of 1585–6 it would explain their absence from the Hariot papers in the British Museum and at Petworth, whose provenance is known. So far no MSS collections deriving from Busby have been found.

[4] It is possible that it was not only an alphabet (i.e. a device for recording the sounds of the Algonquian words) but a glossary of those words he collected (see above, pp. 356, 358, 360, 366) to which Pell referred. It may be suggested (cp. p. 52 above) that Hariot took a dictionary with him in 1585 and entered Carolina Algonquian words opposite what he regarded as their English equivalents.

[5] Clark's note is 'Perhaps because the letters ended in tridents; see Clark's Wood's *Life and Times*, i. 498, and the facsimile'. These are the characters, many of them trident-like in form, of the 'devil's writing' in *Ambrosii...introductio in chaldaicam* (1539), f. 212 v.

[6] Brit. Mus., Add. MS 6789, fo. 523. Holograph.   [7] For 'or'?

[8] Crossed out 'yet'.   [9] Crossed out '& Sᴿ Walter Ral'.   [10] Crossed out 'for'.

[11] These were evidently notes for a more extended discussion, prior to 1606 (which has not been found). That Hariot should have made these astute distinctions indicated that after 1588 he continued to think about the problems involved in successful colonization.

CHAPTER VI

THE FIRST COLONY: JOHN WHITE

FOREWORD

I

The inclusion of a list of drawings, with associated texts, may appear an unusual feature in a documentary collection, yet what follows is not primarily a catalogue of John White's drawings,[1] but an attempt to see what historical evidence they can be made to yield on the Virginia ventures. It is based on the assumption, which the evidence goes some considerable way to prove, that they can be grouped to provide, though naturally with many gaps, a visual commentary on the course of Grenville's expedition through the West Indies to Raleigh's Virginia in 1585 and on the history of the first colony maintained at Roanoke Island during the following year. The arrangement is open to the criticism that it lacks certainty in a number of places,[2] but what is known about the drawings themselves,[3] what White's composite pictures and maps tell us about the individual drawings of birds and fishes, and the extent to which they dovetail into Hariot's analysis (fully illustrated in the previous chapter), all point the same way in the great majority of cases. If there is uncertainty when White made a particular drawing, the reader is given all the available evidence, with the exception of the drawing itself, with which to make up his own mind. All inscriptions contained on the drawings are printed, and texts are added from De Bry's *America*—these are by Thomas Hariot[4]—and from other sources where they are available. In the notes and identifications the question whether the subjects

[1] The revised edition of the *Catalogue of drawings by British artists in the British Museum*, for which the White drawings and derivatives are being listed by Mr P. H. Hulton, will provide such a catalogue. Until it appears, Laurence Binyon's fourth volume (1907) of the original edition should be used.
[2] Cp. pp. 57-8 above.   [3] Pp. 392-8 below.
[4] Cp. pp. 401, 414, 430.

were found along the route traversed by the outward and homeward expeditions or in areas visited by the colonists from Roanoke Island is constantly kept in mind. And this explains, what to some readers may seem superfluous, a certain preoccupation with the fauna and flora of North Carolina.

In the list a sequence has been adopted which divides the items into four groups:

I, nos. 1–4, are preliminaries, mainly from De Bry.

II, nos. 1–15, represent the progress of the expedition through the West Indies between 7 May and 7 June, and reflect in the main the result of visits to Puerto Rico and Hispaniola.

II, nos. 16–31, illustrate the mainly oceanic birds and fishes encountered on the journey between Hispaniola and the Carolina Banks. Since many of these could have been seen earlier on the voyage, or on the homeward run, the arrangement must remain conjectural, but it is given some degree of plausibility by the embellishments on White's more general map (p. 460 below).

II, nos. 32–111, are the product of White's stay in Raleigh's Virginia between 26 May 1585 and 19 June 1586, with the proviso that a small number may possibly belong to 1584 or 1587. Most of them contain evidence associating them with the first colony. None, apart from the maps, clearly indicate that White crossed into what is now the State of Virginia, though he, or Hariot, or both, certainly went there. The items have been arranged with Hariot's notes, or other texts where they exist, so as to give in approximate chronological order the more detailed topographical studies (lacking, unfortunately, any drawings of the fort, houses or Indian village on Roanoke Island) and the ethnological drawings, followed by the flora (quite inadequately represented) and fauna, and lastly the maps, which embodied the cumulation of White's topographical information.

III, nos. 1–7, are drawings which, though not belonging to the Roanoke voyages, had some connexion with them.

IV, nos. 1–11, have no known links with the voyages and are merely entered for the sake of completeness.

In the list the inscription or title on the primary extant version is given first, and subsequent versions, with texts where there are any, follow. As the purpose of the list is to assist historical inquiry, full reference has been made to published lists and reproductions of the drawings.

II

To make the drawings themselves intelligible it is necessary to set out the principal groups which are by White or are derived from his work in some scheme of relationship. This must, in the present state of our knowledge, be a tentative one, so that the following table may not be definitive.

TABLE SHOWING THE RELATIONSHIP BETWEEN
THE VARIOUS GROUPS OF DRAWINGS
BY JOHN WHITE

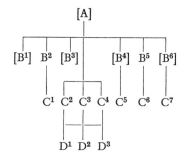

A = the archetype, White's basic collection, not now extant.

B = the sets, or groups, of drawings made by White himself from A, of which only two are now extant.

C = copies, or prints, made by other hands, either direct from A, or from one or other B group.

D = copies made from groups C^{2-4}.

Nothing of the archetype (A) is now known to survive. From it derived Hariot's set (B¹), of the subsequent history of which we know nothing.[1] Our main source is the portfolio of drawings by

[1] Cp. pp. 54-5.

White's hand, which the British Museum acquired in 1866, after it had been in Ireland for nearly a century in the possession of the earls of Charlemont.[1] This (B[2]) has nowhere any reference to White by name, but there is no doubt that all the maps and drawings it contains are his own work. The contemporary title, in White's hand as we must assume, says that the drawings were made in Virginia in 1585—before 17 November if we take it literally.[2] While many of them were, or could have been, made during the outward voyage and in the course of the preliminary reconnaissance from the Carolina Banks during July and August, the maps could not, since a large part of the data had not then been assembled.[3] Moreover, there are also a number of items which do not belong to the 1585 venture at all—Florida Indians copied from Le Moyne; Eskimos, perhaps drawn in England some seven years earlier; Orientals, copied from some costume

[1] Brit. Mus., P. & D. 1906-5-9-1. On 12 March 1788 Edmund Malone wrote to the first earl of Charlemont (Hist. MSS Comm., *Charlemont MSS*, II, 73):

'In Payne's catalogue just published is a book that I thought you would like, but the price being fourteen guineas, I would not venture it without your knowledge. I enclose the title. The drawings are finely executed, many of them whole-length figures of the savage persons discovered in the voyage, and the whole in fine preservation. Payne promised to keep it unsold till I could get your answer; let me know therefore by return of post.'

[*Enclosure.*] '284. The pictures of sundry things collected and counterfeited according to the truth, in the voyage made by Sir W. Raleigh, knight, for the discovery of La Virginea, in the 27th year of the most happie reigne of our soveraigne lady Queene Elizabeth. Seventy-five drawings, coloured, in the original binding. Folio.—Fourteen guineas.'

Payne was the London bookseller, Thomas Payne the elder, and his annual catalogue for 1788 (Brit. Mus. 129. i. 7 (1)) is the earliest known reference to the collection. The original binding has disappeared. Charlemont bought it (he wrote by return on 16 March, 'The book of which you have sent the title must be worth the money if the drawings be well executed. If you think them so, by all means purchase it for me') and it was sold at the dispersal of his library by the third earl in 1865 (Sotheby, *Sale catalogue*, II, viii (1865), lot 228), being bought (*a*) by Henry Stevens, and (*b*) by the British Museum, 1866. It was transferred from the Department of MSS to that of Prints and Drawings in 1906.

[2] Cp. p. 398 below.

[3] Cp. pp. 460-1.

book; and some ancient Picts and Britons, drawn after some chronicle possibly as late as 1588.[1] It is, therefore, a miscellaneous collection, which, however, lacks many of the natural history subjects drawn in association with Hariot, and which is almost certain to have been put together by White for Raleigh, Grenville, or one of the other more significant sponsors of White's activities, probably between 1586 and 1590, even though nothing of its early provenance has yet come to light. Throughout, White, whether drawing from his own experience or copying from others, succeeds in giving a remarkable quality of fidelity to life to almost all his human figures, and a combination of grace and accuracy to the majority of his other drawings. This delicate naturalism sets White apart from all other English draughtsmen of his time, and places him as a significant artist.

A further set (B³), made by John White for Theodor de Bry in 1588 or 1589, is now untraceable. It comprised at least twenty-three American drawings and maps, which are represented by the well-known engravings (C¹) in *America*, pt. i (1590), in which full acknowledgement is made to White and which was, in turn, the source from which the British Museum set (B²) was identified. Compared with the latter, the engravings show a substantial number of variations and there are four items amongst them not represented.[2] It was formerly thought that the elaborations and variations were wholly the work of De Bry and his fellow-engravers, but a closer study shows that White was responsible for a considerable number of the variations from corresponding items in the British Museum set, and makes it quite clear that both derive from the lost archetype.

It is through another portfolio of drawings in the British Museum, which are not in White's hand, that we approach, though not without difficulty and somewhat uncertain conjecture, the archetype most nearly. Between 1 July and 30 October 1709

---

[1] III, nos. 1–7; IV, nos. 1, 3, 5–11, see pp. 462–4 below.
[2] II, nos. 32, 39, 45, 53, see pp. 413, 424, 432, 443 below. There were also five engravings of Picts and Britons represented by White's III, nos. 3–7, see p. 463 below.

John White's Drawings

Dr Hans Sloane drafted a letter to the Abbé Bignon[1] in which the following passage occurs:

> Vous n'ignorez pas que Theodore de Bry a fait un receuil de voyages aux Indes Orientales et Occidentales avec de fort bonnes tailles douces. Les planches de la 1ere partie, qui appartiennent a la Virginie sont tres-belles, et a vous parler franchement si belles et si curieuses que je ne croyois pas qu'elles fussent naturelles, mais que cet illustre graveur y avoit adjouté du sien. Le hazard m'a tiré de cette ereur, car il y a deux ou trois ans, que chez les descendans d'un Peintre et dessinateur nommé White, lequel avoit voyagé avec Sr. Walter Raleigh, je vis le Livre original d'ou toutes ces planches ont esté tirées. Il y en avoit aussi beaucoup d'autres tres-curieuses que Theodore de Bry a negligé de nous donner. Parmi celles ci sont toutes les Plantes, tous les Oiseaux les Poissons &c. Il y en a aussi plusieurs qui regardent les manieres et les moeurs des Indiens, et que j'estime dautant plus curieuses qu'ils etoient naturels avant leur communication avec les Europeans. Theodore de Bry nous dit dans le proeme qu'il a mis au devant de ses planches qu'ils les avoit de White. Ne pouvant pas acheter ce livre je l'ai tout fait copier par un assez habile homme. L'original etoit un peu gaté parce que de jeunes gens s'en servoient pour apprendre a dessiner....

Leaving aside the interesting information that about 1706–7 Sloane was in touch with White's descendants,[2] can we say that he is likely to be referring to the lost archetype? It would certainly seem so, and we should therefore expect to find a collection of copies amongst Sloane's manuscripts. Mr P. H. Hulton has, indeed, found scattered amongst nine volumes of manuscripts[3] seventy-four copies which may, in some way, be associated with White (D[1–3]).[4] Provisionally, it may be suggested that these are the copies referred to in the letter, although some may subsequently have been lost. If this is so we are then left with the volume of drawings which was formerly Sloane MS 5270.[5] This carries an inscription in Sloane's hand claiming that it contains

[1] Brit. Mus., Sloane MS 4069, fos. 112 v.–113. This was discovered by M. Jean Jacquot and transcribed for me by Mr P. H. Hulton, to both of whom I am much indebted.

[2] Cp. pp. 46–7 above.

[3] Brit. Mus., Sloane MSS 5253, 5262–7, 5272, 5289.

[4] With only two doubtful exceptions they can all be associated with drawings in Sloane MS 5270.

[5] Now P. & D. 199. a. 3.

'The originall draughts of yᵉ habits, towns customs &c: of the
West Indians and of the plants birds fishes &c. found in Groenland,
Virginia, Guiana &c. by Mʳ John White who was a Painter &
accompanied Sʳ Walter Raleighe in his voyage. See the preface
to the first part of Theodore de Bry America or the description
of Virginia where some of these draughts are curiously cutt
by that Graver'. The similarity of Sloane's wording to his description of White's 'originals' in the 1709 letter will be obvious.
The first leaf in the collection, moreover, carries also an inscription
in a rather unlettered hand stating: 'There is in this Book a
hundred and 12 Leaues with flowers and Pickters and of fish and
of fowles beside wast Paper this Lent to my soon whit, 11 Aprell
1673.' The drawings, which have now been arranged in their
original order, are almost certainly (apart from a few intruders)
copies by a single hand (or by a single 'school') which is not
White's. Mr P. H. Hulton regards the whole volume as probably
a systematic copy of an earlier portfolio, to which one drawing
and one engraving are probably the only additions. The combination of the 1673 inscription with Sloane's, and of both with the
1709 letter, would suggest that this is the collection of 'originals'
which Sloane saw in 1706–7 and had, up to 1709, been unable to
buy, but which he subsequently acquired from White's descendants. If this is so, we have then reached the position when we
can say that what had been handed down in White's family was
not the archetype, but a copy by another and less skilful hand of
the lost originals. This raises some problems in detail but it is the
only hypothesis which fits the facts as already known.

The materials in the volume fall into three groups (C²⁻⁴). The
first[1] comprises drawings already known through the British
Museum set (B²) and De Bry's engravings, to which two additional items, very closely associated with them, can be added.[2]
They are not copies from B², since they contain some features

[1] II, nos. 4–5, 8–11, 13–14, 21–31, 33, 35, 38, 42, 50–1, 54, see pp. 405, 406–8,
410–13, 416, 419, 423, 429, 439–40, 444.
[2] II, no. 12; IV, no. 2; see pp. 408, 463, cp. also IV no. 4, p. 464.

found elsewhere only in the De Bry engravings,[1] so that their derivation from the common archetype appears reasonably certain. The second group comprises the greater part of the drawings of the birds, fishes and reptiles mentioned by Hariot as having been drawn in Raleigh's Virginia in 1585–6 and not represented elsewhere by drawings in White's hand.[2] This is the most important documentary contribution which the volume has to make to the history of the first colony. The third group (C[4]) consists of drawings not found elsewhere assigned to White and not so far associable with the Roanoke ventures.[3] Some, if not all, of these were copies of drawings by others which, it might appear, White made to include in his own collection. In quality the items in the volume vary from competent, though somewhat lifeless, reproductions to banal caricatures of White's style. Some of the drawings are rubbed or otherwise disfigured, and so the volume might well merit the description 'un peu gaté' of Sloane's letter.

The problems raised by this collection are still far from complete solution, but there may be, perhaps, in Sloane's papers some further clues which will take us a little farther.

Of the remaining specimens of drawings by or after White the most important are those of a butterfly and a number of insects given by White himself to the entomologist Thomas Penny (B[5]),[4] and eventually engraved in Moffet's *Theatrum...insectorum* in 1634 (C[6]). There is no doubt also that John Gerard's engraving of the 'Wysanke' milkweed (C[7])[5] derived from a White drawing (B[6]) differing in detail from that in B[2], although it may not have reached Gerard direct from White. Finally, Richard Hakluyt had at least one drawing (and probably more) by White (B[4]). This is known only as one of a number of rather crude copies of bird drawings which were given to Edward Topsell for his intended book on birds before 1614.[6] As the copy derived from Hakluyt

---

[1] E.g. II, no. 33, see p. 416 below.   [2] II, nos. 56, 58–95, 97–9, 104–5.
[3] They have not been included in the list below (cp. p. 464).
[4] II, nos. 7, 106–8, see pp. 406, 457–60 below.   [5] II, no. 54, see pp. 444–6 below.
[6] 'The Fowles of Heauen', now Huntington Library, Ellesmere MS 1142;
II, nos. 81 (after Hakluyt), 56, 60, 72, 77, 80, see pp. 447–8, 450–2 below.

and a number of others (C^5) are represented in the Sloane volume (C^3) the presumption is that Topsell got them all from Hakluyt, though it is possible that some came to him by a more roundabout route from White.

It will be noted that the drawings which are linked with figures in the engravings for Drake's voyage of 1585–6 are not included in the scheme, since it is impossible to say which originated with John White and which with the unidentified draughtsman of the Drake expedition.[1]

The scheme of relationship here outlined can only be regarded as a provisional one and it can be claimed for it only that it probably fits the existing evidence in the least unsatisfactory way. Lacking proof at a number of points, it is quite possible that it will not withstand the appearance of new evidence, but it may perhaps have some value as a provisional tree for a family of which very little is so far known.

55. THE DRAWINGS OF JOHN WHITE

I. PRELIMINARY MATTER

1. White's title-page.[2]

'The pictures of sondry things collected and counterfeited according to the truth in the voyage made by[3] Sir Walter Raleigh knight, for the discouery of La Virginea. In the 27th yeare of the most happie reigne of our Soueraigne lady Queene Elizabeth.[4] And in the yeare of our Lorde God. 1585.'[5]

---

[1] Cp. pp. 34, 42; II, nos. 7, 8, 25, 26, 29, 30, see pp. 406–7, 411–12 below.

[2] Brit. Mus., P. & D. 1906-5-9-1 (1), written on a small slip of paper, apparently in the same hand, which we may take to be White's, in which the captions on the drawings are written. It is worth noting that no mention is made of White as the artist.

[3] For 'for'. If White wrote the title it is curious that he should have made such a slip.

[4] Running from 17 November 1584 to 16 November 1585.

[5] This might take us, by the English practice, up to 24 March 1586. Some, at least, of the drawings in this volume do not fit within these limitations of date (cp. pp. 393–4, 460–1).

2. De Bry's title-page.[1]

'The true pictures and fashions of the people in that parte of America now called Virginia, discowred by Englismen sent thither in the years of our Lorde 1585. att the speciall charge and direction[2] of the Honourable Sir Walter Ralegh Knigt Lord Warden of the stanneries in the duchies of Corenwal and Oxford[3] who therin hath bynne fauored and auctorised by her Maaiestie and her letters patents.

Translated out of Latin into English by Richard Hackluit.

Diligentlye Collected and Draowne by Ihon White[4] who was sent thiter speciallye[5] and for the same purpose by the said Sir Walter Ralegh the year abouesaid 1585. and also the year 1588.[6] now cutt in copper and first published by Theodore de Bry att his wone chardges.'

3. De Bry's Epistle.[7]

'To the gentle Reader.

Although (frendlye Reader) man by his disobedience, weare depriued of those good Gifts wher with he was indued in his creation, yet he was not berefte of wit to prouyde for hym selfe, not discretion to deuise things necessarie for his vse, excepte suche as appartayne to his soules healthe, as may be gathered by this sauage nations, of whome this present worke intreateth. For

[1] The title-page of the second section of De Bry's *America*, pt. i (1590), in the English version. It also appeared in Latin, French and German.

[2] This description is, surprisingly, correct, while that in no. 1 above is not.

[3] 'Exonia' in the Latin edition, neither being required nor correct.

[4] 'With' in the Latin, French and German editions.

[5] If any reliance can be placed on De Bry, this would suggest that White's selection was due to Raleigh personally and that White was known to him previously.

[6] This would appear to show that De Bry knew of White's 1588 venture. It might suggest that he acquired the drawings from White before his departure from Bideford on 22 April, but that he (De Bry) had left England before news had come of White's unsuccessful return on 22 May (cp. p. 569). Incidentally, it indicates that De Bry had no doubt in his mind that John White, the governor of the 1587 colony who set out to relieve it in 1588, was the same man as the painter (cp. pp. 40–3).

[7] Epistle by Theodor De Bry, sig. ***4 v. As in the remainder of the text corrections made at the end of the volume are used, and words joined by the printer are separated. Otherwise it is given as John Wechel, De Bry's printer, left it.

although they haue noe true knoledge of God nor of his holye worde and are destituted of all lerninge, Yet they passe vs in many thinges, as in Sober feedinge and Dexteritye of witte, in makinge without any instrument of mettall thinges so neate and so fine, as a man would scarclye beleue the same, Vnless the Englishemen Had made proofe Therof by their trauailes into the contrye. Consideringe, Therfore that yt was a thinge worthie of admiration, I was verye willinge to offer vnto you the true Pictures of those people wich by the helfe of Maister Richard Hakluyt of Oxford Minister of Gods Word, who[1] first Incouraged me to publish the worke, I creaued out of the verye original of Maister Ihon White[2] an Englisch paynter who was sent into the contrye by the queenes Maiestye,[3] onlye[4] to draw the description of the place, lyuelye to describe the shapes of the Inhabitants their apparell, manners of Liuinge, and fashions, att the speciall Charges of the worthy knighte, Sir Walter Ralegh, who bestowed noe Small Sume of monnye in the serche and Discouerye of that countrye, From te yeers, 1584,[5] to the ende of The years 1588. Morouer this booke which intreateth of that parte of the new World which the Englishemen call by the name of Virginia I heer sett out in the first place, beinge therunto requested of my

---

[1] The Latin edition adds 'que iam regionum vidit', and this is followed in the French and German editions. Evidently in translating De Bry's own version Hakluyt deleted this misstatement about himself.

[2] On 8 January 1588 Hakluyt delivered dispatches in England, and remained there until March, leaving for Paris about 21 March. On 29 May he was again sent to England and on 27 July reached Paris on his return (Parks, *Hakluyt*, pp. 250–1). Since White was out of England from 22 April to 22 May, it is probable that it was between January and March that De Bry, in England, was told by Hakluyt of White's drawings and was introduced by him to White, who presented him with, or, more probably, sold him a group of replicas from his original set of drawings (cp. p. 394).

[3] Cp. p. 399 above, where White is said to have been sent by Raleigh. No connexion between White and the Queen has yet been traced.

[4] If this statement is to be taken literally White's sole function in 1585–6 was to make drawings, but it is clear that he must have done much of the mapping as well (above, pp. 41, 47–8, 51–6).

[5] The Latin, French and German editions have '1585'. The alteration is again probably due to Hakluyt.

Frends, by Raeson of the memorye of the fresh and late performance ther of, albeyt I haue in hand the Historye of Florida wich should be first sett foorthe because yt was discouured by the Frencheman longe before the discouerye of Virginia, yet I hope shortlye also to publish the same, A Victorye, doubtless so Rare, as I thinke the like hath not ben heard nor seene. I craeued both of them at London, an brought, Them hither to Franckfurt, wher I and my sonnes hauen taken ernest paynes in grauinge the pictures ther of in Copper, seeing yt is a matter of no small importance. Touchinge the stile of both the Discourses, I haue caused yt to bee Reduced into verye Good Frenche and Latin[1] by the aide of verye worshipfull frend of myne. Finallye I hartlye Request thee, that yf any seeke to Contrefaict thes my book, (for in this dayes many are so malicious that they seeke to gayne by other men labours) thow wouldest giue noe credit vnto suche conterfaited Drawghte. For dyuers secret marks lye hiddin in my pictures, which will breede Confusion vnless they bee well obserued.'[2]

4. 1 April 1590. Theodor de Bry's dedicatory epistle to Sir Walter Raleigh.[3]

'To the Right Worthie and Honourable, Sir Walter Ralegh, Knight, Seneschal of the Duchie of Cornewall and Exeter, and L. Warden of the stanneries in Deuon and Cornewell. T. B. wisheth true felictie.

[Raleigh arms, with motto 'Amore et virtute'.]

Sir, seeing that the parte of the Worlde, which is betwene the Florida and the Cap Breton nowe nammed Virginia, to the

[1] This is not precisely correct. The notes to the engravings were originally in Latin and had to be translated into English by Hakluyt and into French by L'Écluse: Hariot's tract was in English and had to be translated into Latin and French by L'Écluse.

[2] The epistle is preceded by an engraving of Adam and Eve in the Garden of Eden. There is no evidence that White had anything to do with the drawing on which it was based.

[3] Theodor De Bry, *America*, pt. i (1590), pp. 3-4. This is his general epistle dedicatory to all three sections of the volume and is followed immediately by his reprint of the 1588 edition of Hariot (cp. pp. 317-18 above). His English is his own and little has been done to straighten it.

honneur of yours most souueraine Layde and Queene Elizabetz, hath ben descouuered by yours meanes. And great chardges. And that your Collonye hath been theer established to your great honnor and prayse, and noe lesser proffit vnto the common welth: Yt is good raison that euery man euertwe[1] him selfe for to showe the benefit which they haue receue of yt. Theerfore, for my parte I haue been allwayes Desirous for to make yow knowe the good will that I haue to remayne still your most humble saeruant. I haue thincke that I cold faynde noe better occasion to declare yt, then takinge the paines to cott in copper (the most diligentye and well that wear in my possible to doe) the Figures which doe leuelye represent the forme and maner of the Inhabitants of the same countrye with theirs ceremonies, sollemne, feastles, and the manner and situation of their Townes, or Villages. Addinge vnto euery figure a brief declaration of the same, to that ende that euerye man cold the better vnderstand that which is in liuelye represented. Moreouer, I haue thinkce that the aforesaid figues wear of greater commendation, If somme Histoire which traitinge of the commodites and fertillitye of the said countrye weare Ioyned with the same, therfore haue I serue miselfe of the rapport which Thomas Hariot hath lattely sett foorth, and haue causse them booth togither to be printed for to dedicated vnto you, as a thiuge[2] which by reigtte dooth allreadye apparteyne vnto you. Therefore doe I creaue that you will accept this little Booke, and take yt In goode partte. And desiringe that fauor that you will receue me in the nomber of one of your most humble seruantz, beschinge the lord to blese and further you in all yours good doinges and actions, and allso to preserue, and keepe you allwayes in good helthe. And soe I comitt you vnto the almyhttie, from Franckfort the first of Apprill 1590.[3]

Your most humble seruant,

THEODORUS DE BRY'

---

[1] For 'exert'? [2] For 'things'.

[3] The Latin edition bears the same date ('Kl. Aprilis'); the German has 3 April, and the French 24 March.

II. LIST OF DRAWINGS, WITH TEXTS, WHICH CAN BE ASSO-
CIATED WITH THE 1585 VIRGINIA VOYAGE AND THE
FIRST COLONY ON ROANOKE ISLAND, 1585-6, OR WITH
SUBSEQUENT VIRGINIA VENTURES

1. Profiles of the islands of Dominica and Santa Cruz.[1]
A. 'The Risinge of the Ilande of Dominica.'[2]
B. 'The Rising of the Ilande of Santicruse.'[3]

2. Fortified camp at Mosquetal (Tallaboa Bay), Puerto Rico.[4]
'The xi[th] Maie the Generall in the Tyger arriued at S[t] Iohns
Iland where he fortified in this manner, toke in fresh water, and
buylt a Pynnes, And then departed from thence the xxiij[th] of the
same moneth. 1585.'[5]

[1] Brit. Mus., P. & D. 1906-5-9-1 (36); Binyon, *Catalogue*, no. 37; Prospectus,
no. 27; Lorant, *New world*, p. [215], [b], [48]. Profile views of the islands as
seen from on shipboard, with a scale of miles, headed 'This scale contaynethe
xxx myles', between the two. The purpose in making them was to provide a
handy means of recognition in steering a course through the islands. Cp. *West
Indies Pilot*, I (1942), 129-32, 211-16.

[2] The course from the Canaries was directed normally towards Dominica and
its recognition was an indication of successful navigation across the Atlantic.
On this occasion the narrator says 'we continued our course for Dominica...
wherewith we fell the 7. day of Maye 1585' (above p. 180), which was probably
the day on which the first sketch for this profile was made.

[3] From Dominica the course lay towards Puerto Rico and the *Tiger* would
have sighted St Croix (Santa Cruz) to starboard. It is not mentioned in the
narrative, but the sketch for the profile was probably made about 9 May, as we
are told that 'the 10. day following wee came to an anker at Cotesa, a little Island
situate neere to the Island of S. John' (above, p. 180).

[4] Brit. Mus., P. & D. 1906-5-9-1 (4); Binyon, *Catalogue*, no. 3; Prospectus,
no. 3; Lorant, *New world*, p. [185], [1]. For the location of the fort and the
documents associated with it see pp. 181, 733-4, 739.

[5] This picture-plan shows the 'Fort' which was constructed between 11 and
13 May (the narrative says they anchored on the 12th, not the 11th). The river
which 'ran by the one side of our forte' is inscribed 'A fresh ryuer'. From it
were constructed a series of trenches and emplacements, running almost due east
to a small lake on the north-east corner of the area enclosed by the encampment.
On the lake are shown seven land-crabs (cp. no. 4 below), a heron, and two
species of duck. The lake-shore was left unprotected, but from its southern end
the entrenchments were carried down to the sea. A small boat, steered by an oar

3. Entrenchment near Cape Rojo, Puerto Rico.[1]

'The forme of a fort which was made by M*aster* Ralfe Lane in a parte of S[t] Iohns Ilande neere Capross where we toke in salt the xxvj[th] of May. 1585.'[2]

and propelled by one pair of oars, is carrying four men with barrels of water across the river just north of the entrenchments, while a party of twelve armed men is emerging from the wood on the north. On the east a long file of men, protected by a party of harquebusiers, is hauling a tree-trunk on a crude truck towards the camp, the narrative telling us that the trees were cut as far as three miles away from the fort and brought back without resistance from the Spaniards. The inscription on the drawing here is 'The manner of drawing in of tymber into the fort for the buylding of a Pynnes'. The entrenchments are continued along the shore with three masked entrances. Riding off-shore—'wee came to an anker...within a Fawlcon shot of the Shoare', the narrative tells us—is the *Tiger*. Inside the camp, on the north, a number of sentinels are posted: this is inscribed 'Northe Syde. M[r] Lanes quarter'. On the northern edge of the woodland inside the camp are the outlines of tents and enclosures, while two horses—'Spanish horses, which wee before had taken', the narrative says—are running in the wood. On the southern edge of the wood are many more tents, hutments and compounds, with the inscription 'The Generalls quarter', i.e. Grenville's. Between the wood and the trenches on the south there is much activity. A fire is burning at the south-east corner and this is probably the site of the forge, built, the Spanish sources say, to make nails, while the pinnace, the construction of which was one reason for building the camp, is lying on the ground bottom-up and nearly completed. Across the river, near its mouth, twenty-five men on foot with a figure on horseback (inscribed 'The Generall') among them, are approaching the fort, some of the men wading the river, while four sentinels welcome them by firing their pieces. This represents Grenville's return to the camp on 22 May after his meeting with the Spaniards to arrange a truce (pp. 182–3). The composition of the drawing indicates that White had experience as a surveyor and was accustomed to the preparation of estate maps. It carries a scale of '40 Paesces', probably the 'geometrical' pace of 5 feet used by John Speed.

[1] Brit. Mus., P. & D. 1906-5-9-1 (5); Binyon, *Catalogue*, no. 4; Prospectus, no. 4; Lorant, *New world*, p. [188], [4]. The outline is reproduced at p. 905 below. It bears a close relationship in its layout to the Roanoke Island fort defences (cp. pp. 905–6). It was probably located at Salinas Bay (p. 184 above).

[2] On 26 May, Ralph Lane, leaving the rest of the ships at anchor in San German Bay, sailed round Cape Rojo, at the south-west tip of Puerto Rico, in a captured Spanish frigate and under the guidance of a Spanish pilot, to look for salt. On shore they found two mounds of salt prepared by the Spaniards (the narrative says one, but the drawing shows two). Lane 'intrenched himselfe vpon the sandes immediatly, compassing one of their salte hils within the trench'. The picture-plan shows the complex lines of trenches and bastions which Lane constructed (which have affinities with the recently-excavated perimeter of the Roanoke fort, pp. 904–6 above). One mound of salt is shown, untouched,

4. 'A lande Crab.'[1]

5. Land Hermit Crabs.

(a) 'Caracol.'[2]

'Caracol.'

'Thes lyue on land neere the Sea syde, and breede in sondry shells when they be empty.'

(b) 'Caracol.'[3]

6. 'Scorpions.'[4]

inside the northern bastion. Sentinels are posted, one of them on top of the second mound inside the main enclosure, where men are tearing down the salt with pickaxes and shovelling it up for others to carry in sacks on their backs to the ship's boat which has been hauled up on the sand through the entrance in the entrenchments. The Spanish prize is anchored off-shore. Twenty-four men can be distinguished. The narrative says Lane had twenty of his own men with him (above, p. 185), but Lane, complaining of the inadequacy of the force Grenville let him have to withstand Don Diego Menéndez Valdés, governor of Puerto Rico, admitted he had twenty-five soldiers and six Spanish prisoners (above, p. 229). Lane's entrenchments, however, frightened off the Spanish force (cp. pp. 162, 229) which came up and he was able to clear the salt and rejoin the rest of the fleet in San German Bay on 29 May.

[1] Brit. Mus., P. & D. 1906-5-9-1 (56); Binyon, *Catalogue*, no. 58; Prospectus, no. 48; Lorant, *New world*, p. [215], [a], [47]. Land Crab, *Cardisoma guanhumi* Latreille, evidently drawn by John White on Puerto Rico in May 1585. He includes a number in the drawing of the camp there (no. 2 above) and one appears in the De Bry engraving of the scene of Indians fishing off the North Carolina coast though it is quite out of place there (no. 46 below). A copy is in Brit. Mus., P. & D. 199. a. 3 (L.B. 3 (20)), and copies of this in turn in Sloane MS 5262, nos. 10, 25.

[2] Brit. Mus., P. & D. 1906-5-9-1 (57 [a–b]); Binyon, *Catalogue*, no. 59; Prospectus, no. 49; Lorant, *New world*, p. [220], [b], [57]. The upper specimen, facing right, is in a long thin shell (*Turritella variegata* Linn.), the lower, facing left, in a snail-like shell (*Natica canrena* Linn.). Both are from the West Indies. The Spanish word *caracol* is for the shells, not the occupants, meaning a periwinkle or other twisted shell. The crabs are Land Hermit Crab, *Coenobita clypeatus* Herbst, from most parts of the West Indies visited by White in May and June 1585. Mistakenly, he puts both the specimens into the Indian fishing-scene (no. 46 below).

[3] Copy in Brit. Mus., P. & D. 199. a. 3 (L.B. 3 (21) [b]); Binyon, *Catalogue*, no. 21. In this copy the specimens are side by side with that in the long shell on the right and that in the round shell on the left. A copy of this is in Sloane MS 5262, no. 19.

[4] Brit. Mus., P. & D. 1906-5-9-1 (73); Binyon, *Catalogue*, no. 73; Prospectus, no. 65; Lorant, *New world*, p. [221], [b], [60]. Scorpions, *Tityus tityinae*, from the West Indies. Of the two studies one is shown on its back, with head to the

7. Fire-flies.

(a) 'A flye which in the night semeth a flame of fyer.'[1]

(b) 'Hanc Cicindelam uná cum icone à Candido pictore peritissimo, qui diligentissimé eam tàm in Hispaniola quam in Virginiâ obseruauit, accepi.'[2]

(c) Fire-flies.[3]

8. Iguana.

(a) 'Igwano. Some of thes are .3. fote in length. and lyue on land.'[4]

left of the drawing, the other facing right and with the tail curled to the left. In Thomas Moffet's 'Insectorum...theatrum', Brit. Mus., Sloane MS 4014, fo. 188, there is a woodcut pasted in the margin which could be after White's second study, but is more likely to have been cut from another book. It is printed in *Insectorum...theatrum* (1634), p. 204, and *Theater of insects* (1658), p. 1049. On p. 208 of the 1634 edition ((1658), p. 1052) American and Hispaniolan Scorpions are discussed, but White is not named as a source of information.

[1] Brit. Mus., P. & D. 1906-5-9-1 (67); Binyon, *Catalogue*, no. 69; Prospectus, no. 59; Lorant, *New world*, p. [214], [b], [46]. Three studies of a fire-fly, (a) top centre, with wings open, (b) left, with wings closed, head to right, (c) right, with wings beginning to open, head to left. This is a West Indian Fire-fly, probably *Pyrophorus noctilucus*. Underneath is a Gadfly (no. 108).

[2] In Thomas Penny's hand. Thomas Moffet, 'Insectorum...theatrum', Brit. Mus., Sloane MS 4014, fo. 109; Lorant, *New world*, p. [220], [c], [58] (without precise reference). They show views (a) and (b) above, (a) being turned with the head to the right, and (b) to the left facing down the page. Both are on separate slips of paper, pasted on. They are by White himself (cp. Raven, *English naturalists*, p. 185).

[3] Woodcuts of 7 (b) in Moffet, *Insectorum theatrum* (1634), p. 112, with text as in MS; and *Theater of insects* (1658), p. 978, where the text is: 'This Cicindele, together with the Figure of it came from a most skilful painter, who had taken strict observation of it both in the lesser Spain and in Virginia. In Hispaniola they are almost all the year long, for they have seldome any winter.' Note the omission of White's name. Moffet goes on ((1634), pp. 112–13; (1658), pp. 978–9) to discuss the glow-worms of Hispaniola, on which White may have given him information. Walter Cope had in 1599 specimens of 'Flies which glow at night in Virginia instead of lights, since there is often no day there for a month' (T. Platter, *Travels*, p. 172).

[4] Brit. Mus., P. & D. 1906-5-9-1 (71); Binyon, *Catalogue*, no. 63; Prospectus, no. 63; Lorant, *New world*, p. [223], [a], [62]. Iguana (*Cyclura* sp.) of the West Indies, detailed identification not being possible. This is the earliest English drawing of the Iguana (the name is of West Indian origin), but the first publication was in the plate of Cartagena in the *Expeditio Francisci Draki* (cp. pp. 34, 42 above and Wright, *Further English voyages*, at p. 54, where it is conveniently reproduced).

(*b*) 'The Gwanoo.'[1]

9. Alligator.

(*a*) 'Allagatto. This being but one moneth old was .3. foote 4. ynches in length. and lyue in water.'[2]

(*b*) Without inscription.[3]

10. Pineapple.

(*a*) 'The Pyne frute.'[4]

(*b*) 'Pine A.'[5]

The figure is identical in posture with White's drawing, though there is a scenic background added in the engraving. Mr Hulton suggests to me, and I have every reason to agree with him, that the probability is that White travelled with Drake's artist from Port Ferdinando to England in June–July 1586 and either copied his drawing of the Iguana or gave him a copy of his own. The English letterpress for the engraving has the note: 'A beast called a Guana bearing this shape and fashion as is here truely purtraicted, it liueth on the land in the woodes and desert places, and is caught by the sauage or Indian people who sell them to the Spaniards, they are of a sad greene collour, and their body of the bignes of a connie [they are larger than a rabbit], they are eaten by the Indians and Spaniardes, and so likewise by vs for a very dilicate meate, in the breeding time the female is full of eggs in great number, and they of all the rest are esteemed the most delicate.'

[1] Copy in Brit. Mus., P. & D. 199. a. 3 (L.B. 3 (17) [a]); Binyon, *Catalogue*, no. 17; of which there is a copy in Sloane MS 5272, no. 22.

[2] Brit. Mus., P. & D. 1906-5-9-1 (72); Binyon, *Catalogue*, no. 74; Prospectus, no. 64; Lorant, *New world*, p. [223], [b], [63]. There is a certain mixture of features in this drawing which makes it impossible to distinguish whether it is an Alligator or a Crocodile (*Crocodylus acutus* Daudin). If it is the former it is more likely to be a West Indian specimen, not the mainland North American Alligator, *Alligator mississippiensis* Daudin. The use of the Spanish term, *El lagarto*, surviving in Spanish-American *lagarto*, would point, though not conclusively, to a West Indian origin. It may be noted that White's inscription is quite wrong and is no guide to his personal observation of this specimen over a period of time (which would tend to place it at Roanoke Island), as it is between one and two years of age. The plate of Santo Domingo in *Expeditio Francisci Draki* (see no. 8 above; Wright, *Further English voyages*, at p. 38) contains a Crocodile, but it is not identical with White's. The English text describes it as 'A strange beast drawne after the life, & is called by our English mariners Aligarta, by the Spaniards Caiman....'

[3] Copy in Brit. Mus., P. & D. 199, a. 3, no. 17 [b]; Binyon, *Catalogue*, no. 17.

[4] Brit. Mus., P. & D. 1906-5-9-1 (41); Binyon, *Catalogue*, no. 43; Prospectus, no. 33; Lorant, *New world*, p. [207], [b], [30]. A single fruit of the Pineapple, *Ananas comosos*.

[5] Copy, without variants, in Brit. Mus., P. & D. 199. a. 3, no. 29; Binyon, *Catalogue*, no. 29.

11. Mammee Apple.
(a) 'Mammea.'[1]
(b) 'Mamea.'[2]

12. Mammee Apple.[3]

13. Banana.
'Platano. or Planten.'[4]

14. Banana.
(a) 'Platano. or Planten.'[5]
(b) 'Platano.'[6]

[1] Brit. Mus., P. & D. 1906-5-9-1 (40 [a]); Binyon, *Catalogue*, no. 42; Prospectus, no. 32; Lorant, *New world*, p. [206], [b], [28]. A single fruit of the Mammee Apple, *Mammea americana*, from the West Indies (cp. pp. 500, 520). Cp. R. Percyvall, *Bibliotheca hispanica* (1591): 'Maméys, m. a fruite in the Indies bigger than a quince hauing a peele as the orenge, and a great stone or kernell in the middle, and the meate verye daintie.'

[2] Copy, without variants, in Brit. Mus., P. & D. 199. a. 3 (L.B. 3 (28) [a]). Another version, which should possibly be a separate item, is in Sloane MS 5289, no. 158. It is green in colour, with the stalk turned to the right, and the inscription is '2 foot 1 inch round. The weight 7 pounds exactly'. There is no direct evidence that it is after White and it may have been drawn from the specimen for Sloane.

[3] Brit. Mus., P. & D. 199. a. 3 (L.B. 3 (28) [b]); Binyon, *Catalogue*, no. 28. Copy of drawing of section of the Mammee Apple, showing two seed-cavities. The original is not known to have survived. It contains no title.

[4] Brit. Mus., P. & D. 1906-5-9-1 (39); Binyon, *Catalogue*, no. 40; Prospectus, no. 40; Lorant, *New world*, p. [205], [26]. Stalk, with bunches of fruit, of the Plantain, *Musa paradisiaca*. Both Hakluyts had suggested that the expedition should carry sugar-canes to plant, the elder indicating that they might be obtained in the West Indies on the way (Taylor, *Hakluyts*, II, 321, 335), and sugar-canes were so carried from either Puerto Rico or Hispaniola to Roanoke Island (pp. 187, 336 below), along with many other plants. But John White was not content with this and took a pictorial record as well. A Spanish prisoner records how on Puerto Rico in May 1585 'They took away with them many banana plants (*muchas plantas de Platanos*), and other fruits which they found along the coast, and made sketches of fruits and trees' (p. 742 below).

[5] Brit. Mus., P. & D. 1906-5-9-1 (40); Binyon, *Catalogue*, no. 41; Prospectus, no. 31; Lorant, *New world*, p. [206], [a], [27]. A single complete fruit of the Plantain, *Musa paradisiaca*, with cut section of a second fruit.

[6] Copy, without variants, in Brit. Mus., P. & D. 199. a. 3 (L.B. 3 (30)); Binyon, *Catalogue*, no. 30; of which Sloane MS 5289, no. 160, is a copy.

15. Flamingo.
'A Flaminco.'[1]

16. Frigate Bird.[2]

17. Tropic Bird.[3]

18. Brown Booby.
'Bobo.'[4]

19. Noddy Tern.
'Tinosa.'[5]

20. Moonfish.
'Polometa. A foote long.'[6]

[1] Brit. Mus., P. & D. 1906-5-9-1 (60); Binyon, *Catalogue*, no. 62; Prospectus, no. 52; Lorant, *New world*, p. [216], [49]. The Flamingo, *Phoenicopterus ruber* Linn., is normally found in the West Indies and Bahamas. It comes to Florida and incidental visitors have reached as far as North Carolina (*Birds of N.C.*, no. 34; H.T.D.). Mrs E. G. Allen (*Trans. American Phil. Soc.*, n.s., XLI, 446) says that this is one of White's drawings which is of special interest to ornithologists for detail and delicacy of execution in the feathers (cp. no. 52 below).

[2] Brit. Mus., P. & D. 1906-5-9-1 (62); Binyon, *Catalogue*, no. 64; Prospectus, no. 54; Lorant, *New world*, p. [219], [a], [54]. The Frigate Bird (or Man-o'-War Bird), *Fregata magnificans* Mathews, a female seen in flight from below. It nests in the West Indies and the Gulf Coast and flies north in summer, sometimes to the North Carolina coast or beyond (*Birds of N.C.*, no. 18; H.T.D.).

[3] Brit. Mus., P. & D. 1906-5-9-1 (65); Binyon, *Catalogue*, no. 67; Prospectus, no. 57 (as *Phaethon americana*); Lorant, *New world*, p. [219], [b], [55]. The Red-billed Tropic Bird, *Phaehon aethereus*, of the West Indies. The yellow-billed species, *P. lepturus catesbyi* Brandt, very rarely comes up the North American coast as far as North Carolina though it breeds in Bermuda (*Birds of N.C.*, no. 11; G. M. Matthews, '*Phaëthon catesbyi* Brandt', in *The Auk*, n.s., XXXII (1915), 195–7.

[4] Brit. Mus., P. & D. 1906-5-9-1 (63); Binyon, *Catalogue*, no. 65; Prospectus, no. 55 (as Brown Gannet, *Sula piscatrix*); Lorant, *New world*, p. [218], [b], [53]. The Brown Booby, *Sula leucogaster leucogaster*, of the West Indies. Cp. 'páxaros bobos' Fernández de Oviedo, *Hist. natural de las Indias*, I (1851), 441.

[5] Brit. Mus., P. & D. 1906-5-9-1 (59); Binyon, *Catalogue*, no. 61; Prospectus, no. 51 (as Noddy Tern, *Anous stolidus*); Lorant, *New world*, p. [217], [a], [50]; E. G. Allen, 'Some sixteenth century paintings of American birds', in *The Auk*, LIII (1936), 17–21, pl. I. The Noddy Tern, *Sterna stolidus*, of the Atlantic coast of the southern United States. It reaches the North Carolina coast but is here best included in the oceanic group.

[6] Brit. Mus., P. & D. 1906-5-9-1 (47); Binyon, *Catalogue*, no. 49; Prospectus, no. 39; Lorant, *New world*, p. [208], [b], [32]. Cp. 'palometas' (modern Spanish equivalent?) in G. Fernández de Oviedo, *Hist. natural de las Indias*, I (1851), 424.

21. Moonfish.
(a) 'Crocobado.'[1]
(b) Without inscription.[2]

22. Grouper.
(a) 'Garopa.'[3]
(b) 'Garopa.'[4]

23. Grouper.
(a) 'Mero.'[5]
(b) 'Mero.'[6]

24. Grunt.
(a) 'Pefe pica.'[7]

Moonfish (or Lookdown), *Selene vomer* Linn. (*Fishes of N.C.*, no. 182; H.T.D.). It is found from Brazil to Massachusetts, but North Carolina specimens are not usually over 6 in. long, so that it probably comes from the West Indies. The pectoral fin is tinted pink and the body and other fins are silver (which has oxidized on the drawing).

[1] Brit. Mus., P. & D. 1906-5-9-1 (49); Binyon, *Catalogue*, no. 51; Prospectus, no. 41; Lorant, *New world*, p. [209], [b], [32]. The name has not been found in Spanish. It is also a specimen of the Moonfish (see above, no. 19), but, though no scale is given, probably a larger specimen. The silvery colour has superimposed on it faint vertical stripes of pink and grey. It is probably also from the West Indies.

[2] Copy in Brit. Mus., P. & D. 199. a. 3 (L.B. 3 (24) [b]); of which Sloane MS 5267, no. 88, is a copy.

[3] Brit. Mus., P. & D. 1906-5-9-1 (48); Binyon, *Catalogue*, no. 50; Prospectus, no. 40; Lorant, *New world*, p. [209], [b], [35]. The name is the Portuguese *garoupa*. This fish is a grouper, most probably the Rock Hind, *Epinephelus ascencionis* Osbeck, which is found abundantly in the West Indies and ranges on the Atlantic coast of North America to North Carolina and beyond.

[4] Copy in Brit. Mus., P. & D. 199. a. 3 (L.B. 3 (22) [b]); of which Sloane MS 5267, no. 104, is a copy.

[5] Brit. Mus., P. & D. 1906-5-9-1 (50); Binyon, *Catalogue*, no. 52; Prospectus, no. 42; Lorant, *New world*, p. [213], [c], [44]. Another grouper, but brownish in colour, with gold underparts, a black spot on ventral fin; caudal fin concave in outline. Probably of genus *Mycteroperca* Gill. and possibly *Mycteroperca venenosa apua* Bloch. The Spanish *Mero* is used for several fishes, but the French *Mérou* is confined to the groupers.

[6] Copy in Brit. Mus., P. & D. 199. a. 3 (L.B. 3 (27) [a]); of which Sloane MS 5267, no. 102, is a copy.

[7] Brit. Mus., P. & D. 1906-5-9-1 (52); Binyon, *Catalogue*, no. 54; Prospectus, no. 44; Lorant, *New world*, p. [212], [c], [41]. Blue-striped Grunt, *Haemuleon sciurus* Shaw, of the West Indies. The letter 'f' should clearly read 's', having

John White's Drawings

(b) 'Peffe Pica.'[1]

25. Soldier-fish.

(a) 'Oio de buey.'[2]

(b) 'Oio Debvey.'[3]

26. Dolphin.

(a) 'Duratho. Of thes some are .5. foote long.'[4]

received its cross-stroke accidentally. The Spanish would then be *Pese pica, Péce pica*=pike-fish, lance-fish? The 'f' was probably intended by White for his characteristic 'f' for 's' (e.g. in Montaigne Pallassi (the first 's'), in map no. 109 below, and cp. nos. 30, 87, 104, 105).

[1] Copy in Brit. Mus., P. & D. 199. a. 3 (L.B. 3 (21) [a]); of which Sloane MS 5267, no. 128, is a copy.

[2] Brit. Mus., P. & D. 1906-5-9-1 (42); Binyon, *Catalogue*, no. 44; Prospectus, no. 34 (as *Holocentrum longipinna*); Lorant, *New world*, p. [212], [b], [40]. Squirrel-fish or Soldier-fish, *Holocentrus ascencionis* Osbeck, which comes up from the West Indies as far north as North Carolina (H.T.D.). Possibly it was thought to be Saupe, *Böops salpa*, from the longitudinal stripes, though the dorsal differs, hence *ojo de buey* = *böops* = ox-eye.

[3] Copy in Brit. Mus., P. & D. 199. a. 3 (L.B. 3 (27) [b]); of which Sloane MS 5267, no. 115, is a copy.

[4] Brit. Mus., P. & D. 1906-5-9-1 (44); Binyon, *Catalogue*, no. 46; Prospectus, no. 36; Lorant, *New world*, p. [209], [c], [36]. Dolphin, *Coryphaena hippurus* Linn., found on both sides of the Atlantic. The name *Dorado* (from its golden glow at night) is still used in Spanish and Portuguese. White shows dolphins chasing flying-fish both off the Bahamas and off South Carolina in his general map (no. 109 below). There is a specially high concentration of dolphins off Cape Hatteras, possibly one of the greatest in the world, where they come to feed on flying-fish (no. 27 below) at the north-eastward deflection of the Gulf Stream (see map at end). 4 ft. in length and 23 lb. is the largest recorded from this area (E. W. Gudger, 'The abundance of the Dolphin, *Coryphaena hippurus*, on the North Carolina coast', in *Jnl. of the Elisha Mitchell Scientific Society*, XLVII (1932), 237-44; *Fishes of N.C.*, no. 194; H.T.D.). The drawing has again the closest of affinities with a figure in a plate in *Expeditio Francisci Draki*, like no. 8 above, this time with one on the plate of San Agustín (Wright, *Further English voyages*, at p. 166). Here White may well have supplied Drake's artist with a copy. The English text reads: 'The liuely purtraicture of a fish called the Dolphin, which is of three seurall coullours: the top of his back and all his fins be blue, all his sides are of light greene, and belly white, his head almost all blue, the taile one parte blue, and the lower parte greene, he is very pleasant to beholde in the sea by day light and in the night he seemed to be of the coullour of gold, he taketh pleasure as other fishes do by swimming by the ship, he is excellent sweete to be eaten, this fish liueth most by chasing of the flying fish and other small fishes, they are caught most commonly by our mariners with harping irons or fisgigs.'

(b) 'Deoratho.'[1]

27. Flying-fish.
(a) 'Bolador. The flyeng fishe.'[2]
(b) 'Boladora.'[3]

28. Remora.
(a) 'Rebeso. Two fote and a halfe long.'[4]
(b) 'Rebeso.'[5]

29. Remora.
(a) 'Rebeso.'[6]
(b) 'Rebosa.'[7]

Richard Maddox had already drawn in his diary of the Fenton voyage the dolphin and flying fish (Brit. Mus., Cotton MS, Appendix xlvii, fo. 22 v.).

[1] Copy, reversed, in Brit. Mus., P. & D. 199. a. 3 (L.B. 3 (25) [a]); of which Sloane MS 5267, no. 68, and possibly no. 82 (described as 'A Dolphin 48 inches long'), are copies.

[2] Brit. Mus., P. & D. 1906-5-9-1 (46); Binyon, *Catalogue*, no. 48; Prospectus, no. 38 (as *Exocoetus evolans*); Lorant, *New world*, p. [211], [38]. Either *Execoetus volitans* or *Parexocoetus brachyptans littoralis* (cp. C. M. Breder, 'Atlantic Ocean flying fishes', in *Bull. Bingham Oceanographic Inst.*, vi, no. 5 (1938), pp. 28, 36). The Spanish name for the flying-fish is now *Pez volador*. The flying-fish concentrate off Cape Hatteras and attract dolphins who prey on them (E. W. Gudger, op. cit.; C. M. Breder, 'Field observations on Flying Fish', in *Zoologica*, ix (New York, 1929), 302, 312; *Fishes of N.C.*, nos. 142–4). Flying-fish chased by dolphins (cp. no. 26 above) are shown twice on White's general map. The figure in the Santiago (Cape Verdes) plate of *Expeditio Francisci Draki* (cp. pp. 34, 42 above, and Wright, *Further English voyages*, at p. 6) has no close affinities with White's drawing. The English text says that they very frequently fell on Drake's ships, and were often chased by the Dolphin and Bonito.

[3] Copy in Brit. Mus., P. & D. 199. a. 3 (L.B. 3 (26)); of which Sloane MS 5267, no. 84, is a copy.

[4] Brit. Mus., P. & D. 1906-5-9-1 (53); Binyon, *Catalogue*, no. 55; Prospectus, no. 45 (as *Echeneis naucrates*); Lorant, *New world*, p. [212], [b], [40]. Dorsal view of Shark-sucker or Remora, *Echeneis naucrates* Linn., reaching 3 ft. in length on the Atlantic coast (*Fishes of N.C.*, no. 320; H.T.D.). The Spanish *Rébeza* ('thick lip') is now superseded by *Rémora*.

[5] Copies in Brit. Mus., P. & D. 199. a. 3 (L.B. 3 (19) [b]), and (L.B. 3 (25) [b]); of which Sloane MS 5267, no. 9, is a copy.

[6] Brit. Mus., P. & D. 1906-5-9-1 (43); Binyon, *Catalogue*, no. 45; Prospectus, no. 35; Lorant, *New world*, p. 213 [b], [43]. Ventral view of the Remora, *Remora remora* Linn.

[7] Copy in Brit. Mus., P. & D. 199. a. 3 (L.B. 3 (19) [a]).

5. JOHN WHITE. 'The arriual of the Englishemen in Virginia.' Engraved by Theodor de Bry.

30. Trigger-fish.

'Pefe porco. Of this, some are .2. fote in length.'[1]

31. Portuguese Man-o'-War.

(*a*) 'This is a lyuing fish, and flote vpon the Sea. Some call them Caruels.'[2]

(*b*) Without inscription.[3]

32. 'The arriual of the Englishemen in Virginia.'[4]

'The sea coasts of Virginia arre full of Ilands, wherby the entrance into the mayne land is hard to finde. For although they

[1] Brit. Mus., P. & D. 1906-5-9-1 (55); Binyon, *Catalogue*, no. 57; Prospectus, no. 47 (as File-fish, *Balistes vetula*); Lorant, *New world*, p. [212], [a], [39]. A copy is in Brit. Mus., P. & D. 199. a. 3 (L.B. 3 (24)); of which copies are in Sloane MS 5267, nos. 44, 51. Queen Trigger-fish, *Balistes vetula* Linn. One is shown by White on his general map (no. 109 below), at sea south-east of Cape Lookout, and he includes several in his drawings of Indians fishing inside the Carolina Sounds (no. 46 below), but these are all too far north for fish of this size, which must have been taken in or near the West Indies. There is again a close connexion between White and the artist of Drake's voyage, whose general map (see pp. 34, 413; Wright, *Further English voyages*, frontispiece) contained the figure of a fish, called a 'Sea Connye' (sea-rabbit) which is nearly the same, reversed, as White's drawing, apart from two variations in the fins; these variations could easily be due to the engraver. Once again, as with no. 24 above, 's' has become 'f', so that the name on the drawing was originally *Pese porco*, *Péce puerco* = pig-fish?

[2] Brit. Mus., P. & D. 1906-5-9-1 (45); Binyon, *Catalogue*, no. 47; Prospectus, no. 37; Lorant, *New world*, p. [210], [37].

A medusa, known as the Portuguese Man-o'-war, hence the name, *Caravella caravella*. It is now known as *Physalia physalis* and is found from the West Indies up the Atlantic coast of North America as far as Massachusetts (*Fishes of N.C.*, p. 220; H.T.D.).

[3] Copy in Brit. Mus., P. & D. 199. a. 3 (L.B. 3 (23)); of which Sloane MS 5262, no. 27, is a copy.

[4] Fig. 5. De Bry, *America*, pt. i, pl. II (Lorant, *New world*, p. [229]), engraving by Theodor De Bry. The drawing is not now extant, but it was evidently based on a sketch similar to that of 1585, only centred farther to the north (cp. p. 215). It is a typical off-shore view, part picture part chart, of the kind favoured by English map-makers (cp. E. Lynam, *English maps and mapmakers* (1944), pp. 13–14, *The mapmaker's art*, pp. 7–8, 46, 57) De Bry has conventionalized his vegetation, figures and ships. The artist and engraver have 'garnished their plot' (cp. p. 53) with six or seven varieties of trees, have shown grape-vines where the 1585 sketch had recorded their presence (pp. 215–17 above), and given us our only representation (a conventionalized one) of the Indian village on Roanoke Island

413

bee separated with diuers and sundrie large Diuision,[1] whiche seeme to yeeld conuenient entrance, yet to our great perill we proued that they wear shallowe, and full of dangerous flatts, and could neuer perce opp into the mayne land, vntill wee made trialls in many places with or small pinness. At lengthe wee fownd an entrance vppon our mens diligent serche therof Affter that wee had passed opp, and sayled ther in for a short space we discouered a mightye riuer fallinge downe into the sownde ouer against those Ilands, which neuertheless wee could not saile opp any thinge far by Reason of the shallewnes, the mouth ther of beinge annoyed with sands driuen in with the tyde therfore saylinge further, wee came vnto a Good bigg yland, the Inhabitante therof as soone as they saw vs began to make a great an[2] horrible crye, as people which neuer befoer had seene men apparelled like vs, and camme a way makinge out crys like wild beasts or men out of their wyts. But beenge gentlye called backe, wee offred the*m* of our wares, as glasses, kniues, babies,[3] and other trifles, which wee thougt they deligted in. Soe they stood still, and perceuinge our Good will and courtesie came fawninge vppon vs, and bade us welcome. Then they brougt vs to their village in the iland called, Roanoac, and vnto their Weroans or Prince, which entertained vs with Reasonable curtesie, althoug the[4] wear amased at the first sight of vs. Suche was our arriuall into the parte of the worlde,[5] which

(cp. pp. 106–7), as well as adding a fish-weir and some figures of Indians. The ships and pinnace are, compared with White's (pp. 403–5, 460–1), of little representational value. The coast runs north from Cape Kenrick (cp. p. 864) to the present Virginia state line, showing as inlets in the Banks 'Hatorasck' (Port Ferdinando), Port Lane (unnamed), 'Trinety harbor', and two further unnamed inlets. The three villages shown are enclosed by palisades.

[1] For 'Diuisions'.   [2] For 'and'.

[3] The French edition has 'poupees'. For one of the dolls see no. 34, pp. 317–18 below.

[4] For 'they'.

[5] That the texts were written by Hariot (if not with as careful a pen as his *Report*) appears from p. 430 below. They were done in Latin, according to De Bry (p. 401 above), and translated into English by Hakluyt, before being maltreated by De Bry's printers. It is strange that, passing through the hands of both Hariot and Hakluyt, the account of the first contacts with Roanoke Island does not fit

we call Virginia, the stature of bodye of wich people, theyr attire, and maneer of lyuinge, their feasts, and banketts, I will particullerlye declare vnto yow.'

33. Pomeiooc.

(a) 'The towne of Pomeiock and true forme of their howses, couered and enclosed some with matts, and some with barcks of trees. All compassed abowt with smale poles stock thick together in stedd of a wall.'[1]

in with what is known of the 1585 expedition, or even with Barlowe's account of the 1584 venture. Perhaps Hariot is using a different story of the earlier voyage from his lost chronicle (cp. p. 387). If so, and if he is being approximately correct, it may be suggested that Amadas made a first attempt to reach Roanoke Island from the north by way of Trinity Harbour, but was turned back by the shoals across the mouths of Albemarle and Currituck Sounds after seeing Indians who made a great fuss of the white men (and originated the 'massacre' story? (cp. p. 81)). If so he later reached the island more decorously from the south by way of Port Ferdinando (cp. pp. 95, 863-4). But why White should have shown the pinnace approaching Roanoke Island from the north (unless De Bry added it) is something of a mystery. (It may, incidentally, be noted that we are presuming that Hariot wrote the notes on seeing a set of the original drawings as supplied by White to De Bry, but it may be that he used a set of early pulls of the engravings, and that De Bry's embellishments may sometimes have misled him.)

[1] Brit. Mus., P. & D. 1906-5-9-1 (8); Binyon, *Catalogue*, no. 7; Prospectus, no. 7; Lorant, *New world*, p. [190], [6]. This drawing (with that of Secoton, no. 37) provides the earliest and most complete evidence on the Algonkian long house in the area of its most southerly extension (see Swanton, *Indians*, pp. 386-439; Flannery, *Analysis*, pp. 63-7). It shows eighteen houses (compare the nine of Roanoke, p. 107, and the thirteen visible in the Secoton picture), of varying sizes, some having an end, a side, or part of a side uncovered. The smaller houses have a door in the gable (see Swanton, *Indians*, pp. 428-30), and the larger show the sleeping benches. One of the largest (see De Bry's 'A') has a distinct roof pattern, ridged instead of arched in section and coming to a peak in the middle: it is described as the 'tempel' (*q.v.*), and suggests southern influence in its construction. The chief's house (De Bry's 'B') is the largest but gives no indication of division into rooms (cp. p. 107 above). Indians in groups stand about: one man splits wood with an axe: one near the top left has a dog (the earliest appearance of this animal in an American drawing so far as is known, cp. p. 357 above): a group (larger than that in no. 42) is shown round a central fire. No vegetation is shown growing. The palisade is close but composed of light poles only. It has an open entrance (cp. Roanoke, p. 107 above) with a path edged with hooped sticks. For the location of the village, probably drawn by White on 12 July 1585, see pp. 191, 870.

(b) Without inscription.[1]

(c) 'The Towne of Pomeiooc.'[2]

'The townes of this contrie are in a maner like vnto those which are in Florida,[3] yet are they not soe stronge nor yet preserued with soe great care. They are compassed abowt with poles starcke faste in the grownd, but they are not verye stronge. The entrance is verye narrowe as may be seene by this picture, which is made accordinge to the forme of the towne of Pomeiooc. Ther are but few howses therin, saue those whiche belonge to the kinge and his nobles. On the one side is their tempel separated from the other howses, and marked with the letter A. yt is builded rownde, and couered with skynne matts, and as yt wear compassed abowt. With cortynes without windowes, and hath noe ligthe but by the doore. On the other side is the kings lodginge[4] marked with the

---

[1] Copy in Brit. Mus., P. & D. 199. a. 3 (L.B. 3 (1)); of which Sloane MS 5253, no. 14, is a copy. This has, outside the stockade, a cornfield on the top left, and a pond at the top right. These features indicate that this copy has affinities with that from which De Bry's engraving was made, rather than with the surviving original (cp. p. 397 above).

[2] De Bry, *America*, pt. i (1590), pl. xix, sigs. C6 v.–C7, with the initials 'T.B.' (Lorant, *New world*, p. 263). De Bry gives to the houses and to the palisade a solidity which they have not got. In general the composition, inside the stockade, follows closely the surviving original, though more precision is given to certain figures (and to their activities); a group of four towards the top right becomes three, a seated figure, and the dog, disappear from near the top left. Outside, much has been added. In the foreground is rather scanty, natural vegetation of a seashore character (which might yield a few identifications of plants), while two paths lead to the opening in the stockade. In the top left part of a cornfield is shown (see below, no. 37), with trees coming down almost to the stockade, a few cultivated sunflowers, and on the top right a pond (De Bry's 'C') with three figures engaged in getting water. The indications from the copy above are that the additions were White's in the version of the drawing with which he supplied De Bry, though the possibility of a few minor inventions by the engraver cannot be discounted.

[3] The comparison is with Le Moyne's drawings and the example is that engraved as De Bry, *America*, pt. ii (1591), no. 30 (Lorant, *New world*, p. 95), clearly a Timucua village, and it is likely that southern influence is to be found in the nature of the stockade, its entrance and possibly the disposition of the houses. The latter (with the possible exception of the temple) are clearly Algonkian in contrast with the round southern types.

[4] 'maison du Seigneur & Superieur' (French version).

letter B. Their dwellinges are builded with certaine potes[1] fastned together, and couered with matts which they turne op[2] as high as they thinke good, and soe receue in the lighte and other. Some are also couered with boughes of trees, as euery man lusteth or liketh best. They keepe their feasts and make good cheer together in the midds of the twone as yt is described in they 17. Figure.[3] When the towne standeth fare from the water they digg a great poude[4] noted with the letter C wherhence they fetche as muche water as they neede.'

34. Woman and child of Pomeiooc.

(a) 'A chiefe Herowans wyfe of Pomeoc. and her daughter of the age of .8. or .10. yeares.'[5]

(b) 'A cheiff Ladye of Pomeiooc.'[6]

---

[1] For 'postes'.   [2] For 'vp'.   [3] See below no. 42, p. 429.

[4] For 'ponde'. The making of ponds or wells is not a culture-trait to which any attention appears to have been given for the southern Algonkian groups.

[5] Brit. Mus., P. & D. 1906-5-9-1 (13); Binyon, *Catalogue*, no. 14; Prospectus, no. 14 (specimen plate); Lorant, *New world*, p. [195], [11]; Brit. Mus., postcard B 429. Probably made at the same time as the drawing of the village (no. 33). The woman's hair is cut in a fringe across the forehead and hangs down on either side of her face, but at the back it is rolled up into a knot. Across the forehead is a headband which could be of decorated skin, but, as it does not appear behind, may be one simulated by tattooing (cp. Swanton, *Indians*, pp. 498, 508–9, 516). There are tattoo marks on her cheeks and chin, and elaborate patterns on her upper arms (cp. Swanton, *Indians*, pp. 522–3; Flannery, *Analysis*, no. 97). Round her neck is painted a three-string necklace with a pendant, while she wears a real three string necklace of rather bluish pearls hanging down nearly to the waist (cp. pp. 423–4 below; Swanton, *Indians*, pp. 488–9, 516–17). Lapped round her waist and reaching to her knees is a fringed skin skirt covering only the front (Strachey's description of it as a 'semicinctum leathern apron' (*Hist. of travell*, p. 72) is the best; cp. Swanton, *Indians*, p. 468 and Flannery, *Analysis*, no. 80). One hand rests on the necklace, the other holds a gourd vessel, identified by Frank G. Speck as a Bottle Gourd (*Lagenaria siceraria* or *L. vulgaris*; *Gourds*, pp. 19–20, cp. pp. 427–9 below) used as a water-container. The child's hair is cut in a fringe in front. She wears a necklace, possibly of copper beads (cp. Swanton, *Indians*, pp. 490–4, and p. 439 below), and a thong round the waist, which is passed through the legs with a pad of moss between and tied at the navel (Swanton, *Indians*, pp. 475–7). She holds a girl doll, dressed in English clothes.

[6] De Bry, *America*, pt. i, pl. VIII (Lorant, *New world*, p. 241), engraving by Theodor de Bry. It adds a background, an island shore looking across an island-

The Roanoke Voyages

'About 20. milles from that Iland, neere the lake of Paquippe, ther is another towne called Pomeioock hard by the sea. The apparell of the cheefe ladyes of that towne differeth but litle from the attyre of those which lyue in Roanoac. For they weare their haire trussed opp in a knott, as the maiden doe which we spake of before,[1] and haue their skinnes pownced[2] in the same manner, yet they weare a chaine of great pearles, or beades of copper, or smoothe bones[3] 5. or 6. fold obout their necks, bearinge one arme in thc same, in the other they carye a gourde full of some kinde of pleasant liquor. They tye deers skinne doubled about them crochinge hygher about their breasts which hange downe before almost to their knees, and are almost altogither naked behinde. Commonlye their yonge daugters of 7. or 8. yeares olde doe wayt vpon them wearinge abowt then a girdle of skinne,[4] which hangeth downe behinde, and is drawen vnder neath betwene their twiste and bownde aboue their nauel with mose[5] of trees betwene that and their skinnes to couer their priuiliers withall.[6] After they be once past 10. yeares of age, they wear deerskinnes as the older sorte doe. They are greatlye Deligted with puppetts[7] and babes[8] which wear brought oute of England.'

35. Old man of Pomeiooc.
(a) 'The aged man in his winter garment.'[9]

studded sound where Indians are fishing from boats. Both figures are sharply Europeanized. Tattooing is added on the woman's calves. The little girl's doll is much more elaborate and she holds in her other hand a rather expensive-looking European rattle.
[1] Cp. no. 38.   [2] Tattooed.
[3] Bone necklaces have not been found referred to elsewhere for this region but beads made of polished pieces of shell which might be mistaken for bone were common later (cp. p. 439 above; Swanton, *Indians*, pp. 481–8).
[4] A string would be more accurate.   [5] Moss, possibly Spanish Moss.
[6] 'couuris par honestete' French.   [7] Dolls.
[8] A mistranslation, or misprint, for 'bells' or 'rattles' (Latin, 'tintinabulis'; French, 'sonnettes').
[9] Brit. Mus., P. & D. 1906-5-9-1 (19); Binyon, *Catalogue*, no. 20; Prospectus, no. 20; Lorant, *New world*, p. [200], [c], [21]. The old man is shown wearing a mantle, a large dressed deer-skin, fringed and slung obliquely on the left shoulder, leaving the left hand clear, and under the right arm, with the top edge turned

(b) Without inscription.[1]

(c) 'An ageed manne in his winter garment.'[2]

'The aged men of Pommeioocke are couered with a large skinne which is tyed vppon their shoulders on one side and hangeth downe beneath their knees wearinge their other arme naked out of the skinne, that they maye be at more libertie. Those skynnes are Dressed with the hair on, and lyned with other furred skinnes. the yonnge men suffer noe hairr at all to growe vppon their faces but assoone as they growe they put them away, but when thy[3] are come to yeeres they suffer them to growe although to say truthe they come opp verye thinne. They also weare their haire bownde op behynde, and, haue a creste on their heads like the others. The contrye abowt this plase is soe fruit full and good, that England is not to bee compared to yt.'

36. Woman of Pomeiooc or Dasemunkepeuc carrying a child.

(a) 'The wyfe of an Herowan of Pomeiooc.'[4]

over to show the hair (not necessarily lined with other fur) on the inside, and reaching below the knee. Hariot's description is otherwise adequate.

[1] Copy, without caption, or variants, in Brit. Mus., P. & D. 199. a. 3 (L.B. 3 (7)); of which Sloane MS 5253, no. 16, is a copy.

[2] De Bry, *America*, pt. i, pl. IX (Lorant, *New world*, p. 243), engraving by Theodor de Bry. Latin, 'Senis Pomeioocensis hiberna vestis'. The mantle is somewhat elaborated to show fur on the inside, and a strip (or tail?) hanging down in front (cp. Beverley, *History and present state* (1947), p. 162; Swanton, *Indians*, pp. 459–60). The main addition is a pair of moccasins (which Swanton, *Indians*, pp. 464–5, and Flannery, *Analysis*, pp. 44–5, failed to notice). No fastenings are visible, though Beverley describes them as tied at the ankle with a running string (op. cit., pp. 162–4). Behind the man, who is standing on an elevated piece of ground, is a view of Pomeiooc village as in no. 33. The entrance (at centre right) is simpler, and there are four cornfields on either side of the village. On the right we have the bird-watcher's hut of the Secoton drawing (no. 37). Beyond the cornfields is a belt of trees, and beyond that the sounds. Either De Bry or White failed to synchronize the topography with the previous versions.

[3] For 'they'. On the rareness of beards, see Flannery, *Analysis*, no. 91; Swanton, *Indians*, p. 498.

[4] Brit. Mus., P. & D. 1906-5-9-1 (15); Binyon, *Catalogue*, no. 16; Prospectus, no. 16; Lorant, *New world*, p. [200], [b], [20]. The discrepancy between this and the De Bry item indicates clearly that while the surviving drawings and the engravings derive from the same originals White was by no means certain of the

(*b*) 'Their manner of careynge ther Childern and atyere of the cheiffe Ladyes of the towne of Dasamonquepeuc.'¹

'In the towne of Dasemonquepeuc distant from Roanoac 4. or 5. milles,² the woemen are attired, and pownced, in suche sorte as the woemen of Roanoac are, yet they weare noe worathes³ vppon their heads, nether haue they their thighes painted with small pricks.⁴ They haue a strange manner of bearing their children, and quite contrarie to ours. For our woemen carrie their children in their armes before their brests, but they taking their sonne by the right hand, bear him on their backs, holdinge the left thighe in their lefte arme after a strange, and conuesnall⁵ fashion, as in the picture is to bee seene.'

37. Secoton.

(*a*) 'Secoton.⁶

identification of his subjects and probably relied on memory for some of his captions when making replicas (cp. no. 50, pp. 439–40). There is no evidence to show which village is meant.

The woman is, like that of no. 34, tattooed on the upper arms; her hair is fringed, hangs round her head, and is not tied up at the back. Her skirt covers her buttocks. The child is naked. Both its arms are over the woman's shoulders from behind: she holds the right hand in front with her right hand, and tucks the left leg under her left arm.

¹ De Bry, *America*, pt. i, pl. x (Lorant, *New world*, p. 245), engraving by Theodor de Bry. Two views, from front and back (probably from White's version), are given against a background as in no. 34.

² As the crow flies this village was about 4 miles from the fort on Roanoke Island (p. 869).   ³ Wreaths or headbands (cp. pp. 417, 423–4, 427, 430, 439).

⁴ In no. 34 the legs too are free of tattooing in the drawing.

⁵ Latin, 'ratione satis mira & peregrina'; French, 'vne facon fort rare & estrange'.

⁶ Brit. Mus., P. & D. 1906-5-9-1 (7); Binyon, *Catalogue*, no. 6; Prospectus, no. 6; Lorant, *New world*, p. [191], [7]; Brit. Mus., postcard B 427. In this picture of an unenclosed village (for its location see p. 871 below) White shows a river or pond at the top centre from which a path leads by the side of the cornfields into the village. The main group of nine houses encloses a small open space in which is a communal fire and from which a broad path or road leads through the middle of the settlement. The house on the right centre, somewhat larger than the rest and probably the chief's, has a small piece of ground enclosed by stakes— either a yard or a private garden. On the path is an eating place with three places set with small as well as large dishes (cp. no. 43). A line of posts marks off the cornfields from the area containing the circle of posts with carved human heads round which a dance is taking place (cp. no. 41), while a group of participants

Their rype corne.[1]

Their greene corne.[2]

Corne newly sprong.[3]

A Ceremony in their prayers with strange iesturs and songs dansing abowt posts carued on the topps lyke mens faces.[4]

Their sittinge at meate.[5]

The place of solemne prayer.[6]

The house wherin the Tombe of their Herounds standeth.'[7]

(*b*) 'The Towne of Secota.'[8]

'Their townes that are not inclosed with poles aire[9] commonlye fayrer. Then such as are inclosed, as appereth in this figure which

crouch in a waiting position on the path. Bottom left is the ceremonial religious fire, and to the left of it a small building probably contains their 'idol' (cp. no. 39) while a larger one holds the remains of their leading men (cp. no. 40). On the top right are the three cornfields, each at a different stage of development with the watch-house intended for keeping birds off the ripe corn (a feature recorded elsewhere only among the Narragansetts (Flannery, *Analysis*, p. 13)). At the top left two other houses are seen under the trees, with the implication that there are others not indicated. It was, with a high degree of probability, drawn by White on 15–16 July 1585 (cp. p. 191 above).

[1] Corn which in the drawing appears rather higher than the adjoining house. For the three successive crops see Hariot, above, p. 338.

[2] Of intermediate height.

[3] Rows of young plants with considerable space between the plants and between the rows. There is no suggestion that any other plants were grown in, or close to, the corn (cp. pp. 342, 422).

[4] This differs from the detailed drawing (no. 41) in having no group of women dancing in the middle of the circle and in having lines of crouching men waiting to participate. There are also eight posts instead of seven.

[5] A long mat (or mats) has by the side two figures whose sex is not clear, eating from a common dish but using two small dishes as well (cp. no. 43, where there is one dish only and those eating are sitting on the mat). Another place is unattended, while one figure eats at the third and a man with a bow stands as if on guard at the bottom. The mats appear to be 2 to 3 feet wide (cp. p. 429).

[6] There is no direct evidence on the precise place fire occupied in the ritual of the Carolina Algonkians, but it is likely to have been a prominent one. It is not unlikely that a virgin fire ceremony was performed at this place (cp. Flannery, *Analysis*, no. 317). It is likely, too, that the posts around the fire were of a permanent character, but it is not clear whether or not they had carved heads.

[7] Cp. no. 40 below.

[8] De Bry, *America*, pt. i (1590), pl. XX (Lorant, *New world*, p. 265), engraving by Theodor de Bry.　　　[9] For 'are'.

liuelye expresseth the towne of Secotam. For the howses are Scattered heer and ther, and they haue gardein [1] expressed by the letter E. wherin groweth Tobacco which the inhabitants call Vppowoc. They haue also groaues wherin thei take deer, and fields vherin [2] they sowe their corne. In their corne fields they builde as yt weare a scaffolde wher on they sett a cottage like to a rownde chaire,[3] signiffied by F. wherin they place one to watche. for there are suche nomber of fowles, and beasts, that vnless they keepe the better watche, they would soone deuoure all ther corne. For which cause the watchman maketh continual cryes and noyse. They sowe their corne with a certaine distance noted by H. other wise one stalke would choke the growthe of another and the corne would not come vnto his rypeurs [4] G. For the leaves therof are large, like vnto the leaues of great reedes. They haue also a seuerall broade plotte C. whear they meete with their neighbours, to celebrate their chiefe solemne feastes as the 18. picture [5] doth declare: and a place D. whear after they haue ended their feaste they make merrie togither.[6] Ouer against this place they haue a rownd plott B. wher they assemble themselues to make their solemne prayers.[7] Not far from which place ther is a lardge buildinge A. wherin are the tombes of their kings and

---

[1] Half-a-dozen houses appear among the trees at the top and centre left; among them Indians are chasing deer and using bows. A large garden plot of tobacco appears below the river at top centre, while a scattered group of sunflowers is seen on the left next to a bed of tobacco. The 'excellent' representations of cultivated sunflowers in this engraving (and in that of Pomeiooc, no. 33) are discussed by C. B. Heiser, 'The sunflower among the North American Indians', in *Proc. American Phil. Soc.*, xcv (1951), pp. 432, 435.

[2] For 'wherin'.

[3] 'vne maisonnette couuerte en demi rond' (French text); 'In aeris tabulatum extruunt. Supra quod aediculam seu tugurium hemicycli in modum tectum' (Latin text). The watch-house, though disproportionately large, does not differ from that in the drawing.

[4] For 'ripeness'.   [5] No. 41.

[6] This would appear rather to be the place where the villagers ate ordinarily. Three places are shown, with three persons eating, one serving and three standing by. Corn cobs, fish and fruits or vegetables appear alongside the large dishes, the smaller being absent (cp. no. 43 below).

[7] At least three of the posts round the fire have carved human faces.

princes, as will appere by the 22. figure[1] likewise they haue garden notted bey the letter I. wherin they vse to sowe pompions.[2] Also a place marked with K. wherin the make a fyre at their solemne feasts,[3] and hard without the towne a riuer L. from whence they fetche their water. This people therfore voyde of all couetousnes lyue cherfullye and att their harts ease. Butt they solemnise their feasts in the nigt, and therfore they keepe verye great fyres to auoyde darkenes, ant[4] to testifie their Ioye.'

38.   Woman of Secoton.

(*a*)   'The wyfe of an Herowan of Secotan.'[5]

(*b*)   Without inscription.[6]

(*c*)   'On of the chieff Ladyes of Secota.'[7]

'The woemen of Secotam are of Reasonable good proportion. In their goinge they carrye their hands danglinge downe,[8] and air dadil[9] in a deer skinne verye excellentlye wel dressed, hanginge

---

[1] No. 40.

[2] A garden with pumpkins is shown down the left side of the newest corn patch: the enclosure attached to the building above is also sown with vegetables of some sort.

[3] The central fire might rather appear to be a permanent communal feature.

[4] For 'and'.

[5] Brit. Mus., P. & D. 1905-5-9-1 (18); Binyon, *Catalogue*, no. 19; *Prospectus*, no. 19; Lorant, *New world*, p. [200], [a], [19]. The woman is standing with folded arms. Her hair is fringed in front, and hangs down the side of her face and at the back. Around her forehead is a headband of, apparently, twisted material (cp. pp. 417, 424; Swanton, *Indians*, pp. 508–9). She is tattooed and has a simulated necklace painted round her neck. (cp. Swanton, *Indians*, p. 532). The nature of the ear-ornament is not too distinct. The skirt is as in no. 36 rather than in no. 34. Probably drawn at the same time as no. 37.

[6] Copy, without variations, Brit. Mus., P. & D. 199. a. 3 (L.B. 3 (8)).

[7] De Bry, *America*, pt. i, pl. IV (Lorant, *New world*, p. 233), engraving by Theodor de Bry. As with no. 36, front and rear views are given, again possibly White's, the skirt appearing in the back view to consist of two fringed skins overlapping and roughly tucked or tied at the back. The ear-ornament is a conventionalized group of beads. The background shows fishing with spears and from canoes, with a wooded mainland beyond.

[8] French, 'les bras croisez ensemble estans enueloppees depuis le dessus du vestre jusques à demi cuisse'.

[9] 'their middle'?

downe from their nauell vnto the mydds of their thighes, which
also couereth their hynder partz. The reste of their bodies are
all bare. The forr parte of their hair is cutt shorte, the reste is not
ouer Longe, thinne, and softe, and falling downe about their
shoulders: They weare a Wrrath[1] about their heads. Their foreheads, cheeks, chynne, armes and leggs are pownced. About their
necks they wear a chaine, ether pricked or paynted. They haue
small eyes, plaine and flatt noses, narrow foreheads, and broade
mowths. For the most parte they hange at their eares chaynes of
longe Pearles, and of some smootht bones.[2] Yet their nayles are
not longe, as the woemen of Florida. They are also deligtted[3]
with walkinge in to the fields, and besides the riuers, to see the
huntinge of deers and catchinge of fische.'

39. Kiwasa.
'Ther Idol Kiwasa.'[4]

'The people of this cuntrie haue an Idol, which they call
Kɪwᴀsᴀ:[5] yt is carued of woode in lengthe 4. foote whose heade

---

[1] French, 'vne guirlande craucelin' (cp. p. 423 above).
[2] Cp. pp. 438–9 below.   [3] For 'delighted'.
[4] De Bry, *America*, pt. i (1590), pl. xxi (Lorant, *New world*, p. 267), without
engraver's initials. It is not represented in this form by a drawing. The figure is
that of a man seated on a two-tier platform covered with mats, with his knees
flexed and apart, with the hands resting on the knees. He is dressed in a sleeveless
jacket of skin, with a folded, fringed skin round the waist and hanging in front,
while he wears leg-pieces on the calves decorated with designs in shells. He has
two loops of beads above each knee, and a four-string necklace. His hair is long,
with an upturned fringe and a top-knot, identical with the Timucua styles in the
engravings of Le Moyne's Florida drawings (*America*, pt. ii). The image is seated
in a circular hut, probably not more than 6 ft. in height and some 6 ft. in diameter.
This is the most suspect of the De Bry engravings, the text fitting in with the
presence of an idol inside the 'temple' (no. 40), and the hair-style and shape of
the hut being almost too closely associable with Le Moyne's drawings, though
the images may indeed prove to be a southern culture-trait not extending north
of Virginia (cp. Swanton, *Indians*, pp. 614–16). Allowing for modifications by
the engraver, the hut could be that near the bottom left in the Secoton drawing
(no. 37); the scale of the Pomeiooc 'temple' was, however, much larger (no. 33).
The hair-style could be a mere formalizing of the rather indefinite appearance of
the head of the image in no. 40.
[5] See p. 888 below.

is like the heades of the people of Florida,[1] the face is of a flesh colour, the brest white, the rest is all blacke, the thighes are also spottet with whitte. He hath a chayne abowt his necke of white beades, betweene which are other Rownde beades of copper which they esteeme more then golde or siluer. This Idol is placed in the temple of the towne of Secotam, as the keper of the kings dead corpses. Somtyme they haue two of thes idoles in theyr churches, and somtine[2] 3. but neuer aboue, which they place in a darke corner wher they shew tetrible.[3] Thes poore soules haue none other knowledge of god although I thinke them verye Desirous to know the truthe. For when as wee knee[l]ed downe on our knees to make our prayers vnto god, they went about to imitate vs, and when they saw we moued our lipps, they also dyd the like. Wherfor that is verye like that they might easelye be brongt[4] to the knowledge of the gospel. God of his mercie grant them this grace.'

40. An ossuary temple.

(a) 'The Tombe of their Cherounes or cheife personages, their flesh clene taken of from the bones saue the skynn and heare of their heads, which flesh is dried and enfolded in matts laide at theire feete. their bones also being made dry, are couered with deare skynns not altering their forme or proportion. With theire Kywash, which is an Image of woode keeping the deade.'[5]

[1] Possibly as the result of the engraver's efforts or even White's. This point might suggest that Hariot's text was written after seeing the engravings, and not the drawings (cp. p. 415 above). The colouring of the image may provide a reason why the Indians at first thought the white men to be supernatural beings (p. 380 above).

[2] For 'somtyme'. [3] For 'terrible'.

[4] For 'brought'.

[5] Brit. Mus., P. & D. 1906-9-5-1 (9); Binyon, *Catalogue*, no. 8; Prospectus, no. 8; Lorant, *New world*, p. [201], [22]. The building is raised on eleven stout timber posts which support a floor which may be of interlaced cane (as a kind of pelmet fringing the floor might suggest) or timber. The upper storey is identical with the houses shown above (nos. 33, 37), a pole framework covered with bark, rush or cane mats, with an arched roof, the mats at the gable

(b) 'The Tombe of their Werowans or Cheiff Lordes.'[1]

'The builde a Scaffolde[2] 9. or 10. foote hihe as is expressed in this figure vnder the tombs of theit[3] Weroans, or cheefe lordes which they couer with matts, and lai the dead corpses of their weroans theruppon in manner followinge. first the bowells are taken forthe. Then layinge downe the skinne, they cutt all the fleshe clean from the bones, which the[4] drye in the sonne, and well dryed the[5] inclose in Matts, and place at their feete. Then their bones (remaininge still fastened together with the ligaments whole and vncorrupted) are couered agayne with leather, and their carcase fashioned as yf their flesh wear not taken away. They

end being thrown back over the roof. Judging by the normal width of mats used (cp. nos. 33, 37) the building would be roughly rectangular in plan. Underneath are two skins for use as mats (for the priest). In the foreground is a small fire. The bodies (ten) are laid side by side on their backs, with the image of the god on the right-hand side facing the gable. It is black, with a white streak on the breast, sitting with hands on knees; the face not clear but the head dressed or covered to give the impression of a hat with a rolled brim, coming to a low peak on top (cp. no. 39). Behind are four mat-covered chests, rectangular in plan, with curved tops (like miniatures of houses). This has been placed in sequence as one of the Secoton group, although it is not certain that it belongs there.

[1] De Bry, *America*, pt. i, pl. xxii (Lorant, *New world*, p. 269), engraving not initialed. Latin, 'Regulorum Sepulcra'. The structure differs only slightly in its interior from the surviving drawing. There are nine bodies instead of ten, giving more room for the image, which is on the left, seated on a ledge, and differing in appearance from that above. On the ground tending the fire is a priest dressed as in no. 44. The main addition is the enclosure of the whole structure inside one of the characteristic long houses, in which the ties by which the pole frame is held together are clearly shown. This makes it plain that the tomb is contained inside the large building on the left foreground in the Secoton village drawing (no. 37) and indicates why no pile-supported buildings are shown or referred to elsewhere in this area, except for the bird-watcher's hut (in no. 37). There is little doubt that this feature was added by White in the drawing he gave De Bry. Building on piles appears to be a southern culture-trait but it is badly documented (cp. Swanton, *Indians*, pp. 408-9, 413-16, 806; Flannery, *Analysis*, pp. 64, 187, 193-4, who thinks it, on very little evidence, to have been a coastal Algonkian invention). It was practised for identical purposes by the Virginia Algonkians (Swanton, *Indians*, pp. 718-19). It is clear that this form of preservation was limited to the chiefs (and just possibly the chief men), inhumation being normal for ordinary burials (ibid., and cp. pp. 367, 373 above).

[2] Latin, 'tabulatum': the height is probably too great.

[3] For 'their'.   [4] For 'they'.   [5] For 'they'.

lapp each corps in his owne skinne after the same in [1] thus handled, and lay yt in his order by the corpses of the other cheef lordes. By the dead bodies they sett their Idol Kiwasa, wher of we spake in the former chapiter: [2] For they are persuaded that the same doth keepe the dead bodyes of their cheefe lordes that nothinge may hurt them. Moreouer vnder the foresaid scaffolde some on of their preists hath his lodginge, which Mumbleth his prayers nighte and day, and hath charge of the corpses. For his bed he hath two deares [3] skinnes spredd on the grownde, yf the wether bee cold hee maketh a fyre to warme by withall. Thes poore soules are thus instructed by natute [4] to reuerence their princes euen after their death.'

41. Indian festival.
(*a*) Without inscription. [5]

---

[1] For 'is'. [2] No. 38.
[3] Latin, 'ferarum pelles'. [4] For 'nature'.
[5] Brit. Mus., P. & D. 1906-5-9-1 (10); Binyon, *Catalogue*, no. 9; Prospectus, no. 9; Lorant, *New world*, pp. [196–7], [12]. Four women and ten men are dancing around the post-circle, while three women embrace in the centre. Details of attire are sometimes difficult to determine on account of off-setting. One of the dancing women (*d*), reckoning clockwise from the bottom, and the three in the centre wear the single apron-skirt (cp. no. 34) as do five men, leaving buttocks and chest bare; one woman (*a*) has a large skin robe suspended from the left shoulder (like the man in no. 43), which leaves the right breast bare; another woman (*k*) has a skin suspended from both shoulders to below her knees in front (and it may cover her back also); while one (*n*) is naked except for a light covering of twigs secured by a waist-band. Seven (including one woman) have a bag (as no. 52) attached to the waist-band, and three men (*f, i* and *m*) have a skin and animal-head breech-cloth (as no. 52), while one (*l*) has apparently a waist-band only. Ten dancers carry gourd rattles (cp. pp. 417, 429), two have arrows, and eight twigs, with undifferentiated but deciduous foliage, in one or both hands. Three men bear marks identifying their status, tribe or totemic clan (cp. no. 53), *b* with three or four downward-pointing arrows (there is a problem of off-setting with *m*) (cp. pp. 443–4 below), *c* with a small animal (sign of his clan, cp. Swanton, *Indians*, pp. 654–61) in a shield, each on the left shoulder-blade, while *m* has two arrows on the right. The men have the hair scraped close at the sides and cockscombed in the centre with large feathers as ornaments, while the women have the hair tied back to the nape of the neck, one only (*a*) having a band round her forehead. The circle is defined by seven posts carved with human heads (women's heads covered by cloaks?) and is about sixteen feet

The Roanoke Voyages

(*b*) 'Their danses which they vse att their hyghe feastes.'[1]

'At a Certayne tyme of the yere they make a great and solemne feaste wherunto their neighbours of the townes adioninge repayre from all parts, euery man attyred in the most strange fashion they can deuise hauinge certayne marks on the backs to declare of what place they bee.[2] The place where they meete is a broade playne,[3] abowt the which are planted in the grownde certayne posts carued with heads[4] like to the faces of Nonnes couered with theyr vayls. Then beeing sett in order they dance singe, and vse the strangest gestures that they can possiblye deuise. Three of the fayrest Virgins, of the companie are in the mydds, which imbrassinge one another doe as yt wear turn abowt in their dancinge. All this is donne after the sunne is sett for auoydinge of heate. When they are weerye of dancinge. they goe oute of the circle, and come in vntill their dances be ended, and they goe to make merrye as is expressed in the 16 figure.'[5]

in diameter (the posts being some seven feet high). Beverley (*History and present state*, p. 196) speaks of a similar circle of 'Posts, with Faces carved on them, and painted' around a temple. Swanton regards the faces as representing 'minor deities of some kind'. The dance evidently forms part of a corn festival—green corn or harvest, the women in the middle being the 'three sisters' of that ritual (this being possibly the only Algonkian source for the ritual, which is found among Iroquoian tribes). Cp. Swanton, *Indians*, pp. 615, 626–8, 742, 748; Flannery, *Analysis*, nos. 270, 287; Beverley, *History and present state*, pp. 221–2. If drawn at Secoton in July (cp. p. 191) the festival must be a green corn one.

[1] De Bry, *America*, pt. i, pl. XVIII (Lorant, *New world*, pp. 260–1), engraving not signed. Latin, 'Virginiensium saltandi ratio solemnibus festis'. The composition is in reverse, with few other major changes from the drawing. Innovations (reckoning the figures counter-clockwise from the bottom) include a chain of beads passing from the left shoulder under the right arm (*a* and *h*); a more cloaklike garment on one of the women (*k*) with a folded-back, fringed collar and reaching below the knees behind and, probably, in front; an apron-skirt of leaves (*g*); a brief girdle made from leaves stuck in the waist-band (*c*); and twigs differentiated into coniferous and deciduous types with possibly reeds (*i*) and yucca (*c*).

[2] Cp. p. 427 and no. 53 below.   [3] In no. 33 it is a fairly confined space.
[4] French 'taillees en marmousets auans la teste': in the sentence reads: 'Amplaigitur est auream in quam conueniunt, circa quam in orbem terrae infixa sunt tigna sculpta monialium velatarum capita experimentia.'
[5] He apparently means pl. XVII (no. 42).

42. Ceremony around a fire.

(*a*) Without inscription.[1]

(*b*) 'Their manner of prainge with Rattels abowt te fyer.'[2]

'When they haue escaped any great danger by sea or lande, or be returned from the warr in token of Ioye they make a great fyer abowt whiche the men and woemen sist[3] together, holdinge a certaine fruite in their hands like vnto a rownde pompion or a gourde, which after they haue taken out the fruits, and the seedes, then fill with smal stons or certayne bigg kernellt[4] to make the more noise, and fasten that vppon a sticke, and singinge after their manner, they make merrie: as myselfe obserued and noted downe at my beinge amonge them. For it is a strange custome, and worth the obseruation.'

43. Man and woman eating.

(*a*) 'Theire sitting at meate.'[5]

[1] Brit. Mus., P. & D. 1906-5-9-1 (11); Binyon, *Catalogue*, no. 10; Prospectus, no. 10; Lorant, *New world*, p. [192], [8]. Ten Indians of both sexes are sitting casually on the ground round a small fire: five of them are holding gourd rattles. A similar, though larger, group is seen in the middle of the village of Pomeiooc (no. 33) but this, perhaps, fits in best with the Secoton drawings. The man at the top centre is conducting some ceremony (cp. Swanton, *Indians*, pp. 747-8). 5 have single apron-skirts, 2 breech-cloths, 3 are probably naked.

[2] De Bry, *America*, pt. i, pl. XVII (Lorant, *New world*, p. 259), engraving by Theodor de Bry. In the French the caption is: 'Feu de ioye es festes solonnelles.' The setting is a sandy ledge beyond which is a sound, with fish-weirs and fishing-canoes. The grouping round the fire is reversed from right to left, while one figure is omitted behind the flame of a large fire. A man and a woman, standing centre left, are added. There are minor variations in costume.

[3] For 'sit'.

[4] Gourd seeds or fruit stones. (Cp. Swanton, *Indians*, pp. 626-7; Flannery, *Analysis* no. 167, who thinks the occurrence of the gourd rattle in this area is probably due to southern influence.)

[5] Brit. Mus., P. & D. 1906-5-9-1 (20); Binyon, *Catalogue*, no. 21; Prospectus, no. 21; Lorant, *New world*, p. [194], [10]. Man on left, woman on right sitting on mat on the ground and eating boiled maize from large, shallow circular wooden dish (cp. pp. 109, 420 above; Swanton, *Indians*, pp. 556-7) with their right hands. The mat is made of cane or reeds (cp. no. 37), in sections about 9-12 in. long, sewn together, and bound (at the end shown on right) with string. The man has his hair shaved at either side, leaving a cockscomb in the middle (cp. nos. 41, 49): a single feather (a turkey's?) is fixed at the back. In his ear he is

(*b*) 'Their sittinge at meate.'[1]

'Their manner of feeding is in this wise. They lay a matt made of bents one[2] the grownde and sett their meate on the mids thcrof, and then sit downe Rownde, the men vppon one side, and the woemen on the other.[3] Their meate is Mayz sodden, in suche sorte as I described yt in the former treatise of[4] verye good taste, deers flesche, or of some other beaste, and fishe. They are verye sober in their eatinge, and drinkinge, and consequentlye verye longe liued because they doe not oppress nature.'

44. A priest.

(*a*) 'One of their Religious men.'[5]

wearing what appears to be a piece of skin, rolled and fringed at both ends (cp. Swanton, *Indians*, pp. 510-11). His fringed mantle is passed over his left shoulder (cp. no. 41). The woman has her hair and her skirt as the woman of Secoton (no. 38). Her three-string necklace of pearls or beads is a short one. No tattooed patterns are visible on either man or woman. In the Secoton drawing (no. 37) the people eating sit on either side of the mats, not on them. This links best, however, with the Secoton group of drawings.

[1] De Bry, *America*, pt. i, pl. xvi (Lorant, *New world*, p. 257), engraving by Theodor de Bry. De Bry adds an outdoor background, which is not necessarily implied in the drawing. There are no significant changes in the dress of the man and woman, but the mat is set more elaborately. From left to right there are added a gourd water-vessel with a cut-out handle at the top which is, at least, not visible in no. 34; a skin bag (cp. nos. 41, 52); a tobacco pipe—the only one in the whole series but very like that excavated at the fort site on Roanoke Island (cp. p. 907)—at the man's right hand; walnuts (cp. p. 330); a fish (like a Striped Bass in appearance); four corn cobs, and a scallop shell. It is highly probable that some or all of these appeared in White's version of this drawing for De Bry.

[2] Rushes or wiry grass. Latin 'Storea scirpea humi strata'; French, 'ioncs ou paille forte'.

[3] It is clearly meant that it is a normal practice for the men and women to eat together. Since the evidence for the men and women eating separately in public among the Virginia Algonkians is strong, Swanton (*Indians*, p. 711) considered that the picture 'represents an Indian in the inner privacy of his family life'. More probably, it represents a distinctive culture-trait of the Carolina Algonkians.

[4] *A briefe and true report*, printed before the engravings. The Latin text has 'eo quo superiore scripsimodo'. Hakluyt, in his translation from the Latin, is here emphasizing that Hariot is the author of the notes.

[5] Brit. Mus., P. & D. 1906-5-9-1 (14); Binyon, *Catalogue*, no. 15; Prospectus, no. 20; Lorant, *New world*, p. [200], [c], [21]. Beverley's description (*Hist. and*

John White's Drawings

(b) 'On of the Religeous men in the towne of Secota.'[1]

'The Priests of the aforesaid Towne of Secota are well stricken in yeers, and as yt seemeth of more experience then the comon sorte. They weare their heare cutt like a creste, on the topps of thier heads as other doe, but the rest are cutt shorte, sauinge those which growe aboue their foreheads in manner of a perriwigge.[2] They also haue somwhat hanginge in their ears. They weare a shorte clocke[3] made of fine hares skinnes quilted with the hayre outwarde.[4] The rest of thier bodie is naked. They are notable enchaunters,[5] and for their pleasure they frequent the riuers, to

present state of Virginia (1947), pp. 164–5) of the Virginia Algonkian priests is a gloss on the engraving and what is said above but it appears to embody some direct observation, the remarks in brackets being my interpolations:

'The Habit of the Indian Priest, is a Cloak made in the form of Woman's Petticoat; but instead of tying it about their middle, they fasten the gatherings about their Neck, and tye it upon the Right Shoulder, always keeping one Arm to use upon occasion. The Cloak hangs even at the bottom, but reaches no further than the middle of the Thigh [there being in the drawing an armhole for the right arm]; but what is most particular in it, is, that it is constantly made of a skin drest soft, with the Pelt or Furr on the outside, and revers'd; insomuch that when the Cloak has been a little worn, the hair falls down in flakes, and looks very shagged, and frightful. The cut of their Hair is likewise peculiar to their Function; for 'tis all shaven close except a thin Crest, like a Cocks-comb which stands bristling up, and runs in a semicircle from the Forehead up along the Crown to the nape of the Neck: They likewise have a border of Hair over the Forehead, which by its own natural strength, and by the stiffning it receives from Grease and Paint, will stand out like the peak of a Bonnet.' [Apart from mention of a skin ear-ornament this completes the description. Cp. Swanton, *Indians*, pp. 477–9.]

[1] De Bry, *America*, pt. i, pl. v (Lorant, *New world*, p. 235), engraving by G. Veen. The figure is duplicated, the back view suggesting ruching of the skins to the low circular neck-band. A fishing scene (varied by an Indian shooting an arrow at a water-bird from a boat) is added as background. The association with Secoton would fit in with nos. 37, 39, 40 above.

[2] Apart from its artificial appearance there was nothing to suggest a peruke.

[3] For 'cloak'.

[4] The rabbit-skins were either of the Marsh Rabbit or the Common Cottontail (p. 355 above). Mr H. W. Krieger writes 'The drawing shows narrow strips of rabbit skin suspended from a neck band. This would indicate a form of suspended warp weaving usual with Indians of the eastern United States. The woodlands Indians cut the rabbit skin "round and round" in a narrow strip that was continuous for a single skin.'

[5] Latin, 'Insignes sunt Magi'. Cp. pp. 378–81, 442.

431

kill with their bowes, and catche wilde ducks, swannes, and other fowles.'

45. Making a dug-out canoe.
'The manner of makinge their boates.'[1]

'The manner of makinge their boates in Virginia is verye wonderfull. For wheras they want Instruments of yron, or other like vnto ours, yet they knowe howe to make them as hand-somelye, to saile with whear they liste in their Riuers, and to fishe with all, as ours. First they choose some longe, and thicke tree, accordinge to the bignes of the boate which they would frame, and make a fyre on the grownd abowt the Roote therof, kindlinge the same by little, and little with drie mosse of trees, and chipps of woode that the flame should not mounte opp to highe, and burne to muche of the lengte of the tree When yt is almost burnt thorough, and readye to fall they make a new fyre, which they suffer to burne vntill the tree fall of yt owne accord. Then burninge of the Topp, and bowghs of the tree in suche wyse that the bodie of the same may Retayne his iust lengthe, they raise yt vppon potes[2] laid ouer cross wise vppon forked posts, at suche a reasonable heighte as they may handsomlye worke vppon yt. Then take they of the barke with certayne shells: thy[3] reserue the, innermost part of the lennke,[4] for the nethermost parte of the boate. On the other side they make a fyre accordinge to the lengthe of the bodye

---

[1] De Bry, *America*, pt. i, pl. xii (Lorant, *New world*, p. 249), engraving by Theodor de Bry, not represented by any extant drawing. The engraving shows a fire burning at the base of a deciduous tree in the top right-hand corner of the engraving. On the upper left an Indian is raking away the embers from the base of a tree which has just been burnt down. Beside the tree is another Indian tending a fire which is being used to burn off the main branches. He has a formalized shell tool in his right hand. In the foreground a partly completed canoe is raised on branches held between two pairs of forked posts. The bark has been removed from the tree, and one end and the top have been neatly (too neatly) squared off. A fire is burning inside the uncompleted canoe and is being tended by an Indian to the right, who is also wielding a formalized shell tool. On the left another Indian is scraping the charred interior of the trunk with what appears to be a large rough piece of stone.   [2] For 'postes'.
[3] For 'they'.   [4] For 'trunke', cp. Latin ed. 'integriorem trunci partem'.

of the tree, sauinge at both the endes. That which they thinke is sufficientlye burned they qu[e]nche and scrape away with shells, and makinge a new fyre they burne yt agayne, and soe they continne somtymes burninge and sometymes scrapinge, vntill the boate haue sufficient bothownes. This god indueth thise sauage people with sufficient reason to make thinges necessarie to serue their turnes.'[1]

46. Fishing scene.
(a) 'The manner of their fishing.'[2]
    'A Cannow.'

[1] Swanton (*Indians*, p. 591) says that this is one of the best descriptions of a method of making canoes which was general throughout the South-east. No mention is made in any of the early English narratives of bark canoes or of rafts in this area. The engraving should be used with White's drawing of a canoe in his fishing scene (no. 46, the boat being accurately reproduced by De Bry). This shows a boat of some 20 ft. long (Barlowe said they could hold twenty, p. 105 above), slightly curved at both ends and with no appreciable differences between bow and stern. There is no ornamentation. Swanton says that cypress was the most popular wood, but that poplar, black walnut, and, in North Carolina, pine were used for boats. Barlowe says pine or pitch trees (p. 104 above), but the latter was not the pitch-pine, which does not grow on the coast. Hariot (pp. 363–4 above) says 'Rakíock' was mainly used. From the description this might well be the Tulip Tree, or alternatively the White Cypress, these being the two largest trees in the coastlands. As drawn by White, the canoe could not have held more than eight persons.

[2] Brit. Mus., P. & D. 1906-5-9-1 (6); Binyon, *Catalogue*, no. 5; Prospectus, no. 5; Lorant, *New world*, p. [189], [5]. The drawing shows a shallow channel through the sounds in which Indians are fishing. In the sky at top left is a Brown Pelican (no. 57), two Trumpeter Swans (no. 58) flying below. At top right is a flight of small water-birds, probably duck, and below nine geese (cp. p. 448 below). The land in the background is low, with a few bushes. On the water (back, right centre) is a fishing-canoe with two Indians. On the left is a straight fish-weir (coming out from the land?) of upright stakes of cane or reed (cp. pp. 360, 365), with two visible lines of binding, which takes a right-angle bend near the edge of the drawing. Protruding on the right is a rectangular fish-trap in which are some seven large and a few smaller fish. One is a skate, probably the Barndoor Skate, *Raja laevis* (*Fishes of N.C.*, no. 15). On the right a few uprights hint at a further weir just out of the picture. Between the weirs are two Indians with long fish-spears (cp. pp. 360–1; Swanton, *Indians*, p. 582) attacking fish: one may be a sturgeon, though the back-plates are not clearly visible (cp. no. 84), and two are certainly Trigger-fish (no. 30, though not appropriate to this area). Of three other fish to the right one is either a Striped Mullet or

The Roanoke Voyages

(b) 'Their manner of fishynge in Virginia.'[1]

'They haue likewise a notable way to catche fishe in their Riuers. for whear as they lacke both yron, and steele, they faste

a Striped Bass (cp. nos. 87, 90): of those to the left, the first is the Hammer-headed Shark, *Sphyrna zygaena* (*Fishes of N.C.*, no. 10), now only a straggler in this area and probably 'imported' from an oceanic drawing, and, near the fish-trap, a Spiny Box-fish (nos. 96–7), three smaller fish not being identifiable, but one whose head is visible near the bow of the canoe being probably a Mud-fish (no. 89). The canoe (with the inscription 'A Cannow'—the word being of West Indian origin and reaching English through Spanish) in centre front has four Indians, wearing only breech-cloths, two sitting at a small fire in the middle of the boat surrounded by fish, one at the stern with a net-pole, 7 or 8 ft. long, with a net at the end made, apparently, with cane and cord, and the fourth at the bow with a short paddle ending in a small, shovel-shaped blade (cp. Barlowe's 'scoops', p. 105 above). A hand-net, with a short handle, a cane rim, and a net of cords in squares is propped up at the stern. Between the canoe and the shore in the foreground is another Hammer-headed Shark and one larger and one smaller fish. At the edge of the water are two shells with Hermit Crabs, both shells and crabs being West Indian (no. 5 above), and a King-crab, *Limulus* (or *Xiphosura*) *polyphemus*, Hariot's 'Seékanauk', p. 361 (see Raven, *English naturalists*, p. 182, and W. T. Calman, 'An early figure of the King-crab, *Limulus polyphemus*', in *Science*, n.s., XXVII (1908), 669, after a modern copy of the fishing scene in British Museum (Natural History)). L'Écluse had a similar specimen (as *Cancer Molluccanus*) engraved for his *Exoticorum*, pp. 106–7, without noting its similarity to that in De Bry. The shore in the foreground contains a number of plants in flower, which should be identifiable, growing down to the water's edge (nos. 54–5 being the only other American plants in the series). The drawing is spoiled as the earliest instance of a North American ecological study by White's contrived additions of West Indian fauna.

[1] De Bry, *America*, pt. i, pl. XIII (Lorant, *New world*, p. 251), engraving by Theodor de Bry. The canoe and its contents are unaltered, but the background is elaborated with three fish-weirs and many fish-spearers and canoes. The fish-trap in the weir on the left has a series of interlocking circular traps, the last ending in a peak. This probably introduces an authentic variant by White, though De Bry's accuracy in reproduction cannot be checked. A canoe is entering the first trap and loading fish with a hand-net. (For fish-weirs see Swanton, *Indians*, pp. 334–5.) Many more fish are given: the White Cat-fish (no. 95 probably) (left centre beyond canoe); the Spotted Sting-ray (*Aëtobatus narinari*, Euphrasen, *Fishes of N.C.*, no. 21) (left, near shore); a water-snake or lizard with two legs (invented?); and a turtle (probably the Diamond-backed Terrapin, no. 103). A West Indian land crab (cp. no. 4) is added to two king-crabs, and the hermit crabs are omitted. The flowers in the foreground have been largely conventionalized. In the boat is another Hammer-headed Shark, a Gar-fish (no. 93) and an eel or snake. De Bry could scarcely have added the fish, etc., if they had not appeared in the drawing White gave him.

vnto their Reedes or longe Rodds, the hollowe tayle of a certain
fishe like to a sea crabbe[1] in steede of a poynte, wehr[2] with by
nighte or day they stricke fishes, and take them opp into their
boates. They also know how to vse the prickles, and prickes of
other fishes. They also make weares, with settinge opp reedes or
twigges in the water, whiche they soe plant[3] one within a nother,
that they growe still narrower, and narrower. as appeareth by this
figure. Ther was neuer seene amonge vs soe cunninge a way to
take fish withall, wherof sondrie sortes as they fownde in their
Riuers vnlike vnto ours. which are also of a verye good taste.
Dowbtless yt is a pleasant sighte to see the people, somtymes
wadinge, and going somtymes sailinge in those Riuers, which are
shallowe and not deepe, free from all care of heapinge opp Riches
for their posteritie, content with heir state, and liuinge frendlye
together of those thinges which god of his bountie hath giuen
vnto them, yet without giuinge hym any thankes according to
his desarte. So sauage is this people, and depriued of the true
knowledge of god. For they haue none other then is mentionned
before in this worke.'[4]

47. Grilling fish.
(a) 'The broyling of thier fish ouer th' flame of fier.'[5]

[1] The King-crab. For the use of spears and hooks see Swanton, *Indians*,
pp. 336–40.
[2] For 'wherewith'.
[3] Latin, 'intertexentes'; French, 'entrelassent', so 'plait'?
[4] The place of fishing in the Indian economy of this area was a vital one,
providing as it did a main source of food, a means of preserving food by drying it
(cp. no. 47), and an article of trade (cp. p. 436 above and Swanton, *Indians*,
p. 252). In method there does not appear to have been an essential difference
between the Carolina Sounds and Chesapeake Bay (cp. Smith, *Works*, passim;
Strachey, *Hist. of travell*, p. 75; Beverley, *Hist. and present state of Virginia*,
pp. 148–9).
[5] Brit. Mus., P. & D. 1906-5-9-1 (11 (b)); Binyon, *Catalogue*, no. 12; Prospectus,
no. 12; Lorant, *New world*, p. [198], [b], [14]. Four forked sticks stuck in the
ground support a rectangular frame with bars across it on which two fish (not
identified) are being grilled whole over a small fire, while two other fish, impaled
on sticks stuck in the ground outside the frame, are also getting some of the fire's
heat.

(b) 'The browyllinge of their fishe ouer the flame.'¹

'After they haue taken store of fishe, they gett them vnto a place fitt to dress yt. Ther they sticke vpp in the grownde 4. stakes in a square roome, and lay 4. potes² vppon them, and others ouer thwart thesame like vnto an hurdle,³ of sufficient heigthe. and layinge their fishe vppon this hurdle, they make a fyre vnderneathe to broile the same, not after the manner of the people of Florida,⁴ which doe but schorte,⁵ and harden their meate in the smoke onlye to Reserue the same duringe all the winter. For this people reseruinge nothinge for store,⁶ thei do broile, and spend away all att once and when they haue further neede, they roste or seethe fresh, as wee shall see heraffter. And when as the hurdle can not holde all the fishes, they hange the Rest by the fyrres⁷ on

---

¹ De Bry, *America*, pt. i, pl. xiv (Lorant, *New world*, p. 253), engraving by Theodor de Bry. An elaborated form. The framework is the same, only on a larger scale. On the left is a man (modelled on the man in no. 49) holding a wooden, two-pronged fork about 4 ft. long (for which I have not seen a parallel): on the right, another man (identically clothed) carries on his back a large basket full of fish, which include a hammer-headed shark and a cat-fish as well as, apparently, a sword-fish—an assorted bag which could scarcely be carried on one man's back. The basket is only about 3 ft. deep and 2 ft. wide, so they cannot have been large specimens. It is carried by a rope over the man's shoulders. While Swanton, *Indians*, p. 603, complains of the 'singular paucity of references to baskets in Virginia and North Carolina', this may not provide a reliable addition to them. It may be conjectured that here White may have added the two men, the second with his basket, but that De Bry perhaps elaborated the basket and its contents.

² For 'posts'.   ³ French, 'en forme de grille'.

⁴ Cp. Hakluyt, *Principal navigations*, x, 436 and Lorant, *New world*, p. 96 (Le Challeux), for 'boucaned' meat and fish.

⁵ Scorch. Cp. Latin, 'qui dumtaxat vstulant & fumo indurant'; French, 'qui ne les font qu'enfumer, & secher'.

⁶ This needs some qualification. From what is said above, some preservation of food (as well as reservation of seed) for the winter took place (pp. 282–3, 354). Trade for copper, stone and dyes took place with the interior (pp. 332–3, 335, 336–7); the saleable assets of the coastal peoples being their dressed deer-skins, mats, shell-beads and pearls, and fish. Farther south, smoked or dried fish was a trade commodity (Swanton, *Indians*, pp. 736–7), and farther north also (Flannery, *Analysis*, no. 53), so it is not unlikely that some at least was bartered inland, and also retained for winter use (though a good deal of fishing could be done through the winter).   ⁷ For 'fire'.

sticks sett vpp in the grounde against the fyre, and then they finishe the rest of their cookerye. They take good heede that they bee not burntt. When the first are broyled they lay others on, that weare. newlye broughte, continuinge the dressinge of their meate in this sorte, vntill they thincke they haue sufficient.'

48. Cooking in a pot over a fire.
(*a*) 'The seething of their meate. in Potts of earth.'[1]
(*b*) 'Their seetheynge of their meate in earthen pottes.'[2]

'Their woemen know how to make earthen vessells[3] with special Cunninge and that so large and fine, that our potters with lhoye[4] wheles can make no better: ant[5] then Remoue them from place to place as easelye as we condoe our brassen kettles. After they haue set them vppon an heape of erthe to stay them from fallinge, they putt wood vnder which being kyndled one of them taketh great care that the fyre burne equallye Rounde abowt. They or their woemen fill the vessel with water, and then putt they in fruite, flesh, and fish, and lett all boyle together like a

---

[1] Brit. Mus., P. & D. 1906-5-9-1 (11 (a)); Binyon, *Catalogue*, no. 11; Prospectus, no. 11; Lorant, *New world*, p. [199], [a], [16]; W. H. Holmes, 'Aboriginal pottery of the eastern United States', in Smithsonian Institution, Bureau of American Ethnology, *Annual report for 1898–9* (1903), p. 26 (in colour). A large earthen pot, with a conical base, is resting directly on the timbers of a small fire. It is almost identical with that excavated by Mr J. C. Harrington at the fort on Roanoke Island (p. 907). It contains, as well as meat, corn cobs and other vegetables.

[2] De Bry, *America*, pt. i, pl. xv (Lorant, *New world*, p. 255), engraving by G. Veen. The pot and fire are much larger, with fish among the vegetables. A man dressed as in no. 49 kneels at the right fanning the flames with what looks like the shell-scraper in plate XII (no. 45) but is probably of bark with a wooden handle: a woman on the left is naked except for a breech-cloth like that worn by the man in no. 52, and she holds in her left hand a wooden spoon or ladle. The latter is possibly White's addition but is not paralleled for this date and could be a European insertion (cp. Swanton, *Indians*, pp. 556–7, from which the inferences would appear fairly evenly balanced; and Flannery, *Analysis*, no. 33, from which the spoon, if authentic, would appear more likely to be made of bark).

[3] Latin, 'figulina vasa'.

[4] The word is doubtful ('theyr'?). Latin, 'vt ne figulus quidem currente rota meliora conficere possit'; French, 'qu'il n'est possible de les faire mieux à la roue'.

[5] For 'and'.

galliemaufrye,[1] which the Spaniarde call, olla podrida. Then they putte yt out into disches, and sett before the companye, and then they make good cheere together. Yet are they moderate in their eatinge wher by they auoide sicknes. I would to god wee would followe their exemple. For wee should bee free from many kynes[2] of diseasyes which wee fall into by sumptwous and vnseasonable banketts, continuallye deuisinge new sawces, and prouocation of gluttonnye to satisfie our vnsatiable appetite.'[3]

49. An Indian, probably Wingina.
(*a*) 'A chiefe Herowan.'[4]
(*b*) 'A cheiff Lorde of Roanoac.'[5]

'The cheefe men of the yland and towne of Roanoac reace[6] the haire of their crounes of theyr heades cutt like a cokes combe, as thes other doe. The rest they wear longe as woemen and truss them opp in a knott in the nape of their necks. They hange pearles stringe copper a[7] threed att their eares, and weare bracelets on their armes of pearles, or small beades of copper or of smoothe

[1] Latin, 'instar lastaurocacabi'; French, 'en forme d'une olla podrida'.
[2] For 'kinds'.
[3] This reveals an ascetic side to Hariot not evident elsewhere.
[4] Brit. Mus., P. & D. 1906-5-9-1 (21); Binyon, *Catalogue*, no. 22; Prospectus, no. 18; Lorant, *New world*, p. [199], [b], [17]. If this is (as in the text to De Bry) a chief of Roanoke Island it cannot be other than Wingina (Pemisapan). His hair is thinned, or shaved, on either side of his head, leaving a roach or cockscomb standing down the middle (cp. Swanton, *Indians*, pp. 501–2; Strachey, *Hist. of travell*, p. 73), and with the long hair behind rolled into a knot (cp. no. 51). His face is not tattooed. An ear ornament of at least nine beads hangs by a loop from the lobe. Round his neck he wears a single short string of pearls, and, on a string, a gorget of copper about 6 in. square suspended from two holes in the top (cp. p. 102 above). On his right wrist he has a bracelet of pearls (cp. Swanton, *Indians*, p. 521). His apron-skirt is a fringed skin with pearls inset in the fringe, brief, and covering only the front.
[5] De Bry, *America*, pt. i, pl. VII (Lorant, *New world*, p. 239), engraving by Theodor de Bry. The figure is duplicated to give a rear view, and both show a double apron-skirt, the buttocks being covered. A background of fishing on the sounds is provided.
[6] For 'rase'. French, 'ont les cheueux...taillez'.
[7] For 'on'.

bone called minsal,[1] nether paintinge nor powncings of them selues, but in token of authoritye, and honor,[2] they wear a chaine of great pearles, or copper beades or smoothe bones abowt their necks, and a plate of copper[3] hinge[4] vpon a stringe. They couer themselues before and behynde, from the nauel vnto the midds of their thighes[5] as the woemen doe with a deers skynne handsomley dressed, and fringed, Moreouer they fold their armes together as they walke, or as they talke one wjth another in signe of wisdome. The yle of Roanoac is verye pleisant, ond[6] hath plaintie of fishe by reason of the Water that enuironeth the same.'

50.   An Indian woman.

(a) 'One of the wyues of Wyngyno.'[7]

(b) 'Of Aquascogoc.'[8]

(c) 'A younge gentill woeman doughter of Secota.'[9]

---

[1] 'bone called minsal' omitted in French text. The word would seem to be an Indian one. Was it bone or beads made of conch shell, the 'roanoak' or 'peak', later used as money? (See Swanton, *Indians*, pp. 481–5; pp. 418, 862.)

[2] Cp. pp. 440–3.   [3] Cp. pp. 102–3, 438.

[4] For 'hung'.

[5] 'from the...thighes' is mistakenly inserted after 'stringe' and is here corrected: note that in the drawing the man is not covered behind.

[6] For 'and'.

[7] Brit. Mus., P. & D. 1906-5-9-1 (17); Binyon, *Catalogue*, no. 18; Prospectus, no. 18; Lorant, *New world*, p. [199], [b], [17]. Her hair and headband are as no. 38. She is painted on the cheeks, chin, wrists, upper arms and calves. Her skirt is as no. 49. She has a short, double-string necklace of black and blue pearls or beads. Her hands rest on her shoulders; her legs are crossed below the knees, thus leading White into the anatomical error of putting her large toe on the outside of her left foot. (Mr H. W. Krieger of the Smithsonian Institution pointed out this, and a number of other details in the drawings, which I should otherwise have failed to notice.) She has an ear-ornament of a blue colour.

[8] Copy, without variants, except for caption, in Brit. Mus., P. & D. 199. a. 3 (L.B. 3 (6)); of which Sloane MS 5253, no. 17, is a copy.

[9] De Bry, *America*, pt. i, pl. VI (Lorant, *New world*, p. 237), engraving by G. Veen. The figure is duplicated. In the rear view the buttocks are covered with a skirt. A background of fishing in the sounds and of an island with a village is added. The discrepancies between one of the wives of the chief Wingina (Pemisapan), a woman of Aquascogoc (not otherwise represented in the series but visited on 13 and 16 July 1585 (p. 191; no. 53)), and the virgin of Secoton

'Virgins of good parentage are apparelled altogether like the woemen of Secota aboue mentionned,[1] sauing that they weare hanginge abowt their necks in steade of a chaine certaine thicke, and rownde pearles, with little beades of copper, or polished bones, betweene them. They pounce their foreheads, cheeckes, armes and legs. Their haire is cutt with two ridges aboue their foreheads, the rest is trussed opp on a knott behinde, they haue broade mowthes, reasonable fair black eyes: they lay their hands often vppon their Shoulders, and couer their brests in token of mayden-like modestye.[2] The reste of their bodyes are naked, as in the picture is to bee seene. They deligt also in seeinge fishe taken in the riuers.'

51.   Indian in war paint.

(*a*) 'The manner of their attire and painting them selues when they goe to their generall huntings or at theire Solemne feasts.'[3]

(*b*) Without inscription.[4]

---

are too obvious to need stressing. In this case they prove that White had no captions on some of his drawings (or did not accept those he had) and so added titles from memory or by invention later.

[1] No. 39 above.

[2] Latin, 'in virginei pudoris signum'.

[3] Brit. Mus., P. & D. 1906-5-9-1(12); Binyon, *Catalogue*, no. 13; Prospectus, no. 13; Lorant, *New world*, p. [193], [9]; Brit. Mus., postcard B 428. The man's hair is dressed as in no. 44 above, but he has a feather stuck upright at his forehead, and two behind each ear. He has red-painted marks on the face, chest (painted necklace and gorgets?), with circles round the nipples, shoulders and upper arms, and calves. He has a copper and bead ear-ornament, a six-string necklace, a two-strand bracelet on the right hand and a skin 'bracer' on the left wrist, wrist-guards being in general use (Swanton, *Indians*, p. 579). He has a slightly more ample apron-skirt than no. 49. The tail hanging down behind is probably that of a puma (cp. p. 357). In his left hand he holds a six-foot bow; and appearing from behind his back on the left is a quiver of woven reeds or cane (being usually of skin, Swanton, *Indians*, p. 579). It is probably held by a thin string over the shoulder. For men at a ceremony similarly dressed see no. 41 above. The communal hunting of deer by means of surrounds is discussed in Swanton, *Indians*, pp. 317-18 (and see pp. 105, 442, 525).

[4] Copy, without variants, in Brit. Mus., P. & D. 199. a. 3 (9); of which Sloane MS. 5253, no. 15, is a copy.

(c) 'A weroan or great Lorde of Virginia.'[1]

'The Princes of Virginia are attyred in suche manner as is expressed in this figure. They weare the haire of their heades long and bynde opp the ende of the same in a knot vnder their eares. Yet they cutt the topp of their heades from the forehead to the nape of the necke in manner of a cokscombe, stirking[2] a faier longe pecher of some berd[3] att the Begininge of the creste vppon their foreheads, and another short one on bothe seides about their eares. They hange at their eares ether thicke pearles, or somwhat els, as the clawe of some great birde, as cometh in to their fansye. Moreouer They ether pownes, or paynt their forehead, cheeks, chynne, bodye, armes, and leggs, yet in another sort then the inhabitantz of Florida.[4] They weare a chaine about their necks of pearles or beades of copper, wich they much esteeme, and ther of wear they also braselets ohn[5] their armes. Vnder their brests about their bellyes appeir certayne spotts, whear they vse to lett them selues bloode, when they are sicke.[6] They hange before them the skinne of some beaste verye feinelye dresset in suche sorte, that the tayle hangcth[7] downe behynde. They carye a quiuer

---

[1] De Bry, *America*, pt. i, pl. III (Lorant, *New world*, p. 231), engraving by Theodor de Bry. The figures are duplicated and differently posed. That on the left, facing front, has his bow in the right hand and an arrow (fletched like a European arrow) in his left, but De Bry has put his 'bracer' on his right wrist instead of his left: the back-viewed figure on the right shows the quiver slung from the waist (which may be correct), the tail hanging also from the waist, a bow in the right hand and an arrow in the left, again with the 'bracer' on the wrong wrist. In both the 'bracer' is emphasized, and is shown decorated with punched holes. A background is added, a group of Indians with bows being seen at the edge of a wood on the left, hunters shooting in the centre and a deer escaping to the woods on the right.

[2] For 'sticking'.   [3] For 'a fair long feather of some bird'.

[4] Cp. the two Florida copies after Le Moyne (III, nos. 1–2, p. 462 below).

[5] For 'on'.

[6] This is the only clear reference to scarification for this area. There are a few for the more northern coastal Algonkian peoples (Flannery, *Analysis*, p. 51), and Catesby's description may cover the Carolina Algonkians as well as more southerly tribes. He says that the cuts were usually made on the calves with the cleansed fang of a rattlesnake (see Swanton, *Indians*, pp. 791–2).

[7] For 'hangeth'. The tail is probably not from the same animal.

made of small rushes holding their bowe readie bent in on hand, and an arrowe in the other, radie to defend themselues. In this manner they goe to warr, or tho[1] their solemne feasts and ban-quetts. They take muche pleasure in huntinge of deer wher of ther is great store in the contrye, for yt is fruit full, pleasant, and full of Goodly woods. Yt hathe also store of riuers full of diuers sorts of fishe. When they go to battel they paynt their bodyes in the most terible manner that their[2] can deuise.'

52. Medicine man.

(*a*) 'The flyer.'[3]

(*b*) 'The Coniuerer.'[4]

'They haue comonlye coniurers[5] or iuglers which vse strange gestures, and often contrarie to nature in their enchantments. For they be verye familiar with deuils, of whome they enquier what their enemys doe, or other suche thinges. They shaue all their

---

[1] For 'to'.   [2] For 'they'.

[3] Brit. Mus., P. & D. 1906-5-9-1 (16); Binyon, *Catalogue*, no. 17; Prospectus, no. 17; Lorant, *New world*, p. [198], [a], [13]; Brit. Mus., postcard B 430. A man in a position for dancing (cp. no. 41). He is wearing a whole dark bird on the right side of his head. This is a culture-trait which Dr Flannery considers suggests a link, through Virginia, with southern New England Algonkian peoples (*Analysis*, no. 95; cp. Strachey, *Hist. of travell*, p. 74). Mrs E. G. Allen (*Trans. American Phil. Soc.*, n.s., XLI, 446) says of this: 'Of special interest to ornithologists is White's drawing of an Indian Flyer who, as a badge of his occupation, wears a bird adorning his head. This shows remarkable detail and delicacy of execution in the feathers.' Round his waist is a thin skin girdle, into which on the right side is tucked a skin bag or pouch. It is apparently made of a number of pieces of skin sewn together, the leather ends of which are made into a fringe (cp. no. 41; Swanton, *Indians*, p. 479). The breech-cloth is a small, unfringed skin with the mask lapped over the girdle and hanging in front (cp. nos. 41, 48; Swanton, *Indians*, p. 478, where an otter-skin is indicated). The title on the drawing is not met with elsewhere but is probably descriptive of his ceremonial dancing abilities.

[4] De Bry, *America*, pt. i, pl. XI (Lorant, *New world*, p. 247), engraving by G. Veen. The figure and its costume do not differ. A background of fishing and of hunting deer in the woods is added.

[5] French, 'enchanteurs'; Latin, 'Praestigitator'. The class of medicine men and soothsayers differed from that of the priests (cp. pp. 380, 430-2; Flannery, *Analysis*, p. 149) and this distinction was uniform amongst the Carolina and Virginia Algonkians but not other coastal Algonkian peoples.

heads sauinge their creste which they weare as other doe, and fasten a small black birde aboue one of their ears as a badge of their office. They weare nothinge but a skinne which hangeth downe from their gyrdle, and couereth their priuityes. They weare a bagg[1] by their side as is expressed in the figure. The Inhabitants giue great credit vnto their speeche, which oftentymes they finde to bee true.'[2]

53. Distinguishing marks used by the Indians.
'The Marckes of sundrye of the Cheif mene of Virginia.'[3]

'The inhabitants of all the cuntrie for the moste parte haue marks rased[4] on their backs, wherby yt may be knowen what Princes subiects they bee, or of what place they haue their originall. For which cause we haue set downe those marks in this figure, and haue annexed the names of the places, that they might more easelye be discerned. Which industrie hath god indued them withal although they be verye sinple, and rude. And to confesse a truthe I cannot remember, that euer I saw a better or quietter people then they. The marks which I obserued amonge them, are heere put downe in order folowinge.

[1] Latin, 'lateri marsupium appendunt'.

[2] Cp. Swanton, *Indians*, pp. 90, 753, 786.

[3] De Bry, *America*, pt. i, pl. XXIII (Lorant, *New world*, p. 271), engraving by Theodor de Bry, there being no corresponding drawing. A man dressed as in no. 51 with bow (the string slack), two arrows, quiver, and 'bracer' on left arm, has on his left shoulder-blade a mark (distinguished as 'F' at the side) and seven other sample marks. They are tribal marks (cp. Swanton, *Indians*, pp. 734–5), or marks of totemic clans (nothing is known of them for the Virginia or North Carolina Algonkians, cp. Swanton, *Indians*, pp. 658–61), or moieties (cp. Swanton, *Indians*, pp. 663, and as 'B' might suggest), or marks of individuals of exceptional rank (as the descriptions of 'A' to 'G' by Hariot would indicate). W. W. Tooker ('The swastika and other marks among the eastern Algonkins', in *American Antiquarian*, XX (1898), 339–49) considers them to be either individual or tribal. The arrow is, he says, a frequent Algonkian sign, and the swastika of 'E' is widely distributed in North America. 'B' may, he thinks, be representational of a pair of pipes or axes crossed, and 'F' of two pairs, the second reversed. White's drawing (no. 41 above) shows some of these in use.

[4] Literally 'scraped'. Those in no. 41 appear to be painted rather than tattooed.

'The marke which is expressed by A. belongeth tho [1] Wingino, the cheefe lorde of Roanoac.

'That which hath B. is the marke of Wingino his sisters husbande.

'Those which be noted with the letters of C. and D. belonge vnto diuerse chefe lordes in Secotam.

'Those which haue the letters E.F.G. are certaine cheefe men of Pomeiooc, and Aquascogoc.' [2]

54. Milkweed.

(a) 'Wysauke. The hearbe which the Sauages call Wysauke wherewith theie cure their woundes which they receeue by the poysoned arroes of their enemyes.' [3]

(b) 'Wisakon.' [4]

(c) Of Indian Swallow woort. Chap. 320. [5]

Wisanck, siue Vincetoxicum Indianum. Indian Swallow wort.

---

[1] For 'to'.

[2] Apart from the doubtful no. 50, this is the only named representation from Aquascogoc.

[3] Brit. Mus., P. & D. 1906-5-9-1 (37); Binyon, *Catalogue*, no. 38; *Prospectus*, no. 28; Lorant, *New world*, p. [204], [25]. Milkweed, showing five pairs of leaves and fruit, with root separate. There are about fourteen species of *Asclepias* in North Carolina (Wells, *Natural gardens*, pp. 389–91), this being *A. syriaca*, the common Milkweed. Medicinally it is known as the pleurisy root, being expectorant and diuretic: it was known also as the silk-weed (cp. pp. 325–6 for other silk-weeds) from the downy coverings of its seeds, while its fibres could be used for textiles by the Indians (though *A. incarnata* was more frequently so used). See Porcher, *Resources*, 2nd ed., pp. 562–5; J. K. Small, *Manual of the south-eastern flora* (1933), pp. 1067–72. The Indian word is from a widely spread Algonkian root meaning bitter and it is, as usual, difficult to identify the plant used very precisely (see p. 900 below, and Huron H. Smith, *Ethnobotany of the Meskwaki*, p. 205).

[4] Copy, without variants, in Brit. Mus., P. & D. 199. a. 3 (L.B. 3 (31)); of which Sloane MS 5289, no. 228, is a copy.

[5] John Gerard, *Herball* (1597), p. 752 (see Wilfrid Blunt, *The art of botanical illustration* (1950), p. 84). This is the only certain contact between John Gerard and the members of the Roanoke expeditions. The engraving (showing the fruit, one pair of leaves—more pointed than in White—and root) could well have been taken from a version of the White drawing, but not that with the present inscription, as Gerard had no details of its medical use by the Indians. It is, however, reasonable, in view of its similarity in appearance, to link it with White. If

John White's Drawings

* The description.

'There groweth in that part of Virginia, or Norembega, where our English men dwelled (intending there to erect a Colony) a kind of *Asclepias*, or Swallow woort, which the Sauages call *Wisanck*: there riseth vp from a single crooked roote one vpright stalke a foote high, slender, and of a greenish colour: wherupon do growe faire broade leaues sharp pointed, with many ribs or nerues running through the same, like those of Ribwoort or Plantaine, set together by couples at certaine distances. The flowers come foorth at the top of the stalks, which as yet are not obserued, by reason the man that brought the seeds and plants heereof did not regard them:[1] after which, there come in place two cods (seldome more) sharpe pointed like those of our Swallowe woort, but greater, stuffed full of most pure silke, of a shining white colour: among which silke appeareth a small long toong (which is the seede) resembling the toong of a birde, or that of the herbe called Adders toong. The cods are not onely full of silke, but euery nerue or sinewe wherewith the leaues be ribbed are likewise most pure silke;[2] and also the pilling of the stems euen as Flaxe is torne from his stalks. This considered; beholde the iustice of God, that as he hath shut vp those people and nations in ifidelitie and nakednes; so hath he not as yet giuen them vnderstanding to couer their nakednes, nor matter wherewith to do the same; notwithstanding the earth is couered with this silke, which daily they tread vnder their feete, which were sufficient to apparell many kingdomes if they were carefully manured, and cherished.

Gerard was one of the City of Raleigh associates in 1589 (cp. p. 570 below) he might well have got the drawing from Raleigh. He seems to have had some information of his own on the 1585–6 venture.

[1] It does not seem that Gerard's knowledge was direct. He has not seen the seeds grown: he could have seen a dried plant. Yet it is more probable that he received nothing more than a drawing and a verbal description. Hariot makes no mention of this plant, unless it is one of his secrets (pp. 336–7).

[2] This is quite distinct from Hariot's grass-silk (pp. 325–6).

★ The place.

'It groweth, as before is rehearsid, in the countries of Norembega, and now called Virginia by the *Honourable* [knight]¹ sir Walter Raleigh, who hath bestowed great summes of monie in the discouerie therof, where are dwelling at this present Englishmen, if neither vntimely death by murdering, or pestilence, corrupt aire, bloodie flixes, or some other mortall sicknes hath not destroied them.²

★ The time.

'It springeth vp, flowreth, and flourisheth both in winter and sommer, as do many, or most of the plants of that countrie.

★ The names.

'The silke is vsed of the people of Pomeioc, and other of the prouinces adioining (being parts of Virginia) to couer the secret parts of maidens that neuer tasted man, as in other places they vse a white kinde of mosse Wisanck:³ we haue thought *Asclepias Virginiana*, or *Vincetoxicum Indianum*, fit and proper names for it: in English Virginia Swallow woort, or the silke woort of Norembega.

★ The nature and vertues.

'A. We finde nothing by report or otherwaies of our owne knowledge, of his phisicall virtues, but onely report of the abundance of most pure silke, wherewith the whole plant is possessed.'⁴

---

¹ Johnson (in his edition of 1633) uses this form.
² An interesting reference to the presumed survival of the 'lost' colony, cp. Hakluyt in *Principal navigations*, II (1599), sig. *3; Taylor, *Hakluyts*, II, 456.
³ Compare pp. 417–18 above.
⁴ Johnson's edition (1633) adds (pp. 898–900) to Gerard's figure and description another of *Apocynum Syriacum Clusii*, 'kept in some gardens by the name of Virginia Silke Grasse', which he takes to be almost identical, and notes the use of its leaves for poultices and of its milk as a purge.

55. Rosegentian.[1]

56. Sandhill Crane.
'Taráwhow. The Crane.'[2]

57. Brown Pelican.
(*a*) 'Alcatrassa.[3] This fowle is of the greatnes of a Swanne. and of the same forme sauing the heade which is in length 16 ynches.' 'Tanboril.'[4]

[1] Brit. Mus., P. & D. 1906-5-9-1 (38); Binyon, *Catalogue*, no. 39; Prospectus, no. 29; Lorant, *New world*, p. [205], [a], [29]. Saltmarsh Rosegentian, *Sabbatia stellaris* Pursh, found abundantly along the coasts of North Carolina and Virginia. It has been authoritatively identified by Mr W. T. Stearn, Department of Botany, Brit. Mus. (N.H.), and the distribution confirmed from the localities represented in the National Herbarium, U.S. National Museum (information from Mr A. C. Smith). The plant is likely to have been drawn by White on account of its medicinal use by the Indians, but for what purpose they used it is not at present clear.

[2] Copy in Brit. Mus., P. & D. 199. a. 3 (L.B. 3 (93)). This is copied in Edward Topsell 'The Fowles of Heauen' (Huntington Library, Ellesmere MS 1142), as 'Tarawkow Konikautes. The Crane of Virginia', with the number '19'. Topsell says nothing of the origin of his drawing (identical in appearance and posture with the above, except for some differences in the drawing of the tail feathers). He introduces it, after some remarks on European Cranes, as follows: 'Peter Martyr writinge of America and the newe found worlde, affirmeth that the Spanyards founde Cranes in Cuba twise as bigge as our vulgar Cranes and Columbus also that he sawe Cranes in Laedesta [?] of redd and scarlett coulours in greate aboundance.' Sandhill Crane, *Megalornis mexicana* Müller, now only an infrequent visitor from Florida (*Birds of N.C.*, p. 111), cp. pp. 96, 358 above. Mrs E. G. Allen (*Trans. American Phil. Soc.*, n.s., XLI, 446) accepts the identification and reproduces the drawing.

[3] Brit. Mus., P. & D. 1906-5-9-1 (58); Binyon, *Catalogue*, no. 60; Prospectus. no. 50; Lorant, *New world*, p. [214], [a], [45]. Decapitated head of the Brown Pelican (*Pelicanus occidentalis carolinensis*). This bird breeds from the West Indies northwards to South Carolina, and winters from Florida southwards to Brazil. A number come from Florida to the North Carolina coast each summer (*Birds of N.C.*, no. 13), so that the specimen may well have been taken there (see one in the drawing of Indians fishing, no. 46). Percyvall, *Bibliotheca Hispanica* (1591), has 'Alcatraces, a kinde of foule like a seamew that feedeth on fish. *Auis quaedam Indica*' (cp. L'Écluse, *Exoticorum* (1605), pp. 106–7). *Alcatraz* was used in English, for example, in the list in Edward Topsell, 'The Fowles of Heauen' (*c.* 1614, Huntington Library, Ellesmere MS 1142), and is still employed locally in the West Indies (Bond, *Field guide to birds of the West Indies*, p. 12).

[4] At the bottom of the drawing, and originally the caption for no. 100 below, showing the drawings to have been on the same sheet and to have been subsequently cut apart.

58. Trumpeter Swan.
'Woanagusso. The Swann.'[1]

59. Common Loon.
'Asanamáwqueo. As bigg as a Goose.'[2]

60. Common Loon.
'Peeáwkoo. As bigg as a Goose.'[3]

61. Bufflehead Duck.
'Weewraamánqueo. As bigg as a Duck.'[4]

62. Surf Scoter.
'Iawéepuwes. Somwhat bigger then a Duck.'[5]

63. Red-breasted Merganser.
'Ovúnziuck. Of the bignes of a Duck.'[6]

64. Gull.
'Kaiauk. A Gull as bigg as a Duck.'[7]

[1] Copy in Brit. Mus., P. & D. 199. a. 3 (L.B. 3 (99)); of which Sloane MS 5265, no. 62, is a copy. Trumpeter Swan, *Cygnus buccinator*, which does not survive in this area (H. K. Coale, 'The present status of the Trumpeter Swan (*Olor buccinator*)', in *The Auk*, n.s., XXXII (1915), 82–90). See two swans in White's 'fishing' drawing, no. 46 above, and cp. Hariot, p. 358 above.

[2] Copy in Brit. Mus., P. & D. 199. a. 3 (L.B. 3 (98)); of which Sloane MS 5265, no. 62, is a copy. Young Common Loon, or Great Northern Diver, *Gavia immer*.

[3] Copy in Brit. Mus., P. & D. 199. a. 3 (L.B. 3 (94)); of which Sloane MS 5265, no. 35, is a copy. This is paralleled in Edward Topsell, 'The Fowles of Heauen' (Huntington Library, Ellesmere MS 1142), as 'Chungent' (which appears to be a poor copy of the above). 'This is also a Virginia water bird....' (Christy and Swanton, cp. p. 59, n. 3, above, both omit this name and bird. I do not know from what Topsell's name derives.) The drawing is, in both cases, too inaccurate for specific determination, but the bird is probably a booby.

[4] Copy in Brit. Mus., P. & D. 199. a. 3 (L.B. 3 (97)); of which Sloane MS 5265, no. 17, is a copy. Bufflehead Duck, *Charitonetta albeola* Linn. (*Birds of N.C.*, no. 65), residing in winter on lakes and open waters.

[5] Copy in Brit. Mus., P. & D. 199. a. 3 (L.B. 3 (95)); of which Sloane MS 5265, no. 12, is a copy. Surf Scoter, *Melanitta perspicillata* Linn. (*Birds of N.C.*, no. 69), which winters on the coast.

[6] Or 'Qvúnziuck.' Copy in Brit. Mus., P. & D. 199. a. 3 (L.B. 3 (96)); of which Sloane MS 5265, no. 20, is a copy. Red-breasted Merganser, *Mergus serrator* Linn. (*Birds of N.C.*, no. 74), a winter visitor to North Carolina, commonest on coast.

[7] Copy in Brit. Mus., P. & D. 199. a. 3 (L.B. 3 (100)); of which Sloane MS 5265, no. 63, is a copy. 'Kaiuk' appears in a list in Edward Topsell, 'The Fowles

John White's Drawings

65. Bald Eagle or Fish Hawk.
'Nahyápuw. The Grype. almost as bigg as an Eagle.'[1]

66. Flicker.
'Quurúcquaneo. A woodpicker. As bigg as a Pigeon.'[2]

67. Woodpecker.
'Memeo. As bigg as a Croo.'[3]

68. Woodpecker.
'Chacháquises. A wodpicker of this bignes.'[4]

69. Woodpecker.
'Maraseequo. A woddpicker of this bignes.'[5]

70. Bird.[6]
'Meemz. Of this bignes.'

of Heauen' (Huntington Library, Ellesmere MS 1142). This may be a young specimen of the Glaucous Gull, *Larus hyperboreus* Gunnerus (*Birds of N.C.*, no. 151), which is, however, a rather rare winter visitor to the North Carolina coast. This makes up nine distinct kinds of sea- or water-bird; Hariot said he had drawings of eight 'strange sorts' of water-fowl (p. 358 above).

[1] Copy in Brit. Mus., P. & D. 199. a. 3 (L.B. 3 (92)); of which Sloane MS 5263, no. 9, is a copy. Southern Bald Eagle, *Haliaetus leucocephalus leucocephalus* Linn. (*Birds of N.C.*, no. 87), or (on account of its light-coloured underparts—they are a brownish white in the drawing) a Fish Hawk or American Osprey, *Pandion haliaetas carolinensis* Gmelin (*Birds of N.C.*, no. 89).

[2] Copy in Brit. Mus., P. & D. 199. a. 3 (L.B. 3 (110)); of which Sloane MS 5263, no. 112, is a copy. Northern Flicker, *Colaptes auratus luteus* Bangs (*Birds of N.C.*, no. 197). Reproduced by E. G. Allen in *Trans. American Phil. Soc.*, n.s., XLI, 447, fig. 18, who says it was first described by Linnaeus after Catesby.

[3] Copy in Brit. Mus., P. & D. 199. a. 3 (L.B. 3 (103)); of which Sloane MS 5263, no. 116, is a copy. Southern Pileated Woodpecker, *Ceaphleus pileatus pileatus* Linn. (*Birds of N.C.*, no. 199).

[4] Copy in Brit. Mus., P. & D. 199. a. 3 (L.B. 3 (105) [b]). Hairy Woodpecker, *Dryobates villosus*.

[5] Copy in Brit. Mus., P. & D. 199. a. 3 (L.B. 3 (101)); of which Sloane MS 5263, no. 121, is a copy. Red-headed Woodpecker, *Melanerpes erythrocephalus* Linn. (*Birds of N.C.*, no. 201).

[6] Copy in Brit. Mus., P. & D. 199. a. 3 (L.B. 3 (105) [a]); of which Sloane MS 5266, no. 151, is a copy. A bird, some 5¼ in. long, is sitting on a leafless twig rising from apparently sandy soil. The beak and back are slate-blue, outlined in a darker shade; the head and neck have brush-strokes of light and dark brown; underparts in light-grey wash, the lines a darker shade; wing-tips and tail grey-brown wash

71. Swallow.
'Weeheépens. The Swallowe.'¹

72. Blue Jay.
'Artamóckes. The linguist. A birde that imitateth and vseth the sounde and tunes almost of all the birdes in the contrie. As bigg as a Pigeon.'²

73. Bird, probably Brown Thresher.
'Poócqueo. Bigger then a Thrush.'³

strengthened with darker shade; legs and feet being blue-grey outlined in black. It is possibly the Blue-grey Gnatcatcher, *Polioptilia cerulea* (information from Dr Herbert Friedmann, U.S. National Museum).

¹ Copy in Brit. Mus., P. & D. 199. a. 3 (L.B. (107) [b]); of which Sloane MS 5266, no. 140, is a copy. American Barn Swallow, *Hirundo erythrogaster* Boddaert (*Birds of N.C.*, no. 224), lacking the white spots on outer tail feathers. It is a common migrant in April–May and August–early September.

² Copy in Brit. Mus., P. & D. 199. a. 3 (L.B. 3 (111)); of which Sloane MS 5263, no. 70, is a copy. Florida Blue Jay, *Cyanocitta cristata cristata* Linn. (*Birds of N.C.*, no. 228). This is represented in Edward Topsell, 'The Fowles of Heauen' (Huntington Library, Ellesmere MS 1142) by the name 'Artamokes' and a ludicrously bad illustration, possibly after this picture, showing the bird with a divided crest, like two horns projecting from either side of the head. His text follows: 'This is a Virginia bird. The description whereof I had from Doctor Bonham. It is the thirde kinde of woode spikers, hauinge a loftie Combe or Creste arisinge at the two Corners behinde and before: The culour of the feathers for the most part blewe from the typpe of the Creste vnto the rump there are some browne blacke feathers and it hath also diuers white spottes The body is white the beake and feete blacke. It is not good for meate, bycause it liueth like other woodspikers vpon flyes spiders and erthworms For this thinge onlie the people of the countrey admire it, and I·doubt whether there be any creature in all the worlde to paralell it: for it imitatheth readilie, all the seuerall voices of other birdes so as Cleopatra Epiphanius or Kinge Mithridates, which had three and twentie languages are not to be compared to this siely birde that can singe with the thrushe, croak with the Rauen, crow with the Cocke mourne with the Turtle, hiss with the Peacocke, and so imitate the residue: for which cause our Countreymen in Virginia doe call it a Linguist as if it had skill in many languages and the people of the countrey call it Artamokes.' (Cp. E. G. Allen, in *Trans. American Phil. Soc.*, n.s., XLI, 448.)

³ Copy in Brit. Mus., P. & D. 199. a. 3 (L.B. 3 (113)); of which Sloane MS 5264, no. 66, is a copy. Probably Brown Thresher, *Taxostoma rufum*. It is represented by 'Poocqueo' (and possibly also by 'Pockway') in Edward Topsell's list in 'The Fowles of Heauen' (Huntington Library, Ellesmere MS 1142).

74. Bird.[1]

75. A Bird.
'Iacháwanjes. Of this biggnes.'[2]

76. Bird.[3]

77. Red-wing.
'Chúwquaréo. The blackbyrd.'[4]

78. Baltimore Oriole.[5]

[1] Copy in Brit. Mus., P. & D. 199. a. 3 (L.B. 3 (112) [a]); of which Sloane MS 5264, no. 103, is a copy. Bird about 6¾ in. long, sitting on branch, the head, back, wings and tail being yellowish brown wash, heavily strengthened with black shading to a yellowish green along the edge of the wing and up the side of the neck towards the crest; the beak being yellowish green outlined in black; the throat grey wash; the underparts grey-white with the brush-strokes in grey; legs and feet being pink, outlines in black. It is possibly an immature specimen of the Maryland Yellowthroat, *Geothlypsis trichas* (information from Dr Herbert Friedmann, U.S. National Museum; *Birds of N.C.*, no. 323).

[2] Copy in Brit. Mus., P. & D. 199. a. 3 (L.B. 3 (104) [a]). It is not evident what the 'j' sound is (cp. p. 887 below). Identified by Dr Friedmann as possibly the Blueheaded Vireo, *Vireo solitarius* Wilson (*Birds of N.C.*, no. 278).

[3] Copy in Brit. Mus., P. & D. 199. a. 3 (L.B. 3 (112) [b]). Bird about 5 in. long on leafless branch, the head, neck, back, wings and tail being in slate-blue wash strengthened with white brush-strokes, the feather lines in a deeper shade of blue; underparts grey-cream (colour of the paper), the brush-strokes grey; legs and feet being blue-grey, the lines black. This may possibly be the Slate-coloured Junco, *Junco hyemalis hyemalis* (information from Dr Herbert Friedmann, U.S. National Museum; *Birds of N.C.*, no. 380).

[4] Copy in Brit. Mus., P. & D. 199. a. 3 (L.B. 3 (107) [a]); of which Sloane MS 5264, no. 91, is a copy. On twig. Eastern Red-wing (or Red-winged Blackbird), *Agelaeius phoeniceus phoeniceus* Linn. (*Birds of N.C.*, no. 334). This is represented in Edward Topsell, 'The Fowles of Heauen' (Huntington Library, Ellesmere MS 1142) above with the 'Chuquareo' (the illustration being a somewhat cruder version of the above) with the note: 'This is a Virginia bird resemblinge our owsell or blacke bird in quantitye & qualitye: for the beake is of a clay colour & the whole body blacke except the forpart of the wings which are a deepe scarlett colour as by the picture you may perceiue.' Cp. Smith, *Works*, p. 60: 'There are woosels [ousels] or blackbirds with red shoulders.'

[5] Copy in Brit. Mus., P. & D. 199. a. 3 (L.B. 3 (106) [b]); of which Sloane MS 5263, no. 87, is a copy. Baltimore Oriole, *Icterus galbula* Linn. (*Birds of N.C.*, no. 336). Appears only as a migrant in the greater part of North Carolina.

79. Grackle.

'Tummaihumenes. Of this bignes.'[1]

80. Cardinal Bird.

'Meesquouns. Almost as bigg as a Parratt.'[2]

81. Towhee.

'Chúwhweeo. Somthing bigger then a Blackbyrd.'[3]

82. Bird.[4]

[1] Copy in Brit. Mus., P. & D. 199. a. 3 (L.B. 3 (102)); of which Sloane MS 5263, no. 96, is a copy. Purple Grackle, *Quisqualis quisqualis*.

[2] Copy in Brit. Mus., P. & D. 199. a. 3 (L.B. 3 (109)); of which Sloane MS 5264, no. 77, is a copy. This is represented in Edward Topsell's 'Fowles of Heauen' (Huntington Library, Ellesmere MS 1142) by the name 'Meessenouns, Virginia', only. Eastern Cardinal Bird, *Richmondena cardinalis cardinalis* Linn. (*Birds of N.C.*, no. 346). This bird was first illustrated, from a live specimen obtained in Italy, by Ulisse Aldrovandi, in his *Ornithologia* (1599) (see E. G. Allen, in *Trans. American Phil. Soc.*, n.s., XLI, 405; Bayard H. Christy, 'The bird itself', in *The Cardinal*, v (1942), 173–86).

[3] Copy in Brit. Mus., P. & D. 199. a. 3 (L.B. 3 (108)); of which Sloane MS 5264, no. 108, and probably Sloane MS 5266, no. 142, are copies. On twig. Red-eyed Towhee, *Pipilo erythrophthalmus erythrophthalmus* Linn. (*Birds of N.C.*, no. 360). Its cry is a series of *che-wink* notes, hence possibly the Indian name. It is in Edward Topsell, 'The Fowles of Heauen' (Huntington Library, Ellesmere MS 1142), as the 'Chuwheeo' (with a good copy of the drawing) and the important note: 'This is also a virginia bird whose picture I receiued from that worthye, industrious, & learned Compiler of nauigations, whose prayses will remaine to the worlds end in the monument of his owne labours, I meane Master Hackluyt. But before I sawe this picture I receiued this breife description from Doctor Bonham. Yt is the greatest Virginian Pye, hauing an ashe coloured beake, but all the body head & necke blacke, except the belly & leggs, which are a compound of white & chessnut. The tayle is very longe, like our english common pyes, & haith vnderneath two white feathers, which because it is proper to that countrye, I haue expressed by that proper name whereby the people there call it.'

[4] Copy in Brit. Mus., P. & D. 199. a. 3 (L.B. 3 (104) [b]); of which Sloane MS 5264, no. 104, is a copy. This shows a bird about 7 in. long pecking a head of maize with multicoloured grains—the latter being the earliest illustration of this type of maize (cp. p. 338 above). The bird has the head, back, wings and tail in brown wash, shading to a darker tone along the top of the back and head, the feather lines being heavily strengthened with dark brown; beneath the wing is a pinkish red, with the underparts in a light wash of blue-grey; the legs and feet brown, outlined in black; the beak a muddy grey. The grains of corn, painted separately, are in blue, yellow-green, dark red body-colour, and grey. The bird may possibly be a female of the Red-eyed Towhee (cp. no. 81 above; information from Dr Herbert Friedmann, U.S. National Museum). Topsell has a Virginia

83. Unidentified bird.[1]

84. Sturgeon.
'Coppáuseo.[2] The Sturgeon. Some 10. 11. 12. or 13. foote in length.'[3]

85. Herring.
'Chaham
Wundúnãham } The hearing .2. foote in length.'[4]

86. Sheepshead.
'Masunnehockeo. The old wyfe, 2. foote in length.'[5]

bird called 'Aushousetta', which is similar, and in a comparable pecking position, without the head of corn (Huntington Library, Ellesmere MS 1142), but there is no description attached.

[1] Copy in Brit. Mus., P. & D. 199. a. 3 (L.B. 3 (106) [a]); of which Sloane MS 5264, no. 105, is a copy. The bird, whose head is turned to the left, is sitting on a honeysuckle branch. The crown of the head, top of back, wings and tail are in light-brown wash, the lines in dark brown; belly and lower back in grey-blue wash with strokes of dark grey; breast, with paper ground and fine brush-strokes in light brown and dark brown; legs and feet grey-blue, outlines in black; beak yellow-green with blue-grey edging. Size as drawn is approximately 7½ in. long. So far this has not been identified as an American or European species. If it is not American the seventeen 'strange sortes' of 'land fowle' of which Hariot records drawings are represented in the collection by numbers 65–82 above (cp. p. 358). In view of its association, however, it seemed best to keep this drawing with the American group until something is known of what it represents.

[2] With the characteristic White 'f' for 's', thus providing a neat proof that these copies (Group C³, see pp. 392, 394–7 above) were made from White's originals.

[3] Copy in Brit. Mus., P. & D. 199. a. 3 (L.B. 3 (128)); of which Sloane MS 5267, no. 95, is a copy. Sharp-nosed Sturgeon, *Acipenser oxyrynchus* Mitchill (*Fishes of N.C.*, no. 26), though the drawing of 9 (for 10 or more) dorsal plates, and the brownish colour of the back might suggest the rarer and smaller Short-nosed Sturgeon, *Acipenser brevirostrum* Le Sueur (ibid., no. 27). Sturgeon formerly ascended the North Carolina rivers in spring in great quantities (cp. Hariot, p. 359 above).

[4] Copy in Brit. Mus., P. & D. 199. a. 3 (L.B. 3 (117)); of which Sloane MS 5267, no. 110, is a copy. The Indian names are probably not alternatives for the same fish, but are likely to apply to distinct kinds: one possibly shad. The drawing is apparently the Branch Herring (or Alewife), *Pomolobus pseudoharengus* Wilson (*Fishes of N.C.*, no. 108), which migrates to the rivers from the sea and the sounds. It is not found south of North Carolina (cp. Hariot, p. 359 above).

[5] Copy in Brit. Mus., P. & D. 199. a. 3 (L.B. 3 (125)). Sloane notes 'Porkfish. Cat. [Catesby]'. Sloane MS 5267, no. 117, is a copy. Sheepshead Bream, *Archosargus probatocephalus* Walbaum (*Fishes of N.C.*, no. 263), found in bays and estuaries from spring to autumn (cp. Hariot, p. 360 above).

87. Mullet.

'Tetszo. The Mullett, some 2 foote in length.'[1]

88. A flat-fish.

'Pashockshin. The Playse. A foote and a halfe in length.'[2]

89. Mud-fish.

'Marangahockes. 3. or 4. foote in length.'[3]

90. Striped Bass.

'Mesíckek. Some 5 or 6 foote in lengthe.'[4]

91. Channel Bass.

'Chigwusso. Some 5. foote in length.'[5]

92. Fish, unidentified.

'Ribuckon. A foote in length.'[6]

[1] Copy in Brit. Mus., P. & D. 199. a. 3 (L.B. 3 (121)). Sloane notes 'Mullet Cat. [Catesby]'. Sloane MS 5267, no. 92, is a copy. A Grey Mullet, possibly the Striped Mullet, *Mugil cephalus* Linn. (*Fishes of N.C.*, no. 155). (Cp. Hariot, p. 360 above.)

[2] Copy in Brit. Mus., P. & D. 199. a. 3 (L.B. 3 (114)); of which Sloane MS 5267, no. 9, is a copy. Probably Southern Flounder, *Paralichthys lethostigmus* Jordan & Gilbert (*Fishes of N.C.*, no. 333). (Cp. Hariot, p. 454 above.) A poor representation.

[3] Copy in Brit. Mus., P. & D. 199. a. 3 (L.B. 3 (115)); of which Sloane MS 5267, no. 119, is a copy. Mud-fish (or Bow-fin), *Amia calva* Linn., found in sluggish waters of the sounds, especially in Albermarle Sound (*Fishes of N.C.*, no. 29, not recording a specimen over 3 ft. long).

[4] Copy in Brit. Mus., P. & D. 119. a. 3 (L.B. 3 (118)); of which Sloane MS 5267, no. 120, is a copy. Striped Bass, *Roccus saxatilis* Walbaum (*Fishes of N.C.*, no. 238): the colour of the back in the drawing is rather bluish instead of olive but there is little doubt about the identification. J. C. Pearson, 'The life history of the Striped Bass, or Rockfish, *Roccus saxatilis* Walbaum', in *Bulletin of the U.S. Bureau of Fisheries*, XLIX [*recte* XLVIII] (1938), 825–51, gives a succinct history of this fish but cannot find any references prior to 1623.

[5] Copy in Brit. Mus., P. & D. 199. a. 3 (L.B. 3 (119)); of which Sloane MS 5267, no. 126, is a copy. Channel Bass, *Sciaenops ocellatus* Linn., found along the Atlantic coast south of New York (*Fishes of N.C.*, no. 276, where a length of 5 ft. and a weight of 75 lb. are recorded).

[6] Copy in Brit. Mus., P. & D. 199. a. 3 (L.B. 3 (116)); of which Sloane MS 5267, no. 127, is a copy. Fish, blue, paling from back to belly; brownish tinge on tail and lower fins; yellowish round gills. A poor representation. This is probably the White Perch, *Morone americana* Gmelin (*Fishes of N.C.*, no. 274).

93. Gar-fish.
'Arasémec. Some 5. or 6. foote in length.'[1]

94. Gar-pike.
'Kowabetteo. Some 5. or 6. foote in length.'[2]

95. Cat-fish.
'Keetrauk. Some 2. foote and a halfe in length.'[3]

96. Spiny Box-fish.
(*a*) 'Gallo.'[4]
(*b*) 'Gallo.'[5]

97. Spiny Box-fish.
'A swelling fish: 8 ynches in lengthe.'[6]

98. Fish, probably Croaker.
'Manchauemec. Some a foote in length.'[7]

[1] Copy in Brit. Mus., P. & D. 199. a. 3 (L.B. 3 (122)); of which Sloane MS 5267, no 80, is a copy. Gar-fish, either *Tylosurus acus* Lacépède (*Fishes of N.C.*, no. 135), a large West Indian gar-fish usually represented off North Carolina by small stragglers (though one of 3 ft. has been taken), or *Tylosurus raphidoma* Ranzoni. De Bry includes one in his engraving of the fishing scene (no. 46, see p. 434 above).

[2] Copy in Brit. Mus., P. & D. 199. a. 3 (L.B. 3 (123)); of which Sloane MS 5267, no. 96, is a copy. Gar-pike, *Lepisosteus osseus* Linn.

[3] Copy in Brit. Mus., P. & D. 199. a. 3 (L.B. 3 (124)); of which Sloane MS 5267, no. 33, is a copy. A cat-fish (a fresh-water fish) most probably the White Cat-fish, *Ameiurus catus* Linn. (*Fishes of N.C.*, no. 33). There are several specimens in De Bry's engraving of no. 46, see p. 434 above.

[4] Brit. Mus., P. & D. 1906-5-9-1 (54); Binyon, *Catalogue*, no. 56; Prospectus, no. 46; Lorant, *New world*, p. [213], [a], [42]. Spiny Box-fish, *Chilomycterus schoepfi* Walbaum, of West Indies (where this may have been found) and the Atlantic coast of North America (see *Fishes of N.C.*, no. 303, as Bur-fish). The Spanish *Gallo* is now used for the Dory, another spiny fish. No. 97 is a copy of another drawing, nearer to the actual colouring, of the same species.

[5] Copy in Brit. Mus., P. & D. 199. a. 3 (L.B. 3 (22) [a]); of which Sloane MS 5267, no. 32, is a copy.

[6] Copy in Brit. Mus., P. & D. 199. a. 3 (L.B. 3 (129)); of which Sloane MS 5267, no. 45, is a copy. Spiny Box-fish, *Chilomycterus schoepfi* Walbaum, as no. 96, above.

[7] Copy in Brit. Mus., P. & D. 199. a. 3 (L.B. 3 (130)); of which Sloane MS 5267, no. 122, is a copy. This is a poor drawing, with indecisive colouring, much

99. Lamprey.
'Kokohockepúweo. The Lampron, a foote in lengthe.'[1]

100. Swell-fish.
(a) ['Tanborel'][2] 'A fresh ryuer fish.'[3]
(b) Without inscription.[4]

101. Loggerhead Turtle.[5]

102. Box Tortoise.
'A land Tort which the Sauages esteeme aboue all other Torts.'[6]

foxed. The back of this fish is brownish with green specks; the belly pinkish, with green flecks; the fins blue (dorsals darker than under-fins); around the mouth it is black, with greenish-purple stripes below mouth. It is probable that this is the Common Croaker, *Micropogon indulatus* Linn (*Fishes of N.C.*, p. 318: cp. Hariot, pp. 359–60 above).

[1] Copy in Brit. Mus., P. & D. 199. a. 3 (L.B. 3 (120)); of which Sloane MS 5267, no. 2, is a copy. Brook Lamprey, or possibly Sea Lamprey, *Petromyzon marinus* Linn. (*Fishes of N.C.*, no. 2), North Carolina being the southern limit of its range. A poor drawing.

[2] Mr Hulton identified traces of the descenders of the letters of this word on no. 100 though the word itself now appears on no. 57 above. It was mistakenly detached when the sheet was cut. The word is apparently the Spanish *tamboril*, a tabor or tambourine, and suitably descriptive of the distended fish.

[3] Brit. Mus., P. & D. 1906-5-9-1 (51); Binyon, *Catalogue*, no. 53; Prospectus, no. 43; Lorant, *New world*, p. [208], [c], [33]. Swell-fish, *Spheroides testudineus* Linn., of West Indies and Atlantic coast of North America; occasionally in North Carolina (*Fishes of N.C.*, no. 301) as Puffer or Rabbit-fish, in streams through salt-marshes near Beaufort. May be from West Indies. Nos. 84–100, seventeen in all, may include all the twelve strange sorts of fish of which Hariot said he had drawings (p. 360 above). If we cut out the Sturgeon, Herring, Oldwife (Sheepshead), Mullet and 'Plaice' (nos. 83–7) mentioned by him we are left with twelve precisely.

[4] Copy in Brit. Mus., P. & D. 199. a. 3 (L.B. 3 (18) [b]); of which Sloane MS 5267, no. 42, is a copy.

[5] Brit. Mus., P. & D. 1906-5-9-1 (69); Binyon, *Catalogue*, no. 71; Prospectus, no. 62 (as Loggerhead, *Thalassochelys caretta*); Lorant, *New world*, p. [224], [64]. Atlantic Loggerhead Turtle, *Caretta caretta caretta*, the only Sea Turtle which breeds on the Carolina Banks, though it has a wide distribution in tropical and sub-tropical seas (H.T.D.; *Amphibians and reptiles of N.C.*, no. 108). Cp. Hariot, p. 362 above. It is worth noting that a figure of a Loggerhead Turtle is included by Drake's artist in the plan of Santo Domingo (cp. pp. 34, 42 above), with a long note on the turtle in the English text, though it is not likely that there was an exchange of drawings, with White in this case.

[6] Brit. Mus., P. & D. 1906-5-9-1 (68); Binyon, *Catalogue*, no. 70; Prospectus, no. 60; Lorant, *New world*, p. [221], [a], [59]. Box Tortoise, *Terrapene carolina carolina* (H.T.D.; *Amphibians and reptiles of N.C.*, no. 114). Cp. Hariot, p. 362 above.

103. Terrapin.[1]

104. Snake.[2]

'Tesicqueo.[3] A kinde of Snake which the Saluages (being rost or sodden) doe eate.[4] Some an ell long.'

105. Skink.[5]

'Memeskson.[6] A foote in length.'

106. Cicada.[7]

'Alae pulcherrimae, argento illitae, naevis*que* fuscis & maculis cum ornatu pictae. externae internis duplo longiores sunt, ma-

---

[1] Brit. Mus., P. & D. 1906-5-9-1 (70); Binyon, *Catalogue*, no. 72; Prospectus, no. 61 (as Terrapin, *Malacoclemmys terapin*), with specimen plate; Lorant, *New world*, p. [222], [61]. Diamond-back Terrapin, *Malaclemys terrapin* sub.sp., of North Carolina (H.T.D.; *Amphibians and reptiles of N.C.*, nos. 124-5), found in salt-marshes north and south of Cape Hatteras. Cp. Hariot, p. 362 above.

[2] Copy in Brit. Mus., P. & D. 199. a. 3 (L.B. 3 (127)); of which Sloane MS 5272, no. 52, is a copy. It cannot be accurately identified from the drawing, but the colouring would indicate that it is a Scarlet King-snake, *Lampropeltis triangulum elapsoides*, or the closely related Milk-snake, *L. triangulum triangulum*, the former known from North Carolina southwards and the latter from North Carolina northwards to Maine on the eastern seaboard (information from Dr Doris M. Cochran, U.S. National Museum; *Amphibians and reptiles of N.C.*, nos. 95, 99).

[3] With the characteristic White 'f' for 's' (cp. nos. 24, 30, 87, 105).

[4] Snake-eating is recorded of the Virginia Algonkians by Strachey (*Hist. of travell*, p. 80). Here it is likely to represent a culture-trait of the Carolina Algonkians, and as such is not elsewhere on record, though snake-eating was common in the south-east (cp. Flannery, *Analysis*, p. 25; Swanton, *Indians*, pp. 252, 295).

[5] Copy in Brit. Mus., P. & D. 199. a. 3 (L.B. 3 (126)); of which Sloane MS 5272, no. 45, is a copy. This is the Skink, genus *Eumeces*, of which three species, *fasciatus* (cp. *Amphibians and reptiles of N.C.*, no. 64), *inexpectatus* and *laticeps*, have been recorded from the coastal region visited by the colonists (information from Dr Doris M. Cochran, U.S. National Museum).

[6] The first 's' is the characteristic White 'f' (cp. nos. 24, 30, 87, 104).

[7] Known only from Moffet. The lower drawing on 'Insectorum...theatrum', Brit. Mus., Sloane MS 4014, fo. 124 v., where the text occurs, may be that referred to. Woodcut and text in *Insectorum...theatrum* (1634), p. 128, and in *Theater of insects* (1658), pp. 990-1 where the translation is: 'the wings very curious, of a silver colour, and painted with dusky spots and specks very trim, the outermost twice as long as the innermost, and more various: the dark brown is more rarely seen, which Ludovicus Armacus [*sic*] a very diligent Chirurgeon, brought from Guinea, and gave to Pennius [Thomas Penny]: also Mr. White a rare Painter,

457

gisq*ue* variegatae. Fusca rarior vide*tur*, quam ex Guinea Ludo-
uicus Atmarus Chirurgus diligentissimus Pennio dedit. Dedit illi
aliam ex Virginiâ portatam Candidus, pictor non incele*bris*;
cinerei o*mn*ino coloris, (fortè Graecorum τέρφην) sed proportione
cum primis simili alas utrasq*ue* habet argenteas, sed neutiq*uam*
(ut prima͞e illae virides) maculatas.'

107.   Swallow-tail Butterfly.
(*a*)   Without inscription.[1]
(*b*)   'Mamankanois.'[2]
(*c*)   'Mamankanois[3]

Hanc è Virginiâ Americanâ Candidus ad me Pictor detulit
1587[4]

Diurna Papilio prima,[5] omniu*m* maxima maxima*m* partem

gave him another brought forth from Virginie, it was all of an ash-colour, (it
may be what the Greeks call τέρφην) but it was like the former in proportion,
it hath both its wings silver coloured, but not at all spotted as the former green
ones were.' Noted by Raven (*English naturalists*, p. 128). The Greek name is from
τέρφας (Aelian, *Nat. Anim.*, x. 44), in a Byzantine form τέρφην. (I am indebted
to Mr W. R. Smyth and Miss N. M. Holley for the references.)

[1] Brit. Mus., P. & D. 1906-5-9-1 (66); Binyon, *Catalogue*, no. 68; Prospectus,
no. 58; Lorant, *New world*, p. [220], [a], [56]. Tiger Swallow-tail Butterfly,
Papilio turnus.   [2] Copy in Brit. Mus., P. & D. 199. a. 3 (L.B. 3 (18) [a]).

[3] This word is in a different hand from the remainder. Original drawing by
White in Thomas Moffet, 'Insectorum...theatrum', Brit. Mus., Sloane MS
4014, fo. 96.

[4] This hand is Thomas Penny's, and the inscription has been used to argue
that White brought the drawing back from his 1587 voyage. It will be remembered that White returned on 8 November and met Raleigh on the 20th, presumably in London (pp. 538, 563 above). By English reckoning 1587 ran on to
24 March 1588. On the other hand, there is nothing in the inscription to make
it impossible that this was a drawing made by White in 1585-6 and of which he
gave a copy to Penny before he left Portsmouth on 26 April (cp. W. J. Holland,
'The first picture of an American butterfly', in *Scientific Monthly*, xxix (1929),
45-8, where the drawing was reproduced for the first time, his *Butterfly book*,
rev. ed., New York, 1931, pp. 304-7, and pl. lxxvii, and R. G. Adams, 'An effort
to identify John White', in *American Historical Review*, xli (1935-6), 87-91).

[5] Brit. Mus., Sloane MS 4014, fo. 95 v. It is printed in Moffet's *Insectorum...
theatrum* (1634), p. 88 [*recte* 98], where a woodcut of the butterfly, without
inscription, appears.

flauescit, iis locis partibusq*ue* exceptis, que hic attramento denigrantur. Quinetiam extremi illi internarum alarum globuli coelicolore*m* spirant: ut genuinis Sapphyris consitum putares. Oculi chrysolythum referunt, magnitudinem formamq*ue* adeo ad normam exculptam hîc exhibemus, ut plura de ijs attexere non sit necessum.'

(*d*) 'The first Day-Butterfly[1] being the greatest of all, for the most part all yellowish, those places and parts excepted which are here blacked with ink. Moreover, the roundles of the inner wings are sky-colour, insomuch that you would think they were set with Saphire stones; the eyes are like the Chysolite: the bignesse and form is so exactly set forth in the figure, that there need no more to be said of it.'

108   Gadfly.

(*a*) 'A dangerous byting flye.'[2]

(*b*) 'Duas Asilorum[3] rariores species Pennius descripsit, quarum unam ex Virginia Indorum Candidus, alteram ex Russia Elmerus chirurgus diligens ad eum misit. Virginiensis maximam muscam capite subrubentem magnitudine aequat: & ad formam ejus proximé accedit, nisi quod caput nigrum, argentea*m* linea*m* á scapulis ad os pertracta*m*, & oculos nigriores majoresq*ue* obtinet. stimulus illi in ore longus & robustus, scapulae ex fusco nigricantes, et duas argenteas alas emittentes. Ad caudam sex vel septem habet incisuras subalbidi coloris, reliquo corpore subnigricante. Volatus celeri-

---

[1] As translated in Moffet, *Theater of insects* (1658), p. 967, where the woodcut is again reproduced.

[2] Brit. Mus., P. & D. 1906-5-9-1 (67); Binyon, *Catalogue*, no. 69; Prospectus, no. 59; Lorant, *New world*, p. [214], [b], [46], noted by Raven (*English naturalists*, p. 182). This is on the same sheet as the Fire-flies (no. 7). It is not precisely identifiable (*Tabanus* sp.), possibly *T. rufofrater*.

[3] Thomas Moffet, 'Insectorum...theatrum', Brit. Mus., Sloane MS 4014, fo. 63. Neither of the two drawings on this folio is White's, but the second drawing on fo. 69 v. is identified as his by Mr P. H. Hulton.

tate neminem muscarum metuit, plurimas Vincit. Venter ex cinereo lutescente, dilué Virescit.'

(*c*) Gadfly.[1]

109. Map of Eastern North America from Florida to Chesapeake Bay.[2]

[1] Thomas Moffet, *Insectorum...theatrum* (1634), p. 60, with woodcuts of the drawings and text as in MS; also *Theater of insects* (1658), p. 936, where the text is: 'Pennius [Thomas Penny] hath set down 2 very rare kindes of Asili, one of which was sent him out of Virginia by White, the other out of Russia by Elmer a Chirurgeon for a great present. That out of Virginia was full as big as the biggest Flies, having a reddish head, and very like in shape too, but only that the head was black, and had from the shoulders a white streak drawn to the mouth, having also bigger and blacker eyes. He had in his mouth a long sting and very strong, his shoulder of a blackish brown colour, from whence came forth two wings of a silver colour, to the tail downward, it had six or seven joynts or fissures, of a whitish colour, all the rest of the body blackish. In swiftnesse of flight inferiour to none, surpassing the most; his belly was between an ash and yellow colour, or a pale green.'

[2] Fig. 6. Brit. Mus., P. & D. 1906-5-9-1-(2); Binyon, *Catalogue*, no. 1; Prospectus, no. 1; Lorant, *New world*, pp. [186–7]; Hakluyt, *Principal navigations*, VIII (1904), at p. 400. Size 370 × 472 mm. The map is a composite with at least four elements: (*a*) a Spanish map which included the Bahamas (cp. that of Diogo Homem of 1568 in Wright, *English voyages to the Caribbean*), and which contributes, from the bottom of the map, the following names: Moyagora (Mariguana), Iabo (Great Inagua or Acklin Is.), Iani (Long Is.), Gvanima (combination of Cat Is. and Eleuthera), Cigateo (Great Abaco), Bahama; (*b*) Jacques le Moyne's map of Florida (in De Bry, *America*, pt. ii, pl. 1 (Lorant, *New world*, pp. [186–7]) and in a version now lost but partly incorporated in M. Lescarbot, *Histoire de la nouvelle France* (ed. W. L. Grant and H. P. Biggar, I, Champlain Soc., 1907) which contributed the following names (reading south from the Gulf shore and north from the southern tip of the peninsula): TERRA [F]LORIDA, [Baye des] perles, R. de Ianpones, [B. de la] Haulte, OATCHAQVA, [   ]raburg, [C:] de Rapare, Baye de sa Ponce, Port de Repoy, Secrope, R. d. la Paix, Baye des Iles, CATOS [Calos?], Les Martirs, C: DE FLORIDE, Coste des Feuz, Les Iardinetz, C: Canaueral, C: de Mont, C: de Francoys, R: des Daufins, SATVRIONA [Satouriona], Carline [La Caroline], Machiaca [Mathiaqua], R: de May, VTINA [grand Outina], R. de Seine, R. de Somme, R. de Loyre, R. de Charente, R. de Garonne, [M]ontaigne Pallassi [Montagne de Palassi], R: de Gironde, MACEOV [Macou], R: Belle [R. Bette], R. Grande, ADVSTA MAION [Audusta], Port Royal, Toupa, STALAME HOIA, C: de S. Helene, R: Iordain (the alternatives in brackets are from the Lescarbot version): the coast is made to bear due east from Port Royal, with great consequent distortion, while from R: Iordain to Cape Fear the coast is purely conjectural; (*c*) the map, no. 110 below, made by White and Hariot, the omitted names being noted (pp. 848, 854–72 below); it does not indicate any northern shore to Chesapeake Bay;

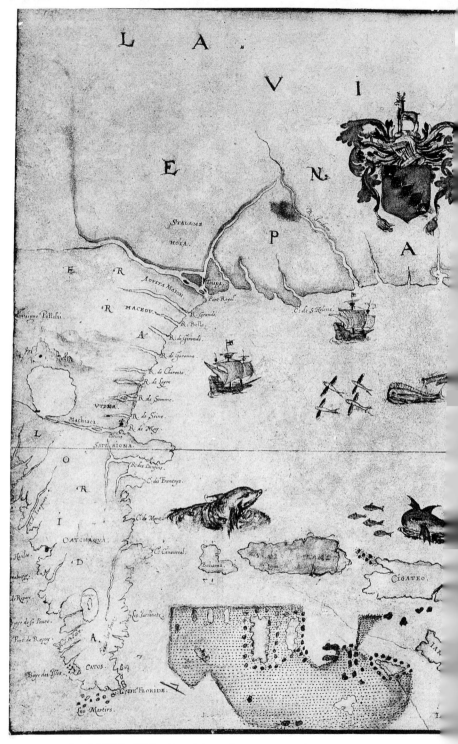

6. JOHN WHITE. Map of Eastern North America from
Florida to Chesapeake Bay.

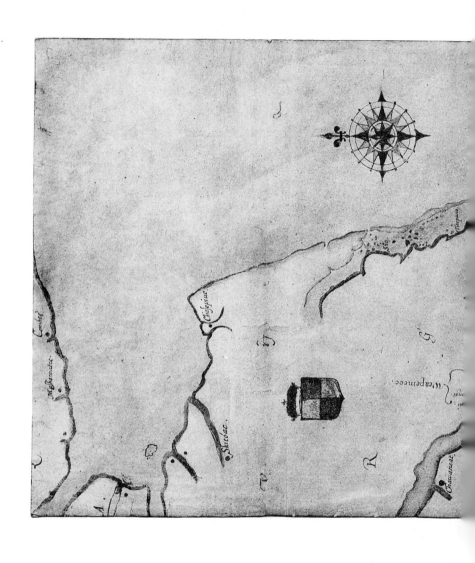

7. JOHN WHITE. Map of Eastern North America from Cape Lookout to Chesapeake Bay.

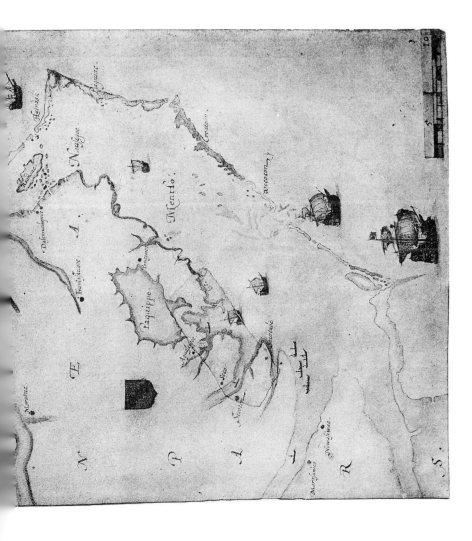

110. Map of Eastern North America from Cape Lookout to Chesapeake Bay.[1]
'La Virginea Pars.'

(*d*) John Dee's 1580 map (see *Principal navigations*, VIII, end) which contributes NORAM[BEGA], a promontory with islands in the same latitude as the opening of Chesapeake Bay, and La Be[rmuda] nearly half-way down on the right of the map (which has here been trimmed). Raleigh's achievement appears on LA VIRGENIA PARS. Ships are shown at sea, sailing north, past Port Royal; a vessel is anchored at Wococon, and another at Port Ferdinando, while one ship is sailing eastwards from the Bahamas and another westwards just north of Bermuda. The ocean is liberally 'garnished', with sea-monsters, though the large, toothed whales (probably), porpoises, dolphins (shown chasing flying-fish in two places), and trigger-fish were not invented. The scale of latitudes is very defective and was certainly not inspired by Hariot. Hakluyt may have had something to do with its composition, or, alternatively, it may have inspired him to invite Ortelius in 1590 to put together his materials on western North America with a view to incorporating with them what was available in England (from White and Le Moyne) on the east and so bringing out a new map of North America as a whole (cp. Ortelius to Jacob Cole, 25 August 1590, in Ortelius, *Epistulae*, ed. J. H. Hessels, p. 443). The new map was first put together on the Molyneux globe 1592 (cp. pp. 850–1).

[1] Fig. 7. Brit. Mus. P. & D. 1906-5-9-1 (3); Binyon, *Catalogue*, no. 2; Prospectus, no. 2; Lorant, *New world*, p. [186]; Hakluyt, *Principal navigations*, VIII (1904), at p. 320. The topographical details are fully discussed below (pp. 847–8, 854–72) and the names are all represented on the map at end. The map measures 480 × 235 mm. It contains a scale of leagues. Above Weapemeoc are the Royal arms (now damaged): near Lake Paquippe are Raleigh's arms (cp. above). Outside the Banks one fairly large ship is seen approaching Wococon Island, while another, larger, in its wake has rounded Cape Lookout which White probably knew as Cape Fear (cp. p. 868 below). A pinnace is shown crossing Pamlico Sound from Wococon to the Pamlico River, and another pinnace appears about to enter the River. Further north in the sound a third pinnace is making its way from the inlet north of Cape Hatteras (Chacandepeco) towards Roanoke Island. A fourth is seen at the head of Albemarle Sound. Off Port Ferdinando a medium-sized vessel is seen lying at anchor. Indian canoes are shown on the Neuse, Pamlico, and Pungo Rivers, in Roanoke Sound, and in Albemarle Sound. The map has been patched, probably on account of a defect in the paper, in the area around Pamlico River, but the drawing is not interrupted. Offsetting in this map is not serious.

111. Map of Eastern North America from Cape Lookout to Chesapeake Bay.[1]

'Americae pars, Nunc Virginia dicta primum ab Anglis inuenta sumptibus Domini Walteri Raleigh Equestris ordinis viri Anno Domini .M.D.LXXXV regni vero Sereniss*imae* nostrae Reginae Elizabethae XXVII Hujus vero Historia peculiari Libro discripta est, additis Indiginarum Iconibus Autore Ioanne With Sculptore Theodoro de Bry, Qui et excud*et*.'

III. DRAWINGS WHICH HAVE SOME INDIRECT CONNEXION WITH THE ROANOKE VOYAGES

1. 'Of Florida.'[2]
2. 'Of Florida.'[3]

[1] Fig. 8. De Bry, *America*, pt. i, pl. i. It has close links with no. 110, but it goes much farther west. Part of these western discoveries represent areas visited or heard of by Lane and omitted in no. 110; some, like the mountains in which the Roanoke River rises, are conjectural. Conventional signs are adopted for villages (making them all 'enclosed', cp. pp. 215–17, 415, 420 above), Indian figures and trees being added to 'garnish' the map. Ships are shown in different positions from those in no. 110, the emphasis being shifted to Chesapeake Bay where four ships have entered or are about to do so. This, together with revisions of nomenclature (see pp. 849–50 below) and some additions, indicates that it carries certain improvements by White of *c.* 1587–8, but the proportions between the banks, sounds and mainland have been altered, the engraving is often conventional, and the effect of authenticity given in the other map is often lost.

[2] Man. Brit. Mus., P. & D. 1906-5-9-1 (22); Binyon, *Catalogue*, no. 23; Prospectus, no. 23; Brit. Mus., postcard B 431; Lorant, *New world*, p. [203], [24]. If the conclusions above (p. 189) are correct this cannot have been made from life by White on his outward voyage in 1585. Binyon and Lorant have noted that this and the following item closely resemble the Indians in De Bry's engravings of Le Moyne's Florida drawings (*America*, pt. II, pls. I–II, VIII, XI, XV, XVII, XXVI, XXVII; Lorant, pp. 37, 39, 51, 57, 65, 71, 87, 89). The ornaments and arms, and, especially, the style of hair-dressing, indicate the subject clearly as a member of the Timucua group of tribes of the St John's River, Florida (see Swanton, *Indians*, pp. 179, 193–4). It seems certain that White adapted this from a lost original of Le Moyne's, but, seeing the latter's tendency to Europeanize Indian figures and faces (cp. a Le Moyne original in Lorant, p. 32), it is probable that White modified the features in accordance with those he had seen in North Carolina.

[3] Woman. Brit. Mus., P. & D. 1906-5-9-1 (23); Binyon, *Catalogue*, no. 24; Prospectus, no. 24; Brit. Mus., postcard B 432; Lorant, *New world*, p. [202], [23]. See note 2 above, and compare with De Bry's engravings (*America*, pt. ii, pls. xx, xxxix; Lorant, pp. 75, 113).

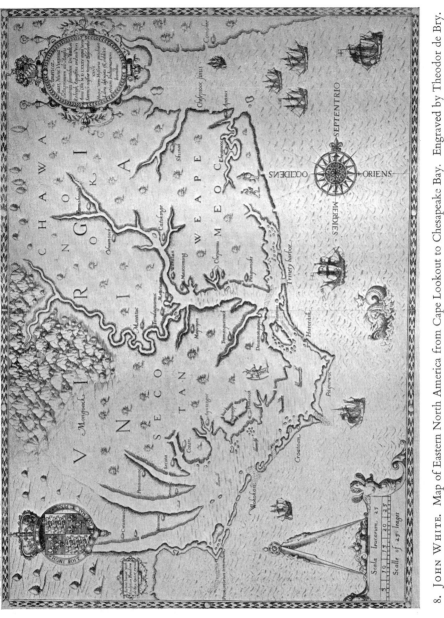

8. JOHN WHITE. Map of Eastern North America from Cape Lookout to Chesapeake Bay. Engraved by Theodor de Bry.

3. (*a*) 'A Pict warrior.'[1]   (*b*) 'A British warrior.'[2]

4. (*a*) 'A woman neighbour vnto the Picts.'[3]
   (*b*) 'A British woman.'[4]

5. (*a*) 'A Pict warrior.'[5]   (*b*) 'A British warrior.'[6]

6. (*a*) 'A woman Pict.'[7]   (*b*) 'A British woman.'[8]

7. (*a*) 'A warrior neighbour of the Picts.'[9]
   (*b*) 'A British warrior.'[10]

IV. DRAWINGS NOT ASSOCIATED WITH THE
ROANOKE VOYAGES

1. An Eskimo man.[11]

2. An Eskimo man.[12]

---

[1] Brit. Mus., P. & D. 1906-9-5-1 (24); Binyon, *Catalogue*, no. 25.
[2] Engraved. De Bry, *America*, pt. i [sect. 3], 'Som picture of the Pictes...', fig. i.
[3] Brit. Mus., P. & D. 1906-5-9-1 (25); Binyon, *Catalogue*, no. 26.
[4] De Bry, *America*, pt. i [sect. 3], fig. ii.
[5] Brit. Mus., P. & D. 1906-5-9-1 (26); Binyon, *Catalogue*, no. 27.
[6] De Bry, *America*, pt. i [sect. 3], fig. iii.
[7] Brit. Mus., P. & D. 1906-5-9-1 (27); Binyon, *Catalogue*, no. 28.
[8] De Bry, *America*, pt. i [sect. 3], fig. iv.
[9] Brit. Mus., P. & D. 1906-5-9-1 (28); Binyon, *Catalogue*, no. 29.
[10] De Bry, *America*, pt. i [sect. 3], fig. v. De Bry evidently obtained the drawings for his plates from White at the same time as those of America. He printed them, with an engraving of Adam and Eve, in which White had no hand, to show that the ancient Britons were not dissimilar in appearance and dress to the North American Indians (cp. John Aubrey, 'They were 2 or 3 degrees I suppose less salvage than the Americans', *Wiltshire collections* (1862), p. 5). The White drawings, probably after a chronicle, differ from the engravings. The latter were subsequently used as type-figures of ancient Britons by Speed and others (cp. T. D. Kendrick, *British antiquity* (1950), pp. 122–4. He reproduces two of the drawings and two engravings). Comparable drawings of *c.* 1575 are in Lucas de Heere's 'Corte Besschryvinge van England, Scotland, ende Irland', Brit. Mus., Additional MS 28330.
[11] Brit. Mus., P. & D. 1906-5-9-1 (33); Binyon, *Catalogue*, no. 30; Prospectus, no. 25; copy in Brit. Mus., P. & D. 199. a. 3 (L.B. 3 (11)); of which there is a copy in Sloane MS 5253, no. 9.
[12] As no. 1, but back view. Copy. Brit. Mus., P. & D. 199. a. 3 (L.B. 3 (10)); of which there is a copy in Sloane MS 5253, no. 10. Compare De Bry's treatment of nos. 36, 38, 44, 49–51 above.

3. An Eskimo woman and child.[1]

4. An English boat attacked by Eskimos.[2]

5. Common Roller.[3]

6. Hoopoe.[4]

7. A man, probably Turkish.[5]

8. A woman, probably Turkish.[6]

9. A man, probably Uzbek.[7]

10. A man, possibly Levantine.[8]

11. A woman, possibly Levantine.[9]

[1] Brit. Mus., P. & D. 1906-5-9-1 (34); Binyon, *Catalogue*, no. 31; Prospectus, no. 26; copy in Brit. Mus., P. & D. 199. a. 3 (L.B. 3 (12)); of which there is a copy in Sloane MS 5253, no. 15.

[2] Copy. Brit. Mus., P. & D. 199. a. 3 (L.B. 3 (13)); Binyon, *Catalogue*, no. 13. No original is known, but there is a copy in Sloane MS 5253, no. 8. The style is White's. The execution (additional pen-work, etc.) makes it clear it is not an original. Mr Hulton regards nos. 1–3 as likely to have been made in England from Eskimos brought by Frobisher in 1578, but this drawing would not fit such an interpretation.

[3] Brit. Mus., P. & D. 1906-5-9-1 (64); Binyon, *Catalogue*, no. 66; Prospectus, no. 56; Lorant, *New world*, p. [217], [b], [51]. The Common Roller, *Corasias garrulus*.

[4] Brit. Mus., P. & D. 1906-5-9-1 (61); Binyon, *Catalogue*, no. 63; Prospectus, no. 53; Lorant, *New world*, p. [218], [a], [52]. The Hoopoe, *Upopa epops*, for the early description of which in England see Raven, *English naturalists*, pp. 88, 177, 197, 332. There is a drawing of a somewhat similar crested bird in Sloane MS 5263, no. 143, but with much too short a beak to be anything but a very bad copy of a drawing of a hoopoe. It may, however, be after an otherwise unknown White drawing.

[5] Brit. Mus., P. & D. 1906-5-9-1 (31); Binyon, *Catalogue*, no. 32.

[6] Brit. Mus., P. & D. 1906-5-9-1 (32); Binyon, *Catalogue*, no. 33.

[7] Brit. Mus., P. & D. 1906-5-9-1 (33); Binyon, *Catalogue*, no. 34.

[8] Brit. Mus., P. & D. 1906-5-9-1 (34); Binyon, *Catalogue*, no. 35.

[9] Brit. Mus., P. & D. 1906-5-9-1 (35); Binyon, *Catalogue*, no. 36. This group (nos. 7–11) all derives, Mr Hulton informs me, from one or more costume books and there are a number of analogies to the figures in published works. It is possible that there should follow here the group of drawings in Brit. Mus., P. & D. 199. a. 3 (L.B. 3 (2–5, 32–91)), classed as C⁴ above (pp. 392, 397). There is a copy of some lilies (L.B. 3 (77)) in Sloane MS 5289, no. 211. All are omitted from the list in view of the uncertainty of their connexion with White.

CHAPTER VII

THE 1586 VENTURES

But let that man with better sence aduize
  That of the world least part to vs is red:
  And dayly how through hardy enterprize,
  Many great Regions are discouered,
  Which to late age was neuer mentioned.
  Who euer heard of th'Indian Peru?
  Or who in venturous vessell measured
  The Amazons huge riuer now found trew?
Or fruitfullest Virginia who did euer vew?
           Faerie Queene, bk. ii, proem st. 2 [1]

He that wins gold, let him wear it.
    Letter from San Lucar, 24 July/3 August 1586 [2]

NARRATIVE

The circumstances, previously related, under which the first colony came to an end, played a great part in determining the fate of the Roanoke enterprises. An experiment without precedent, Lane's colony was on the whole a success rather than a failure. It proved that Englishmen could remain for nearly a year on American soil. This was a considerable step forward in the colonizing process. But that Lane should return without having made contact with the relief expeditions, was a very severe blow to the prospects of future investment in the ventures which Raleigh sponsored.

Raleigh failed to send Lane the essential supplies which he lacked owing to the damage the *Tiger* received. True, he fitted out a ship of 100 tons and supplied it. (It could have been the *Lion*.) But he did not succeed in getting it to sea early in 1586. The date of the

---

[1] *The Faerie Queene. Book Two*, ed. Edwin Greenlaw, 1933 (*The works of Edmund Spenser*. A variorum edition. Edd. E. Greenlaw, C. G. Osgood and F. M. Padelford. Johns Hopkins Press).

[2] Letter from an English agent urging that 'our reprisal men' should attack the Indies fleets (*Cal. S.P. Foreign, 1586–8*, pt. i, p. 57).

465

queen's letter to Lane (20 March)[1] may perhaps represent the date round about which it was expected to clear. In fact Hakluyt says[2] it did not sail until after Easter (3 April), and reached Port Ferdinando sometime after 19 June. The length of the passage—comparable with that of 1585—suggests that a call was made in the West Indies, as in 1584 and 1585, though it apparently arrived a little earlier than either of these expeditions. Yet Lane had it firmly fixed in his mind that it would come by Easter,[3] although it had not yet been demonstrated, so far as can be ascertained, that winds and currents would enable this to be done. We may conclude tentatively then that the promise to send a supply ship to arrive so early was unwise, but that its appearance before the end of June was not exceptionally late and that Lane's departure with Drake arose from circumstances—mainly his relations with the Indians—of which Raleigh could have no knowledge at home. It is ironical, however, that the whole sequence of colonization was destroyed, inadvertently, by Drake.

Raleigh's supply ship was only the forerunner of a much larger expedition which Grenville was preparing at Bideford. Of those preparations we know little. The venture appears to have found more support in North Devon than at Court. An attempt by Carew Raleigh to raise money from the Merchant Adventurers of Exeter[4] in January failed. About the same time some 65 tuns of wine were taken off a French ship, the *Susanne*, at Southampton for the supply of Raleigh's ships.[5] By 16 April Grenville was ready to sail,[6] but his fly-boat (probably the *Roebuck*) and his frigate, which might well have been that taken in the Mona passage in 1585, were unable to cross Bideford Bar, and may even have sustained some damage in attempting to do so. It was therefore some time after 27 April, possibly 2 May,[7] before the squadron left Bideford. Some ships from Plymouth may have joined it.[8]

[1] Document no. 60, p. 474 below.   [2] P. 477 below.
[3] Cp. p. 261 above.   [4] Document no. 56, p. 471 below.
[5] Document no. 61, pp. 474-5 below.   [6] Document no. 62, pp. 475-6 below.
[7] Cp. pp. 476, 788 below.   [8] P. 756.

Besides two large vessels, there were four or five smaller ones with some 400 men.[1] The squadron soon began to encounter merchant ships coming from Spain. One, an English ship, the *Angel* of Topsham, was stopped and Grenville took some wine and oil belonging to Breton merchants out of her before letting her go free.[2] Then, a few days later, on 8/18 May, off Cape Finisterre, a number of other vessels were sighted, two of which Grenville boarded and took. One was a Norman ship, either the *Brave* or the *Peter*,[3] and the other was the *Julian* of St Brieuc, of some 60 tons, Peter Godbecin master, bound from San Lucar to Dunkirk with a mixed cargo. Deciding to send them back to England, Grenville had some of the goods taken from the *Angel* transferred to the *Julian*, which he put in charge of Richard Willett of Bideford, who brought her to Appledore.[4] Later, meeting with a Dutch fly-boat, the *Martin Johnson* of Amsterdam, bound for Spain, Grenville took her also, distributed her cargo amongst his ships, and incorporated her in his squadron, claiming that Low Countries' ships trading with the enemy and bringing butter, bacon and cheese for the Spanish fleet were lawful prizes.[5]

Whatever the rights and wrongs of these prize-takings were, they undoubtedly helped Grenville on his way, though they had weakened his force by two prize crews sent back to England. By this time Grenville was very conscious he was late and so he sailed

[1] Cp. pp. 787–8, 482 below (Pedro Diaz saying there were six vessels in all and Peter Godbecin seven). We lack any certain evidence of their names, but the fact that John Norris of Barnstaple was a subscriber may lend some significance to the grant to him of letters of reprisal on 23 October 1585 for the *Pelican*, *Prudence* (110 tons), and *Jesus* of Barnstaple, and the *Elizabeth* of Topsham, and on 3 November 1585 for the *Speedwell* of Dartmouth (Andrews, 'Elizabethan privateering', pp. 311, 316; Brit. Mus., Lansdowne MS 115, f. 196; P.R.O., H.C.A. 25/1, pkt. 4), as some of them may well have gone with Grenville.

[2] P. 481.

[3] Document no. 65, p. 482 below, describes her as Norman. She could have been the *Peter* (p. 483), or, more probably, the *Brave* of Fécamp, 30 tons, Adam Mannier master, brought to Appledore by Melchior Yeo (p. 564).

[4] Document no. 65, p. 482 below.

[5] Document no. 66, pp. 484–8 below. Her cargo seems to have been mainly linens.

direct for Madeira to shorten substantially his voyage to Virginia. He made a call at Porto Santo for water but was, according to Diaz,[1] courageously resisted, and had to clear without obtaining any. He then sailed for Virginia, arriving at Port Ferdinando about a fortnight after Raleigh's supply ship had gone.

When this was it is not possible to say precisely. Hakluyt tells us[2] that Raleigh's ship arrived 'Immediatly' after Lane's men left with Drake. Her men then spent some time looking for the colonists up and down the country before departing. If we take her as having arrived between 20 and 25 June, she may have gone at the end of the month or during the first week of July. It does not seem likely that the three men left behind by Lane[3] were found, but there is a trace of some incident which occurred while she was there in the finding by Grenville of the hanged bodies of an Englishman and an Indian[4] which are not likely to have been left since Lane's time. This is all we know, except that Hakluyt tells us she brought her stores back to England. It seems like bad management, since Grenville was known to be on his way and she might have awaited him. Perhaps, like Lane's, her men became too impatient.

So much then for the first supply ship. Grenville arrived, Hakluyt tells us,[5] 'about fourteene or fifteene dayes after' she had gone. This would bring us, most probably, to the end of the second, or into the third, week of July. Grenville should not have taken more than 75 days out—which would bring him to 15 July—and probably less. But it is possible he took longer, as about 8/18 August eight sail were said[6] to have appeared off the Spanish post at Santa Elena (32° 20' N. lat.), five being described as large and three small. The smaller ones entered the harbour, sounded the bar and went out again, then they all left. No comparable squadron of English vessels is known to have been in American waters about this time, though it is possible they were French. If Grenville

---

[1] Pp. 788–9 below.   [2] Document no. 64, p. 479 below.
[3] P. 307 above.   [4] P. 790 below.
[5] P. 479 below.   [6] Wright, *Further English voyages*, p. 203.

reached the American coast so far south as this, and at this time, our chronology of his arrival at Port Ferdinando would require revision.

Late as he was, Grenville determined to search for the settlers. Hakluyt tells us[1] that he led several expeditions himself and that he explored parts where he had not been in 1585. This may merely mean that he went up Albemarle Sound and possibly entered the Chowan or Roanoke Rivers, or it may even suggest that he, too, explored some part of Chesapeake Bay. Unfortunately we know no details. The Roanoke Indians, we gather from Diaz,[2] kept carefully out of his way. He caught three only. Being escorted to the ships, two got away, but from the third[3] enough was learnt to make it clear that Lane had gone with Drake. Grenville's subsequent actions cast some doubt on his judgment. Having some 300 to 400 men with him, and presumably reasonable stores, he could have left a colony comparable in size with Lane's either at the fort or at a more favourable spot, or else he could have abandoned the whole enterprise. Instead, he took the half-measure of leaving a small holding party behind. It was apparently put under a man Diaz calls Master Cofar (Coffin?) and another called Chapman. It numbered fifteen or eighteen, was given four pieces of iron ordnance, and supplies for one or two years.[4] In view of the evidence of Indian hostility which Grenville had, this was very rash, but he may have argued wrongly from the small number of Indians who showed themselves near the fort that there was no danger, though he had personal knowledge of what the Indian population had been in 1585. It is not unlikely that his real reason for paying less attention than he ought to have done to the problems of the settlement was that he wished to set out on the track of the *flota* in hopes of repeating his success of 1585 and picking off prizes.

If this reasoning is correct, it is likely that he sailed round about the same time as he had done the previous year, i.e. about 25 August.

---

[1] Pp. 479–80 below. [2] P. 790 below.
[3] Pp. 495, 790 below. [4] Cp. pp. 480, 528, 791 below.

But he did not succeed in finding any Spaniards,[1] and had reached the Azores when his men fell seriously ill, whether with scurvy or fever we do not know. Diaz says about thirty-four died. So, turning about, he made a long voyage to Newfoundland for fresh supplies. Landing at St Francis Bay, they refreshed themselves and presumably caught some fish, but we do not know whether they arrived too late to get other stores from the fishing vessels. Then Grenville made again for the Azores, taking there a bark with passengers, a cargo of hides at Villa Franca, and, with another English privateer, a ship from Puerto Rico off Terceira.[2] How many of his own squadron still accompanied him we cannot tell. He himself came back to Bideford with one prize, apparently the last taken, in December.[3]

With three Dutch and two Spanish prizes Grenville is likely to have paid both his own way and that of the supply ship, even though he had to restore some of his gains to the French and Dutch.[4] But the results, so far as the colonizing project was concerned, were inconclusive and somewhat discouraging. Lane having come home in July, Grenville had little to report except that he had kept the door open for further expeditions, but he had not yet demonstrated that continuous settlement was either possible or profitable.

White picked up the following year some information[5] about the loss of Grenville's colonists. The Roanoke Indians ambushed them on the island, calling out two for a friendly parley, turning on them and killing one, the remaining ten fighting their way to the shore and getting clear in their boat while their house was burning.[6]

---

[1] The fleet had left Havana on 1/11 August, and, encountering bad weather, lost seven out of thirty ships before entering San Lucar on 26 October/5 November (Wright, *Further English voyages*, p. lxvi).

[2] Cp. pp. 494, 792 below. She may well have been a straggler—one of those considered lost by stress of weather—from Juan de Guzman's fleet.

[3] Document no. 70, p. 494 below.

[4] Cp. pp. 480–8, 564 below.   [5] Document no. 77, pp. 528–9 below.

[6] Probably the building inside the entrenchments, but possibly one of the houses outside, cp. pp. 528, 902–3 below.

They picked up four others a little way along the beach and made for the small island between Port Ferdinando and Port Lane in the Banks. From there they eventually departed and were not seen again. So much the friendly Croatoan Indians told White. Lane's three deserted men were the first 'lost colonists': these fourteen made up the first 'lost colony'. The short-sightedness of Grenville's interim arrangement on Roanoke Island was illustrated by this tragedy.

56. 16 JANUARY 1586.

AN ATTEMPT TO RAISE SUBSCRIPTIONS IN EXETER[1]

16 Jan., 1585. 'At this Courte there were certaine Articles brought in by our deputie[2] which were deliuered hime by Master Carewe Rawleigh[3] touchinge a pretended voiage to Wyngandacoia and a noate of the marchantable and other comodities there founde, which beinge published and reade, our deputie did move the Companie to be venturers that waie. Wherevnto the Companie did answere That forasmuche as they were adventurers already with Master Audrian Gilberte in a voyage vnto China[4] they will not aduenture anie more in anie suche voiages vntill they see that voiage ended or some successe thereof'.

---

[1] Printed by William Cotton, *An Elizabethan guild of the city of Exeter*, pp. 81–2, from 'Act book of the Merchant Adventurers of Exeter, 1558–1603', in the possession of the Incorporation of the Weavers, Tuckers and Shearmen of Exeter, Tuckers' Hall, Fore street, Exeter. I am indebted to Mr G. E. Madge, Victoria Inn, Union Road, Exeter, reader of the society, for information on the present location of the 'Act Book', and to Dr. J. A. Youings for checking it.

[2] Apparently the deputy of the governor, Thomas Chapell.

[3] This is the only evidence that subscriptions were invited from corporate bodies for the Roanoke voyages, and the most direct link found between Carew Raleigh, Sir Walter's elder brother, and the expeditions. The Merchant Adventurers had agreed in January 1584 to invest in Peckham's project (Quinn, *Gilbert*, II, 481–3).

[4] It would appear that this was an engagement to participate in the second expedition of 1586, rather than in that of the previous year, by John Davis under Adrian Gilbert's patent of 1584. Cotton (*An Elizabethan guild of the city of Exeter*, pp. 82–4, 149) gives further information on the money subscribed to the Davis expeditions.

57.   31 JANUARY [1586].

WILLIAM CAMDEN TO ABRAHAM ORTELIUS[1]

Sir Richard Grenvile is preparing for a voyage to Winandichoa, which is also called Virginia, which is above Florida at a latitude of 35°[2] and where, last year, he left a small colony of Englishmen[3]....London, the day before the calends of February, old style.

58. $\dfrac{\text{19 FEBRUARY}}{\text{1 MARCH}}$ 1586.

DEDICATION BY MARTIN BASANIER TO SIR WALTER RALEIGH[4]

I am assured that further familiarity [with your studies in navigation] will give you not only pleasure and contentment, but will

---

[1] Extract, Latin, translated (J. H. Hessels, ed., *Abrahami Ortelii epistulae* (1887), pp. 334–5).

[2] The first reasonably accurate location for the colony sent out of England, so far as we know (cp. pp. 7–8). It was not precise enough for Ortelius, who tried, later in the year, to fix its position on the map (pp. 488, 496 below).

[3] 'exiguam Anglor*um* coloniam...reliquit'. Camden apparently regarded it as too small.

The letter goes on to say that nothing has been heard of Sir Francis Drake since he left the Canaries, that Bernard Drake (soon to die of fever at Exeter) was preparing a voyage to the East Indies by way of the Cape (did he mean Cavendish, or did Cavendish take over Bernard Drake's plan?), and that the first expedition sent by Adrian Gilbert had returned with prospects of a northerly passage.

[4] Extract, translated, from the dedication to Sir Walter Raleigh, René de Laudonnière, *L'histoire notable de la Floride...mis en lumière par M[artin] Basanier* (Paris, Guillaume Auvray), sig. A2 v.–A3 (reprinted in Taylor, *Hakluyts*, II, 350–2). Besides the epistle dedicatory, the prefatory matter includes (*a*) Latin verses to Raleigh by 'I. Auratus Poeta & Interpres regius', (*b*) four lines of verse to Raleigh by 'M. Basanierius', the theme, though a conventional type of compliment, is the same as that of Guilio Cesare Stella's *Columbeidos* (London, 1585), also addressed to Raleigh (cp. pp. 491–2 below). It reads:

'Ad Egregii viri Walteri Raleghi Indicam nouam coloniam.

    Tempore Diluuii teras diuina colomba
    Detexit nobis ramo viridantis Oliuae.
    Alter & illa Columba Columbus, & ipse Raleghus
    Tertia, Virginiae cui virgo terra reperta est.'

(*c*) an anagram on the letters W.R. by Basanier, and eight lines of Latin verse on Raleigh by Hakluyt (sig. A4 v.–B1).

make you still more ardent and desirous to continue the fine and noble exploits which have already won you an incomparable triumph in honour and glory. And in this also because you have not spared your great possessions or your own person or anything else which appertains to a man who makes profession of honour and *virtú* and have followed the very path trodden by our ancestors when they have desired to profit their realms, immortalize their names and, in the end, attain to the glory of God. These are the three principal points to which the man of honour and *virtú* ought infallibly to aspire, and in which you have, by a firm and laudable constancy, daily persevered with increase of honour and profit to your nation. Witnesses of fresh and recent memory in that respect are the two voyages made in the two years last past[1] towards the west, in which you and other of your friends have employed at least 60,000 crowns,[2] to this effect that, from the report of signal and trustworthy persons,[3] you have there discovered certain islands and land between Florida and Cape Breton. This has now, in honour of your most virtuous and serene queen, been named Virginea, where the seigneur Greenuill has established your colony, an exploit certainly most laudable and not less profitable to a commonwealth....Paris, 1 March 1586.

[1] In 1584 and 1585.

[2] The *écu* was worth three *livres tournois* and its conventional value was 5s. The earliest exchange figure in N. W. Posthumus, *Nederlandsche prijsgeschiedenis* (Leiden, 1943), p. 590, is for 1619 when the *écu* was only 3s. 4d. Henri Hauser, *Recherches et documents sur l'histoire des prix en France* (Paris, 1936), p. 24, gives the *livre tournois* of 1580 as worth 15.70 francs of 1928, which would bring the *écu* to nearly 8s. H. A. Innis (*The cod fisheries*, pp. 27-9) gives figures of 2.91 : 1 as the gold rates of the *écu sol* and the pound sterling, 1552-1601, making the *écu* about 7s. At 6s. 8d. the figure above would be £20,000. This was almost certainly given him by Hakluyt and is a high, but possible, figure for total expenditure 1584-5, but not by Raleigh personally (cp. pp. 220-1). Raleigh had his own share in mind when he wrote to Leicester from the Court on 29 March 1586: 'Your Lordshipe doth well vnderstand my affection towardes Spayn and how I haue consumed the best part of my fortune hating the tirrannus sprosperety [*sic*] of that estate' (Brit. Mus., Harleian MS 4994, fo. 2; Edwards, *Ralegh*, II, 33).

[3] An early reflection of the reports of Grenville and the letters of Ralph Lane.

59. $\frac{6}{16}$ MARCH 1586.

NEWS FROM ANTWERP[1]

We hear from Spain that the Red Indians have killed four hundred English at Satuga[2]...Antwerp, March 16, 1586.

60. 20 MARCH 1586.

QUEEN ELIZABETH'S LETTER TO RALPH LANE[3]

xx° die Martij [1585]....

An other [lettre] vnto Ralph Lane declaring her Ma*iestes* well lyking of his enterprice & his constancie in the same—nil.[4]

61. [APRIL 1586.]

MEMORANDUM OF THE FRENCH AMBASSADOR TO THE LORD TREASURER, LORD HIGH ADMIRAL AND SIR FRANCIS WALSINGHAM AT THEIR LAST MEETING[5]

A ship laden with 65 tuns of wine[6] has been taken within the harbour of Hamptone. The merchant, owner of the vessel, after having made inquiry and search for the same, found a good part

---

[1] Extract, translated, *Fugger news-letters*, 2nd ser., ed. V. von Klarwill, p. 102 (see p. 218 above).

[2] Neither the place nor the incident is identifiable, but the item shows how English activities in America were attracting interest (cp. Setubal, p. 752). I am doubtful about 'Red Indians' as a translation, but I have not seen the original.

[3] Signet Office Docquet Book, Ind. 6800, fo. 57 v. No full draft of this letter has been found. It was clearly the queen's reply to Lane's lost letter to her from Virginia (cp. p. 222 above), intended to be sent by Raleigh's supply ship (pp. 477–9 below). As Lane had left Roanoke Island with Drake it is unlikely that he ever received the letter.

[4] No fee being charged for issuing the signet letters.

[5] Extract, translated. State Papers, Foreign, France, S.P. 78/15, 150 (*Cal. S.P. Foreign, 1585–6*, p. 698). The ambassador was the newly arrived G. de l'Aubespine, Sieur de Chateauneuf, the Lord Treasurer Lord Burghley, and the Lord High Admiral Lord Charles Howard.

[6] Another memorial from Chateauneuf to Walsingham, 26 April/6 May 1586 (S.P. 78/15, 112; *Cal. S.P. Foreign, 1585–6*, p. 584), gives the vessel's name as the *Susanne* of Mechez sur Gironde, with Gascony wine for Mathurin Gaultier and Geoffrey Periere. The affair is said to have taken place three or four months ago, i.e. about January 1586, when Grenville's second expedition was in preparation.

of the said wine. Instead of it being restored to him, Sir John Gilbert and Martin Wetz,[1] servant to Monsieur de Raley, have taken 21 tuns of it, saying that it was for provisioning the ships of the said Sir [Walter] Raley, without having given him a penny. And Sir John Semer has taken of it 10 or 12 tuns for which he has paid with the same money as the said Gilbert,[2] together with several others who have taken some, the names of whom the judge of admiralty[3] has.

[*Margin:*] The lords order[4] in respect of the said wine that the said judge of the admiralty take the names of those who have had of it, to the end they may be constrained to pay for it or restore it, but notwithstanding he makes no accounting although he has the names of those that had it.

62. 16 APRIL 1586.

GRENVILLE ATTEMPTS TO CROSS BIDEFORD BAR[5]

16 April year aforesaid [1586] Sir Richard Greynuylle sailed ouer the barr with his flee boat and friget[6] but for want of sufficient

---

[1] Apparently Martin White of Plymouth, Raleigh's factor (cp. pp. 44, 218).

[2] S.P. 78/15, 112, says that even after being presented with letters from the privy council Gilbert and Seymour refused to pay, saying the wines 'were for the provisioning of the ships of Sir [Walter] Ralley', a marginal note adding that 'Monsieur Raulegh' would give satisfaction, though two years later Chateauneuf was still complaining that Raleigh had never paid for sixteen tuns of wine seized for him on this occasion (30 July/8 Aug. 1588, *Cal. S.P. Foreign, July–Dec. 1588*, p. 88). Fitzwilliam of Ratley also had wine in 1586 for which he would not pay. If Raleigh was having this wine taken up under his commission of 1585 (pp. 156–7), he was probably overstepping his powers, as it extended only to Devon, Cornwall and Bristol so far as we know.

[3] Dr Julius Caesar.

[4] Order by the lords of the privy council.

[5] Diary of Philip Wyot, 1586–1608, printed in J. R. Chanter, *Sketches of the literary history of Barnstaple*, p. 91. The diary of the town clerk of Barnstaple was last heard of in the hands of Mr Alfred James (William Matthews, *British diaries, 1442–1942* (Univ. of California Press, 1950)).

[6] The fly-boat is in all probability the *Roebuck*, but the frigate is not the *Tiger* (cp. p. 193 above and Rowse, *Grenville*, p. 233). She is more likely to be the 'La: a frigott' (*Lady=Nuestra Señora*) brought as a prize by Grenville which in turn may possibly be identified with the frigate taken in the Mona Channel in

water one the barr being neare vpon neape, he left his ship. This Sir Richard Greynuylle pretended his goinge[1] to Wyngandecora, where he was last year.

63. THE DEPUTY LIEUTENANTS OF CORNWALL TO THE PRIVY COUNCIL[2]

...Finallie we aduertise that Sir Richard Greneuill nowe being reddye to depart to the sea, hath signefied vnto vs that he haith left the charge of the 300 men wherof he was by your lordships appointed capteyn, vnto Degorye Grenvile, Iohn Facye,[3] and Iohn Blighe gentlemen his pettye captayns, and to his kinsman George Grenevile as their capteyn, whome by the aucthorities comitted vnto vs we do for the present necessitie confirme and allow so to be, vntill it shall please your lordships therin otherwise to directe.... At Liskerd the xxvij[th] of Aprill 1586.

    Your honors most humble to be comaunded

Wyllyam Mohun   Fra: Godolphin

R. Edgecumb

May 1585 (cp. p. 483), and it is possible she became in turn the *Virgin God Save Her* (cp. p. 486). Diaz gives the tonnage of one ship as 150 and that of the rest (making six in all) as between 60 and 100. It is not unlikely that one at least of the letters of reprisal issued to Raleigh on 18 February 1586 ('2. bonds of Sir Walter Raleghs—1000. lib. a pece, dated 18. febr. 1585', The Lord High Admiral to William Hareward, H.C.A. 25/3, pkt. 9, last item), was for the use of Grenville's expedition, though Raleigh had other ships privateering this year also.

A map, dated 14 March 1591[-2], in Brit. Mus., Additional MS 12505, fos. 481-2, shows 'The barre of barstaple' and the limits of 'The ordynary full sea'.

[1] Meaning 'intended to go'. He finally left, according to Diaz, on 2 May (cp. p. 788 below).

[2] S.P. 12/188, 42 (see Rowse, *Grenville*, p. 232). This is the latest certain date on which Grenville is said to have been in England.

[3] In fact he accompanied Grenville as master of one of his vessels (cp. p. 486 below).

64. THE 1586 VOYAGES.[1]

The third voyage made by a Ship, sent in the yeere 1586. to the reliefe of the Colonie planted in Virginia, at the sole charges of Sir Walter Raleigh.

In the yeere of our Lord, 1586. sir Walter Raleigh at his owne charge prepared a ship of 100. tunnes,[2] fraighted with all maner of things in most plentiful maner for the supplie and relief of his Colonie then remaining in Virginia: but before they set saile from England, it was after Easter,[3] so that our Colonie halfe dispaired of the comming of any supplie, wherefore euery man prepared for himselfe, determining resolutely to spend the residue of their life time in that countrey, and for the better performaunce of this their determination, they sowed, planted, and set such things as were necessarie for their reliefe in so plentifull a manner, as might haue suffised them two yeeres without any further labor: thus trusting to their owne haruest they passed the summer till the tenth of Iune, at which time their corne which they had sowed was within one fortnight of reaping, but then it happened,[4] that Sir Frauncis Drake in his prosperous returne from the sacking of Saint Domingo, Cartagena, and Saint Augustines determined in his way

---

[1] Hakluyt, *Principall navigations* (1589), pp. 747–8; III (1600), 265, collated with VIII (1904), 346–8. This is the only narrative of the American voyages in Hakluyt which is not a first-hand account. The natural assumption is that Hakluyt found himself, when he came to compile the *Principall navigations*, without any account of the two voyages made in 1586. He had already Lane's and Bigges's stories of the end of the first colony, and White's journal for 1587, while he would also remember in outline what had happened in 1586. Hariot's chronicle, apparently including a history of these voyages, was evidently not at Hakluyt's disposal (cp. p. 387 above). It seems probable, therefore, that he wrote this himself, though it is surprising that he did not obtain a more detailed account for his second edition.

[2] The ship has not been identified, though it may be noted that she was of the same tonnage as the *Lion* (p. 179 above).

[3] Easter in 1586 was on 3 April. If Grenville sailed between 27 April and 2 May (p. 276) this vessel cannot have anticipated him by many days.

[4] It is improbable that this was a chance decision by Drake, and is likely to have been planned before he left England (pp. 250–1 above).

homewarde to visit his countrymen the English Colonie then remayning in Virginia: so passing along the coastes of Florida, he fell with the partes, where our English Colony inhabited, and hauing espyed some of that company, there he ankered, and went alande where he conferred with them of their state and welfare, and howe thinges had past with them: they aunswered him that they liued all, but hitherto in some scarsitie, and as yet coulde here of no supplye out of England: therefore they requested him that he would leaue with them some two or three shippes, that if in some reasonable time they heard not out of England, they might then return themselues: which hee agreed to: whilest some were then writing their letters to send into England, and some others making reportes of the accidentes of their trauels each to other, some on lande, some on boord, a great storme arose, and droue the most of their fleete from their ankers to Sea, in which shippes, at that instant were the chiefest of the English Colony: the rest on land perceiuing this, hasted to those three sayles which were appointed to be left there, and for feare they should be left behinde, left[1] all thinges so confusedly,[2] as if they had bene chased from thence by a mightie armie, and no doubt so they were, for the hande of God came vpon them for the crueltie, and outrages committed by some of them against the natiue inhabitantes of that Countrie.[3]

---

[1] 'they left', Hakluyt, III (1600), 265.

[2] There is nothing in this account of the end of the first colony that could not have been based on Lane and Bigges (pp. 288–94, 300–3), apart from the statement that after the storm there were still three ships with the colonists at Port Ferdinando, which were to have been left with them. In fact only the *Francis* was to have been left behind, and she had sailed during or just after the storm (pp. 291–2 above). But Hakluyt's recollection of his sources, if he was the writer, may not have been too clear.

[3] This view fits in with that expressed by Hariot in the *Briefe and true report* (above, p. 381), which was in Hakluyt's hands early in 1588. It accords also with his own earlier opinion, based on the desirability of maintaining trade, that good relations with the Indians were to be cultivated (Taylor, *Hakluyts*, II, 318), though he was to modify this view later (below, p. 552).

Immediatly after the departing of our English Colonie out of this paradise of the worlde, the shippe[2] aboue mentioned sent and set forth at the charges of Sir Walter Ralegh, and his direction, arriued at Hatorask, who after some time spent in seeking our Colony vp in the Countrie, and not finding them, returned with all the aforesayd prouision into England.[3]

Iune.[1]

About fourteene or fifteene daies after the departure of the aforesayd shippe, Sir Richard Grindfield[4] Generall of Virginia, accompanied with three shippes[5] well appointed for the same voyage arriued there, who not finding the aforesayd ship according to his expectation, nor hearing any newes of our English Colony, there seated,[6] and left by him, Anno 1585. him selfe trauailing vp into diuers places of the Countrey, as well to see if he could here any newes of the Colony left there by him the yere before, vnder the charge of Master Lane his deputie, as also to discouer some places of the Countrie:[7] but after some time spent therein[8] not hearing any newes of them, and finding the place[9]

Sir Richard Grindfields third voyage.

---

[1] Not in Hakluyt, III (1600), who has 'This ship arriued in Virginia'.

[2] Drake sailed with the colonists on 18 or 19 June (above pp. 294, 302), so that the arrival of Raleigh's ship can probably be put before the end of June.

[3] The very vague statement of what was done and found suggests that the writer merely learnt that the ship, after visiting Roanoke, still retained her stores on her return.

[4] Hakluyt, III (1600), 265, spells Grenville's name 'Grinuile'. The account of Grenville's visit suggests that the writer had some more specific information than on the voyage of the first supply ship, but had no detailed narrative before him at the time of writing. His time of arrival is discussed on pp. 468–9 above. Grenville, by making for Madeira instead of the Canaries, evidently hoped to save time. His breaking-off of his quarrel with the inhabitants of Porto Santo and his sailing direct for the North American coast indicates that, though he could not resist delaying to take prizes, he realized the need for expedition (below p. 789).

[5] There seems no reason to doubt that Grenville had seven or eight ships in his squadron when he reached Madiera and that all of these accompanied him to Virginia (pp. 482, 788–9 below).

[6] Diaz describes more specifically what Grenville found (p. 790 below).

[7] It is unlikely that Grenville travelled very far from Roanoke, and it is evident that the Indians did their best to keep out of his way (pp. 790–1 below). On the one Indian caught and brought back, see p. 495 below.

[8] According to Diaz, Grenville stayed fourteen days (p. 792 below).

[9] 'places', Hakluyt, III (1600), 265.

which they inhabited desolate, yet vnwilling to loose the possession of the Countrie, which Englishmen had so long helde: after good deliberation he determined to leaue some men behinde to retaine possession of the Country: whereupon he landed 15. men[1] in the Ile of Roanoake furnished plentifully with all maner of prouision for two yeeres,[2] and so departed for England.

Not long after he fell with the Isles of Açores, on some of which Ilandes he landed, and spoyled the Townes of all such thinges as were worth cariage, where also he tooke diuers Spanyardes:[3] with these, and many other exploytes done by him in this voyage, as well outwarde as homeward, he returned into England.[4]

65. FRENCH SHIPS AND GOODS TAKEN BY GRENVILLE

(*a*) 3 August 1586. Libel on behalf of Francis James, John Bedell and Reginald Pereficey,[5] merchants of Morleis[6] in Brittany against Richard Willett of Bydeforde, for the ship, the *Julian* of St Brian[7] and her goods, amounting to 79 tons, 1 pipe, worth £294. 2*s.*, of which a certain quantity (listed in the schedule) belonged to Peter Godbecin, master of the *Julian*, and the mariners of the ship, which was bound from San Lucar to Dunkerke.

(*b*) 12 August 1586. Deposition of Peter Godbecin,[8] of 'Sancto

---

[1] Hakluyt, III (1600), 265, adds in margin 'Fifteene men more left in Virginia'. The same figure is given in White's account of the 1587 expedition (p. 528 below), but Diaz says it was eighteen, two of whom were called Cofar (Coffin) and Chapman (p. 791 below), and as his is direct evidence it may be the more reliable.

[2] Diaz says Grenville left with them four pieces of artillery and supplies for eighteen men for one year (p. 791 below).

[3] This omits all mention of the mishaps of Grenville's ship which, with much sickness on board, put back to Newfoundland to re-victual. Nor is the mention of Grenville's raids on the Azores necessarily accurate. Diaz records only the raid on the careened ship from which a cargo of hides was taken. It might, however, be the result of a blurred recollection of Grenville's fight with the inhabitants of Porto Santo (Madiera) on the way out (pp. 788–9, 792 below).

[4] Grenville returned about 16/26 December (pp. 494, 792 below).

[5] Abstract. P.R.O., H.C.A. 24/54, no. 193.

[6] Morlaix.   [7] St Brieuc.

[8] Extracts. H.C.A. 13/26. He signs himself Gwichelot Godbesin. There are two cases intertwined in this action. The one is for the recovery of the *Julian* and

Brio'[1] of Brittany, sailor, who answers 'that this ex*amina*te beinge at Cales in Spayne did there see in Aprill laste the articulate shippe the Angill of Opsham[2] laden with sundry goodes by Iohn Piddeen a Brittayne, for whose accompte the same was laden he knoweth nothing'. Otherwise he knows nothing, 'Savinge he sayethe the said shippe was bounde for Opsham in this Realme of Englande of this ex*amina*tes knowledge For this ex*amina*te departed from Spayne in company of the said shippe'. He says 'That the articulate Richard Willett on the xviij[th] day of May laste accordinge to the stile of Fraunce[3] was at the seas in a shippe of warre in company of Sir Richard Greinfeilde knighte of this ex*amina*tes knowledge for the same day he and others aborded and tooke this ex*amina*te and his shippe the Iulian laden with oyles and other goodes bound for Dunkercke, and the same day or the nexte the said Richard Willett came on borde this ex*amina*tes said shippe of this ex*amina*tes perfecte remembrance.' He answers also 'that the nexte day[4] after this ex*amina*te was taken by the said Sir Richard Greinfeilde and Willett and companye, the said Richard called this ex*amina*te on borde his shippe the Admirall and bade him be mery and gave him a cuppe of wyne and asked him if he knewe Iohn Biddekyn[5] who answered Yea, and Sir Richard replied here ys of his wynes I tooke him a fewe dayes paste and if yt had not byn for an Englishe man that was in his shippe I would haue lefte him nothinge And whiles this ex*amina*te was in the said shippe he sawe the same Richard Willett goyng and com*m*yng and geving

---

her lading, the other for the recovery of goods belonging to Perificey and Noblett which were on the *Angel* of Topsham, were taken by Grenville, and were, it was alleged, brought by Willett on the *Julian* to England. I am indebted to Dr K. R. Andrews for this and for several of the following items.

[1] St Brieuc.

[2] The *Angel* of Topsham. A Spanish embargo on English shipping in Spain had been in force since May 1585 so that Grenville was rightly suspicious of the ship. Under what circumstances she was allowed to leave Spain is not known.

[3] 8 May Old Style, which helps to tie Grenville's departure from England to the first week in May.

[4] 9/19 May.

[5] Possibly the same as the John Piddeen mentioned above.

as one of his Councell and company.' He cannot answer more, 'Savinge that the said Willett and companye beinge vij shippes togeather¹ took likewise a Norman shippe comminge from Spayne the same day this examinate was taken.'²

(*c*) 9 October 1586. Additional 'positions' on the part of Richard Willett,² who denies he came on board the *Julian* the day she was taken or within two days, or meddled with the goods on board. Further, he denies that after coming to Appledore he carried a barrel of wine belonging to the master, Peter Godbecin, to Bideford 'before the captaine came from London',³ or broke bulk in other ways. But there was a barrel of his own wine on board which he took out, having taken it from his own ship and placed it in the *Julian* 'when he toke charge of her to bringe her to England'. He denies that certain goods on the *Julian* belonged to the master, and that she had 79 tons weight of merchandise on board when she was unloaded at Bideford and Appledore; the ship was not above the burden of 60 tons and could not have carried so much.

(*d*) 14 October 1586. Allegation on behalf of Richard Willett,⁴ who maintains the *Julian* was lawful prize taken under letters of reprisal. Her lading of 60 tons was divided according to the orders of the lord high admiral to Sir John Gilbert, vice-admiral of Devon, and others, 6 tons going to the lord admiral,⁵ 11 tons to John Norris (assigned to him as an adventurer),⁶ 35 tons to

---

¹ Diaz (p. 787 below) says six.
² Diaz mentions that a second ship was taken but does nothing to identify her. She is likely to have been either the *Brave* or the *Peter* (cp. pp. 564, 483, 788, below).
³ He presumably means a representative of Raleigh and Grenville who would look after the distribution of prize goods.
⁴ Abstract. H.C.A. 24/54, no. 160.
⁵ This was the tenth (in kind) due to the lord admiral.
⁶ He is described in another case (ibid. nos. 180, 183; H.C.A. 13/26, 11 Aug. 1586, John Slocombe) as John Norris of Barnstaple, merchant, trading to Bilbao. His *Falcon's Flight* sailed under Captain William Irish in 1590, so that he may have had some concern with the Virginia projects of that year (cp. p. 581 below).

Sir Walter Rawley and Sir Richard Grenfeilde,[1] while Willett got 8 tons and a pipe worth £31. 9s. at £3. 14s. the ton.[2]

(e) 1 December 1586. Decree,[3] signed by Dr Julius Caesar, in favour of Reginald Perificey and Peter Noblett, merchants, of Morleis in Brittany, against Richard Willett of Bydeford for 6 tuns of 'Sheris' wines (valued at £20) and 6 hogsheads of oil (valued at £7. 10s.) taken from the *Angell* of Toppesham, bound from Cales in Spain.

(f) 'The *Queenes* custom of goods brought in by commission of reprisall 28 Aprilis 1590.'[4]

'Barnestable

Sir Richard Greynvile in ye La: [Lady?] a frigott	050. 10. 0[5]
Sir Richard in ye Iohn of Amsterdame	005. 0. 0
Aldred Stockama in ye sonday of Bediforde	19.
H. Shaply in ye falcones flighte[6]	002. 11. 4
Sir Richard Greynvile in ye Iohn of Bedyford[7]	005. 14. 6
Richard Willett in ye Peter & in ye Iulian	151. 12. 0'[8]

[1] This was a very high proportion (over 58%) for the principal adventurers to obtain, the normal proportions (after the tenths and customs had been deducted) were one-third each to the owners, victuallers and crew.

[2] This would make the total value of the prize goods £220. This made a total of 59 tons, 1 pipe, and left nothing for the crew, and so his figures are highly suspect.

[3] Abstract. H.C.A. 24/54, no. 126.

[4] Extracts from Caesar's notes on prizes, running from November 1585 to April 1590. Brit. Mus., Lansdowne MS 144, f. 27. It is by no means clear that they are complete, or that the items are in strict chronological order (though some attempt was evidently made to maintain a sequence).

[5] This could well be one of Grenville's 1585 prizes (cp. pp. 184, 475 above). To get the value of the prize cargo as declared for customs it is usual to multiply by 20, which would give £1005 in this case.

[6] Belonged to John Norris in 1590 (p. 482).

[7] Three items omitted.

[8] It is tempting to regard this item (showing a prize-cargo worth some £3032) as belonging to 1586, in which case the *Peter* might well be the second French prize. But the entry is likely to be for a later year, and, if so, it shows the *Julian* was being used as privateer. The cargo is, in any case, too valuable to have come with Willett in 1586 (cp. n. 2 above).

66. THE CASE OF A DUTCH SHIP TAKEN BY GRENVILLE
(*a*)   27 FEBRUARY 1587.

SIR RICHARD GRENVILLE TO DR JULIUS CAESAR[1]

Good master Doctor I do vnderstonde by my servaunt and others
howe troblesome some causes which partely concerne me haue
bene vnto you, and withall your good will professed towardes me
for the which albeit hetherto I haue not bene so gratefull vnto you
as I sholde, yet in the endd I trust to be found neither vnmindfull
nor vnthankfull to so good a frende/ There is lately come into
thies partes a factor of one Lemmons[2] with a Comission from your
Courte of thadmiraltie to demaunde certeyne goodes which he
pretendeth to haue made proofe of in your Courte, but it manifestly
apeareth that Lemon intrudeth himself as a common dealer in like
causes, vpon somme intelligence that he hath gotten that such a
shippe is comme into my handes and theron at happe hazarde hathe
made some vniuste proofe of somthing as by his factors instructions
apeareth, for neither knoweth he the iuste quantetie of the goodes,
nor the prises, by the which meanes he is enforced to send to his
master to vnderstonde the same (as I doubt not but his master hath
sence sent into holland to haue the promotion of this cause).   But
to acquaint you in friendly and iuste sorte with the cause I can
aprove[3] that the goodes which lemon wold make claime vnto,
were belonging to Spanishe fleminges, consigned to Ledgers[4] in
Spaine, there residente, & other sent to be Ledger there, which
course I thinke the States[5] (relinquishing the governement and
their subiection to the King of Spaine) wold never alowe of,
Besides this they caried some good proportion of victuall for the
Spanish fleete.[6] as butter bacon cheese, wherby it maie apeare vnto

---

[1] Brit. Mus., Lansdowne MS 158, fos. 48–49 v (see R. Granville, *History of the
Granville family*, pp. 93–4; Rowse, *Grenville*, pp. 248–9).

[2] Michael Leman, who acted as an agent for merchants of Holland and Zeeland
in a number of admiralty cases; he is mentioned in the case of the *Hope* of Flushing
(James Lancaster, defendant), 21 October 1590 (H.C.A. 3/21).

[3] Prove.   [4] Lodgers? or Leaguers?   [5] The United Provinces.

[6] The two fleets Santa Cruz was preparing (p. 721). The ship is the 'Flemish
flyboat bound for San Lucar', taken on the outward voyage in May 1586, its cargo

all men that thies gooddes do rather belonge to such as are wholy
Spanishe then ony waies assured to this estate/ And that I can make
good proofe herof as of other like coulored dealinge of thies men
to this estate, and their states there, in the processe of this cause it
shall furder apeare, yet not withstonding on my Lord Admiralles
favorable *lettres* in their cause whose hon*our* shall commaunde
bothe my liefe and all that I possesse in he[r] service, I can be
content to deale well with Lemmon, in such sort as I may for this
shippe being taken by som*me* of my company, that acount, hath
neve[r] come to my sight w*h*ich Lemon demaundeth/ And that
w*h*ich hath com*me* hath bene so spoiled with wette and other sea
accident*e*s, as it amounteth not by farre to that qualitie and quantitie, that is Imagined, & yo*u* knowe how hardly such a company
as men in like actions must vse at sea wilbe kept from spoile of such
thing*e*s as com*me* to their fingers,[1] And my selfe hath bene offered
the one halfe for the other even by Douchemen*n*, wherfore seing
thies spanishe flemin[ges] haue so vnequall a cause as in pleadinge
for my selfe, I muste and will make it apeare, I hartely praie yo*u*
in my iuste cause to geve me that favo*ur* that a trewe Inglishe
Subiect to her m*a*iestie as his countrey shall deserve, of the w*h*ich
as from yo*ur* owne inclinac*i*on I doubt not/ So shall yo*u* governe
and comaunde me in ony thinge as yo*ur* poore frende[2]/ Thus
hauing laid open the estate of this cause vnto yo*u* as to him who
I am p*er*swaded is my very good frende in ony my iust accions
assuringe yo*u* that I will not be vnmindfill of yo*ur* courtezies
towardes me with my very hartie comendacons I praing yo*u* to
p*ar*don my boldnes with yo*u*, I comitte yo*u* to the protection of the
almightie/ Bedyforde[3] this .27. of february 1586/

Your asured loving frend

R: Greynuile

distributed and the vessel itself added to the squadron for the Virginia voyage
(Wright, *Further English voyages*, p. 238; p. 788 below).   [1] Cp. p. 597.

[2] It is not clear whether this is simply arrogance or a hint that he would be
prepared to bribe Caesar if necessary.

[3] Bideford. According to Diaz (p. 793), he had gone to London after his return
in December 1586 in order to help in the preparation of White's expedition.

[*Holograph. Addressed:*] To the worshippfull my very lovinge frende m*a*ster Doctor Caesar Iudge of the Admiraltie yeve thics [*Endorsed* (*in another hand*):] 27° februarii, 1586. Sir Richard Grenefield abowt an hulke of Amsterdam.

(*b*) [*c.* JUNE 1587.]

ORDER IN THE HIGH COURT OF ADMIRALTY[1]

An order taken and made in her Ma*i*estes highe Courte of the Admiralty of England by the Right worshipful m*a*ster Doctor Cesar Iudge thereof W*illia*m Hareward Register of the same being presente betwene Sir Richard Greinfeild Knighte, Arthure Facy Captayne & Iohn Facy M*a*ster[2] on thone partie And Michaell Lemon the lawfull Procurator and Attorney of Peter Lengens, Adrian Cornelison, Achar Slot, and Peter Vandennore, marchants of Amsterdam, owners & proprietaries of the goods laden in the Marten Johnson,[3] & also of Marten Flam of Amsterdam and Walter Buys of Middleborough and their companie marchants on the other partie by the mutual consente and assent of both parties in maner and forme followinge viz*t* Whereas Captayne Arthur Facy and his company in May 1586[4] took at the sea the Martyn Johnson with the goodes hereunder mentioned

3 drifatts cont*aining* 719 peeces Ienes fu*s*tians

1 chest ropeing

12 peeces browne hollandes and

This date shows that he had returned before the end of February. Dr K. R. Andrews informs me that in H.C.A. 25/2, pkt. 5 (now classed as 'unfit') letters of reprisal were granted to Grenville for the *Virgin God Save Her*, the *Roebuck* and a pinnace on 2 February 1587.   [1] H.C.A. 14/24, 176.

   [2] John Facy was to have been left at home (p. 476 above). It is not clear whether Arthur and John Facy were in this instance captain and master respectively of the ship which took the Dutchman, or were in command of the prize crew which took her over, but they were clearly both on the Virginia voyage.

   [3] This was the fly-boat bound for San Lucar which was taken to Virginia by Grenville, according to Pedro Diaz (cp. p. 788 below). Nothing is said in the documents on this case about the return of the ship by Grenville. It is not improbable that she was given back on his return to England so soon as Michael Leman began to pursue the case on behalf of the owners and shippers.

   [4] The date coincides with that in Diaz's deposition (cp. p. 788 below).

25 peeces hollandes some whole rome some halfe and 12 li. of
fine flax.

6 barrells cont*aining* xij⁰ lis fyne flax.

one packe with 40 sayes

7 peeces striped canvas

one barrels of iron nayles

First I doe order and decree that Sir Richard Greinvile knight
and Arthur Facy and company at or before the firste of Auguste
next ensewinge shall deliver to the said Michaell Lemon his
executors or assignes at the nowe dwellinge house of Iohn Applinge
in Exceter¹ merchante two entire parts of all the said severall
goodes beinge devided into three parts / The said Lemon allowinge
xii^li in money towardes the Customs of the said goodes² in such
sorte conditioned as they came to the handes of the said Sir Richard
Greinfeilde And in case eany of the said goodes happen at the tyme
appoynted for their delivery to the said Lemon to be ympaired
wasted or decayed since the takinge of them by the said Facies and
company That then the said Sir Richard shall supply and make
good and pay to the said Lemon the iuste valewe of the goodes or
soe muche for the same as the decay shall amounte vnto.³

And further whereas the said Arthure and Iohn Facye and their
cumpanye in Marche last⁴ tooke a Flyboate called the Redd Lyon

¹ John Aplyn, Merchant Adventurer of Exeter, was in 1586 a subscriber to
John Davis's voyage of that year (cp. W. Cotton, *An Elizabethan guild of the city
of Exeter*, pp. 49, 83).

² At the usual 5%, this would indicate a total value for the goods of £240.
The decree amounts in fact to a concession to the Dutch to trade with Spain, but
under penalty, in this case of one-third of the value of the goods taken. Later
a passport system was instituted, under which a limited number of Dutch ships
were permitted to trade with Spain.   ³ Cp. pp. 484–5.

⁴ 1587, a quite distinct case. In this instance the Dutch were not so easily
satisfied. On 4 June he is said to be still detaining woad in spite of letters from the
Lord High Admiral and from Walsingham (Lansdowne MS 145, fo. 178).
A fortnight later Caesar reports that, Grenville having been ordered to hand over
the woad, there is nothing further outstanding against him. Nevertheless, Leman
was still pursuing Grenville for redress in this same case three years later (H.C.A.
13/28, 30 Oct. 1590). For these references I am indebted to Dr K. R. Andrews.
The case of the *Red Lion* provides a link between Arthur Facy's activities in 1586
and 1587 and his doings as captain of the *Brave* in 1588.

laden with 2660 kintalls of greene woade appertaining to the above-named Marten Flam Walter Buys and companie I doe of likewise order and decre with the consent of the parties aforesaid, That the said Lemon shall have all the said oad savinge 350 kintalls, And alsoe shall receave and have as parte of the said goods for his parte nine tonnes demie at Rye. And yf anye more be deliverid owte of the said shipp I doe also order and decre that the same shalbe made good to the said Lemon as [well?] by the said Sir Richard as [by the said Arthure and Iohn Facye?]. And that the said Michaell Leymon shall geve full and sufficient aucthority to such persons as Sir Richard Greinfeild Knighte shall name for the recovery of the said goodes at the proper coste and chardges of the said Sir Richard.

67. $\frac{20}{30}$ SEPTEMBER 1586.[1]

ABRAHAM ORTELIUS TO JACOB COLE (ORTELIANUS)[1]

...your letter was most pleasing to me as were the hand-drawn, coloured pictures enclosed. I did not know you were so skilled in this art. To quote your own words, I do not care about colours, plain drawings do quite well enough.[2] I am lost in wonder at 'that harbour of the Carthaginians, an outstanding work of nature'.[3] Unless I am mistaken it shows in this American region 'a most loyal roadstead of ships'. That geographical map will sometime be of use to me. As to this district is it that which the English discovered, in the true sense of that word—Virginia, or one different from that?[4] If another, I should like to know by what name this is called.[5]...30 September 1586. Antwerp.

[*Addressed:*] Domino Jacobo Colio, Londinum.

[1] Extract. Latin, translated. Brit. Mus., Harleian MS 6994, f. 39. I am indebted to Mr P. H. Hulton, Mr J. L. Nevinson and Mr W. R. Smyth for this version.
[2] Cp. a similar statement in Hessels, ed., *Abrahami Ortelii...epistulae*, p. 614.
[3] Cp. Virgil, *Aeneid*, bk. ii, line 23.
[4] 'this district' is clearly that discovered under Raleigh's auspices. But Camden had given Ortelius both names for it some eight months before (p. 472 above).
[5] Cole duly sent the information and was thanked by Ortelius (p. 496 below).

The 1586 Ventures

68. 12 OCTOBER 1586.

For after that you had seasoned your primer yeares at Oxford[2] in knowledge and learning, a good ground and a sure foundation to build therevpon all your good actions, you trauelled into France, and spent there a good part of your youth in the warres and martiall seruices.[3] And hauing some sufficient knowledge and experience therein, then after your returne from thense, to the end you might euerie waie be able to serue your prince and commonweale, you were desirous to be acquainted in maritimall affaires. Then you, togither with your brother[4] sir Humfreie Gilbert, trauelled the seas, for the search of such countries, as which if they had beene then discouered, infinit commodities in sundrie respects would haue insued, and whereof there was no doubt, if the fleet then accompanieng you, had according to appointment followed you, or your self had escaped the dangerous sea fight,[5] when manie of your companie were slaine, and your ships therewith also sore

---

[1] Extract from John Hooker's dedication to Sir Walter Raleigh of 'The Irish historie...by Giraldus Cambrensis', in Holinshed, *Chronicles*, II (1587), 2nd numeration, sigs. A 3–A 4. Miss Eleanor Rosenberg ('Giacopo Castelvetro, Italian publisher in Elizabethan London, and his patrons', in *Huntington Library Quarterly*, VI (1942–3), 119–48) considers this dedication to be part of a systematic publicity campaign for the Virginia enterprise, arranged by Richard Hakluyt. She fails to establish any link between Hakluyt and Hooker (though p. 552 below may contain a reference to this edition of Giraldus), and what she says is unlikely. Hooker knew Raleigh's family and, as chamberlain of Exeter, Raleigh himself; and any priming he needed most likely came from Raleigh. (It will be noted above (pp. 493–4) that Hakluyt himself asked Raleigh what he would like him to put into his proposed dedication to him of Peter Martyr's *Decades*.) It is not impossible, however, that Hooker had seen a copy of Hakluyt's 'Discourse of western planting'.

[2] For the duration of Raleigh's residence at Oriel College see C. S. Emden, *Oriel papers* (1948), pp. 9–21, where the conclusion would appear at least probable that he did not go to Oxford until 1572 (after his French adventures) and left sometime in 1574 to enter Lyons Inn before his admission to the Middle Temple on 27 February 1575.

[3] Raleigh's French service apparently began in 1569 and ended in 1572 (W. Spedding, *Ralegh* (1899), pp. 9–11, and Emden, above: with Hakluyt's reference, p. 545).   [4] Half-brother, having the same mother.

[5] This mysterious episode (1578–9) is discussed above, pp. 80–1, and in Quinn, *Gilbert*, I, 44–5.

battered and disabled. And albeit this hard beginning (after which followed the death of the said woorthie knight your brother) was a matter sufficient to haue discouraged a man of a right good stomach and value from anie like seas attempts;[1] yet you, more respecting the good ends, wherevnto you leuelled your line for the good of your countrie, did not giue ouer, vntill you had recouered a land, and made a plantation of the people of your owne English nation in *Virginia*, the first English colonie that euer was there planted,[2] to the no little derogation of the glorie of the Spaniards, & an impeach to their vaunts; who bicause with all cruel immanitie, contrarie to all naturall humanitie, they subdued a naked and a yeelding people, whom they sought for gaine and not for anie religion or plantation of a commonwelth, ouer whome to satisfie their most greedie and insatiable couetousnesse, did most cruellie tyrannize, and most tyranicallie and against the course of all human nature did scorch and rost them to death, as by their owne histories

Spanish brags. dooth appeare.[3] These (I saie) doo brag and vaunt, that they onelie haue drawne strange nations and vnknowne people, to the obedience of their kings, to the knowledge of christianitie, and to the inriching of their countrie, and thereby doo claime the honor to be due to themselues onelie and alone. But if these your actions were well looked into, with such due consideration as apperteineth, it shall be found much more honorable in sundrie respects, for the aduancement of the name of God, the honour of the prince, and the benefit of the common wealth. For what can be more pleasant to God, than to gaine and reduce in all christianlike manner, a lost people to the knowledge of the gospell, and a true christian religion,

[1] Hooker passes over Raleigh's investment in Gilbert's last voyage (Quinn, *Gilbert*, I, 84).   [2] In 1585 under Lane.

[3] This distorted picture of the nature and methods of Spanish expansionism as a contrast to the beneficent aims of English colonizers, though not wholly untrue, is typical of much Elizabethan propaganda against Spain. It received a greatly increased impetus from the translation (by M.S.) of Bartolomé de las Casas, *Brevisima relación de la destruycion de las Indias* (1552), as *The Spanish colonie, or brief chronicle of the acts and gestes of the Spaniardes in the West Indies* (1583), which is here referred to, and which was used by Raleigh in his *Report of the truth of the fight about the Iles of Açores* (1591).

than which cannot be a more pleasant and a sweet sacrifice, and a more acceptable seruice before God?[1] And what can be more honorable to princes, than to inlarge the bounds of their kingdoms without iniurie, wrong, & bloudshed; and to frame them from a sauage life to a ciuill gouernment, neither of which the Spaniards in their conquests haue performed?[2] And what can be more beneficiall to a common weale, than to haue a nation and a kingdome to transferre vnto the superfluous multitude of frutelesse and idle people (heere at home dailie increasing) to trauell, conquer, and manure another land, which by the due intercourses to be deuised, may and will yeeld infinit commodities?[3] And how well you doo deserue euerie waie in following so honorable a course, not we our selues onelie can witnesse, but strange nations also doo honour you for the same: as dooth appeare by the epistle of *Basslmerus* of France, to the historie of Florida:[4] and by *Iulius Caesar* a citizen of Rome in his epistle to his book intituled *Cullombeados.*[5] It is well knowne, that it had beene no lesse easie for you,

[1] On the missionary motive cp. pp. 126–7, 372, 376; Taylor, *Hakluyts*, II, 214–18, 318. For a general discussion see Louis B. Wright, *Religion and empire, 1558–1625* (Chapel Hill, 1943), pp. 3–56.

[2] The political and economic aspects of civilizing the North American Indians are discussed by Christopher Carleill, Sir George Peckham, and the two Richard Hakluyts in Quinn, *Gilbert*, II, 357, 361, 452–3, 468; Taylor, *Hakluyts*, II, 246–9, 267, 313–14; and see pp. 138, 371–2, 381 above.

[3] The under-employment motive also is generally stressed (see p. 127 above; Quinn, *Gilbert*, I, 160–1; II, 361, 461–3; Taylor, *Hakluyts*, II, 233–9, 269–70, 319, 326).

[4] Martin Basanier's dedication to Raleigh of *L'histoire notable de la Floride*, dated 1 March 1586, N.S. (see pp. 472–3 above), which was undoubtedly inspired by Hakluyt as publicity for the Virginia enterprises.

[5] Guilio Cesare Stella, *Columbeidos, libri priores duo* (Londini apud Iohannem Wolfium, 1585), with a dedicatory epistle to Raleigh. The poem is a eulogy of Columbus and the dedication says that it is published for the first time in England in honour of Raleigh's 'heroic attempts' to emulate him in sending an expedition to the New World. It is agreed by Miss Rosenberg (loc. cit.) and by the late Miss K. T. Butler ('Giacomo Castelvetro, 1546–1616', in *Italian Studies*, v (1950), 1–42) that the poem is edited and introduced by the refugee protestant Italian author Giacomo Castelvetro, but the latter maintains that the dedication shows that he did not know Raleigh and 'indeed its whole tone is rather that of a bid for patronage' (p. 11), while Miss Rosenberg considers it part, even if a minor

than for such as haue beene aduanced by kings, to haue builded great houses, purchased large circuits, and to haue vsed the fruits of princes fauours, as most men in all former and present ages haue doone; had you not preferred the generall honour and commoditie of your prince and countrie before all priuat gaine and commoditie: wherby you haue beene rather a seruant than a commander to your owne fortune.[1] And no doubt the cause being so good, and the attempt so honorable, but that God will increase your talent, and blesse your dooings, and euerie good man will commend and further the same. And albeit the more noble enterprises a man shall take in hand the more aduersaries he shall haue to depraue and hinder the same: yet I am persuaded, as no good man shall haue iust cause, so there is none so much carried with a corrupt mind, nor so enuious of his countries honour, nor so bent against you, that he will derogate the praise and honour due to so worthie an enterprise;[2] and that so much the sooner, bicause you haue indured so manie crosses,[3] and haue through so much enuiengs and mis-

part, of an inspired campaign (by Hakluyt) on behalf of the Virginia venture. She goes on to say (p. 129): 'Hooker's well-intentioned but confused references to "Bassimerus" and "Julius Caesar" are incomprehensible as mere slips on the part of so careful a scholar, if he had himself perused the dedications to which he refers. But they became understandable if we conceive of Hooker as working hastily from notes and Hakluyt's suggestions for the passage.' This does not seem a justifiable inference. '*Bassimerus*' is an obvious printer's error for '*Basanierus*' which is what Hooker might well have written for Basanier (see p. 472 above), while he would have been delighted to refer to a contemporary Italian as '*Iulius Caesar*' (for after all was the judge of the admiralty not of that name?). Hooker's pedantic habit of mind is, in fact, well illustrated by just these references. (In this discussion I am indebted to Miss Norah H. Evans.)

[1] This puts in more general terms what Basanier and Hakluyt said more specifically about Raleigh's financial contributions to the ventures (pp. 472–3), but it is a genuine tribute from one who was very critical of the get-rich-quick activities of the privateers and other overseas speculators (cp. Document no. 50, pp. 312–13 above).

[2] Again, in general terms, this reflects the criticism and opposition, especially from Lane's colonists since their return in July, which Hakluyt and Hariot were to rebut more systematically (cp. pp. 320–4, 514).

[3] Especially the return of Lane's colonists with Drake, but possibly also that of the supply ship (p. 479), of whose return to a south-western port Hooker is likely to have heard. Grenville was still at sea when this dedication was written.

fortunes perseuered in your attempts, which no doubt shall at last by you be performed when it shall please him, who hath made you an instrument of so worthie a worke.....Exon.[1] October 12. 1586.

69. 30 DECEMBER 1586.

RICHARD HAKLUYT TO SIR WALTER RALEIGH[2]

I heare nothinge from you of the acceptation of my dedication of that noble historie of the eight decades of Peter Martyr, which wil cost mee fortie frenche crownes[3] and five monethes travayle with that which is to come before yt be finished, which wilbe aboute the begininge of March.[4] Yf her maiestie haue of late advanced you, I wold be gladde to be acquaynted with your titles, and if there be any thinge else that you wold haue mentioned in the epistle dedicatorie, you shal doe wel to let mee vnderstand of yt betymes.

Your mappe answerable vnto the Spanish voyage of Antonio de Espeio,[5] vppon occasion of business vnlooked for, hath bin hitherto differred by Andrewe Home the Portingale, the prince of the Cosmographers of this age.[6] But within this moneth you shall not fayle of yt God willinge, and that in better sorte for the longer staying for yt.[7]

Yf you proceed, which I longe much to knowe,[8] in your entre-

---

[1] Exeter, of which Hooker was chamberlain.

[2] Bodleian Library, Clarendon MSS, Addenda 307, fos. 2–3 v, extracts; printed in Taylor, *Hakluyts*, II, 355-6. This letter is the only surviving example of the correspondence received by Raleigh relating to the Roanoke enterprises. There is no indication of how Edward Hyde, earl of Clarendon, acquired it.

[3] Equivalent to about £14 (see p. 473 above). Hakluyt is evidently hoping to receive at least this sum from Raleigh.   [4] See pp. 513-15 below.

[5] Hakluyt had recently published Espejo in Spanish in Paris (pp. 549–50 below).

[6] Professor Taylor believes that this is the 'secret mappe of those partes made in Mexico' in 1585 which in 1599 was in Hariot's possession (*Hakluyts*, II, 355), but is not now, apparently, extant. André Homem had been cosmographer to Francis I and Charles IX.

[7] If the Homem map was delivered within the next three months, it, or a copy, was probably carried by White's expedition which left in May (p. 517).

[8] Hakluyt will have known of the return of the first colony in July, and, almost certainly, of the fruitless voyage of Raleigh's supply ship (above, p. 479), but he cannot yet have heard of Grenville's return in December (for the date, see p. 494 below), with the news that he had left a holding party at Roanoke.

prise of Virginia, your best planting wilbe aboute the bay of the Chesepians, to which latitude Peter Martyr, and franciscus lopez de Gomara the Spaniard[1] confesse that our Gabot[2] and the English did first discover: which the Spaniardes here after cannot deny vs whensoever wee shalbe at Peace with them. And your voyage of Antonio de Espeio bringeth you to rich syluer mynes vp in the countre in the latitude of 37.½.[3]...Paris the 30th of December .1586.[4] R[ichard] H[akluyt].

[*Addressed:*] To the right worshipful and worthy knyght Sir Walter Ralegh giuc these with spede./ At the Courte or at Durham house./

70. DECEMBER 1586.

GRENVILLE RETURNS FROM VIRGINIA[5]

In december[6] this year Sir Richard Greynfeld came home bringing a prise with him, laden with sugar, ginger & hyds.[7]

---

[1] Francisco López de Gómara, in his *História general de los Indias occidentales* (1552), fo. xx.

[2] López de Gómara conflates the discoveries of John and Sebastian Cabot, attributing them to the latter (see J. A. Williamson, *Voyages of the Cabots* (1929), pp. 77–8).

[3] Hakluyt is probably not basing his view on Lane's recommendations (above, pp. 261–3, 274–5), but on the illusion, to which the Spaniards were to cling (below, pp. 827–32), that Chesapeake Bay would provide easy access to the mines of New Mexico.

[4] It is not clear whether Hakluyt is using New or Old Style dating (cp. pp. 155). If the former, the letter should be double-dated 20/30 December.

[5] Diary of Philip Wyot, 1586–1608, in J. R. Chanter, *Sketches of the literary history of Barnstaple*, p. 92 (see above, pp. 475–6).

[6] Pedro Diaz (p. 792 below) gives the date of arrival as 26 December. If this is reliable, and the dating is New Style, Grenville's return was on 16 December.

[7] This is, with a high degree of probability, the vessel from Puerto Rico taken by Grenville at the Azores on its way home. Its cargo would not be appropriate to any of his other prizes (cp. pp. 480–8, 792).

The 1586 Ventures

71. 1588–9.

ENTRIES IN BIDEFORD PARISH REGISTER[1]

[a]   Anno Domini 1588 Christnynges....

Raleigh,[2] A Wynganditoian... xxvij day of March[3]

[b]   Anno Domini 1589 Burynges....

Rawly A man of Wynganditoia the vij[th] day of Aprile sepultus fuit[4]

72. [1586–7.]

RALEIGH'S PRESENT TO THE EARL OF NORTHUMBER-
LAND[5]

To Sir Walter Rawlys man that brought his Lordship a bed of cedar or cypress, 10s.[6]

[1] I am indebted to Dr. J. A. Youings and Major William Ascott, O.B.E., for checking these entries for me.

[2] He was probably the Indian from Roanoke Island captured by Grenville in 1586 (p. 790 below).

[3] Rowse, *Grenville*, p. 241, gives 'Sunday, 26 March 1588', but, in 1588, 26 March was a Tuesday and 27 March a Wednesday.

[4] The deaths of his servant Lawrence and his daughter Rebecca about the same time (also recorded in the register) might suggest that some infectious disease had broken out in Sir Richard Grenville's household at Bideford.

[5] Hist. MSS Comm., *6th rep.*, pt. i [5], p. 227 (from the account roll for 1586 to February 1587 of Henry Percy, 9th earl of Northumberland (1564–1632), from the MSS of the duke of Northumberland at Syon House). It probably dates from after Northumberland's return from the Netherlands in 1586.

[6] The suggestion is that this bed may have been made from timber brought from Virginia in 1585 or 1586, and that the earl's steward was unfamiliar with the timber of which it was made. Hariot (for whose references to cedar or cypress see p. 364 above) later lived at Syon House, in whose grounds there are now fine specimens of trees which Hariot described, namely the Swamp Cypress (*Taxodium distichum*) and the Sweet Gum (*Liquidambar styraciflua*).

73. $\dfrac{9}{19}$ JANUARY 1587.

ABRAHAM ORTELIUS TO JACOB COLE (ORTELIANUS).[1]

My thanks to you my dearest nephew, for your diligence and care in searching out the site of Wigandecua,[2] which I understand from the fragment of the map[3] sent to you, and which I have had back from you.[4]...Thank you. Antwerp, 19 January 1587, new style.

[1] Latin. Extract, translated (J. H. Hessels, ed., *Abrahamus Ortellii epistulae* (1887), p. 346.) Cole ('Jacobus Colius Carbo', otherwise Ortelianus) was living in London.

[2] Ortelius had already heard the name from Camden (p. 472 above).

[3] 'tabul*ae*'. The fragment was probably part of the map of America from the 1585 edition of the *Theatrum orbis terrarum* which Ortelius was engaged in revising.

[4] Ortelius had his new map engraved in the same year, 1587, and it was probably on sale as a single sheet in that year. The only alteration he made in the coastline was to insert an inlet, running east and west, just north of his 'C. de arenas' (thus bringing it into line with John Dee's map of 1580), together with the name 'WINGANDEKOA' as a regional or tribal name below the cape. The map was not, however, included in his atlas until 1590 (*Theatrum.* Additamentum IV), contemporaneously with the much more informative map in De Bry, which, however, nowhere contained the name as it had by then been discarded (cp. pp. 853–4).